Lecture Notes in Computer Science 12470

More information about this subseries at http://www.springer.com/series/7408

Bruno C. d. S. Oliveira (Ed.)

Programming Languages and Systems

18th Asian Symposium, APLAS 2020
Fukuoka, Japan, November 30 – December 2, 2020
Proceedings

 Springer

Editor
Bruno C. d. S. Oliveira (iD)
University of Hong Kong
Hong Kong, Hong Kong

ISSN 0302-9743   ISSN 1611-3349   (electronic)
Lecture Notes in Computer Science
ISBN 978-3-030-64436-9   ISBN 978-3-030-64437-6   (eBook)
https://doi.org/10.1007/978-3-030-64437-6

LNCS Sublibrary: SL2 – Programming and Software Engineering

This Springer imprint is published by the registered company Springer Nature Switzerland AG
The registered company address is: Gewerbestrasse 11, 6330 Cham, Switzerland

Preface

This volume contains the papers presented at the 18th Asian Symposium on Programming Languages and Systems (APLAS 2020), held online during November 30 – December 2, 2020. APLAS 2020 was originally meant to be held in Fukuoka City, Japan, but due to the COVID-19 epidemic, it was changed to an online event.

APLAS aims to stimulate programming language research by providing a forum for the presentation of the latest results and the exchange of ideas in programming languages and systems. APLAS is based in Asia but is an international forum that serves the worldwide programming languages community.

This year we solicited contributions in the forms of regular research papers and tool papers. Among others, solicited topics include: semantics, logics, and foundational theory; design of languages, type systems, and foundational calculi; domain-specific languages; compilers, interpreters, and abstract machines; program derivation, synthesis, and transformation; program analysis, verification, model-checking; logic, constraint, probabilistic, and quantum programming; software security; concurrency and parallelism; tools and environments for programming and implementation; and applications of SAT/SMT to programming and implementation.

We also continued employing a light double-blind reviewing process adopted recently by APLAS with an author-response period. More precisely, we had a two-stage reviewing process. Each paper received at least three reviews before the author-response period, which was followed by a one-week Program Committee (PC) discussion, taking into account initial impressions of the papers as well as the author responses.

This year we received 46 submissions, out of which 19 papers (17 regular papers and 2 tool papers) were accepted after thorough reviews and discussions by the PC. We were also honored to include three invited talks by distinguished PL researchers:

- Luca Cardelli (University of Oxford, UK) on "Integrated Scientific Modeling and Lab Automation"
- Hidehiko Masuhara (Tokyo Institute of Technology, Japan) on "Object Support for GPU Programming: Why and How"
- Nadia Polikarpova (University of California San Diego, USA) on "Generating Programs from Types"

I am indebted to many people who helped make APLAS 2020 possible. First and foremost, I sincerely thank the PC, who have spent a lot of time and effort throughout the entire reviewing process. I am also grateful for the sub-reviewers and expert reviewers for their thorough and constructive reviews. I thank Masahiro Yasugi (Kyushu Institute of Technology, Japan) who served as a general chair and worked out every detail of the conference well in advance. This year's APLAS was especially challenging to prepare due to the complications of moving to and organizing an online event.

I am also grateful to AAFS Executive Committee (especially Wei-Ngan Chin, National University of Singapore, Singapore, and Atsushi Igarashi, Kyoto University, Japan) who provided a lot of helpful advice and thank them for their leadership. I thank the previous APLAS PC chair, Anthony Widjaja Lin (TU Kaiserslautern, Germany) for his helpful advice and resources. Finally, I thank Eelco Visser and Elmer van Chastelet for their very helpful conf.researchr.org conference management system, as well as Eddie Kohler for his very helpful HotCRP conference management system.

October 2020   Bruno C. d. S. Oliveira

Organization

General Chair

Masahiro Yasugi   Kyushu Institute of Technology, Japan

General Vice-chair

Kento Emoto   Kyushu Institute of Technology, Japan

Local Arrangement Chair

Ryosuke Sato   The University of Tokyo, Japan

Remote Arrangement Chair

Tomoharu Ugawa   The University of Tokyo, Japan

Workshop Chair

Atsushi Igarashi   Kyoto University, Japan

Program Chair

Bruno C. d. S. Oliveira   The University of Hong Kong, Hong Kong

Program Committee

Edwin Brady	University of St Andrews, UK
Soham Chakraborty	IIT Delhi, India
Shigeru Chiba	The University of Tokyo, Japan
Andreea Costea	National University of Singapore, Singapore
Silvia Crafa	University of Padova, Italy
Pierre-Evariste Dagand	LIP6, CNRS, France
Mila Dalla Preda	University of Verona, Italy
Cristina David	University of Bristol, UK
Benjamin Delaware	Purdue University, USA
Jeremy Gibbons	University of Oxford, UK
Ichiro Hasuo	National Institute of Informatics, Japan
Sam Lindley	Heriot-Watt University and The University of Edinburgh, UK
James McKinna	The University of Edinburgh, UK
Madhavan Mukund	Chennai Mathematical Institute, India

Hakjoo Oh	Korea University, South Korea
Florian Rabe	University of Erlangen-Nuremberg, Germany
Sukyoung Ryu	KAIST, South Korea
Tom Schrijvers	KU Leuven, Belgium
Ilya Sergey	Yale-NUS College and National University of Singapore, Singapore
Marco Servetto	Victoria University of Wellington, New Zealand
Wouter Swierstra	Utrecht University, The Netherlands
Alwen Tiu	The Australian National University, Australia
Sam Tobin-Hochstadt	Indiana University Bloomington, USA
Janis Voigtländer	University of Duisburg-Essen, Germany
Meng Wang	University of Bristol, UK
Nicolas Wu	Imperial College London, UK
Yizhou Zhang	University of Waterloo, Canada
Tijs van der Storm	CWI, University of Groningen, The Netherlands

Additional Reviewer

Robert Rand

Abstracts of Invited Talks

Integrated Scientific Modeling and Lab Automation

Luca Cardelli

University of Oxford, UK
luca.a.cardelli@gmail.com

Abstract. The cycle of observation, hypothesis formulation, experimentation, and falsification that has driven scientific and technical progress is lately becoming automated in all its separate components. However, integration between these automated components is lacking. Theories are not placed in the same formal context as the (coded) protocols that are supposed to test them: neither description knows about the other, although they both aim to describe the same process. We develop integrated descriptions from which we can extract both the model of a phenomenon (for possibly automated mathematical analysis), and the steps carried out to test it (for automated execution by lab equipment). This is essential if we want to carry out automated model synthesis, falsification, and inference, by taking into account uncertainties in both the model structure and in the equipment tolerances that may jointly affect the results of experiments.

Object Support for GPU Programming: Why and How

Hidehiko Masuhara

Tokyo Institute of Technology, Japan
`masuhara@is.titech.ac.jp`

Abstract. General-purpose computing on graphics processing units (GPGPU) is now widely used in many application domains. However, programming for GPGPU is challenging due to its peculiar performance characteristics and still being done either in low-level languages or through libraries (e.g., those for matrix computation and machine learning). This talk discusses the performance challenges of using objects in GPGPU programming from the viewpoint of memory management, and the efficient mechanisms to support objects.

Generating Programs from Types

Nadia Polikarpova

UC San Diego, USA
npolikarpova@eng.ucsd.edu

Abstract. Program synthesis is a promising approach to automating low-level aspects of programming by generating code from high-level declarative specifications. But what form should these specifications take? In this talk I will advocate for using types as input to program synthesis. Types are widely adopted by programmers, they can vary in expressiveness and capture both functional and non-functional properties, and finally, type checking is often fully automatic and compositional, which helps the synthesizer find the right program. I will describe two type-driven program synthesizers we developed. The first one is Synquid, a synthesizer for recursive functional programs that uses expressive refinement types as a specification mechanism. The second one is Hoogle+, which relies on more mainstream Haskell types and generates code snippets by composing functions from Haskell libraries.

Contents

Program Analysis and Verification

A Set-Based Context Model for Program Analysis 3
Leandro Fachinetti, Zachary Palmer, Scott F. Smith, Ke Wu,
and Ayaka Yorihiro

Declarative Stream Runtime Verification (hLola). 25
Martín Ceresa, Felipe Gorostiaga, and César Sánchez

Formal Verification of Atomicity Requirements for Smart Contracts 44
Ning Han, Ximeng Li, Guohui Wang, Zhiping Shi, and Yong Guan

Types

Neural Networks, Secure by Construction: An Exploration
of Refinement Types 67
Wen Kokke, Ekaterina Komendantskaya, Daniel Kienitz, Robert Atkey,
and David Aspinall

A New Refinement Type System for Automated vHFL$_\mathbb{Z}$ Validity Checking. . . . 86
Hiroyuki Katsura, Naoki Iwayama, Naoki Kobayashi,
and Takeshi Tsukada

Behavioural Types for Memory and Method Safety in a Core
Object-Oriented Language 105
Mario Bravetti, Adrian Francalanza, Iaroslav Golovanov, Hans Hüttel,
Mathias S. Jakobsen, Mikkel K. Kettunen, and António Ravara

Syntactically Restricting Bounded Polymorphism for Decidable Subtyping. . . . 125
Julian Mackay, Alex Potanin, Jonathan Aldrich, and Lindsay Groves

Semantics

An Abstract Machine for Strong Call by Value. 147
Małgorzata Biernacka, Dariusz Biernacki, Witold Charatonik,
and Tomasz Drab

Certified Semantics for Relational Programming 167
Dmitry Rozplokhas, Andrey Vyatkin, and Dmitry Boulytchev

Algebraic and Coalgebraic Perspectives on Interaction Laws. 186
Tarmo Uustalu and Niels Voorneveld

Program Generation, Transactions and Automation

Stack-Driven Program Generation of WebAssembly   209
  Árpád Perényi and Jan Midtgaard

Banyan: Coordination-Free Distributed Transactions over
Mergeable Types.   231
  Shashank Shekhar Dubey, K. C. Sivaramakrishnan,
  Thomas Gazagnaire, and Anil Madhavapeddy

Automatically Generating Descriptive Texts in Logging Statements:
How Far Are We?.   251
  Xiaotong Liu, Tong Jia, Ying Li, Hao Yu, Yang Yue, and Chuanjia Hou

Synthesis and Program Transformation

Parameterized Synthesis with Safety Properties.   273
  Oliver Markgraf, Chih-Duo Hong, Anthony W. Lin, Muhammad Najib,
  and Daniel Neider

Relational Synthesis for Pattern Matching   293
  Dmitry Kosarev, Petr Lozov, and Dmitry Boulytchev

REFINITY to Model and Prove Program Transformation Rules   311
  Dominic Steinhöfel

Debugging, Profiling and Constraint Solving

A Counterexample-Guided Debugger for Non-recursive Datalog.   323
  Van-Dang Tran, Hiroyuki Kato, and Zhenjiang Hu

A Symbolic Algorithm for the Case-Split Rule in String
Constraint Solving.   343
  Yu-Fang Chen, Vojtěch Havlena, Ondřej Lengál, and Andrea Turrini

P^3: A Profiler Suite for Parallel Applications on the Java Virtual Machine. . .   364
  Andrea Rosà and Walter Binder

Author Index   373

Program Analysis and Verification

A Set-Based Context Model
for Program Analysis

Leandro Fachinetti[1], Zachary Palmer[2(✉)], Scott F. Smith[1], Ke Wu[1],
and Ayaka Yorihiro[3]

[1] Johns Hopkins University, Baltimore, USA
[2] Swarthmore College, Swarthmore, USA
zachary.palmer@swarthmore.edu
[3] Cornell University, Ithaca, USA

Abstract. In program analysis, the design of context models is an understudied topic. This paper presents a study of context models for higher-order program analyses and develops new approaches. We develop a context model which equates control flows with the same *set* of call sites on the program stack, guaranteeing termination without the arbitrary cutoffs which cause imprecision in existing models. We then selectively polyinstantiate these contexts to avoid exponential growth.

We evaluate this model and existing models across multiple higher-order program analysis families. Existing demand-driven analyses cannot support the set model, so we construct a demand-driven analysis, Plume, which can. Our experiments demonstrate that the set-based model is tractable and expressive on representative functional programs for both forward- and demand-driven functional analyses.

Keywords: Program analysis · Control flow · Data flow · Context sensitivity · Higher-order · Object-oriented

1 Introduction

In higher-order program analysis, there exists a fundamental tension between context sensitivity and field sensitivity (also called structure-transmitted data dependence [41]). Context sensitivity relates to how the analysis accounts for the calling context of a function while analyzing the function's body. Field sensitivity relates to how the analysis aligns constructions and destructions as it explores structured data: for instance, whether it can accurately project a field from a constructed record or, equivalently, look up a non-local variable captured in closure. Context and field sensitivity inform each other: an analysis lacking in context sensitivity may lead to spurious data flows despite perfect field sensitivity. Any analysis which is perfectly context- and field-sensitive has been shown to be undecidable [29] so, for an analysis tool to guarantee termination, some concessions must be made.

A common approach is to preserve field sensitivity by approximating context sensitivity using an abstract model. When introducing one of the first

© Springer Nature Switzerland AG 2020
B. C. d. S. Oliveira (Ed.): APLAS 2020, LNCS 12470, pp. 3–24, 2020.
https://doi.org/10.1007/978-3-030-64437-6_1

higher-order program analyses, kCFA, Shivers wrote about context models: "Choosing a good abstraction that is well-tuned to typical program usage is not a topic that I have explored in depth, although it certainly merits study." [33, p. 34] The choice of context models is a critical factor in analysis precision and running time, but explorations of this question have been largely confined to truncated call strings à la kCFA [4,12,18,19,23,38,39]. Recent work has explored selective approaches to polyinstantiation [16,37] and using different context models for parts of the same program [17,21,22], but these approaches must still contend with a crucial weakness: in kCFA-like models, polyinstantiation of a saturated context will lose the oldest call site. This conflates that call site's control flows with those of other call sites and weakens the analysis.

Alternative models of control flow exist in the space of object-oriented alias analyses. The context and field sensitivity problems can be reduced to matched parenthesis problems, so they can be modeled as a linear conjunctive language (LCL) [26] reachability problem. While that problem is undecidable, performant and relatively precise approximations have been recently developed [41]. Unfortunately, it is not clear what information is lost in these approximations or which programs would be affected by using LCL reachability in an analysis.

Another recent technique, synchronized pushdown systems (SPDS) [34], involves making *no* concessions on either context sensitivity or field sensitivity but treating them as separate problems. The resulting analysis performs well on traditional object-oriented programs. But functional programs rely heavily upon the interplay of data and interprocedural control flow and we show that this approach is problematic for those programs (see Sect. 4.3).

In contrast with the kCFA-like models, we propose not to discard old call site information at all. Instead, we represent calling contexts as the *set* of call sites on the program stack. This identifies calls appearing at the same site but retains information about the entire sequence of calls, preventing the conflation of control flows in the k-limited models described above. This precision introduces a problem: because the set stores *call sites* rather than *called functions*, a recursive function calling itself at n sites may create 2^n different contexts, all of which analyze the same recursive function. We address this by selectively polyinstantiating contexts in a fashion similar to context tunneling [16].

We evaluate these techniques both in terms of precision and performance. Evaluating the precision of a *component* of a program analysis is a challenge: it is difficult to separate the effects of the component from how it interacts with the surrounding analysis. Our evaluation is a *reproducability* experiment: we test a Cartesian product of program analyses and context models, demonstrating that the k-cutoff and set-based context models exhibit the same difference in behavior across those analyses. Given that these differences are reproducible in different analyses, we ascribe them to the context model.

For the reproducability experiment's result to apply broadly, the analyses must be significantly different. We perform the experiment on three analyses. The first two are ADI, a state-of-the-art functional analysis [4], and an analysis similar to mCFA [24] in the style of object-oriented CFA analyses.

For the third analysis, we desired to use a higher-order analysis in a *demand-driven* style. Demand-driven analyses differ from forward-running analyses in that they only look up values on demand rather than propagating abstract heaps throughout the program. Demand-driven analyses were originally developed for first-order programs [5,13,15,28,30–32] where they were shown to achieve good performance/expressiveness trade-offs. Unfortunately, previous higher-order demand-driven analyses [6,7,9,27,34,35] do not support set-based context models. We develop a new demand-driven higher-order program analysis, Plume, to support set-based contexts and selective polyinstantiation. We prove that Plume is sound, decidable, and strictly more expressive than DDPA [6], a previous analysis in this class.

We describe Plume, set-based context models, and selective polyinstantiation in Sect. 2. We formalize Plume in Sect. 3. Precision and performance testing are discussed in Sect. 4 and Sect. 5. (The full performance evaluation as well as the proofs of Plume's soundness and decidability appear in a supplemental report [8]). Section 6 discusses related and future work; we conclude in Sect. 7.

2 Overview

This section gives an overview of Plume, set-based context models and selective polyinstantiation. Although our examples focus on the Plume analysis, set-based context models and selective polyinstantiation are applicable to other analyses as well. We discuss their use in other analyses in later sections.

2.1 Shallow A-Normalized Lambda Calculus

Throughout this paper, we will focus on a shallow A-normalized lambda calculus. The grammar for this language appears in Fig. 1. An expression is a list of clauses to be executed in sequence; the result is the last assigned variable in that sequence.

Call site annotations Θ are used for selective polyinstantiation; we discuss them in Sect. 2.4 below.

$e ::= [c, \ldots]$	*expressions*	$v ::= f$	*values*
$c ::= x = b$	*clauses*	$f ::= \mathbf{fun}\ x\ \text{->}\ (e)$	*functions*
$b ::= f \mid x \mid x\ x\ \Theta$	*clause bodies*	$\Theta ::= [\theta, \ldots]$	*call site annotation lists*
$x ::= (identifiers)$	*variables*	$\theta ::= @x$	*call site annotations*
$E ::= [x = v, \ldots]$	*environments*		

Fig. 1. Grammar of analyzed language

We require that all programs are *alphatized*: all clauses define a unique variable. This creates a bijection between variable names and program points, simplifying the theory and presentation. We include more language features in the implementation evaluated in Sects. 4 and 5.

2.2   Plume by Example

Plume is a *demand-driven* program analysis inspired by DDPA [6]. Plume proceeds by incrementally constructing a *contextual control flow graph* (CCFG). This structure tracks control flow in a context-sensitive manner by associating a calling context with each graph node. DDPA does not include context information in CFG nodes. The CCFG is the only data structure in Plume; there are no stores or program states. Plume iteratively expands call sites, effectively inlining function bodies into the CCFG.

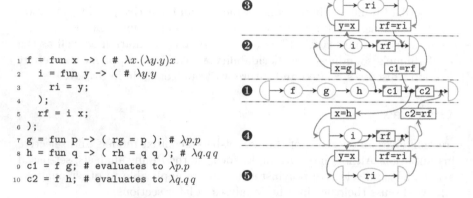

```
1  f = fun x -> ( # λx.(λy.y)x
2    i = fun y -> ( # λy.y
3      ri = y;
4    );
5    rf = i x;
6  );
7  g = fun p -> ( rg = p ); # λp.p
8  h = fun q -> ( rh = q q ); # λq.q q
9  c1 = f g; # evaluates to λp.p
10 c2 = f h; # evaluates to λq.q q
```

Fig. 2. Identity example: ANF   **Fig. 3.** Identity example: CCFG result

Consider the example program in Fig. 2. f is simply an η-converted identity function. The functions defined in g and h are never called; they are simply used as distinct values for discussion. In the execution of the program, the call assigned to variable c1 will return g; the call assigned to variable c2 will return h.

Constructing the CCFG. Plume's CCFG initially consists only of the middle row of nodes (marked ❶) representing top-level program points. Because the analysis is demand-driven, we are not concerned with f, g, and h: they are value assignments and, if those values are required, we will look them up on demand.

The first function call appears at c1. We start by tracing *backward* from c1 to find the called function. We pass two clauses—h = ... and g = ...—which do not define f and so are skipped. We then discover variable f and its function.

We next add the second row of nodes (marked ❷). The top line is the body of the f function; the two nodes below are *wiring* nodes that represent the call's parameter and return data flows.

This is why the analysis does not require a store: values may be established on demand by retracing these control flow edges.

The call site rf is now reachable via non-call nodes. Expanding rf yields the top row of nodes (marked ❸).

The call site c2 becomes reachable so, like before, we identify f as the called function. We do not reuse the previous f subgraph: because this call occurs at a distinct site, we create a new subgraph. This subgraph appears in the second-to-last row in the diagram (marked ❹). Finally, we expand the call site rf, adding the nodes in the last row (marked ❺).

The completed CCFG is Plume's result and can be used to perform lookups. To look up c2 from the end of the program, for instance, we move backward through the graph and encounter c2=rf; our lookup therefore reduces to finding the value of rf from that node. Moving backward from c2=rf, we discover rf=ri, changing our goal to finding the value of ri. This process proceeds through ri=y , y=x, and x=h, eventually leading us to the function defined on line 8.

This example does not show the lookup of a non-local variable. This is a delicate process in demand-driven analyses and is solved in Plume with a *stack* of lookup variables, a technique originally developed for DDPA [6]. We discuss this approach in Appendix A in the supplemental material [8] for reasons of space.

2.3   Models of Context Sensitivity

Multiple passes over a program point allow different calls of a function to be distinguished. These passes manifest in Plume as copies of the function in the CCFG; in other analyses, they may manifest as additional program states, edges in an automaton, or similar structures. A decidable program analysis must limit how many times it analyzes each program point to keep these structures finite.

One typical finitization approach is to associate each function call with a calling context derived from the circumstances under which the function is called. In kCFA [33], for instance, calling contexts are a list of the k most recent call sites visited by the program. In polyvariant P4F [12], calling contexts are represented by the call site from which we have most recently returned. DDPA [6] and Plume, like many program analyses, are parametric in the model of calling context used. We use Σ to denote a context model and use Σ_k to denote the model in which contexts are the top k call sites of the stack.

```
1  o = fun x -> ( r = x x;  )
2  z = o o;  # (λx.x x)(λx.x x)
```

Fig. 4. Ω-combinator: ANF

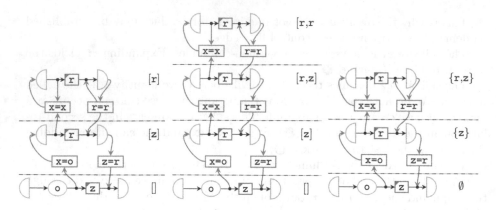

Fig. 5. 1Plume CCFG   **Fig. 6.** 2Plume CCFG   **Fig. 7.** SetPlume CCFG

One contribution of this paper is the development of a tractable analysis using a *set-based* context model denoted Σ_{Set}, which represents contexts as the set of *all* call sites on the call stack. Σ_{Set} addresses a weakness of traditional k-cutoff models: recursion. Consider the non-terminating Ω-combinator program in Fig. 4 analyzed by Plume using Σ_1 (which we call 1Plume). The generated CCFG appears in Fig. 5. Initially, the calling context is empty: the top level of the program is not generated from any calls. When the first r call site is expanded, it introduces nodes associated with the context [r]. (The context for groups of nodes appears to the right.) The z is dropped from this context because the list is limited to size 1. When the second r call site is expanded, we also associate that call with [r], reusing the subgraph associated with this context.

By the time a program analysis begins to reuse resources in recognition of the recursive call, we have lost all information about where the recursive call started. In the final context of the CCFG, [r], the call site z is no longer present. If the same recursive function were called in multiple locations, all such calls would eventually converge on the [r] context and their control flows would be conflated. As illustrated in Fig. 6, increasing k does nothing to prevent this: the context [r,r] has similarly lost all information before the recursive call.

Recent developments in object-oriented k-cutoff models mitigate this problem in a variety of ways. Context tunneling [16] is the most relevant to this case: at each call, we can decide whether to polyinstantiate the context as above or to proceed with the context we already have. This technique is almost identical in expressiveness to selective polyinstantiation, which we discuss below. Instead of applying this technique to prevent information loss, however, we use the set-based context model (which loses none of this information) and apply this technique to support performance.

The CCFG in Fig. 7 is generated by Plume using Σ_{Set} (which we call Set-Plume); SetPlume does not conflate recursive calls in this way. While this CCFG initially appears to be the same as the one generated by 1Plume, the contexts associated with each node retain every call site encountered since the top level of the program. As a consequence, calls to the same function at different sites will not be conflated. This is critical to allow recursive polymorphic functions such as List.map to be analyzed correctly.

SetPlume is not the first program analysis to retain the context of recursive calls by eshewing k-limited context. LCL reachability-based analyses [41] have a similar approximation which tracks the call stack even more precisely at the expense of some data flow information. However, most state-of-the-art analyses use a k-cutoff model [4,18] or rely upon an externally generated CFG [34,35].

2.4 Selective Polyinstantiation

Σ_{Set} distinguishes calls to recursive functions at different call sites by retaining information about where the recursive function was called. Unlike Σ_k, there is no point at which polyinstantiation loses information. As a result, Σ_{Set} is vulnerable to an exponential expansion of contexts. We address this issue using a selective polyinstantiation technique similar to the context tunneling work mentioned above.

Consider a recursive function whose body contains n recursive call sites (e.g. an expression interpreter). This recursive function may

```
1  fact0 = fun self -> (
2    factfn = fun n -> (
3      factret =
4        ifzero n then (
5          factret1 = 1;
6        ) else (
7          n' = n - 1;
8          selfself = self self @self;
9          factn' = selfself n' @n;
10         fact = factn' * n;
11 ); ); );
12 fact = fact0 fact0 @self;
13 x = 5;
14 fact5 = fact x;
```

Fig. 8. Factorial example: extended ANF

be called through any combination of the n recursive sites, leading to 2^n possible contexts. This is clearly intractable. Further, it is a waste of effort: the analysis is only more precise if different recursive calls yield different (abstract) values, and the inference of polymorphic recursion is known to be undecidable [14].

Our strategy is to be selective: when a function calls itself, we choose not to polyinstantiate it. The challenge is that, while Σ_{Set} correctly identifies and avoids polyinstantiation for recurring *call sites*, it does not identify recursive *functions*. To identify a recursive call, we must take into account both the position of call site and the function being called there. We explicitly mark each call site with the identities of those functions which should *not* be polyinstantiated if they are called in that location.

Consider the self-passing factorial program written in Fig. 8 in an extended ANF. The only contexts generated during the analysis of this program in Set-Plume will be $\emptyset$ and {fact5} despite the fact that there are several other function calls in the program. Upon reaching line 8, for instance, the analysis looks up self and discovers that the function being called is the one assigned to fact0. Because the ANF is alphatized, the name of the function's parameter, self, uniquely identifies it in the program. The annotation @self indicates that, if this function is called on line 8, it should *not* be polyinstantiated. As a result, this call site is wired to the body of that function associated with the current context, {fact5}, rather than to a new copy. These annotations are often automatically inferrable: the performance benchmark programs evaluated in Appendix D of the supplement [8] are written in an ML-like surface language *without* annotations and are then machine translated to an annotated ANF.

Selective polyinstantiation is almost equivalent in expressiveness to context tunneling. Both systems determine whether or not to polyinstantiate based upon the pairing of call site and called function. This choice is driven here by annotations and in the context tunneling work by a global relation. (Selective polyinstantiation can differentiate between call sites within the same method while context tunneling cannot, but this distinction seems unlikely to be useful.) There are two key differences between this work and context tunneling. First: the context tunneling paper [16] uses a data-driven machine learning algorithm to generate its pairwise relation; by comparison, we use a simple lexical annotator here. Second: the motivations differ. The data-driven algorithm is used to prevent the k-limited context from losing precision; here, we apply the technique to mitigate performance concerns. Selective polyinstantiation also shares some properties with earlier work [37] which eliminate provably redundant polyinstantiations, although that work is not applicable to the set-based context model discussed here.

Note that this approach is not limited to Σ_{Set} or to Plume. Selective polyinstantiation is similar to context tunneling [16], which has been applied to k-limited context models to prevent new, unimportant context information from supplanting old, important context information. Here, polyinstantiation is used to prevent a blow-up in complexity instead.

3   Formalizing Plume

We now formally define the Plume analysis. As outlined in Sect. 2.2, the analysis proceeds in two steps. First, the program is embedded into an initial CCFG; second, we perform a full closure of the CCFG using information from a demand-driven value lookup algorithm. There is no store or heap; all values are looked up by following the CCFG backward from the point of interest. We define the analysis in three parts: the initial embedding and corresponding preliminary definitions (Sect. 3.1), the demand-driven lookup function (Sect. 3.2), and the CCFG closure algorithm (Sect. 3.3).

3.1   Preliminary Definitions

We begin by abstracting the target program. We define "hatted" analogs for each grammar term in Fig. 1: $\hat{e}$ for abstract expressions, $\hat{c}$ for abstract clauses, and so on. We denote the abstraction of a concrete expression as $\alpha(e) = \hat{e}$. For convenience, we define RV as a function returning the last defined variable in an expression and use || to denote list concatenation.

Recall that a CCFG is a *contextual* control flow graph; it contains context information. We begin by defining a general notion of context model, Σ.

Definition 1. *A context model Σ is a triple $\langle \hat{C}, \epsilon, \oplus \rangle$ where*

- *$\hat{C}$ is a set whose elements, denoted $\hat{C}$, are calling contexts.*
- *ϵ, the "empty context", is an element of $\hat{C}$.*
- *For all $\hat{C} \in \hat{C}$ and all $\hat{c}$, $\hat{C} \oplus \hat{c} = \hat{C}'$ and $\hat{C}' \in \hat{C}$.*

We formalize the k-cutoff and set models of Sect. 2 as follows:

Definition 2.

- $\Sigma_k = \langle \hat{C}, [], \oplus \rangle$ *where $\hat{C}$ contains all lists of $\hat{c}$ of length up to k and* $[\hat{c}_n, \ldots, \hat{c}_1] \oplus \hat{c}_0 = [\hat{c}_{k-1}, \ldots, \hat{c}_0]$.
- $\Sigma_{\mathsf{Set}} = \langle \hat{C}, \emptyset, \oplus \rangle$ *where $\hat{C}$ is the power set of all $\hat{c}$ and $\hat{C} \oplus \hat{c} = \hat{C} \cup \{\hat{c}\}$.*

Each context model defines a distinct Plume variant; for instance, we give Plume using Σ_{Set} the name SetPlume. Throughout the remainder of this section, we assume some fixed context model meeting the conditions of Definition 1.

$$\hat{a} ::= \hat{c} \mid \hat{x} \overset{@\hat{e}}{=} \hat{x} \mid \hat{x} \overset{\mathcal{D}\hat{e}}{=} \hat{x} \mid \textsc{Start} \mid \textsc{End} \qquad \textit{annotated clauses} \qquad \hat{\eta} ::= \langle \hat{a}, \hat{C} \rangle \qquad \textit{CCFG nodes}$$
$$\hat{V} ::= \{\hat{v}, \ldots\} \qquad\qquad\qquad\qquad\qquad\qquad \textit{value sets} \qquad\quad \hat{g} ::= \hat{\eta} \ll \hat{\eta} \qquad \textit{CCFG edges}$$
$$\hat{X} ::= [\hat{x}, \ldots] \qquad\qquad\qquad\qquad\qquad \textit{variable lookup stacks} \qquad \hat{G} ::= \{\hat{g}, \ldots\} \qquad \textit{CCFG's}$$

Fig. 9. Analysis grammar

Given a context model, the remaining constructs required for the Plume analysis appear in Fig. 9. A CCFG $\hat{G}$ is a set of edges between contextual control flow points $\hat{\eta}$, each of which is a pairing between a program point and the calling context in which that program point is visited. To work with these graphs, we introduce the following notation:

Definition 3. *We use the following notational sugar for CCFG graph edges:*

- *$\hat{a}_1 \ll \ldots \ll \hat{a}_n$ abbreviates $\{\hat{a}_1 \ll \hat{a}_2, \ldots, \hat{a}_{n-1} \ll \hat{a}_n\}$.*
- *$\hat{a}' \ll \{\hat{a}_1, \ldots, \hat{a}_n\}$ (resp. $\{\hat{a}_1 \ldots \hat{a}_n\} \ll \hat{a}'$) denotes $\{\hat{a}' \ll \hat{a}_1, \ldots, \hat{a}' \ll \hat{a}_n\}$ (resp. $\{\hat{a}_1 \ll \hat{a}', \ldots, \hat{a}_n \ll \hat{a}'\}$).*
- *We write $\hat{a} \lll \hat{a}'$ to mean that $(\hat{a} \ll \hat{a}') \in \hat{G}$ for $\hat{G}$ understood from context.*

Using the above, we define the initial state of the CCFG as just the clauses of the main program, with no function calls (yet) wired in.

Definition 4. *The initial embedding of an expression into a CCFG,* $\widehat{\mathrm{EMBED}}(e)$, *is the graph* $\hat{G} = \langle \mathrm{START}, \epsilon \rangle \ll \langle \hat{c}_1, \epsilon \rangle \ll \ldots \ll \langle \hat{c}_n, \epsilon \rangle \ll \langle \mathrm{END}, \epsilon \rangle$ *where* $\alpha(e) = [\hat{c}_1, \ldots, \hat{c}_n]$.

For example, the subgraph labeled ❶ in Fig. 3 is the initial embedding of the Fig. 2 expression.

3.2   The Lookup Function

Plume does not require an explicit representation of the heap. Instead, we look up the value of each variable when it is needed by starting from the point where it is *used* and tracing backward through the CCFG to the point where it is *defined*.

Given a CCFG $\hat{G}$, we formalize variable lookup as a relation $\hat{G}, \langle \hat{a}, \hat{C} \rangle \vdash \hat{X} \rightarrowtail \hat{v}$ which indicates that the value $\hat{v}$ may be discovered by reducing the lookup stack $\hat{X}$ from program point $\hat{a}$ in calling context $\hat{C}$. For instance, if lookup of variable $\hat{x}$ from the end of the program produces value $\hat{v}$, we may write "$\hat{G}, \langle \mathrm{END}, \epsilon \rangle \vdash [\hat{x}] \rightarrowtail \hat{v}$". (As mentioned briefly in Sect. 2.2 and illustrated in Appendix A in the supplemental material [8], we use a *stack* of variables to facilitate looking up non-local (i.e. closure-captured) variables.) Note that the provided program point $\hat{a}$ is assumed *not* to have executed yet; each time we step backward through the graph, we are undoing the effect of the preceding clause.

We formally define this relation as follows:

Definition 5. $\hat{G}, \hat{\eta} \vdash \hat{X} \rightarrowtail \hat{v}$ *holds iff there is a proof using the rules of Fig. 10.*

Given a position $\hat{\eta}$ in the CCFG $\hat{G}$ and a lookup stack $\hat{X}$, the rules in Fig. 10 describe which transitions are legal during lookup. Any valid path through the CCFG to locate a variable definition corresponds to a proof in that system.

The Alias rule indicates that, when looking for variable $\hat{x}$ and about to undo the assignment $\hat{x}=\hat{x}'$, we can reduce our lookup to finding the value of $\hat{x}'$ from that point. The Value Discovery rule indicates that, when stepping back to $\hat{x}=\hat{v}$ while looking for $\hat{x}$, our lookup is complete: $\hat{v}$ is the answer. The Function Enter Non-Local and Value Discard rules represent the beginning and end (respectively) of the lookup of a closure-captured variable, using the stack to retain the variable while finding the definition site of the closure. The other two function rules represent a value flowing into or out of a function (and update the current lookup variable appropriately); the Skip rule handles clauses which do not have an impact on the current lookup.

In Sect. 2.2 we informally described the lookup of the value of c2 of Fig. 2 from the end of the program; formally that lookup corresponds to a proof of $\hat{G}, \langle \mathrm{END}, \epsilon \rangle \vdash [\texttt{c2}] \rightarrowtail (\texttt{fun p -> } \ldots)$ in the lookup system of Fig. 10, for $\hat{G}$ being the CCFG of Fig. 3.

VALUE DISCOVERY
$$\frac{\langle \hat{x} = \hat{v}, \hat{C} \rangle \lll \hat{\eta}}{\hat{G}, \hat{\eta} \vdash [\hat{x}] \rightarrowtail \hat{v}}$$

VALUE DISCARD
$$\frac{\hat{\eta}' = \langle \hat{x} = \hat{f}, \hat{C} \rangle \quad \hat{\eta}' \lll \hat{\eta} \quad \hat{G}, \hat{\eta}' \vdash \hat{X} \rightarrowtail \hat{v}}{\hat{G}, \hat{\eta} \vdash [\hat{x}] \,||\, \hat{X} \rightarrowtail \hat{v}}$$

ALIAS
$$\frac{\hat{\eta}' = \langle \hat{x} = \hat{x}', \hat{C} \rangle \quad \hat{\eta}' \lll \hat{\eta} \quad \hat{G}, \hat{\eta}' \vdash [\hat{x}'] \,||\, \hat{X} \rightarrowtail \hat{v}}{\hat{G}, \hat{\eta} \vdash [\hat{x}] \,||\, \hat{X} \rightarrowtail \hat{v}}$$

FUNCTION ENTER PARAMETER
$$\frac{\hat{\eta}' = \langle \hat{x} \overset{\hat{\text{Qc}}}{=} \hat{x}', \hat{C} \rangle \quad \hat{\eta}' \lll \hat{\eta} \quad \hat{G}, \hat{\eta}' \vdash [\hat{x}'] \,||\, \hat{X} \rightarrowtail \hat{v}}{\hat{G}, \hat{\eta} \vdash [\hat{x}] \,||\, \hat{X} \rightarrowtail \hat{v}}$$

FUNCTION ENTER NON-LOCAL
$$\frac{\hat{\eta}' = \langle \hat{x}'' \overset{\hat{\text{Qc}}}{=} \hat{x}', \hat{C} \rangle}{\hat{\eta}' \lll \hat{\eta} \quad \hat{x}'' \neq \hat{x} \quad \hat{c} = (\hat{x}_f \; \hat{x}_v \; \hat{\Theta}) \quad \hat{G}, \hat{\eta}' \vdash [\hat{x}_f, \hat{x}] \,||\, \hat{X} \rightarrowtail \hat{v}}{\hat{G}, \hat{\eta} \vdash [\hat{x}] \,||\, \hat{X} \rightarrowtail \hat{v}}$$

FUNCTION EXIT
$$\frac{\hat{\eta}' = \langle \hat{x} \overset{\hat{\text{Dc}}}{=} \hat{x}', \hat{C} \rangle \quad \hat{\eta}' \lll \hat{\eta} \quad \hat{G}, \hat{\eta}' \vdash [\hat{x}'] \,||\, \hat{X} \rightarrowtail \hat{v}}{\hat{G}, \hat{\eta} \vdash [\hat{x}] \,||\, \hat{X} \rightarrowtail \hat{v}}$$

SKIP
$$\frac{\hat{\eta}' = \langle \hat{x}'' = \hat{b}, \hat{C} \rangle \quad \hat{\eta}' \lll \hat{\eta} \quad \hat{x}'' \neq \hat{x} \quad \hat{G}, \hat{\eta}' \vdash [\hat{x}] \,||\, \hat{X} \rightarrowtail \hat{v}}{\hat{G}, \hat{\eta} \vdash [\hat{x}] \,||\, \hat{X} \rightarrowtail \hat{v}}$$

Fig. 10. Abstract value lookup

3.3 CCFG Closure Construction

Given a CCFG, the lookup function allows us to determine the values that variables may have. We can use this to in turn deductively close over the CCFG: we add to the CCFG when we discover new control flows based upon looking up values of variables. In this way, CCFG closure and value lookup work in tandem: closure grows the CCFG based upon lookup, that growth increases the set of values that lookup provides, closure grows the CCFG further, and so on.

When a function application is reached with a novel function-argument pair, we add its body to the graph and add edges wiring that body around the call site, effectively inlining that function as described in Sect. 2.2. We pair each of the function's clauses with the calling context $\hat{C}$ in which they will be executed. Below, we formalize this process as a function: it creates an edge from each predecessor of the call site ($\text{PREDS}(\hat{\eta})$) to a parameter wiring node ($\langle \hat{x}_0 \overset{\hat{\text{Qc}}}{=} \hat{x}_1, \hat{C}' \rangle$), connects that wiring node to the body of the function via a sequence of edges, adds an edge from the body to a return wiring node ($\langle \hat{x}_2 \overset{\hat{\text{Dc}}}{=} \text{RV}(\hat{c}_n), \hat{C}' \rangle$), and then draws edges from that return wiring node to the call site's successors ($\text{SUCCS}(\hat{\eta})$). We delegate the choice of calling context $\hat{C}'$ to the caller of the wiring function.

Definition 6. *Let* $\widehat{\text{WIREFUN}}(\hat{\eta}, \mathtt{fun}\ \hat{x}_0\ \text{->}\ ([\hat{c}_1, \ldots, \hat{c}_n]), \hat{x}_1, \hat{x}_2, \hat{C}') =$

$\quad\text{PREDS}(\hat{\eta}) \ll \langle \hat{x}_0 \overset{\underset{Q\hat{c}}{}}{=} \hat{x}_1, \hat{C}' \rangle \ll \langle \hat{c}_1, \hat{C}' \rangle \ll \ldots \ll \langle \hat{c}_n, \hat{C}' \rangle \ll \langle \hat{x}_2 \overset{\underset{\text{RV}(\hat{c}_n), \hat{C}'}{}}{=}$

$\quad \ll \text{SUCCS}(\hat{\eta})$

where $\hat{\eta} = \langle \hat{c}, \hat{C} \rangle$, $\text{PREDS}(\hat{\eta}) = \{\hat{\eta}' \mid \hat{\eta}' \lll \hat{\eta}\}$, *and* $\text{SUCCS}(\hat{\eta}) = \{\hat{\eta}' \mid \hat{\eta} \lll \hat{\eta}'\}$.

We describe a call site which can be reached via a control flow from the beginning of the program (and therefore must be analyzed) as *active*:

Definition 7. *The predicate* $\widehat{\text{ACTIVE?}}(\hat{\eta}', \hat{G})$ *holds iff path* $\text{START} \ll \hat{\eta}_1 \ll \ldots \ll \hat{\eta}_n \ll \hat{\eta}'$ *appears in* $\hat{G}$ *such that no* $\hat{\eta}_i$ *is of the form* $\langle \hat{x}{=}\hat{x}'\ \hat{x}''\ \hat{\Theta}, \hat{C} \rangle$.

We are now ready to define the closure construction.

CONTEXTUAL APPLICATION

$$\frac{\hat{\eta} = \langle \hat{c}, \hat{C} \rangle \quad \hat{c} = (\hat{x}_1 {=} \hat{x}_2\ \hat{x}_3\ \hat{\Theta}) \quad \widehat{\text{ACTIVE?}}(\hat{\eta}, \hat{G}) \quad \hat{G}, \hat{\eta} \vdash [\hat{x}_2] \rightarrowtail \hat{f}}{\hat{G}, \hat{\eta} \vdash [\hat{x}_3] \rightarrowtail \hat{v} \quad \hat{f} = \mathtt{fun}\ \hat{x}_4\ \text{->}\ (\hat{e}) \quad Q\hat{x}_4 \notin \hat{\Theta} \quad \hat{C}' = \hat{C} \oplus \hat{c}}$$
$$\overline{\hat{G} \Longrightarrow^1 \hat{G} \cup \widehat{\text{WIREFUN}}(\hat{\eta}, \hat{f}, \hat{x}_3, \hat{x}_1, \hat{C}')}$$

ACONTEXTUAL APPLICATION

$$\frac{\hat{\eta} = \langle \hat{c}, \hat{C} \rangle \quad \hat{c} = (\hat{x}_1 {=} \hat{x}_2\ \hat{x}_3\ \hat{\Theta}) \quad \widehat{\text{ACTIVE?}}(\hat{\eta}, \hat{G})}{\hat{G}, \hat{\eta} \vdash [\hat{x}_2] \rightarrowtail \hat{f} \quad \hat{G}, \hat{\eta} \vdash [\hat{x}_3] \rightarrowtail \hat{v} \quad \hat{f} = \mathtt{fun}\ \hat{x}_4\ \text{->}\ (\hat{e}) \quad Q\hat{x}_4 \in \hat{\Theta}}$$
$$\overline{\hat{G} \longrightarrow^1 \hat{G} \cup \widehat{\text{WIREFUN}}(\hat{\eta}, \hat{f}, \hat{x}_3, \hat{x}_1, \hat{C})}$$

Fig. 11. Control flow graph closure construction

Definition 8. *We define* $\hat{G} \Longrightarrow^1 \hat{G}'$ *to be the least relation satisfying the rules in Fig. 11. We write* $\hat{G}_0 \Longrightarrow^* \hat{G}_n$ *to denote* $\hat{G}_0 \Longrightarrow^1 \ldots \Longrightarrow^1 \hat{G}_n$. *We write* $\Longrightarrow^!$ *to denote the transitive closure of* $\Longrightarrow^1$.

To understand the rules in this definition, consider a function-argument pair at a call site. We must select a calling context $\hat{C}$ to ascribe to the call. The rules are otherwise similar: given an active call site for which values can be found for both the function ($\hat{x}_2$) and argument ($\hat{x}_3$), we wire the body of the called function around the call site ($\hat{x}_1$) using the wiring function defined above. The only difference regards $\hat{\Theta}$ and $\hat{C}$. Since the program is alphatized, all function parameters are unique, so we identify each function by its parameter ($\hat{x}_4$). If the parameter appears in a call site annotation in $\hat{\Theta}$, we do *not* polyinstantiate the call site (the Acontextual Application rule); if the parameter *does not* appear in the annotations, then we *do* (the Contextual Application rule).

3.4   Soundness and Decidability

The Plume analysis defined above is both sound and decidable. Here, soundness means that the lookup relation $\hat{G}, \hat{\eta} \vdash \hat{X} \rightarrowtail \hat{v}$ is always an over-approximation: if a value can exist at runtime, then the lookup relation holds for its abstract counterpart. Soundness is demonstrated in Appendix C.1 in the supplemental material [8] in two parts: first by showing the operational semantics in Appendix B in the supplemental material [8] equivalent to a *graph-based* operational semantics and then by showing the Plume analysis to be an abstraction of the latter. Decidability proceeds by upper bounding the size of the CCFG and then by a counting argument. This proof appears in Appendix C.2 in the supplemental material [8].

4   Evaluation of Precision

In this section, we evaluate the precision of the analysis techniques presented in this paper. We perform this evaluation in three parts:

1. We directly compare Plume to DDPA, a closely-related functional analysis.
2. We compare the context models Σ_k and Σ_{Set} and evaluate the precision impact of selective polyinstantiation. We do so via a reproducability experiment involving multiple functional analyses.
3. We consider another state-of-the-art analysis technique—synchronized pushdown systems [34]—and discuss how it may apply to functional programs.

All higher-order program analyses evaluated in this section are available as supplementary material associated with this submission.

4.1 kPlume $\geq$ kDDPA

DDPA [6], like Plume, is a demand-driven higher-order functional program analysis. Both analyses iteratively construct a CFG and use on-demand lookups rather than explicit value stores. Unlike Plume, DDPA uses an *acontextual* control flow graph (ACFG); calling contexts are represented as an extra parameter in lookup. The ACFG in DDPA is much smaller than the CCFG of Plume, but (1) the graph closure rules of DDPA perform all lookups irrespective of context and (2) the caching structures necessary to make DDPA efficient are of the same size complexity as Plume's CCFG.

Like Plume, DDPA is parametric in its context model, but DDPA is more restrictive and cannot support Σ_{Set}. With list-based models, the analyses are directly comparable and kPlume is *more precise* than kDDPA. Formally,

Theorem 1. *For any program $\hat{e}$ and any natural number k, let $\dot{G}$ be the ACFG produced for $\hat{e}$ by kDDPA and let $\hat{G}$ be the CCFG produced for $\hat{e}$ by kPlume. Then, for any variable $\hat{x}$ and program point $\hat{c}$ in e, every value produced by lookup on $\hat{G}$ in kPlume is also produced by lookup on $\dot{G}$ in kDDPA.*

For space, the proof of this Theorem appears in Appendix C.3 in the supplemental material [8]. As kPlume subsumes kDDPA, we elide kDDPA from the remainder of this discussion.

4.2   Comparing Context Models

We now focus not on Plume or any one analysis but instead upon the effect that context models and selective polyinstantiation have on functional program analyses in general. We cannot simply compare two analyses: it would be unclear how the choice of analysis affected the result. We cannot even do so while holding the rest of the analysis theory constant (e.g. comparing kPlume vs. SetPlume) as the results may only pertain to the theory in question (e.g. Plume).

To draw conclusions about context sensitivity models independent of the program analysis, we examine the *reproducibility* of changes as the program analysis itself is varied. We compare pairs of program analysis from a variety of analysis families; each analysis in a pair differs from its counterpart only by context sensitivity model, while each pair differs from the other pairs significantly. We contend that, if changing the context sensitivity model of an analysis produces an effect which is consistent across all pairs, it is reasonable to ascribe this effect to the context model rather than to the program analyses. This conclusion is more reliable the larger the differences are between the analysis families. We therefore conduct our experiments on the following families of program analyses:

- Plume, the demand-driven functional program analysis family in this paper.
- ADI, a state-of-the-art forward functional program analysis family [4].
- mADI, a modification of [4] using techniques from mCFA [24] to more closely match object-oriented program analysis behavior.

We chose ADI to represent a series of higher-order program analyses that include P4F [12], AAC [19], PDCFA [18], CFA2 [39], and others. ADI is the most recent of the series and its precision is the state-of-the-art. ADI's reference implementation does not include a notion of context sensitivity so, for these experiments, we use a purpose-built implementation of ADI over the same ANF language used by Plume. This artifact yields two analyses, kADI and SetADI, with context sensitivity models identical to kPlume and SetPlume.

We also modified ADI to produce an analysis family called mADI that models the precision of object-oriented CFA-based analyses [24]. The main distinction is in how non-local variables are handled when constructing a closure: ADI stores a reference to the non-local while mADI stores a fresh copy of its value. As a result, mADI is *less precise* than ADI but *more performant*. mADI is to ADI what mCFA [24] is to kCFA. Just as with ADI, we define two variants of mADI with different context models: kmADI uses Σ_k and SetmADI uses $\Sigma_{\mathtt{Set}}$. (Note that the ADI paper [4] only used a list model).

Functional Test Cases. Presently, no standard suite of functional precision benchmarks exist. For this experiment, we developed a series of small programs which are representative of common functional programming patterns:

- **rec-ident**, two calls to a recursive identity function. This function recurses, decrementing a counter to zero, and then returns its argument. It is called once with an integer and again with a boolean.

- **list-2map**, which generates an integer list in a loop and then maps over that list twice. The first mapper is (+1); the second mapper is (==0).
- **nest-pairmap**, which uses a homogeneous pair mapping function to increment the elements of a pair (as in: pairmap (pairmap inc)((0,1), (1,0))) or to convert them to boolean values.
- **foldl-2L2F**, which performs two left folds on two distinct lists. The first list (of integers) is summed; the second list (of booleans) is "and-ed".
- **foldl-2L1F**, which generates the same lists as foldl-2L2F using a single mapping function with case analysis.
- **foldl-1L2F**, which folds over a single list of integers twice. The first fold sums the list; the second fold produces true iff the list contains no zeroes.

Each of the tests above calls a function on two types of primitive data: integers and booleans. For each of the above programs, we ran each analysis both with selective polyinstantiation annotations and without them. (k-limited analyses without selective polyinstantiation are presented here for completeness but are not representative of the state of the art.) A test passes if the analysis can distinguish integers from booleans in every case.

For analyses not using k-cutoff models, we indicate whether the test passed (denoted ✓) or failed (denoted ✗) by the above criteria. For analyses using k-cutoff models, we give the minimum value of k necessary for the test to pass (or ✗ if no such k exists). In real programs, the two function calls to be distinguished do not necessarily appear side by side. To simulate this, we η-converted the two call sites some number of times d; thus, d appears in the results in places where the number of η conversions affects the choice of k.

Analysis	kPlume		SetPlume		kADI		SetADI		kmADI		SetmADI		Boomerang	Bmg. SPDS
Annot.?	yes	no	yes	no	yes	no	yes	no	yes	no	yes	no	n/a	n/a
rec-ident	$1+d$	✗	✓	✓	$1+d$	✗	✓	✓	$1+d$	✗	✓	✓	✓	✓
list-2map	$2+d$	✗	✓	✓	$2+d$	✗	✓	✓	$2+d$	✗	✓	✓	✓	✗
nest-pairmap	$3+d$	$3+d$	✗	✗	$3+d$	$3+d$	✗	✗	$3+d$	$3+d$	✗	✗	✗	✗
foldl-2L2F	$2+d$	✗	✓	✓	$2+d$	✗	✓	✓	$2+d$	✗	✓	✓	✓	✗
foldl-2L1F	$2+d$	✗	✓	✓	$2+d$	✗	✓	✓	$2+d$	✗	✓	✓	✓	✗
foldl-1L2F	$2+d$	✗	✓	✓	$2+d$	✗	✓	✓	$2+d$	✗	✓	✓	✓	✗

Fig. 12. Precision of analyses on functional test cases

Functional Test Results. The results of our experiments appear in Fig. 12. (Note that Boomerang and Boomerang SPDS analyses are not list-vs-set and are discussed below.) Some clear patterns emerge from these results.

First and foremost: the differences between the Σ_k and Σ_{Set} context models are reproducible across all three analysis families. Each family's four-column group is identical. This degree of similarity suggests that the change in behavior is, in fact, due to the context model.

Second: selective polyinstantiation had no impact on the precision of Σ_{Set}. This is intuitive as these functions do not exhibit polymorphic recursion. In agreement with previous work [16], selective polyinstantiation *improved* the Σ_k analyses. This is because Σ_k may lose information on polyinstantiation; Σ_{Set} does not.

Third: Σ_{Set} fails on `nest-pairmap`. In this example, Σ_k required three call sites worth of context: one for the outer `pairmap` call, one for the inner `pairmap` call (which served as the outer call's mapping function), and one to call the element mapping function itself. Because this test was not recursive, no annotations were present. Σ_{Set} failed on this example because it conflated the calls to the two mappers (the inner `pairmap` function and the element mapper), as they occurred at the same call site (within `pairmap` itself). Σ_k succeeded here because it admits duplicate call sites in its contexts.

In conclusion, the precisions of Σ_{Set} and Σ_k are incomparable: each has advantages over the other. Σ_{Set} succeeds unconditionally in most cases; selective polyinstantiation merely improves performance. Σ_k without selective polyinstantiation unsurprisingly fails in all recursive cases; with selective polyinstantiation, it succeeds on every case (including `pairmap`). But annotated Σ_k is still fragile because k must be large enough to accommodate d, the number of polyinstantiations between the two calls' nearest ancestor, which cannot be determined at analysis time.

4.3   Synchronized Pushdown Systems

Two types of precision are key to higher-order program analyses: context sensitivity (specifically with respect to interprocedural control flow) and so-called "field sensitivity" or "structure-transmitted data dependence" (such as which values were stored in a particular record or object field). Any analysis with perfect precision in both of these forms is known to be undecidable [29], so program analyses must decide which concessions to make. In SetPlume, for instance, context sensitivity is approximated with a set while field sensitivity is handled by the variable lookup stack $\hat{X}$, which is represented by the stack of a pushdown automaton in our implementation and not approximated.

Boomerang SPDS [34] uses a *synchronized pushdown system*: both context and field sensitivity are represented without approximation but in separate pushdown automata. Boomerang SPDS's separation of these concerns showed promise but functional programs rely upon the interplay between control and data flow, so we chose to run the examples from the previous section on these two analyses to investigate their precision on common functional-style code.

The Boomerang analysis family artifacts perform analysis of at-scale Java programs and not our ANF grammar, so we translated each of our examples by hand. These translations attempt to preserve the control flow of the original program while minimizing the number of program points introduced.

Our results from running these experiments appears in the rightmost two columns of Fig. 12 above. The original Boomerang analysis bears a striking resemblance to the behavior of set-based context models on these examples. Boomerang SPDS, on the other hand, failed on every example except for rec-ident. This is unsurprising in retrospect: Boomerang SPDS intentionally disregards interactions between interprocedural calls and structured data flow.

This interaction does not appear in rec-ident (as there is no structured data) but is critical in every other example; indeed, that type of interaction is common in functional programs and in related higher-order object-oriented design patterns such as the Visitor Pattern. Contrary to suppositions in the SPDS paper [34], these results suggest that the SPDS technique is *not* appropriate for higher-order programming patterns in functional languages.

4.4   Threats to Validity

Test Cases. There does not presently exist a standard functional test suite for analysis precision. The test cases presented here represent common functional programming patterns but are not numerous or complete.

Translations. The conclusions regarding the Boomerang family of analyses rely upon translations of functional programming idioms to Java. We only make claims regarding the Boomerang analysis technique with respect to existing functional programming languages and not with respect to the object-oriented languages for which those analyses were designed.

5   Summary of Performance

We subjected the analysis techniques in this paper to two forms of preliminary performance experiments: one which used typical functional microbenchmarks from previous work [12] and another which used pumped versions of pathological patterns to simulate use at scale. We leave experiments on programs from the wild to future work. The details of these experiments appear in Appendix D in the supplemental material [8] for reasons of space; we summarize them here.

We applied each of SetPlume, kPlume, P4F [12], and Boomerang SPDS to each microbenchmark; kPlume is most similar to SetPlume and so most directly demonstrates the impact of Σ_{Set}. P4F and Boomerang SPDS are recent state-of-the-art analyses. We used P4F in lieu of 1ADI as they are theoretically similar and the P4F artifact has been used in previously published benchmarks.

SetPlume performs comparably or favorably to the other analyses in the microbenchmarks and pumped examples with one significant exception: a regular expression matching program. This program makes use of continuation passing, effectively hiding self-reference from our annotator and thus preventing selective polyinstantiation from occurring. In the remaining cases, SetPlume performs well; indeed, in the analysis of a brute-force SAT solving program, SetPlume completes the analysis while both P4F and Boomerang SPDS trigger thirty-minute timeouts. While more thorough and realistic benchmarks remain to be conducted, we conclude that set-based context models with selective polyinstantiation show promise as a practical tradeoff between precision and performance.

6 Related Work

6.1 Context Models

The higher-order program analysis community has long known that, in practice, the widely-used kCFA context model [4,12,18,19,23,33,38,39] is imprecise and slow [39, p.25], issues that have been the biggest impediments in the adoption of higher-order analyses. The closest to a systematic study of context models in the higher-order analysis literature is *Allocation Characterizes Polyvariance* [11], but the main intent of that paper is to identify a layer of abstraction between context models (what they call *polyvariance techniques*) and the AAM [38] underlying analysis technique; the paper is not concerned with *evaluating* the context models empirically to determine how tractable they are in practice.

Object-oriented analysis research has explored the choice of context model further. Recent efforts have explored how to avoid polyinstantiation [16,37] and how to vary polyvariance models within a singe analysis run [17,21,22]. These analyses are still brittle in a way, as polyinstantiating a saturated context still loses information. However, they preserve the ordered property of k-cutoff models and so can often correctly handle the `pairmap` example in Sect. 4.2.

Other context models have been explored for object-oriented analyses, both in theory [2] and in practice [3,20,25]. The experiments in these papers confirm the weaknesses of the k-limited context models and point at better alternatives, including a context model based on the arguments of a method call (the *Cartesian Product Algorithm* [1]), and a context model based on the object whose method is called (termed *object sensitivity* [25]).

mCFA [24] simulates running kCFA in an object-oriented program. mCFA inspired the mADI analysis we used in our evaluation (Sect. 4).

To the best of our knowledge the set-based context model introduced in this paper is novel in the literature of both higher-order and object-oriented analysis.

6.2 Selective Polyinstantiation

As mentioned in Sect. 2.4, selective polyinstantiation is most similar to context tunneling [16]. It also bears some resemblance to *Polymorphic Splitting* [40]. Both selective polyinstantiation and polymorphic splitting involve annotating the analyzed program to direct decisions on polymorphism. In selective polyinstantiation, the annotations occur at *call sites* and indicate functions for which the analysis *should not* be polymorphic. In polymorphic splitting, by contrast, the annotations occur at function *definitions* and indicate where the analysis *should* be polymorphic. The selective polyinstantiation technique prevents building spurious contexts and can be adapted to other underlying analysis techniques. Polymorphic splitting is an analysis technique in and of itself.

6.3   Analysis Techniques

DDPA. DDPA [6] is an ancestor of Plume. The difference between Plume and DDPA is in how they handle context: Plumes' context is stored in the CCFG while DDPA's context is reconstructed during lookup. This has two consequences. First, all Plume lookups include context, making Plume more precise than DDPA (Sect. 4.1). Second, because Plume does not reconstruct contexts, it is more permissive than DDPA and allows set-based models to be defined.

Demand CFA. Beyond DDPA, the technique closest to Plume is Demand CFA [10]. Plume has the advantage of context sensitivity while Demand CFA does not. However, Plume builds a full CCFG to answer localized lookups; Demand CFA may need to construct only a small part of the CFG for some lookups.

Other Higher-Order Analysis Techniques. Unlike most other higher-order analysis techniques [4,12,18,19,23,24,33,38,39], Plume does not maintain an abstraction of the heap (sometimes also called a *store* elsewhere in the literature); Plume reconstructs only the relevant parts of the heap on demand with a lookup function over the CFG. Some other higher-order analysis techniques feature something called a *pushdown abstraction*, which yields perfect call–return alignment [12,18,19,39] (though not perfect context sensitivity), but Plume only aligns calls and returns up to the precision of its context model.

Boomerang. The Boomerang family of analyses consists of two object-oriented alias analyses for Java: the original Boomerang [35] and the recently-defined "synchronized pushdown system" variant [34] called Boomerang SPDS. These analyses do not model context sensitivity using a model of the form Σ. The Boomerang analysis computes control flow in tandem with IFDS [30] and uses additional iterations to address non-distributive flow problems; Boomerang SPDS instead models control flow using a pushdown system which is intentionally separated from the modeling of field-sensitive data flow. The SPDS technique is not specific to Boomerang; it has been applied to the IDEal taint analysis [36] and has shown promise as a performance improvement there. All evaluations of these theories prior to this paper have been on traditional object-oriented code.

Other Object-Oriented Analysis Techniques. The idea of reconstructing the heap on demand was inspired by first-order demand-driven CFL-reachability analyses [30], and DDPA was the first analysis to bring this technique to a higher-order setting. The primary challenge of that setting is the interdependence between control-flow and data-flow: no CFG is available a priori and so one must be built as the analysis proceeds. Another challenge is lookup of closure-captured variables: previous attempts to bring the technique to a higher-order setting [9] lost precision in those cases, but Plume and DDPA are both able to preserve precision by performing a series of subordinate lookups.

Recent analyses based on linear conjunctive language (LCL) reachability [41] bear some resemblance to Plume in that they reduce lookup to an automaton reachability question. While Plume is related to CFL reachability analyses [30], this recent work reduces to the undecidable problem of LCL reachability and then uses a computable approximation algorithm. Both classes of analysis approach context- and field-sensitivity as an approximation of reachability on a two-stack pushdown automaton; one avenue of future work is to determine if LCL reachability can be applied to Plume-style analyses.

7   Conclusions

This paper introduced set-based context sensitivity. This addresses the weakness of k-limiting models – that polyinstantiation can cause information loss – without compromising field sensitivity or separating it into a distinct problem. To make set-based models practical, we applied selective polyinstantiation, an adaptation of techniques used in k-limiting model research. This technique prevents recursive functions from triggering the worst case performance of the set-based model.

To demonstrate the viability of these techniques, we have formally defined Plume, a demand-driven higher-order program analysis which supports them, and implemented several analysis artifacts. Our experiments show that, for representative functional examples, several set-based, selectively polyinstantiated analyses are superior in precision to their k-cutoff counterparts. We have also demonstrated that analyses using these techniques yield performance comparable with state-of-the-art analyses on typical functional benchmarks.

References

1. Agesen, O.: The Cartesian product algorithm: simple and precise type inference of parametric polymorphism. In: ECOOP (1995)
2. Besson, F.: CPA beats ∞-CFA. In: Proceedings of the 11th International Workshop on Formal Techniques for Java-like Programs (2009)
3. Bravenboer, M., Smaragdakis, Y.: Strictly declarative specification of sophisticated points-to analyses. In: OOPSLA (2009)
4. Darais, D., Labich, N., Nguyen, P.C., Horn, D.V.: Abstracting definitional interpreters. CoRR (2017)
5. Duesterwald, E., Gupta, R., Soffa, M.L.: A practical framework for demand-driven interprocedural data flow analysis. TOPLAS **19**(6), 992–1030 (1997)
6. Facchinetti, L., Palmer, Z., Smith, S.: Higher-order demand-driven program analysis. TOPLAS **41**, 1–53 (2019)
7. Facchinetti, L., Palmer, Z., Smith, S.F.: Relative store fragments for singleton abstraction. In: Static Analysis (2017)
8. Fachinetti, L., Palmer, Z., Smith, S.F., Wu, K., Yorihiro, A.: Appendices to a set-based context model for program analysis (2020). https://www.cs.swarthmore.edu/~zpalmer/publications/supplemental/aplas2020-supplement.pdf
9. Fähndrich, M., Rehof, J., Das, M.: Scalable context-sensitive flow analysis using instantiation constraints. In: PLDI (2000)
10. Germane, K., McCarthy, J., Adams, M.D., Might, M.: Demand control-flow analysis. In: Enea, C., Piskac, R. (eds.) VMCAI 2019. LNCS, vol. 11388, pp. 226–246. Springer, Cham (2019). https://doi.org/10.1007/978-3-030-11245-5_11
11. Gilray, T., Adams, M.D., Might, M.: Allocation characterizes polyvariance: a unified methodology for polyvariant control-flow analysis. In: ICFP (2016)

12. Gilray, T., Lyde, S., Adams, M.D., Might, M., Van Horn, D.: Pushdown control-flow analysis for free. In: POPL (2016)
13. Heintze, N., Tardieu, O.: Demand-driven pointer analysis. In: PLDI (2001)
14. Henglein, F.: Type inference with polymorphic recursion. TOPLAS **15**(2), 253–289 (1993)
15. Horwitz, S., Reps, T., Sagiv, M.: Demand interprocedural dataflow analysis. In: SIGSOFT (1995)
16. Jeon, M., Jeong, S., Oh, H.: Precise and scalable points-to analysis via data-driven context tunneling. Proc. ACM Program. Lang. **2**(OOPSLA), 29 (2018)
17. Jeong, S., Jeon, M., Cha, S., Oh, H.: Data-driven context-sensitivity for points-to analysis. Proc. ACM Program. Lang. **1**(OOPSLA), 1–28 (2017)
18. Johnson, J.I., Sergey, I., Earl, C., Might, M., Van Horn, D.: Pushdown flow analysis with abstract garbage collection. JFP **24**(2–3), 218–283 (2014)
19. Johnson, J.I., Van Horn, D.: Abstracting abstract control. In: DLS (2014)
20. Lhoták, O., Hendren, L.: Evaluating the benefits of context-sensitive points-to analysis using a BDD-based implementation. TOSEM **18**(1), 31–353 (2008)
21. Li, Y., Tan, T., Møller, A., Smaragdakis, Y.: Precision-guided context sensitivity for pointer analysis. Proc. ACM Program. Lang. **2**(OOPSLA), 141:1–141:29 (2018)
22. Li, Y., Tan, T., Møller, A., Smaragdakis, Y.: Scalability-first pointer analysis with self-tuning context-sensitivity. In: Proceedings of the 2018 26th ACM Joint Meeting on European Software Engineering Conference and Symposium on the Foundations of Software Engineering, ESEC/FSE 2018 (2018)
23. Might, M.: Environment Analysis of Higher-order Languages. Ph.D. thesis (2007)
24. Might, M., Smaragdakis, Y., Van Horn, D.: Resolving and exploiting the k-CFA paradox: illuminating functional vs. object-oriented program analysis. In: PLDI (2010)
25. Milanova, A., Rountev, A., Ryder, B.G.: Parameterized object sensitivity for points-to analysis for Java. TOSEM **14**(1), 1–41 (2005)
26. Okhotin, A.: Conjunctive grammars. J. Autom. Lang. Comb. **6**, 519–535 (2001)
27. Rehof, J., Fähndrich, M.: Type-base flow analysis: from polymorphic subtyping to CFL-reachability. In: POPL (2001)
28. Reps, T.: Shape analysis as a generalized path problem. In: PEPM (1995)
29. Reps, T.: Undecidability of context-sensitive data-dependence analysis. TOPLAS **22**(1), 162–186 (2000)
30. Reps, T., Horwitz, S., Sagiv, M.: Precise interprocedural dataflow analysis via graph reachability. In: POPL (1995)
31. Reps, T.W.: Demand interprocedural program analysis using logic databases. In: Ramakrishnan, R. (ed.) Applications of Logic Databases. SECS, vol. 296, pp. 163–196. Springer, Boston (1995). https://doi.org/10.1007/978-1-4615-2207-2_8
32. Saha, D., Ramakrishnan, C.R.: Incremental and demand-driven points-to analysis using logic programming. In: PPDP (2005)
33. Shivers, O.G.: Control-flow Analysis of Higher-order Languages. Ph.D. thesis, uMI Order No. GAX91-26964 (1991)
34. Späth, J., Ali, K., Bodden, E.: Context-, flow-, and field-sensitive data-flow analysis using synchronized pushdown systems. Proc. ACM Program. Lang. **3**(POPL), 1–29 (2019)
35. Späth, J., Do, L.N.Q., Ali, K., Bodden, E.: Boomerang: demand-driven flow- and context-sensitive pointer analysis for Java. In: ECOOP (2016)
36. Späth, J., Ali, K., Bodden, E.: Ideal: efficient and precise alias-aware data-flow analysis. PACMPL **1**(OOPSLA), 1–27 (2017)

37. Tan, T., Li, Y., Xue, J.: Making k-object-sensitive pointer analysis more precise with still k-limiting. In: Rival, X. (ed.) SAS 2016. LNCS, vol. 9837, pp. 489–510. Springer, Heidelberg (2016). https://doi.org/10.1007/978-3-662-53413-7_24
38. Van Horn, D., Might, M.: Abstracting abstract machines. In: ICFP (2010)
39. Vardoulakis, D., Shivers, O.: CFA2: a context-free approach to control-flow analysis. In: Gordon, A.D. (ed.) ESOP 2010. LNCS, vol. 6012, pp. 570–589. Springer, Heidelberg (2010). https://doi.org/10.1007/978-3-642-11957-6_30
40. Wright, A.K., Jagannathan, S.: Polymorphic splitting: an effective polyvariant flow analysis. TOPLAS **20**(1), 166–207 (1998)
41. Zhang, Q., Su, Z.: Context-sensitive data-dependence analysis via linear conjunctive language reachability. In: POPL (2017)

Declarative Stream Runtime Verification (hLola)

Martín Ceresa[1], Felipe Gorostiaga[1,2,3]($\boxtimes$), and César Sánchez[2]

[1] CIFASIS, Rosario, Argentina
[2] IMDEA Software Institute, Pozuelo de Alarcón, Spain
felipe.gorostiaga@imdea.org
[3] Universidad Politécnica de Madrid, Madrid, Spain

Abstract. Stream Runtime Verification (SRV) is a formal dynamic analysis technique that generalizes runtime verification algorithms from temporal logics like LTL to stream monitoring, allowing the computation of richer verdicts than Booleans (quantitative values or even arbitrary data). The core of SRV algorithms is a clean separation between temporal dependencies and data computations. In spite of this theoretical separation previous engines include ad-hoc implementations of just a few data types, requiring complex changes in the tools to incorporate new data types.

In this paper we present a solution as a Haskell embedded domain specific language that is easily extensible to arbitrary data types. The solution is enabled by a technique, which we call *lift deep embedding*, that consists in borrowing general Haskell types and embedding them transparently into an eDSL. This allows for example the use of higher-order functions to implement static stream parametrization. We describe the Haskell implementation called HLOLA and illustrate simple extensions implemented using libraries, which would require long and error-prone additions in other ad-hoc SRV formalisms.

1 Introduction

In this paper we study the problem of implementing a truly generic Stream Runtime Verification (SRV) engine, and show a solution using an embedded domain specific language (eDSL) based on borrowing very general types from the host language into the SRV language and then applying a deep embedding.

Runtime Verification (RV) [2,20,26] is an area of formal methods for reactive systems that analyses dynamically one trace of the system at a time. Compared to static techniques like model checking [8] RV sacrifices completeness to obtain an applicable and formal extension of testing and debugging. Monitors are generated from formal specifications which then inspect a single trace of execution

This work was funded in part by Madrid Regional Government project "S2018/TCS-4339 (BLOQUES-CM)" and by Spanish National Project "BOSCO (PGC2018-102210-B-100)".

© Springer Nature Switzerland AG 2020
B. C. d. S. Oliveira (Ed.): APLAS 2020, LNCS 12470, pp. 25–43, 2020.
https://doi.org/10.1007/978-3-030-64437-6_2

at a time. Early RV languages were based on logics like LTL [27] or past LTL adapted for finite paths [3,12,21]. Other approaches followed, based on regular expressions [36], rule based languages [1], or rewriting [34]. These specification languages come from static verification, where decidability is key to obtain algorithmic solutions to decision problems like model checking. Therefore, the observations and verdicts are typically Boolean values.

Stream Runtime Verification [10,35] starts from the observation that most monitoring algorithms for logics from static verification can be generalized to richer observations and outcomes (verdicts), by generalizing the datatypes of the individual internal operations of the monitors. Languages for SRV, pioneered by LOLA [10], describe monitors declaratively via equations that relate streams of input and streams of output, offering a clean separation between the time dependencies and the concrete operations. The temporal part is a sequence of operations on abstract data, mimicking the steps of the algorithms for temporal logics. Each individual operation can then be performed on a datatype implementation, obtaining monitors for arbitrary data. Offset expressions allow us to refer to stream values in different moments of time, including future instants (that is, SRV monitors need not be causal).

Most previous SRV developments [9,16,18,25] focus on efficiently implementing the temporal engine, promising that the clean separation between time and data allows incorporating off-the-shelf datatypes easily. However, in practice, adding a new datatype requires modifying the parser, the internal representation, and the runtime system that keeps track of offset expressions and partially evaluated expressions. Consequently, these tools only support a limited hard-wired collection of datatypes. In this paper, we give a general solution to this problem via a Haskell eDSL, resulting in the language HLOLA[1], whose engine implements a generic SRV monitoring algorithm that works for general datatypes.

Typically, a DSL is designed as a complete language, first defining the types and terms of the language (this is, the underlying theory), which is then implemented—either as an eDSL or as a standalone DSL—, potentially mapping the types of the DSL into types of the host. However, our intention with HLOLA is to have a language where datatypes are not decided upfront but can be added on demand without requiring any re-implementation. For this reason, HLOLA borrows (almost) arbitrary types from the host system and then embeds all these borrowed types, so HLOLA is agnostic from the stream types (even types added in the future). Even though this technique has been somewhat part of the folklore of modern Haskell based eDSLs (e.g. [40]), this is a novel approach to build runtime verification engines. We called this technique a *lift deep embedding*, which consists of (1) lifting the types and values of the host language into the generic DSL using generic programming, and (2) deep embedding the resulting concrete DSL into the host language. This technique allows us to incorporate Haskell datatypes into HLOLA, and enables the use of many features from the host language in the DSL. For example, we use higher-order functions to describe transformations that produce stream

---

[1] Available open source at http://github.com/imdea-software/hlola.

declarations from stream declarations, obtaining static parameterization for free. In turn, libraries collect these transformers, which allows defining in a few lines new logics like LTL, MTL, etc. or quantitative semantics for these logics. Haskell type-classes allow us to implement *simplifiers* which can compute the value of an expression without resolving all its sub-expressions first. If the unevaluated sub-expressions contain future offset references, the engine may anticipate verdicts ahead of time. Implementing many of these in previous SRV systems has required to re-invent and implement features manually (like macro expansions or ad-hoc parameterization). We use polymorphism both for genericity (to simplify the engine construction) and to enable the description of generic stream specifications, which, again, is not allowed by previous SRV engines. Finally, we also exploit features present in Haskell to offer IO for many stream datatypes for free.

Related Work. SRV was pioneered by LOLA [10] for monitoring synchronous systems only supporting Integers and Booleans. Copilot [31] is a Haskell implementation that offers a collection of building blocks to transform streams into other streams, but Copilot does not offer explicit time accesses (and in particular future accesses). LOLA 2.0 [16] extends LOLA with special constructs for runtime parameterization and real-time features. TeSSLa [9] and Striver [18] are two modern SRV approaches that target real-time event streams. All these languages still support only limited hard-wired datatypes.

RV and SRV overlap with other areas of research. Synchronous languages –like Esterel [5] or Lustre [19]– are based on data-flow. These languages force causality because their intention is to describe systems and not observations or monitors, while SRV removes the causality assumption allowing the reference to future values. In Functional Reactive Programming (FRP) [13] reactive behaviors are defined using the building blocks of functional programming. An FRP program describes a step of computation, a reaction when new input values (events) are available, thus providing implicitly the dependency of the output streams at the current point from input streams values. Again, the main difference is that FRP programs do not allow explicit time references and that the dependencies are causal (after all, FRP is a programming paradigm). In comparison, FRP allows immediately all the features of the programming language without needing the solution proposed in this paper. It would be interesting to study the opposite direction that we solve in this paper: how to equip FRP with explicit times and non-causal future references. Also, FRP does not typically target resource calculation, while this is a main concern in RV (and in SRV).

Contributions. In summary, the contributions of the paper are: (1) An implementation of SRV, called HLOLA, based on an eDSL that exploits advanced features of Haskell to build a generic engine. A main novelty of HLOLA as an SRV implementation is the use of a lift deep embedding to gain very general types without costly implementations. Section 3 describes the runtime system of HLOLA. (2) An implementation of many existing RV specification languages (including LTL, MT-LTL and MTL) in HLOLA, which illustrates the simplicity of extending the language. This is shown in Sect. 4. (3) A brief empirical evaluation, which suggests that the HLOLA engine executes using only the theoretically predicted resources, shown in Sect. 5.

2 Preliminaries

We briefly introduce SRV using LOLA (see [35]) and then present the features of Haskell as a host language that we use to implement HLOLA.

2.1 Stream Runtime Verification: Lola

Intuitively speaking, LOLA is a specification language and a monitoring algorithm for synchronous systems. LOLA programs describe monitors by expressing, in a declarative manner, the relation between output streams and input streams. Streams are finite sequences of values, for example, a Boolean stream is a sequence of Boolean values. The main idea of SRV is to cleanly separate the temporal dependencies from the data computation.

For the data, monitors are described declaratively by providing one expression for each output stream. Expressions are terms from a multi-sorted first order theory, given by a first-order signature and a first-order structure. A theory is a finite collection of interpreted *sorts* and a finite collection of interpreted function symbols. Sorts are interpreted in the sense that each sort is associated with a *domain*, for example the domain of sort *Bool* is the set of values {*true, false*}. For the purpose of this paper we use sorts and types interchangeably, as we use Haskell types to implement LOLA sorts. Function symbols are interpreted, meaning that f is both (1) a constructor to build terms; and (2) a total function (the interpretation) used to evaluate and obtain values of the domain of the return sort. For example, natural numbers uses two sorts (*Nat* and *Bool*), constant function symbols 0, 1, 2, ... of sort *Nat*, and *True* and *False* of type *Bool*, as well as functions +, *, $\cdots$ *Nat* × *Nat* → *Nat* and predicates <, ⩽, ..., that are symbols that return *Bool*. We assume that our theories include equality, and also that for every sort T there is a ternary function if · then · else · that returns a value of sort T given a Boolean and two arguments of sort T. We use $e : T$ to represent that e has sort T.

Given a set Z of (typed) *stream variables*, *offset expressions* are $v[k, d]$ where v is a stream variable, $d : T$ is a constant and k is an integer number. For example, $x[-1, false]$ is an *Bool* offset expression and $y[+3, 5]$ is a *Nat* offset expression. The intended meaning of $v[k, d]$ is to represent, at time n, the value of the stream v at time $n + k$. The second argument d indicates the default value to be used beyond the time limits. When it is clear from the context, we use v to refer to the offset expression $v[0]$ (that does not need a default value). The set of *stream expressions* over a set of variables Z (denoted $Expr(Z)$) is the smallest set containing Z and all offset expressions of variables of type Z, that is closed under constructor symbols of the theory used. For example $(x[-1, false] \lor x)$ and $(y + y[+3, 5] * 7)$ are stream expressions.

A LOLA *specification* consists of a set $\{s_1, s_2 \ldots\}$ of input stream variables and a set $\{t_1, t_2 \ldots\}$ of output stream variables, and one *defining expression* $t_i = exp_i$ per output variable over the set of input and output streams, including t_i itself.

Example 1. The following is a LOLA specification with input stream variable s : *Bool* and output stream variable *once_s* : *Bool*:

```
input  bool s
output bool once_s = once_s [-1,false] || s
```

This example corresponds to the LTL formula $\diamondsuit s$. The following specification counts how many times s was *True* in the past (toint is the function that returns 0 for *False* and 1 for *True*):

```
output int n_once_s = n_once_s [-1,0] + toint(s)
```

A valuation of a specification associates a stream of length N to each of its stream variables, all of which are of the same length. Given a stream σ_i for each input stream variable s_i and a stream τ_i for each output stream variable t_i in a specification, every expression e can be assigned a stream $[\![e]\!]$ of length N. For every $j = 0 \ldots N - 1$:

- $[\![c]\!](j) = c$ for constants;
- $[\![s_i]\!](j) = \sigma_i(j)$ and $[\![t_i]\!](j) = \tau_i(j)$ for stream variables;
- $[\![f(e_1, \ldots, e_n)]\!](j) = f([\![e_1]\!](j), \ldots, [\![e_n]\!](j))$; and
- $[\![v[k,d]]\!](j) = [\![v]\!](j + k)$ if $0 \leqslant j + k < N$, and $[\![v[k,d]]\!](j) = d$ otherwise.

We say that a valuation is an evaluation model, if $[\![t_i]\!] = [\![e_i]\!]$ for each output variable t_i, that is, if every output stream satisfies its defining equation. The dependency graph is the graph of offset dependencies between variables, and can be used to rule out cycles in specifications to guarantee that every specification has a unique output for every input.

One very important aspect of SRV is its ability to analyze specifications and automatically calculate the necessary resources. A monitor is *trace-length independent* if it operates with an amount of memory (and of processing time per input event) that does not depend on the length of the trace. Many logics admit trace-length independent algorithms for their past fragments, like for example LTL and TLTL [3] and MTL [38]. The notion of *efficient monitorability* in SRV [10,35], defined as the absence of positive (future) cycles in the dependency graph, guarantees a trace-length independent monitor. The dependency graph can also be used to build efficient runtime systems, by determining when a value stream variable is guaranteed to be resolved (the latency) and when a value can be removed because it will no longer be necessary (the back-reference). See [35] for longer formal definitions.

2.2   Haskell as a Host Language for an eDSL

An *embedded Domain Specific Language* [23] (eDSL) is a DSL that can be used as a language by itself, and also as a library in its host programming language. An eDSL inherits the language constructs of its host language and adds domain-specific primitives. In this work we implemented HLOLA as an eDSL in Haskell. In particular, we use Haskell's features as host language to implement static parameterization (see Sect. 3.4), a technique that allows the programmatic definition of specifications. This is used to extend HLOLA to support many temporal logics proposed in RV. Other SRV implementations, in their attempt to offer expressive data theories in a standalone tool, require a long and costly implementation of features that are readily available in higher-order expressive languages like Haskell. Using an eDSL, we can effectively focus our development efforts on the temporal aspects of LOLA.

We describe in the next section the *lift deep embedding*, which allows us to lift Haskell datatypes to LOLA and then to perform a single deep embedding for all lifted datatypes. This technique fulfills the promise of a clean separation of time and data and eases the extensibility to new data theories, while keeping the amount of code at a minimum. Additionally, using eDSLs brings benefits beyond data theories, including leveraging Haskell's parsing, compiling, type-checking, and modularity. The drawback is that specifications have to be compiled with a Haskell compiler, but once a specification is compiled, the resulting binary is agnostic of the fact that an eDSL was used. Therefore, any target platform supported by Haskell can be used as a target of HLOLA. Moreover, improvements in the Haskell compiler and runtime systems will be enjoyed seamlessly, and new features will be ready to be used in HLOLA.

Haskell [28] is a pure statically typed functional programming language that has been reported to be an excellent host language for eDSLs [17]. Functions are values, and function application is written simply as a blank space without parentheses, which helps eDSLs look cleaner. Haskell also allows custom parametric polymorphic datatypes, which eases the definition of new data theories, and enables us to abstract away the types of the streams, effectively allowing the expression of generic specifications.

Haskell's ecosystem provides a plethora of frameworks for generic programming [22]. In particular, our engine implementation uses the *Typeable* class to incorporate new types without modification. However, we do not perform any kind of traversal over generic data, we employ the *Typeable* class as a mechanism to hide concrete types and implement heterogeneous lists. Members of the *Typeable* class have an associated type representation, which can be compared, and therefore employed to define a *Dynamic* datatype (which hides a *Typeable* datatype), and to define a type-safe cast operation. New datatypes developed by the active Haskell community can be incorporated immediately into HLOLA. The datatype members of the *Typeable* class encompass all sorts that are used in practice in SRV.

Haskell is declarative and statically typed, just like LOLA. In LOLA, functions are functions in the mathematical sense, that is, they do not have side effects.

LOLA does not make assumptions about when these functions will be called, and guarantees that a function yields the same result when applied to the same arguments twice. This is aligned with the Haskell purity of (total) functions.

Another feature that improves syntax readability is Haskell type classes, which allows overloading methods. We can redefine functions that are typically native in other languages, such as Boolean operators ($\vee$) and ($\wedge$), and the arithmetic operators ($+$), ($-$) and ($*$), as well as define and use custom infix operators. Such definitions are possible by extensions made by the de-facto Haskell compiler, GHC [29]. Haskell has let-bindings, list comprehensions, anonymous functions, higher-order, and partial function application, all of which improves specification legibility. Finally, HLOLA uses Haskell's module system to allow modular specifications and to build language extensions.

3   Implementation

3.1   Language Design

We model input and output stream variables using:

- *Input Stream* declarations, which model LOLA's input variables simply as a *name*. During evaluation, the engine can look up a name in the environment and fetch the corresponding value at a required time instant.
- *Output Stream* declarations, which model output streams in LOLA. These declarations bind the name of the stream with its *Expression*, which represents the defining expression of a LOLA output stream.

Revisiting the LOLA specification in Example 1, in HLOLA, s will be an *Input Stream* declaration and *once_s* an *Output Stream* declaration.

We seek to represent many theories of interest for RV and to incorporate new ones transparently, so we abstract away concrete types in the eDSL. For example, we want to use the theory of *Boolean* without adding the constructors that a usual deep embedding would require. To accomplish this goal we revisit the very essence of functional programming. Every expression in a functional language—as well as in mathematics—is built from two basic constructions: *values* and *function applications*. Therefore, to implement our SRV engine we use these two constructions, plus two additional stream access primitives to capture offset expressions. The resulting datatype is essentially a de-functionalization [33] of the applicative interface. There is a limitation that some Haskell datatypes cannot be handled due to the use of *Dynamic* and *Typeable*, which we introduce within the engine to get a simple way to implement generic programming while preserving enough structure. However, this is not a practical limitation to represent theories and sorts of interests for monitoring.

We define expressions in Haskell as a parametric datatype *Expr* with a polymorphic argument *domain*. An $e :: Expr\ domain$ represents an expression e over the domain *domain*. The generic *domain* is automatically instantiated at static time by the Haskell compiler, effectively performing the desired lifting of Haskell datatypes to types of the theory in HLOLA. For example, the use of *Expr Int* will make the compiler instantiate *domain* as *Int*. The resulting concrete *Expressions* constitute a typical deeply embedded DSL. We call this two step technique a *lift deep embedding*. This technique avoids defining a constructor for all elements in the data theory, making the incorporation of new types transparent.

Here we present in more detail the *Expr* construction in Haskell. The first two constructors (**Leaf** and **App**) are the *data constructions* of the language, which are aligned with the notions of de-functionalization mentioned above, and allow encoding terms from a LOLA theory seamlessly. The other two constructors (**Now** and (**:@**)) represent the offset expressions:

- The constructor **Leaf** :: *Typeable a* $\Rightarrow$ *a* $\rightarrow$ *Expr a* models an element of the theory.
- The constructor **App** :: (*Typeable a*, *Typeable b*, *Typeable* (*b* $\rightarrow$ *a*)) $\Rightarrow$ *Expr* (*b* $\rightarrow$ *a*) $\rightarrow$ *Expr b* $\rightarrow$ *Expr a* represents the application of a *function Expression* to a *value Expression*.
- A term **Now** :: *Stream a* $\rightarrow$ *Expr a* represents the value of a stream in the current instant.
- The *at* infix constructor, (**:@**) :: *Stream a* $\rightarrow$ (*Int*, *Expr a*) $\rightarrow$ *Expr a* models future and past offset expressions, specifying the default value to use if the access falls off the trace

These constructions allow us to lift operations from domain values to *Expressions* directly. For example, we can create an *Expression* that represents the sum of two *Expr Int* without defining a dedicated type of *Expression*.

Similarly, we define the *Stream* declarations in Haskell as a parametric datatype *Stream* with a polymorphic argument *domain*.

- The **Input** :: (*FromJSON a*, *Read a*, *Typeable a*) $\Rightarrow$ *String* $\rightarrow$ *Stream a* constructor represents an input stream, and associates the name of the stream to the type of its values.
- The **Output** :: *Typeable a* $\Rightarrow$ (*String*, *Expr a*) $\rightarrow$ *Stream a* constructor represents an output stream, and associates the name of the stream to the type of its values and its defining *Expression*, of the same type.

The LOLA specification from Example 1 can be written in HLOLA as follows:

```
once_s :: Stream Bool
once_s = Output ("once_s", App (App (Leaf (∨)) prevOnce_s) (Now s))
   where s = Input "s"
         prevOnce_s = once_s :@ (−1, False)
```

The expression of *once_s* takes the application of the (data theory) function ($\vee$) to the value of *once_s* at -1, using *False* as the default value, and applying the result to the current value of *s*. We define the infix operator (**=:**) that builds an output stream from a name and an expression, and override the Boolean operator $\vee$; and the HLOLA *Output Stream* declaration looks almost like a LOLA expression:

$$once\_s = \texttt{"once\_s"} =: once\_s :@ (-1, \textit{False}) \vee \textbf{Now}\ s$$

3.2 Static Analysis

Not every grammatically correct LOLA specification is valid. Some errors like syntactic errors, missing references and type mismatches can be checked by the Haskell compiler. But to guarantee that a specification is well-defined we also need to examine the dependency graph to check that it does not contain closed paths of weight zero. This will ensure that the value of a stream at any point does not depend on itself. We first convert every *Expression a* and *Stream a* to their equivalent *Expression* and *Stream* declaration of *Dynamic*, so *Stream* declarations and *Expressions* of different types can be mixed and used in the same specification. Then we obtain the dependency graph by traversing the stream definitions in the specification recursively. One drawback of this approach is that the Haskell type-system can no longer track the original type of an expression, but this step is made after Haskell has type-checked the specification, guaranteeing that the engine is forgetting the type information of a well-typed specification. The engine keeps the information on how to parse the input streams and how to show output values given a stream name, safely casting from and into *Dynamic*, and avoiding type mismatches when converting from dynamically-typed objects. We make the following claim:

Claim. Every conversion from a Dynamic *Expression* within the HLOLA engine returns a value *Expression* of the expected type.

The proof of this claim can be done using Liquid Haskell [39] and is ongoing research beyond the scope of this paper. Assuming the claim above, a runtime type error can only be produced when processing an input event whose value is not of the expected type.

During this stage, the tool also calculates the minimum weight of the paths in the dependency graph, a non-positive value that we call *minimum back reference* and note *minBackRef*, along with the maximum weight of the edges, which we call *latency* and note *maxLatency*. The dependency graph of the specification in Example 1 is shown on the right. The *minBackRef* is -1, because *once_s* depends on the previous value of itself, and the *maxLatency* is 0 because there are no references to future values of streams. The values of *minBackRef* and *maxLatency* indicate that the engine will only keep the values of the streams at the present and previous instants.

3.3 Runtime System

We now describe some key internal datatypes used in the implementation of the execution engine. An *Instant* is a map that binds the name of a stream to an

Expression. Given a specification with m streams $s_1, \ldots, s_m$, an *Instant* can be interpreted as a vector of size m. A *Sequence* is an ordered collection of *Instants*, one of which is said to be "in focus". The *Instants* in the past of the one in focus are stored in the *Sequence* in an array of size $(maxLatency - minBackRef)$, which limits the amount of memory that the engine can consume. On the other hand, the *Instants* in the future of the one in focus are stored as a list. Even though this list can be (implicitly) as long as the full trace, the elements in the list will not actually exist in memory until they are needed to compute a value, due to the laziness of Haskell evaluation. We can think of a *Sequence* as a matrix of expressions, where each column is an *Instant* vector, and one of them is in focus. The evaluation of a specification with m streams over n instants is conceptually an $n \times m$ matrix.

Given a specification and a list of values, we first create a *Sequence* with an empty past and the focus on the first instant. In this *Sequence*, the value of the cell (s_i, n) in the *Sequence* matrix for an *input* stream s_i and instant n, is a **Leaf** containing the value read for the stream of s_i at time instant n. Similarly, the value of every *output* stream t_j and instant n is the defining *Expression* for t_j in the specification, waiting to be specialized and evaluated. Note that these values do not actually exist in memory until they are needed. The goal of the engine is to compute a **Leaf** expression (this is, a ground value) at every position in the matrix, particularly for output streams.

Starting from the initial state, the engine will solve every output stream at the instant in focus, and then move the focus one step forward. This algorithm guarantees that all elements in the past of the focus are leaves. The figure on the right illustrates the

$$
\begin{array}{c} \\ s_1 \\ \vdots \\ s_k \\ t_1 \\ \vdots \\ t_m \end{array}
\begin{array}{c} 1 \qquad\qquad 2 \qquad\qquad 3 \quad \ldots \quad n \\
\left(\begin{array}{ccccc}
\textbf{Leaf}_{1,1} & \textbf{Leaf}_{1,2} & \textbf{Leaf}_{1,3} & \ldots & \textbf{Leaf}_{1,n} \\
\vdots & \vdots & \vdots & \ddots & \vdots \\
\textbf{Leaf}_{k,1} & \textbf{Leaf}_{k,2} & \textbf{Leaf}_{k,3} & \ldots & \textbf{Leaf}_{k,n} \\
\textbf{Leaf}_{k+1,1} & \textbf{Leaf}_{k+1,2} & e_{1,3} & \ldots & e_{1,n} \\
\vdots & \vdots & \vdots & \ddots & \vdots \\
\textbf{Leaf}_{k+m,1} & \textbf{Leaf}_{k+m,2} & e_{m,3} & \ldots & e_{m,n}
\end{array} \right) \\
\qquad\qquad\qquad\qquad \triangle
\end{array}
$$

Sequence of an execution at time instant 3, where some of the output expressions $e_{1,3} \ldots e_{m,n}$ can be leaves too. At the end of the execution, the focus will be on the last column of the matrix, and all the elements in the matrix will be leaves.

The output streams will be calculated and output incrementally while new data is retrieved for the input streams. The engine will block when it needs the value of an input stream that has not been provided yet. These characteristics of the Haskell runtime system allow the monitor to run online processing events from the system under analysis on the fly, or offline over dumped traces.

A language that offers means to define new datatypes must not only provide the constructs to define them, but it also must implement the encoding and decoding of custom datatypes. Extensible encoding and decoding of datatypes in the theory is not trivial and might account for a large portion of the codebase. As an eDSL, HLOLA can rely upon Haskell's facilities to define how to encode and decode *Typeable* datatypes, sometimes even automatically from their definitions.

This class encompasses many of the datatypes that are used in practice to encode values (observations and verdicts) when monitoring systems.

Input events are fed to HLOLA in JSON format, where each line is a string representation of a JSON object with one field per input stream. The types of the input streams have to be instances of the *FromJSON* class, meaning that a value of the corresponding type can be constructed from a serialized JSON *Object*. Output streams must be instances of the *ToJSON* class, which means that we can get a JSON *Object* from a value of the corresponding type.

Haskell allows defining custom datatypes via the **data** statement. Once defined, these types can be used just like any other type in Haskell. Most of the times, we can use Haskell's **deriving** mechanism to make our custom types instances of the corresponding classes, if needed. Sect. 4 contains examples of custom datatypes for input values.

3.4 Additional Features

The use of Haskell as a host language eases the implementation of many useful features of SRV in HLOLA. We show here two examples: anticipation and parameterized streams.

Anticipation. Input event streams represent the trace of observations of a system, and output streams encode a property to be evaluated dynamically. The principle of *anticipation*, as presented in [11], states that once every (infinite) continuation of a finite trace leads to the same verdict, then the finite trace can safely evaluate to this verdict. This principle can be trivially implemented when functions know all their arguments, but it is not always possible to anticipate what the output of the function will be when some of the arguments will only be known in the future. Nevertheless, there are cases where a function can be evaluated with just a subset of its arguments. This property of some functions can be used to compute their values as soon as all the relevant information is retrieved, avoiding waiting for input values that are not strictly necessary to evaluate the function. This idea effectively brings us closer to strict anticipation as defined above.

The circumstances under which a function can be computed with missing arguments is data-specific information. Typical SRV implementations provide simplifications for some functions in the covered theories, but do not offer a way to provide new simplifications to their theories. Instead, we provide a framework to keep the simplifications extensible. To allow the use of functions off-the-shelf as well as simplifiable functions, we define a new datatype and a class of which the Haskell function constructor $(\rightarrow)$ is an instance, shown below:

    data *LFunction a b* = *Pure* $(a \rightarrow b)$ | *Simplifier* $(Maybe\ a \rightarrow Maybe\ b)$

    class *ILFunction x* **where** *toLFunction* :: $x\ a\ b \rightarrow LFunction\ a\ b$

    instance *ILFunction* $(\rightarrow)$ **where** *toLFunction* = *Pure*

We then generalize the type of the function application constructor **App** :: *Expression* $(f\ b\ a) \rightarrow Expression\ b \rightarrow Expression\ a$, under the constraint that f be a member of the class *ILFunction*. In this way, users of the eDSL can define their own simplifiable functions using the *Simplifier* constructor, or just use off-the-shelf functions seamlessly; which will automatically be applied the *Pure* constructor by the compiler.

The language is shipped with simplifiers for the Boolean operators $\lor$ and $\land$; as well as the if · then · else · operator and some numeric operators. These simplifiers have great impact in temporal logics with references to the future, where values can often be resolved at an instant with the information retrieved up to that point—without the need to wait until all future values are resolved. We show the simplifiers for the if · then · else · operator in the extended version of the paper [6].

Parameterized Streams. Static parametrization is a feature of some SRV systems which allows instantiating an abstract specification. This is useful to reuse repetitive specifications and capture the essence of a stream definition, abstracting away the specific values. Sect. 4 shows how this feature is used to concisely implement several monitoring languages as libraries in HLOLA. This feature is implemented in Lola2.0 [15] as well as in TeSSLa [9] using an ad-hoc macro feature in the tool chain. Here we show how static parametrization can be obtained directly using Haskell features. Consider again the specification of $\diamondsuit s$ shown in Example 1:

> *once_s* :: *Stream Bool*
> *once_s* = "once_s" =: *once_s* :@ $(-1, False) \lor$ **Now** s

If we want to define a stream to compute $\diamondsuit r$, we would have to define a stream *once_r* whose definition is almost identical to the definition of *once_s*. This leads to code duplication and hard to maintain specifications.

Instead of defining an output stream *once_s* specifically for s, we aim to write a general stream *once* parameterized by a Boolean stream. We can use Haskell as a macro system to programmatically define specifications, effectively implementing static parameterization.

Example 2. The definition of *once* in HLOLA using static parameterization is:

> *once* :: *Stream Bool* $\to$ *Stream Bool*
> *once* s = "once" <: s =: *once* s :@ $(-1, False) \lor$ **Now** s

Note that we simply abstracted away the occurrences of s. To avoid name clashes among different instantiations of *once*, we concatenate the string "once" with the name of the argument stream s, by using the operator <:. Static parametrization is used extensively to implement libraries as described in the next section.

4   Extensible Libraries in HLola

One of the benefits of implementing an eDSL is that we can reuse the library system of the host language to modularize and organize the code. The Haskell module system allows importing third parties libraries, as well as developing new libraries; HLOLA ships with some predefined theories and stream-specific libraries. In this section we show an overview of the stream-specific libraries.

Past-LTL. The operators of Past-LTL [4] can be described using the LOLA specification language (e.g. ◇ from Example 2). Given two Boolean streams p and q, the Boolean stream p *'since'* q is *True* if q has ever been *True*, and p has been *True* since the last time q became *True*. One can simply **import** *Lib.LTL* and then define streams like: *property = yesterday* (p *'since'* q).

Example 3. We show an example of a Past-LTL property for a sender/receiver model taken from [4]: $\Box(snd.state = waitForAck \rightarrow \ominus\boxminus snd.state \neq waitForAck)$. Using HLOLA, we define a type to represent the possible states of the sender, deriving a *FromJSON* instance to use it as the type of an input stream *sndrState*:

data *SndrState = Get | Send | WaitForAck* **deriving** (*Generic, Read, FromJSON, Eq*)

Then, we define the property as a Boolean output stream:

sndrState :: Stream SndrState
sndrState = **Input** `"senderState"`

sndrNotWaiting :: Stream Bool
sndrNotWaiting = `"sndrNotWaiting"` *=:* **Now** *sndrState /* *==* **Leaf** *WaitForAck*

prop :: Stream Bool
prop = **let** *sndrWaitingAck =* **Now** *sndrState ===* **Leaf** *WaitForAck*
              startedWaiting = yesterday (*historically sndrNotWaiting*)
        in `"prop"` *=: sndrWaitingAck* *'implies'* **Now** *startedWaiting*

MTL. Metric Temporal Logic [24] is an extension of LTL with time constraints that give upper and lower bounds on the temporal intervals. The stream *until* is parameterized by two integers, which are the boundaries of the interval, and two Boolean streams to model the formula $p\,\mathcal{U}_{[a,b]}\,q$. We use recursion to programmatically define the *Expression* of *until*, which will be unfolded at compile time for the dependency graph sanity check. This expansion can be observed in the dependency graph of a specification that uses *until*, for example, *property = until* $(-1,1)$ p q, which checks that a stream p is *True* until q is *True* in the interval $(-1,1)$, which is shown on the right.

In [32], Reinbacher et al. introduce Mission-Time LTL, a projection of LTL for systems which are bounded to a certain mission time. They propose a translation of each LTL operator to its corresponding MTL operator, using $[0, mission_t]$ as the temporal interval, where

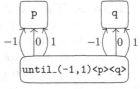

$mission_t$ represents how the duration of the mission. The ability of HLOLA to monitor MTL can be used to monitor Mission-Time LTL through this translation.

Example 4. We show an example of an MTL property taken from [30]: $\Box(alarm \rightarrow (\Diamond_{[0,10]} allclear \lor \Diamond_{[10,10]} shutdown))$.

This property uses MTL to establish deadlines between environment events and the corresponding system responses. In particular, the property assesses that an *alarm* is followed by a *shutdown* event in exactly 10 time units unless *all clear* is sounded first. We consider three Boolean input streams *alarm*, *allclear* and *shutdown*—which indicate if the corresponding event is detected—and define an output stream that captures whether the property holds:

$alarm =$ **Input** `"alarm"` :: *Stream Bool*
$allclear =$ **Input** `"allclear"` :: *Stream Bool*
$shutdown =$ **Input** `"shutdown"` :: *Stream Bool*

prop :: *Stream Bool*
$prop =$ `"prop"` $=:$ **Now** *alarm* '*implies*' **Now** *willClear* $\lor$ **Now** *willShutdown*
    where $willClear = eventually\ (0, 10)\ allclear$
        $willShutdown = eventually\ (10, 10)\ shutdown$

5   Implementation and Empirical Evaluation

The implementation of HLOLA requires no code for the parser and type checker, since it reuses those from the Haskell compiler. The table below shows the number of lines for the full HLOLA implementation.

Language and input		Engine		Syntax		Libraries	
Files: ./	LoC	Files: Engine/	LoC	Files: Syntax/	LoC	Files: Lib/	LoC
DecDyn.hs	87	Engine.hs	176	Booleans.hs	37	LTL.hs	21
InFromFile.hs	51	Focus.hs	39	HLPrelude.hs	3	MTL.hs	29
Lola.hs	62			Num.hs	26	Pinescript.hs	41
StaticAnalysis.hs	78			Ord.hs	18	Utils.hs	13
Total	278	**Total**	215	**Total**	102	**Total**	104

In summary, the core of the tool has 493 lines, while the utils account for 206 lines, giving a total of 699 lines. This compares to the tens of thousands of lines of a parser and runtime system of a typical stand-alone tool. In the rest of this section we summarize how using Haskell enables the use of available tools, and then report on an empirical evaluation of HLOLA.

Haskell Tools. The use of Haskell as a host language allows us to use existing tools to improve HLOLA specifications, such as LiquidHaskell and QuickCheck.

Liquid Haskell [39] enriches the type system with refinement types that allow more precise descriptions of the types of the elements in a Haskell program. In our case we can use Liquid Haskell to express specifications with more precision. For example, we can prevent a specification that adds the last n elements from being used with a negative n:

`{- nsum :: Stream Int -> Nat -> Stream Int -}`
$nsum$ :: *Stream Int* $\rightarrow$ *Int* $\rightarrow$ *Stream Int*
$nsum\ s\ n =$ `"n_sum"` $<:\ s\ <:\ n\ =:\ nsum\ s\ n$:@ $(-1, 0) +$ **Now** $s - s$:@ $(-n, 0)$
Then, given a stream r of type *Stream Int* we can attempt to define a stream s that computes the sum of the last 5 values on stream r as $s = nsum\ r\ 5$.

Running LiquidHaskell with `--no-termination` allows the recursive definition of n over this specification, which yields no error, but running LiquidHaskell on $s' = nsum\ r\ (-1)$ produces a typing error.

QuickCheck [7] is a tool to perform random testing of Haskell programs, which we can easily use for HLOLA specifications. For example, we can assess that the first instant at which a Boolean stream p is *False* is exactly one instant after the last instant at which $\boxminus p$ is *True*, increasing our confidence on the implementation of the Past-LTL $\boxminus$ operator.

Empirical Evaluation. We report now on an empirical evaluation performed to assess whether the engine behaves as theoretically expected in terms of memory usage. The hardware platform over which the experiments were run is a MacBook Pro with MacOS Catalina Version 10.15.4, with an Intel Core i5 at 2,5 GHz and 8 GB of RAM.

The first two *Stream* declarations calculate if an input *Boolean* stream p is periodic with period n. This is a simple, yet interesting property to assess in embedded systems. We specify this property in two different ways. In the first *Stream* declaration, we define a single stream which compares the current value of p with its value n instants before:

$booleanPeriodWidth :: Int \to Stream\ Bool$
$booleanPeriodWidth\ n =$ `"periodic_width"` $=:$ **Now** $p === p :@ (-n, \mathbf{Now}\ p)$

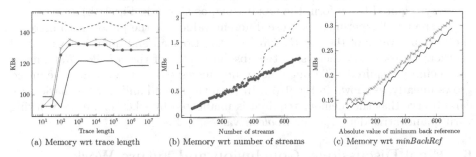

(a) Memory wrt trace length   (b) Memory wrt number of streams   (c) Memory wrt *minBackRef*

Fig. 1. Empirical evaluation

The data of this experiment is represented by the solid, unmarked black curves in Fig. 1 (a) and (c).

In the second *Stream* declaration, we programmatically create $n + 1$ streams *carrier i*, with $i = 0 \ldots n$ defined as a function that compares its argument with the value of p i instants before, which is bound by the partially applied equality function:

$booleanPeriodHeight :: Int \to Stream\ Bool$
$booleanPeriodHeight\ n =$ `"periodic_height"` $=:$ **Now** $(carrier\ n)\ \langle \star \rangle$ **Now** p
   where
      $carrier\ 0 =$ `"carrier_prd"` $<:\ 0 =: (\equiv)\ \langle \$ \rangle$ **Now** p
      $carrier\ n =$ `"carrier_prd"` $<:\ n =: carrier\ (n-1) :@ (-1, \mathbf{Leaf}\ (const\ True))$

The data of this experiment is represented by the solid, circle-marked red curves in Fig. 1 (a) and (b).

We also run a quantitative version of this n-period checker, whose value is 100 at a given instant if p at that instant is equal to the value of p n instants ago; 50 if it is equal to the value of p $n-1$ or $n+1$ instants ago; 25 if it is equal to the value of p $n-2$ or $n+2$ instants ago; and 0 otherwise. Note that this specification has a value closer to 100 when the specification is closer to being periodic, and closer to 0 when the specification is further from being periodic. This example illustrates how HLOLA can be used to define quantitative semantics of temporal logics, which is an active area of research in Runtime Verification. In this case we also define a version with a single stream (represented by the solid, cross-marked brown curves in Fig. 1 (a) and (c)), and a version with auxiliary streams, each of which has an offset of -1 at most (represented by the dashed blue curves in Fig. 1 (a) and (b)).

In the first experiment, we run all four specifications over traces with synthetic inputs of varying length. The results are shown in Fig. 1 (a), which suggest that the memory required is approximately constant, indicating that the memory used is independent of the trace length, and that monitors run in constant space, as theoretically predicted.

In the second experiment, we vary the period n to asses how the number of streams affects the memory usage for both period checkers. The outcome suggests that increasing the number of streams only impacts linearly on the memory required to perform the monitoring, as shown in Fig. 1 (b).

In the third experiment, we use different values for the period n to increase the absolute value of the *minBackRef* for the Boolean and quantitative period checkers to asses how increasing the absolute value of the *minBackRef* affects the memory required. The outcome again suggests that the memory required grows linearly, as shown in Fig. 1 (c). In both the second and third scenarios, we can observe that the memory required is unaffected by whether we are working with quantitative datatypes or *Boolean* values.

6   Final Discussions, Conclusion and Future Work

Final Discussions. One alternative to *Typeable* is to use modular datatypes and evaluators [37]. However, this would break our goal of transparently borrowing datatypes in the lift deep embedding, by forcing HLOLA data sorts to be defined manually as Haskell datatypes.

Resource analysis is a central concern in RV and, in fact, in all real-time and critical systems. For example, aviation regulation forbids the use of runtime environments with garbage collection for critical systems. But this is still an option for soft-critical applications, where HLOLA has successfully been applied to improve mission software of autonomous UAVs [41]. As future work we plan to generate embeddable C code from a restricted version of HLOLA, using the Ivory framework [14] (see Copilot [31]).

An eDSL like HLOLA is a library within the host language, and can be used as a theory within HLOLA reflectively. This feature can greatly simplify writing specifications, used for example to express predictive Kalman filters as in [41] or quantitative semantics of STL and MTL.

Conclusions. We have presented HLOLA, an engine for SRV implemented as a Haskell eDSL. We use the notion of lift deep embedding—folklore in advanced eDSLs (see [40])—in a novel way to fulfill the SRV promise of a clean separation between the temporal engine and the data manipulated, allowing the transparent incorporation of new types. Using Haskell makes readily available features like static parameterization—which allows implementing many logics with Boolean and quantitative semantics—, otherwise programmed in an ad-hoc manner in other SRV tools. The resulting system HLOLA is very concise. A well-known drawback of using an eDSL is that errors are usually cryptic. We are currently working on a front-end restriction of the language that enables better error reporting, while still allowing expert users to use all the advanced features.

Current work includes extending HLOLA to support time-stamped event streams, which allows monitoring real-time event sequences as in [18]. This extension will be to Striver [18] like HLOLA is to LOLA. From the point of view of exploiting Haskell further, future work includes using LiquidHaskell more aggressively to prove properties of specifications and memory bounds, as well as proving formally the claim that our use of *Dynamic* is safe. We are also working on using QuickCheck to generate test traces from specifications and on studying how to use model-based testing to improve the test suites obtained.

References

1. Barringer, H., Goldberg, A., Havelund, K., Sen, K.: Rule-based runtime verification. In: Steffen, B., Levi, G. (eds.) VMCAI 2004. LNCS, vol. 2937, pp. 44–57. Springer, Heidelberg (2004). https://doi.org/10.1007/978-3-540-24622-0_5
2. Bartocci, E., Falcone, Y. (eds.): Lectures on Runtime Verification. LNCS, vol. 10457. Springer, Cham (2018). https://doi.org/10.1007/978-3-319-75632-5
3. Bauer, A., Leucker, M., Schallhart, C.: Runtime verification for LTL and TLTL. ACM Trans. Softw. Eng. Methodol. **20**(4), 14 (2011)
4. Benedetti, M., Cimatti, A.: Bounded model checking for past LTL. In: Garavel, H., Hatcliff, J. (eds.) TACAS 2003. LNCS, vol. 2619, pp. 18–33. Springer, Heidelberg (2003). https://doi.org/10.1007/3-540-36577-X_3
5. Berry, G.: The foundations of Esterel. In: Proof, Language, and Interaction: Essays in Honour of Robin Milner, pp. 425–454. MIT Press (2000)
6. Ceresa, M., Gorostiaga, F., Sanchez, C.: Declarative stream runtime verification (hLola) (2020)
7. Claessen, K., Hughes, J.: QuickCheck: a lightweight tool for random testing of Haskell programs. In: Proceedings of the ICFP 2000, pp. 268–279. ACM (2000)
8. Clarke, E.M., Grunberg, O., Peled, D.A.: Model Checking. MIT Press, Cambridge (1999)
9. Convent, L., Hungerecker, S., Leucker, M., Scheffel, T., Schmitz, M., Thoma, D.: TeSSLa: temporal stream-based specification language. In: Massoni, T., Mousavi, M.R. (eds.) SBMF 2018. LNCS, vol. 11254, pp. 144–162. Springer, Cham (2018). https://doi.org/10.1007/978-3-030-03044-5_10

10. D'Angelo, B., et al.: LOLA: runtime monitoring of synchronous systems. In: Proceedings of the TIME 2005, pp. 166–174. IEEE (2005)
11. Dong, W., Leucker, M., Schallhart, C.: Impartial anticipation in runtime-verification. In: Cha, S.S., Choi, J.-Y., Kim, M., Lee, I., Viswanathan, M. (eds.) ATVA 2008. LNCS, vol. 5311, pp. 386–396. Springer, Heidelberg (2008). https://doi.org/10.1007/978-3-540-88387-6_33
12. Eisner, C., Fisman, D., Havlicek, J., Lustig, Y., McIsaac, A., Van Campenhout, D.: Reasoning with temporal logic on truncated paths. In: Hunt, W.A., Somenzi, F. (eds.) CAV 2003. LNCS, vol. 2725, pp. 27–39. Springer, Heidelberg (2003). https://doi.org/10.1007/978-3-540-45069-6_3
13. Eliot, C., Hudak, P.: Functional reactive animation. In: Proceedings of the ICFP 2007, pp. 163–173. ACM (1997)
14. Elliott, T., et al.: Guilt free ivory. SIGPLAN Not. **50**(12), 189–200 (2015)
15. Faymonville, P., Finkbeiner, B., Schirmer, S., Torfah, H.: A stream-based specification language for network monitoring. In: Falcone, Y., Sánchez, C. (eds.) RV 2016. LNCS, vol. 10012, pp. 152–168. Springer, Cham (2016). https://doi.org/10.1007/978-3-319-46982-9_10
16. Faymonville, P., Finkbeiner, B., Schledjewski, M., Schwenger, M., Stenger, M., Tentrup, L., Torfah, H.: StreamLAB: stream-based monitoring of cyber-physical systems. In: Dillig, I., Tasiran, S. (eds.) CAV 2019. LNCS, vol. 11561, pp. 421–431. Springer, Cham (2019). https://doi.org/10.1007/978-3-030-25540-4_24
17. Gill, A.: Domain-specific languages and code synthesis using Haskell. CACM **57**, 42–49 (2014)
18. Gorostiaga, F., Sánchez, C.: Striver: stream runtime verification for real-time event-streams. In: Colombo, C., Leucker, M. (eds.) RV 2018. LNCS, vol. 11237, pp. 282–298. Springer, Cham (2018). https://doi.org/10.1007/978-3-030-03769-7_16
19. Halbwachs, N., Caspi, P., Pilaud, D., Plaice, J.: LUSTRE: a declarative language for programming synchronous systems. In: Proceedings of the POPL 1987, pp. 178–188. ACM Press (1987)
20. Havelund, K., Goldberg, A.: Verify your runs. In: Meyer, B., Woodcock, J. (eds.) VSTTE 2005. LNCS, vol. 4171, pp. 374–383. Springer, Heidelberg (2008). https://doi.org/10.1007/978-3-540-69149-5_40
21. Havelund, K., Roşu, G.: Synthesizing monitors for safety properties. In: Katoen, J.-P., Stevens, P. (eds.) TACAS 2002. LNCS, vol. 2280, pp. 342–356. Springer, Heidelberg (2002). https://doi.org/10.1007/3-540-46002-0_24
22. Hinze, R., Jeuring, J., Löh, A.: Comparing approaches to generic programming in Haskell. In: Backhouse, R., Gibbons, J., Hinze, R., Jeuring, J. (eds.) SSDGP 2006. LNCS, vol. 4719, pp. 72–149. Springer, Heidelberg (2007). https://doi.org/10.1007/978-3-540-76786-2_2
23. Hudak, P.: Building domain-specific embedded languages. ACM Comput. Surv., **28**(4es) (1996)
24. Koymans, R.: Specifying real-time properties with metric temporal logic. R.-Time Syst. **2**(4), 255–299 (1990)
25. Leucker, M., Sánchez, C., Scheffel, T., Schmitz, M., Schramm, A.: TeSSLa: runtime verification of non-synchronized real-time streams. In: Proceedings of the SAC 2018, pp. 1925–1933. ACM (2018)
26. Leucker, M., Schallhart, C.: A brief account of runtime verification. J. Log. Algebraic Program. **78**(5), 293–303 (2009)
27. Manna, Z., Pnueli, A.: Temporal Verification of Reactive Systems: Safety. Springer, New York (1995). https://doi.org/10.1007/978-1-4612-4222-2

28. Marlow, S.: Haskell language report (2010)
29. Marlow, S., Peyton Jones, S.: The Glasgow Haskell Compiler. Lulu, The Architecture of Open Source Applications, vol. 2, January 2012
30. Ouaknine, J., Worrell, J.: Some recent results in metric temporal logic. In: Cassez, F., Jard, C. (eds.) FORMATS 2008. LNCS, vol. 5215, pp. 1–13. Springer, Heidelberg (2008). https://doi.org/10.1007/978-3-540-85778-5_1
31. Pike, L., Goodloe, A., Morisset, R., Niller, S.: Copilot: a hard real-time runtime monitor. In: Barringer, H., et al. (eds.) RV 2010. LNCS, vol. 6418, pp. 345–359. Springer, Heidelberg (2010). https://doi.org/10.1007/978-3-642-16612-9_26
32. Reinbacher, T., Rozier, K.Y., Schumann, J.: Temporal-logic based runtime observer pairs for system health management of real-time systems. In: Ábrahám, E., Havelund, K. (eds.) TACAS 2014. LNCS, vol. 8413, pp. 357–372. Springer, Heidelberg (2014). https://doi.org/10.1007/978-3-642-54862-8_24
33. Reynolds, J.C.: Definitional interpreters for higher-order programming languages. High. Order Symb. Comput. 11(2), 363–397 (1998)
34. Roşu, G., Havelund, K.: Rewriting-based techniques for runtime verification. Autom. Softw. Eng. 12(2), 151–197 (2005)
35. Sánchez, C.: Online and offline stream runtime verification of synchronous systems. In: Colombo, C., Leucker, M. (eds.) RV 2018. LNCS, vol. 11237, pp. 138–163. Springer, Cham (2018). https://doi.org/10.1007/978-3-030-03769-7_9
36. Sen, K., Roşu, G.: Generating optimal monitors for extended regular expressions. ENTCS 89(2), 226–245 (2003)
37. Swierstra, W.: Data types à la carte. J. Funct. Program. 18(4), 423–436 (2008)
38. Thati, P., Roşu, G.: Monitoring algorithms for metric temporal logic specifications. Electron. Notes Theor. Comput. Sci. 113, 145–162 (2005)
39. Vazou, N., Seidel, E.L., Jhala, R.: LiquidHaskell: experience with refinement types in the real world. In: Proceedings of the Haskell 2014, pp. 39–51. ACM (2014)
40. Westphal, O., Voigtländer, J.: Implementing, and keeping in check, a DSL used in e-learning. In: Nakano, K., Sagonas, K. (eds.) FLOPS 2020. LNCS, vol. 12073, pp. 179–197. Springer, Cham (2020). https://doi.org/10.1007/978-3-030-59025-3_11
41. Zudaire, S., Gorostiaga, F., Sanchez, C., Schneider, G., Uchitel, S.: Assumption monitoring using runtime verification for UAV temporal task plan executions. Under submission (2020)

Formal Verification of Atomicity Requirements for Smart Contracts

Ning Han[1], Ximeng Li[1,3]($\boxtimes$), Guohui Wang[2], Zhiping Shi[1], and Yong Guan[3]

[1] Beijing Key Laboratory of Electronic System Reliability and Prognostics,
Capital Normal University, Beijing, China
15238483068@163.com, shizp@cnu.edu.cn
[2] Beijing Engineering Research Center of High Reliable Embedded System,
Capital Normal University, Beijing, China
ghwang@cnu.edu.cn
[3] Beijing Advanced Innovation Center for Imaging Theory and Technology,
Capital Normal University, Beijing, China
{lixm,guanyong}@cnu.edu.cn

Abstract. Smart contracts are notoriously vulnerable to bugs and loopholes. This is due largely to an unusual combination of features: reentrant calls, transfer-triggered code execution, the way exceptions are propagated, etc. Numerous validation techniques have been developed to ensure the safety and security of smart contracts. An important class of problems dealt with is related to the atomic performance of actions such as contract calls and state updates. In this paper, we examine the major existing atomicity-related criteria for the safety and security of smart contracts. We then propose an atomicity criterion and argue about its advantages. Furthermore, we develop a Hoare-style program logic that is capable of verifying the fulfillment of safety requirements by smart contracts, including the satisfaction of the proposed criterion. The program logic is developed and proven sound for a core Solidity-like language, which supports reentrant calls, ether transfers, and exception handling.

1 Introduction

Blockchains are distributed digital ledgers containing records of user data and activities [33]. The blockchain technology provides multiple desired features such as distributed consensus, decentralized management and control, the difficulty in corrupting data and fake data, the traceability of provenance, etc. This technology has the potential to play a key role in the effective and efficient management of trust relationship in the information era.

Since the advent of Ethereum [32], programmability has become an indispensable feature of blockchain systems. Programs implementing smart contracts [30] can be written to define the logic of transactions over a blockchain system. Programmability greatly eases the development of a wide spectrum of blockchain applications, ranging from digital currency to online gaming.

B. C. d. S. Oliveira (Ed.): APLAS 2020, LNCS 12470, pp. 44–64, 2020.
https://doi.org/10.1007/978-3-030-64437-6_3

There has been a high level of activity in the development of smart contracts. However, a great number of bugs and loopholes have been found to exist in the smart contracts deployed. These bugs and loopholes put on-chain digital assets at stake [1,5]. The safety and security problems of smart contracts have led to extensive recent efforts related to the validation of smart contracts (as recently surveyed in [31]). The bulk of the existing work is focused on bug detection and verification [3,7,9,11,12,15,17,20,22,24–27,34], semantic foundation [6,13, 16,18,19,21], or language design [8,10,28]. Relatively little attention has been directed to the discussion about the safety and security requirements themselves. The mis-specification of requirements and criteria could lead to undetected flaws or false alarms, even if the analysis is sound and precise with respect to the specified requirements.

An important class of requirements for the safety and security of smart contracts is the atomicity of operations – a group of related operations should be performed in an all-or-nothing fashion. A typical problem is as follows. A contract may fail to transfer an amount of ether, yet deduct this amount from its book-keeping records, leading to locked funds. Atomicity problems also arise in other scenarios than related to digital currency. Consider a contract that may update the sales figures of a product, without updating its stock. Atomicity problems significantly harm the integrity of the business logics of smart contracts.

In this paper, we propose an atomicity criterion (Sect. 2) that can be used to specify the updates to state variables and the performance of function calls that must happen in sync, in smart contract transactions. The criterion is flexible to use because it supports the specification of which ones of all the potential variable updates and function calls in a smart contract are of concern. Hence, the criterion can be tailored to capture application-specific atomicity requirements.

Currently, the bulk of the existing techniques for the source-level verification of smart contracts does not come with an emphasis on soundness with respect to a concrete language semantics. In this work, we devise a Hoare-style program logic (Sect. 4) for the verification of smart contracts, covering the atomicity criterion we propose, as well as other safety criteria. We establish the soundness of the program logic with respect to a Solidity-like language (Sect. 3), for which we carefully formulate the typing disciplines and a formal semantics.

The main contributions of this paper are:

1. an atomicity criterion for smart contracts supporting the specification of the state updates, as well as function calls, that must happen in atomic batches,
2. a Hoare-style program logic supporting the source-level verification of safety requirements on smart contracts, especially the proposed atomicity criterion.

The proposed program logic provides the vocabulary for referring to, and reasoning about the initial and current values of state variables, the builtin balances of accounts, the caller address, the amount of ether transfered with calls, the presence of successful calls within and between contracts, and the presence of uncaught exceptions. It employs forward-style inference rules for assignments to variables and mapping elements, which provides a basis for automation. It uses contract invariants to capture the effect of calls with reentry possibilities.

Both the proposed atomicity criterion and program logic are illustrated (Sect. 5) using examples of practical relevance, including a batch-transfer function for the refund of smart contract users. For space reasons, the detailed formal definitions of the smart contract language and the proofs of the theoretical results are given in the addendum of this paper.

2   Atomicity Criteria for Smart Contracts

We introduce the proposed atomicity criterion with the help of a simple example. We then discuss major related atomicity criteria in the literature. We use the smart contract language defined in the present work for this discussion, to avoid potential confusion arising from the switch between different languages.

```
fun withdraw(; b:U256) ret x:U256
{
    b := bal;
    if (b = 0) { throw };
    bal := 0;
    try { caller.transfer(b) }
    catch { bal := b; err := err + 1 }
}
```

Fig. 1. The function withdraw

The smart contract function withdraw in Fig. 1 allows a fixed amount of ether to be withdrawn once. In this function, bal is a state variable belonging to the overall contract. It records the amount of ether that can be withdrawn (i.e., the balance). This amount is retrieved in the local variable b, which is declared after the ; in the first line. If a previous withdrawal has already succeeded (b = 0 in the conditional), then the call ends with an exception. Otherwise, the bookkeeping balance bal is zeroed, and the amount of ether to be withdrawn is transfered to the caller. Exceptions occurring in the transfer are caught and handled by resetting bal to its initial value, and incrementing the state variable err. This state variable is used to log the number of errors occurring with the ether withdrawal attempts by calling the function withdraw.

A key point about the safety of the function withdraw is that the actual transfer of ether is kept in sync with the update of the bookkeeping balance bal. More concretely, when the execution of withdraw is completed, the transfer has been successfully performed, if and only if bal has been updated to zero.

There are two further aspects to be noted about withdraw in Fig. 1. Firstly, when stating the atomicity requirement, it is more convenient to be concerned with the overall value change of the variable bal (e.g., to zero) than with the execution of a specific assignment to bal (e.g., $bal := b$). That is, it is more convenient to consider semantic updates (i.e., overall value changes) of state variables, rather than syntactic updates (e.g., particular assignments to state variables) of them. Secondly, although err is also a state variable of the contract like bal is, the update of err is not supposed to happen in sync with the update of bal. Hence, the atomicity of a transaction does not imply that the update of all the state variables should happen in one atomic batch.

In this work, we deal with the formal verification of the following atomicity criterion for smart contracts.

For a number of semantic updates to specific state variables, as well as calls to specific functions, either all of them happen or none of them happen, in the execution of a smart contract function.

For the execution of `withdraw` in Fig. 1, it can be shown that either *bal* is updated, the builtin balance [32] of the contract is updated, and the call to transfer is also successfully performed, or none of the above happens.

Related Atomicity Criteria. In the literature, there are two major criteria used to detect atomicity problems in smart contracts that are related to ours.

The first criterion is to check whether write accesses to state variables happen only after successful ether transfers (e.g., [22]). The rationale is that if a transfer fails, the builtin balance of the contract does not change, and, hence, no bookkeeping by means of updating a state variable should be attempted. This criterion is simple to understand, and can be efficiently implemented. On the other hand, this criterion is not met by the function `withdraw`. This is because a write to the state variable *bal* (*bal* := *b*) happens even if the transfer fails. However, it is inappropriate to report this write as causing an atomicity problem, because overall the bookkeeping in *bal* is kept in sync with actual ether transfer, and with the builtin balance. In fact, the utility of the write *bal* := *b* in the function `withdraw` is different than that considered when adopting the criterion in [22]. This write is not for deducting an amount from the recorded balance to reflect ether transfer, but for canceling out the effect of an earlier deduction.

The second criterion is a security property called atomicity [16]. To see if a smart contract satisfies atomicity, one considers two executions of the contract, started in states that differ only in the gas value. If the two executions end with different values for some declared state variable(s), then it is required that the values of all the state variables should be the same as in the beginning, in at least one execution. Hence, the only allowed form of interference that the gas value has on the state is the suspension of changes to all state variables atomically. This atomicity property addresses a noninterference concern that is not addressed by our criterion. On the other hand, this property is not satisfied by the function `withdraw`. This is because if there is an insufficient amount of gas initially, causing the transfer in `withdraw` to fail, then the change to the value of *bal* is suspended, but the change to *err* is not. However, it is inappropriate to report this update of *err* as causing an atomicity problem, because this update is used to implement the logging functionality, and it does not cause the builtin balance of the contract to be out of sync with the bookkeeping balance.

Remark 1. In the motivating example, we use an exception-handling programming construct. Language features like this are introduced with Solidity version 0.6. Nevertheless, if the try ... catch ... were replaced by an if statement whose conditional checks whether a low-level call implementing the transfer succeeds or not, the essence of the example would remain.

3   Smart Contract Language

We consider a simplified programming abstraction for smart contracts. There is a blockchain system that contains a number of user accounts. Each account has an address, maintains its balance in the native digital currency of the blockchain, contains a storage that maps the state variables to their values, and contains a smart contract. Although we do not aim for a formalization of the computation model that is absolutely precise for Ethereum, we use "ether" to refer to the native digital currency, to aid the intuition of a reader familiar with Ethereum.

$$
\begin{aligned}
\theta &::= \mathsf{U160} \mid \mathsf{U256} \mid \mathsf{bool} \\
tp &::= \theta \mid \theta_1 \to \theta_2 \\
l &::= v : \theta \quad (\text{where } v \in \mathbb{N} \cup \{tt, ff\}) \\
tvs &::= x_1 : \theta_1, \ldots, x_n : \theta_n \\
tpvs &::= x_1 : tp_1, \ldots, x_n : tp_n \\
e &::= l \mid x \mid x\langle e \rangle \mid e_1 \, aop \, e_2 \mid e_1 \, cop \, e_2 \mid e_1 \, bop \, e_2 \mid \\
&\quad\ \ \mathsf{this} \mid \mathsf{caller} \mid \mathsf{callval} \mid \mathsf{balance} \mid \mathsf{adr}(c) \\
S &::= \mathsf{skip} \mid e_1 := e_2 \mid \mathsf{if} \, (e) \, \{S\} \mid \mathsf{while} \, (e) \, \{S\} \mid S_1; S_2 \mid \\
&\quad\ \ e_\mathsf{a}.f(e_1, \ldots, e_n) \to x \mid e_\mathsf{a}.\mathsf{transfer}(e) \mid \mathsf{throw} \mid \mathsf{try} \, \{S_1\} \, \mathsf{catch} \, \{S_2\} \\
fd &::= \mathsf{fun} \, f(tvs_1; tvs_2) \, \mathsf{ret} \, x : \theta \, \{S\} \\
fbd &::= \mathsf{fun} \, (tvs) \, \{S\} \\
ctr &::= \mathsf{contract} \, c \, \{ \, \mathsf{var} \, tpvs \, fd_1 \, \ldots \, fd_m \, fbd \, \} \\
ctrs &::= [ctr_1, \ldots, ctr_n]
\end{aligned}
$$

Fig. 2. The syntax of the smart contract language

3.1   Syntax

We define a smart contract language with the syntax in Fig. 2. A *basic type* θ can be U160 that represents 160-bit addresses of user accounts, U256 that represents 256-bit unsigned integers, or the Boolean type bool. A *type tp* can be a basic type, or a mapping type $\theta_1 \to \theta_2$. A *literal l* can be a Boolean literal, or a numeral with value v and type θ. A *basic typed variable list tvs* is a list of variables each associated with a basic type. A *typed variable list tpvs* is a list of variables each associated with a type.

An *expression e* can be a literal, a variable reference, the expression $x\langle e \rangle$ that is used to retrieve the value for the key e in the mapping x or to update this value, an arithmetic operation, a comparative operation, a Boolean operation, the retrieval of the address of a contract ($\mathsf{adr}(c)$), or one of the operations retrieving state information about the current execution. The expression this retrieves the address of the currently executing contract. The expression caller retrieves the address of the caller contract (i.e., the contract calling the currently executing function). The expression callval retrieves the amount of ether transfered along with the call. The expression balance retrieves the ether balance of the currently executing contract.

A *statement* S can be an assignment, a branching construct, a looping construct, a sequential composition, or one of the constructs with strong association to smart contract programming. The statement $e_a.f(e_1, \ldots, e_n) \rightarrow x$ invokes the function with identifier f in the contract at the address e_a, passing n expressions as arguments, and putting the return value in the local variable x. The statement $e_a.\mathsf{transfer}(e)$ transfers the amount e of ether to the address e_a. The statement throw throws an exception. The statement try $\{S_1\}$ catch $\{S_2\}$ catches exceptions resulting from a call or a throw in S_1, and handles them in S_2.

A *function definition fd* contains a list tvs_1 of formal parameters, a list tvs_2 of local variables, a typed return variable, and a statement S that is the function body. A *fallback function* in a contract is executed when a call is made to a non-existing function in the contract, or after the contract receives ether. The definition of a fallback function *fbd* consists only of a list tvs of local variables and a function body. The fallback functions in our language resemble the fallback functions in Solidity [2].

A *contract ctr* consists of a contract identifier c, a typed variable list (with state variables), a list of function definitions, and a fallback function definition. Finally, *ctrs* models a list of contracts deployed together. A contract in *ctrs* may refer to another contract in the same list using the identifier of the latter.

We use Tp to represent the set of types, use L to represent the set of literals, use Var to represent the set of variables, use C to represent the set of contract identifiers, use Ctr to represent the set of contracts, and use Fid to represent the set of function identifiers. We adhere mostly to the rule that the initial letters for the names of sets are in upper case, and the initial letters for the meta-variables represents the individual elements are in lower-case. The only exception is the use of the meta-variable S for individual statements.

The language design reflects a number of key features of Ethereum smart contracts – the differentiation of local variables and state variables, mappings, ether transfer with post-processing at the receiver, exception handling, etc. Intra-contract and inter-contract calls are supported through the unified construct $e_a.f(e_1, \ldots, e_n) \rightarrow x$. If the address of the callee equals that of the current contract, then an internal call is made; otherwise an external call is made.

3.2   Semantics

We present the key facts about the static semantics (i.e., type system) and dynamic semantics of our smart contract language.

Static Semantics. The type system establishes the judgment

$$\vdash ctrs$$

This judgment says that the list *ctrs* of contracts is well-typed. The main requirements are that the contract identifiers should be pairwise distinct, and that each contract ctr in the list should be typable. The typability of each individual contract is captured by the judgment

$$ctrs \vdash ctr$$

In a contract ctr, the declaration of state variables with their types induces a *storage typing environment* in the set $Var \rightarrow Tp \cup \{\bot\}$. We denote this storage typing environment by $ste\text{-}of(ctr)$. In a function with the identifier $f_\bot \in Fid \cup \{\bot\}$ in the contract ctr ($f_\bot = \bot$ for the fallback function), the declaration of the formal parameters, local variables, and the return variable induces a *local typing environment* in the set $Var \rightarrow (L \cup \{\bot\})$. We denote this local typing environment by $lte\text{-}of(ctr, f_\bot)$. To establish $ctrs \vdash ctr$, the statements and expressions in the contract ctr are typed under $ste\text{-}of(ctr)$ and $lte\text{-}of(ctr, f_\bot)$.

Remark 2. A key reason for the contract ctr to be typed with a given list of contracts ($ctrs$) is the following. For a function call in the code of ctr, if the target contract of the call is specified by the contract identifier (i.e., $\mathsf{adr}(c).f(e_1, \ldots, e_n) \rightarrow x$), then the type system checks that c is in the set of contract identifiers of $ctrs$. Moreover, the existence of a function whose signature matches the call is statically checked in the target contract. Hence, the invocation of the fallback function in the target contract at runtime is avoided.

Dynamic Semantics. We define a big-step semantics for our smart contract language. We introduce the semantic domains and the main judgment below.

Let $\mathbb{N}_k$ represent the subset of natural numbers up to $2^k - 1$. Let $\mathcal{D} := \{\mathbb{N}_{256}, \mathbb{N}_{160}, \{tt, ff\}\}$. Let $SVal := \bigcup \mathcal{D} \cup \bigcup_{A_1, A_2 \in \mathcal{D}} (A_1 \rightarrow A_2)$ be the set of *structured values*. We model the status of an account by an *account state* in the set $ASt := \mathbb{N}_{256} \times Ctr \times (Var \rightarrow SVal)$. For each $ast \in ASt$, ast is of the form (bal, ctr, st), where bal represents the balance of the account, ctr represents the smart contract of the account, and st represents the storage of the account. We model the state of the blockchain by *world states* in the set $WSt := \mathbb{N}_{160} \rightarrow ASt \cup \{\bot\}$. Each address value is mapped to an optional account state by a world state wst. We model the context for the current call by *execution environments* in the set $EE := \mathbb{N}_{160} \times \mathbb{N}_{160} \times \mathbb{N}_{256}$. For each $ee \in EE$, ee is of the form (ths, clr, cvl), where ths represents the address of the currently executing contract, clr represents the address of the caller contract, and cvl represents the amount of ether transfered with the current call. We record the values of the local variables of an executing function by local states in the set $LSt := Var \rightarrow (L \cup \{\bot\})$. Hence, each variable is mapped to an optional literal. That is, a local state lst records the types of the variables alongside their values. We model the deployment of contracts at addresses by *address environments* in the set $H := C \rightarrow \mathbb{N}_{160}$. This set is ranged over by η. We use the dot-notation to reference a component of a tuple. For instance, we refer to the balance of an account by $ast.bal$.

The evaluation of statements is represented by the judgment

$$\langle S, lst, wst, ee \rangle \rightarrow_\eta (lst', wst', cs)_{flg}$$

This judgment says: the evaluation of the statement S in the local state lst, the world state wst, the execution environment ee, and the address environment η results in the local state lst', the world state wst', the set cs of successful calls, and the Boolean flag flg indicating the existence of uncaught exceptions. More concretely, cs is a subset of

$$\{ call(v, v', f_\perp) \mid v, v' \in \mathbb{N}_{160} \wedge f_\perp \in Fid \cup \{\perp\}\}$$

Here, $call(v, v', f_\perp)$ represents a successful call from the account at the address v to the account at the address v'. The $f_\perp$ is an optional function identifier for the intended callee. In case $f_\perp = \perp$, a transfer is intended.

3.3   Preservation of Types by Evaluation

We show that types and the observance of types by the values of variables are preserved by evaluation.

We write $ste \blacktriangleright st$ to express that the storage type environment ste is consistent with the storage st. Intuitively, each state variable is mapped under st to a value (which could be a function value) in the range of its type according to ste. We write $lte \triangleright lst$ to express that the local type environment lte is consistent with the local state lst. Intuitively, each local variable is mapped under lst to a value in the range of its type according to lte.

We write $wf(ctr, f_\perp, lst, wst)$ to express that the values of all local variables, parameters and the return variable of the function identified by $f_\perp$ in the contract ctr as recorded in lst, and the values of all state variables (of any contract) as recorded in wst, are consistent with the types of these variables, and that each contract in wst is well-typed under some list fds of contracts.

$wf(ctr, f_\perp, lst, wst) :=$

   $lte\text{-}of(ctr, f_\perp) \triangleright lst \wedge$

   $(\forall v \in \mathbb{N}_{160} : \forall ast : wst(v) = ast \Rightarrow ste\text{-}of(ast.ctr) \blacktriangleright ast.st \wedge \exists ctrs : ctrs \vdash ast.ctr)$

We then have the following result.

Theorem 1. *If $wf(ctr, f_\perp, lst, wst)$ holds, $ctr = wst(ee.ths).ctr$ holds, $S = stmt\text{-}of(ctr, f_\perp)$ holds, and $\langle S, lst, wst, ee \rangle \rightarrow_\eta (lst', wst', cs)_{flg}$ can be derived, then $wf(ctr, f_\perp, lst', wst')$ holds.*

Here, $stmt\text{-}of(ctr, f_\perp)$ gives the body of the function identified by $f_\perp$ in the contract ctr. The theorem indicates that if a well-typed function is executed to completion, and the values of local and state variables observe their types initially, then the local and state variables still have the same types that are observed by their values in the end.

4 Program Logic

The program logic for our smart contract language establishes Hoare-style judgments for the functions of smart contracts. It explicitly records the presence of successful calls via dedicated terms, and implicitly keeps track of the presence of state updates via logical variables. In this manner, it supports the reasoning about whether specific calls and state updates are performed in atomic batches.

4.1 The Assertions

We consider the following language for formulating the assertions in the program logic. These assertions are used as the pre-conditions and post-conditions for statements and functions, as well as the invariants for contracts.

$$\underline{t} ::= \nu \mid w \mid x \mid x^c \mid \mathfrak{b} \mid \kappa \mid u \mid \mathit{ths} \mid \mathit{clr} \mid \mathit{cvl} \mid \varepsilon$$
$$t ::= \underline{t} \mid \bar{c} \mid t_1 \, aop \, t_2 \mid \underline{t}(t) \mid t[t_1 : t_2] \mid (t_1, t_2, f_\perp)$$
$$\phi ::= t_1 \, cop \, t_2 \mid \phi_1 \, bop \, \phi_2 \mid \exists \underline{t} : \phi$$

A *basic term* $\underline{t}$ can be a value[1] (ν), an auxiliary variable (w), a local variable (x), a state variable annotated with the identifier of its contract (x^c), the variable $\mathfrak{b}$ representing a mapping from account addresses to balances, the variable κ representing a mapping from triples ($\nu_1, \nu_2, f_\perp$) to Boolean values for the presence of successful calls from the account at address ν_1 to the account at address ν_2, targeting the function identified by $f_\perp$, a logical variable u representing the value of a program variable, $\mathfrak{b}$ or κ, at a fixed program point, ths representing the address of the currently executing contract, clr representing the address of the caller, cvl representing the call value, or ε signalling an uncaught exception.

A *term* t can be a basic term, the term $\bar{c}$ for the address of the contract with identifier c, an arithmetic operation on terms, $\underline{t}(t)$ for the application of $\underline{t}$ on t, $t[t_1 : t_2]$ for the update of t (that represents a function) at point t_1 to t_2, or a triple $(t_1, t_2, f_\perp)$ consisting of a source contract address, a destination contract address, and an optional function identifier for a call. Whether such a call has been successfully performed is represented by $\kappa(t_1, t_2, f_\perp)$.

An *assertion* ϕ can be a comparison of two terms, a Boolean operation on two assertions, or an assertion with a quantified basic term.

We use ε as syntactical sugar for $\varepsilon = \mathit{tt}$, and use $\neg \varepsilon$ as syntactical sugar for $\varepsilon = \mathit{ff}$. For an assertion ϕ, we use $\neg \phi$ as syntactical sugar for $((0 = 0) \, \mathit{xor} \, \phi)$, and we use $\forall \underline{t} : \phi$ as syntactical sugar for $\neg(\exists \underline{t} : \neg \phi)$.

We write $\mathit{lvs}(\phi)$ for the set of logical variables in the assertion ϕ. We write $\mathit{svs}(a_1, \ldots, a_n)$ for the set of state variables (of the form x^c for some x and c) in any of $a_1, \ldots, a_n$. We write $\mathit{vs}(a_1, \ldots, a_n)$ for the set of variables in any of $a_1, \ldots, a_n$. Here, each a_i is an assertion or a term. We precede a set of variables with $\exists$ to represent a series of existential quantifications over the variables in this set. We write $\phi[t_1/\underline{t}_1, \ldots, t_n/\underline{t}_n]$ for the simultaneous substitution of $t_1, \ldots, t_n$ for $\underline{t}_1, \ldots, \underline{t}_n$, in ϕ, where $\underline{t}_1, \ldots, \underline{t}_n$ are pair-wise distinct.

---

[1] We allow function values in the assertions, and, hence, ν is used rather than v.

We write $[e]_X^c$ for the term or assertion corresponding to the expression e. Here, c is the identifier of the contract in which e resides, and X is the set of local variables of the function in which e resides. We define $[x]_X^c := x$ if $x \in X$, and $[x]_X^c := x^c$ if $x \notin X$. We define $[x\langle e \rangle]_X^c := x^c([e]_X^c)$, where the right-hand side represents the application of x^c on $[e]_X^c$. The definition of $[e]_X^c$ on other expressions are relatively straightforward.

4.2   The Inference System

We write Δ to represent a function that takes each contract identifier c and function identifier f to a pair $([x_1, \ldots, x_n, x], (\Phi, \Phi'))$. Here, $x_1, \ldots, x_n$ are the formal parameters of the function identified by f in c, and x is the return variable of this function. Furthermore, Φ and Φ' are the *pre-condition* and *post-condition* of this function, respectively. We restrict the local variables of a function that are used in its pre-condition to the formal parameters. We restrict the local variables of a function that are used in its post-condition to the return variable.

The *invariant* I for a contract satisfies: If I holds before any function of the contract is called, then I holds after the function finishes executing. Furthermore, we assume that the only basic terms contained in the invariant for a contract with the contract identifier c are the state variables of the contract, logical variables, $\mathfrak{b}$, and κ, where $\mathfrak{b}$ is only used in the term $\mathfrak{b}(\overline{c})$, and κ is only used in terms $\kappa(\overline{c}, t, f_\perp)$ for some t and $f_\perp$. Hence, after the contract with identifier c makes a call, the values for the terms involving $\mathfrak{b}$ and κ in I can only change when the contract is re-entered.

The logical judgment for statements is

$$I, \Delta \vdash_X^c \{\phi\}\ S\ \{\phi'\}$$

The judgment says that under I and Δ, if the pre-condition ϕ holds when starting to evaluate the statement S, and the evaluation terminates, then the post-condition ϕ' holds on termination. The statement S is part of the contract with identifier c, with accesses to local variables in X.

The inference rules for statements that are neither calls nor transfers are shown in Fig. 3. The two rules for assignments are formulated to support forward reasoning [14]. For the rule about assignments to variables x, the post-condition says that there exists some initial value w for x, such that the pre-condition holds for this value, and an equality holds between the two sides of the assignment, provided that the expression e is evaluated using the value of w for x. The premise of this rule requires that w should be fresh for ϕ. The rule for assignments to mappings embodies similar intuition. The rule for sequential compositions $S_1; S_2$ derives a post-condition that reflects the post-state can either be an exceptional post-state of S_1, or the post-state of S_2 in case S_1 finishes normally. The rule for try $\{S_1\}$ catch $\{S_2\}$ employs the pre-condition $\phi''[tt/\varepsilon] \wedge \neg\varepsilon$ for S_2, where ϕ'' is the post-condition for S_1. The substitution erases the information about the exception from S_1 because the exception is caught. The conjunction with $\neg\varepsilon$ signals to S_2 that there is no current exception. The remaining rules in Fig. 3 can be understood following intuition from standard Hoare logic [4].

$$\frac{w \notin vs(\phi)}{I, \Delta \vdash_X^c \{\phi\} \; x := e \; \{\exists w : \phi[w/[x]_X^c] \wedge [x]_X^c = [e]_X^c[w/[x]_X^c] \wedge \neg \varepsilon\}}$$

$$\frac{w \notin vs(\phi) \quad \phi' = \exists w : \phi[w/x^c] \wedge x^c = w[[e_1]_X^c[w/x^c] : [e_2]_X^c[w/x^c]] \wedge \neg \varepsilon}{I, \Delta \vdash_X^c \{\phi\} \; x\langle e_1 \rangle := e_2 \; \{\phi'\}}$$

$$\frac{I, \Delta \vdash_X^c \{\phi\} \; S_1 \; \{\phi''\} \quad I, \Delta \vdash_X^c \{\phi'' \wedge \neg \varepsilon\} \; S_2 \; \{\phi'\}}{I, \Delta \vdash_X^c \{\phi\} \; S_1; S_2 \; \{\phi'' \wedge \varepsilon \vee \phi'\}}$$

$$\frac{I, \Delta \vdash_X^c \{\phi \wedge [e]_X^c\} \; S \; \{\phi'\}}{I, \Delta \vdash_X^c \{\phi\} \; \text{if} \; (e) \; \{S\} \; \{\phi' \vee \phi \wedge \neg [e]_X^c \wedge \neg \varepsilon\}}$$

$$\frac{I, \Delta \vdash_X^c \{\phi \wedge [e]_X^c\} \; S \; \{\phi\}}{I, \Delta \vdash_X^c \{\phi\} \; \text{while} \; (e) \; \{S\} \; \{\phi \wedge \neg [e]_X^c \wedge \neg \varepsilon \vee \phi \wedge \varepsilon\}}$$

$$\frac{I, \Delta \vdash_X^c \{\phi\} \; S_1 \; \{\phi''\} \quad I, \Delta \vdash_X^c \{\phi''[tt/\varepsilon] \wedge \neg \varepsilon\} \; S_2 \; \{\phi'\}}{I, \Delta \vdash_X^c \{\phi\} \; \text{try} \; \{S_1\} \; \text{catch} \; \{S_2\} \; \{\phi'' \wedge \neg \varepsilon \vee \phi'\}}$$

$$\frac{}{I, \Delta \vdash_X^c \{\phi\} \; \text{skip} \; \{\phi\}} \qquad \frac{}{I, \Delta \vdash_X^c \{\phi\} \; \text{throw} \; \{\phi[f\!f/\varepsilon] \wedge \varepsilon\}}$$

$$\frac{I, \Delta \vdash_X^c \{\phi_1'\} \; S \; \{\phi_2'\} \quad \phi_1 \Rightarrow \phi_1' \quad \phi_2' \Rightarrow \phi_2}{I, \Delta \vdash_X^c \{\phi_1\} \; S \; \{\phi_2\}}$$

Fig. 3. The inference rules for statements (part 1)

The inference rules for call statements are presented in Fig. 4. The first rule describes the case where the identifier (c') of the target contract is known. In the premise, it is checked that the pre-condition Φ of the callee function should hold with substitutions of the argument expressions for the formal parameters, as well as the substitutions in δ, under the pre-condition ϕ of the call. Here, the substitutions in δ take the execution environment used for the evaluation of Φ to that of the callee. In the conclusion of this rule, the condition ϕ' in the post-condition describes the states reached if the call succeeds. In ϕ', it is stated that there is some return value w, and some set of successful calls described by the function w', for which the post-condition Φ' holds in the execution environment of the callee. In addition, the final mapping κ for the successful calls is as w', except that the success of the current call from $\bar{c}$ to $\overline{c'}$ targeting f is also recorded. The additional conditions in ϕ' state that the pre-conditions ϕ and Φ hold in the post-state, if the updated variables are re-mapped to some appropriate values (e.g., their values in the pre-state). The inclusion of these conditions enables information to be passed directly, or via the logical variables shared by Φ and Φ', from the pre-state to the post-state. The second rule in Fig. 4 describes how to reason about a call for which the identifier of the target contract is unavailable. In the post-condition, ϕ' describes the post-states reached after the call succeeds. The first disjunct of ϕ' describes post-states reached without any successful

$$\Delta(c', f) = ([x_1, \ldots, x_n, x'], (\Phi, \Phi')) \qquad \delta = [\overline{c'}/ths][\overline{c}/clr][0/cvl]$$

$$\frac{\phi \wedge \neg \varepsilon \;\Rightarrow\; \exists lvs(\Phi) : \Phi[[e_1]^c_X/x_1, \ldots, [e_n]^c_X/x_n]\delta \quad vs(\Phi') \cap \{w, w'\} = \emptyset}{lvs(\phi) \cap lvs(\Phi) = \emptyset \qquad (\bigcup_i vs([e_i]^c_X)) \cap \{ths, clr, cvl\} = \emptyset}$$

$$I, \Delta \vdash^c_X \{\phi\}\; \mathsf{adr}(c').f(e_1, \ldots, e_n) \to x\; \{\phi' \wedge \neg \varepsilon \vee \phi[ff/\varepsilon] \wedge \varepsilon\}$$

where $\phi' = \exists lvs(\Phi)$:

$$\begin{pmatrix} \exists \mathfrak{b} : \exists \kappa : \exists svs(\phi, \Phi, [e_1]^c_X, \ldots, [e_n]^c_X) : \exists x : \\ \phi \wedge \Phi[[e_1]^c_X/x_1, \ldots, [e_n]^c_X/x_n]\delta \\ \wedge\, \exists w, w' : \Phi'[w/x'][w'/\kappa]\delta \wedge x = w \wedge \kappa = w'[(\overline{c}, \overline{c'}, f) : tt] \end{pmatrix}$$

$$\frac{lvs(\phi) \cap lvs(I) = \emptyset \quad \phi \wedge \neg \varepsilon \;\Rightarrow\; \exists lvs(I) : I \quad vs(\phi) \cap \{w, w'\} = \emptyset}{I, \Delta \vdash^c_X \{\phi\}\; e_a.f(e_1, \ldots, e_n) \to x\; \{\phi' \wedge \neg \varepsilon \vee \phi[ff/\varepsilon] \wedge \varepsilon\}}$$

where $\phi' = $

$$\begin{pmatrix} \exists w : \exists w' : \exists (svs(\phi) \setminus \{x^c \mid x \in Var\}) : \exists x : \\ \phi[w/\mathfrak{b}][w'/\kappa] \wedge \mathfrak{b}(\overline{c}) = w(\overline{c}) \wedge \\ \kappa \stackrel{c,1}{=} w'[[e_a]^c_X[w/\mathfrak{b}], f : tt] \wedge \kappa \stackrel{c,2}{=} w' \end{pmatrix} \vee$$

$$\exists lvs(I) : \exists w :$$

$$\begin{pmatrix} (\exists svs(\phi, I, [e_a]^c_X) : \exists \mathfrak{b} : \exists x : (\exists \kappa : \phi \wedge I) \wedge w = [e_a]^c_X) \\ \wedge\, \exists w' : I[w'/\kappa] \wedge \kappa = w'[(\overline{c}, w, f) : tt] \end{pmatrix}$$

Fig. 4. The inference rules for statements (part 2)

$$\kappa \stackrel{c,1}{=} w'[t, f_\perp : tt] \;:=$$

$$\begin{pmatrix} \kappa(\overline{c}, t, f_\perp) = tt \wedge \\ \forall w'', f'_\perp : (w'' \neq t \vee f'_\perp \neq f_\perp) \Rightarrow \kappa(\overline{c}, w'', f'_\perp) = w'(\overline{c}, w'', f'_\perp) \end{pmatrix}$$

$$\kappa \stackrel{c,2}{=} w' \;:=\; (\forall w'', f'_\perp : \kappa(w'', \overline{c}, f'_\perp) = w'(w'', \overline{c}, f'_\perp))$$

Fig. 5. The definitions of $\kappa \stackrel{c,1}{=} w'[t, f_\perp : tt]$ and $\kappa \stackrel{c,2}{=} w'$

reentrance to the current contract. It reflects the fact that the state variables of the current contract still have their initial values after the call, and the mapping of successful calls is related to the initial mapping w' as $\kappa \stackrel{c,1}{=} w'[[e_a]^c_X[w/\mathfrak{b}], f : tt] \wedge \kappa \stackrel{c,2}{=} w'$. The two conjuncts of this condition are defined according to Fig. 5. Hence, the condition $\kappa \stackrel{c,1}{=} w'[[e_a]^c_X[w/\mathfrak{b}], f : tt] \wedge \kappa \stackrel{c,2}{=} w'$ says that there is a successful call from the current contract to the callee, and otherwise the successful calls from the current contract, or to the current contract, are the same as before. The second disjunct of ϕ' describes the post-states reached after successful reentrance to the current contract during the call. The invariant I of the current contract is used to establish the post-condition. It is stated that there is some function w' describing the presence of all successful calls immediately before the return of the current call, such that I is satisfied for w', and the new

$$\Delta(c', f) = ([], (\Phi, \Phi')) \quad \delta = [\overline{c'}/ths][\overline{c}/clr] \quad lvs(\phi) \cap lvs(\Phi) = \emptyset$$

$$\begin{pmatrix} c \neq c' \wedge (\phi \wedge \neg\varepsilon) \wedge [e]^c_X \leq \mathsf{b}(\overline{c}) \wedge \mathsf{b}(\overline{c'}) + [e]^c_X < 2^{256} \Rightarrow \\ \exists lvs(\Phi) : \Phi[\mathsf{b}[\overline{c} : \mathsf{b}(\overline{c}) - [e]^c_X, c' : \mathsf{b}(\overline{c'}) + [e]^c_X]/\mathsf{b}]\delta[[e]^c_X/cvl] \end{pmatrix}$$

$$vs([e]^c_X) \cap \{ths, clr, cvl\} = \emptyset \quad vs(\phi, \Phi, \Phi') \cap \{w, w', w_0, w_1\} = \emptyset$$

$$\overline{I, \Delta \vdash^c_X \{\phi\}\ \mathsf{adr}(c').\mathsf{transfer}(e)\ \{\phi' \wedge \neg\varepsilon \vee \phi[ff/\varepsilon] \wedge \varepsilon\}}$$

where $\phi' = \exists lvs(\Phi) : \exists w :$

$$\begin{pmatrix} \exists w_0 : \exists w_1 : \exists \kappa : \exists svs(\phi, \Phi, [e]^c_X) : \\ w = [e]^c_X[w_0/\mathsf{b}] \wedge \phi[w_0/\mathsf{b}] \wedge \Phi[w_1/\mathsf{b}]\delta[w/cvl] \wedge \\ w_1 = w_0[\overline{c} : w_0(\overline{c}) - w, \overline{c'} : w_0(\overline{c'}) + w] \\ \wedge \exists w' : \Phi'[w'/\kappa]\delta[w/cvl] \wedge \kappa = w'[(\overline{c}, \overline{c'}, \bot) : tt] \wedge c \neq c' \end{pmatrix}$$

$$lvs(\phi) \cap lvs(I) = \emptyset \quad vs(\phi, I) \cap \{w, w', w_0, w_1\} = \emptyset$$

$$\begin{pmatrix} \overline{c} \neq [e_a]^c_X \wedge (\phi \wedge \neg\varepsilon) \wedge [e]^c_X \leq \mathsf{b}(\overline{c}) \wedge \mathsf{b}([e_a]^c_X) + [e]^c_X < 2^{256} \\ \Rightarrow \exists lvs(I) : I[\mathsf{b}[\overline{c} : \mathsf{b}(\overline{c}) - [e]^c_X, [e_a]^c_X : \mathsf{b}([e_a]^c_X) + [e]^c_X]/\mathsf{b}] \end{pmatrix}$$

$$\overline{I, \Delta \vdash^c_X \{\phi\}\ e_a.\mathsf{transfer}(e)\ \{\phi' \wedge \neg\varepsilon \vee \phi[ff/\varepsilon] \wedge \varepsilon\}}$$

where $\phi' =$

$$\begin{pmatrix} \exists w : \exists w' : \exists(svs(\phi) \setminus \{x^c \mid x \in Var\}) : \\ \phi[w/\mathsf{b}][w'/\kappa] \wedge \overline{c} \neq [e_a]^c_X[w/\mathsf{b}] \wedge \mathsf{b}(\overline{c}) = w(\overline{c}) - [e]^c_X[w/\mathsf{b}] \wedge \\ \kappa \overset{c,1}{=} w'[[e_a]^c_X[w/\mathsf{b}], \bot : tt] \wedge \kappa \overset{c,2}{=} w' \end{pmatrix} \vee$$

$$\exists lvs(I) : \exists w :$$

$$\begin{pmatrix} \exists w_0 : \exists w_1 : \exists svs(\phi, I, [e_a]^c_X, [e]^c_X) : \\ (\exists \kappa : \phi[w_0/\mathsf{b}] \wedge I[w_1/\mathsf{b}]) \wedge w = [e_a]^c_X[w_0/\mathsf{b}] \wedge \overline{c} \neq w \wedge \\ w_1 = w_0[\overline{c} : w_0(\overline{c}) - [e]^c_X[w_0/\mathsf{b}], w : w_0(w) + [e]^c_X[w_0/\mathsf{b}]] \end{pmatrix}$$

$$\wedge \exists w' : I[w'/\kappa] \wedge \kappa = w'[(\overline{c}, w, \bot) : tt]$$

Fig. 6. The inference rules for statements (part 3)

set of successful calls is as described by w', except that the call from the current contract to the target contract should be added (last line of the second disjunct).

The inference rules for transfer statements are presented in Fig. 6. The rules for transfers come with a case distinction in whether the identifier of the target contract is explicitly specified in the transfer statement. If the identifier of the target contract is explicitly specified, the pre-condition and post-condition of the callee function (i.e., the fallback function of the target contract) are leveraged in reasoning about the transfer. Otherwise, the invariant of the current contract is used. In the premise of the rule for the transfer statement $\mathsf{adr}(c').\mathsf{transfer}(e)$, it is checked that the precondition of the callee function is implied by the fact that the transfer is performed towards a different contract than the current one, the precondition of the transfer, and the fact that the transfered amount can be supplied by the caller and does not cause any overflow of the callee's balance. In the conclusion of this rule, the condition ϕ' describes the states reached in case the transfer succeeds. In ϕ', it is stated that there exists some call value w (i.e., the amount of ether transfered to the callee), and some mapping w' for the successful calls that have been performed on completion of the callee function, such that the post-condition Φ' of the callee holds. The successful calls that have been performed after the returning of the callee are as those after the completion of the callee, except that the current transfer has also succeeded. It is also stated that the identifier of the current contract is different than the identifier of the target contract (in case the transfer succeeds). The remaining part of ϕ' says that there exists mappings w_0 and w_1 for the account balances immediately before the transfer is performed, and immediately before the execution of the callee function, respectively, such that the pre-condition ϕ of the transfer holds if the balances of the accounts are in accordance with w_0, and the pre-condition Φ of the callee function holds if the balances of the accounts are in accordance with w_1. The rule for the transfer statement $e_a.\mathsf{transfer}(e)$ is analogous to the rule for the transfer statement $\mathsf{adr}(c').\mathsf{transfer}(e)$ in the treatment of account balances. In addition, the rule for the transfer statement $e_a.\mathsf{transfer}(e)$ is analogous to the rule for the call statement $e_a.f(e_1, \ldots, e_n) \rightarrow x$ in the treatment of the two different cases regarding the presence of reentrance into the current contract.

Based on the verification of statements, functions and fallback functions can be verified against their specifications. Furthermore, a given contract ctr can be verified against the specifications of its functions in Δ, using an invariant I for the contract ctr. This gives rise to an instance of the judgment $I, \Delta \vdash ctr$. Ultimately, a given set of smart contracts can be verified against the specifications of their functions in Δ. This results in an instance of the judgment $\Delta \vdash ctrs$.

The program logic devised in the above lays a solid foundation for the verification of safety properties for smart contracts. Some of the logic rules have relatively involved formulations. To overcome the tediousness of using these rules in the reasoning tasks, a semi-automated tool can be implemented to conduct verification based on the specification of contract invariants and loop invariants.

4.3   Soundness

The soundness of our program logic relies on a notion of satisfaction of assertions in states. We interpret the assertions in *assertion states* of the form $\sigma := (lst, wst, ee, cs, flg, \zeta)$. The first five components are all from the semantic judgment for statements. The last component, ζ, is a function that gives the values of the auxiliary variables w, as well as the logical variables u in the assertions. The interpretation result is written $[\![\phi]\!]_{\mathrm{asst}}(\sigma)$, which is a truth value.

We articulate the notion that a function semantically satisfies its specification that consists of a pre-condition and a post-condition. More concretely, we write $ctrs \models \{\Phi\}\ (ctr, f_\perp)\ \{\Phi'\}$ to express that under the following five conditions

1. $wf(ctr, f_\perp, lst, wst)$,
2. $\forall x \in nprms\text{-}of(ctr, f_\perp) : \exists \theta : lst(x) = d(\theta) : \theta$,
3. $\eta(cid(ctr)) = ee.ths \wedge \forall i : wst(\eta(cid(ctrs!i))).ctr = ctrs!i$,
4. $\langle stmt\text{-}of(ctr, f_\perp), lst, wst, ee \rangle \rightarrow_\eta (lst', wst', cs)_{f\!f}$,
5. $[\![\Phi]\!]_{\mathrm{asst}}(lst, wst, ee, cs_0, f\!f, \zeta) = tt$,

it holds that $[\![\Phi']\!]_{\mathrm{asst}}(lst', wst', ee, cs_0 \cup cs, f\!f, \zeta) = tt$.

Intuitively, the main requirement of $ctrs \models \{\Phi\}\ (ctr, f_\perp)\ \{\Phi'\}$ is that if the execution of the function with the identifier $f_\perp$ in the smart contract ctr starts in a state that satisfies the condition Φ (Condition 5), and the execution finishes without uncaught exceptions (Condition 4), then the ending state satisfies the condition Φ'. Condition 1 requires that the execution of the function should be started in local and world states in which the values of variables are consistent with their types (see Sect. 3.3). Condition 2 requires that the initial local state should map each local variable to the default value for its (basic) type, unless the variable is a parameter. Here, the default value for the basic type θ is written $d(\theta)$, which is defined as 0 for the basic types U160 and U256, and defined as $f\!f$ for the basic type bool. Condition 3 is a sanity condition on the address environment η used in the evaluation. It requires that the identifier of the currently executing contract should be mapped to the address of the current contract (*ee.ths*). Additionally, it requires that the identifier of each given contract should be mapped to an account address where the code of the contract can be found.

We have the following theorem about the soundness of the program logic.

Theorem 2. *If* $\vdash$ *ctrs and* $\Delta \vdash$ *ctrs can be derived, ctr is in ctrs, and* $\Delta(ctr, f_\perp) = (xs, (\Phi, \Phi'))$ *for some xs, then we have ctrs* $\models \{\Phi\}\ (ctr, f_\perp)\ \{\Phi'\}$.

Hence, if a given series of smart contracts are well-typed, and these contracts pass the verification using the program logic, then each function (or fallback function) of each given contract semantically satisfies its specification.

With the assertion language in Sect. 4.1, Theorem 2 supports the sound deductive verification of general safety requirements for smart contracts at the source-level. When logical variables are used in Φ and Φ' to help express the presence of semantic updates to state variables, and the term κ is used to help express the presence of successful calls, the sound reasoning about the satisfaction of the atomicity criterion proposed in Sect. 2 is supported (see Sect. 5).

5   Atomicity Verification

Firstly, we evaluate our technique using the example in Fig. 1 that was intuitively discussed to motivate our work. Secondly, we consider a more involved example with atomicity requirements verified on a function refunding a group of users.

Verifying Atomicity for Ether Withdrawal. Suppose a smart contract *ctr* has identifier c, and it consists of the function `withdraw` of Fig. 1, and a fallback function with the code if $(bal = 0)$ {throw}.

Suppose Δ has the domain $\{(c, \texttt{withdraw}), (c, \perp)\}$. Furthermore, suppose

$$\Delta(c, \texttt{withdraw}) := (\,[\,], (bal^c = u_1 \wedge \mathfrak{b} = u_2,\ bal^c \neq u_1 \Leftrightarrow \mathfrak{b}(\bar{c}) \neq u_2(\bar{c}))\,)$$
$$\Delta(c, \perp) := (\,[\,], (f\!f, tt)\,)$$

Then, it can be established that $\Delta \vdash [ctr]$, using the invariant

$$I = (bal^c = 0 \wedge \mathfrak{b}(\bar{c}) = u)$$

for the contract *ctr*. This invariant states that if the state variable *bal* has value 0 before calling either function of the contract *ctr*, then *bal* still has the value 0, and the builtin balance of the contract remains the same (via the logical variable *u*), after the callee function finishes executing. If *bal* and *err* are both declared with the type U256 in the contract *ctr*, then we also have ⊢ [*ctr*]. This enables the establishment of the following result using Theorem 2.

$$[ctr] \models \{bal^c = u_1 \wedge \mathfrak{b} = u_2\} \; (ctr, \mathtt{withdraw}) \; \{bal^c \neq u_1 \Leftrightarrow \mathfrak{b}(\overline{c}) \neq u_2(\overline{c})\}$$

This result indicates that if we start the execution of the function `withdraw` in a legal initial state (i.e., with the values of *b* and *x* observing the type U256, and the value of *b* being 0), and the execution finishes normally, then *bal* is semantically updated if and only if the builtin balance of the contract is updated. If the execution ends exceptionally, then there is no effect on the states. This means that the fact established in the above applies for all possible executions started from legal initial states for the function `withdraw`. These include both the executions that end normally, and the executions that end exceptionally.

Thus, it is verified that the function `withdraw` always performs the actual transfer and the bookkeeping in an atomic batch.   □

```
fun refund( ; i:U256) ret x:U256 {
  if (lock != 0) { throw };
  lock := 1; i := 0;
  while (i < num) {
    if (bals⟨addr⟨i⟩⟩ > 0) {
      try { addr⟨i⟩.transfer(bals⟨addr⟨i⟩⟩); bals⟨addr⟨i⟩⟩ := 0 }
      catch { skip }
    };
    i := i + 1
  };
  lock := 0
}
```

Fig. 7. The function `refund`

Verifying Per-account Atomicity for Batch Transfer. We consider a more involved example, where a contract *ctr* with identifier *c* consists of the function `refund` in Fig. 7, and a fallback function with code if (*lock* != 0) {throw}.

Via a `while` loop, the function `refund` transfers the amount *bals*⟨*addr*⟨*i*⟩⟩ of ether to the user account at address *addr*⟨*i*⟩, for each *i* from 0 to *num* − 1. To avoid reentrance, the state variable *lock* is used. Each time a transfer is made, *lock* has the value 1. Hence, an exception is thrown if the receiver attempts at a call back to `refund` or the fallback function of the contract *ctr*.

The rationale of the function `refund` is to refund as many users as possible in a single execution. The transfer to a specific user may fail, without affecting the transfer to a different user. Hence, it cannot be guaranteed in general that all the transfers happen in an atomic batch. Nevertheless, it is crucial to ensure that for each individual user, the transfer and the setting of the bookkeeping balance to 0 (with $bals\langle addr\langle i\rangle\rangle := 0$) must happen together.

This atomicity requirement can be verified using the proposed program logic. With the pre-condition

$$\forall r : 0 \leq r < num^c \Rightarrow (bals^c(addr^c(r)) = u(r) \wedge \kappa(\overline{c}, addr^c(r), \bot) = f\!f)$$

for the function refund, the post-condition

$$\forall r : 0 \leq r < num^c \Rightarrow (bals^c(addr^c(r)) \neq u(r) \Leftrightarrow \kappa(\overline{c}, addr^c(r), \bot) = tt)$$

can be derived. This indicates that the bookkeeping balance for the r-th user is semantically updated, if and only if a transfer to the r-th user succeeds. $\square$

The two examples given in this section are both about atomicity requirements on a single smart contract, in a scenario involving ether transfer. In general, the usage scope of the proposed program logic is not limited to the verification of requirements on a single smart contract, or ether-related scenarios. This is because pre-conditions and post-conditions involving any state variables of multiple smart contracts that are deployed together can be specified. For instance, in a retailing scenario, if the information about the products and their current stock are managed in two different smart contracts, the proposed program logic can be used to verify that the registration of a product in one of the smart contracts must happen together with the initialization of its stock in the other. Last but not least, the usage scope of the proposed program logic goes beyond the verification of atomicity requirements. This is because the Hoare-style pre-conditions and post-conditions support the verification of partial correctness in general.

6   Related Work

Design and Formalization of Smart Contract Languages. To support the sound verification of smart contracts, there have been a number of developments on the formalization of smart contract languages.

In [13], a calculus called Featherweight Solidity is defined to closely model the core of the Solidity language. The calculus supports contract creation and single inheritance, which are not supported by our language. In [6], a minimal calculus for Solidity contracts is formalized. The formalization contains an explicit model of transactions and blockchains, while our formalization is focused on the execution of a single transaction. Neither work deals with the verification of smart contracts beyond type checking. On the other hand, we provide a discussion of atomicity-related requirements on smart contracts, and devise a program logic for the source-level verification of smart contracts.

In [34] and [21], formalizations of large fragments of Solidity are provided, with a big-step semantics, and a small-step semantics, respectively. Both formalizations are mechanized – the first in the Coq proof assistant, and the second in the K Framework. In [16,18,19], the bytecode language of the Ethereum virtual machine is formalized. These works are mostly focused on the semantic foundation for smart contracts, without looking much into verification problems.

The work [28] does not formalize an existing smart contract language, but proposes a new language for the safe programming of smart contracts. This is an intermediate language with strong safety guarantees provided by its type system. Light-weight static analyses are defined to address some of the verification issues. The design of a new language simplifies the verification of smart contracts.

Formal Validation of Smart Contracts. There have been extensive research efforts into the formal validation of smart contracts. The consideration of soundness is featured by a small fragment of the existing developments.

In [26], a technique based on software model checking is proposed for the automated verification of Ethereum smart contracts. The approach is sound in general. However, there is no mentioning of a formal semantics on which soundness arguments are based. In [17], a tool for the source-level verification of Solidity contracts is presented. Semi-automated deductive verification is performed, but the verification does not appear to be based on solid semantic foundation.

Several developments exist on the analysis and verification of Ethereum smart contracts in low-level and intermediate-level languages. In [15] and [27], static analysis techniques and tools for the sound checking of EVM bytecode are presented. In [22], a verification technique for the LLVM intermediate representation of smart contracts is developed. Our development differs from these existing ones both in the language level targeted, and in the verification approach taken.

Finally, in [3], a program logic is formalized in the Isabelle proof assistant for the deductive verification of EVM bytecode. The program logic is proven sound based on the semantic foundation provided in [19]. On the down side, it is relatively difficult to specify the desired properties and auxiliary information needed for a proof, while working with low-level code. In consideration of this issue, [23] proposes to conduct theorem proving based verification of Ethereum smart contract at the level of the Ethereum intermediate language Yul.

Program Verification via Matching Logics. In [29], an approach and tool for verifying programs directly based on an operational semantics is proposed. The work builds on matching logic. It has a language-agnostic proof system using a unified representation of both the language semantics and the program correctness specifications. This approach has proven to be effective for real-world programming languages. If the approach is taken for the verification of smart contracts, there will be no need to develop a program logic and prove its correspondence with the semantics. On the other hand, the specification of the correctness assertions and the intermediate assertions (e.g., contract invariants and loop invariants) in matching logic patterns is expected to be more verbose on average than that in the proposed program logic. There will also be the need for an operational semantics in which the calls to contracts with unknown code is specified abstractly. It remains to be an interesting topic to evaluate the approach of [29] in the formal verification of smart contracts, and to figure out about the impact of the underlying logic (language-specific program logic VS language-agnostic matching logic) on the conceptual complexity in reasoning about smart contracts and on the efficiency of verifiers that can be implemented.

7   Conclusion

Atomicity guarantees are crucial for the integrity of smart contracts. We propose an atomicity criterion that supports the characterization of semantic updates to variables, and enables the flexible specification of the operations that are supposed to be performed in atomic batches. We devise a Hoare-style program logic that supports the sound verification of the proposed atomicity criterion on smart contracts specifically, and partial correctness properties of smart contracts in general. The program logic is devised for a core Solidity-like programming language supporting the use of local and state variables, mappings, intra-contract and inter-contract calls, ether transfers, and the handling of exceptions. We illustrate the advantages of the proposed atomicity criterion, and the effectiveness of the program logic, using examples with practical relevance.

In the contract invariants of the proposed program logic, the Boolean conditions that are preserved as well as which state variables are unaffected by arbitrary executions of a smart contract can be expressed. However, the specification of the constraints on the value changes of state variables is not supported. In future work, we plan to further improve the expressiveness of the contract invariants, and extend our development to handle contract creation.

Acknowledgments. This work was supported by the National Natural Science Foundation of China (61877040, 61876111, 62002246), and the general project numbered KM202010028010 of Beijing Municipal Education Commission.

References

1. Ethereum smart contract best practices - known attacks. https://consensys.github.io/smart-contract-best-practices/known_attacks/
2. Solidity. https://solidity.readthedocs.io/en/v0.6.10/
3. Amani, S., Bégel, M., Bortin, M., Staples, M.: Towards verifying Ethereum smart contract bytecode in Isabelle/HOL. In: CPP 2018, pp. 66–77 (2018)
4. Apt, K.R.: Ten years of Hoare's logic: a survey - part 1. ACM Trans. Program. Lang. Syst. **3**(4), 431–483 (1981)
5. Atzei, N., Bartoletti, M., Cimoli, T.: A survey of attacks on Ethereum smart contracts (SoK). In: Maffei, M., Ryan, M. (eds.) POST 2017. LNCS, vol. 10204, pp. 164–186. Springer, Heidelberg (2017). https://doi.org/10.1007/978-3-662-54455-6_8
6. Bartoletti, M., Galletta, L., Murgia, M.: A minimal core calculus for Solidity contracts. CoRR, abs/1710.09437 (2019)
7. Beckert, B., Herda, M., Kirsten, M., Schiffl, J.: Formal specification and verification of Hyperledger Fabric chaincode. In: SDLT 2018 (2018)

8. Bernardo, B., Cauderlier, R., Pesin, B., Tesson, J.: Albert, an intermediate smart-contract language for the Tezos blockchain. CoRR, abs/2001.02630 (2020)
9. Bhargavan, K., Delignat-Lavaud, A., Fournet, C., et al.: Formal verification of smart contracts: Short paper. In: PLAS@CCS 2016, pp. 91–96 (2016)
10. Blackshear, S., Cheng, E., Dill, D.L., et al.: Move: a language with programmable resources (2020). https://developers.libra.org/
11. Chang, J., Gao, B., Xiao, H., Sun, J., Cai, Y., Yang, Z.: sCompile: critical path identification and analysis for smart contracts. In: Ait-Ameur, Y., Qin, S. (eds.) ICFEM 2019. LNCS, vol. 11852, pp. 286–304. Springer, Cham (2019). https://doi.org/10.1007/978-3-030-32409-4_18
12. Chen, T., Zhang, Y., Li, Z., et al.: TokenScope: automatically detecting inconsistent behaviors of cryptocurrency tokens in Ethereum. In: CCS 2019, pp. 1503–1520 (2019)
13. Crafa, S., Pirro, M.D., Zucca, E.: Is Solidity solid enough? In: FC 2019, pp. 138–153 (2019)
14. Gordon, M., Collavizza, H.: Forward with Hoare. In: Roscoe, A.W., Jones, C.B., Wood, K.R. (eds.) Reflections on the Work of C.A.R. Hoare, pp. 101–121. Springer, London (2010). https://doi.org/10.1007/978-1-84882-912-1_5
15. Grishchenko, I., Maffei, M., Schneidewind, C.: Foundations and tools for the static analysis of Ethereum smart contracts. In: Chockler, H., Weissenbacher, G. (eds.) CAV 2018. LNCS, vol. 10981, pp. 51–78. Springer, Cham (2018). https://doi.org/10.1007/978-3-319-96145-3_4
16. Grishchenko, I., Maffei, M., Schneidewind, C.: A semantic framework for the security analysis of Ethereum smart contracts. In: Bauer, L., Küsters, R. (eds.) POST 2018. LNCS, vol. 10804, pp. 243–269. Springer, Cham (2018). https://doi.org/10.1007/978-3-319-89722-6_10
17. Hajdu, Á., Jovanovic, D.: solc-verify: a modular verifier for Solidity smart contracts. In: VSTTE 2019, pp. 161–179 (2019)
18. Hildenbrandt, E., Saxena, M., Rodrigues, N., et al.: KEVM: a complete formal semantics of the Ethereum virtual machine. In CSF 2018, pp. 204–217 (2018)
19. Hirai, Y.: Defining the Ethereum virtual machine for interactive theorem provers. In: FC 2017, pp. 520–535 (2017)
20. Jiang, B., Liu, Y., Chan, W.K.: ContractFuzzer: fuzzing smart contracts for vulnerability detection. In: ASE 2018, pp. 259–269 (2018)
21. Jiao, J., Lin, S., Sun, J.: A generalized formal semantic framework for smart contracts. In: FASE 2020, pp. 75–96 (2020)
22. Kalra, S., Goel, S., Dhawan, M., Sharma, S.: ZEUS: analyzing safety of smart contracts. In: NDSS 2018 (2018)
23. Li, X., Shi, Z., Zhang, Q., Wang, G., Guan, Y., Han, N.: Towards verifying Ethereum smart contracts at intermediate language level. In: Ait-Ameur, Y., Qin, S. (eds.) ICFEM 2019. LNCS, vol. 11852, pp. 121–137. Springer, Cham (2019). https://doi.org/10.1007/978-3-030-32409-4_8
24. Luu, L., Chu, D., Olickel, H., et al.: Making smart contracts smarter. In: CCS 2016, pp. 254–269 (2016)
25. Nikolic, I., Kolluri, A., Sergey, I., et al.: Finding the greedy, prodigal, and suicidal contracts at scale. In: ACSAC 2018, pp. 653–663 (2018)
26. Permenev, A., Dimitrov, D., Tsankov, P., et al.: VerX: safety verification of smart contracts. In: S&P 2020 (2020)
27. Schneidewind, C., Grishchenko, I., Scherer, M., Maffei, M.: eThor: practical and provably sound static analysis of Ethereum smart contracts. arXiv, arXiv:2005.06227 (2020)

28. Sergey, I., Nagaraj, V., Johannsen, J., et al.: Safer smart contract programming with Scilla. In: OOPSLA 2019, pp. 1–30 (2019)
29. Stefanescu, A., Park, D., Yuwen, S., et al.: Semantics-based program verifiers for all languages. In: OOPSLA 2016, pp. 74–91 (2016)
30. Szabo, N.: Smart contracts (1994). https://nakamotoinstitute.org/formalizing-securing-relationships/
31. Tolmach, P., Li, Y., Lin, S.-W., et al.: A survey of smart contract formal specification and verification. CoRR, arXiv:2008.02712 (2020)
32. Wood, G.: Ethereum: a secure decentralised generlised transaction ledger. https://gavwood.com/paper.pdf
33. Yaga, D., Mell, P., Roby, N., Scarfone, K.: Blockchain technology overview. Technical report, NISTIR 8202 (2018)
34. Zakrzewski, J.: Towards verification of Ethereum smart contracts: a formalization of core of Solidity. In: VSTTE 2018, pp. 229–247 (2018)

Types

Neural Networks, Secure by Construction
An Exploration of Refinement Types

Wen Kokke[1,2(✉)], Ekaterina Komendantskaya[1], Daniel Kienitz[1],
Robert Atkey[3], and David Aspinall[2]

[1] Heriot-Watt University, Edinburgh, UK
wen.kokke@ed.ac.uk, {ek19,dk50}@hw.ac.uk
[2] University of Edinburgh, Edinburgh, UK
david.aspinall@ed.ac.uk
[3] Strathclyde University, Glasgow, UK
robert.atkey@strath.ac.uk

Abstract. We present StarChild and Lazuli, two libraries which leverage refinement types to verify neural networks, implemented in F* and Liquid Haskell. Refinement types are types augmented, or *refined*, with assertions about values of that type, *e.g.* "integers greater than five", which are checked by an SMT solver. Crucially, these assertions are written in the language itself. A user of our library can refine the type of neural networks, *e.g.* "neural networks which are robust against adversarial attacks", and expect F* to handle the verification of this claim for any specific network, without having to change the representation of the network, or even having to learn about SMT solvers.

Our initial experiments indicate that our approach could greatly reduce the burden of verifying neural networks. Unfortunately, they also show that SMT solvers do not scale to the sizes required for neural network verification.

Keywords: Neural networks · Verification · Refinement types

1 Introduction

Deep neural networks—or simply *neural networks*—is an umbrella term for a range of machine learning algorithms that, given numeric data instances as an input, construct a *non-linear function* or *classifier* that separates these data instances into classes. When a suitable classifier is found, it can be used to classify new, unseen data—or at least, that's the hope. Data instances can be pixel data for images, numeric encodings of the words from a lexicon for text analysis, or generally any n features of interest, viewed as a point in an n-dimensional real space. There are numerous applications of neural networks: in computer vision,

The work was funded by the National Cyber Security Center, UK. Grant *SecConn-NN: Neural Networks with Security Contracts*—*towards lightweight, modular security for neural networks.*

B. C. d. S. Oliveira (Ed.): APLAS 2020, LNCS 12470, pp. 67–85, 2020.
https://doi.org/10.1007/978-3-030-64437-6_4

Fig. 1. (Left) Image from MNIST [16] dataset, which is correctly classified as 0 by a given neural network. (Center) A small perturbation applied to the image. (Right) Resulting noisy image classified by the same neural network as a 3 with 92% confidence.

natural language processing, data mining, to name but a few. As neural networks move into domains where safety and security are important—*e.g.* autonomous cars, conversational agents, governance—the problem of their verification comes to the forefront.

Neural network verification is a notoriously difficult problem. Firstly, neural networks rely on data for training, testing, and often for verification. This data may be incomplete, noisy, or deliberately *poisoned*. Secondly, finding a suitable classifier is a mathematically complex task. There is a continuum of suitable classifiers in a continuous real space, and the search space may be prohibitively large, and an optimal classifier may not even exist. Finally, neural networks are difficult to interpret. Even if a reasonably accurate classifier is found, we do not understand all its latent properties. This is particularly true for classifiers that work with data of high dimensionality.

The very features that we value in neural networks (adaptivity and the ability to generalise from noisy data) becomes a source of safety and security threats. Neural networks are known to be vulnerable to *adversarial attacks* [10,19,21,22,25] (specially crafted inputs that can create an unexpected and possibly dangerous output) and suffer from *catastrophic forgetting* [20].

One approach to the verification of complex problems is *lightweight verification*, which means to:

1. verify only the properties that *matter* [9],
2. embed verification in the implementation, and
3. employ proof automation where possible.

In neural network verification, one property that matters is *adversarial robustness*, commonly characterised as the deviation in the neural network's outputs given perturbations of its inputs, checked for some set of inputs [11,13,23]. For datasets with relatively low inner-class variation, like MNIST [16], we can pick our sample images either randomly or by hand, and define perturbations using some valid transformations like rotation, scaling, and translation. For example, we could pick the image on the left of Fig. 1 as a sample image for the class zero, and verify whether, given a certain range of perturbations defined by a suitable distance function, we can guarantee that the perturbed image is still classified as 0. Such method would not cover unanticipated perturbations, *e.g.* since we did

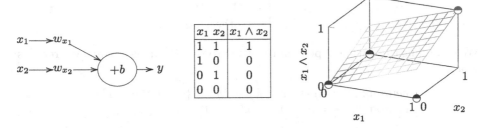

Fig. 2. (Left) Perceptron shown graphically as a neural network. (Center) Dataset for perceptron. (Right) Dataset as points in the three-dimensional space, with a linear classifier for the data.

not think of noise, the image on the right of Fig. 1 is not covered by our safety guarantees. This is not the only possible interpretation of the "neural network verification problem", but it is by far the most common. We will therefore use it throughout the paper.

We are primarily interested in exploring the space of solutions for (2) and (3). Since neural networks are "just" functions, we seek to embed verification constraints on inputs and outputs in the types of these functions, and then use the facilities of refinement type checking—with SMT solver integration—to automate all tedious proofs. In this paper, we explore this space using F* [24] and Liquid Haskell [27] and test whether contemporary, off-the-shelf programming language technologies are suitable for neural network verification, and to analyse the benefits and limitations of using refinement types. We hope the reader will find this study useful, by employing our ideas, avoiding the pitfalls we encountered, and perhaps filling the gaps in contemporary programming language technologies.

1.1 Example: Verifying the AND-Gate

Let's use a simple example to illustrate the use of our library: a perceptron for the logical AND-gate [17]. It has two inputs, a single, fully-connected layer, and one output, and its training set is the truth table for Boolean conjunction (see Fig. 2).

The *perceptron* is a gradient descent algorithm that approximates the linear function:

$$\text{neuron} : (x_1 : \mathbb{R}) \rightarrow (x_2 : \mathbb{R}) \rightarrow (y : \mathbb{R})$$
$$\text{neuron } x_1 \ x_2 = b + w_{x_1} \times x_1 + w_{x_2} \times x_2$$

that separates the data points into two classes, as shown in Fig. 2. The constants w_{x_1} and w_{x_2} are called the *weights* of the neuron, and b its bias. The gradient descent algorithm searches for suitable values for these constants, e.g.:

$$\text{neuron } x_1 \ x_2 = -0.9 + 0.5x_1 + 0.5x_2$$

Often, perceptrons involve an activation function, which is applied to the result of the linear function. Here, we use the *threshold function S*. We discuss other activation functions in Sect. 4.

$$S\ x = \begin{cases} 1, & \text{if } x \geq 0 \\ 0, & \text{otherwise} \end{cases}$$

We can refine the output type of our new neuron function, as S only ever returns 0 or 1:

$$\text{neuron} : (x_1 : \mathbb{R}) \rightarrow (x_2 : \mathbb{R}) \rightarrow (y : \mathbb{R}\ \{y = 0 \vee y = 1\})$$
$$\text{neuron } x_1\ x_2 = S\ (-0.9 + 0.5x_1 + 0.5x_2)$$

Let's verify that the neural network returns the "correct" values for inputs which lie within some distance ϵ of 1 and 0. Let's call these values *truthy* and *falsey*:

$$\text{truthy } x = |1 - x| \leq \epsilon$$
$$\text{falsey } x = |0 - x| \leq \epsilon$$

We can request that F* checks whether our neural network is correct by refining the type of neuron, *e.g.* by requiring that the output be 1 if both inputs are truthy. If neuron does not satisfy this property, test will not type check:

$$\text{test} : (x_1 : \mathbb{R}\ \{\text{truthy } x_1\}) \rightarrow (x_2 : \mathbb{R}\ \{\text{truthy } x_2\}) \rightarrow (y : \mathbb{R}\ \{y = 1\})$$
$$\text{test} = \text{neuron}$$

The user can implement the network *directly* in F*. Alternatively, if they have a pre-existing neural network in, *e.g.* Python, they can *export* the network to F*, as a Python library to export networks is included in both StarChild and Lazuli. For instance, we can use a Python library to find a suitable function for the data in Fig. 2, and export our model to F* to obtain the following code:

```
val model : network (*with*) 2 (*inputs*) 1 (*output*) 1 (*layer*)
let model = NLast // ← makes single-layer network
  { weights    = [[0.5R]; [0.5R]]
  ; biases     = [−0.9R]
  ; activation = Threshold }
```

Let's verify that it is correct for, *e.g.* $\epsilon = 0.1$, in F*:

```
let eps      = 0.1R
let truthy x = 1.0R - eps ≤ x && x ≤ 1.0R + eps
let falsey x = 0.0R - eps ≤ x && x ≤ 0.0R + eps

val test : (x₁ : R{truthy x₁}) → (x₂ : R{truthy x₂})
         → (y  : vector R 1 {y ≡ [1.0R]})
let test x₁ x₂ = run model [x₁; x₂]
```

Refinement types, used in this manner, seem to be a natural fit. The "burden" of verifying the AND-gate in our approach is minuscule. Once written, the user can reuse the code for test to verify different neural networks that use similar verification conditions, and develop a codebase of reusable verification conditions.

As a benefit of using F*, any model specified using StarChild, and any other F* program, is usable in refinements, and F* takes care of the translation to the SMT logic for us! For instance, when F* checks the function test, it passes the definition and the refinements on the inputs and output to the SMT solver, and only accepts the function if the SMT solver does. It *does not* check the networks output for all inputs within distance ϵ—this wouldn't be feasible, as there are uncountably many, and even accounting for the maximum precision of floating-point numbers, the search space is vast.

F* translates programs to the SMT logic by normalising them, translating constructs to their SMT equivalents where possible, and keeping the rest as uninterpreted functions. For instance, test normalises to:

```
let test x₁ x₂ = if x₁×0.5R + x₂×0.5R - 0.9R ≥ 0.0R then 1.0R else 0.0R
```

The normalised version can be translated directly to the SMT logic, together with the type refinements for test. This generates the following SMT query—simplified for readability—in SMTLIB2 Lisp [5]:

```
(define-fun neuron ((x₁ Real) (x₂ Real)) Real
  (ite (>= (- (+ (* x₁ 0.5) (* x₂ 0.5)) 0.9) 0.0) 1.0 0.0))
(define-fun truthy ((x Real)) Bool (and (<= 0.9 x) (<= x 1.1)))
(assert (∀ ((x₁ Real) (x₂ Real))
  (=> (and (truthy x₁) (truthy x₂)) (= (neuron x₁ x₂) 1.0))))
(check-sat)
```

As it turns out, this particular query is satisfiable, which you can verify with your favourite SMTLIB2-compatible solver. Therefore, our neural network is robust around truthy inputs!

1.2 Contributions

We make several contributions:

- We introduce two libraries, StarChild[1] for F*, and Lazuli[2] for Liquid Haskell. These libraries allow users to conveniently and modularly define and verify neural networks (Sect. 2).
- We illustrate that both F* and Liquid Haskell are suitable for the lightweight verification of neural networks (Sect. 2).
- We describe an approach for translating Keras [6] models, *e.g.* generated in Python, to StarChild and Lazuli (Sect. 2.2).
- We describe an approach for automating proofs involving non-linear activation functions, by piecewise-linearisation. SMT queries using non-linear functions such as the exponential function are not generally supported, and problems involving such functions are generally undecidable. However, all deep neural networks use non-linear activation functions, such as Sigmoid or Softmax (Sect. 4)
- We show that both training and testing using piecewise-linear approximations of non-linear activation functions is possible, and results in only a negligible decrease in performance (Sect. 4).

---

[1] https://github.com/wenkokke/starchild.
[2] https://github.com/wenkokke/lazuli.

- Finally, we describe several problems that we believe cannot be overcome without substantial improvements in both the programming languages, *e.g.* F* and Liquid Haskell, and in SMT solvers. These are problems of scale, and limitations that arise from the incomplete implementation of real-valued expressions in F*, and the lack of normalisation of refinements in Liquid Haskell. We suggest possible solutions for the future (Sect. 5).

Neural network verification is a growing area of research, with several tools on the market, e.g. Marabou [13], ERAN [23], DLV [11], PAROT [3], to name a few. It is not our goal to produce another competing tool, hence the missing benchmarking against these. Instead, our goal is to establish programming language principles for incorporating these tools into a more abstract framework, which may open ways of embedding neural net verification into future multi-component projects.

2   An Overview of StarChild

Neural networks are functions on vectors of real numbers. Hence, the StarChild library consists mostly of an F* implementation of basic linear algebra (implemented in `StarChild.LinearAlgebra`). A second module contains an implementation of dimension-safe neural networks, following Grenade[3] and the "dependently-typed" Haskell bindings for TensorFlow[4,5] (implemented in `StarChild.Network`).

The linear algebra module defines the types of length-indexed real vectors and matrices, using F*'s implementation of real numbers (implemented in `FStar.Real`), and using refinements of F*'s implementation of lists for both vectors and matrices, where the refinement adds a length-index.

The module further defines standard operations on vectors and matrices: maps and folds, the dot product, and matrix multiplication (see Fig. 3). We reuse the list implementations of these functions when possible, but often F* needs us to redefine functions, *e.g.* `map1`, to verify the length-index.

Finally, the module defines common distance metrics on vectors, which can be used in verification constraints. However, not all distance metrics can be represented in the SMT logic. For instance, Euclidean distance uses the square root function, which is non-linear. Instead, we opt to use the squared Euclidean distance (see Fig. 3).

The neural network module defines the structure of neural networks. A neural network is a non-empty list of layers, where the number of outputs of each layer matches the number of inputs of the next layer. The network type has three parameters—the number of inputs, outputs, and layers. Just like with lists, there are two ways to construct a network. `NLast` defines a single-layer network, whose number of inputs and outputs correspond to those of the layer. `NStep` adds a layer

---

[3] https://github.com/HuwCampbell/grenade.
[4] https://hackage.haskell.org/package/tensor-safe.
[5] https://github.com/helq/tensorflow-haskell-deptyped.

```
type vector 'a n    = v:list 'a {length v ≡ n}
type matrix 'a r c = vector (vector 'a c) r

val dot : #n:N // Dot product
          → xs:vector ℝ n → ys:vector ℝ n → ℝ
let dot #n xs ys = sum (map2 (fun x y → x × y) xs ys)

val vAv : #n:N // Vector addition
          → xs:vector ℝ n → ys:vector ℝ n → vector ℝ n
let vAv #n xs ys = map2 (fun x y → x + y) xs ys

val vXm : #r:N → #c:N // Vector-matrix multiplication
          → xs:vector ℝ r → yss:matrix ℝ r c → vector ℝ c
let rec vXm #r #c xs yss = match xs, yss with
  | [], [] → replicate 0.0R
  | (x :: xs), (ys :: yss) →
    vAv #c (scale #c x ys) (vXm #(r - 1) #c xs yss)

val mXm : #i:N → #j:N → #k:N // Matrix-matrix multiplication
          → matrix ℝ i j → matrix ℝ j k → matrix ℝ i k
let mXm #i #j #k xss yss = map (fun xs → vXm #j #k xs yss) xss

val sed : #n:N // Squared Euclidean distance
          → xs:vector ℝ n → ys:vector ℝ n → ℝ≥0
let sed #n xs ys =
  sum≥0 #n (map2 #ℝ #ℝ #ℝ≥0 #n (fun x y → (x − y) × (x − y)) xs ys)
```

Fig. 3. Linear algebra functions in StarChild.

to the front of a network, where the number of inputs of new layer becomes the number of inputs of the network, and the number of outputs of the new layer has to correspond to the old number of inputs of the network:

```
type network (i:N>0) (o:N>0) : n:N → Type =
  | NLast : l:layer i o → network i o 1
  | NStep : #n:N>0 → #h:N>0
            → l:layer i h → ls:network h o n → network i o (n + 1)
```

We use $\mathbb{N}_{>0}$ to denote the refined type of positive natural numbers, and similarly, $\mathbb{R}_{>0}$ and $\mathbb{R}_{\geq0}$ to denote the positive and non-negative real numbers.

Each fully-connected layer consists of a matrix of weights, whose dimensions correspond to the number of inputs and outputs of the layer, a vector of biases, whose length corresponds to the number of outputs of the layer, and the name of an activation function:

```
type layer (i:N>0) (o:N>0) =
  { weights    : matrix ℝ i o
  ; biases     : vector ℝ o
  ; activation : activation }
```

```
val lsigmoid : ℝ → ℝ
let lsigmoid x = let v = 0.25R × x + 0.5R in
                if v < 0.0R then 0.0R else
                if 1.0R < v then 1.0R else v

val lexp : ℝ → ℝ_{>0}
let lexp x = if x ≤ − 1.0R then 0.00001R else
             if x ≥ 1.0R then 5.898R × x − 3.898R else x + 1.0R

val norm : #n:ℕ_{>0} → vector ℝ_{>0} n → vector ℝ n
let norm #n xs = map1 #ℝ_{>0} #ℝ #n (fun x → x / sum_{≥0} #n xs) xs

val lsoftmax : #n:ℝ_{>0} → vector ℝ n → vector ℝ n
let lsoftmax #n xs = norm (map1 #ℝ #ℝ_{>0} #n lexp xs)
```

Fig. 4. Naive piecewise-linear approximations of the Sigmoid and Softmax functions in the StarChild library.

Our current implementation supports four common activation functions:

```
type activation : Type =
  | Linear   // linear(x) = x
  | ReLU     // relu(x) = max(0, x)
  | Sigmoid  // sigmoid(x) = 1/(1+e^{-x})
  | Softmax  // softmax(x̄)_i = e^{x_i} / ∑_{j=1}^{k} e^{x_j}
```

The linear and ReLU functions are straightforward to define, although the FStar.Real module is rather sparse, and lacks functions for, *e.g.* minimum, maximum, negation, *etc.*:

```
val linear : ℝ → ℝ
let linear x = x // i.e. identity function
val relu : ℝ → ℝ
let relu x = if x ≤ 0.0R then x else 0.0R
```

However, the Sigmoid and Softmax functions are non-linear functions, and cannot be translated directly to the SMT logic. Our solution is to use piecewise-linear approximations of these functions. Since F* does not allow us to fine-tune the translation to the SMT logic, we implement these directly in F*. In Fig. 4, we present two naive implementations of piecewise-linear approximations for the Sigmoid and Softmax functions. We discuss a more principled approach to generating linear approximations in Sect. 4.

To run a StarChild network, we simply run each layer successively, feeding the output of one layer into the next:

```
val run : #i:ℕ_{>0} → #o:ℕ_{>0} → #n:ℕ_{>0}
        → ls:network i o n → xs:vector ℝ i
        → Tot (vector ℝ o) (decreases n)
let rec run #i #o #n ls xs = match ls with
  | NLast l    → run_layer l xs
  | NStep l ls → run ls (run_layer l xs)
```

We annotate the function with a totality annotation, which lets F* verify the recursion terminates by checking that the number of layers decreases.

We run a layer by performing the computations described in Sect. 1.1: we multiply the inputs by the weights, add the bias, and run the activation function:

```
val run_layer : #i:ℕ>0 → #o:ℕ>0
                → l:layer i o → xs:vector ℝ i → vector ℝ o
let run_layer #i #o l xs =
  run_activation #o l.activation (vAv #o l.biases (vXm #i #o xs l.weights))
```

Finally, we run an activation function by matching the name, *e.g.* Sigmoid, up with the appropriate definition, *e.g.* lsigmoid:

```
val run_activation : #n:pos → a:activation → xs:vector ℝ n → vector ℝ n
let run_activation #n a xs =
  match a with
  | Linear  → xs
  | ReLU    → map1 relu xs
  | Sigmoid → map1 lsigmoid xs
  | Softmax → lsoftmax xs
```

2.1   A Note on Lazuli

The Liquid Haskell counterpart to StarChild, Lazuli, follows a similar architecture, and shares the module and function names whenever possible. Any differences are due to quirks of F* or Liquid Haskell.

When implementing dimension-safe vector arithmetic in Liquid Haskell, it is convenient to store the dimensions of a vector or matrix in the structure itself, hence, in Lazuli, vectors and matrices are refined record types. For instance, a vector is a record which stores a list and an integer, with a type refinement requiring that integer is exactly equal to the length of the list.

Liquid Haskell allows us to fine-tune the translation of functions to the SMT language, hence, if the user wants to, they could translate the standard Softmax function to the linearised Softmax *only* during verification. This has consequences for the safety guarantees, however, as the verified network no longer corresponds *exactly* to the executed network.

Finally, Liquid Haskell does not support normalisation prior to the translation to the SMT logic. Instead, Liquid Haskell supports *refinement reflection* [28], in which Haskell functions are translated to SMT equalities which encode their reduction behaviour. This offloads the burden of normalisation to the SMT solver. Unfortunately, SMT solvers perform exploratory search, in which they use these equations in *both* directions, *i.e.* they expand as well as reduce. Hence, they are much less efficient at reduction, and consequently, at the time of writing Lazuli is significantly slower than StarChild.

2.2   The Convenience of Keras Models

We don't have any illusions that training networks in F* or Liquid Haskell will be the preferred method, or even feasible, in the near future. Therefore, it is important to integrate our libraries with existing methods. For this reason, we implemented a Python library for converting Keras [6] models to StarChild and Lazuli, which we bundle with StarChild and Lazuli as convert.py.

3   Verifying A "Real" Example: MNIST

In this section, we describe our experiences using StarChild to verify a neural network trained on MNIST.

The MNIST dataset contains 28×28 images of the handwritten digits "0" to "9". Hence, an input consists of 748 pixels, and an output is—conventionally—a probability distribution over the 10 classes, created by the Softmax function. This leaves us to determine the number of hidden layers, their sizes, and their activation functions. For instance, we could opt for a 128-node hidden layer using the ReLU activation function:

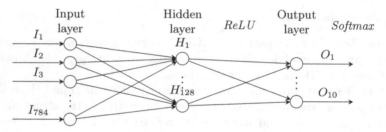

Unfortunately, this model has $784 \times 128 + 128 + 128 \times 10 + 10 = 101770$ constant parameters and 784 input parameters. Worse, it has 3 fully-connected layers, meaning that each input parameter occurs at least $128 \times 10 = 1280$ times in the SMT query, and constant parameters occur several times in accordance to the layer they are in. This is a *huge* query from an SMT solving perspective, and it would overwhelm any SMT solver. However, this is not a large network from a machine learning perspective. We discuss this matter further in Sect. 5.

For now, we seek to make verification with an SMT solver tractable. One option is to reduce the dimensionality of the input, and reduce the size of the network. If used with care, this usually only leads to modest decreases in model accuracy. We use *principal component analysis* (PCA) to reduce the size of the input vectors to 25, and reduce the size of the hidden layer to 10. This model has *far fewer* parameters, $25 \times 10 + 10 + 10 \times 10 + 10 = 370$, yet it only suffers a loss of 2 percentage points in test accuracy (see Fig. 9). Note that verifying the correctness of the smaller model gives us no formal guarantees about the correctness of the larger model. Hence, using this approach, we are forced to deploy the smaller, less accurate model. Figure 5 shows the F* code for the smaller MNIST network, imported from Keras using the library described in Sect. 2.2.

Unlike in Sect. 1.1, vectors in Fig. 5 are wrapped in an assertion (**let** v = ... **in assert_norm** (length v = n); v). There are two assertion keywords, **assert** and **assert_norm**. These assertions have no runtime significance. Instead, one can think of them as functions with the refined type (b:bool {b $\equiv$ true}) $\rightarrow$ (). That is to say, assertions take an argument of type bool and verify, using an SMT solver, that it is true.

By default, terms are translated to the SMT logic *unnormalised*, similar to Liquid Haskell (see Sect. 2.1). After all, terms may grow enormously through normalisation. Using **assert_norm** forces F* to normalise terms before querying the SMT solver. Without it, F* offloads the burden of term reduction to the SMT solver. Unfortunately, SMT solvers do exploratory search, and are much less efficient at reduction. Worse, F* encodes a notion of fuel into translated terms, meaning function definitions can only be unfolded a set number of times, determined by the command-line argument --max-fuel (default 8). Beyond that, programs fail to type check.

Let's verify the model is robust for class "0" in an ϵ-ball $\mathbb{B}(\hat{x})$ around a sample input $\hat{x}$, $\mathbb{B}(\hat{x}, r) = \{x \in \mathbb{R}^n : ||\hat{x} - x||_2 \leq r\}$. First, we pick an input vector representing the digit "0", and convert it to F*:

```
val sample_in : vector ℝ 25
let sample_in = let v = [7.394R; −0.451R; ...; 0.199R]
                in assert_norm (length v = 25); v
```

Then, we run the Keras model on the input, and convert the output to F*:

```
val sample_out: vector ℝ 10
let sample_out = let v = [0.998R; 0.000R; ...; 0.000R]
                 in assert_norm (length v = 10); v
```

For readability, we elide several elements from each vector, and limit the precision of the floating-point numbers.

With these two definitions in hand, we can define our verification condition. The idea is that, for all inputs within a certain distance ϵ_1 from our sample input, the neural network output should be within a certain ϵ_2 from the sample output. Let $\epsilon_1 = 0.01$ and $\epsilon_2 = 1$:

```
let _ = assert_norm (∀ (x:vector ℝ 25). (sed #25 sample_in x < 0.01R)
    ⟹ (sed #10 sample_out (run m x) < 1.0R))
```

Note that the function sed (squared Euclidean distance) is defined in Fig. 3. While type checking, F* verifies that our verification condition holds. Crucially, it wouldn't be possible to verify this by testing.

Once again, the "burden" of verification in our approach is rather small, as it takes only a handful of lines of code to formulate the verification conditions, and the code which checks them. Unfortunately, even for this modest model, verification of complex conditions takes an *infeasibly long* amount of time. We address this problem in Sect. 5.

```
val layer_0 : layer 25 10
let layer_0 =
  { weights = (let v = [ (let v = [−0.64R; 0.19R; ...; 0.54R; 0.78R]
                             in assert_norm (length v = 10); v)
                         ; (let v = [0.79R; 0.53R; ...; −1.00R; 0.82R]
                             in assert_norm (length v = 10); v)
                         ...
                         ; (let v = [−0.33R; −0.44R; ...; −0.20R; −0.04R]
                             in assert_norm (length v = 10); v) ]
                   in assert_norm (length v = 25); v)
  ; biases = (let v = [0.15R; 1.28R; ...; 1.03R; 0.32R]
                 in assert_norm (length v = 10); v)
  ; activation = ReLU }

val layer_1 : layer 10 10
let layer_1 =
  { weights = (let v = [ (let v = [0.00R; −0.87R; ...; −0.99; 0.26R]
                             in assert_norm (length v = 10); v)
                         ; (let v = [−0.50R; −1.28R; ...; 0.65R; 0.62R]
                             in assert_norm (length v = 10); v)
                         ...
                         ; (let v = [0.50R; −0.49R; ...; −0.73R; −0.34R]
                             in assert_norm (length v = 10); v) ]
                   in assert_norm (length v = 10); v)
  ; biases = (let v = [−0.41R; −0.41R; ...; 1.08R; 0.15R]
                 in assert_norm (length v = 10); v)
  ; activation = Softmax }

val model : network 25 10 2
let model = NStep layer_0 (NLast layer_1)
```

Fig. 5. StarChild model generated from Keras.

4   Piecewise-Linear Approximations Made Easy

In this section, we discuss non-linear activation functions, and automatic linearisation. Deep neural networks require the use of non-linear functions between each layer—the composition of two linear functions is itself a linear function, and hence any deep neural network which uses only linear activation functions is equivalent to a shallow neural network.

Unfortunately, SMT solvers do not generally support non-linear arithmetic, and where they do, the solvers are slower and less reliable. At the time of writing, F* uses the Z3 solver [18]. Z3 uses Dual Simplex [7] to solve linear real arithmetic. It also supports a fragment of non-linear real arithmetic—specifically, multiplications—and solves this using a conflict resolution procedure based on cylindrical algebraic decomposition [12]. However, the addition of multiplication

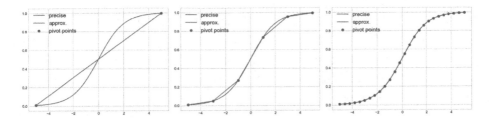

Fig. 6. Linearisation of the Sigmoid function over the interval $I = [-5, 5]$ with $n = 1$, $n = 5$, and $n = 25$ line segments.

is not enough to cover the non-linear activation functions used in deep learning, which often use exponents, logarithms, and trigonometric functions. The only solver we are aware of that supports these functions out of the box is MetiTarski [2]. However, the MetiTarski documentation reads "Beyond 4 or 5 continuous variables, there is very little hope for MetiTarski in finding a proof." Since our smallest possible "real" problem involves 25 continuous variables, we have very little hope that MetiTarski will prove useful to us.

We approximate non-linear activation functions using piecewise-linear approximations, *i.e.* several connected line segments. We refer to this as "linearisation". For instance, in Fig. 4 we used two handwritten piecewise-linear approximations for the Sigmoid and the exponential functions. This approach is a little crude, and manual linearisation is time consuming. Instead, we have developed an algorithm for automatic linearisation of a function $\sigma : \mathbb{R} \to \mathbb{R}$ over an interval I using n line segments:

1. We split the interval I into n equal-sized sub-intervals $I_1, \ldots, I_n$.
2. For each sub-interval I_i:
   (a) Let $l_i = \min I_i$ and $u_i = \max I_i$.
   (b) We draw a line segment of the form $f_i(x) = m_i x + b_i$, with slope m_i and y-intercept b_i, from the minimum $(l_i, \sigma(l_i))$ to the maximum $(u_i, \sigma(u_i))$.
3. Finally, we connect all line segments f_i. The result is a piecewise-linear approximation for σ over the interval I.

The parameter n determines the granularity. In Fig. 6, we show the linear approximation of the Sigmoid function for different values of n.

How should a piecewise-linear approximation behave outside of the interval I? We have three simple options:

1. We can extrapolate the first and last line segments beyond the interval boundaries.
2. We can return the minimum point, $\sigma(\min I)$, for inputs below the interval, and return the maximum point, $\sigma(\max I)$, for inputs above the interval.
3. We can combine (1) and (2). We start by extrapolating, following (1), and allow the user to specify lower and upper bounds, where we switch to returning the constant minimum and maximum, following (2).

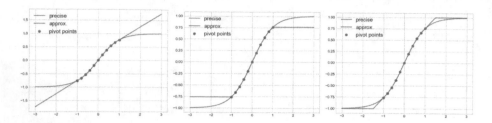

Fig. 7. Linearisation of the tanh-function over the interval $[-1, 1]$ with $n = 10$ with three different bounding methods: extrapolation, constant values, and the user-defined combination.

The first option is unsound, as it may result in cases where the codomain of the piecewise-linear approximation is not a subset of the codomain of the approximated function. For instance, the piecewise-linear approximation of the exp-function may return values < 0 for a sufficiently small input. The second option is sound, albeit a bit crude. The third option combines the best of (1) and (2), but requires manual tweaking. In Fig. 7, we show examples of these methods for the tanh-function.

Piecewise-linear functions are not continuously differentiable, as they are non-differentiable at each point where two line segments meet. For instance, the ReLU function relu(x) is not differentiable at $x = 0$, since the left derivative at $x = 0$ is 0, and the right derivative at $x = 0$ is 1. The same applies to our linearised functions. However, ReLUs are widely used, and are differentiated by arbitrarily choosing the derivative at $x = 0$ as either 0 or 1. Therefore, we have two options for training our networks:

1. We train our network with non-linear activation functions, but verify it and run it with piecewise-linear approximations.
2. We train our network with piecewise-linear approximations.

The first option has the advantage that we train with smooth, continuously differentiable activation functions. However, we train and verify with different architectures. As long as we verify and run the same object, this is not a problem for safety. It does raise a question: what is the effect of running a model trained with non-linear functions on a linearised architecture?

In Fig. 8, we present the loss in test accuracy, as a result of transferring weights trained with the precise tanh function to networks with piecewise-linear approximations. If the tanh function is approximated with at least 3 line segments, the drop in accuracy is marginal.

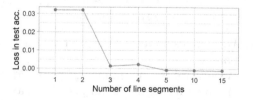

Fig. 8. Loss from weight transfer (tanh).

Hidden activation	Output activation	Training accuracy	Test accuracy	Training time (sec.)
Fully-connected network trained on MNIST (with PCA 25)				
relu	softmax	0.973	0.968	7.6
tanh	softmax	0.968	0.963	7.7
linear tanh	linear softmax	0.964	0.960	18.1
Convolutional network trained on MNIST				
relu	softmax	0.999	0.991	50.7
linear tanh	linear softmax	0.993	0.985	106.8
Convolutional network trained on CIFAR-10				
tanh	softmax	0.811	0.704	115.6
relu	softmax	0.925	0.782	115.1
linear tanh	linear softmax	0.769	0.702	243.9

Fig. 9. Performance for two networks trained on MNIST and one on CIFAR-10. For the linearised hidden activations, we use 3 segments. For the exp-function in piecewise-linear softmax, we use 10 segments. We extrapolate the first and last line segments.

The second option has the advantage that we train and verify with the same architecture. Therefore, we do not incur the drop in accuracy which we expect from option (1). However, it does raise a different question: what is the effect of training with linearised activation functions, which have non-smooth gradients? We train a fully-connected and a convolutional neural network on the MNIST dataset and a convolutional neural network on the CIFAR-10 dataset [14]. Each architecture is trained with either the precise tanh and Softmax functions, or with their piecewise-linear approximations ($n = 5$). Since we did not observe any difference with respect to the different bounding methods, we only report the result for the extrapolation method. In Fig. 9, we show the results for these experiments. The drop in train and test accuracy of the fully-connected neural network trained and tested with linearised activation functions is marginal. For comparison we also train a convolutional neural network, and we observe that this model with linearised activations functions performs only slightly worse than a state-of-the-art model with ReLU activations.

5 Lessons Learned

Refinement Types for Neural Network Verification. StarChild and Lazuli are flexible and lightweight libraries. They support the dimension-safe construction of neural networks. They support the lightweight verification of neural networks, in which neural networks and their verification conditions be written in the same language. Finally, they provide us with a user-friendly interface to SMT solvers, which means that merely *stating* the verification conditions is enough—the host language does the verification as part of type checking.

Training and Verification in the Same Language. We hope to extend our libraries with the ability to *train* as well as verify networks. However, there are several barriers to this. For F*, the main barrier is that code cannot be executed, but instead must be extracted to OCaml or F#. For Haskell, there already exist several Haskell-bindings for TensorFlow. However, at the time of writing, Liquid Haskell only verifies Haskell source, and not runtime objects such as neural network models. Hence, we would have to either extend Liquid Haskell with the ability to verify runtime objects, or convert the trained models to Haskell code. The former would constitute a significant contribution to Liquid Haskell, and the latter, while much simpler to implement, has very few advantages over our current approach.

Training networks using Keras made our work significantly easier, and importing the models to our libraries was an easy task. There is already existing work importing pre-trained models to theorem provers for the purposes of verification, e.g. MLCert in Coq [4]. Our approach to importing models differs from MLCert: we translate floating-point numbers to F* reals, whereas MLCert translates them to bit-vectors.

Whether or not we integrate training into our libraries in the future, we believe that interfacing with the Python machine learning ecosystem will remain important for the foreseeable future.

Linearisation. The method presented for scalable automatic linearisation in Sect. 4 works remarkably well. Our experiments show that it is possible to use piecewise-linear approximations of non-linear functions both during training and at runtime without a serious loss in accuracy. This is important, as non-linear real arithmetic with exponentials, logarithms, and trigonometric functions is undecidable, and therefore, it is unlikely that any future SMT solver will be able to efficiently decide problems of this sort.

Our current method of linearisation is crude, in that it splits the interval into sub-intervals of equal length. Often, a much better approximation is possible by varying the lengths of the sub-intervals.

Scalability and Size Reduction. F* and Liquid Haskell offer to translate any program to the SMT logic. Unfortunately, this generality comes with a cost. In Fig. 10, we present a benchmark for the verification of the n-ary AND gate, *i.e.* the network which returns 1 if, and only if, each of its n inputs is 1. The verification task is to check whether the network returns the correct answer for each of four sample inputs. There are two curves for StarChild. One in which we use **assert**, and one in which we use **assert_norm**. Both are exponential. On the contrary, the line for Z3 does not exceed $1s$. Hence, it seems F* introduces an exponential factor in its encoding.

Unfortunately, while the curve for Z3 is encouraging, it does not scale to more complex conditions, such as the robustness conditions discussed in Sect. 3. Most solvers for linear real arithmetic simply do not scale to the size and complexity needed to check robustness conditions for even modest neural networks. There are several existing lines of work which attempt to address this problem. Marabou [13] uses a modification of the Simplex algorithm which more efficiently decides problems with piecewise-linear functions (such as ReLU). DeepPoly [23] uses abstract interpretations. Kwiatkowska [15] gives an overview of the progress in this area.

However, we consider the problem of scalable verification somewhat orthogonal to our goals. We seek to integrate existing solvers with programming languages in ways which make neural network verification as lightweight as possible. We used Z3 and other SMTLIB2-compatible solvers because these solvers have existing integration with programming languages. For future work, we plan to look into integrating Marabou with a dependently-typed programming language, and abandon generality in favour of generating efficient queries specific to the neural network domain.

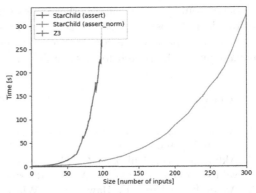

Fig. 10. Verification time for n-ary AND.

Soundness of the Proposed Approach. We did not prove, or attempt to prove, that neural network transformations, such as size reduction (Sect. 3) or linearisation (Sect. 4) preserves the semantics of the network. Our assumption is that the verified network is deployed in practice, and we do not extend safety guarantees to the full precision network.

Whether or not this approach is practically feasible deserves further attention. There are multiple papers in the machine learning community that show that reduced size networks are feasible, and even desirable. There are a rising number of implementations of neural networks on special purpose hardware, *e.g.* using FPGAs [26]), mobile phones [1], and special-purpose robotics hardware that require compression techniques. Ensuring that reduced-size networks perform sufficiently similar to the original networks is an optimisation problem that has been considered in the literature, and is beyond the limits of this study. However, we do provide a more detailed discussion of effects of linearisation in Sect. 4, as it is less well-studied in the literature.

Continuous Training and Verification. In Sect. 1, we discussed why lightweight verification is appropriate for neural network verification. However, there is one novel feature of neural network verification, as opposed to the verification of conventional programs. Usually, we assume that the object we verify is uniquely defined, often hand-written, and therefore needs to be verified as-is. Neural networks are different—often there is a continuum of models that can serve as suitable classifiers. Given the task of verifying a neural network, we are no longer required to think of the object as immutable. This opens up new possibilities, where we can feed information from the verification process back into the training process. In fact, some papers in machine learning have already started to explore this fact [8].

Seen from this angle, methods such as dimensionality reduction and linearisation do not pose a threat to the soundness of our verification methods, but instead are a part of the conversation between the training and the verification mechanism in the search for a suitable, safe classifier.

References

1. Abadi, M., et al.: TensorFlow: Large-scale machine learning on heterogeneous distributed systems (2016)
2. Akbarpour, B., Paulson, L.C.: MetiTarski: an automatic theorem prover for real-valued special functions. J. Autom. Reason. **44**(3), 175–205 (2009)
3. Ayers, E.W., Eiras, F., Hawasly, M., Whiteside, I.: PaRoT: a practical framework for robust deep neural network training. In: Lee, R., Jha, S., Mavridou, A. (eds.) NFM 2020. LNCS, vol. 12229, pp. 63–84. Springer, Cham (2020). https://doi.org/10.1007/978-3-030-55754-6_4
4. Bagnall, A., Stewart, G.: Certifying true error: machine learning in Coq with verified generalisation guarantees. In: AAAI (2019)
5. Barrett, C., Stump, A., Tinelli, C., et al.: The SMT-LIB standard: version 2.0. In: Proceedings of the 8th International Workshop on Satisfiability Modulo Theories, Edinburgh, England, vol. 13, p. 14 (2010)
6. Chollet, F., et al.: Keras (2015). https://keras.io
7. Dutertre, B., de Moura, L.: A fast linear-arithmetic solver for DPLL(T). In: Ball, T., Jones, R.B. (eds.) CAV 2006. LNCS, vol. 4144, pp. 81–94. Springer, Heidelberg (2006). https://doi.org/10.1007/11817963_11
8. Fischer, M., Balunovic, M., Drachsler-Cohen, D., Gehr, T., Zhang, C., Vechev, M.T.: DL2: training and querying neural networks with logic. In: Proceedings of the 36th International Conference on Machine Learning, ICML 2019, vol. 97, pp. 1931–1941. PMLR (2019)
9. Fisher, K., Launchbury, J., Richards, R.: The HACMS program: using formal methods to eliminate exploitable bugs. Phil. Trans. R. Soc. A. **375**, 20150401 (2017)
10. Goodfellow, I.J., Shlens, J., Szegedy, C.: Explaining and harnessing adversarial examples. arXiv preprint arXiv:1412.6572 (2014)
11. Huang, X., Kwiatkowska, M., Wang, S., Wu, M.: Safety verification of deep neural networks. In: Majumdar, R., Kunčak, V. (eds.) CAV 2017. LNCS, vol. 10426, pp. 3–29. Springer, Cham (2017). https://doi.org/10.1007/978-3-319-63387-9_1
12. Jovanović, D., de Moura, L.: Solving non-linear arithmetic. ACM Commun. Comput. Algebra **46**(3/4), 104 (2013)
13. Katz, G., et al.: The Marabou framework for verification and analysis of deep neural networks. In: Dillig, I., Tasiran, S. (eds.) CAV 2019. LNCS, vol. 11561, pp. 443–452. Springer, Cham (2019). https://doi.org/10.1007/978-3-030-25540-4_26
14. Krizhevsky, A., Hinton, G., et al.: Learning multiple layers of features from tiny images. Technical report, Citeseer (2009)
15. Kwiatkowska, M.Z.: Safety verification for deep neural networks with provable guarantees (invited paper). In: Fokkink, W., van Glabbeek, R. (eds.) CONCUR 2019, LIPIcs, vol. 140, pp. 1:1–1:5. Schloss Dagstuhl - Leibniz-Zentrum für Informatik (2019)

16. LeCun, Y., Cortes, C., Burges, C.: Mnist handwritten digit database. ATT Labs [Online]. http://yann.lecun.com/exdb/mnist. Accessed Feb 2010
17. McCulloch, W., Pitts, W.: A logical calculus of the ideas immanent in nervous activity. Bull. Math. Biophys. **5**, 115–133 (1943)
18. de Moura, L., Bjørner, N.: Z3: an efficient SMT solver. In: Ramakrishnan, C.R., Rehof, J. (eds.) TACAS 2008. LNCS, vol. 4963, pp. 337–340. Springer, Heidelberg (2008). https://doi.org/10.1007/978-3-540-78800-3_24
19. Papernot, N., McDaniel, P.D., Swami, A., Harang, R.E.: Crafting adversarial input sequences for recurrent neural networks. In: Brand, J., Valenti, M.C., Akinpelu, A., Doshi, B.T., Gorsic, B.L. (eds.) 2016 IEEE Military Communications Conference, MILCOM 2016, Baltimore, MD, USA, 1–3 November 2016. pp. 49–54. IEEE (2016)
20. Parisi, G., et al.: Continual lifelong learning with neural networks: a review. Neural Netw. **113**, 54–71 (2019)
21. Pertigkiozoglou, S., Maragos, P.: Detecting adversarial examples in convolutional neural networks. CoRR abs/1812.03303 (2018). http://arxiv.org/abs/1812.03303
22. Serban, A.C., Poll, E.: Adversarial examples - A complete characterisation of the phenomenon. CoRR abs/1810.01185 (2018). http://arxiv.org/abs/1810.01185
23. Singh, G., Gehr, T., Püschel, M., Vechev, M.T.: An abstract domain for certifying neural networks. PACMPL **3**(POPL), 41:1–41:30 (2019)
24. Swamy, N., et al.: Dependent types and multi-monadic effects in F*. In: Proceedings of the 43rd Annual ACM SIGPLAN-SIGACT Symposium on Principles of Programming Languages, POPL 2016. ACM Press (2016)
25. Szegedy, C., et al.: Intriguing properties of neural networks. arXiv preprint arXiv:1312.6199 (2013)
26. Umuroglu, Y., et al.: FINN: a framework for fast, scalable binarized neural network inference. In: Proceedings of the 2017 ACM/SIGDA International Symposium on Field-Programmable Gate Arrays, FPGA 2017, Monterey, CA, USA, 22–24 February 2017, pp. 65–74 (2017)
27. Vazou, N.: Liquid Haskell: Haskell as a Theorem Prover. Ph.D. thesis, University of California, San Diego, USA (2016)
28. Vazou, N., et al.: Refinement reflection: complete verification with SMT. Proc. ACM Program. Lang. **2**(POPL), 1–31 (2018)

A New Refinement Type System for Automated $\nu\text{HFL}_\mathbb{Z}$ Validity Checking

Hiroyuki Katsura[1]([✉]) [iD], Naoki Iwayama[1], Naoki Kobayashi[1] [iD], and Takeshi Tsukada[2] [iD]

[1] The University of Tokyo, Bunkyo City, Japan
{katsura,iwayama,koba}@kb.is.s.u-tokyo.ac.jp
[2] Chiba University, Chiba, Japan
tsukada@math.s.chiba-u.ac.jp

Abstract. Kobayashi et al. have recently shown that various verification problems for higher-order functional programs can naturally be reduced to the validity checking problem for $\text{HFL}_\mathbb{Z}$, a higher-order fixpoint logic extended with integers. We propose a refinement type system for checking the validity of $\nu\text{HFL}_\mathbb{Z}$ formulas, where $\nu\text{HFL}_\mathbb{Z}$ is a fragment of $\text{HFL}_\mathbb{Z}$ without least fixpoint operators, but sufficiently expressive for encoding safety property verification problems. Our type system has been inspired by the type system of Burn et al. for solving the satisfiability problem for HoCHC, which is essentially equivalent to the $\nu\text{HFL}_\mathbb{Z}$ validity checking problem. Our type system is more expressive, however, due to a more sophisticated subtyping relation. We have implemented a type-based $\nu\text{HFL}_\mathbb{Z}$ validity checker RETHFL based on the proposed type system, and confirmed through experiments that RETHFL can solve more instances than Horus, the tool based on Burn et al.'s type system.

1 Introduction

Kobayashi et al. [8,17] have recently shown that various verification problems for higher-order functional programs can naturally be reduced to the validity checking problem for $\text{HFL}_\mathbb{Z}$, an extension of HFL [16] with integers. In this paper, we focus on a fragment of $\text{HFL}_\mathbb{Z}$ called $\nu\text{HFL}_\mathbb{Z}$, which is a fragment of $\text{HFL}_\mathbb{Z}$ without least fixpoint operators, and propose an automated method for solving the validity checking problem (which, in turn, serves as an automated method for higher-order program verification, thanks to the reduction mentioned above). The fragment $\nu\text{HFL}_\mathbb{Z}$ is sufficiently expressive for encoding safety properties of programs. A validity checker for $\nu\text{HFL}_\mathbb{Z}$ can also be used as a building block for a validity checker for full $\text{HFL}_\mathbb{Z}$, as briefly discussed in [17], and worked out for the first-order fixpoint logic [7].

To see the connection between program verification and $\nu\text{HFL}_\mathbb{Z}$ validity checking, let us consider the following ML program.

© Springer Nature Switzerland AG 2020
B. C. d. S. Oliveira (Ed.): APLAS 2020, LNCS 12470, pp. 86–104, 2020.
https://doi.org/10.1007/978-3-030-64437-6_5

```
let rec sum n k =
    if n <= 0 then k n
    else sum (n - 1) (fun r -> k (n + r))
let main m = sum m (fun r -> assert(r >= m))
```

This program calculates the sum of integers from 1 to n, and then asserts that the value is no less than n. Suppose that we wish to verify that the assertion never fails for any integer n. By using the reduction of Kobayashi et al. [8], the verification problem can be reduced to the validity checking problem for the following νHFL$_\mathbb{Z}$ formula.

$$\psi := \forall m.(\nu\text{Sum}.\lambda n.\lambda k.$$
$$(n \leq 0 \Rightarrow k\ n) \wedge$$
$$(n > 0 \Rightarrow \text{Sum}\ (n-1)\ (\lambda r.k\ (n+r)))$$
$$)\ m\ (\lambda r.r \geq m) \tag{1}$$

Here, the part $\nu\text{Sum}.\lambda n.\cdots$ denotes the greatest predicate such that $\text{Sum} = \lambda n.\cdots$. A detailed explanation is deferred to Sect. 2, but the reader should be able to notice the close correspondence between the program and the formula above: for example, the part $(n \leq 0 \Rightarrow \cdots) \wedge (n > 0 \Rightarrow \cdots)$ corresponds to the conditional expression in the program.

In this paper, we propose a refinement type system for proving the validity of a νHFL$_\mathbb{Z}$ formula, and develop an automated procedure for refinement type inference. In our refinement type system, the type of propositions is refined to a type of the form $\bullet\langle\theta\rangle$, which is the type of propositions that hold whenever θ holds; in other words, if a proposition ψ has type $\bullet\langle\theta\rangle$, then θ is an underapproximation of ψ (with respect to the order false $<$ true). For example, νHFL$_\mathbb{Z}$ formula $x \geq 0$ has type $\bullet\langle x > 0\rangle$ because $x > 0 \Rightarrow x \geq 0$ holds.

Our type system has been inspired by that of Burn et al. [2] for proving the satisfiability of Higher-order Constrained Horn Clauses (HoCHC), a higher-order extension of Constrained Horn Clauses (CHC) [1]. In fact, the HoCHC satisfiability problem[1] is essentially the same as the νHFL$_\mathbb{Z}$ validity checking problem (in the sense that for any HoCHC C, there exists a νHFL$_\mathbb{Z}$ formula ψ_C such that C is satisfiable if and only if ψ_C is valid, and vice versa). The main difference between our type system and theirs is in the subtyping relation. We introduce more sophisticated subtyping relations, which makes the resulting subtyping relation complete with respect to the semantic subtyping relation. In contrast, the subtyping relation in Burn et al.'s system is too conservative, which makes their type system too weak; in fact, as confirmed through experiments, there are many νHFL$_\mathbb{Z}$ formulas whose validity can be proved in our type system but the satisfiability of the corresponding HoCHC cannot be proved in Burn et al.'s type system.

An alternative existing approach to automatically proving the validity of a νHFL$_\mathbb{Z}$ formula is a combination of (pure) HFL model checking and predicate

---

[1] Throughout the paper, we assume integer arithmetic as the underlying constraint language of HoCHC.

abstraction [5]. Though our type-based approach is less powerful in theory than the model checking approach, ours tends to be faster, as confirmed by our experiments. Thus, we consider that the two approaches are complementary.

The rest of this paper is structured as follows. Section 2 reviews the definition of $\nu\text{HFL}_\mathbb{Z}$. Section 3 presents our refinement type system for $\nu\text{HFL}_\mathbb{Z}$ and proves the soundness of the type system and the relative completeness of the subtyping relation. Section 4 discusses the relationship between our type system for $\nu\text{HFL}_\mathbb{Z}$ and Burn et al.'s one for HoCHC. Section 5 presents an automated method for $\nu\text{HFL}_\mathbb{Z}$ validity checking based on our type system. Section 6 reports an implementation and experimental results. Section 7 discusses related work, and Sect. 8 concludes the paper.

2   Preliminaries: $\nu\text{HFL}_\mathbb{Z}$

We review the syntax and semantics of $\nu\text{HFL}_\mathbb{Z}$ [8], which is a simply-typed higher-order logic with arithmetic operations and the greatest fixed-point operator.

2.1   Syntax

The logic $\nu\text{HFL}_\mathbb{Z}$ is simply typed. The syntax of *simple types* is given by:

$$\rho ::= \bullet \mid \eta \to \rho \qquad \text{and} \qquad \eta ::= \rho \mid \textbf{Int}.$$

The type $\bullet$ is for propositions and **Int** is for integers. The types are constructed from these atomic types and the function type constructor $\to$. The above syntax restricts occurrences of **Int** only to argument positions. The reason will be explained in the next subsection.

The syntax of $\nu\text{HFL}_\mathbb{Z}$ formulas is given by:

$$\psi \quad ::= \quad n \mid \psi_1 \text{ op } \psi_2 \mid \textbf{p}(\psi_1, \cdots, \psi_n) \mid \textbf{tt} \mid \textbf{ff} \mid \psi_1 \vee \psi_2 \mid \psi_1 \wedge \psi_2 \mid \forall X : \textbf{Int}.\psi$$
$$\mid \quad X \mid \lambda X : \eta.\psi \mid \psi_1 \psi_2 \mid \nu X : \rho.\psi$$

where n ranges over integers, **op** over basic binary operations on integers (such as summation and multiplication), **p** over basic predicates on integers (such as equality), and X over variables. The constructors in the first line are standard; those in the second line are those from the simply-typed λ-calculus (i.e. variable X, abstraction $\lambda X : \eta.\psi$ and application $\psi_1 \psi_2$) and the greatest fixed-point operator $\nu X : \rho.\psi$. The occurrences of X in $\forall X : \textbf{Int}.\psi$, $\lambda X : \eta.\psi$ and $\nu X : \rho.\psi$ are binding occurrences. We shall not distinguish α-equivalent terms. We shall often omit the type annotations. Lower case letters such as x, y and z are sometimes used as variables of type **Int**.

The typing rules are straightforward. A *judgment* is a triple $\Gamma \vdash_H \psi : \eta$, where Γ is a *(simple) type environment* (i.e. finite map from variables to simple types). The type system is basically the simply-typed λ-calculus with typed constants

$$n : \textbf{Int} \qquad op : \textbf{Int} \to \textbf{Int} \to \textbf{Int} \qquad p : \textbf{Int} \to \cdots \to \textbf{Int} \to \bullet$$
$$\textbf{tt}, \textbf{ff} : \bullet \qquad \vee, \wedge : \bullet \to \bullet \to \bullet$$

and the following additional typing rules:

$$\frac{\Gamma, X : \textbf{Int} \vdash_H \psi : \bullet}{\Gamma \vdash_H \forall X : \textbf{Int}.\psi : \bullet} \quad \text{and} \quad \frac{\Gamma, X : \rho \vdash_H \psi : \rho}{\Gamma \vdash_H \nu X : \rho.\psi : \rho}.$$

The complete list of typing rules can be found in [6]. In the sequel, we shall consider only well-typed formulas.

A closed formula of type $\bullet$ is called a *sentence*.

Example 1. Let ψ be the νHFL$_\mathbb{Z}$ formula defined by

$$\psi \quad := \quad \nu X : \textbf{Int} \to \bullet.\, \lambda y : \textbf{Int}.\, y \neq 0 \wedge X\,(y+1).$$

The meaning of this formula can be intuitively understood as follows. Since it is a fixed-point, (the meaning of) this formula must be a solution of the equation

$$X \quad = \quad \lambda y.\, y \neq 0 \wedge X\,(y+1).$$

More specifically it is the greatest solution, where a predicate A is greater than B if $\forall n \in \mathbf{Z}.(A\,n \Rightarrow B\,n)$.

A more intuitive way to guess the greatest solution is to iteratively apply the equation. Since (the meaning of) ψ satisfies the above equation, one has

$$\begin{aligned} \psi\,n \quad &= \quad (n \neq 0) \wedge \psi\,(n+1) \quad = \quad (n \neq 0) \wedge (n+1 \neq 0) \wedge \psi\,(n+2) \quad = \quad \cdots \\ &= \quad (n \neq 0) \wedge (n+1 \neq 0) \wedge \cdots \wedge (n+k \neq 0) \wedge \ldots. \end{aligned}$$

This informal argument shows that $\psi\,n$ must be false for every $n \leq 0$. The greatest solution is obtained by letting $\psi\,n$ be true if $\psi\,n$ does not have to be false by this argument based on expansion of the definition. Hence $\psi\,n$ is true for every $n > 0$. □

2.2 Semantics

A type η is interpreted as a poset $\mathcal{D}_\eta$ and a formula ψ of type η as an element of $\mathcal{D}_\eta$. The formal definition is as follows.

The poset $\mathcal{D}_\eta = (\mathcal{D}_\eta, \sqsubseteq_\eta)$ is defined by induction on η:

$$\begin{aligned} \mathcal{D}_\bullet &= \{\top, \bot\} \quad \sqsubseteq_\bullet = \{(\bot, \bot), (\bot, \top), (\top, \top)\} \\ \mathcal{D}_\textbf{Int} &= \mathbb{Z} \quad \sqsubseteq_\textbf{Int} = \{(n, n) \mid n \in \mathbb{Z}\} \\ \mathcal{D}_{\eta \to \rho} &= \{f \in \mathcal{D}_\eta \to \mathcal{D}_\rho \mid \forall x, y.(x \sqsubseteq_\eta y \Rightarrow f(x) \sqsubseteq_\rho f(y))\} \\ \sqsubseteq_{\eta \to \rho} &= \{(f, g) \mid \forall x \in \mathcal{D}_\eta.f(x) \sqsubseteq_\rho g(x)\}. \end{aligned}$$

We note that $\mathcal{D}_{\eta \to \rho}$ is not the set of all functions but *monotone* functions. Observe that $\mathcal{D}_\rho$ is a complete lattice (i.e., for each subset $A \subseteq \mathcal{D}_\rho$, the greatest lower bound $\bigsqcap A$ of A exists). The interpretation $\mathcal{D}_{\mathbf{Int}}$ is not a complete lattice, and this is why we distinguish **Int** from other simple types.

For a simple type environment Γ, we write $[\![\Gamma]\!]$ for the set of functions that maps a variable X in (the domain of) Γ to an element of $\mathcal{D}_{\Gamma(X)}$. We call an element of $[\![\Gamma]\!]$ a *valuation*. Valuations are ordered by the point-wise ordering.

The interpretation $[\![\psi]\!]$ of a formula $\Gamma \vdash_H \psi : \eta$ is a *monotone* function from $[\![\Gamma]\!]$ to $\mathcal{D}_\eta$. It is defined by induction on ψ. For example,

$$[\![\nu X : \rho.\psi]\!](\chi) \quad := \quad \bigsqcap \{v \in \mathcal{D}_\rho \mid v \sqsubseteq_\rho [\![\psi]\!](\chi[X \mapsto v])\}$$

where $\chi[X \mapsto v]$ is the valuation defined by $\chi[X \mapsto v](X) = v$ and $\chi[X \mapsto v](Y) = \chi(Y)$ $(X \neq Y)$. The right-hand-side of the above definition is an explicit formula that calculates the greatest fixed-point of the mapping $v \mapsto [\![\psi]\!](\chi[X \mapsto v])$. The well-definedness and correctness of this explicit formula is ensured by the facts that $\mathcal{D}_\rho$ is a complete lattice and that $v \mapsto [\![\psi]\!](\chi[X \mapsto v])$ is monotone. We omit other cases since they are straightforward; see [6] for the complete definition.

We write the interpretation of a sentence ψ as $[\![\psi]\!]$ since it is independent of a valuation (as a sentence has no free variable). If $[\![\psi]\!](\emptyset) = \top$, then the sentence ψ is *valid* and we write $\models \psi$. The $\nu HFL_\mathbb{Z}$ *validity checking problem* is the problem of checking whether a given sentence is valid. Note that this problem is undecidable in general.

Example 2. Let us consider the following formula νHFL$_\mathbb{Z}$ formula:

$$\phi := \forall m.(\nu \text{Sum}.\lambda n.\lambda k.$$
$$(n > 0 \vee k\ n) \wedge$$
$$(n \leq 0 \vee \text{Sum}\ (n-1)\ (\lambda r.k\ (n+r)))$$
$$)\ m\ (\lambda r.r \geq m).$$

This formula is essentially the same as the example in Introduction (Sect. 1) except that $\Rightarrow$ is replaced with other connectives (since $\Rightarrow$ is not in νHFL$_\mathbb{Z}$). The relationship between this formula and the safety verification of the program at the beginning of Introduction can be now explained as follows.

The reduction of the program corresponds to the β-reduction, the expansion of Sum (cf. Example 1), and some trivial rewriting of formulas such as $(0 \neq 0) \vee \delta \longrightarrow \delta$. The safety verification asks whether the program fails in some finite steps. If the program fails, then the corresponding rewriting of the formula shows that the formula is false. If there is no such rewriting, the formula is true as expected since the greatest fixed-point is true "by default" (cf. Example 1). $\square$

3 Refinement Type System

This section introduces a refinement type system, which our validity checker is based on. The refinement type system introduced in this section is inspired by and closely related to that of Burn et al. [2]. This section focuses on our refinement type system; a comparison of the two systems is the topic of the next section.

3.1 Syntax of Refinement Types

Our type system uses refinement types to describe properties of formulas. Here we define the syntax and semantics of refinement types.

The syntax of *refinement types* is given by the following grammar:

arithmetic expressions $\mathbf{a} ::= n \mid x \mid \mathbf{op}(\mathbf{a}_1, \cdots, \mathbf{a}_n)$

constraint formulas $\theta ::= \mathbf{tt} \mid \mathbf{ff} \mid \mathbf{p}(\mathbf{a}_1, \cdots, \mathbf{a}_n) \mid \theta_1 \wedge \theta_2 \mid \theta_1 \vee \theta_2$

extended constraint formulas $\Theta ::= \theta \mid \Theta_1 \wedge \Theta_2 \mid \exists x.\Theta$

refinement types $\tau ::= \bullet\langle\theta\rangle \mid x : \mathbf{Int} \to \tau \mid \tau_1 \to \tau_2$.

The occurrence of x in $x : \mathbf{Int} \to \tau$ is a binding occurrence. We shall not distinguish between α-equivalent refinement types.

Each refinement type τ describes a property on formulas and semantic elements of a simple type ρ. This relationship is formalized as the *refinement relation*, which is defined by the following rules:

$$\frac{}{\bullet\langle\theta\rangle :: \bullet} \qquad \frac{\tau :: \rho}{(x : \mathbf{Int} \to \tau) :: (\mathbf{Int} \to \rho)} \qquad \frac{\tau_1 :: \rho_1 \quad \tau_2 :: \rho_2}{(\tau_1 \to \tau_2) :: (\rho_1 \to \rho_2)}.$$

For every refinement type τ, there exists a unique simple type ρ such that $\tau :: \rho$. We write $\Gamma \vdash \tau :: \rho$ if $\tau :: \rho$ and $\mathrm{fv}(\tau) \subseteq \{x \mid \Gamma(x) = \mathbf{Int}\}$.

The meaning of arithmetic expressions and constraint formulas should be obvious. We explain the intuitive meaning of refinement types. If $\tau :: \rho$, then τ is for formulas of simple type ρ that satisfies a certain property.

A formula ψ of type $\bullet$ has the refinement type $\bullet\langle\theta\rangle$ if θ implies ψ. More precisely, the type judgement $\psi : \bullet\langle\theta\rangle$ means "if θ holds, then the interpretation of ψ is $\top$." The simplest example is $\bullet\langle\mathbf{tt}\rangle$; if $\psi : \bullet\langle\mathbf{tt}\rangle$, then the interpretation of ψ is $\top$. Another extreme example is $\bullet\langle\mathbf{ff}\rangle$; $\psi : \bullet\langle\mathbf{ff}\rangle$ holds for every formula ψ of simple type $\bullet$ since the condition $\mathbf{ff}$ never holds. Both ψ and θ may contain free variables. For example, $\psi : \bullet\langle x > 0\rangle$ holds if the interpretation of $\psi[n/x]$ is $\top$ for every $n > 0$.

The meaning of the refinement type $\tau_1 \to \tau_2$ is similar to the standard function type. A formula ψ has type $\tau_1 \to \tau_2$ just if $\psi\phi : \tau_2$ for every formula ϕ of type τ_1.

The meaning of $x : \mathbf{Int} \to \tau$ is similar to the above case, but τ can refer to the argument x in this case. For example, $x : \mathbf{Int} \to \bullet\langle x > 0\rangle$ is for formulas ψ of simple type $\mathbf{Int} \to \bullet$ such that $\psi n : \bullet\langle n > 0\rangle$ for every n.[2] In other words, it is a type for predicates that are true on every positive integer.

It is worth emphasising that a refinement type describes a situation in which a formula should be *true*. It does not say anything about a situation in which a formula should be *false*. Therefore the constantly true function $\lambda X : \rho.\mathbf{tt}$ has all refinement type τ such that $\tau :: \rho \to \bullet$. So a (valid) refinement type judgement $\psi : \tau$ gives an underapproximation of ψ.

---

[2] Equivalently, $\psi x : \bullet\langle x > 0\rangle$, provided that ψ has no free occurrence of x.

3.2 Semantics of Refinement Types

In order to clarify the informal definition of the meaning of refinement types given above, we formalize the semantics of refinement types. For a refinement type $\tau :: \rho$, we give two interpretations. In the first interpretation, the refinement type is interpreted as the subset $(\!|\tau|\!) \subseteq \mathcal{D}_\rho$ of semantic elements that satisfies τ. This is a direct formarization of the above discussed meaning of refinement types. In the second interpretation, the refinement type is seen as an element $\gamma_\tau \in \mathcal{D}_\rho$. As expected, the two interpretations are closely related: we have $(\!|\tau|\!) = \{v \in \mathcal{D}_\rho \mid \gamma_\tau \sqsubseteq_\rho v\}$.

We give some auxiliary definitions. The interpretation $[\![\theta]\!]$ of constraint formulas θ is straightforward as constraint formulas can be seen as $\nu\mathrm{HFL}_\mathbb{Z}$ formulas. It is a map from valuations α on free variables of θ to $\mathcal{D}_\bullet = \{\bot, \top\}$. The interpretation can be naturally extended to extended constraint formulas by $[\![\exists x.\Theta]\!](\alpha) := \bigsqcup_{v \in \mathbb{Z}}[\![\Theta]\!](\alpha[x \mapsto v])$.

The first interpretation $(\!|\tau|\!)$ of a refinement type $\Gamma \vdash \tau :: \rho$ is a function from valuations $\alpha \in [\![\Gamma]\!]$ to subsets $(\!|\tau|\!)(\alpha) \subseteq \mathcal{D}_\rho$ of the interpretation of ρ. It is defined by induction on the structure as follows:

$$(\!| \bullet \langle \theta \rangle |\!)(\alpha) := \begin{cases} \{\top\} & (\text{if } \alpha \models \theta) \\ \{\bot, \top\} & (\text{if } \alpha \not\models \theta) \end{cases}$$

$$(\!|x : \mathbf{Int} \to \tau|\!)(\alpha) := \{f \in \mathcal{D}_{\mathbf{Int} \to \rho} \mid \forall v \in \mathcal{D}_{\mathbf{Int}}.\ f(v) \in (\!|\tau|\!)(\alpha[x \mapsto v])\}$$

$$(\!|\tau_1 \to \tau_2|\!)(\alpha) := \{f \in \mathcal{D}_{\rho_1 \to \rho_2} \mid \forall v \in (\!|\tau_1|\!)(\alpha).\ f(v) \in (\!|\tau_2|\!)(\alpha)\}.$$

This is basically a direct translation of the informal semantics discussed in the previous subsection.

The second interpretation γ_τ is a map from $[\![\Gamma]\!]$ to $\mathcal{D}_\rho$, inductively defined by

$$\gamma_{\bullet\langle\theta\rangle}(\alpha) := \begin{cases} \top_\bullet & (\text{if } \alpha \models \theta) \\ \bot_\bullet & (\text{if } \alpha \not\models \theta) \end{cases}$$

$$\gamma_{x:\mathbf{Int}\to\tau}(\alpha) := \left[\mathcal{D}_{\mathbf{Int}} \ni v \ \mapsto\ \gamma_\tau(\alpha[x \mapsto v])\right]$$

$$\gamma_{\tau_1\to\tau_2}(\alpha) := \left[\mathcal{D}_{\rho_1} \ni v \ \mapsto\ \begin{cases} \gamma_{\tau_2}(\alpha) & (\text{if } \gamma_{\tau_1}(\alpha) \sqsubseteq_{\rho_1} v) \\ \bot_{\rho_2} & (\text{otherwise}) \end{cases}\right]$$

where we assume $(\tau_1 \to \tau_2) :: (\rho_1 \to \rho_2)$ in the last case. Here $\top_\rho$ and $\bot_\rho$ are the greatest and least element of $\mathcal{D}_\rho$. The element $\gamma_\tau(\alpha)$ is the minimum element in $(\!|\tau|\!)(\alpha)$.

Lemma 1. *Assume $\Gamma \vdash \tau :: \rho$ and $\alpha \in [\![\Gamma]\!]$. Then*

$$\forall v \in \mathcal{D}_\rho.\left[v \in (\!|\tau|\!)(\alpha) \iff \gamma_\tau(\alpha) \sqsubseteq_\rho v\right].$$

$$\frac{\Delta(x) = \tau}{\Delta \vdash x : \tau} \quad \text{(RVar)}$$

$$\frac{\Delta, x : \mathbf{Int} \vdash \psi : \bullet\langle\theta\rangle \quad x \notin \mathbf{fv}(\theta)}{\Delta \vdash \forall x^{\mathbf{Int}}.\psi : \bullet\langle\theta\rangle} \quad \text{(RAllI)}$$

$$\frac{\Delta \vdash \psi : x : \mathbf{Int} \to \tau}{\Delta \vdash \psi\,\mathbf{a} : [\mathbf{a}/x]\tau} \quad \text{(RAppI)}$$

$$\overline{\Delta \vdash \mathbf{p}(\mathbf{a}_1, \cdots, \mathbf{a}_n) : \bullet\langle \mathbf{p}(\mathbf{a}_1, \cdots, \mathbf{a}_n)\rangle} \quad \text{(RPred)}$$

$$\frac{\Delta \vdash \psi_1 : \bullet\langle\theta_1\rangle \quad \Delta \vdash \psi_2 : \bullet\langle\theta_2\rangle}{\Delta \vdash \psi_1 \wedge \psi_2 : \bullet\langle\theta_1 \wedge \theta_2\rangle} \quad \text{(RAnd)}$$

$$\frac{\Delta \vdash \psi_1 : \tau_1 \to \tau_2 \quad \Delta \vdash \psi_2 : \tau_1}{\Delta \vdash \psi_1\,\psi_2 : \tau_2} \quad \text{(RApp)}$$

$$\frac{\Delta \vdash \psi_1 : \bullet\langle\theta_1\rangle \quad \Delta \vdash \psi_2 : \bullet\langle\theta_2\rangle}{\Delta \vdash \psi_1 \vee \psi_2 : \bullet\langle\theta_1 \vee \theta_2\rangle} \quad \text{(ROr)}$$

$$\frac{\Delta, X : \tau \vdash \psi : \tau}{\Delta \vdash \nu X.\psi : \tau} \quad \text{(RGfp)}$$

$$\frac{\Delta \vdash \psi : \tau_1 \quad \Delta; \mathbf{tt} \vdash \tau_1 \prec \tau_2}{\Delta \vdash \psi : \tau_2} \quad \text{(RSub)}$$

$$\frac{\Delta, x : \mathbf{Int} \vdash \psi : \tau}{\Delta \vdash \lambda x.\psi : x : \mathbf{Int} \to \tau} \quad \text{(RAbsI)}$$

$$\frac{\Delta, x : \tau_1 \vdash \psi : \tau_2}{\Delta \vdash \lambda x.\psi : \tau_1 \to \tau_2} \quad \text{(RAbs)}$$

Fig. 1. Refinement typing rules

$$\frac{\Delta \models \Theta \wedge \theta_2 \Rightarrow \theta_1}{\Delta; \Theta \vdash \bullet\langle\theta_1\rangle \prec \bullet\langle\theta_2\rangle} \quad \text{(S-Bool)}$$

$$\frac{\Delta, x : \mathbf{Int}; \Theta \vdash \tau_1 \prec \tau_2}{\Delta; \Theta \vdash x : \mathbf{Int} \to \tau_1 \prec x : \mathbf{Int} \to \tau_2} \quad \text{(S-IntFun)}$$

$$\frac{\Delta; \Theta \wedge \mathbf{rty}(\tau_2') \vdash \tau_1' \prec \tau_1 \quad \Delta; \Theta \vdash \tau_2 \prec \tau_2'}{\Delta; \Theta \vdash \tau_1 \to \tau_2 \prec \tau_1' \to \tau_2'} \quad \text{(S-Fun)}$$

Fig. 2. Subtyping rules

3.3 Typing Rules

Now we define our refinement type system by giving the typing rules.

A *refinement type environment* Δ is a finite map from a subset of variables to refinement types or **Int**. We write $\Delta :: \Gamma$ if the domains of Δ and Γ coincide and $\Delta(X) :: \Gamma(X)$ for every X in the domain. Here we assume **Int** :: **Int**.

A *refinement type judgement* is a triple $\Delta \vdash \psi : \tau$. We shall only consider a refinement type judgement that refines a simple type judgement. That means, when we consider $\Delta \vdash \psi : \tau$, we implicitly assume a simple type judgement $\Gamma \vdash_H \psi : \rho$ and refinement relations $\Delta :: \Gamma$ and $\Gamma \vdash \tau :: \rho$.

Figure 1 shows typing rules of the refinement type system. We explain some key rules. The rule RAnd says that $\theta_1 \wedge \theta_2$ is an underapproximation of $\psi_1 \wedge \psi_2$ if θ_i is an underapproximation of ψ_i for $i = 1, 2$. The rule RAppI substitutes the actual argument $\mathbf{a}$ for x in τ. The rule RGfp is the standard coinductive (i.e. greatest) fixed-point rule, saying that the fixed-point $\nu X.\psi$ has type τ if ψ has type τ under the assumption that X has type τ. The most important rule for this paper is RSub, which allows us to construct a derivation of $\Delta \vdash \psi : \tau_2$ from that of $\Delta \vdash \psi : \tau_1$ under a certain assumption. We explain this rule in more detail.

The rule RSub refers to the subtyping judgement $\Delta; \Theta \vdash \tau_1 \prec \tau_2$, defined by the *subtyping rules* listed in Fig. 2. Among the rules in Fig. 2, S-Fun is the only nontrivial rule. Similar to the standard subtyping rule for function types, it concludes $\tau_1 \to \tau_2 \prec \tau_1' \to \tau_2'$ from $\tau_1' \prec \tau_1$ and $\tau_2 \prec \tau_2'$. A notable point is that the assumption for $\tau_1' \prec \tau_1$ is strengthened by $\mathbf{rty}(\tau_2')$, which is defined by the following equations:

$$\mathbf{rty}(\bullet\langle\theta\rangle) := \theta \qquad \mathbf{rty}(x{:}\mathbf{Int} \to \tau) := \exists x.\mathbf{rty}(\tau) \quad \text{and} \quad \mathbf{rty}(\tau_1 \to \tau_2) := \mathbf{rty}(\tau_2).$$

A key property of $\mathbf{rty}(\tau)$ is the following lemma.

Lemma 2. *Assume $\Gamma \vdash \tau :: \rho$ and $\alpha \in [\![\Gamma]\!]$. If $\alpha \not\models \mathbf{rty}(\tau)$, then $(\![\tau]\!)(\alpha) = \mathcal{D}_\rho$.*

This means that, if $\mathbf{rty}(\tau)$ is false, then τ_2 is the trivial property that all elements satisfy. Therefore, to show that $\tau \prec \tau'$, we can assume without loss of generality that $\mathbf{rty}(\tau')$ holds because otherwise $\tau \prec \tau'$ trivially holds. This explains why we can assume $\mathbf{rty}(\tau_2')$ in the premise of S-Fun.[3]

The significance of the assumption $\mathbf{rty}(\tau_2')$ in S-Fun is demonstrated by the next example.

Example 3. Recall the formula ψ in Introduction (Sect. 1) and Example 2:

$$\forall m.(\nu\mathrm{Sum}.\lambda n.\lambda k.(n > 0 \vee k\,n) \wedge (n \leq 0 \vee \mathrm{Sum}\,(n{-}1)\,(\lambda r.k(r{+}n))))\,m\,(\lambda r.r \geq m).$$

We would like to show that $\vdash \psi : \bullet\langle\mathbf{tt}\rangle$, which implies the validity of ψ as we shall see. The most interesting part is the typing of $(\nu\mathrm{Sum}.\ldots)$:

$$\vdash (\nu\mathrm{Sum}.\ldots) \; : \; n : \mathbf{Int} \to (x : \mathbf{Int} \to \bullet\langle x \geq n\rangle) \to \bullet\langle\mathbf{tt}\rangle.$$

Let Δ be the refinement type environment:

$$\mathrm{Sum} : \big(n{:}\mathbf{Int} \to (x{:}\mathbf{Int} \to \bullet\langle x \geq n\rangle) \to \bullet\langle\mathbf{tt}\rangle\big), \quad n{:}\mathbf{Int}, \quad k{:}\big(x{:}\mathbf{Int} \to \bullet\langle x \geq n\rangle\big).$$

It suffices to show:

$$\Delta \vdash (n > 0 \vee k\,n) \wedge (n \leq 0 \vee \mathrm{Sum}\,(n-1)\,(\lambda r.k(r+n))) \; : \; \bullet\,\langle\mathbf{tt}\rangle.$$

We have:

$$
\cfrac{
  \cfrac{\vdots}{(n > 0 \vee k\,n) : \bullet\langle\mathbf{tt}\rangle}
  \qquad
  \cfrac{
    n \leq 0 : \bullet\langle n \leq 0\rangle
    \qquad
    \cfrac{\vdots}{\mathrm{Sum}\,(n-1)\,(\lambda r.k(r+n)) : \bullet\langle n > 0\rangle}
  }{
    (n \leq 0 \vee \mathrm{Sum}\,(n-1)\,(\lambda r.k(r+n))) : \bullet\langle\mathbf{tt}\rangle
  }
}{
  (n > 0 \vee k\,n) \wedge (n \leq 0 \vee \mathrm{Sum}\,(n-1)\,(\lambda r.k(r+n))) \; : \; \bullet\,\langle\mathbf{tt}\rangle
}
$$

where we omit $\Delta \vdash$ from each judgement and implicitly rewrite $\bullet\langle n \leq 0 \vee n > 0\rangle$ to $\bullet\langle\mathbf{tt}\rangle$. Since the left judgement is easy to show, we focus on the right judgement.

We have

$$\Delta \vdash \mathrm{Sum}\,(n-1) \; : \; (r : \mathbf{Int} \to \bullet\langle r \geq n - 1\rangle) \to \bullet\langle\mathbf{tt}\rangle$$

---

[3] A reader may wonder why we do not assume $\mathbf{rty}(\tau_2')$ in the other premise. This is because the subtyping judgements $\Delta; \Theta \vdash \tau_2 \prec \tau_2'$ and $\Delta; \Theta \wedge \mathbf{rty}(\tau_2') \vdash \tau_2 \prec \tau_2'$ are equivalent in the sense that the derivability of one of them implies the other's. We chose the simpler judgement.

$$\dfrac{\dfrac{\Delta, r : \mathbf{Int} \models n > 0 \wedge r \geq n - 1 \Rightarrow r \geq 0}{\Delta, r : \mathbf{Int}; n > 0 \vdash \bullet\langle r \geq 0\rangle \prec \bullet\langle r \geq n-1\rangle}}{\Delta; n > 0 \vdash r : \mathbf{Int} \to \bullet\langle r \geq 0\rangle \prec r : \mathbf{Int} \to \bullet\langle r \geq n-1\rangle} \qquad \dfrac{\Delta \models n > 0 \Rightarrow \mathbf{tt}}{\Delta; \mathbf{tt} \vdash \bullet\langle \mathbf{tt}\rangle \prec \bullet\langle n > 0\rangle}$$

$$\Delta; \mathbf{tt} \vdash (r : \mathbf{Int} \to \bullet\langle r \geq n-1\rangle) \to \bullet\langle \mathbf{tt}\rangle \prec (r : \mathbf{Int} \to \bullet\langle r \geq 0\rangle) \to \bullet\langle n > 0\rangle$$

Fig. 3. A derivation of a subtyping judgement used in Example 3

but this is not immediately usable since

$$\Delta \nvdash (\lambda r.k(r+n))) \ : \ r : \mathbf{Int} \to \bullet\langle r \geq n - 1\rangle.$$

Actually this judgement is *invalid*[4]: the type of k requires that $r + n \geq n$ but $r \geq n - 1$ is not sufficient for this when $n \leq 0$. Therefore one needs subtyping.

Figure 3 proves a subtyping judgement. Note that the assumption $n > 0$ plays a crucial role in the left branch of the derivation. Since $\Delta \vdash (\lambda r.k(r+n)))$: $(r : \mathbf{Int} \to \bullet\langle r \geq 0\rangle)$ is easily provable, we have completed the proof.

$\square$

3.4 Soundness and Completeness

This subsection defines the semantic counterpart of (sub)typing judgements, and discuss soundness and completeness of the refinement type system.

The interpretation of a refinement type environment $\Delta :: \Gamma$ is the subset $[\![\Delta]\!] \subseteq [\![\Gamma]\!]$ defined by

$$[\![\Delta]\!] \quad := \quad \{\alpha \in [\![\Gamma]\!] \mid \forall X \in \mathrm{dom}(\Gamma).\, \alpha(X) \in [\![\Delta(X)]\!](\alpha)\}.$$

We write $[\![\Delta; \Theta]\!]$ for the set of valuations $\{\alpha \in [\![\Delta]\!] \mid \alpha \models \Theta\}$.

The semantic counterpart of (sub)typing judgements are defined as follows:

$$\Delta; \Theta \models \tau \prec \tau' \quad :\Longleftrightarrow \quad (\!(\tau)\!)(\alpha) \subseteq (\!(\tau')\!)(\alpha) \text{ for every } \alpha \in [\![\Delta; \Theta]\!]$$
$$\Delta \models \psi : \tau \quad :\Longleftrightarrow \quad [\![\psi]\!](\alpha) \in (\!(\tau)\!)(\alpha) \text{ for every } \alpha \in [\![\Delta]\!].$$

The (sub)typing rules are sound with respect to the semantics of judgements.

Theorem 1 (Soundness)

- *If $\Delta; \Theta \vdash \tau_1 \prec \tau_2$, then $\Delta; \Theta \models \tau_1 \prec \tau_2$.*
- *If $\Delta \vdash \psi : \tau$, then $\Delta \models \psi : \tau$.*

Proof. By induction on the derivations. See [6]. $\square$

By applying Soundness to sentences, one can show that a derivation in the refinement type system witnesses the validity of a sentence.

---

[4] The formal definition of the validity of a refinement type judgement will be defined in the next subsection.

Corollary 1. *Let ψ be a $\nu HFL_{\mathbb{Z}}$ sentence. If $\vdash \psi : \bullet\langle tt \rangle$, then $\models \psi$.*

A remarkable feature is completeness. Although the type system is not complete for typing judgements, it is complete for subtyping judgements.

Theorem 2 (Completeness of subtyping). *If $\Delta; \Theta \models \tau_1 \prec_\rho \tau_2$, then $\Delta; \Theta \vdash \tau_1 \prec_\rho \tau_2$.*

Proof (Sketch). By induction on the structure of simple type ρ. Here we prove only the case $\rho = \rho_1 \to \rho_2$. A complete proof can be found in [6].

In this case $\tau = \tau_1 \to \tau_2$ and $\tau' = \tau_1' \to \tau_2'$. Assume that $\Delta; \Theta \models \tau \prec \tau'$. We prove $\Delta; \Theta \models \tau_2 \prec \tau_2'$ and $\Delta; \Theta \wedge \mathbf{rty}(\tau_2') \models \tau_1' \prec \tau_1$. Then $\Delta; \Theta \vdash \tau \prec \tau'$ follows from the induction hypothesis and S-Fun.

We prove $\Delta; \Theta \models \tau_2 \prec \tau_2'$. Let $\alpha \in [\![\Delta; \Theta]\!]$ and $v \in (\![\tau_2]\!)(\alpha)$ and define $f \in (\![\tau_1 \to \tau_2]\!)(\alpha)$ by $f(x) := v$. By the assumption, $f \in (\![\tau_1' \to \tau_2']\!)(\alpha)$. Since $\top_{\rho_1} \in (\![\tau_1']\!)(\alpha)$, we have $f(\top_{\rho_1}) = v \in (\![\tau_2']\!)(\alpha)$. Since $v \in (\![\tau_2]\!)(\alpha)$ is arbitrary, we obtain $(\![\tau_2]\!)(\alpha) \subset (\![\tau_2']\!)(\alpha)$.

We prove $\Delta; \Theta \wedge \mathbf{rty}(\tau_2') \models \tau_1' \prec \tau_1$. Assume for contradiction that $\Delta; \Theta \wedge \mathbf{rty}(\tau_2') \not\models \tau_1' \prec \tau_1$. Then, there exist $\alpha \in [\![\Delta; \Theta \wedge \mathbf{rty}(\tau_2')]\!]$ and $g \in (\![\tau_1']\!)(\alpha)$ such that $g \notin (\![\tau_1]\!)(\alpha)$. By Lemma 1, we have the minimal element $\gamma_{\tau_1 \to \tau_2}(\alpha)$ in $(\![\tau_1 \to \tau_2]\!)(\alpha)$, which belongs to $(\![\tau_1' \to \tau_2']\!)(\alpha)$ by the assumption. Since $g \in (\![\tau_1']\!)(\alpha)$, we have $\gamma_{\tau_1 \to \tau_2}(\alpha)(g) \in (\![\tau_2']\!)(\alpha)$. One can prove that $\alpha \models \mathbf{rty}(\tau_2')$ implies $\bot_{\rho_2} \notin (\![\tau_2']\!)(\alpha)$ and thus $\gamma_{\tau_1 \to \tau_2}(\alpha)(g) \neq \bot_{\rho_2}$. On the other hand, from the definition of the minimal element $\gamma_{\tau_1 \to \tau_2}(\alpha)$ and the assumption $g \notin (\![\tau_1]\!)(\alpha)$, we have $\gamma_{\tau_1 \to \tau_2}(\alpha)(g) = \bot_{\rho_2}$, a contradiction. $\qquad\square$

4 Relationship with Higher-Order Constrained Horn Clauses

Our work is closely related to the work on *Higher-order constrained Horn clauses* (HoCHC for short) [2]. HoCHC has been introduced by Burn et al. [2] as a higher-order extension of the standard notion of constrained Horn clauses. They also gave a refinement type system that proves the satisfiability of higher-order constrained Horn clauses. The satisfiability problem of higher-order constrained Horn clauses is equivalent to the validity problem of $\nu HFL_{\mathbb{Z}}$, and the refinement type system of Burn et al. [2] is almost identical to ours, *except for the crucial difference in the subtyping rules*. Below we discuss the connection and the difference between our work on their work in more detail; readers who are not familiar with HoCHC may safely skip the rest of this section.

4.1 The Duality of $\nu HFL_{\mathbb{Z}}$ and HoCHC

A HoCHC is of the form[5] $\psi \implies Z$, where ψ is a $\nu HFL_{\mathbb{Z}}$ formula that does not contain the fixed-point operator ν and Z is a variable X or the constant

---

[5] The syntax of HoCHC is modified in a way that emphasises the relationship to $\nu HFL_{\mathbb{Z}}$.

ff whose simple type is the same as ψ. The formula ψ in HoCHC may have free variables that possibly include X. A valuation α *satisfies* the HoCHC if $[\![\psi]\!](\alpha) \sqsubseteq [\![Z]\!](\alpha)$. A *solution* of a set of HoCHCs is a valuation that satisfies all given HoCHCs. Burn et al. [2] studied the *HoCHC satisfiability problem*, which asks whether a given finite set of HoCHC has a solution.

The HoCHC satisfiability problem can be characterized by using the least fixed-points. Assume a set of HoCHCs $\mathcal{C} = \{\psi_0 \Longrightarrow \mathbf{ff}, \psi_1 \Longrightarrow X_1, \ldots, \psi_n \Longrightarrow X_n\}$, where $X_1, \ldots, X_n$ are pairwise distinct variables. The HoCHCs $\{\psi_1 \Longrightarrow X_1, \ldots, \psi_n \Longrightarrow X_n\}$ has the minimum solution, say α, and $\mathcal{C}$ has a solution if and only if $[\![\psi_0]\!](\alpha) = \bot$ for the minimum solution α.

The connection to the νHFL$_\mathbb{Z}$ validity problem becomes apparent when we consider the dual problem. Given a ν-free formula ψ, we write $\overline{\psi}$ for the *dual* of ψ obtained by replacing $\wedge$ with $\vee$, **ff** with **tt**, atomic predicates $\mathbf{p}(\vec{\mathbf{a}})$ with its negation $\neg\mathbf{p}(\vec{\mathbf{a}})$ and a variable X with the dual variable $\overline{X}$. Then $\mathcal{C}$ has a solution if and only if so does

$$\{\overline{\psi}_0 \Longleftarrow \mathbf{tt}, \ \overline{\psi}_1 \Longleftarrow \overline{X}_1, \ \ldots, \ \overline{\psi}_n \Longleftarrow \overline{X}_n\}.$$

This dual problem has a characterisation using the greatest fixed-points: it has a solution if and only if $[\![\overline{\psi}_0]\!](\alpha) = \top$ where α is the *greatest* solution α of $\{\overline{\psi}_1 \Longleftarrow \overline{X}_1, \ldots, \overline{\psi}_n \Longleftarrow \overline{X}_n\}$. Since the greatest solution satisfies $\overline{\psi}_i = \overline{X}_i$ for every i, it can be represented by using the greatest fixed-point operator ν of νHFL$_\mathbb{Z}$. By substituting $\overline{X}_i$ in $\overline{\psi}_0$ with the νHFL$_\mathbb{Z}$ formula representation of the greatest solution α, one obtains a νHFL$_\mathbb{Z}$ formula ϕ. Now $\mathcal{C}$ has a solution if and only if $[\![\phi]\!] = \top$, that means, ϕ is valid.

4.2 The Similarity and Difference Between Two Refinement Type Systems

The connection between HoCHC and νHFL$_\mathbb{Z}$ allows us to compare the refinement type system for HoCHC of Burn et al. [2] with our refinement type system for νHFL$_\mathbb{Z}$. In fact, as mentioned in Introduction, this work is inspired by their work. Our refinement type system is almost identical to that of Burn et al. [2], but there is a significant difference. The subtyping rule for function types in their type system corresponds to:

$$\frac{\Delta; \Theta \vdash \tau_1' \prec \tau_1 \qquad \Delta; \Theta \vdash \tau_2 \prec \tau_2'}{\Delta; \Theta \vdash \tau_1 \to \tau_2 \prec \tau_1' \to \tau_2'}.$$

The difference from S-Fun is that $\mathbf{rty}(\tau_2')$ cannot be used to prove $\tau_1' \prec \tau_1$. Because of this difference, our refinement type system is strictly more expressive than that of Burn et al. [2]. Their refinement type system cannot prove the (judgement corresponding to the) subtyping judgement in Example 3, namely,

$$\Delta; \mathbf{tt} \vdash ((r\!:\!\mathbf{Int} \to \bullet\langle r \geq n-1\rangle) \to \bullet\langle\mathbf{tt}\rangle) \prec ((r\!:\!\mathbf{Int} \to \bullet\langle r \geq 0\rangle) \to \bullet\langle n > 0\rangle);$$

recall that $\mathbf{rty}((r : \mathbf{Int} \to \bullet\langle r \geq 0\rangle) \to \bullet\langle n > 0\rangle) = (n > 0)$ is crucial in the derivation of the subtyping judgement in Example 3. In fact, their type system cannot prove that the sentence in Example 3 is valid.

The difference is significant from both theoretical and practical view points. Theoretically our change makes the subtyping rules complete (Theorem 2). Practically this change is needed to prove the validity of higher-order instances. We will confirm this claim by experiments in Sect. 6.

5   Type Inference

This section discusses a type inference algorithm for our refinement type system in Sect. 3. The type system is based on constraint generation and solving. The constraint solving procedure simply invokes external solvers such as Spacer [9], HoIce [3] and PCSAT [12]. In what follows, we describe the constraint generation algorithm and discuss the shape of generated constraints.

5.1   Constraint Generation

The constraint generation algorithm adopts the template-based approach. For each subformula $\Gamma \vdash \phi : \rho$ of a given sentence $\vdash \psi : \bullet$, we prepare a refinement type template, which is a refinement type with predicate variables. For example, if $\Gamma = (X : \rho', y : \mathbf{Int}, Z : \rho'')$ and $\rho = \mathbf{Int} \to (\mathbf{Int} \to \bullet) \to \mathbf{Int} \to \bullet$, then the template is $a : \mathbf{Int} \to (b : \mathbf{Int} \to \bullet\langle P(y, a, b)\rangle) \to c : \mathbf{Int} \to \bullet\langle Q(y, a, c)\rangle$. The ideas are: (i) for each occurrence of type $\mathbf{Int}$, we give a fresh variable of type $\mathbf{Int}$ (in the above example, a, b and c), and (ii) for each occurrence of type $\bullet$, we give a fresh predicate variable (in the above example, P and Q). The arity of each predicate variable is the number of integer variables available at the position. Recall that the scope of x in $(x : \mathbf{Int} \to \tau)$ is τ.

Then we extract constraints. For example, assume that

$$\frac{x : \mathbf{Int} \vdash \phi_1 : (\mathbf{Int} \to \bullet) \to \bullet \qquad x : \mathbf{Int} \vdash \phi_2 : \mathbf{Int} \to \bullet}{x : \mathbf{Int} \vdash \phi_1 \phi_2 : \bullet}$$

is a part of the simple type derivation of the input sentence. Then the refinement type templates for ϕ_1 and ϕ_2 are

$$(y : \mathbf{Int} \to \bullet\langle P(x, y)\rangle) \to \bullet\langle Q(x)\rangle \quad \text{and} \quad z : \mathbf{Int} \to \bullet\langle R(x, z)\rangle,$$

respectively. The refinement type system requires that

$$x : \mathbf{Int}; \mathbf{tt} \vdash (z : \mathbf{Int} \to \bullet\langle R(x, z)\rangle) \prec (y : \mathbf{Int} \to \bullet\langle P(x, y)\rangle),$$

from which one obtains a constraint $x : \mathbf{Int}, z : \mathbf{Int}; \mathbf{tt} \models P(x, z) \Rightarrow R(x, z)$, or more simply $\forall x, z. [P(x, z) \implies R(x, z)]$.

Example 4. Recall the formula ψ in Example 1:

$$\psi \quad := \quad \nu X.\, \lambda y.\, y \neq 0 \wedge X\,(y + 1) \quad : \quad \mathbf{Int} \to \bullet.$$

We generate constraints for the sentence $\forall z.\, (z \leq 0) \vee \psi z$. The refinement type template for ψ is $y : \mathbf{Int} \to \bullet\langle P(z, y)\rangle$.

The first constraint comes from the subtyping judgement filling the gap between

$$\cfrac{z : \mathbf{Int} \vdash z \leq 0 : \bullet\langle z \leq 0\rangle \qquad \cfrac{z : \mathbf{Int} \vdash \psi : y : \mathbf{Int} \to \bullet\langle P(z,y)\rangle}{z : \mathbf{Int} \vdash \psi\,z : \bullet\langle P(z,z)\rangle}}{z : \mathbf{Int} \vdash (z \leq 0) \vee \psi\,z : \bullet\langle (z \leq 0) \vee P(z,z)\rangle}$$

and $z : \mathbf{Int} \vdash (z \leq 0) \vee \psi\,z : \bullet\langle \mathbf{tt}\rangle$. The required subtyping judgement is $z : \mathbf{Int}; \mathbf{tt} \vdash \bullet\langle (z \leq 0) \vee P(z,z)\rangle \prec \bullet\langle \mathbf{tt}\rangle$, from which one obtains

$$\forall z \in \mathcal{D}_{\mathbf{Int}}.\quad \mathbf{tt} \implies z \leq 0 \vee P(z,z).$$

The second constraint comes from the gap between

$$\cfrac{\cdots \vdash y \neq 0 : \bullet\langle y \neq 0\rangle \qquad \cfrac{\cdots \vdash X : (y' : \mathbf{Int} \to \bullet\langle P(z,y')\rangle)}{\cdots \vdash X\,(y+1) : \bullet\langle P(z,(y+1))\rangle}}{\begin{array}{c} z : \mathbf{Int}, X : (y' : \mathbf{Int} \to \bullet\langle P(z,y')\rangle), y : \mathbf{Int} \vdash \\ (y \neq 0 \wedge X\,(y+1)) : \bullet\langle (y \neq 0) \wedge P(z,(y+1))\rangle \end{array}}$$

and the requirement $z : \mathbf{Int}, X : y{:}\mathbf{Int} \to \bullet\langle P(z,y)\rangle, y : \mathbf{Int} \vdash (y \neq 0 \wedge X\,(y+1)) : \bullet\langle P(z,y)\rangle$. The second constraint is

$$\forall y, z \in \mathcal{D}_{\mathbf{Int}}.\quad P(z,y) \implies P(z,y+1).$$

These two constraints are sufficient for the validity of $\forall z.\,(z \leq 0) \vee \psi\,z$.   □

Remark 1. The constraint generation procedure is *complete* with respect to the typability: $\vdash \psi : \bullet\langle \mathbf{tt}\rangle$ is derivable for the input sentence if and only if the generated constraints are satisfiable. However it is not complete with respect to the validity since the refinement type system is not complete with respect to the validity.   □

5.2   Shape of Generated Constraints

Constraints obtained by the above procedure are of the from

$$\forall \tilde{x}.\quad P_1(\tilde{x}_1) \wedge \cdots \wedge P_n(\tilde{x}_n) \wedge \theta \implies Q_1(\tilde{y}_1) \vee \cdots \vee Q_m(\tilde{y}_m).$$

Here P_i and Q_j are predicate variables and θ is a constraint formula. If $m \leq 1$, then this is called a *constrained Horn clause* (*CHC* for short). Following [12], we call the general form pCSP. We invoke external solvers such as Spacer [9], HoIce [3] and PCSAT [12] to solve the satisfiability of generated constraints.

PCSAT [12] accepts the constraints of the above form, so it can be used as a backend solver of the type inference. However PCSAT is immature at present compared with CHC solvers, some of which are quite efficient. By this reason, we use CHC solvers such as Spacer [9] and HoIce [3] as the backend solver if the constraints are CHCs.

It is natural to ask when generated constraints are CHCs. We give a convenient sufficient condition on input νHFL$_\mathbb{Z}$ formulas. We say a formula is *tractable* if for every occurrence of disjunctions $(\psi_1 \vee \psi_2)$, at least one of ψ_1 and ψ_2 is an atomic formula. For example, $((F\,x) \wedge (G\,y)) \vee (b = 2)$ is tractable because $b = 2$ is atomic, and $((F\,x) \wedge (b = 2)) \vee (G\,y)$ is not. If the input formula is tractable, the constraint generation algorithm generates CHCs.

In the context of program verification, the safety property verification of higher-order programs are reducible to the validity problem of tractable formulas. In fact, the reduction given in [8] satisfies this condition. Therefore the translation in [8] followed by our type-based validity checking reduces the safety property verification to CHCs, for which efficient solvers are available.

6   Implementation and Experiments

6.1   Implementation

We have implemented a νHFL$_{\mathbb{Z}}$ validity checker RETHFL based on the inference on the proposed refinement type system. RETHFL uses, as its backend, CHC solvers HoIce [3] and Spacer [9], and pCSP solver PCSAT [12]. In the experiments reported below, unless explicitly mentioned, HoIce is used as the backend solver. We have also implemented a functionality to disprove the validity when a given formula is untypable, as discussed below. For this functionality, Eldarica [4] is used to obtain a resolution proof of the unsatisfiability of CHC.

A Method to Disprove the Validity of a νHFL$_{\mathbb{Z}}$ Formula. Since our reduction from the typability of a νHFL$_{\mathbb{Z}}$ formula ψ to the satisfiability of CHC or pCSP is complete, we can conclude that ψ is untypable if the CHC or pCSP obtained by the reduction is unsatisfiable. That does not imply, however, that the original formula ψ is invalid, due to the incompleteness of the type system. Therefore, when a CHC solver returns "unsat", we try to disprove the validity of the original formula. To this end, we first use Eldarica [4] to obtain a resolution proof of the unsatisfiability of CHC, and estimate how many times each fixpoint formula should be unfolded to disprove the validity of the νHFL$_{\mathbb{Z}}$ formula. Below we briefly explain this idea through an example.

Example 5. Let us consider the following formula:

$$\forall n.n < 0 \vee (\nu X.(\lambda y.y = 1 \vee (y \geq 1 \wedge X\ (y - 1)))) \ n.$$

By preparing a refinement type template $y : \mathbf{Int} \to \bullet\langle P_X(y) \rangle$ for X, we obtain the following constraints:

$$\forall x \in \mathcal{D}_{\mathbf{Int}}. \ \mathbf{tt} \Rightarrow P_X(x) \vee x < 0$$
$$\forall x \in \mathcal{D}_{\mathbf{Int}}. \ P_X(x) \Rightarrow x = 1 \vee (x \geq 1 \wedge P_X(x - 1)),$$

which correspond to the CHC:

$$\forall x \in \mathcal{D}_{\mathbf{Int}}. \ x \geq 0 \Rightarrow P_X(x) \qquad \forall x \in \mathcal{D}_{\mathbf{Int}}. \ P_X(x) \wedge x \neq 1 \wedge x < 1 \Rightarrow \mathbf{ff}$$
$$\forall x \in \mathcal{D}_{\mathbf{Int}}. \ P_X(x) \wedge x \neq 1 \Rightarrow P_X(x - 1)$$

This set of CHC is unsatisfiable, having the following resolution proof:

$$\frac{0 \geq 0 \Rightarrow P_X(0) \quad P_X(0) \wedge 0 \neq 1 \wedge 0 < 1 \Rightarrow \mathbf{ff}}{0 \geq 0 \wedge 0 \neq 1 \wedge 0 < 1 \Rightarrow \mathbf{ff} \, (= \mathbf{ff})}$$

Here, the two leaves of the proof have been obtained from the first two clauses by instantiating x to 0. Since the second clause is used just once in the proof, we can estimate that a single unfolding of X is sufficient for disproving the validity of the formula. We thus expand the fixpoint formula for X once and check whether the following resulting formula holds by using an SMT solver:

$$\forall n.n < 0 \vee (n = 1 \vee (n \geq 1 \wedge \mathbf{tt})).$$

The SMT solver returns 'No' in this case; hence we can conclude that the original νHFL$_\mathbb{Z}$ formula is invalid.

6.2   Experiments

We have conducted experiments to compare RETHFL with:

- Horus [2]: a HoCHC solver based on refinement type inference [2].
- PAHFL [5]: a νHFL$_\mathbb{Z}$ validity checker [5] based on HFL model checking and predicate abstraction.

The experiments were conducted on a Linux server with Intel Xeon CPU E5-2680 v3 and 64 GB of RAM. We set the timeout as 180 s in all the experiments below.

Comparison with Horus [2]. We prepared two sets of benchmarks A and B. Both benchmark sets A and B consist of νHFL$_\mathbb{Z}$ validity checking problems and the corresponding HoCHC problems. Benchmark set A comes from the HoCHC benchmark for Horus [2], and we prepared νHFL$_\mathbb{Z}$ versions based on the correspondence between HoCHC and νHFL$_\mathbb{Z}$ discussed in Sect. 4. Benchmark set B has been obtained from safety verification problems for OCaml programs. Benchmark set A has 8 instances, and benchmark set B has 56 instances. In the experiments, we used Spacer as the common backend CHC solver of RETHFL and Horus.

The result is shown in Fig. 4. In the figure, "Unknown" means that Horus returned "unsat", which implies that it is unknown whether the program is safe, due to the incompleteness of the underlying refinement type system. RETHFL could solve 8 instances correctly for benchmark set A, and 46 instances for benchmark set B. In contrast, Horus could solve 7 instances correctly for benchmark set A, and only 18 instances for benchmark set B; as already discussed, this is mainly due to the difference of the subtyping relations of the underlying type systems. The running times were comparable for the instances solved by both RETHFL and Horus.

Comparison with PAHFL [5]. We used two benchmark sets I and II. Benchmark set I is the benchmark set of PAHFL [5] consisting of νHFL$_\mathbb{Z}$ validity

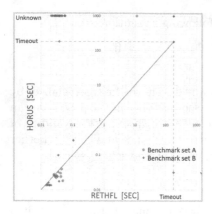

Fig. 4. Comparison with Horus [2].

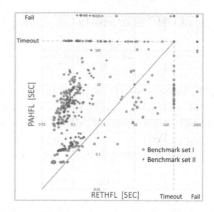

Fig. 5. Comparison with PAHFL [5].

checking problems, which have been obtained from the safety property verification problems for OCaml programs [13]. Since the translation used to obtain νHFL$_\mathbb{Z}$ formulas is tailor-made for and works favorably for PAHFL, we also used benchmark set II, which consists of the original program verification problems [13]; for this benchmark set, RETHFL and PAHFL use their own translations to νHFL$_\mathbb{Z}$ formulas.

The results of the two experiments are shown in Fig. 5. In the figure, "Fail" means that the tool terminated abnormally, due to a problem of the backend solvers, or a limitation of our current translator from OCaml programs to νHFL$_\mathbb{Z}$ formulas. For benchmark set I, RETHFL and PAHFL solved 205 and 217 instances respectively. For benchmark set II, RETHFL and PAHFL solved 247 and 217 instances respectively. Thus, both systems are comparable in terms of the number of solved instances. As for the running times, our solver outperformed PAHFL for most of the instances.

We also compared our solver with PAHFL by using 10 problems reduced from higher-order non-termination problems, which were used in [10]. While PAHFL could solve 4 instances, our solver could not solve any of them in 180 s. This is mainly due to the bottleneck of the underlying pCSP solver; developing a better pCSP solver is left for future work.

7   Related Work

Burn et al. [2] introduced a higher-order extension of CHC (HoCHC) and proposed a refinement type system for proving the satisfiability of HoCHC. As already discussed in Sect. 4, the HoCHC satisfiability problem is essentially equivalent to the νHFL$_\mathbb{Z}$ validity problem. Our type system is more expressive than Burn et al.'s type system due to more sophisticated subtyping rules. We have confirmed through experiments that our νHFL$_\mathbb{Z}$ solver RETHFL outperforms their HoCHC solver Horus in terms of the number of solved instances.

Iwayama et al. [5] have recently proposed an alternative approach to νHFL$_\mathbb{Z}$ validity checking, which is based on a combination of (pure) HFL model checking, predicate abstraction, and counterexample guided abstraction refinement. In theory, their method is more powerful than ours, since theirs can be viewed as a method for inferring refinement *intersection* types. In practice, however, their solver PAHFL is often slower and times out for some of the instances which RETHFL can solve. Thus, both approaches can be considered complementary.

Kobayashi et al. [7] have shown that a validity checker for a first-order fixpoint logic can be constructed on top of the validity checker for the ν-only fragment of the first-order logic. We expect that the same technique can be used to construct a validity checker for full HFL$_\mathbb{Z}$ on top of our νHFL$_\mathbb{Z}$ validity checker RETHFL.

There are other refinement type-based approach to program verification, such as Liquid types [11,15] and F* [14]. They are not fully automated in the sense that users must provide either refinement type annotations or qualifiers [11] as hints for verification, while our method is fully automatic. Also, our νHFL$_\mathbb{Z}$-based verification method can deal with (un)reachability in the presence of both demonic and angelic branches, while most of the type-based verification methods including those mentioned above can deal with reachability in the presence of only demonic branches.

8   Conclusion

We have proposed a refinement type system for νHFL$_\mathbb{Z}$ validity checking, and developed an automated procedure for refinement type inference. Our refinement type system is more expressive than the system by Burn et al. [2] thanks to the refined subtyping relation, which is sound and relative complete with respect to the semantic subtyping relation. We have confirmed the effectiveness of our approach through experiments. Future work includes an improvement of the backend pCSP solver (which is the current main bottleneck of our approach), and an extension of the method to deal with full HFL$_\mathbb{Z}$, based on the method for the first-order case [7].

Acknowledgments. We would like to thank anonymous referees for useful comments. This work was supported by JSPS Kakenhi JP15H05706, JP20H00577, and JP20H05703.

References

1. Bjørner, N., Gurfinkel, A., McMillan, K., Rybalchenko, A.: Horn clause solvers for program verification. In: Beklemishev, L.D., Blass, A., Dershowitz, N., Finkbeiner, B., Schulte, W. (eds.) Fields of Logic and Computation II. LNCS, vol. 9300, pp. 24–51. Springer, Cham (2015). https://doi.org/10.1007/978-3-319-23534-9_2
2. Burn, T.C., Ong, C.L., Ramsay, S.J.: Higher-order constrained horn clauses for verification. Proc. ACM Program. Lang. **2**(POPL), 11:1–11:28 (2018). https://doi.org/10.1145/3158099

3. Champion, A., Chiba, T., Kobayashi, N., Sato, R.: ICE-based refinement type discovery for higher-order functional programs. In: Beyer, D., Huisman, M. (eds.) TACAS 2018. LNCS, vol. 10805, pp. 365–384. Springer, Cham (2018). https://doi.org/10.1007/978-3-319-89960-2_20

4. Hojjat, H., Rümmer, P.: The ELDARICA horn solver. In: Proceedings of FMCAD 2018, pp. 1–7. IEEE (2018). https://doi.org/10.23919/FMCAD.2018.8603013

5. Iwayama, N., Kobayashi, N., Tsukada, T.: Predicate abstraction and CEGAR for νHFL$_\mathbb{Z}$ validity checking (2020). Draft

6. Katsura, H., Iwayama, N., Kobayashi, N., Tsukada, T.: A new refinement type system for automated νHFL$_\mathbb{Z}$ validity checking (2020). A longer version of this paper, http://www.kb.is.s.u-tokyo.ac.jp/~katsura/papers/aplas20.pdf

7. Kobayashi, N., Nishikawa, T., Igarashi, A., Unno, H.: Temporal verification of programs via first-order fixpoint logic. In: Chang, B.-Y.E. (ed.) SAS 2019. LNCS, vol. 11822, pp. 413–436. Springer, Cham (2019). https://doi.org/10.1007/978-3-030-32304-2_20

8. Kobayashi, N., Tsukada, T., Watanabe, K.: Higher-order program verification via HFL model checking. In: Ahmed, A. (ed.) ESOP 2018. LNCS, vol. 10801, pp. 711–738. Springer, Cham (2018). https://doi.org/10.1007/978-3-319-89884-1_25

9. Komuravelli, A., Gurfinkel, A., Chaki, S.: SMT-based model checking for recursive programs. Formal Methods Syst. Des. **48**(3), 175–205 (2016). https://doi.org/10.1007/s10703-016-0249-4

10. Kuwahara, T., Sato, R., Unno, H., Kobayashi, N.: Predicate abstraction and CEGAR for disproving termination of higher-order functional programs. In: Kroening, D., Păsăreanu, C.S. (eds.) CAV 2015. LNCS, vol. 9207, pp. 287–303. Springer, Cham (2015). https://doi.org/10.1007/978-3-319-21668-3_17

11. Rondon, P.M., Kawaguchi, M., Jhala, R.: Liquid types. In: Gupta, R., Amarasinghe, S.P. (eds.) Proceedings of the PLDI 2008, pp. 159–169. ACM (2008). https://doi.org/10.1145/1375581.1375602

12. Satake, Y., Unno, H., Yanagi, H.: Probabilistic inference for predicate constraint satisfaction. In: Proceedings of the AAAI, vol. 34, pp. 1644–1651 (2020). https://doi.org/10.1609/aaai.v34i02.5526

13. Sato, R., Iwayama, N., Kobayashi, N.: Combining higher-order model checking with refinement type inference. In: Proceedings of PEPM 2019, pp. 47–53 (2019). https://doi.org/10.1145/3294032.3294081

14. Swamy, N., et al.: Dependent types and multi-monadic effects in F*. In: 43rd ACM SIGPLAN-SIGACT Symposium on Principles of Programming Languages (POPL), pp. 256–270. ACM (2016). https://www.fstar-lang.org/papers/mumon/

15. Vazou, N., Seidel, E.L., Jhala, R., Vytiniotis, D., Jones, S.L.P.: Refinement types for Haskell. In: Jeuring, J., Chakravarty, M.M.T. (eds.) Proceedings of the 19th ACM SIGPLAN International Conference on Functional Programming, Gothenburg, Sweden, 1–3 September 2014, pp. 269–282. ACM (2014). https://doi.org/10.1145/2628136.2628161

16. Viswanathan, M., Viswanathan, R.: A higher order modal fixed point logic. In: Gardner, P., Yoshida, N. (eds.) CONCUR 2004. LNCS, vol. 3170, pp. 512–528. Springer, Heidelberg (2004). https://doi.org/10.1007/978-3-540-28644-8_33

17. Watanabe, K., Tsukada, T., Oshikawa, H., Kobayashi, N.: Reduction from branching-time property verification of higher-order programs to HFL validity checking. In: Proceedings of PEPM 2019, pp. 22–34 (2019). https://doi.org/10.1145/3294032.3294077

Behavioural Types for Memory and Method Safety in a Core Object-Oriented Language

Mario Bravetti[1] , Adrian Francalanza[2] , Iaroslav Golovanov[3],
Hans Hüttel[3] , Mathias S. Jakobsen[3], Mikkel K. Kettunen[3],
and António Ravara[4]($\boxtimes$)

[1] Dipartimento di Informatica, Universitá di Bologna, Bologna, Italy
[2] Department of Computer Science, University of Malta, Msida, Malta
[3] Institut for Datalogi, Aalborg Universitet, Aalborg, Denmark
[4] NOVA-LINCS and NOVA School of Science and Technology, Caparica, Portugal
aravara@fct.unl.pt

Abstract. We present a type-based analysis ensuring memory safety and object protocol completion in the Java-like language Mungo. Objects are annotated with usages, typestates-like specifications of the admissible sequences of method calls. The analysis entwines usage checking, controlling the order in which methods are called, with a static check determining whether references may contain null values. It prevents null pointer dereferencing in a typestate-aware manner and memory leaks and ensures that the intended usage protocol of every object is respected and completed. The type system admits an algorithm that infers the most general usage with respect to a simulation preorder. The type system is implemented in the form of a type checker and a usage inference tool.

1 Introduction

The notion of reference is central to object-oriented programming, which is thus particularly prone to the problem of *null-dereferencing* [18]: a recent survey [30, Table 1.1] analysing questions posted to StackOverflow referring to java.lang exception types notes that, as of 1 November 2013, the most common exception was precisely null-dereferencing. Existing approaches for preventing null-dereferencing require annotations, *e.g.* in the form of pre-conditions or type qualifiers, together with auxiliary reasoning methods. For instance, Fähndrich and Leino [12] use type qualifiers with data flow analysis to determine if fields are used safely, while Hubert *et al.* rely on a constraint-based flow analysis [20]. Recently, type qualifiers to prevent issues with null pointers were adopted in mainstream languages, like nullable types in C#, Kotlin, and Swift, and option

Work partially supported by the EU H2020 RISE programme under the Marie Skłodowska-Curie grant agreement No. 778233 (BehAPI), the UK EPSRC grant EP/K034413/1 (ABCD), and by NOVA LINCS (UIDB/04516/2020) via FCT.

B. C. d. S. Oliveira (Ed.): APLAS 2020, LNCS 12470, pp. 105–124, 2020.
https://doi.org/10.1007/978-3-030-64437-6_6

types in OCaml, Scala, and Java. These approaches rely on programmer intervention, what can be viewed as a limitation, since the absence of null-dereferencing does not come "for free", just as a consequence of a program being well-typed.

Static analysis tools that are "external" with respect to the type-system, like the Checker framework [10] or the Petri Net based approach in [8], can be used to check the code once it is in a stable state. However, both type qualifiers and "external" static analyses suffer from a common problem: they are restrictive and require additional explicit checks in the code (*e.g.*, if-then-else statements checking for null), resulting in a "defensive programming" style.

On the contrary, by including the analysis *as part of the type system*, one obviates the need for additional annotations and auxiliary reasoning mechanisms. For instance, the Eiffel type system [24] now distinguishes between attached and detachable types: variables of an attached type can never be assigned a void value, which is only allowed for variables of detachable type. However, enriching the type system in this way is not enough, in that *it is the execution of a method body that typically changes the program state*, causing *object fields* to become *nullified*. The *interplay* between *null-dereferencing* and the *order in which methods of an object are invoked* is therefore important. A recent manifestation of this is the bug found in Jedis [32], a Redis [33] Java client, where a close method could be called even after a socket had timed out [32, Issue 1747]. One should therefore see an object as following a *protocol* describing the *admissible sequences of method invocations*. The intended protocol can, thus, be expressed as a *behavioural type* [3,6,21]: our idea is to use such types to ensure no null-dereferencing via static type checking.

There are two main approaches to behavioural type systems. The notion of *typestates* originates with Strom and Yemini [29]; the idea is to annotate the type of an object with information pertaining to its current state. Earlier work includes that of Vault [11], Fugue [9] and Plaid [2,31]. In the latter, an object-oriented language, the programmer declares for each class *typestates* (the significant states of objects) and annotates each method with (statically checked) pre and post-conditions. Pre-conditions declare typestates that enable the method; post-conditions define in which typestate the method execution leaves the object. One has also to declare in these assertions the states of fields and parameters. Garcia *et al.* [14] describe a gradual typestate system following the approach of Plaid and combining access permissions with gradual types [28] to also control aliasing in a robust way. The other approach taken is that of *session types* [19]. This originated in a π-calculus setting where the session type of a channel is a protocol that describes the sequence of communications that the channel must follow. Channels are *linear*: they are used exactly once with the given protocol, and evolve as a result of each communication that it is involved in.

1.1 Our Approach

The approach of Gay *et al.* [15], adopted in this paper, combines the two approaches above to behavioural types: the type of a class C is endowed with a *usage type* denoting a behaviour that any instance of C must follow. Consider the class File in Listing 1.1 [1]; the usage defined on lines 4–8 specifies the

admissible sequences of method calls for any object instance of File. The usage is
a set of defining equations where Init is the initial *variable* (denoting a typestate).
It tells the object must first be opened, going then into typestate Check (another
usage variable) where only the method isEOF can be called. When isEOF is called
the continuation of the protocol depends on the method result: if it returns EOF
one can only close the file and the protocol is completed (denoted by **end**); if it
returns NOTEOF one can read and check again. This ensures that all methods
of a File object are called according to the safe order declared.

```
enum FileStatus { EOF , NOTEOF }                                           1
                                                                           2
class File {                                                               3
  { Init = {open ; Check}                                                  4
    Check = {isEOF ;                                                       5
              ⟨EOF: {close ; end} , NOTEOF: {read ; Check}⟩               6
          }                                                                7
  }                                                                        8
                                                                           9
  void open (void x) { ... }                                             10
  FileStatus isEOF (void x) { ... }                                      11
  Char read (void x) { ... }                                             12
  void close (void x) { ... }                                            13
}                                                                         14
```

Listing 1.1. An example class describing files

In Listing 1.2 an additional class FileReader is introduced. Its usage type,
at line 18, requires that the init() method is called first, followed by method
readFile().

```
class FileReader {                                                       17
  { Init = {init ; {readFile ; end}}}                                    18
                                                                         19
  File file ;                                                           20
                                                                         21
  void init () { file = new File }                                      22
                                                                         23
  void readFile () {                                                     24
    file .open (unit );                                                 25
    loop:  switch (file .isEOF ()) {                                    26
             EOF: file .close ()                                        27
             NOTEOF: file .read (); continue loop                       28
         }                                                              29
  }                                                                     30
}                                                                       31
```

Listing 1.2. An example class intended for reading files

Class FileReader uses class File for its field file declared at line 20: method
calls on file will have to follow the usage type of File. Indeed, since FileReader

class usage imposes to call method init before method readFile, we have that FileReader class code correctly deals with objects of class File: first method init code creates a File object inside field file, then method readFile code follows File usage for such an object, by first opening it, entering a loop (lines 26 to 29) to read until its end, and closeing it. So, in general, type checking of a class (as FileReader) entails checking that: assuming the usage type of the class is followed, all fields (e.g. file) are correctly dealt with according to the usage type of their class (e.g. the usage of File). Moreover, since methods on field file are called by code of method readFile only, and since, by considering for FileReader class typestates, we know that such method can only be performed after the init method, no null-dereferencing can occur when FileReader class code is executed. In spite of this, previous work considering typestates and no null-dereferencing checking would not allow to type check the FileReader class. For example the above mentioned approach of [2,14,31] would require the programmer, besides declaring typestates imposing init to be performed before method readFile, to explicitly annotate readFile method with a precondition stating that file cannot be null. Such annotations are quite demanding to the programmer and sometimes even redundant. When an object is in a given typestate (e.g. when readFile is enabled) the values of its fields are, implicitly, already constrained (file cannot be null). Therefore type-checking based on a typestate-aware analysis of FileReader class code (i.e., assuming that the usage type of the class is followed) makes it possible to guarantee no null-dereferencing without any additional annotation. Typestate-aware analysis of null-dereferencing is one of the novel contributions of this paper.

The type system for Mungo (a Java-like language) [23] depends on *linearity* and *protocol fidelity*. Linearity requires that, once an object reference is written to a variable/field whose type is a class with a usage, it can be read from that variable/field at most once (it can also be passed around or written to other variables/fields instead). This avoids aliasing while permitting compositional reasoning via the type system, making it possible to statically verify that objects follow the intended protocol. Protocol fidelity requires that usage of a class is followed when calling methods on a variable/field whose type is that class. Checking protocol compliance merely by such a simple form of protocol fidelity, however, does not suffice to correctly perform all checks guaranteeing correctness of our example. For instance, protocol fidelity in [23] permits:

- Omitting file = **new** File in the body of method init at line 22. However, even if one follows the prescribed protocol of FileReader by invoking first init and then readFile, one gets a null-dereferencing when calling open on file.
- Adding file = **null** after file = **new** File at line 22. This results not only in getting a null-dereferencing, as above, but also in losing the reference to the created object before its protocol is completed, due to object memory being released only at the end of its protocol.
- Adding file = **new** File at line 27 before calling close. This result in the loss of the reference to the previous object stored in file that has not yet completed its protocol.

Therefore, the Mungo type system in [23] does *not* provide guarantees ruling out null-dereferencing and loss of references. In particular, three unpleasant behaviours are still allowed: (*i*) null-assignment to a field/parameter containing an object with an incomplete typestate; (*ii*) null-dereferencing (even null.m() is accepted); (*iii*) using objects without completing their protocol and without returning them. Moreover the type system in [23] is based on a mixture of type checking and type inference that makes it not fully compositional – to be, type checking a class should not depend on type checking other classes; without it, the complexity of the type analysis would not depend only on the structure of the class being typechecked but also on that of other classes.

1.2   Contributions

In this paper we present the first "pure" behavioural type-checking system for Mungo that handles all these important unsolved issues. This constitutes (to our knowledge) the *first compositional behavioural type system* for a realistic object-oriented language that *rules out null-dereferencing and memory leaks* as a by-product of a safety property, *i.e.,* protocol fidelity, and of a (weak) liveness property, *i.e.,* object *protocol completion* for terminated programs. In particular it is the first type system that checks null-dereferencing in a *typestate-aware* manner. Note that, while protocol fidelity is an expected property in behavioural type systems, this does not hold for properties like: *protocol completion* for a mainstream-like language or *memory safety*, i.e., no null-dereferencing/memory leaks. Notably our type system:

- Makes it possible to analyze source code of individual classes *in isolation* (by just relying on usages of other classes which are part of their public information, thus respecting correct encapsulation principles).
- Is based on a more complex notion of protocol fidelity, w.r.t. the type system in [23], that includes a special typestate for variables/fields representing the null value and encompasses typestate-aware null-dereferencing checking.
- Is based on requiring protocol completion for terminated programs and references that are lost (e.g. by means of variable/field re-assignment or by not returning them).
- Is compositional and uses type checking only, i.e. a term is typable if its immediate constituents are (unlike [23] which uses a mixture of type checking and type inference).
- Admits an algorithm for *principal usage inference*. For any class, the algorithm correctly infers the largest usage that makes the class well-typed.

The typing-checking system and the usage inference system presented herein as (rule based) inductive definitions, were implemented (in Haskell) to allow to test not only the examples presented ahead, but also more elaborate programs – a suit of examples and the code implementing both systems is available at GitHub [1]. A new version of Mungo following our approach is also available at https://github.com/jdmota/java-typestate-checker.

Table 1. Syntax of Mungo

$$D ::= \text{enum L } \{\vec{l}\} \mid \text{class C } \{\mathcal{U}, \vec{M}, \vec{F}\}$$
$$F ::= z \; f$$
$$M ::= t \; m(t \; x)\{e\}$$
$$v ::= \text{unit} \mid \text{true} \mid \text{false} \mid l \mid \text{null}$$
$$r ::= x \mid f \mid \text{this}$$
$$e ::= v \mid r \mid \text{new C} \mid f = e \mid r.m(e) \mid e; e$$
$$\mid k : e \mid \text{continue } k \mid \text{if (e) \{e\} else \{e\}}$$
$$\mid \text{switch (r.m(e)) } \{l_i : e_i\}_{i_i \in L}$$

$$b ::= \text{void} \mid \text{bool} \mid L$$
$$z ::= b \mid C$$
$$t ::= b \mid C[\mathcal{U}]$$
$$u ::= \{m_i; w_i\}_{i \in I} \mid X$$
$$w ::= u \mid \langle l_i : u_i \rangle_{l_i \in L}$$
$$E ::= X = u$$
$$\mathcal{U} ::= u^{\vec{E}}$$

Due to space restrictions, we omit in this paper some rules and results. The complete formal systems are presented and described in detail in http:// people.cs.aau.dk/~hans/APLAS20/typechecking.pdf and http://people.cs.aau. dk/~hans/APLAS20/inference.pdf.

2 The Mungo Language

Mungo is a typed Java-like language in the style of Featherweight Java [22] that contains usual object-oriented and imperative constructs; the name also refers to its associated programming tool developed at Glasgow University [23,34]. The Mungo language is a subset of Java that extends every Java class with a typestate specification. The syntax of Mungo is given in Table 1. A *program* $\vec{D}$ is a sequence of *enumeration declarations*, introducing a set of n labels $\{l_1, \ldots, l_n\}$, for some natural $n > 0$, identified by a name $L \in$ **ENames**, followed by a sequence of *class declarations* where $C \in$ **CNames** is a class name, $\vec{M}$ a set of methods, $\vec{F}$ a set of fields, and $\mathcal{U}$ a usage. A program $\vec{D}$ is assumed to include a main class, called Main, with a single method called main having void parameter/return type and usage type $\mathcal{U} = \{\text{main; end}\}^\varepsilon$. In the examples we used a set of defining equations to specify usages, indicating which variable is the initial one. In the formal syntax we omit the initial variable—a usage is just an expression u with a set of defining equations $\vec{E}$ as superscript $(u^{\vec{E}})$. The usage in line 18 of Listing 1.2 is thus written as $\{\text{init}; RF\}^E$, with $E = \{RF = \{\text{readFile; end}\}\}$.

Fields, classes and methods are annotated with *types*, ranged over by t. The set of base types **BTypes** contains the void type (that of value unit), the type bool of values, and enumerations types, ranged over by L, for sets of labels. Typestates $C[\mathcal{U}] \in$ **Typestates** are a central component of the behavioural type system, where C is a class name and $\mathcal{U}$ is a *usage*, specifying the admissible sequences of method calls allowed for an object. In our setting typestates are used to type *non-uniform objects* [27], instead of the usual class type (*i.e.*, we write $C[\mathcal{U}]$ instead of just C). A *branch* usage $\{m_i; w_i\}_{i \in I}$ describes that any one of the methods m_i can be called, following which the usage is then w_i. We let end denote the *terminated*, empty usage – a branch with $I = \emptyset$. The usage {readFile; end} is a simple example of a terminating branch usage. A *choice* usage $\langle l_i : u_i \rangle$ specifies that the usage continues as u_i depending on a label l_i. This is useful when the flow of execution depends on the return value of a method. The usage in line 6 of Listing 1.1 is an example of a choice usage. Recursive usages allow for iterative behaviour. A defining equation $X = u$ specifies the behaviour of the usage variable X, which can occur in u or in any of the other equations.

The set **Values** is ranged over by v and contains boolean values, unit, labels, and null. References ranged over by r describe how objects are accessed – as method parameters ranged over by $x \in \mathbf{PNames}$, as field names ranged over by $f \in \mathbf{FNames}$ or as the enclosing object, this. Values and references are expressions. To follow a linear discipline, reading either a field or a parameter containing an object nullifies the reference (as the object is passed somewhere else). Moreover, assigning objects to references is only possible if they contain null or if their protocol is terminated. Expressions also include standard method calls $r.m(e)$. Methods have exactly one argument; the extension to an arbitrary number of arguments is straightforward. Sequential compositions is denoted by $e; e'$, conditionals are if (e) $\{e_1\}$ else $\{e_2\}$, and there is a restricted form of selection statements, switch $(r.m(e))$ $\{l_i : e_i\}_{i_i \in L}$, that branches on the result of a method call that is supposed to return a label (an example of this construct is in lines 26–29 of Listing 1.2).

Iteration in Mungo is possible by means of jumps. This lets us give more expressive behavioural types as mutual recursions in nested loops [23]. Expressions can be labelled as $k : e$, where k must be a unique label; the execution can then jump to the unique expression labelled k by evaluating the expression continue k (an example of this construct is in lines 26 and 28 of Listing 1.2). We require that labelled expressions are well-formed: in a labelled expression $k : e$, the label k is bound within e, and all occurrences of continue k must be found in this scope; moreover, in e, continue cannot be part of the argument of a method call; the expression on the right side of an assignment or on the left of a sequential composition must not be a continue expression; finally, within $k : e$ there must be at least a branch, considering all if and switch expressions possibly included in the code e, that does not end up in continue k (if there is no if and switch, e must not end up in continue k). This last condition rules out pathological infinite behaviours such as $k :$ if (true) {continue k} {continue k} and $k :$ continue k.

A method named m is declared as $t_2 \, m(t_1 \, x)\{e\}$, where t_2 denotes the return type of m, while the argument type is t_1. The body of m is an expression e. Classes in Mungo are instantiated with new C. When an object is created all its fields are initialised to null. Assignment is always made to a field inside the object on which a method is evaluated (fields are considered private). For an object to modify a field in another object, it must use a method call.

We introduce a dot-notation that refers directly to components of a class definition; we let $C.\mathsf{methods}_{\vec{D}} \stackrel{\text{def}}{=} \vec{M}$, $C.\mathsf{fields}_{\vec{D}} \stackrel{\text{def}}{=} \vec{F}$ and $C.\mathsf{usage}_{\vec{D}} \stackrel{\text{def}}{=} \mathcal{U}$.

To describe (partially) evaluated expressions, we extend the syntax to include *run-time expressions* and values:

$$v:: = \cdots \mid o$$
$$e:: = \cdots \mid \mathsf{return}\{e\} \mid \mathsf{switch}_{r.m}\ (e)\{l_i : e_i\}_{l_i \in L}$$

The $\mathsf{return}\{e\}$ construct encapsulates the ongoing evaluation of a method body e. We also introduce a general switch construct that allows arbitrary expressions and thus the partial evaluation of this construct.

3   The Type System

Our type system is a sound approximation of the reduction relation (*c.f.*, Sect. 4) and rejects programs that "may go wrong" [26]. We return to this type safety result as Theorem 2 in Sect. 5. The main intentions behind our type system are to ensure that every object will follow its specified protocol, that no null pointer exceptions are raised, and no object reference is lost before its protocol is completed. The system lets us type classes separately and independently of a main method or of client code. Following Gay et al. [15], when we type a class, we type its methods according to the order in which they appear in the class usage. This approach to type checking is crucial. For suppose we call a method m of an object o that also has a field containing another object o'. This call will not only change the typestate of o (admitting the method was called at a moment allowed by the usage). The call can also change the state of o', since the code of method m may contain calls to methods found in o'. With the type-checking system we present herein, we take an important step further: by giving a special type to null and make a careful control of it in the typing rules, we manage to prevent memory leaks and detect previously allowed null-pointer exceptions.

Example 1. Recall the FileReader class in Listing 1.2. Its usage requires calling first method init to guarantee that field file gets a new File object. Then the usage of FileReader requires calling the method readFile which then call methods on file according to its usage (*cf.* Listing 1.1): first open then iterate testing for end-of-file (using the method isEOF), reading while this is not the case. Failure to follow the usage of FileReader and, for instance, calling readFile without having called init first causes null-dereferencing. The behavioural type system of Mungo presented herein prevents this, alleviating the programmer from having to consider all possible negative situations that could lead to errors for each method. Usages are also simpler than the (sometimes redundant) assertions required by Plaid [2,14,31] and the defensive programming style required by tools such as Checker [10] is not needed.   ∎

Typing program definitions $\overrightarrow{D}$ requires judgements like $\vdash \overrightarrow{D}$. Rule TPROG (below) says a program is well-typed if each of its enumeration and class declarations are well-typed; in turn declarations require judgements $\vdash_{\overrightarrow{D}} D$, saying an enumeration is well-typed if all labels in the set do not occur in any other enumeration declaration (labels are uniquely associated with a type L – rule TEnum omitted) and a class is well-typed if its usage is well-typed.

Judgements for typing class usages are of the form

$$\Theta; \Phi \vdash_{\vec{D}} C[\mathcal{U}] \triangleright \Phi'$$

where Φ is a *field typing environment* assigning types to fields of the class C (Φ' is the corresponding result of the typing derivation, reflecting the changes in the typestates of objects stored in the fields) and Θ is an environment assigning field type environments to usage equation variables, to deal with recursive behaviour, as explained below. The judgement also considers the program definition $\vec{D}$ in which the class occurs, but since it never changes in a type derivation, we will not refer it in the rules henceforth presented (a subset of all rules; the omitted ones are in the technical reports referred at the end of Sect. 1). The judgement takes Θ, Φ, $\vec{D}$, and $C[\mathcal{U}]$ as input and if there is a derivation, it outputs Φ'.

Rule TClass uses an empty usage variable type environment and a field typing environment assigning *initial* types to the fields of the class: since when a new object is created, all its fields of a class type are initialised with null, their respective type in the initial field typing environment is $\bot$ (to control dereferencing), a new type not available to the programmer – we extend the syntax of types with it (see below). So,

$$\vec{F}.\text{inittypes} \triangleq \{f \mapsto \text{inittype}(z) \mid z\ f \in \vec{F}\}$$

where $\text{inittype}(b) \triangleq b$ and $\text{inittype}(C) \triangleq \bot$. Moreover, following the class usage $\mathcal{U}$ must result in a *terminated* field typing environment Φ, *i.e.*, fields with class types must have either usage end or type $\bot$. The judgement $\Theta; \Phi \vdash C[\mathcal{U}] \triangleright \Phi$, discussed below, makes use of the method set $\vec{M}$ via $C.\text{methods}$.

$$(\text{TProg}) \ \frac{\forall D \in \vec{D}.\vdash_{\vec{D}} D}{\vdash \vec{D}} \qquad (\text{TClass}) \ \frac{\emptyset; \vec{F}.\text{inittypes} \vdash C[\mathcal{U}] \triangleright \Phi \quad \text{terminated}(\Phi)}{\vdash_{\vec{D}} \text{class } C\{\mathcal{U}, \vec{F}, \vec{M}\}}$$

Linear and Terminated Types. Values have a type that can be either a base type b, $\bot$, the type of null, or "general" typestates $C[\mathcal{U}]$, with U now being either branch or choice usages.

$$W ::= w^{\vec{E}} \qquad U ::= \mathcal{U}|W \qquad t ::= b|C[U]|\bot$$

An important distinction in our type system is the one between linear and non-linear types, as it is this distinction that makes the type system able to detect potential null dereferencings and memory leaks.

A type t is *linear*, written $\text{lin}(t)$, if it is a class type $C[U]$ with a usage U that is different from end. This use of linearity forces objects to be used only by a single "client", thus preventing interference in the execution of its protocol.

$$\text{lin}(t) \triangleq \exists C, U . t = C[U] \land U \neq \text{end}$$

All other types are non-linear, and we call such types *terminated*.

Table 2. Typing class usage definitions

$$I \neq \emptyset \qquad \forall i \in I. \ \exists \Phi''.$$

$$\text{TCBR} \ \frac{\{\text{this} \mapsto \Phi\}; (\emptyset \cdot (\text{this}, [x_i \mapsto t_i'])) \vdash e_i : t_i \rhd \{\text{this} \mapsto \Phi''\}; (\emptyset \cdot (\text{this}, [x_i \mapsto t_i''])) \ \wedge \ \text{terminated}(t_i'') \wedge t_i \ m_i(t_i' \ x_i)\{e_i\} \in C.\text{methods} \wedge \Theta; \Phi'' \vdash C[w_i^{\vec{E}}] \rhd \Phi'}{\Theta; \Phi \vdash C[\{m_i; w_i\}_{i \in I}^{\vec{E}}] \rhd \Phi'}$$

$$\text{TCCH} \ \frac{\forall l_i \in L \ . \ \Theta; \Phi \vdash C[u_i^{\vec{E}}] \rhd \Phi'}{\Theta; \Phi \vdash C[\langle l_i : u_i \rangle_{l_i \in L}^{\vec{E}}] \rhd \Phi'} \qquad\qquad \text{TCEND} \ \frac{}{\Theta; \Phi \vdash C[\text{end}^{\vec{E}}] \rhd \Phi}$$

$$\text{TCVAR} \ \frac{}{(\Theta, [X \mapsto \Phi]); \Phi \vdash C[X^{\vec{E}}] \rhd \Phi'} \qquad\qquad \text{TCREC} \ \frac{(\Theta, [X \mapsto \Phi]); \Phi \vdash C[u^{\vec{E}}] \rhd \Phi'}{\Theta; \Phi \vdash C[X^{\vec{E} \uplus \{X=u\}}] \rhd \Phi'}$$

Typing class usages requires the rules in Table 2. Each one applies to a different constructor of usages: rule TCEND is a base case: end does not change the field environment. Rules TCREC and TCVAR are used to type a class with respect to a recursive usage X, which is well-typed if the class C can be well-typed under the body u of X defined in $\vec{E}$ (note that in the premise of TCREC, the defining equation for X does not occur); rule TCVAR handles recursion variables appearing in usages, associating a type with the variable in the environment. Rule TCCH deals with choice usages, requiring all possible evolutions to lead to the same usage to guarantee determinism. Finally, the important rule TCBR deals with (non-terminated) branch usages: for each method m_i mentioned, its body e_i is checked with its return type t_i; and the initial type t_i' of the parameter x, declared in the method signature; following the effect of executing the method body, yields the resulting type t_i'' of x and the resulting type of this.

Example 2. Recall the class File from Listing 1.1. To type it, we inspect its usage. As it starts as a branch, we apply TCBR and check that the body of method open is well-typed and move on to check usage Check. As it is a recursion variable, we use TCREC; we now have a branch usage where we check that the body of method isEOF is well-typed, using rule TCCH. If the method returns EOF, we then check method close and terminate with rule TCEND; if it returns NOTEOF, we check method read and finish the type-checking process (the derivation ends) since we find again the recursion variable Check. Both cases result in identical field typing environments. ∎

Typing expressions requires rules for values, with atomic and composite constructors. Our semantics is stack-based and introduces run-time extensions to the language. In the type system, the counterpart of the stack is an environment that plays a limited role in typing the language we show herein but is essential for typing code resulting from computational steps (details in the technical report).

Let the *object field environment* Λ record the type information for fields in objects and $S = [x \mapsto t]$ be a parameter type environment.

The key element when typing the programmer's code is the pair (o, S), where o is the main object. Type judgements are of the form

$$\Lambda; (o, S) \vdash_{\vec{D}}^{\Omega} e : t \triangleright \Lambda'; (o, S')$$

Their intended meaning is as follows: evaluating e in the initial environments Λ and S will produce final typing environments Λ' and S', results yield only if the derivation succeeds. Here Ω is a label environment that is used to map a label k to a pair of environments (Λ, S), Ω is only used in continue expressions and is therefore omitted in most rules (as well as $\vec{D}$). Since typing environments are functions, $\Lambda\{o \mapsto t\}$, for instance, denotes the result of a substitution, *i.e.*, the environment equal to Λ everywhere but in the image of o, that is now t.

When typing values, unit has type void, null has type $\bot$, and the boolean values have type Bool where the initial and final environments in the judgements do not change. Typing a parameter is similar to typing (reading) a field, so we only describe the latter here. The rules are presented below. The rule TOBJ handles object typing and it says that once we type an object, corresponding to reading it, we remove it from the object type environment.

$$(\text{TOBJ}) \quad \frac{}{\Lambda\{o \mapsto t\}; (o', S) \vdash o : t \triangleright \Lambda; (o', S)}$$

TNoLFLD describes how to type non-linear parameters and fields: no updates happen to the environments. The rule TLINFLD deals with linear parameters and fields: after typing the value, the linear parameter or field is updated to the type $\bot$ (to prevent aliasing) in either the parameter stack environment or field type environment (only the rules for fields are presented, as those for parameters are similar).

$$(\text{TLINFLD}) \quad \frac{t = \Lambda(o).f \quad \text{lin}(t)}{\Lambda; (o, S) \vdash f : t \triangleright \Lambda\{o.f \mapsto \bot\}; (o, S)}$$

$$(\text{TNoLFLD}) \quad \frac{\neg\text{lin}(t)}{\Lambda\{o.f \mapsto t\}; (o, S) \vdash f : t \triangleright \Lambda\{o.f \mapsto t\}; (o, S)}$$

The key atomic constructors are the creation of objects and assignment to fields and parameters. The typing rules are given below; we omit the rule typing assignment to parameters, as it is similar to that of fields.

$$(\text{TNEW}) \ \Lambda; (o, S) \vdash \text{new } C : C[C.\text{usage}] \triangleright \Lambda; (o, S)$$

$$(\text{TFLD}) \quad \frac{C = \Lambda(o).\text{class} \qquad \text{agree}(C.\text{fields}(f), t')}{\Lambda; (o, S) \vdash e : t' \triangleright \Lambda', o.f \mapsto t; (o, S') \qquad \neg\text{lin}(t)}{\Lambda; (o, S) \vdash f = e : \text{void} \triangleright \Lambda'\{o.f \mapsto t'\}; (o, S')}$$

The assignment rules are designed to avoid overwriting fields containing objects with incomplete protocols. To that purpose we use a binary predicate agree that only holds if both arguments are the same base type or class type.

$$\text{agree}(z, t) \overset{\text{def}}{=} z = t \vee \exists C. \ z = C \wedge (t = \bot \vee \exists U. \ t = C[U])$$

Notice that in rule (TFLD) null agrees with any class type declared in the program only if the field does not contain an object with a linear type.

Example 3. Consider a field f declared in the program with some class type C. Rule (TFLD) only lets us assign to f if its type is not linear, *i.e.*, it must be either $\perp$ or $C[\text{end}]$. So, f either contains null or an object with a terminated protocol. The **agree** predicate lets us assign to f either null or, more significantly, any object with a usage (that in the subsequent code will be followed, as the rules we present below show). In particular, one can assign new C to f.   ∎

To type a method call on a field using the rule (TCALLF) (the rule for typing method calls on parameters is similar) first the type environments must be updated by typing the argument and then the usage of the callee object must offer the method. Usages have a labelled transition semantics. Transitions are of the form $u \xrightarrow{m} u'$ and $u \xrightarrow{l} u'$ and defined by the rules below.

$$(\text{Branch}) \quad \frac{j \in I}{\{m_i : w_i\}_{i \in I}^{\vec{E}} \xrightarrow{m_j} w_j^{\vec{E}}} \qquad (\text{Unfold}) \quad \frac{u^{\vec{E} \cup \{X = u\}} \xrightarrow{m} \mathcal{W}}{X^{\vec{E} \cup \{X = u\}} \xrightarrow{m} \mathcal{W}}$$

$$(\text{Sel}) \quad (\langle l_i : u_i \rangle_{l_i \in L})^{\vec{E}} \xrightarrow{l_i} u_i^{\vec{E}}$$

The rule (TRET) for typing return is not surprising: once the environments are updated by typing the expression e, we remove from the object environment the last entry, with the identity of the caller and the type of the value in the parameter identifier, given that this type is terminated (to prevent memory leaks and dangling objects with incomplete protocols).

Note that the body of the method is not typed in this rule, since it was handled at the class declaration.

$$(\text{TCallF}) \quad \frac{\begin{array}{c} \Lambda; (o, S) \vdash e : t \rhd \Lambda'\{o.f \mapsto C[\mathcal{U}]\}; (o, S') \\ t' \ m(t \ x)\{e'\} \in C.\text{methods}_{\vec{B}} \qquad \mathcal{U} \xrightarrow{m} \mathcal{W} \end{array}}{\Lambda; (o, S) \vdash f.m(e) : t' \rhd \Lambda'\{o.f \mapsto C[\mathcal{W}]\}; (o, S')}$$

$$(\text{TRet}) \quad \frac{\Lambda; \Delta \vdash_{\vec{B}} e : t \rhd \Lambda'; \Delta' \qquad \Delta' = \Delta'' \cdot (o', [x \mapsto t']) \qquad \text{terminated}(t')}{\Lambda; \Delta \cdot (o, S) \vdash_{\vec{B}} \text{return}\{e\} : t \rhd \Lambda'; \Delta'' \cdot (o, S)}$$

Example 4. Recall class File from Listing 1.1. Rule (TCALLF) states that in order for a call of the close method to be well-typed, there must be a transition labelled with close. This method call thus fails to typecheck under usage Init.   ∎

We conclude this section presenting the typing rules for control structures. The rule TSEQ for sequential composition requires the left expression not to produce a linear value (that would be left dangling): $e; e'$ is well-typed only if the type of e is not linear. Moreover, e' is typed with the environments resulting from typing e (*i.e.*, we take into account the evolution of the protocols of objects in e).

The rules TLAB and TCON for labelled expressions allows environments to change during the evaluation of continue-style loops. However, if a continue expression is encountered, the environments must match the original environments, in order to allow an arbitrary number of iterations. Since (o, S) is not relevant, we refer it as Δ.

$$(\text{TSEQ}) \quad \frac{\Lambda; (o,S) \vdash e : t \rhd \Lambda''; (o, S'') \quad \neg\text{lin}(t) \quad \Lambda''; (o, S'') \vdash e' : t' \rhd \Lambda'; (o, S')}{\Lambda; (o, S) \vdash e; e' : t' \rhd \Lambda'; (o, S')}$$

$$(\text{TLAB}) \quad \frac{\Omega' = \Omega, k : (\Lambda, \Delta)}{\Lambda; \Delta \vdash^{\Omega'} e : \text{void} \rhd \Lambda'; \Delta'}{\Lambda; \Delta \vdash^{\Omega} k : e : \text{void} \rhd \Lambda'; \Delta'} \qquad (\text{TCON}) \quad \frac{\Omega' = \Omega, k : (\Lambda, \Delta)}{\Lambda; \Delta \vdash^{\Omega'} \text{continue } k : \text{void} \rhd \Lambda'; \Delta'}$$

In Subsect. 1.1 a class FileReader was introduced with a loop repeated in Listing 1.3. Even though calling the close method leaves the field in another state than calling read, the code is well typed. The reason is that after calling read, the field is left in the initial state when entering the loop, and another iteration occurs. When calling close the loop is ended. Hence the only resulting state for the field after the loop, is File[end].

```
[...]                                                              26
file.open(unit)                                                    27
loop: switch(file.isEOF()) {                                       28
        EOF: file.close() (*@\label{lst:code:2}@*)                 29
        NOTEOF: file.read();                                       30
                continue loop                                      31
    }                                                              32
[...]                                                              33
```

Listing 1.3. Loop from class FileReader

4   The Dynamic Semantics of Mungo

The operational semantics of Mungo is a reduction relation and uses a stack-based binding model, the semantic counterpart of that of the type system.

Expressions transitions are relative to a program definition $\overrightarrow{D}$ with the form

$$\vdash_{\overrightarrow{D}} \langle h, env_S, e \rangle \to \langle h', env_S', e' \rangle$$

A *heap* h records the bindings of object references. In the heap, every object reference o is bound to some pair $(C[\mathcal{W}], env_F)$ where $C[\mathcal{W}]$ is a typestate and $env_F \in \textbf{Env}_\textbf{F}$ is a field environment. A *field environment* is a partial function $env_F : \textbf{FNames} \rightharpoonup \textbf{Values}$ that maps field names to the values stored in the fields. Given a heap $h = h' \uplus \{o \mapsto (C[\mathcal{W}], env_F)\}$, we write $h\{\mathcal{W}'/h(o).\text{usage}\}$ to stand for the heap $h' \uplus \{o \mapsto (C[\mathcal{W}'], env_F)\}$[1]; $h\{v/o.f\}$ for $h' \uplus \{o \mapsto (C[\mathcal{W}], env_F\{f \mapsto v\})\}$; and we use the notation $h\{o.f \mapsto C[\mathcal{W}]\}$

---

[1] We use $\uplus$ to denote disjoint union.

to denote the heap $h' \uplus \{o \mapsto (C[W'], env'_F)\}$ where $env'_F = env_F\{f \mapsto C[W]\}$. Moreover, if $h = h' \uplus \{o \mapsto \_\}$ then $h \backslash \{o\} = h'$ and when $o \notin \text{dom}(h)$, $h \backslash \{o\} = h$. Finally, we say a heap is *terminated* if for all objects in its domain, their usages are terminated.

The *parameter stack* env_S records to the bindings of formal parameters. It is a sequence of bindings where each element (o, s) contains an object o and a parameter instantiation $s=[x \mapsto v]$. In a parameter stack $env_S \cdot (o, s)$ we call the bottom element o the *active object*. Often, we think of the parameter stack as defining a function. The domain $\text{dom}(env_S)$ of the parameter stack env_S is the multiset of all object names on the stack. The range of the parameter stack $\text{ran}(env_S)$ is the multiset of all parameter instantiations on the stack. We refer to the attributes of an object o bound in heap h, where $h(o)=\langle C[W], env_F \rangle$, as:

$$h(o).\text{class} \stackrel{\text{def}}{=} C \qquad h(o).\text{env}_F \stackrel{\text{def}}{=} env_F$$

$$h(o).\text{usage} \stackrel{\text{def}}{=} W \qquad h(o).f \stackrel{\text{def}}{=} env_F(f) \qquad h(o).\text{fields} \stackrel{\text{def}}{=} \text{dom}(env_F)$$

The Transition Rules. Linearity also appears in the semantics, and the linearity requirement is similar to that of the type system. Here, a value v is said to be linear w.r.t. a heap h written $\text{lin}(h, v)$ iff v has type $C[U]$ and $U \neq \text{end}$. If the field denotes a terminated object or a ground value, field access is *unrestricted*.

Below we show the most important transition rules. The rules for reading linear fields illustrate how linearity works in the semantics. In LDEREF we update a linear field or parameter to null after we have read it, while the rule UDEREF tells us that the value contained in an unrestricted fields remains available.

$$\text{(UDEREF)} \quad \frac{h(o).f = v \quad \neg\text{lin}(v, h)}{\vdash_{\vec{D}} \langle h, (o, s) \cdot env_S, f \rangle \rightarrow \langle h, (o, s) \cdot env_S, v \rangle}$$

$$\text{(LDEREF)} \quad \frac{h(o).f = v \quad \text{lin}(v, h)}{\vdash_{\vec{D}} \langle h, (o, s) \cdot env_S, f \rangle \rightarrow \langle h\{\text{null}/o.f\}, (o, s) \cdot env_S, v \rangle}$$

$$\text{(UPD)} \quad \frac{h(o).f = v' \quad \neg\text{lin}(v', h)}{\vdash_{\vec{D}} \langle h, (o, s) \cdot env_S, f = v \rangle \rightarrow \langle h\{v/o.f\}, (o, s) \cdot env_S, \text{unit} \rangle}$$

$$\text{(LBL)} \quad \vdash_{\vec{D}} \langle h, env_S, k : e \rangle \rightarrow \langle h, env_S, e\{k : e/\text{continue } k\} \rangle$$

$$\text{(CALLF)} \quad \frac{env_S = (o, s) \cdot env'_S \qquad o' = h(o).f}{\vdash_{\vec{D}} \langle h, env_S, f.m(v) \rangle \rightarrow \langle h\{W/h(o').\text{usage}\}, (o', [x \mapsto v]) \cdot env_S, \text{return}\{e\} \rangle}$$

$$\text{(RET)} \quad \frac{v \neq v' \Rightarrow \neg\text{lin}(v', h)}{\vdash_{\vec{D}} \langle h, (o, [x \mapsto v']) \cdot env_S, \text{return}\{v\} \rangle \rightarrow \langle h, env_S, v \rangle}$$

The rule LBL shows how a loop iteration is performed by substituting instances of continue k with the expression defined for the associated label. In CALLF the premise describes how an object must follow the usage described by its current typestate. A method m can only be called if the usage of the object allows an m transition and the result of this evaluation is that the usage of the object is updated and the next evaluation step is set to the method body

e by wrapping the expression in a special return$\{e\}$ statement; this is a run-time extension of the syntax that lets us record method calls waiting to be completed. The RET rule describes how a value is returned from a method call, by unpacking the return statement into the value, while popping the call stack. For details on the run-time syntax, see the technical report.

5   Results About the Type System

The first important result is the soundness of the type system, as usual shown in two steps: subject-reduction and type-safety. So, firstly, well-typed programs remain well-typed during execution. In our setting this means that when a well-typed configuration reduces, it leads to a configuration that is also well-typed. A configuration is well-typed if its bindings match the type information given: The heap matches the field typing environment Λ, the stack Δ in the type system matches the stack from the semantics, the objects mentioned in the type system match those of e, the expression e itself is well typed and the field type environment Λ is compatible with the program $\vec{D}$. If this is the case, we write $\Lambda, \Delta \vdash_{\vec{D}} \langle h, env_S, e \rangle : t \triangleright \Lambda'$. Let Δ and Δ' be sequences of object type and parameter type environments, defined as $\Delta = envT_O \cdot envT_S$. An object type environment $envT_O$ maps object names to typestates.

$$envT_O : \textbf{ONames} \rightharpoonup \textbf{Typestates}$$

A parameter type environment $envT_S$ is a sequence of pairs $(o, [x \mapsto t])$ mapping an object o to a parameter binding $[x \mapsto t]$.

To prove Theorem 1, we need typing rules for the dynamic syntax. Rule (TRET) is one such rule; it also becomes central when proving Theorem 3.

$$\text{(TRET)} \quad \frac{\Lambda; \Delta \vdash_{\vec{D}} e : t \triangleright \Lambda'; \Delta' \qquad \Delta' = \Delta'' \cdot (o', \lfloor x \mapsto t' \rfloor) \qquad \text{terminated}(t')}{\Lambda; \Delta \cdot (o, S) \vdash_{\vec{D}} \text{return}\{e\} : t \triangleright \Lambda'; \Delta'' \cdot (o, S)}$$

The rule tell us that a return$\{e\}$ expression is well-typed if the expression body e is well-typed and the method parameter used in the expression body is terminated after the execution. The final type environment is one, in which the parameter stack environment does not mention the called object and its associated parameter. The intention is that this mirrors the modification of the stack environment in the semantics as expressed in the reduction rule (RET).

Theorem 1 (Subject reduction). *Let $\vec{D}$ be such that $\vdash \vec{D}$ and let $\langle h, env_S, e \rangle$ be a configuration. If $\vdash_{\vec{D}} \langle h, env_S, e \rangle \rightarrow \langle h', env'_S, e' \rangle$ then:*

$\exists \Lambda, \Delta \;.\; \Lambda, \Delta \vdash_{\vec{D}} \langle h, env_S, e \rangle : t \triangleright \Lambda'; \Delta'$ *implies*
$\exists \Lambda^N, \Delta^N \;.\; \Lambda^N, \Delta^N \vdash_{\vec{D}} \langle h', env'_S, e' \rangle : t \triangleright \Lambda''; \Delta'$, *where $\Lambda'(o) = \Lambda''(o)$ and o is the active object in the resulting configuration.*

Secondly, a well-typed program will never go wrong. In our case, this means that a well-typed program does not attempt *null-dereferencing*, and all method calls follow the specified usages. We formalize the notion of run-time error via a predicate and write $\langle h, env_S, e \rangle \longrightarrow_{err}$ whenever $\langle h, env_S, e \rangle$ has an error. Rules (NC-1) and (NC-2) describe two cases of null-dereferencing that occur when the object invoked by method m has been nullified.

$$\text{(NC-1)} \quad \frac{h(o).f = \text{null}}{\langle h, (o, s) \cdot env_S, f.m(v) \rangle \longrightarrow_{err}}$$

$$\text{(NC-2)} \quad \langle h, (o, [x \mapsto \text{null}]) \cdot env_S, x.m(v) \rangle \longrightarrow_{err}$$

Theorem 2 (Type safety). *If* $\Lambda; \Delta \vdash_{\vec{D}} \langle h, env_S, e \rangle \; : \; t \triangleright \Lambda'; \Delta'$ *and* $\langle h, env_S, e \rangle \to^* \langle h', env'_S, e' \rangle$ *then* $\langle h', env'_S, e' \rangle \not\longrightarrow_{err}$

The second important result concerning type-checking is that well-typed terminated programs do not leave object protocols incomplete. It is a direct consequence of requiring in rule TClass the field typing environment to be terminated and of the fact that the only active object is the main one, o_{main}, which have the end usage).

Theorem 3 (Protocol Completion). *Let* $\vdash \vec{D}$. *For all reachable configurations* $\langle h, env_S, e \rangle_{\vec{D}}$ *such that* $\langle h, env_S, e \rangle \not\to$, *we have* $env_S = (o_{main}, s_{main})$, $e = v$, *and moreover,* terminated(h).

6 Usage Inference

In this section, we outline a usage inference algorithm and present results for the inferred usages. The algorithm infers usages from class declarations in order to improve usability: it allows programmers to abstain from specifying usages for all class declarations and facilitates type checking with less usages annotations in the source program. The algorithm works on an acyclic graph of dependencies between class declarations. This dependency graph defines the order in which inference takes place, where the usage for a class C can only be inferred if the usages of its fields have been explicitly declared or previously inferred.

The inference algorithm returns a usage for any given class declaration. It considers how method call sequences of the class affect its field typing environments by using the type rules defined in Table 2. The process can be described by the following three steps: **Step 1.** Extract allowed method sequences. **Step 2.** Filter non-terminating sequences. **Step 3.** Convert sequences into usages.

Step 1 is the most interesting since it establishes the possible sequences of method calls in relation to the type system by using a transition relation $\to$ given by rule (CLASS) shown below. This rule states that a method call m initiated from field typing environment Φ and results in Φ' is allowed if the method body is well-typed and its parameter is terminated at the end. The (CLASS) rule, when applied to a class declaration, defines a transition system where field typing environments are states and transitions between them are method calls.

$$(\text{CLASS}) \quad \frac{\begin{array}{c} \{\text{this} \mapsto \Phi\}; \emptyset \cdot (\text{this}, [x \mapsto t]) \vdash^{\emptyset} e : t' \triangleright \{\text{this} \mapsto \Phi'\}; \emptyset \cdot (\text{this}, [x \mapsto t'']) \\ t' \; m(t \; x) \; \{e\} \in C.\text{methods} \qquad\qquad \neg\text{lin}(t'') \end{array}}{\Phi \xrightarrow{m} \Phi'}$$

Note that the premise of the (CLASS) rule is similar to the premise of (TCBR) and that a method transition is only available if the method body is well typed according to (TCBR). From the transition system defined by $\rightarrow$, we filter out all transitions that cannot reach a terminated environment, since these environments will result in protocols that cannot terminate.

Example 5. Recall the FileReader example from Listing 1.2. We wish to infer the usage for the FileReader class. Since the class has a field of type File, the usage of the File class must be known. The inference algorithm starts from the initial field typing environment $\{\text{file} : \bot\}$. Using the (CLASS) rule we see that only the method body of init is well typed in the initial field typing environment, thus updating the field typing environment $\{\text{file} : \text{File}[\mathcal{U}]\}$. The procedure is then repeated for the updated environment where a call to readFile is now possible. The field is now terminated and the algorithm proceeds to convert the transition system into a usage. This conversion is done by representing each state of the transition system as a usage variable and each transition as a branch usage. The resulting usage for class FileReader is: $X\{X=\{\text{init};X'\} \; X'=\{\text{readFile};\text{end } \text{readFile};X\}\}$ ∎

A correctly inferred usage, in our case, is the *principal usage* for a class declaration. A principal usage is the most permissible usage hence it includes the behaviours of all usages that well-type a class. In other words, the most permissible usage allows all sequences of method calls, for a class declaration, that do not lead to null-dereferencing errors and can terminate. We define principality in terms of a simulation ordering $\sqsubseteq$ where the principal usage can simulate any usage that would make the class well typed. Let R be a binary relation on usages. We call R a usage simulation iff for all $(\mathcal{U}_1, \mathcal{U}_2) \in R$ we have that:

1. If $\mathcal{U}_1 \xrightarrow{m} \mathcal{U}_1'$ then $\mathcal{U}_2 \xrightarrow{m} \mathcal{U}_2'$ such that $(\mathcal{U}_1', \mathcal{U}_2') \in R$
2. If $\mathcal{U}_1 \xrightarrow{l} \mathcal{U}_1'$ then $\mathcal{U}_2 \xrightarrow{l} \mathcal{U}_2'$ such that $(\mathcal{U}_1', \mathcal{U}_2') \in R$

We say that $\mathcal{U}$ is a subusage of $\mathcal{U}'$, written $\mathcal{U} \sqsubseteq \mathcal{U}'$, if for some usage simulation R we have $(\mathcal{U}, \mathcal{U}') \in R$. Principal usages are always recursive since there is no difference between a field typing environment at the initial state and at the end as all fields are non-linear in accordance with protocol completion. A method sequence that results in a terminated environment can be repeated any number of times and remain well typed. To allow usages to express termination or repetition, we allow a limited form of non-determinism to choose between end and repeating the protocol, as in the definition of X' above. If $\mathcal{U}_I$ is the inferred usage for a class C, then C is well-typed with this usage. Moreover, the inferred usage is principal wrt. usage simulation.

Theorem 4 (Principality). *If $\mathcal{U}_I$ is the inferred usage for class C, then $\mathcal{U}_I$ is the largest usage for C that makes C well typed. That is, $\vdash_{\vec{D}} class\ C\{\mathcal{U}_I, \vec{F}, \vec{M}\}$ and $\forall \mathcal{U}.\vdash_{\vec{D}} class\ C\ \{\mathcal{U}, \vec{F}, \vec{M}\} \implies \mathcal{U} \sqsubseteq \mathcal{U}_I$.*

7   Conclusions and Future Work

In this paper we present a behavioural type system for the Mungo language, also implemented in the form of a type-checker. Every class is annotated with usages that describe the protocol to be followed by method calls to object instances of the class. Moreover, object references can only be used in a linear fashion. The type system provides a formal guarantee that a well-typed program will satisfy three important properties: memory-safety, and object protocol fidelity and object protocol completion. Behavioural types are essential, as they allow variables of class type to have a type that evolves to $\perp$, which is the only type inhabited by the null value. This is in contrast to most type systems for Java like languages that do not let types evolve during a computation and overload null to have any type.

Furthermore, a contribution that is novel and in contrast to other typestate-based approaches is that it is possible to infer usages from a class description. We have implemented a tool that can infer the most general usage wrt. a simulation preorder that makes the class well-typed.

In our type system, variables obey a very simple protocol of linearity: They must be written to once, then read once (otherwise they return a null value). The current version of the Mungo tool [23] allows for a representation of fields that can be used k times for $k > 1$ by having k field variables that are each used once. A natural extension of the system is therefore to allow for a richer language of safe variable protocols. An approach currently under investigation is to use ideas from the work on behavioural separation of Caires and Seco [7], by Franco et al. on SHAPES [13] and that of Militão et al. [25].

To be able to type a larger subset of Java than what Mungo currently allows, further work also includes adding inheritance to the language in a type-safe manner. Inheritance is common in object oriented programming, and would allow Mungo to be used for a larger set of programs. This is particularly important, since classes in languages like Java always implicitly inherit from the class Object. However, Grigore has shown that type checking for Java in the presence of full subtyping is undecidable [17]. Therefore, in further work, we need to be extremely careful when introducing subtyping into our system. Moreover, notice that this would require defining subtyping for class usages, a form of behavioural/session subtyping [4,5,16].

References

1. https://github.com/MungoTypesystem/Mungo-Typechecker/ExamplePrograms/
2. Aldrich, J.: The Plaid programming language (2010)

3. Ancona, D., et al.: Behavioral types in programming languages. Found. Trends Program. Lang. **3**(2–3), 95–230 (2016)
4. Bravetti, M., Carbone, M., Zavattaro, G.: Undecidability of asynchronous session subtyping. Inf. Comput. **256**, 300–320 (2017)
5. Bravetti, M., Carbone, M., Zavattaro, G.: On the boundary between decidability and undecidability of asynchronous session subtyping. Theoret. Comput. Sci. **722**, 19–51 (2018)
6. Bravetti, M., Zavattaro, G.: Process calculi as a tool for studying coordination, contracts and session types. J. Logical Algebraic Methods Program. **112**, 100527 (2020)
7. Caires, L., Seco, J.C.: The type discipline of behavioral separation. In: The 40th Symposium on Principles of Programming Languages, POPL 2013, pp. 275–286. ACM (2013)
8. de Boer, F.S., Bravetti, M., Lee, M.D., Zavattaro, G.: A petri net based modeling of active objects and futures. Fundamenta Informaticae **159**(3), 197–256 (2018)
9. DeLine, R., Fähndrich, M.: Typestates for objects. In: Odersky, M. (ed.) ECOOP 2004. LNCS, vol. 3086, pp. 465–490. Springer, Heidelberg (2004). https://doi.org/10.1007/978-3-540-24851-4_21
10. Dietl, W., Dietzel, S., Ernst, M.D., Muslu, K., Schiller, T.W.: Building and using pluggable type-checkers. In: Proceedings of the 33rd International Conference on Software Engineering, ICSE 2011, pp. 681–690. ACM (2011)
11. Fähndrich, M., DeLine, R.: Adoption and focus: practical linear types for imperative programming. In: Proceedings of PLDI 2002, pp. 13–24. ACM (2002)
12. Fähndrich, M., Leino, K.R.M.: Declaring and checking non-null types in an object-oriented language. In: Proceedings of OOPSLA 2003, pp. 302–312. ACM (2003)
13. Franco, J., Tasos, A., Drossopoulou, S., Wrigstad, T., Eisenbach, S.: Safely abstracting memory layouts. CoRR, abs/1901.08006 (2019)
14. Garcia, R., Tanter, É., Wolff, R., Aldrich, J.: Foundations of typestate-oriented programming. Trans. Program. Lang. Syst. **36**(4), 1–44 (2014)
15. Gay, S.J., Gesbert, N., Ravara, A., Vasconcelos, V.T.: Modular session types for objects. Logical Methods Comput. Sci. **11**(4), 1–76 (2015)
16. Gay, S.J., Hole, M.: Subtyping for session types in the pi calculus. Acta Informatica **42**(2–3), 191–225 (2005)
17. Grigore, R.: Java generics are turing complete. In: Proceedings of POPL 2017, pp. 73–85. ACM (2017)
18. Hoare, T.: Null references: the billion dollar mistake (2009)
19. Honda, K.: Types for dyadic interaction. In: Best, E. (ed.) CONCUR 1993. LNCS, vol. 715, pp. 509–523. Springer, Heidelberg (1993). https://doi.org/10.1007/3-540-57208-2_35
20. Hubert, L., Jensen, T., Pichardie, D.: Semantic foundations and inference of non-null annotations. In: Barthe, G., de Boer, F.S. (eds.) FMOODS 2008. LNCS, vol. 5051, pp. 132–149. Springer, Heidelberg (2008). https://doi.org/10.1007/978-3-540-68863-1_9
21. Hüttel, H., et al.: Foundations of session types and behavioural contracts. ACM Comput. Surv. **49**(1), 1–36 (2016)
22. Igarashi, A., Pierce, B.C., Wadler, P.: Featherweight java: a minimal core calculus for Java and GJ. Trans. Program. Lang. Syst. **23**(3), 396–450 (2001)
23. Kouzapas, D., Dardha, O., Perera, R., Gay, S.J.: Typechecking protocols with Mungo and StMungo: a session type toolchain for Java. Sci. Comput. Program. **155**, 52–75 (2018)

24. Meyer, B.: Ending null pointer crashes. Commun. ACM **60**(5), 8–9 (2017)
25. Militão, F., Aldrich, J., Caires, L.: Aliasing control with view-based typestate. In: Proceedings of the 12th Workshop on Formal Techniques for Java-Like Programs, FTFJP 2010. ACM (2010)
26. Milner, R.: A theory of type polymorphism in programming. J. Comput. Syst. Sci. **17**, 348–375 (1978)
27. Nierstrasz, O.: Regular types for active objects. In: Proceedings of the 8th Conference on Object-Oriented Programming Systems, Languages, and Applications (OOPSLA 1993), pp. 1–15. ACM (1993)
28. Siek, J., Taha, W.: Gradual typing for objects. In: Ernst, E. (ed.) ECOOP 2007. LNCS, vol. 4609, pp. 2–27. Springer, Heidelberg (2007). https://doi.org/10.1007/978-3-540-73589-2_2
29. Strom, R.E., Yemini, S.: Typestate: a programming language concept for enhancing software reliability. IEEE Trans. Softw. Eng. **12**(1), 157–171 (1986)
30. Sunshine, J.: Protocol programmability. PhD thesis, Carnegie Mellon University, Pittsburgh, PA, USA (2013). AAI3578659
31. Sunshine, J., Stork, S., Naden, K., Aldrich, J.: Changing state in the plaid language. In: Companion to OOPSLA 2011, pp. 37–38. ACM (2011)
32. The Jedis Project: Jedis (2011–2019). https://github.com/xetorthio/jedis/
33. The Redis Project: Redis (2011–2019). https://redis.io/
34. Voinea, A.L., Dardha, O., Gay, S.J.: Typechecking Java protocols with [St]Mungo. In: Gotsman, A., Sokolova, A. (eds.) FORTE 2020. LNCS, vol. 12136, pp. 208–224. Springer, Cham (2020). https://doi.org/10.1007/978-3-030-50086-3_12

Syntactically Restricting Bounded Polymorphism for Decidable Subtyping

Julian Mackay[1]($\boxtimes$)(iD), Alex Potanin[1](iD), Jonathan Aldrich[2](iD), and Lindsay Groves[1](iD)

[1] Victoria University of Wellington, Wellington, New Zealand
{julian,alex,lindsay}@ecs.vuw.ac.nz
[2] Carnegie Mellon University, Pittsburgh, USA
jonathan.aldrich@cs.cmu.edu

Abstract. Subtyping of Bounded Polymorphism has long been known to be undecidable when coupled with contra-variance. While decidable forms of bounded polymorphism exist, they all sacrifice either useful properties such as contra-variance (Kernel $F_{<:}$), or useful metatheoretic properties ($F_{<:}^{\top}$). In this paper we show how, by syntactically separating contra-variance from the recursive aspects of subtyping in System $F_{<:}$, decidable subtyping can be ensured while also allowing for both contra-variant subtyping of certain instances of bounded polymorphism, and many of System $F_{<:}$'s desirable metatheoretic properties. We then show that this approach can be applied to the related polymorphism present in $D_{<:}$, a minimal calculus that models core features of the Scala type system.

Keywords: Polymorphism · Language design · Functional languages · Object oriented languages

1 Introduction

Bounded polymorphism (or bounded quantification) is a powerful and widely used language construct that introduces a form of abstraction for types. Where functions provide an abstraction of behaviour for values, bounded polymorphism provides an abstraction of behaviour for types. A motivating example is an ordering for numbers, comparing two numbers, and returning -1 if the first is smaller than the second, 0 if the two numbers are equal, and 1 if the first is larger than the second. Below we provide such the signature for ord using no particular language syntax.

```
def ord : [A <. Number] A -> A -> Integer
```

The type A is unimportant except in that A is some subtype of Number (the upper bound on A). Ideally we would like ord to be defined abstractly for any value that could be considered a Number, and not have to write a separate function for

© Springer Nature Switzerland AG 2020
B. C. d. S. Oliveira (Ed.): APLAS 2020, LNCS 12470, pp. 125–144, 2020.
https://doi.org/10.1007/978-3-030-64437-6_7

Integer, Natural, and Real. ord is quantified over type A which is bounded by Number.

Bounded polymorphism has been adopted by many different languages, and is not exclusive to any specific paradigm. Haskell is an instance of bounded polymorphism in a functional setting. In Haskell, bounds take the form of type classes that values must conform to [17]. In an object oriented language, Java Generics provide a form of bounded polymorphism for both method and class definitions. Scala exists in both the function and object oriented paradigms, and includes generics similar to that of Java (only more flexible), but adds abstract type members on top, further complicating matters.

Unfortunately, several forms of bounded polymorphism have been shown to exhibit undecidable subtyping. To the surprise of many at the time, Pierce [13] demonstrated that subtyping in System $F_{<:}$, a typed λ-calculus with subtyping and bounded polymorphism, was undecidable by a reduction to the halting problem. More recently, and to perhaps less surprise, subtyping of Java Generics was also shown to be undecidable [8]. Hu and Lhoták [9] showed subtyping of $D_{<:}$, a minimal calculus, capturing parts of the Scala type system, was undecidable by a reduction to an undecidable fragment of System $F_{<:}$. Mackay et al. [10] developed two decidable variants on Wyvern, a programming language closely related to Scala. Mackay et al. focused on recursive types in Scala, but touched on bounded polymorphism.

If subtyping in languages with relatively wide usage is undecidable, then one might ask the question: how important is decidable subtyping in practice? Unfortunately, undecidability means that type checking of certain programs will not terminate, and will potentially crash without any error message indicating the problem. In writing a compiler, one fix to this problem might be to enforce a maximal depth on proof search, or to simply timeout during type checking. These are unsatisfying solutions, as not only might they create some false negatives, but they also won't be able to provide the programmer much guidance on debugging their program. Thus, while presumably rare, the potential problems are severe.

Not all forms of bounded polymorphism are undecidable, and there have been attempts at identifying fragments of bounded polymorphism that are both decidable and expressive. With regard to System $F_{<:}$, the most notable instances of these are perhaps Kernel $F_{<:}$ and $F_{<:}^{\top}$ (technically Kernel $F_{<:}$ existed prior to questions of decidability). All restrictions sacrifice some aspect of the language, and exclude some category of program from the language. Both Kernel $F_{<:}$ and $F_{<:}^{\top}$ exclude useful behaviour, or in the case of $F_{<:}^{\top}$ introduce undesirable properties to the language (this will be addressed in Sect. 2).

In this paper we show how simple syntactic restrictions can allow for decidable forms of bounded polymorphism that are easy to type check, allow for informative error messages, all while retaining many of the useful properties of typing in System $F_{<:}$: subtype transitivity, type safety, and minimal typing. We then demonstrate that this approach can be extended to the related calculus $D_{<:}$. The novelty of our approach lies in its simplicity. Simple syntactic restrictions allow for relatively simple extensions to existing type checkers, and can help keep metatheory simple. Simplicity of metatheory is particularly useful in the context of $D_{<:}$, a type system that arises from a family of type systems that are notoriously nuanced in their theoretical foundations [15].

2   The Undecidability of Bounded Polymorphism in System $F_{<:}$

Bounded polymorphism was formalized in System $F_{<:}$ by Cardelli [4], and shown to be undecidable by Pierce [13]. System $F_{<:}$ introduces bounded polymorphism to the simply typed λ-calculus by way of a universally quantified syntactic form with the following typing rule.

$$\frac{\Gamma, (\alpha \leqslant \tau_1) \vdash t \: : \: \tau_2}{\Gamma \vdash \Lambda(\alpha \leqslant \tau_1).t \: : \: \forall(\alpha \leqslant \tau_1).\tau_2}$$

That is, term t, with type τ_2, is quantified over some type, represented by α, whose upper bound is τ_1. The undecidability of subtyping in System $F_{<:}$ was demonstrated by a reduction of subtyping to the halting problem. The reduction relies on the contra-variance in the subtyping rule for bounded polymorphism given below.

$$\frac{\Gamma \vdash \tau_2 <: \tau_1 \qquad \Gamma, (\alpha \leqslant \tau_2) \vdash \tau_1' <: \tau_2'}{\Gamma \vdash \forall(\alpha \leqslant \tau_1).\tau_1' <: \forall(\alpha \leqslant \tau_2).\tau_2'} \quad \text{(S-All)}$$

As can be seen above, subtyping of bounded polymorphism in System $F_{<:}$ allows for contra-variance on the polymorphic type bound. Kernel $F_{<:}$, a variant of System $F_{<:}$, has been shown to be decidable in its subtyping [14]. Kernel $F_{<:}$ removes the contra-variance of the S-ALL rule above, and instead enforces invariance on the bound.

$$\frac{\Gamma, (\alpha \leqslant \tau) \vdash \tau_1 <: \tau_2}{\Gamma \vdash \forall(\alpha \leqslant \tau).\tau_1 <: \forall(\alpha \leqslant \tau).\tau_2} \quad \text{(S-All-Kernel)}$$

While decidable, S-ALL-KERNEL is unsatisfying as it excludes desirable behaviour. Ideally, we would like the ord function, from Sect. 1, to be usable in positions that require a more specific type such as Integer. Suppose we want to parameterize an Integer sorting algorithm on not just the list, but the ordering too.

```
def sort (compare : [A <: Integer] A -> A -> Integer,
          l : List[Integer]) : List[Integer]
```

We would like to be able to call the above sort function with ord.

```
assert(sort(ord, [1, 8, 2, -10]) == [-10, 1, 2, 8])
```

Castagna and Pierce [5] attempted to introduce such variance in a safe way by proposing $F_{<:}^{\top}$ with the following subtyping rule for bounded polymorphism.

$$\frac{\Gamma \vdash \tau_2 <: \tau_1 \qquad \Gamma, (\alpha \leqslant \top) \vdash \tau_1' <: \tau_2'}{\Gamma \vdash \forall(\alpha \leqslant \tau_1).\tau_1' <: \forall(\alpha \leqslant \tau_2).\tau_2'} \quad (\text{S-All}^{\top})$$

$$
\begin{array}{llll}
\tau ::= \\
\quad \top & top & \tau \to \tau & arrow \\
\quad \alpha & variable & \forall(\alpha \leqslant \tau).\tau & all
\end{array}
$$

Fig. 1. System $F_{<:}$ Type Syntax

Unfortunately, while decidable, $F_{<:}^{\top}$ sacrifices minimal typing. That is, it is possible to write a term in $F_{<:}^{\top}$ that can be typed with two different, and unrelated types [6]. A lack of minimal typing means that the typing algorithm for $F_{<:}^{\top}$ is not complete.

3   Separating Recursion and Contra-Variance in System $F_{<:}$

In this section we present a variant of System $F_{<:}$ that introduces a syntactic restriction on bounded polymorphism to achieve decidable subtyping. We start by introducing the type syntax of System $F_{<:}$ in Fig. 1. Since we are only concerned with subtyping, and not typing, we only present the type syntax. The term syntax and typing rules can be found in the accompanying technical report. Further, throughout the rest of this paper, we refer to several different definitions of subtyping and typing. To distinguish between these differences, we annotate the judgment. We have already mentioned three different subtyping definitions, and differentiate them here

- Subtyping for System $F_{<:}$ as defined by Cardelli et al. [4] is indicated as $\Gamma \vdash \tau_1 <: \tau_2$.
- Subtyping for Kernel $F_{<:}$ is indicated as $\Gamma \vdash \tau_1 <:^K \tau_2$.
- Subtyping for $F_{<:}^{\top}$ is indicated as $\Gamma \vdash \tau_1 <:^\top \tau_2$.

A type in System $F_{<:}$ is either the top type ($\top$), a bounded type variable (α), an arrow type ($\tau \to \tau$), or a universally quantified type ($\forall(\alpha \leqslant \tau).\tau$) i.e. bounded polymorphism. Note: in the literature, polymorphism can mean several different language features, however in this paper, unless stated otherwise, we use it as short hand to refer to bounded polymorphism of the form in System $F_{<:}$.

In Fig. 2 we define the subtyping of $F_{<:}^N$, a normal form of subtyping in System $F_{<:}$, defined by Pierce [13]. Subtyping is bounded above by $\top$ ($\text{S}^N\text{-Top}$)

and explicitly reflexive in the case of type variables (S^N-RFL). A type super-types a type variable if it supertypes its upper bound (S^N-VAR). Subtyping of arrow types is contra-variant with respect to its argument type, and covariant with respect to its return type (S^N-ARR). Finally, subtyping of bounded poly-morphism is contra-variant with respect to the type bounds, and covariant with respect to the type bodies.

Achieving a decidable variant of System $F_{<:}$ follows a simple idea: we restrict contra-variance of type bounds to only types that do not themselves contain bounded polymorphism. In Fig. 3 we introduce a separated variant for the syntax of System $F_{<:}$ called $F^R_{<:}$. In $F^R_{<:}$, types containing no bounded polymorphism are identified by ρ. Their only difference from more general types is a lack of bounded polymorphism. A restricted type, ρ, is either $\top$, a restricted type variable γ, or an arrow type. We keep the generalized form of type variables, α, for convenience. We now define a restricted subtyping relation using the rule set in Fig. 4.

$$\Gamma \vdash \tau <:^N \top \quad (S^N\text{-TOP}) \qquad\qquad \Gamma \vdash \alpha <:^N \alpha \quad (S^N\text{-RFL})$$

$$\frac{(\alpha \leqslant \tau') \in \Gamma \quad \Gamma \vdash \tau' <:^N \tau}{\Gamma \vdash \alpha <:^N \tau} \; (S^N\text{-VAR}) \qquad \frac{\Gamma \vdash \tau_2 <:^N \tau_1 \quad \Gamma \vdash \tau'_1 <:^N \tau'_2}{\Gamma \vdash \tau_1 \to \tau'_1 <:^N \tau_2 \to \tau'_2} \; (S^N\text{-ARR})$$

$$\frac{\Gamma \vdash \tau_2 <:^N \tau_1 \qquad \Gamma, (\alpha \leqslant \tau_2) \vdash \tau'_1 <:^N \tau'_2}{\Gamma \vdash \forall(\alpha \leqslant \tau_1).\tau'_1 <:^N \forall(\alpha \leqslant \tau_2).\tau'_2} \; (S^N\text{-ALL})$$

Fig. 2. System $F_{<:}$ Subtyping

$\tau ::=$	**$F^R_{<:}$ Type**	$\alpha ::=$	**Type Variable**
$\top$	*top*	υ	*unrestricted*
α	*variable*	γ	*restricted*
$\tau \to \tau$	*arrow*	$\rho ::=$	**Restricted Type**
$\forall(\gamma \leqslant \rho).\tau$	*restricted all*	$\top$	*top*
$\forall(\upsilon \leqslant \tau).\tau$	*all*	γ	*variable*
		$\rho \to \rho$	*arrow*

Fig. 3. $F^R_{<:}$ Type Syntax

The subtyping of $F^R_{<:}$ defined in Fig. 4 replaces the S^N-ALL rule with two rules: S^R-ALL-KERNEL and S^R-ALL. S^R-ALL-KERNEL is exactly the rule for subtyping of bounded polymorphism found in Kernel $F_{<:}$, that is, for $\forall(\alpha \leqslant \tau_1).\tau'_1$ to subtype $\forall(\alpha \leqslant \tau_2).\tau'_2$, τ_1 and τ_2 must be syntactically equivalent. Contra-variance is allowed only in cases where the type bounds are of the form

$\gamma \leqslant \rho$, and thus do not themselves include bounded polymorphism. This is captured by the rule S^R-ALL.

The result of this restriction is that subtyping may only introduce new instances of bounded polymorphism into the context if they are common to both types.

3.1 Subtype Decidability

In order to prove subtype decidability, we define a finite measure on types under a context $(\mathcal{M}(\Gamma, \tau))$, along with an ordering $(\mathcal{M}(\Gamma_1, \tau_1) < \mathcal{M}(\Gamma_2, \tau_2))$. We subsequently demonstrate that for any calls to a subtype algorithm for $F^R_{<:}$, all resulting subtype calls are strictly smaller that the original call.

$$\Gamma \vdash \tau <:^R \top \quad (S^R\text{-}\text{TOP}) \qquad \Gamma \vdash \alpha <:^R \alpha \quad (S^R\text{-}\text{RFL})$$

$$\frac{(\alpha \leqslant \tau') \in \Gamma \quad \Gamma \vdash \tau' <:^R \tau}{\Gamma \vdash \alpha <:^R \tau} \ (S^R\text{-}\text{VAR}) \qquad \frac{\Gamma \vdash \tau_2 <:^R \tau_1 \quad \Gamma \vdash \tau_1' <:^R \tau_2'}{\Gamma \vdash \tau_1 \to \tau_1' <:^R \tau_2 \to \tau_2'} \ (S^R\text{-}\text{ARR})$$

$$\frac{\Gamma, (\alpha \leqslant \tau) \vdash \tau_1 <:^R \tau_2}{\Gamma \vdash \forall(\alpha \leqslant \tau).\tau_1 <:^R \forall(\alpha \leqslant \tau).\tau_2} \ (S^R\text{-}\text{ALL-KERNEL})$$

$$\frac{\Gamma \vdash \rho_2 <:^R \rho_1 \quad \Gamma, (\gamma \leqslant \rho_2) \vdash \tau_1 <:^R \tau_2}{\Gamma \vdash \forall(\gamma \leqslant \rho_1).\tau_1 <:^R \forall(\gamma \leqslant \rho_2).\tau_2} \ (S^R\text{-}\text{ALL})$$

Fig. 4. $F^R_{<:}$ Subtyping

Indexed Types. Before we define our measure $\mathcal{M}$, we introduce an indexing on type variables and types, along with a related invariant on typing contexts.

We index type variables with a natural number, indicating their position in a context. This is represented as a superscript on type variables: α^n under context Γ is the $(n + 1)$th type variable introduced to Γ (the first type variable introduced to Γ being indexed by 0). We extend this indexing to types in the form of an upper bound on type variable indices: τ^n under context Γ indicates that for all α^i occurring in τ^n, $i < n$. Generally the index n is not important, and so we only include it when relevant. We further define a simple form of well-formedness:

Definition 1 (Type Variable Well-Formedness). *A type τ^n is well-formed under context Γ (written $\Gamma \vdash \tau^n$ wf) if and only if $n \leq |\Gamma|$.*

We now use this to define a well-formedness property that we assume on all typing contexts:

Definition 2 (Typing Context Well-Formedness). *A typing context Γ is well-formed (written Γ wf) if and only if for all $(\alpha^n \leqslant \tau^i) \in \Gamma$ we have $i < n$.*

That is, a type bound τ in a typing context Γ may only contain occurrences of type variables that were already in Γ when τ was added to it.

Note that indices on types are not unique, and are only an upper bound on type variable occurrences. i.e. if we are able to write τ^n, and $n < m$, then we are equally able to write τ^m. Finally, we use this to define an indexing on typing contexts.

Definition 3 (Indexed Typing Context)

$$\Gamma^n \triangleq \{(\alpha^i \leqslant \tau) | (\alpha^i \leqslant \tau) \in \Gamma \text{ and } i \leq n\}$$

$$
\begin{aligned}
\mathcal{D}(\Gamma, \alpha) &= 1 + \mathcal{D}(\Gamma', \tau) & \mathcal{D}(\Gamma, \top) &= 0 \\
&\text{where } \Gamma = \Gamma', (\alpha \leqslant \tau), \Gamma'' & \mathcal{D}(\Gamma, \forall(\alpha \leqslant \tau_1).\tau_2) &= 0 \\
\mathcal{D}(\Gamma, \tau_1 \to \tau_2) &= 1 + max(\mathcal{D}(\Gamma, \tau_1), \mathcal{D}(\Gamma, \tau_2))
\end{aligned}
$$

Fig. 5. Quantification depth: the depth of the next instance of bounded polymorphism.

$$
\begin{aligned}
\mathcal{Q}(\top) &= 0 & \mathcal{Q}(\emptyset) &= \emptyset \\
\mathcal{Q}(\alpha) &= 0 & \mathcal{Q}(\Gamma) &= \mathcal{Q}(\tau) + \mathcal{Q}(\Gamma') \\
\mathcal{Q}(\tau_1 \to \tau_1) &= \mathcal{Q}(\tau_1) + \mathcal{Q}(\tau_2) & &\text{where } \Gamma = \Gamma', (\alpha \leqslant \tau) \\
\mathcal{Q}(\forall(\alpha \leqslant \tau_1).\tau_2) &= 1 + \mathcal{Q}(\tau_1) + \mathcal{Q}(\tau_2) & \mathcal{Q}(\Gamma, \tau^n) &= \mathcal{Q}(\Gamma^n) + \mathcal{Q}(\tau^n)
\end{aligned}
$$

Fig. 6. Quantification size: the number of instances of bounded polymorphism in a type.

A Finite Measure on Types. $\mathcal{M}(\Gamma, \tau)$ is defined as a lexicographic ordering on the quantification size and the quantification depth of τ under Γ. Note: we use quantification here to refer to bounded polymorphism, i.e. "*all*" types of the form $\forall(\alpha \leqslant \tau_1).\tau_2$. We define $\mathcal{M}$ using two simpler measures:

1. $\mathcal{D}(\Gamma, \tau)$ (see Fig. 5): the depth at which the next instance of bounded polymorphism occurs in τ, and
2. $\mathcal{Q}(\Gamma, \tau)$ (see Fig. 6): the number of instances of bounded polymorphism in τ under context Γ.

$\mathcal{D}$, or quantification depth is defined in Fig. 5 as the maximum depth at which the next quantification type occurs. $\mathcal{D}$ is also necessarily finite, since it is bounded by the sizes the context Γ and type τ. Note: we assume a simple well-formedness property, that type variables in the context only refer to types lower down in the context, this allows us to disregard Γ'' in the definition of $\mathcal{D}(\Gamma, \alpha)$.

$\mathcal{Q}(\tau)$, or quantification size of a type is defined in Fig. 6 as the number of syntactic instances of quantification within some τ. It is simple to demonstrate that $\mathcal{Q}$ is finite, as it is bound by the (finite) size of τ. We then define $\mathcal{Q}(\Gamma, \tau)$, as the quantification size of both the type τ, and all types in the context Γ. Since context arising from type checking must be finite, it follows that $\mathcal{Q}(\Gamma, \tau)$ must also be finite.

$$\mathcal{M} = \mathcal{Q} \times \mathcal{D}$$

$$and$$
$$(q_1, d_1) < (q_2, d_2) \iff q_1 < q_2 \text{ or} \quad\quad (1)$$
$$q_1 = q_2 \text{ and } d_1 < d_2 \ (2)$$

Fig. 7. Lexicographic ordering on quantification size and depth.

Finally, we define $\mathcal{M}(\Gamma, \tau)$ along with an ordering in Fig. 7. $\mathcal{M}(\Gamma, \tau)$ is defined as $(\mathcal{Q}(\Gamma, \tau), \mathcal{D}(\Gamma, \tau))$. The key property of $\mathcal{M}$ that guarantees subtype decidability, is the fact that restricted types have no bounded polymorphism as subterms, i.e.

Property 1 (Quantification Size of Restricted Types in $F^R_{<:}$.)

$$\forall \rho, \mathcal{Q}(\rho) = 0$$

Proof of Decidability. Since the subtyping defined in Fig. 4 is syntax-directed, the inversion of the rules themselves represent an algorithm for subtyping of $F^R_{<:}$. This means that we need not define an algorithm, and are only required to reason about the conclusions of the rules and their premises. We define $\text{subtype}_{F^R_{<:}}$ as the algorithm obtained by inverting the rules in Fig. 4. Theorem 1 provides a proof of decidability of subtyping in $F^R_{<:}$.

Theorem 1 (Subtype Decidability of $F^R_{<:}$.). *For all Γ, τ_1, and τ_2, $\text{subtype}_{F^R_{<:}}(\Gamma, \tau_1, \tau_2)$ is guaranteed to terminate.*

Proof. Termination of $\text{subtype}_{F^R_{<:}}$ is easy to demonstrate by showing that $\mathcal{M}$ represents a strictly decreasing measure on subtyping. That is, for any subtype check

$$\text{subtype}_{F^R_{<:}}(\Gamma, \tau_1, \tau_2)$$

for any resulting calls

$$\text{subtype}_{F^R_{<:}}(\Gamma', \tau_1', \tau_2')$$

we have

$$\mathcal{M}(\Gamma', \tau_1') + \mathcal{M}(\Gamma', \tau_2') < \mathcal{M}(\Gamma, \tau_1) + \mathcal{M}(\Gamma, \tau_2)$$

Since $\text{subtype}_{F^R_{<:}}$ is defined as the inversion of the rules in Fig. 4, the above property is demonstrated by showing that the size of the premises (as measured by $\mathcal{M}$) of each rule is strictly smaller than the size of the conclusion. In most cases it is fairly simple to demonstrate this invariant, however in the cases of S^R-VAR and S^R-ALL, the result is not necessarily so obvious.

Case 1 (S^R-VAR*).*

$$\frac{(\alpha \leqslant \tau') \in \Gamma \qquad \Gamma \vdash \tau' <:^R \tau}{\Gamma \vdash \alpha <:^R \tau} \quad (S^R\text{-VAR})$$

The only sub-proof that we need demonstrate our invariant for is $\Gamma \vdash \tau' <:^R \tau$. That is, we need to show that

$$(\mathcal{Q}(\Gamma, \tau') + \mathcal{Q}(\Gamma, \tau), \mathcal{D}(\Gamma, \tau') + \mathcal{D}(\Gamma, \tau)) < (\mathcal{Q}(\Gamma, \alpha) + \mathcal{Q}(\Gamma, \tau), \mathcal{D}(\Gamma, \alpha) + \mathcal{D}(\Gamma, \tau))$$

Since $\mathcal{Q}(\Gamma, \tau)$ and $\mathcal{D}(\Gamma, \tau)$ fall on both sides of the ordering, it is sufficient to show that
$$(\mathcal{Q}(\Gamma, \tau'), \mathcal{D}(\Gamma, \tau')) < (\mathcal{Q}(\Gamma, \alpha), \mathcal{D}(\Gamma, \alpha))$$

Γ is in fact an ordered list of type variable bounds, and thus $(\alpha \leqslant \tau') \in \Gamma$ is equivalent to asserting that there exists some Γ' and Γ'' such that $\Gamma = \Gamma', (\alpha \leqslant \tau'), \Gamma''$. Now from the definition of $\mathcal{D}$ we have that

$$\mathcal{D}(\Gamma, \alpha) = 1 + \mathcal{D}(\Gamma', \tau')$$

Therefore, clearly $\mathcal{D}(\Gamma, \alpha) > \mathcal{D}(\Gamma', \tau')$, and since Γ (and thus Γ') is ordered all variables in τ' are mapped within Γ', and $\mathcal{D}(\Gamma, \tau') = \mathcal{D}(\Gamma', \tau')$, giving us

$$\mathcal{D}(\Gamma, \alpha) > \mathcal{D}(\Gamma, \tau')$$

Since $\mathcal{D}$ is decreasing, in order to show that our invariant is obeyed, we need only show that $\mathcal{Q}$ is not increasing, i.e. $\mathcal{Q}(\Gamma, \alpha) \not< \mathcal{Q}(\Gamma, \tau')$. We make use of the well-formedness of typing contexts that we defined in Definition 2. That is, whenever we retrieve a type bound from a well-formed typing context, the index of that type bound is strictly smaller than that of the associated type variable. Suppose that α above is indexed by some n By definition

$$\mathcal{Q}(\Gamma, \alpha^n) = \mathcal{Q}(\Gamma^n) + \mathcal{Q}(\alpha^n)$$

Further, by Definition 2 we know there exists some i such that $i < n$ and

$$\mathcal{Q}(\Gamma, \tau^i) = \mathcal{Q}(\Gamma^i) + \mathcal{Q}(\tau^i)$$

Since $i < n$ and $n \leq n$, by Definition 3 we know that

$$\Gamma^i \cup \{(\alpha^n \leqslant \tau^i)\} \subseteq \Gamma^n$$

Therefore,

$$\mathcal{Q}(\Gamma^n) \geq \mathcal{Q}(\Gamma^i) + \mathcal{Q}(\tau^i)$$

and finally we get

$$\mathcal{Q}(\Gamma^n) + \mathcal{Q}(\alpha^n) \geq \mathcal{Q}(\Gamma^i) + \mathcal{Q}(\tau^i)$$

Case 2 (S^R-ALL).

$$\frac{\Gamma \vdash \rho_2 <:^R \rho_1 \qquad \Gamma, (\gamma \leqslant \rho_2) \vdash \tau_1 <:^R \tau_2}{\Gamma \vdash \forall(\gamma \leqslant \rho_1).\tau_1 <:^R \forall(\gamma \leqslant \rho_2).\tau_2} \quad (S^R\text{-ALL})$$

Firstly, it is simple to show that

$$\mathcal{M}(\Gamma, \rho_1) + \mathcal{M}(\Gamma, \rho_2) < \mathcal{M}(\Gamma, \forall(\gamma \leqslant \rho_1).\tau_1) + \mathcal{M}(\Gamma, \forall(\gamma \leqslant \rho_2).\tau_2)$$

Secondly, the key observation is that by Property 1 we know that

$$\mathcal{Q}(\rho_1) = \mathcal{Q}(\rho_2) = 0$$

As a result we also have that

$$\mathcal{Q}(\Gamma, (\gamma \leqslant \rho_2) = \mathcal{Q}(\Gamma))$$

Thus we have

$$\mathcal{Q}(\Gamma, (\gamma \leqslant \rho_2), \tau_1) + \mathcal{Q}(\Gamma, (\gamma \leqslant \rho_2), \tau_2) = \mathcal{Q}(\Gamma, \tau_1) + \mathcal{Q}(\Gamma, \tau_2)$$

It is thus simple to show that

$$\mathcal{Q}(\Gamma, \tau_1) + \mathcal{Q}(\Gamma, \tau_2) < \mathcal{Q}(\Gamma, \forall(\gamma \leqslant \rho_1).\tau_1) + \mathcal{Q}(\Gamma, \forall(\gamma \leqslant \rho_2).\tau_2)$$

and subsequently we get the desired result.

3.2   Properties of $\mathbf{F}_{<:}^R$

One of the most useful aspects of $F_{<:}^R$, is that it represents a subset of System $F_{<:}$. That is, not only is any type τ in $F_{<:}^R$ also a type in System $F_{<:}$, but subtyping in $F_{<:}^R$ implies subtyping in System $F_{<:}$, and typing in $F_{<:}^R$ implies typing in System $F_{<:}$. This means that $F_{<:}^R$ inherits several useful properties of System $F_{<:}$ metatheory.

In this Section, we discuss some of the properties of $F_{<:}^R$, and in doing so, we refer to both the typing judgment, and operational semantics. These are identical to those of System $F_{<:}$, and so are not given here, but are provided in the accompanying technical report [1]. As with subtyping, we often need to refer to several different forms of typing, and we make this distinction by annotating the judgment appropriately. Typing in System $F_{<:}$ is indicated as $\Gamma \vdash \tau_1 : \tau_2$, and in $F_{<:}^R$ as $\Gamma \vdash \tau_1 :^R \tau_2$.

Subtype Transitivity. Unlike other variants on System $F_{<:}$ [9], $F_{<:}^R$ retains the subtype transitivity of System $F_{<:}$.

Theorem 2 (Subtype Transitivity in $\mathbf{F}_{<:}^R$). *For all τ_1, τ_2, and τ_3, if $\Gamma \vdash \tau_1 <:^R \tau_2$ and $\Gamma \vdash \tau_2 <:^R \tau_3$, then $\Gamma \vdash \tau_1 <:^R \tau_3$.*

Proof. Subtype transitivity is proven as part of more general theorem that includes narrowing of the typing context. i.e. we prove the following properties mutually hold:

$$\frac{\Gamma \vdash \tau_1 <:^R \tau_2 \quad \Gamma \vdash \tau_2 <:^R \tau_3}{\Gamma \vdash \tau_1 <:^R \tau_3} \ (\text{Trans}) \qquad \frac{\Gamma_1, (\alpha \leqslant \tau), \Gamma_2 \vdash \tau_1 <:^R \tau_2 \quad \Gamma_1 \vdash \tau' <:^R \tau}{\Gamma_1, (\alpha \leqslant \tau'), \Gamma_2 \vdash \tau_1 <:^R \tau_2} \ (\text{Narrowing})$$

The proof can be found in the associated technical report [1].

Subtyping in $F^R_{<:} \subset$ Subtyping in System $F_{<:}$. $F^R_{<:}$ is not a significant change to the semantics of bounded polymorphism from System $F_{<:}$, in fact subtyping in $F^R_{<:}$ is a subset of subtyping in System $F_{<:}$. That is any subtyping that can be derived in $F^R_{<:}$ can also be derived in System $F_{<:}$.

Theorem 3 ($F^R_{<:} \subset$ System $F_{<:}$). *For all Γ, τ_1, and τ_1, if $\Gamma \vdash \tau_1 <:^R \tau_2$ then $\Gamma \vdash \tau_1 <:^N \tau_2$.*

Proof. The result is easily reached by noting that every rule in Fig. 4 has a counterpart in Fig. 2 that is at least as permissive.

This is a useful property because it implies that existing type checkers need only introduce syntactic checks at key points (when checking subtyping between polymorphic types with different bounds), and do not need significant modifications to the subtyping algorithm.

Subtyping in Kernel $F_{<:} \subset$ Subtyping in $F^R_{<:}$. $F^R_{<:}$ represents a super-set of Kernel $F_{<:}$ in terms of subtyping. This provides a useful lower bound on expressiveness. Any valid Kernel $F_{<:}$ program is also a valid $F^R_{<:}$ program.

Theorem 4 (Kernel $F_{<:} \subset F^R_{<:}$). *For all Γ, τ_1, and τ_1, if $\Gamma \vdash \tau_1 <:^K \tau_2$ then $\Gamma \vdash \tau_1 <:^R \tau_2$.*

Proof. The result arises from the fact that the S^R-Kernel-All rule in Fig. 4 is the exact rule for bounded polymorphism in Kernel $F_{<:}$. Thus, subtyping in $F^R_{<:}$ is at least as expressive than subtyping in Kernel $F_{<:}$.

Type Safety. As subtyping in $F^R_{<:}$ is a subset of subtyping in System $F_{<:}$, and the two calculi have otherwise identical typing, it follows that every well-typed program in $F^R_{<:}$ is well-typed in System $F_{<:}$. It is thus unsurprising that given System $F_{<:}$'s type safety, and that the two calculi have identical operational semantics, any well-typed $F^R_{<:}$ program is guaranteed to not get stuck. In other words, $F^R_{<:}$ is type safe.

Theorem 5 (Type Safety). *For all Γ, t and τ, if $\Gamma \vdash t :^R \tau$, then reduction of t is guaranteed to not get stuck.*

Proof. The result arises immediately from the type safety of System $F_{<:}$, and the result in Theorem 3.

Minimal Typing. As mentioned in Sect. 2 $F_{<:}^{\top}$ [5] is another variant of System $F_{<:}$ that allows for subtyping of bounded polymorphism that is both decidable and contra-variant on type bounds. We also mentioned that typing in $F_{<:}^{\top}$ is not minimal [6], and thus some terms can be typed with two different types that are not related by subtyping. Specifically, in $F_{<:}^{\top}$, the term $t = \Lambda(X \leqslant \text{Int}).\lambda(x : X).x$ can be shown to have both the type $\tau_1 = \forall(X \leqslant \text{Int}).X \to X$, and the type $\tau_2 = \forall(X \leqslant \text{Int}).X \to \text{Int}$. In $F_{<:}^{\top}$, these two types are unrelated, and have no lower bound. The implications of this lack of minimality are that the standard typing algorithm for System $F_{<:}$ is not complete for $F_{<:}^{\top}$, and will assign t one type, but not the other, and any usage where t is required to be typed with both types will not type check.

The reason for the loss of minimal typing in $F_{<:}^{\top}$ is due to a "rebounding" of type variables during subtyping to $\top$. Subtyping of the body of a polymorphic type is done with reduced type information as the bound of the type variable is treated as $\top$, hiding the relationship between the type variable and its bound.

A central motivation in designing $F_{<:}^{R}$ is to provide reliable and expected behaviour to type checkers, that allows for understandable error messages in type checking. The loss of minimal typing does not provide these assurances. For instance, it seems reasonable to expect that in the example above, τ_1 should subtype τ_2, and if it doesn't a satisfying reason should be provided by the type checker. Subtyping in $F_{<:}^{R}$ does not perform the same "rebounding", and as a result does not suffer from the same loss of minimal typing.

$$\tau ::=$$

$\top$	*top*	$x.L$	*selection*
$\bot$	*bottom*	$\{L : \tau \ldots \tau\}$	*declaration*
$\forall(x : \tau).\tau^x$	*function*		

Fig. 8. $D_{<:}$ Type Syntax

Theorem 6 (Minimal Typing). *For all Δ, Γ, t, τ_1, and τ_2, if $\Delta; \Gamma \vdash t :^R \tau_1$ and $\Delta; \Gamma \vdash t :^R \tau_2$, then there exists some τ, such that $\Delta; \Gamma \vdash t :^R \tau$, $\Delta; \Gamma \vdash \tau <:^R \tau_1$, and $\Delta; \Gamma \vdash \tau <:^R \tau_2$.*

Proof. The proof can be found in the associated technical report [1].

4   Separating $D_{<:}$

$D_{<:}$ is a calculus related to System $F_{<:}$ that includes abstract type members and dependent functions, and serves to model core aspects of the Scala type system. The syntax of $D_{<:}$ is given in Fig. 8, and at first glance does not immediately resemble that of System $F_{<:}$. Most noticeably, $D_{<:}$ does not include any type variables. The expressiveness of $D_{<:}$ derives from being able to capture System $F_{<:}$ using path types ($x.L$) and dependent function types ($\forall(x : \tau_1).\tau_2$).

A type in $D_{<:}$ is either $\top$, $\bot$, a type declaration $\{L : \tau_1 \ldots \tau_2\}$, a selection type $x.L$, or a dependent function type $\forall(x : \tau_1).\tau_2^x$.

In $D_{<:}$, type declarations $(\{L : \tau_1 \ldots \tau_2\})$ define a type. Given a path x to the type definition, the defined type can be used by selection on the path: $x.L$. That is, if value x has type $\{L : \tau_1 \ldots \tau_2\}$, then $x.L$ refers to the defined type, where τ_1 is the lower bound, and τ_2 the upper bound. This is useful when combined with the dependent function types of $D_{<:}$. The return types of functions in $D_{<:}$ can be dependent on the argument. This dependence is indicated in the syntax by a super-script of the variable identifying the argument. i.e. $\forall(x : \tau_1).\tau_2^x$ indicates that x is free in τ_2.

$D_{<:}$ subtyping is defined in Fig. 9, and is indicated by $\Gamma \vdash \tau_1 <:^D \tau_2$. Subtyping is bound above by $\top$ (TOP) and below by $\bot$ (BOT). Subtyping is explicitly reflexive (RFL). Selection types subtype their upper bounds (SEL1), and super type their lower bounds (SEL2). Subtyping of type declarations are contra-variant with respect to the lower bounds, and covariant with respect to their upper bounds (BND). Finally, subtyping of dependent function types is contra-variant with respect to the argument types, and covariant with respect to the return types, with the return types being dependent on the arguments (ALL).

Coupling type declarations together with dependent function types allows for similar functionality to $F_{<:}$. That is, we can use the encoding below to capture bounded polymorphism from System $F_{<:}$ in $D_{<:}$.

$$[\![\top]\!] \triangleq \top \quad (1) \qquad [\![\tau_1 \rightarrow \tau_2]\!] \triangleq \forall(x_\alpha : [\![\tau_1]\!]).[\![\tau_2]\!]^{x_\alpha} \qquad (3)$$

$$[\![\alpha]\!] \triangleq x_\alpha.A \;(2) \qquad [\![\forall(\alpha \leqslant \tau_1).\tau_2]\!] \triangleq \forall(x_\alpha : \{A : \bot \ldots [\![\tau_1]\!]\}).[\![\tau_2]\!]^{x_\alpha} \;(4)$$

$$\Gamma \vdash \tau <:^D \top \quad (\text{TOP}) \qquad \Gamma \vdash \bot <:^D \tau \quad (\text{BOT}) \qquad \Gamma \vdash \tau <:^D \tau \quad (\text{RFL})$$

$$\frac{\Gamma(x) = \{L : \tau_1 \ldots \tau_2\}}{\Gamma \vdash x.L <:^D \tau_2} \;(\text{SEL1}) \qquad \frac{\Gamma(x) = \{L : \tau_1 \ldots \tau_2\}}{\Gamma \vdash \tau_1 <:^D x.L} \;(\text{SEL2})$$

$$\frac{\begin{array}{c}\Gamma \vdash \tau_1 <:^D \tau_2 \\ \Gamma \vdash \tau_2 <:^D \tau_3\end{array}}{\Gamma \vdash \tau_1 <:^D \tau_3} \;(\text{TRANS}) \qquad \frac{\begin{array}{c}\Gamma \vdash \tau_2 <:^D \tau_1 \\ \Gamma, (x : \tau_2) \vdash \tau_1' <:^D \tau_2'\end{array}}{\Gamma \vdash \forall(x : \tau_1).\tau_1' <:^D \forall(x : \tau_2).\tau_2'} \;(\text{ALL})$$

$$\frac{\Gamma \vdash \tau_2 <:^D \tau_1 \qquad \Gamma \vdash \tau_1' <:^D \tau_2'}{\Gamma \vdash \{L : \tau_1 \ldots \tau_1'\} <:^D \{L : \tau_2 \ldots \tau_2'\}} \;(\text{BND})$$

Fig. 9. $D_{<:}$ Subtyping

The above encoding is in fact not enough to demonstrate the undecidability of $D_{<:}$ due to the fact that subtyping of System $F_{<:}$ types is not equivalent to subtyping of their encoding in $D_{<:}$. That is, while the following holds:

$$\Gamma \vdash \tau_1 <:^N \tau_2 \Rightarrow [\![\Gamma]\!] \vdash [\![\tau_1]\!] <:^D [\![\tau_2]\!]$$

the inverse does not.

$$[\![\Gamma]\!] \vdash [\![\tau_1]\!] \ <:^D \ [\![\tau_2]\!] \ \not\Rightarrow \ \Gamma \vdash \tau_1 \ <:^N \ \tau_2$$

The reasons for this are due to the fact that functions in System $F_{<:}$ are unrelated to polymorphic types, but in $D_{<:}$ they are both captured using dependent function types. A simple counter-example to the inverse are the types $\forall(\alpha \leqslant \top).\top$ and $\top \rightarrow \top$. Both polymorphic types and arrow types in System $F_{<:}$ are encoded as dependent function types, and $[\![\forall(\alpha \leqslant \top).\top]\!]$ subtypes $[\![\top \rightarrow \top]\!]$, however, it is clear that $\forall(\alpha \leqslant \top).\top$ does not subtype $\top \rightarrow \top$. The full proof for this was demonstrated by Hu and Lhoták [9]. This result does not affect the undecidability result for $D_{<:}$, as the proof of undecidability in System $F_{<:}$ does not rely on arrow types. Pierce's [13] proof of undecidability uses a subset of System $F_{<:}$ that does not include arrow types, and thus while the encoding of System $F_{<:}$ into $D_{<:}$ is not complete, it is possible to define a complete encoding of the fragment of System $F_{<:}$ that is undecidable. We leave the details of this to Hu and Lhoták [9].

Figure 10 presents the syntax for $D_{<:}^R$, a separated variant of $D_{<:}$. $D_{<:}^R$ introduces a similar separation on syntax to that of $F_{<:}^R$. Where $F_{<:}^R$ places a restriction on the bounds of type variables, $D_{<:}^R$ places a restriction on the bounds of type members. That is, we distinguish restricted type definitions from unrestricted ones. A restricted type definition ($\{R \ : \rho_1 \ldots \rho_2\}$) is a type definition that does not contain any dependent function types in either the upper or lower bound. As with $F_{<:}^R$ This restriction is indicated by restricted types (ρ). Note: restricted types are only separated from dependent function types, and not function types in general. As we have already mentioned, dependent functions in $D_{<:}$ capture both abstraction over values and abstraction over types, while in System $F_{<:}$, bounded polymorphism only captures abstraction over types. To this end, we allow restricted types in $D_{<:}^R$ to include non-dependent function types ($\forall(x : \tau_1).\tau_2$) that can be identified by the absence of the variable super-script indicating the return type is dependent on the argument type.

$\tau ::=$	$D_{<:}^R$ **Type**
$\top$	*top*
$\bot$	*bottom*
$\{U : \tau \ldots \tau\}$	*declaration*
$\{R : \rho \ldots \rho\}$	*restricted declaration*
$x.L$	*selection*
$\forall(x : \tau).\tau^x$	*dependent function*

$L ::=$	**Type Label**
U	*unrestricted*
R	*restricted*
$\rho ::=$	$D_{<:}^R$ **Restricted Type**
$\top$	*top*
$\bot$	*bottom*
$\{L : \rho \ldots \rho\}$	*declaration*
$\forall(x : \rho).\rho$	*function*
$x.R$	*selection*

Fig. 10. $D_{<:}^R$ Type Syntax

$$\Gamma \vdash \tau \ <:^R \ \top \quad (\text{Top}^R) \qquad \Gamma \vdash \bot \ <:^R \ \tau \quad (\text{Bot}^R) \qquad \Gamma \vdash x.L \ <:^R \ x.L \quad (\text{Rfl}^R)$$

$$\frac{\Gamma(x) = \{L \ : \tau_1 \ldots \tau_2\}}{\Gamma \vdash x.L \ <:^R \ \tau} \ \ \frac{\Gamma \vdash \tau_2 \ <: \ \tau}{} \quad (\text{Sel1}^R) \qquad \frac{\Gamma(x) = \{L \ : \tau_1 \ldots \tau_2\}}{\Gamma \vdash \tau \ <:^R \ x.L} \ \ \frac{\Gamma \vdash \tau \ <: \ \tau_1}{} \quad (\text{Sel2}^R)$$

$$\frac{\Gamma \vdash \tau_2 \ <:^R \ \tau_1 \qquad \Gamma \vdash \tau_1' \ <:^R \ \tau_2'}{\Gamma \vdash \{L \ : \tau_1 \ldots \tau_1'\} \ <:^R \ \{L \ : \tau_2 \ldots \tau_2'\}} \quad (\text{Bnd}^R)$$

$$\frac{\Gamma, (x : \tau) \vdash \tau_1 \ <:^R \ \tau_2}{\Gamma \vdash \forall(x : \tau).\tau_1^x \ <:^R \ \forall(x : \tau).\tau_2^x} \quad (\text{All-Kernel}^R)$$

$$\frac{\Gamma \vdash \rho_2 \ <:^R \ \rho_1 \qquad \Gamma, (x : \rho_2) \vdash \tau_1 \ <:^R \ \tau_2}{\Gamma \vdash \forall(x : \rho_1).\tau_1'^x \ <:^R \ \forall(x : \rho_2).\tau_2'^x} \quad (\text{All}^R)$$

Fig. 11. $D^R_{<:}$ Subtyping

4.1 Restricted Subtyping in $D^R_{<:}$

Subtyping for $D^R_{<:}$ is defined in Fig. 11. There are several differences between the restricted form of subtyping and that of $D_{<:}$. As with bounded polymorphism in $F^R_{<:}$, subtyping of dependent function types in $D^R_{<:}$ can be proven using one of two rules: (i) KERNEL-ALL^R, a subtype rule that enforces invariance on the argument type, and (ii) ALL^R, a subtype rule that allows covariance on function argument types of the form ρ.

$$\begin{aligned}
\mathcal{D}(\Gamma, x.L) \quad &= 1 + max(\mathcal{D}(\Gamma, \tau_1), \mathcal{D}(\Gamma, \tau_2)) \\
&\text{where } \Gamma \vdash x \ : \ \{L \ : \tau_1 \ldots \tau_2\} \\
\mathcal{D}(\Gamma, \forall(x : \tau_1).\tau_2) &= 1 + max(\mathcal{D}(\Gamma, \tau_1), \mathcal{D}(\Gamma, \tau_2))
\end{aligned} \qquad \begin{aligned}
\mathcal{D}(\Gamma, \top) \quad &= 0 \\
\mathcal{D}(\Gamma, \bot) \quad &= 0 \\
\mathcal{D}(\Gamma, \forall(x : \tau_1).\tau_1^x) &= 0
\end{aligned}$$

Fig. 12. Quantification Depth: the depth of the next dependent function type.

Subtyping in $D^R_{<:}$ also differs from standard $D_{<:}$ subtyping in how reflexivity and transitivity are formalized. Explicit subtype reflexivity in $D^R_{<:}$ is restricted to type selections $(x.L)$. This is similar to the modification $F^N_{<:}$ makes to traditional System $F_{<:}$.

Subtype Transitivity. As in $F^N_{<:}$, the explicit transitivity rule, TRANS, is removed. Transitivity rules are generally difficult to design an algorithm for as it is not always clear what to choose for the middle type (τ_2 in Trans). To try and recapture some level of transitivity, we modify the subtype rules for upper and lower bounds by introducing a level of transitivity (see SEL1^R and SEL2^R

in Fig. 11). This mirrors the difference in transitivity between the $F_{<:}^N$ version of System $F_{<:}$ subtyping, and the original definition of Cardelli [4], where the explicit transitivity rule was removed, and replaced with a modified rule for type variable subtyping that accounted for transitivity. In the $F_{<:}^N$ (and $F_{<:}^R$) rule set, general transitivity is provable as a property of subtyping. Unfortunately the same cannot be said for $D_{<:}^R$. Subtyping in $D_{<:}^R$ is not transitive.

The reason for the loss of transitivity is due to the relationship between the upper and lower bounds of type definitions: there is no requirement that the lower bound subtypes the upper bound. Precursor calculi to $D_{<:}$ attempted to enforce this invariant, but due to a complex set of reasons, this is not generally possible in the presence of another Scala feature: intersection types. A critical insight of previous work on the DOT calculus, is that ill-formed type bounds not necessarily unsound [2,3,16] since ultimately at run-time, any type bounds must be fulfilled by some value (a witness), and only well-formed bounds may be fulfilled. The details are interesting, but are fairly complex and so we do not address them further.

4.2 Subtype Decidability in $D_{<:}^R$

The subtype decidability argument for $D_{<:}^R$ is much like that of $F_{<:}^R$: We define an ordering on the number of dependent function types and the depth of a type down to the next dependent function type. We define the measures $\mathcal{D}$ and $\mathcal{Q}$ in Figs. 12 and 13. As with $F_{<:}^R$, the finite measure of $D_{<:}^R$ the lexicographic ordering:

$$\mathcal{M} = \mathcal{D} \times \mathcal{Q}$$

$$
\begin{aligned}
\mathcal{Q}(\top) &= 0 \\
\mathcal{Q}(\alpha) &= 0 \\
\mathcal{Q}(\forall(x:\tau_1).\tau_2) &= \mathcal{Q}(\tau_1) + \mathcal{Q}(\tau_2) \\
\mathcal{Q}(\forall(x:\tau_1).\tau_2^x) &= 1 + \mathcal{Q}(\tau_1) + \mathcal{Q}(\tau_2)
\end{aligned}
\qquad
\begin{aligned}
\mathcal{Q}(\Gamma) &= \mathcal{Q}(\tau) + \mathcal{Q}(\Gamma') \\
&\text{where } \Gamma = \Gamma', (\alpha \leqslant \tau) \\
\mathcal{Q}(\Gamma, \tau^n) &= \mathcal{Q}(\Gamma^n) + \mathcal{Q}(\tau^n)
\end{aligned}
$$

Fig. 13. Quantification Size: the number of dependent function types in a $D_{<:}^R$ type.

We can now prove subtype decidability for $D_{<:}^R$ using much the same logic as we did for $F_{<:}^R$. We define a subtype algorithm for $D_{<:}^R$: $\text{subtype}_{D_{<:}^R}$. As with $\text{subtype}F_{<:}^R$, $\text{subtype}_{D_{<:}^R}$ is the inversion of the rule set in Fig. 11. A sketch of the proof of decidability is given below.

Theorem 7 (Subtype Decidability of $D_{<:}^R$). *For all Γ, τ_1, and τ_2, $\text{subtype}_{D_{<:}^R}(\Gamma, \tau_1, \tau_2)$ is guaranteed to terminate.*

Proof. As with the proof of subtype decidability for $F_{<:}^R$, it is fairly simple to demonstrate that for any call $\text{subtype}_{D_{<:}^R}(\Gamma, \tau_1, \tau_2)$, by the measure $\mathcal{M}$, any resulting calls to $\text{subtype}_{D_{<:}^R}$ are strictly smaller.

4.3 Type Safety

Subtyping in $D_{<:}^R$ is a subset of subtyping in $D_{<:}^R$, and as with $F_{<:}^R$, this affords $D_{<:}^R$ many of the properties of $D_{<:}$. Type safety is one such property, and arises immediately from Theorem 8 below.

Theorem 8 ($D_{<:}^R \subset D_{<:}$). *For all Γ, τ_1, and τ_1, if $\Gamma \vdash \tau_1 <:^R \tau_2$ then $\Gamma \vdash \tau_1 <:^D \tau_2$.*

Proof. The result follows directly from the fact that for every rule in Fig. 11, there is an corresponding rule in Fig. 9 that is at least as permissive. □

4.4 Expressiveness

The expressiveness of $D_{<:}^R$ is still an open question, and can only properly be addressed in an empirical way. It is worth noting that our definition of $D_{<:}^R$ is similar in its conception to $F_{<:}^R$, in that we take care to only place restrictions on the use of *dependent* function types, and not function types in general. Argument types may still refer to function types that do not meaningfully modify the context. In fact, $D_{<:}^R$ is actually still too strict, and could potentially be relaxed further in its definition. There is no reason that subtyping of non-dependent function types need to have the same restrictions placed on them as dependent function types. It is likely possible that we could extend the subtyping in Fig. 11 with the following rule.

$$\frac{\Gamma \vdash \tau_2 <:^R \tau_1 \qquad \Gamma, (x : \tau_2) \vdash \tau_1' <:^R \tau_2'}{\Gamma \vdash \forall(x : \tau_1).\tau_1' <:^R \forall(x : \tau_2).\tau_2'} \quad (\text{ALL2}^R)$$

While at first glance the above rule looks like it might re-introduce undecidability, note that the return types do not depend on the argument type: that is they lack the super-script ^{x}. In this case, while we are still introducing differing types to the context, they are not referred to in the return types, and so are of no consequence. Such a rule is not without potential problems however. It is not immediately clear what the above rule would mean for other properties of $D_{<:}^R$.

5 Related Work

5.1 Strong $F_{<:}$ and Strong $D_{<:}$

Hu and Lhoták [9], defined decidable variants of System $F_{<:}$ and $D_{<:}$ named Strong $F_{<:}$ and Strong $D_{<:}$ respectively. Their approach introduces a second typing context to subtyping, one for each type, giving subtyping the following form.

$$\Gamma_1 \gg \tau_1 <: \tau_2 \ll \Gamma_2$$

Hu and Lhoták refer to this as "stare-at subtyping". Type bounds in τ_1 are appended to Γ_1, while type bounds in τ_2 are appended to Γ_2. This separation of contexts ensures that there is no problematic "rebounding" [13] that might lead to an expansive context. There are however some short comings to this technique, specifically subtype transitivity is lacking in both type systems. Below we demonstrate an instance of subtype transitivity that is lost in Strong $F_{<:}$.

$$A = \forall(\alpha \leqslant \top).\alpha \qquad B = \forall(\alpha \leqslant \text{Int}).\alpha \qquad C = \forall(\alpha \leqslant \text{Int}).\text{Int}$$

While it can be shown that both A subtypes B and B subtypes C in Strong $F_{<:}$, the transitive case cannot be derived, i.e. $A \not<: C$. During subtyping of bounded polymorphism in Strong $F_{<:}$ (and Strong $D_{<:}$), two typing contexts are maintained, each updated with the bounds of the relevant type. While subtype reflexivity of type variables allows α to subtype α when deriving $A <: B$, this is not so when attempting to derive $A <: C$. This is not an especially complex example, and is a subtyping that programmers might expect to hold.

Using a syntactic separation we are able to retain subtype transitivity in $F^R_{<:}$. The trade off is that we exclude a specific class of programs. These programs, however, can be identified syntactically, and thus $F^R_{<:}$ enables the type checker to better guide programmers in fixing their error.

While we have already mentioned that $D^R_{<:}$ is not indeed transitive, this is due to the potential for "bad bounds" on type definitions, and the problems associated with ensuring "good bounds". $D^R_{<:}$ does not exclude the types of transitivity seen in Strong $D_{<:}$ which lacks transitivity, not only due to the "bad bounds" problem, but also for the same reasons Strong $F_{<:}$ does. More specifically, the subtyping $A <: C$ can be derived in $F^R_{<:}$. Similarly, the equivalent example in $D_{<:}$ is not derivable in Strong $D_{<:}$, but is derivable in $D^R_{<:}$.

5.2   Wyvern

Mackay et al. [10] defined two decidable variants of Wyvern [11,12], a language related to Scala, featuring type members, dependent function types, recursive types, and a limited form of intersection types called type refinements. Their variants of Wyvern were named Wyv_{fix} and Wyv_{self}, and took different approaches to ensuring decidability.

Interestingly, Wyv_{fix} introduces essentially the same double headed form of subtyping that Hu and Lhoták [9] did. An independent discovery, Mackay et al. [10] use the double headed subtyping form in a slightly different setting with the same purpose. While the Strong Kernel $D_{<:}$ of Hu and Lhoták [9] does not include recursive types or any form of intersection types, Wyv_{fix} does. Wyv_{fix} suffers from the same loss of transitivity that Strong Kernel $D_{<:}$ does, and as such prohibits several useful forms of expressiveness.

Wyv_{self} does not use a double headed form, and rather makes use of a Material/Shape separation inspired by the work of Greenman et al. [7]. Wyv_{self} does not allow for contra-variance on the argument types of dependent functions.

6   Conclusion

In this paper we have presented $F_{<:}^R$, a variant of System $F_{<:}$ that is decidable in its subtyping, while retaining several of the desirable qualities of System $F_{<:}$. Our approach is largely in the form of a syntactic restriction on types, rather than a significant departure from the semantics of subtyping bounded polymorphism. Further, we have shown that this approach can be applied to another related calculus, $D_{<:}$, to get $D_{<:}^R$, a type system that models core concepts of Scala. $D_{<:}^R$ does not sacrifice certain instances of transitivity and expressiveness that other similar designs in the past have.

In future work, we hope to show that this approach can be further applied to the much more complex DOT calculus, by incorporating intersection types and recursive types. Further, the expressiveness of these restrictions is still an open question. While there are many languages that incorporate bounded polymorphism similar to System $F_{<:}$, it is not clear how many of them allow for bounded polymorphism within type bounds, the pattern that $F_{<:}^R$ restricts. What is yet harder to say is what the restrictions of $D_{<:}^R$ mean for Scala. As we have noted, the Scala type system potentially suffers from more undecidability issues than just those related to dependent function types, recursive types in Scala are also a source of undecidability [10], and so $D_{<:}^R$ does not ensure decidability of Scala's type system.

To settle the question of expressiveness, it would be valuable to conduct an empirical survey of existing languages with bounded polymorphism to determine either (i) how many of them already restrict the usage of bounded polymorphism in the way that $F_{<:}^R$ and $D_{<:}^R$, or (ii) how many of them are permit such patterns, but are not in practice used by the respective programming communities.

References

1. Syntactically restricting bounded polymorphism for decidable subtyping. Technical report (2020). https://doi.org/10.5281/zenodo.4039832
2. Amin, N., Moors, A., Odersky, M.: Dependent object types. In: 19th International Workshop on Foundations of Object-Oriented Languages (2012)
3. Amin, N., Rompf, T., Odersky, M.: Foundations of path-dependent types. In: Proceedings of the 2014 ACM International Conference on Object Oriented Programming Systems Languages and Applications, OOPSLA 2014 (2014)
4. Cardelli, L., Martini, S., Mitchell, J.C., Scedrov, A.: An extension of system F with subtyping. In: Ito, T., Meyer, A.R. (eds.) Theor. Aspects Comput. Softw., pp. 750–770. Springer, Berlin Heidelberg, Berlin, Heidelberg (1991)
5. Castagna, G., Pierce, B.C.: Decidable bounded quantification. In: Proceedings of the 21st ACM SIGPLAN-SIGACT Symposium on Principles of Programming Languages, POPL 1994 (1994)
6. Castagna, G., Pierce, B.C.: Corrigendum: decidable bounded quantification. In: Proceedings of the 22nd ACM SIGPLAN-SIGACT Symposium on Principles of Programming Languages, POPL 1995 (1995)
7. Greenman, B., Muehlboeck, F., Tate, R.: Getting F-bounded polymorphism into shape. In: Proceedings of the 35th ACM SIGPLAN Conference on Programming Language Design and Implementation, PLDI 2014 (2014)

8. Grigore, R.: Java generics are turing complete. In: Proceedings of the 44th ACM SIGPLAN Symposium on Principles of Programming Languages, POPL 2017 (2017)

9. Hu, J.Z.S., Lhoták, O.: Undecidability of D<: and its decidable fragments. In: Proceedings of the ACM on Programming Languages (POPL) (2019)

10. Mackay, J., Potanin, A., Aldrich, J., Groves, L.: Decidable subtyping for path dependent types. In: Proceedings of the ACM on Programming Languages (POPL) (2019)

11. Nistor, L., Kurilova, D., Balzer, S., Chung, B., Potanin, A., Aldrich, J.: Wyvern: a simple, typed, and pure object-oriented language. In: Proceedings of the 5th Workshop on MechAnisms for SPEcialization, Generalization and inHerItance. MASPEGHI 2013 (2013)

12. Omar, C., Kurilova, D., Nistor, L., Chung, B., Potanin, A., Aldrich, J.: Safely composable type-specific languages. In: Jones, R. (ed.) ECOOP 2014. LNCS, vol. 8586, pp. 105–130. Springer, Heidelberg (2014). https://doi.org/10.1007/978-3-662-44202-9_5

13. Pierce, B.C.: Bounded quantification is undecidable. In: Proceedings of the 19th ACM SIGPLAN-SIGACT Symposium on Principles of Programming Languages, POPL 1992 (1992)

14. Pierce, B.C.: Types and Programming Languages. The MIT Press, Massachusetts (2002)

15. Rapoport, M., Kabir, I., He, P., Lhoták, O.: A simple soundness proof for dependent object types. In: Proceedings of the ACM on Object-Oriented Programming, Systems, Languages, and Applications (OOPSLA) (2017)

16. Rompf, T., Amin, N.: Type soundness for dependent object types (dot). In: Proceedings of the 2016 ACM SIGPLAN International Conference on Object-Oriented Programming, Systems, Languages, and Applications, OOPSLA 2016 (2016)

17. Wadler, P., Blott, S.: How to make ad-hoc polymorphism less ad hoc. In: Proceedings of the 16th ACM SIGPLAN-SIGACT Symposium on Principles of Programming Languages, POPL 1989 (1989)

Semantics

An Abstract Machine for Strong
Call by Value

Małgorzata Biernacka⬥, Dariusz Biernacki⬥, Witold Charatonik⬥,
and Tomasz Drab⁽✉⁾⬥

Institute of Computer Science, University of Wrocław, Wrocław, Poland
{mabi,dabi,wch,tdr}@cs.uni.wroc.pl
https://ii.uni.wroc.pl/~mabi, https://ii.uni.wroc.pl/~dabi,
https://ii.uni.wroc.pl/~wch, https://ii.uni.wroc.pl/~tdr

Abstract. We present an abstract machine that implements a full-reducing (a.k.a. strong) call-by-value strategy for pure λ-calculus. It is derived using Danvy et al.'s functional correspondence from Crégut's KN by: (1) deconstructing KN to a call-by-name normalization-by-evaluation function akin to Filinski and Rohde's, (2) modifying the resulting normalizer so that it implements the right-to-left call-by-value function application, and (3) constructing the functionally corresponding abstract machine.

This new machine implements a reduction strategy that subsumes the fireball-calculus variant of call by value studied by Accattoli et al. We describe the strong strategy of the machine in terms of a reduction semantics and prove the correctness of the machine using a method based on Biernacka et al.'s generalized refocusing. As a byproduct, we present an example application of the machine to checking term convertibility by discriminating on the basis of their partially normalized forms.

Keywords: λ-calculus · Abstract machines · Reduction strategies · Normalization by evaluation · Reduction semantics.

1 Introduction

Full-reducing (also known as strong) normalization strategies in the lambda calculus have so far received relatively little attention compared to weak strategies that provide foundations for functional programming languages, such as OCaml (implementing call by value) or Haskell (implementing call by need). However, recent advances in proof technology and the use of proof assistants based on dependently typed lambda calculus for complex verification efforts propel the design and study of strong reduction strategies, and of their corresponding efficient realizations on a machine [2,7,18].

This research is supported by the National Science Centre of Poland, under grant number 2019/33/B/ST6/00289.

B. C. d. S. Oliveira (Ed.): APLAS 2020, LNCS 12470, pp. 147–166, 2020.
https://doi.org/10.1007/978-3-030-64437-6_8

Abstract machines provide a convenient computation model that mediates between the specific reduction strategy in the calculus and its practical implementations. The first machine for strong normalization of lambda terms is due to Crégut [11]. This machine implements normal-order strategy [17], i.e., a hybrid strategy that iterates call by name (CbN), and necessarily extends reduction to open terms and reduces under lambda abstractions—unlike machines for weak strategies that operate on closed terms and stop at lambdas. Similarly to strong CbN, one can define strong call by value (CbV) as an iteration of weak CbV, carefully generalizing the notion of value to open terms [1]. A normalization function realizing strong CbV was proposed by Grégoire & Leroy and implemented in their virtual machine extending the ZAM machine [18]. Another virtual machine for strong CbV was derived by Ager et al. [5] from Aehlig and Joachimski's normalization function [4]. Recently, a strong call-by-need strategy has been proposed by Kesner et al. [7], and the corresponding abstract machine has been derived by Biernacka et al. [9]. On the other hand, there is a line of work done by Accattoli et al. who study computational complexity of abstract machines, in particular in the context of a weak CbV strategy that operates on open terms, as an intermediate step towards an efficient machine for strong CbV [2].

Many abstract machines are devised or tailored by hand, and their correctness is far from obvious. Alternatively, Danvy et al. initiated a derivational approach that allows to obtain abstract machines from preexisting semantic artefacts for specific strategies by applying well-defined transformations in a systematic way.

Danvy et al.'s functional correspondence [6] is a two-way semantics-preserving derivation method that relates higher-order evaluators and abstract machines. More precisely, following Reynolds' recipe of applying a CPS translation and defunctionalization to a higher-order evaluator expressed in a functional meta-language, it leads to an implementation, in the same meta-language, of the corresponding abstract machine [23]. However, the two program transformations can be inverted and, as first observed by Danvy [12], starting with an implementation of an abstract machine, one can obtain a higher-order compositional evaluator, in the style of a valuation function of denotational semantics [25], that abstractly and concisely embodies the low-level intricacies of the machine, typically scattered all over the transition rules. Such an evaluator can then be locally modified according to one's needs and a new abstract machine can be derived from it. This approach has proven extremely successful at numerous occasions and it appears to be considerably more systematic and effective than groping for the right changes directly at the level of the abstract machine.

The goal of this work is to derive an abstract machine that can be seen as a strong CbV counterpart of Crégut's machine for normal order which avoids needless reevaluation of function arguments. Rather than directly tweaking the KN machine we propose to take a systematic approach following Danvy's recipe and (1) we first deconstruct KN into a compositional evaluator, (2) we then modify this evaluator accordingly to account for CbV, and (3) from the new evaluator we derive a new abstract machine. Our meta-language is a small subset of OCaml [20].

In the process, we identify the reduction semantics of the rrCbV variant of a strong CbV strategy in the pure lambda calculus which we also present. In the terminology of Biernacka et al.'s, this is a hybrid strategy that uses three kinds of contexts, and it subsumes as a substrategy the weak right-to-left strategy of Accattoli et al.'s fireball calculus. As an application of the machine we also show how to check convertibility of terms by their partial normalization where we can stop the machine and compare computed prefixes of normal forms. Thus, the contributions of this paper include:

1. a full systematic derivation of the machine from a CbV evaluator,
2. a presentation of an abstract machine for strong CbV that is a counterpart of Crégut's KN machine,
3. a reduction semantics for a strong CbV strategy,
4. an application of the machine to convertibility checking.

Outline. In Sect. 2 we recall the KN machine and present the NbE function obtained by its deconstruction. In Sect. 3 we present the machine derived from the evaluator, and in Sect. 4 the corresponding reduction semantics. In Sect. 5 we prove the correctness of the machine with respect to the semantics, and in Sect. 6 we conclude.

Supplementary Materials. The full derivations can be found at https:// bitbucket.org/pl-uwr/scbv-machine.

2   Deconstruction of the KN Machine

In this section we highlight the endpoints of the derivation: the KN machine, and the resulting evaluator obtained from an OCaml encoding of the machine. The main steps in the derivation are: disentangling the abstract machine into a defunctionalized form, refunctionalizing the stacks of the machine into continuations, mapping the continuation-passing evaluator to direct style, and refunctionalizing the closures the direct-style evaluator operates on into their functional representation [12]. All these transformations are described in detail in the supplementary materials.

2.1   Specification of the KN Machine

Crégut's KN machine is shown in Fig. 1. Due to the lack of space we do not discuss its architecture here; we refer the reader to the original paper [11] (which also includes a nice introduction to de Bruijn indices and levels) or to a more modern presentation in [17]. We also discuss all transitions of the machine in our supplementary materials.

The presentation here is slightly optimized compared to the original, and it coincides (on closed terms) with later presentation introduced by Munk [21]. The machine is in strong bisimulation with the original one, but the latter threads

Syntax:

$$Terms \ni T ::= n \mid T_1 \, T_2 \mid \lambda T$$
$$T_N ::= T \mid V(n)$$
$$Closures \ni C ::= [T_N, E]$$
$$Envs = Closures^* \ni E ::= \bullet \mid C :: E$$
$$Frames \ni F ::= \Box \, [T, E] \mid \lambda \Box \mid T \, \Box$$
$$Stacks = Frames^* \ni S ::= \bullet \mid F :: S$$
$$Confs \ni K ::= \langle T_N, E, S, m \rangle \mid \langle S, T, m \rangle$$

Initial state (for closed terms):

$$I_{KN} : T \mapsto \langle T, \bullet, \bullet, 0 \rangle$$

Transition rules:

$$\langle T_1 \, T_2, E, S_1, m \rangle \rightarrow \langle T_1, E, \Box \, [T_2, E] :: S_1, m \rangle \tag{1}$$
$$\langle \lambda T, E, \Box \, [T', E'] :: S_1, m \rangle \rightarrow \langle T, [T', E'] :: E, S_1, m \rangle \tag{2}$$
$$\langle \lambda T, E, S_2, m \rangle \rightarrow \langle T, [V(m+1), \bullet] :: E, \lambda \Box :: S_2, m+1 \rangle \tag{3}$$
$$\langle 0, [T, E] :: E', S_1, m \rangle \rightarrow \langle T, E, S_1, m \rangle \tag{4}$$
$$\langle n+1, C :: E, S_1, m \rangle \rightarrow \langle n, E, S_1, m \rangle \tag{5}$$
$$\langle V(n), E, S_1, m \rangle \rightarrow \langle S_1, m-n, m \rangle \tag{6}$$
$$\langle \bullet, T_{nf}, 0 \rangle \rightarrow T_{nf} \tag{7}$$
$$\langle \Box \, [T', E'] :: S_1, T_{neu}, m \rangle \rightarrow \langle T', E', T_{neu} \, \Box :: S_1, m \rangle \tag{8}$$
$$\langle \lambda \Box :: S_2, T_{nf}, m \rangle \rightarrow \langle S_2, \lambda T_{nf}, m-1 \rangle \tag{9}$$
$$\langle T_{neu} \, \Box :: S_1, T_{nf}, m \rangle \rightarrow \langle S_1, T_{neu} \, T_{nf}, m \rangle \tag{10}$$

Fig. 1. Rules for the KN machine

more redundant information: the parameter m in configurations is exactly the number of lambda frames in the current stack and need not be saved in stack frames.

The machine operates on lambda terms with de Bruijn indices used to represent bound variables in the standard way. Things get more complicated when we want to reduce open terms or reduce under lambdas, where we need to care for free variables. In the KN machine this is done using de Bruijn levels which represent the number of enclosing lambda abstractions from the root of the term to the current variable occurrence, and such *abstract variables* are formed with a different constructor $V(n)$. The machine normalizes terms according to the normal-order strategy that extends CbN to reduce open terms and under lambdas. It can be seen as an extension of the Krivine machine for CbN [19].

2.2 Shape Invariant

The machine specification can be seen as a function explicitly written in trampolined style [15], where each transition dispatches by a single pattern matching on the term or on the stack component of the configuration. Stacks are sequences of frames that are constructed when traversing the term in search of a next redex. However, this "flat" representation allows more stacks to be formed than are reachable in a machine run from the initial empty stack. In order to reason about the machine correctness, one needs to identify the precise structure of reachable stacks. Crégut expresses this shape invariant by a regular expression [11] but it can also be expressed simply by the context grammar using two kinds of stacks S_1, S_2:

$$S_1 ::= \Box\,[T, E] :: S_1 \mid S_2$$
$$S_2 ::= \bullet \mid \lambda\Box :: S_2 \mid T_{neu}\,\Box :: S_1$$

where T_{neu} denotes terms in neutral form. Neutral and normal forms are constructed according to the following grammar:

$$\text{Normal forms} \ni T_{nf} ::= \lambda T_{nf} \mid T_{neu}$$
$$\text{Neutral terms} \ni T_{neu} ::= n \mid T_{neu}\,T_{nf}$$

García-Pérez and Nogueira [16] underline the importance of establishing the shape invariant for refunctionalization step of the functional correspondence and characterize evaluation contexts of the normal-order strategy by an outside-in context grammar.[1] Below we present the grammar of normal-order contexts for the λ-calculus, i.e., leftmost-outermost contexts. We can see that the machine stacks correspond to the inside-out representation of contexts: S_1 represents L-contexts encoding the weak CbN strategy while S_2 represents A-contexts of the strong extension of CbN. The grammar of outside-in contexts is, on the other hand, more natural for top-down decomposition. Both L^{io} and L^{oi} represent the same L-contexts family but with reversed order of frames in the lists. We elaborate on the connection between the two kinds of representations in Sect. 4 when we discuss the strong CbV strategy.

inside-out contexts	outside-in contexts

$$L^{io} ::= \Box\,T :: L^{io} \mid A^{io} \qquad\qquad B^{oi} ::= \Box\,T :: B^{oi} \mid T_{neu}\,\Box :: L^{oi} \mid \bullet$$
$$A^{io} ::= \bullet \mid \lambda\Box :: A^{io} \mid T_{neu}\,\Box :: L^{io} \qquad L^{oi} ::= \lambda\Box :: L^{oi} \mid B^{oi}$$

2.3 Compositional Evaluator

The evaluator derived through the functional correspondence from the encoding of the abstract machine of Fig. 1, after some tidying to underline its structure,

---

[1] This family can be also defined in terms of an order on contexts [3].

```
(* syntax of the lambda-calculus with de Bruijn indices *)
type index = int
type term  = Var of index | Lam of term | App of term * term

(* semantic domain *)
type level = int
type glue  = Abs of (sem -> sem) | Neutral of term
 and sem   = level -> glue

(* reification of semantic objects into normal forms *)
let rec reify (d : sem) (m : level) : term =
  match d m with
  | Abs f ->
    Lam (reify (f (fun m' -> Neutral (Var (m'-m-1))))(m+1))
  | Neutral a ->
    a

(* sem -> sem as a retract of sem *)
let to_sem (f : sem -> sem) : sem =
  fun _ -> Abs f
let from_sem (d : sem) : sem -> sem =
  fun d' -> fun m ->
    match d m with
    | Abs f -> f d' m
    | Neutral a -> Neutral (App (a, reify d' m))

(* interpretation function *)
let rec eval (t : term) (e : sem list) : sem =
  match t with
  | Var n -> List.nth e n
  | Lam t' -> to_sem (fun d -> eval t' (d :: e))
  | App (t1, t2) -> from_sem (eval t1 e)
                             (fun m -> eval t2 e m)

(* NbE: interpretation followed by reification *)
let nbe (t : term) : term = reify (eval t []) 0
```

Fig. 2. An OCaml implementation of the higher-order compositional evaluator corresponding to the KN machine: an instance of normalization by evaluation for normal-order β-reduction in the λ-calculus.

is shown in Fig. 2. The evaluator implements an algorithm that follows the principles of normalization by evaluation [14], where the idea is to map a λ-term to an object in the meta-language from which a syntactic normal form of the input term can subsequently be read off. Actually, what we have mechanically obtained from KN is an OCaml implementation of a domain-theoretic residualizing model of the λ-calculus, in which the recursive type **sem** is an encoding of a reflexive domain D of interpretation, isomorphic to $\mathcal{N} \to ((D \to D) + \Lambda^{neu}_{\perp})_{\perp}$

(where $\mathcal{N}$ and Λ^{neu} are discrete CPOs of natural numbers and neutral terms, respectively). In particular, to_sem and from_sem encode continuous functions $\phi : (D \rightarrow D) \rightarrow D$ and $\psi : D \rightarrow (D \rightarrow D)$, respectively, such that $\psi \circ \phi = id$, establishing that $D \rightarrow D$ is a retract of D [14], which guarantees that β-convertible terms are mapped to the same semantic object. The interpretation function eval is completely standard, except for the η-expansion in the clause for application which comes from the fact that the derivation has been carried out in an eager meta-language. The reification function reify mediates between syntax and semantics in the way known from Filinski and Rohde's work [14] on NbE for the untyped λ-calculus.

As a matter of fact, what we have obtained through the functional correspondence from KN is very close to what Filinski and Rohde invented (and proved correct using domain-theoretic tools). The difference lies in the semantic domain which in their case was represented (in SML) by the type that in OCaml would read as

```
type sem = Abs of ((unit -> sem) -> sem)
         | Neutral of (level -> term)
```

from which we can see that the de Bruijn level is only needed to construct a neutral term and otherwise redundant (an observation confirmed by the definition of to_sem we have derived). With this domain of interpretation function arguments are explicitly passed as thunks. From the reduction strategy point of view, the normalizer of Fig. 2 (and KN) implements a two-stage normalization strategy: first reduce a term to a weak normal form (function eval) and then normalize the result (function reify). Seen that way, the two constructors of type sem represent the two possible kinds of weak normal forms.

For the record, we have derived an alternative abstract machine for normal-order reduction starting with Filinski and Rohde's NbE. This machine differs from KN in that it processes neutral terms in a separate mode and with an additional kind of stack. In the next section, we modify our NbE so that it accounts for CbV function applications.

In his MSc thesis, Munk also presents selected steps of a deconstruction of KN into a NbE [21]. However, he goes through a step in which de Bruijn levels are moved from the stack to closures in the environment. This step has not been formally justified and the resulting NbE is quite different from Filinski and Rohde's or from ours.

3   Construction of a Call-by-Value Variant

In this section we derive a call-by-value variant of the Crégut abstract machine. This is done by modifying the evaluator of Fig. 2 such that it accounts for CbV, and then inverting the transformations on the path from the abstract machine to the evaluator.

Call by value is a family of strategies where arguments of a function are evaluated (to a weak normal form) before being passed to the function. This way

```
type sem = Abs of (sem -> sem) | Neutral of (level -> term)

let rec reify (d : sem) (m : level) : term =
  match d with
  | Abs f ->
    Lam (reify (f (Neutral (fun m' -> Var (m'-m-1))))(m+1))
  | Neutral l ->
    l m

let to_sem (f : sem -> sem) : sem = Abs f

let from_sem (d : sem) : sem -> sem =
  fun d' ->
    match d with
    | Abs f ->
      f d'
    | Neutral l ->
      Neutral (fun m -> let n = reify d' m in App (l m, n))

let rec eval (t : term) (e : sem list) : sem =
  match t with
  | Var n -> List.nth e n
  | Lam t' -> to_sem (fun d -> eval t' (d :: e))
  | App (t1, t2) -> let d2 = eval t2 e
                    in from_sem (eval t1 e) d2

let nbe (t : term) : term = reify (eval t []) 0
```

Fig. 3. An OCaml implementation of the modified higher-order compositional evaluator: an instance of normalization by evaluation for a call-by-value β-reduction in the λ-calculus.

one avoids needless recomputation of arguments that are used more than once. A possible approach to a strong variant of such a strategy is the *applicative order* (a.k.a. leftmost-innermost) reduction [26], where the arguments are evaluated to the strong normal form. Here, however, we aim at a different, two-stage strategy, analogous to the one embodied in KN and in the normalizer of Fig. 2, which is a conservative extension of the standard CbV: the arguments are first evaluated to a weak normal form, then the function is applied and only then the resulting weak normal form is further reduced to the strong normal form. In order to obtain one fixed member of the family, we follow [2] and choose the right-to-left order of evaluation of arguments (we also choose the right-to-left order of normalization in inert terms, see Sect. 4).

3.1 Call-by-Value Evaluator

In call by value, function arguments are evaluated before the application takes place. To reflect this design choice in the evaluator, we modify the domain of interpretation:

```
type sem = Abs of (sem -> sem)
         | Neutral of (level -> term)
```

where an argument passed to a function is no longer a thunk, but a preevaluated value in the semantic domain. Here, the two constructors correspond to two kinds of weak normal forms: λ-abstraction and inert term, as presented in Sect. 4. All the other changes in the evaluator are simple adjustments to this modification. An OCaml implementation of the modified evaluator is shown in Fig. 3, where we arbitrarily decided to evaluate function application right to left (witness the explicit sequencing of computations with `let` in the clause for application in `eval`) and similarly for generating neutral terms (again, with `let` in `from_sem`).[2]

This normalizer could subsequently be given a domain-theoretic treatment, using the same techniques as the ones applied by Filinski and Rohde to their call-by-name normalizer [14] – an interesting endeavour that would offer one possible way of revealing the precise meaning of the modified normalizer. Here, instead, we take advantage of the functional correspondence and we derive a semantically equivalent abstract machine that we then analyse and we identify the reduction strategy it implements and inherits from the underlying NbE of Fig. 3.

The machine we derived from the evaluator has been subject to further optimizations before we arrived at the version presented in the next section. In particular, the de Bruijn level m has been moved from application frames of the stack to a dedicated register in the configurations of the machine. This modification requires a more careful bookkeeping of the level and, most notably, it has to be decremented when the machine leaves the scope of a lambda, just as in KN of Fig. 1. We also flattened the stack structure to be represented by a single list of frames, instead of by a pair of mutually inductive list-like structures. The final machine is then close in style to KN and can be seen as its call-by-value variant.

3.2 Abstract Machine

The machine obtained by derivation from the NbE evaluator is presented in Fig. 4. There are syntactic categories of lambda terms T in de Bruijn notation, machine representations of weak normal forms W, inert terms I, environments E, stack frames F, stacks S and configurations K. Weak normal forms are either closures consisting of a lambda abstraction and an environment or inert terms. Inert terms are either abstract variables $V(n)$ or inert terms applied to a weak normal

---

[2] While it would be possible to directly use Filinski and Rohde's NbE to obtain the evaluator of this section, our goal was to reveal and adjust the evaluator underlying KN, and the precise relation between KN and Filinski and Rohde's NbE has not been revealed prior to this work.

form. Just as in the KN machine, here n is de Bruijn level (not to be confused with de Bruijn index in the grammar of terms T). Weak normal forms represent the intermediate values that are passed to functions as arguments through the environment and subsequently reduced further to normal form. Environments are just sequences of weak normal forms; they represent mappings that assign nth element of the sequence to the variable with de Bruijn index n. As usual, stacks represent evaluation contexts.

Syntax:

$$Terms \ni T ::= n \mid T_1 \, T_2 \mid \lambda T$$
$$Wnfs \ni W ::= [\lambda T, E] \mid I$$
$$Inerts \ni I ::= V(n) \mid I \, W$$
$$Envs \ni E ::= \bullet \mid W :: E$$
$$Frames \ni F ::= [T, E] \, \Box \mid \Box \, W \mid \Box \, T \mid \lambda\Box \mid I \, \Box$$
$$Stacks \ni S ::= \bullet \mid F :: S$$
$$Confs \ni K ::= \langle T, E, S, m \rangle_\varepsilon \mid \langle S, W, m \rangle_c \mid \langle S, T, m \rangle_s$$

Transition rules:

$$T \mapsto \langle T, \bullet, \bullet, 0 \rangle_\varepsilon \tag{0}$$
$$\langle T_1 \, T_2, E, S_1, m \rangle_\varepsilon \to \langle T_2, E, [T_1, E] \, \Box :: S_1, m \rangle_\varepsilon \tag{1}$$
$$\langle \lambda T, E, S_1, m \rangle_\varepsilon \to \langle S_1, [\lambda T, E], m \rangle_c \tag{2}$$
$$\langle 0, W :: E, S_1, m \rangle_\varepsilon \to \langle S_1, W, m \rangle_c \tag{3}$$
$$\langle n + 1, W :: E, S_1, m \rangle_\varepsilon \to \langle n, E, S_1, m \rangle_\varepsilon \tag{4}$$
$$\langle [T, E] \, \Box :: S_1, W, m \rangle_c \to \langle T, E, \Box \, W :: S_1, m \rangle_\varepsilon \tag{5}$$
$$\langle \Box \, W :: S_1, [\lambda T, E], m \rangle_c \to \langle T, W :: E, S_1, m \rangle_\varepsilon \tag{6}$$
$$\langle \Box \, W :: S_1, I, m \rangle_c \to \langle S_1, I \, W, m \rangle_c \tag{7}$$
$$\langle S_3, [\lambda T, E], m \rangle_c \to \langle T, V(m + 1) :: E, \lambda\Box :: S_3, m + 1 \rangle_\varepsilon \tag{8}$$
$$\langle S_2, I \, W, m \rangle_c \to \langle I \, \Box :: S_2, W, m \rangle_c \tag{9}$$
$$\langle S_2, V(n), m \rangle_c \to \langle S_2, m - n, m \rangle_s \tag{10}$$
$$\langle I \, \Box :: S_2, T_{nf}, m \rangle_s \to \langle \Box \, T_{nf} :: S_2, I, m \rangle_c \tag{11}$$
$$\langle \lambda\Box :: S_3, T_{nf}, m \rangle_s \to \langle S_3, \lambda T_{nf}, m - 1 \rangle_s \tag{12}$$
$$\langle \Box \, T_{nf} :: S_2, T_{neu}, m \rangle_s \to \langle S_2, T_{neu} \, T_{nf}, m \rangle_s \tag{13}$$
$$\langle \bullet, T_{nf}, 0 \rangle_s \mapsto T_{nf} \tag{14}$$

Fig. 4. Rules for KNV, a call-by-value variant of KN

There are three kinds of configurations corresponding to three modes of operation: in configurations $\langle \cdot, \cdot, \cdot, \cdot \rangle_\varepsilon$ the machine evaluates some subterm to a weak normal form; in $\langle \cdot, \cdot, \cdot \rangle_c$ it continues with a computed weak normal form and in $\langle \cdot, \cdot, \cdot \rangle_s$ it continues with a computed (strong) normal form. Let us discuss the transitions. For the moment we ignore the indices in stacks; we think of S_1, S_2 and S_3 as arbitrary members of the syntactic category S of stacks. Similarly, T_{neu} and T_{nf} are arbitrary terms. These indices will become relevant in the next section.

Transitions (0)–(6) implement a right-to-left version of the well-known CEK machine [13] in a formulation similar to [6], but using de Bruijn indices. The initial transition (0) loads the term to be evaluated to a configuration with the empty environment and empty stack on de Bruijn level 0. Transitions (1)–(4) operate on configurations of the form $\langle T, E, S, m \rangle_{\mathcal{E}}$ that are meant to evaluate the term T within the environment E in the context represented by S to a weak normal form (wnf). In the case of application $T_1 \ T_2$, transition (1) calls the evaluation of T_2 and pushes a closure pairing T_1 with the current environment to the stack. Note that this implements the first of our right-to-left choices of the order of reduction. A lambda abstraction in (2) is already in wnf, so we change the mode of operation to a configuration of the form $\langle S, W, m \rangle_{\mathcal{C}}$. Transitions (3) and (4) simply read a value of a variable from the environment (which always returns a wnf) and change the mode of operation.

Configurations of the form $\langle S, W, m \rangle_{\mathcal{C}}$ continue with a wnf W in a context represented by S. There are two goals in these configurations: the first is to finish the evaluation (to wnfs) of the closures stored on the stack according to the weak call-by-value strategy; the second is to reduce W to a strong normal form. This is handled by rules (5)–(10), where rules (5) and (6) are responsible for the first goal, and rules (7)–(10) for the second. In rule (5) the stack contains a closure, so we start evaluating this closure and push the already computed wnf to the stack; when this evaluation reaches a wnf, rules (6) or (7) apply. If the wnf is a lambda abstraction, transition (6) implements a β-contraction. Otherwise it is an inert term; in this case rule (7) reconstructs the application of this inert term to the wnf popped from the stack (which gives another wnf). Rules (8)–(10) are applied when there are no more wnfs on the top of the stack; here we pattern-match on the currently processed wnf W. If W is a closure, transition (8) pushes the elementary context $\lambda\Box$ to the stack, increments the de Bruijn level $(m + 1)$, adds the abstract variable $V(n)$ to the environment and starts the evaluation of the body. If W is an application $I \ W'$, rule (9) delays the normalization of I by pushing it to the stack and continues with W'; note that this implements the second of our right-to-left choices of the order of reduction. Finally, if W is an abstract variable with index n at level m, we reach a normal form; rule (10) computes the final index of the variable and changes the mode of operation to a configuration of the form $\langle S, T, m \rangle_{\mathcal{S}}$.

Configurations of the form $\langle S, T, m \rangle_{\mathcal{S}}$ continue with a (strong) normal form T in a context represented by S (recall that the grammar of normal forms is presented in Sect. 2.2). The goal in these configurations is to finish the evaluation of inert term stored on the stack and to reconstruct the final term. This is handled by transitions (11)–(14); the choice of the transition is done by pattern-matching on the stack. If there is an inert term I on the top of the stack, rule (11) pushes the already computed normal form on the stack and calls normalization of I by switching the mode of operation to $\langle S, W, m \rangle_C$. Otherwise there is a $\lambda\square$ frame or a previously computed normal form on the top of the stack; in these cases transitions (12) and (13) reconstruct the term accordingly. Finally, when the stack is empty, transition (14) unloads the final result from a configuration.

The machine is pure in a sense that it does not use mutable state nor other computational effects so it can be directly implemented in a pure functional language. Thanks to that all structures of the machine are persistent data structures with their advantages (cf. [22]). It differs from machines of [2] in that its implementation does not perform on-the-fly α-conversion nor does it use pointers explicitly. Assuming *uniform cost criteria* for arithmetic operations, the cost of dispatch and of each transition is constant.

3.3   Shape Invariants

As in the case of the KN machine, not all sequences of stack frames represent valid contexts that can occur in a reachable configuration of the machine from Fig. 4. We define the syntactic category K_{wf} of well-formed configurations with the following grammar.

$$S_1 ::= [T, E] \, \square :: S_1 \mid \square \, W :: S_1 \mid S_3$$
$$S_2 ::= \square \, T_{nf} :: S_2 \mid S_3$$
$$S_3 ::= \bullet \mid \lambda\square :: S_3 \mid I \, \square :: S_2$$
$$K_{wf} ::= \langle T, E, S_1, m \rangle_{\mathcal{E}} \mid \langle S_1, W, m \rangle_C \mid \langle S_2, I, m \rangle_C \mid \langle S_2, T_{neu}, m \rangle_S \mid \langle S_3, T_{nf}, m \rangle_S$$

A simple induction on the length of evaluation gives the following lemma.

Lemma 1. *For all initial terms T, all configurations reachable from T are well-formed.*

One can note that there is no invention in designing syntactic categories W and I which correspond to grammars of weak normal forms and inert terms. They are products of defunctionalization which is a part of mechanization carried out via functional correspondence. More interestingly, all shape invariants can be derived. It is enough to use a separate grammar for normal forms in the higher-order normalizer. Through derivation this grammar is imprinted on the grammars of stacks and configurations.

3.4   An Application: Streaming of Expressions

Here we show a method for early discovering that two terms are not β-convertible, i.e., that they do not have equal normal forms. Grégoire and Leroy show in [18] that the comparison of normal forms can be short-circuited when enough data is computed. Our idea is to run the machine on both terms as long as partial results are the same. If the machine completes the computation on both terms and the computed normal forms are equal, the terms are β-convertible. But whenever it sees partial results that are different for the two input terms, we immediately know that the two terms do not have equal normal forms, without actually completing the computation. In some cases it allows to give an answer even on divergent terms. To get a partial result it is enough to interrupt the machine after transitions (8) and (11) when it pushes $\lambda\square$ and $\square\, T_{nf}$ frames, respectively, on the stack. This method is implemented in the accompanying code.

$$(T_1\, T_2)[i := T] = T_1[i := T]\, T_2[i := T]$$
$$(\lambda T_1)[i := T] = \lambda(T_1[i+1 := T])$$

$$n[i := T] = \begin{cases} n & : n < i \\ \uparrow^i_{\geq 0} T & : n = i \\ n - 1 & : n > i \end{cases}$$

$$\uparrow^i_{\geq k} (T_1\, T_2) = \uparrow^i_{\geq k} T_1 \uparrow^i_{\geq k} T_2$$
$$\uparrow^i_{\geq k} \lambda T = \lambda\uparrow^i_{\geq k+1} T$$

$$\uparrow^i_{\geq k} n = \begin{cases} n + i & : n \geq k \\ n & : n < k \end{cases}$$

$$(\lambda T_1)T_2 \to_\beta T_1[0 := T_2]$$
$$C[T_1] \overset{C}{\to}_\beta C[T_2] \quad \text{if } T_1 \to_\beta T_2$$

Fig. 5. β-contraction and β-reduction for terms with de Bruijn indices

As an example, consider the terms $\lambda x.\lambda y.\Omega$ and $\lambda x.(x\ \lambda y.\Omega)\, x$ (using standard notation with names). Even if the evaluation of these terms never terminates, we can detect different partial results and determine that these two terms cannot have equal normal forms. By running our machine we learn that the normal form of the former term (if it exists) starts with $\lambda x.\lambda y.\square$ while the the normal form of the latter (if it exists) starts with $\lambda x.\square\ x$.

This application is not specific to KNV and a similar procedure can be implemented based on KN. However, as is usual with CbV vs CbN, KNV in general performs better by avoiding reevaluation (to weak normal form) of function arguments.

4   Reduction Semantics for Strong CbV

A reduction semantics is a form of small-step operational semantics with an explicit representation of reduction contexts, i.e., of locations in a term where the computation can take place. Roughly, reduction contexts can be thought to represent terms with a hole. The atomic computation step is defined by a rewriting relation on terms, often called the contraction relation. For example, in our source language, the lambda calculus with de Bruijn indices, the reduction semantics can be formally defined as in Fig. 5, where the contraction relation is $\to_\beta$, and one-step reduction is defined as contraction in context $\overset{C}{\to}_\beta$, where reduction contexts C describe the specific reduction strategy. For example, if we take C to be L from Sect. 2.2, then we obtain the normal-order strategy. The notation $C[T]$ denotes the term reconstructed by *plugging* the term T in the hole of the context C.

In uniform strategies the grammar of reduction contexts is defined using only one nonterminal (as in CbN or CbV), while *hybrid* strategies use more than one nonterminal (as in normal order). The strong CbV strategy is another example of a hybrid strategy, one with three nonterminals leading to three kinds of contexts, each describing a separate substrategy.

As already observed in Sect. 2.2, shape invariants of the machine stack naturally lead to reduction contexts of the strategy realized by the machine. For the case of the KNV machine, stack invariants translate to grammar of contexts shown in Fig. 6 (left). Equivalently, they can be translated to an automaton, whose transitions are labelled with terms (as opposed to their machine representations), where the syntactic categories of terms in weak normal form and inert terms in the lambda calculus are

$$\text{Weak normal forms } \mathbf{Wnfs} \ni T_W ::= \lambda T \mid T_I$$
$$\text{Inert terms } \mathbf{Inerts} \ni T_I ::= n \mid T_I \, T_W$$

The grammar generates all stacks in syntactic categories S_1, S_2, S_3 in an inside-out manner: the automaton reading a stack from left to right moves from the hole of the represented context towards the topmost symbol. By reversing the arrows in the automaton we obtain an outside-in grammar (Fig. 6 right). A context nonterminal (its kind) in inside-out grammars denotes the kind of the hole, whereas in outside-in grammars it denotes the kind of the context generated by that nonterminal.

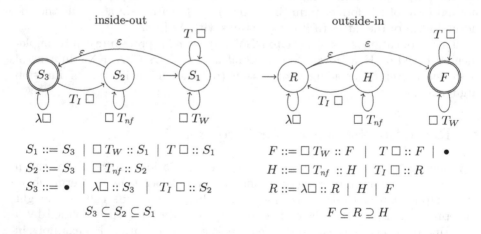

Fig. 6. Reduction semantics: automata and grammars of contexts

To complete the reduction semantics of strong CbV we have to specify a contraction relation. We simply read it from transition (6), where environments storing delayed substitution consist of structures representing weak normal forms.

Thus our contraction is β-contraction restricted to a variant where an argument has to be in weak normal form. We call it βwnf-contraction:

$$(\lambda T)T_W \twoheadrightarrow_{\beta wnf} T[0 := T_W]$$

The substrategy corresponding to the F nonterminal in Fig. 6 and βwnf-contraction can be recognized as the right-to-left weak strategy of the *fireball calculus* considered in [2]. It is known that this strategy is deterministic and reduces terms to weak normal forms. Our strong strategy corresponds to the nonterminal R (the starting symbol in the grammar); it contains the substrategy F and thus it is a conservative extension of the right-to-left call-by-value strategy.

In our strategy arguments of functions are evaluated in the right-to-left order. Similarly, arguments of inert terms are evaluated in the same order—thus we can refer to the strategy as *twice right-to-left call-by-value, rrCbV*. This is an arbitrary choice; three other options are possible. Some of these options, like lrCbV leave place for optimizations: after completing the weak right-to-left reduction the stack contains a sequence of arguments in weak normal form, which are then composed to build an inert term that is immediately decomposed to the very same sequence of weak normal forms before normalizing them with the strong left-to-right strategy. An optimized machine could refocus directly to strong reduction of arguments on stack instead of rebuilding an inert term and decomposing it again.

Strong CbV, as weak CbV, is an *incomplete strategy*, i.e., some normalizable terms may loop forever, e.g., $K \, I \, \Omega$.[3] Nevertheless, it allows to compute values of recursive functions.

Example 1. Consider the term $\lambda(K \, I \, \Omega)$. We can decompose it uniquely into a context $\lambda(K \, I \, \Box)$ and a subterm Ω forming a βwnf-redex. The context in the inside-out representation is $K \, I \, \Box \, :: \, \lambda\Box \, :: \, \bullet$ and it satisfies the S_1 constraints. In the outside-in representation it is $\lambda\Box \, :: \, K \, I \, \Box \, :: \, \bullet$ and conforms with the grammar R. Here S_1 and R are initial nonterminals in the grammars of contexts defined in Fig. 6. Thus $\lambda(K \, I \, \Omega)$ loops in the rrCbV strategy.

On the contrary, in term $\lambda(K \, I \, \lambda\Omega)$ the subterm $\lambda\Omega$ fits the T_W grammar and $\lambda(\Box \, \lambda\Omega)$ is a correct context of rrCbV. Thus $\lambda(K \, I \, \lambda\Omega)$ reduces to λI in two steps.

5   Correctness

In this section we show the correctness of the derived machine: it *traces* [10] (i.e., exactly implements, in a step-by-step manner) the reduction semantics. Before stating the formal theorem we need some definitions.

---

[3] Where $K = \lambda x.\lambda y.x$, $I = \lambda x.x$, $\Omega = (\lambda x.x \, x) \, (\lambda x.x \, x)$, using standard notation with names.

5.1   Decoding of Machine Representations

Terms. In the proof of correctness we have to translate lambda terms to machine configurations and back. The encoding of a term to a configuration is given by transition (0) in Fig. 4. The translation in the other direction is more involved. We start by defining two functions: $[\![\cdot, \cdot]\!]_W : Wnfs \to \mathbb{N} \to \mathbf{Wnfs}$ decoding the machine representations of weak normal forms and the function $[\![\cdot, \cdot]\!]_I :$ $Inerts \to \mathbb{N} \to \mathbf{Inerts}$ decoding the representations of inert terms. The formal definitions of these functions are given in extended version of this paper [8]. The second parameter, which is a de Bruijn level, is needed to decode an abstract variable. The function $[\![\cdot, \cdot, \cdot]\!]_T : Terms \to Envs \to \mathbb{N} \to Terms$ decodes machine representations of arbitrary terms.

Stacks. Intuitively, a stack should be decoded to an evaluation context. However, we are going to prove a termination result, for which we need an intermediate representation: lists of *annotated frames*. The annotation $\{\cdot\}_w$ in $\{T\}_w \square$ indicates that the term T occurring in a context $T \square$ is known to be in weak normal form; similarly $\{\cdot\}_n$ in $\square \{T\}_n$ indicates that T is known to be in strong normal form.

$$AnnFrms \ni C ::= T \square \mid \square T \mid \{T\}_w \square \mid \square \{T\}_n \mid \lambda\square$$
$$AnnFrms^* \ni L ::= \bullet \mid C :: L$$

The function $[\![\cdot]\!]_S : Stacks \to AnnFrms^*$ decodes stacks by decoding term representations in stack frames and adding frame annotations.

Annotated Decompositions. A configuration of the machine encodes, among others, a decomposition of a term into its subterm and a surrounding context.

Example 2. Consider a fragment of evaluation of the term $\lambda 00$ (which is $\lambda x.xx$ in de Bruijn notation). We adopt here the OCaml notation for lists, so $[1; \lambda\square]$ is the same as $1 :: \lambda\square :: \bullet$.

$$\langle [\square \ V(1); \ \lambda\square], V(1), 1\rangle_C \xrightarrow{(7)} \langle [\lambda\square], V(1) \ V(1), 1\rangle_C \xrightarrow{(9)}$$

$$\langle [V(1) \ \square; \ \lambda\square], V(1), 1\rangle_C \xrightarrow{(10)} \langle [V(1) \ \square; \ \lambda\square], 0, 1\rangle_S \xrightarrow{(11)}$$

$$\langle [\square \ 0; \ \lambda\square], V(1), 1\rangle_C$$

Here both stacks $[\square \ 0; \ \lambda\square]$ and $[\square \ V(1); \ \lambda\square]$ represent the same context $\lambda(\square \ 0)$, so the first and the last configuration in this sequence gives the same decomposition of $\lambda 00$ to the subterm 0 in the context $\lambda(\square \ 0)$. In order to capture the fact that the machine does not fall into an infinite loop, even if it considers the same decomposition more than once, we introduce a more informative notion of *annotated decomposition*. We introduce annotations for terms that allow to distinguish between arbitrary terms and terms in weak or strong normal form.

$$AnnTerms \ni A ::= T \mid \{T\}_w \mid \{T\}_n$$
$$AnnDcmp \ni D ::= A :: L$$

Configurations. Configurations are first decoded to annotated decompositions with function $[\![\cdot]\!]_K : Confs \to AnnDcmp$ and then to terms by function plug : $AnnDcmp \to Terms$. The latter function ignores all annotations.

5.2 Formal Correctness Result

We are now ready to state the result formally as the following theorem.

Theorem 1. *KNV traces the twice right-to-left strong CbV strategy, i.e.:*

1. *The function* $\text{plug}([\![\cdot]\!]_K) : Confs \to Terms$ *is a surjection.*
2. *For each machine transition* $K \to K'$, *either* $\text{plug}([\![K]\!]_K) = \text{plug}([\![K']\!]_K)$ *(i.e., the two configurations represent different decompositions of the same term), or* $\text{plug}([\![K]\!]_K)$ *reduces to* $\text{plug}([\![K']\!]_K)$ *in the strategy.*
3. *There are no silent loops in the machine, i.e., no infinite sequences of transitions* $K_0 \to \ldots \to K_n \to \ldots$ *such that* $\text{plug}([\![K_i]\!]_K) = \text{plug}([\![K_{i+1}]\!]_K)$ *for all* i.
4. *For all terms* T, T', *if* T *reduces to* T' *according to the strategy, then for each* K *such that* $\text{plug}([\![K]\!]_K) = T$ *there exists a sequence of machine transitions* $K \to \ldots \to K'$ *such that* $\text{plug}([\![K']\!]_K) = T'$.

The proof of this theorem is more tedious than sophisticated. We provide a sketch in the extended version of this article [8]. Point 1 is a simple observation that for any term T the corresponding initial configuration is decoded to T. For point 2, a simple case analysis gives that all transitions $\overset{\neq(6)}{\to}$ leave the decoding of the configurations unchanged. The fact that $\overset{(6)}{\to}$ implements βwnf-contraction is technically more involved, but not surprising.

Probably the most interesting part concerns point 3, which implies that the machine always finds a redex in a finite number of steps. We present the main intuitions here, leaving formal details in the extended version. We start by introducing a strict partial order on annotated terms and frames. For all terms $T_1, \ldots, T_7$ we set

$$T_1 < T_2 \,\square < \square\, T_3 < \{T_4\}_{\mathsf{w}} < \{T_5\}_{\mathsf{w}}\,\square < \square\, \{T_6\}_{\mathsf{n}} < \lambda\square < \{T_7\}_{\mathsf{n}}$$

Then we extend this order to the reversed lexicographic extension $<_{rlex}$ of $<$ on annotated decompositions: $D_1 <_{rlex} D_2$ iff $D_1^R <_{lex} D_2^R$ where D^R denotes the reverse of D and $<_{lex}$ is the standard lexicographic extension of $<$. Since a given term may have only finitely many corresponding annotated decompositions that cannot grow forever, there are no silent loops.

Example 3. The following is the sequence of decodings of configurations from Example 2. Note that this sequence is strictly increasing in the $<_{rlex}$ order.

$$[\{0\}_{\mathsf{w}};\, \square\, 0;\, \lambda\square] \overset{(7)}{\to} [\{0\ 0\}_{\mathsf{w}};\, \lambda\square] \overset{(9)}{\to} [\{0\}_{\mathsf{w}};\, \{0\}_{\mathsf{w}}\,\square;\, \lambda\square] \overset{(10)}{\to}$$

$$[\{0\}_{\mathsf{n}};\, \{0\}_{\mathsf{w}}\,\square;\, \lambda\square] \overset{(11)}{\to} [\{0\}_{\mathsf{w}};\, \square\, \{0\}_{\mathsf{n}};\, \lambda\square]$$

5.3 Corollaries

Since all the transformations used in the derivation are meaning-preserving, we can informally state that: For every closed term T and its OCaml representation t, the computation `eval t [] 0` in the call-by-value normalizer of Fig. 3 returns a `sem` value iff T reaches weak normal form in the strategy. Similarly the computation `nbe t` returns a `term` value `t'` iff T reaches a normal form T' in the strategy, and `t'` is an OCaml representation of T'.

6 Conclusion and Future Work

We presented the first systematic derivation of an abstract machine KNV that implements the strong CbV strategy for normalization in the lambda calculus. The derivation starts from the KN machine for normal-order reduction and uses off-the-shelf tools to transform semantic artefacts in a sequence of steps that constitute the so-called functional correspondence, as a two-way derivation recipe. We also presented the reduction semantics for the strong CbV strategy that can be read off the obtained machine, and that is an example of a hybrid strategy with three kinds of reduction contexts. As an example application of the machine, we illustrated how it can be used for convertibility checking, e.g., in proof assistants based on dependent type theory.

In [2], the authors introduced a time complexity criterion for an abstract machine: a machine is called a *reasonable implementation* of a given strategy if it can simulate n reduction steps in a number of transitions that is polynomial in n and in the size of the initial term. It is easy to observe that KNV is not a reasonable implementation of strong CbV due to the size explosion problem. Consider, e.g., the following term family e_n where c_n denotes the nth Church numeral:

$$\omega := \lambda x.x\ x \qquad\qquad e_n := \lambda x.c_n\ \omega\ x$$

Each e_n reduces to its normal form in the number of steps linear in n, but the size of this normal form is exponential in n. Since KNV never reuses structures constructed before, it has to introduce each of the exponentially many constructors in a separate step. Therefore, it is not a reasonable implementation. We intend to construct a modified version of KNV that will critically rely on sharing of intermediate results. We conjecture that such a modification is both necessary and sufficient to achieve a reasonable implementation of strong CbV. We also believe that the present development is a crucial stepping stone in this undertaking and that it offers all the necessary tools. In particular, sharing, in more than one flavour, can be most naturally introduced at the level of the evaluator of Fig. 3 and the resulting abstract machine will be a reflection of this modification through the functional correspondence.

Acknowledgements. We thank Filip Sieczkowski and the anonymous reviewers for their helpful comments on the presentation of this work.

References

1. Accattoli, B., Guerrieri, G.: Open call-by-value. In: Igarashi, A. (ed.) APLAS 2016. LNCS, vol. 10017, pp. 206–226. Springer, Cham (2016). https://doi.org/10.1007/978-3-319-47958-3_12
2. Accattoli, B., Guerrieri, G.: Abstract machines for open call-by-value. Sci. Comput. Program. **184** (2019). https://doi.org/10.1016/j.scico.2019.03.002
3. Accattoli, B., Lago, U.D.: (Leftmost-outermost) beta reduction is invariant, indeed. In: Logical Methods in Computer Science, vol. 12 (2016). https://doi.org/10.2168/LMCS-12(1:4)2016
4. Aehlig, K., Joachimski, F.: Operational aspects of untyped normalization by evaluation. Math. Struct. Comput. Sci. **14**, 587–611 (2004)
5. Ager, M.S., Biernacki, D., Danvy, O., Midtgaard, J.: From interpreter to compiler and virtual machine: a functional derivation. Technical report BRICS RS-03-14, DAIMI, Department of Computer Science, Aarhus University, Aarhus, Denmark, March 2003
6. Ager, M.S., Biernacki, D., Danvy, O., Midtgaard, J.: A functional correspondence between evaluators and abstract machines. In: Miller, D. (ed.) Proceedings of the Fifth ACM-SIGPLAN International Conference on Principles and Practice of Declarative Programming (PPDP 2003), pp. 8–19. ACM Press, Uppsala, August 2003
7. Balabonski, T., Barenbaum, P., Bonelli, E., Kesner, D.: Foundations of strong call by need. PACMPL **1**(ICFP), 20:1–20:29 (2017). https://doi.org/10.1145/3110264
8. Biernacka, M., Biernacki, D., Charatonik, W., Drab, T.: An abstract machine for strong call by value. CoRR abs/2009.06984 (2020). https://arxiv.org/abs/2009.06984
9. Biernacka, M., Charatonik, W.: Deriving an abstract machine for strong call by need. In: Geuvers, H. (ed.) 4th International Conference on Formal Structures for Computation and Deduction, FSCD 2019, 24–30 June 2019, Dortmund, Germany. LIPIcs, vol. 131, pp. 8:1–8:20. Schloss Dagstuhl - Leibniz-Zentrum für Informatik (2019). https://doi.org/10.4230/LIPIcs.FSCD.2019.8
10. Biernacka, M., Charatonik, W., Zielinska, K.: Generalized refocusing: from hybrid strategies to abstract machines. In: Miller, D. (ed.) 2nd International Conference on Formal Structures for Computation and Deduction, FSCD 2017, 3–9 September 2017, Oxford, UK. LIPIcs, vol. 84, pp. 10:1–10:17. Schloss Dagstuhl - Leibniz-Zentrum fuer Informatik (2017). https://doi.org/10.4230/LIPIcs.FSCD.2017.10
11. Crégut, P.: Strongly reducing variants of the Krivine abstract machine. High.-Order Symb. Comput. **20**(3), 209–230 (2007). A preliminary version was presented at the 1990 ACM Conference on Lisp and Functional Programming
12. Danvy, O.: A rational deconstruction of Landin's SECD machine. In: Grelck, C., Huch, F., Michaelson, G.J., Trinder, P. (eds.) IFL 2004. LNCS, vol. 3474, pp. 52–71. Springer, Heidelberg (2005). https://doi.org/10.1007/11431664_4
13. Felleisen, M., Friedman, D.P.: Control operators, the SECD machine, and the λ-calculus. In: Wirsing, M. (ed.) Formal Description of Programming Concepts III, pp. 193–217. Elsevier Science Publishers B.V. (North-Holland), Amsterdam (1986)
14. Filinski, A., Rohde, H.K.: Denotational aspects of untyped normalization by evaluation. Theor. Inform. Appl. **39**(3), 423–453 (2005). A preliminary version was presented at FOSSACS 2004

15. Ganz, S.E., Friedman, D.P., Wand, M.: Trampolined style. In: Lee, P. (ed.) Proceedings of the 1999 ACM SIGPLAN International Conference on Functional Programming. SIGPLAN Notices, vol. 34, no. 9, pp. 18–27. ACM Press, Paris, September 1999
16. García-Pérez, A., Nogueira, P.: On the syntactic and functional correspondence between hybrid (or layered) normalisers and abstract machines. Sci. Comput. Program. **95**, 176–199 (2014)
17. García-Pérez, Á., Nogueira, P.: The full-reducing Krivine abstract machine KN simulates pure normal-order reduction in lockstep: a proof via corresponding calculus. J. Funct. Program. **29**, e7 (2019). https://doi.org/10.1017/S0956796819000017
18. Grégoire, B., Leroy, X.: A compiled implementation of strong reduction. In: Wand, M., Jones, S.L.P. (eds.) Proceedings of the Seventh ACM SIGPLAN International Conference on Functional Programming (ICFP 2002), Pittsburgh, Pennsylvania, USA, 4–6 October 2002, pp. 235–246. ACM (2002). https://doi.org/10.1145/581478.581501
19. Krivine, J.L.: A call-by-name lambda-calculus machine. High.-Order Symb. Comput. **20**(3), 199–207 (2007)
20. Leroy, X., Doligez, D., Frisch, A., Garrigue, J., Rémy, D., Vouillon, J.: The OCaml system, release 4.10. INRIA, Rocquencourt, France, February 2020. https://caml.inria.fr/pub/docs/manual-ocaml/
21. Munk, J.: A study of syntactic and semantic artifacts and its application to lambda definability, strong normalization, and weak normalization in the presence of state. Master's thesis, DAIMI, Department of Computer Science, Aarhus University, Aarhus, Denmark, May 2007. BRICS research report RS-08-3
22. Okasaki, C.: Purely Functional Data Structures. Cambridge University Press, Cambridge (1999)
23. Reynolds, J.C.: Definitional interpreters for higher-order programming languages. High.-Order Symb. Comput. **11**(4), 363–397 (1998). Reprinted from the Proceedings of the 25th ACM National Conference (1972), with a foreword [24]
24. Reynolds, J.C.: Definitional interpreters revisited. High.-Order Symb. Comput. **11**(4), 355–361 (1998)
25. Schmidt, D.A.: Denotational Semantics: A Methodology for Language Development. Allyn and Bacon Inc., Boston (1986)
26. Sestoft, P.: Demonstrating lambda calculus reduction. In: Mogensen, T.Æ., Schmidt, D.A., Sudborough, I.H. (eds.) The Essence of Computation. LNCS, vol. 2566, pp. 420–435. Springer, Heidelberg (2002). https://doi.org/10.1007/3-540-36377-7_19

Certified Semantics for Relational Programming

Dmitry Rozplokhas[1,3], Andrey Vyatkin[2], and Dmitry Boulytchev[2,3]($\boxtimes$)

[1] Higher School of Economics, Saint Petersburg, Russia
[2] Saint Petersburg State University, Saint Petersburg, Russia
dboulytchev@math.spbu.ru
[3] JetBrains Research, Saint Petersburg, Russia

Abstract. We present a formal study of semantics for the relational programming language MINIKANREN. First, we formulate a denotational semantics which corresponds to the minimal Herbrand model for definite logic programs. Second, we present operational semantics which models interleaving, the distinctive feature of MINIKANREN implementation, and prove its soundness and completeness w.r.t. the denotational semantics. Our development is supported by a COQ specification, from which a reference interpreter can be extracted. We also derive from our main result a certified semantics (and a reference interpreter) for SLD resolution with cut and prove its soundness.

1 Introduction

In the context of this paper, we understand "relational programming" as a puristic form of logic programming with all extra-logical features banned. Specifically, we use MINIKANREN as an exemplary language; MINIKANREN can be seen as a logical language with explicit connectives, existentials and unification, and is mutually convertible to the pure logical subset of PROLOG.[1] Unlike PROLOG, which relies on SLD-resolution, most MINIKANREN implementations use a monadic *interleaving search*, which is known to be complete [15]. MINIKANREN is designed as a shallow DSL which may help to equip the host language with logical reasoning features. This design choice has been proven to be applicable in practice, and there are more than 100 implementations for almost 50 languages.

Although there already were attempts to define a formal semantics for MINIKANREN, none of them were capable of reflecting the distinctive property of MINIKANREN's search—*interleaving* [18]. Since this distinctive search strategy is essential for the specification of the language and its extensions, the description of almost all development on miniKanren was not based on formal semantics. The introductory book on MINIKANREN [12] describes the language by means of

---

The reported study was funded by RFBR, project number 18-01-00380.

[1] A detailed PROLOG-to-MINIKANREN comparison can be found here: http://minikanren.org/minikanren-and-prolog.html.

B. C. d. S. Oliveira (Ed.): APLAS 2020, LNCS 12470, pp. 167–185, 2020.
https://doi.org/10.1007/978-3-030-64437-6_9

$$
\begin{aligned}
\mathcal{C} &= \{C_i^{k_i}\} & \text{constructors with arities} \\
\mathcal{T}_X &= X \cup \{C_i^{k_i}(t_1, \ldots, t_{k_i}) \mid t_j \in \mathcal{T}_X\} & \text{terms over the set of variables } X \\
\mathcal{D} &= \mathcal{T}_\varnothing & \text{ground terms} \\
\mathcal{X} &= \{x, y, z, \ldots\} & \text{syntactic variables} \\
\mathcal{A} &= \{\alpha, \beta, \gamma, \ldots\} & \text{semantic variables} \\
\mathcal{R} &= \{R_i^{k_i}\} & \text{relational symbols with arities} \\
\mathcal{G} &= \mathcal{T}_\mathcal{X} \equiv \mathcal{T}_\mathcal{X} & \text{unification} \\
&\quad \mathcal{G} \wedge \mathcal{G} & \text{conjunction} \\
&\quad \mathcal{G} \vee \mathcal{G} & \text{disjunction} \\
&\quad \textbf{fresh } \mathcal{X} . \mathcal{G} & \text{fresh variable introduction} \\
&\quad R_i^{k_i}(t_1, \ldots, t_{k_i}), \; t_j \in \mathcal{T}_\mathcal{X} & \text{relational symbol invocation} \\
\mathcal{S} &= \{R_i^{k_i} = \lambda\, x_1^i \ldots x_{k_i}^i . g_i;\} \; g & \text{specification}
\end{aligned}
$$

Fig. 1. The syntax of the source language

an evolving set of examples. In a series of follow-up papers [1,7,13–15,30] various extensions of the language were presented with their semantics explained in terms of a SCHEME implementation. We argue that this style of semantic definition is fragile and not self-sufficient since it relies on concrete implementation languages' semantics and therefore is not stable under the host language replacement. In addition, the justification of important properties of the language and specific relational programs becomes cumbersome.

In this paper, we present a formal semantics for core MINIKANREN and prove some of its basic properties. First, we define denotational semantics similar to the least Herbrand model for definite logic programs [23]; then we describe operational semantics with interleaving in terms of a labeled transition system. Finally, we prove soundness and completeness of the operational semantics w.r.t the denotational one. We support our development with a formal specification using the COQ proof assistant [4], thus outsourcing the burden of proof checking to the automatic tool and deriving a certified reference interpreter via the extraction mechanism. As a rather straightforward extension of our main result, we also provide a certified operational semantics (and a reference interpreter) for SLD resolution with cut, a new result to our knowledge; while this step brings us out of purely relational domain, it still can be interesting on its own.

2   The Language

In this section, we introduce the syntax of the language we use throughout the paper, describe the informal semantics, and give some examples.

The syntax of the language is shown in Fig. 1. First, we fix a set of constructors $\mathcal{C}$ with known arities and consider a set of terms $\mathcal{T}_X$ with constructors as functional symbols and variables from X. We parameterize this set with an alphabet of variables since in the semantic description we will need *two* kinds of variables. The first kind, *syntactic* variables, is denoted by $\mathcal{X}$. The second kind, *semantic* or *logic* variables, is denoted by $\mathcal{A}$. We also consider an alphabet of *relational symbols* $\mathcal{R}$ which are used to name relational definitions. The central syntactic category in the language is *goal*. In our case, there are five types of goals: *unification* of terms, conjunction and disjunction of goals, fresh variable introduction, and invocation of some relational definition. Thus, unification is used as a constraint, and multiple constraints can be combined using conjunction, disjunction, and recursion. The final syntactic category is a *specification* $\mathcal{S}$. It consists of a set of relational definitions and a top-level goal. A top-level goal represents a search procedure which returns a stream of substitutions for the free variables of the goal. The definition for a set of free variables for both terms and goals is conventional; as "**fresh**" is the sole binding construct the definition is rather trivial. The language we defined is first-order, as goals can not be passed as parameters, returned or constructed at run time.

We now informally describe how relational search works. As we said, a goal represents a search procedure. This procedure takes a *state* as input and returns a stream of states; a state (among other information) contains a substitution that maps semantic variables into the terms over semantic variables. Then five types of scenarios are possible (depending on the type of the goal):

- Unification "$t_1 \equiv t_2$" unifies terms t_1 and t_2 in the context of the substitution in the current state. If terms are unifiable, then their MGU is integrated into the substitution, and a one-element stream is returned; otherwise the result is an empty stream.
- Conjunction "$g_1 \wedge g_2$" applies g_1 to the current state and then applies g_2 to each element of the result, concatenating the streams.
- Disjunction "$g_1 \vee g_2$" applies both its goals to the current state independently and then concatenates the results.
- Fresh construct "**fresh** $x \cdot g$" allocates a new semantic variable α, substitutes all free occurrences of x in g with α, and runs the goal.
- Invocation "$R_i^{k_i}(t_1,...,t_{k_i})$" finds a definition for the relational symbol $R_i^{k_i} = \lambda x_1 \ldots x_{k_i} \cdot g_i$, substitutes all free occurrences of a formal parameter x_j in g_i with term t_j (for all j) and runs the goal in the current state.

We stipulate that the top-level goal is preceded by an implicit "**fresh**" construct, which binds all its free variables, and that the final substitutions for these variables constitute the result of the goal evaluation.

Conjunction and disjunction form a monadic [32] interface with conjunction playing role of "**bind**" and disjunction the role of "**mplus**". In this description, we swept a lot of important details under the carpet—for example, in actual implementations the components of disjunction are not evaluated in isolation, but both disjuncts are evaluated incrementally with the control passing from one disjunct to another (*interleaving*) [18]; the evaluation of some goals can be additionally deferred (via so-called "*inverse-η-delay*") [13]; instead of streams the implementation can be based on "**ferns**" [8] to defer divergent computations, etc. In the following sections, we present a complete formal description of relational semantics which resolves these uncertainties in a conventional way.

As an example consider the following specification. For the sake of brevity we abbreviate immediately nested "**fresh**" constructs into the one, writing "**fresh** $x\ y\ \ldots \cdot g$" instead of "**fresh** x. **fresh** y. $\ldots g$".

```
append° = λ x y xy .                      revers° = λ x xr .
  ((x ≡ Nil) ∧ (xy ≡ y)) ∨                  ((x ≡ Nil) ∧ (xr ≡ Nil)) ∨
  (fresh h t ty .                           (fresh h t tr .
    (x ≡ Cons (h, t))  ∧                      (x ≡ Cons (h, t))  ∧
    (xy ≡ Cons (h, ty)) ∧                     (append° tr (Cons (h, Nil)) xr) ∧
    (append° t y ty));                        (revers° t tr));

revers° x x
```

Here we defined[2] two relational symbols—"$append^o$" and "$revers^o$",—and specified a top-level goal "$revers^o$ x x". The symbol "$append^o$" defines a relation of concatenation of lists—it takes three arguments and performs a case analysis on the first one. If the first argument is an empty list ("Nil"), then the second and the third arguments are unified. Otherwise, the first argument is deconstructed into a head "h" and a tail "t", and the tail is concatenated with the second argument using a recursive call to "$append^o$" and additional variable "ty", which represents the concatenation of "t" and "y". Finally, we unify "Cons (h, ty)" with "xy" to form a final constraint. Similarly, "$revers^o$" defines relational list reversing. The top-level goal represents a search procedure for all lists "x", which are stable under reversing, i.e. palindromes. Running it results in an infinite stream of substitutions:

$\alpha \mapsto$ Nil
$\alpha \mapsto$ Cons $(\beta_0,$ Nil$)$
$\alpha \mapsto$ Cons $(\beta_0,$ Cons $(\beta_0,$ Nil$))$
$\alpha \mapsto$ Cons $(\beta_0,$ Cons $(\beta_1,$ Cons $(\beta_0,$ Nil$)))$
. . .

where "α" is a *semantic* variable, corresponding to "x", "β_i" are free semantic variables. Therefore, each substitution represents a set of all palindromes of a certain length.

3 Denotational Semantics

In this section, we present a denotational semantics for the language we defined above. We use a simple set-theoretic approach analogous to the least Herbrand model for definite logic programs [23]. Strictly speaking, instead of developing it from scratch we could have just described the conversion of specifications into definite logic form and took their least Herbrand model. However, in that case, we would still need to define the least Herbrand model semantics for definite logic programs in a certified way. In addition, while for this concrete language the conversion to definite logic form is trivial, it may become less trivial for its extensions (with, for example, nominal constructs [7]) which we plan to do in future.

---

[2] We respect here a conventional tradition for MINIKANREN programming to super-script all relational names with "^{o}".

We also must make the following observations. First, building inductive denotational semantics in a conventional way amounts to constructing a complete lattice and a monotone function and taking its least fixed point [31]. As we deal with a first-order language with only monotonic constructs (conjunction/disjunction) these steps are trivial. Moreover, we express the semantics in CoQ, where all well-formed inductive definitions already have proper semantics, which removes the necessity to justify the validity of the steps we perform. Second, the least Herbrand model is traditionally defined as the least fixed point of a transition function (defined by a logic program) which maps sets of ground atoms to sets of ground atoms. We are, however, interested in *relational* semantics which should map a program into n-ary relation over ground terms, where n is the number of free variables in the topmost goal. Thus, we deviate from the traditional route and describe the denotational semantics in a more specific way.

To motivate further development, we first consider the following example. Let us have the following goal:

x ≡ Cons (y, z)

There are three free variables, and solving the goal delivers us the following single answer:

$\alpha \mapsto$ Cons (β, γ)

where semantic variables α, β and γ correspond to the syntactic ones "x", "y", "z". The goal does not put any constraints on "y" and "z", so there are no bindings for "β" and "γ" in the answer. This answer can be seen as the following ternary relation over the set of all ground terms:

$$\{(\text{Cons } (\beta,\gamma), \beta, \gamma) \mid \beta \in \mathcal{D}, \gamma \in \mathcal{D}\} \subseteq \mathcal{D}^3$$

The order of "dimensions" is important, since each dimension corresponds to a certain free variable. Our main idea is to represent this relation as a set of total functions

$$\mathfrak{f} : \mathcal{A} \mapsto \mathcal{D}$$

from semantic variables to ground terms. We call these functions *representing functions*. Thus, we may reformulate the same relation as

$$\{(\mathfrak{f}(\alpha), \mathfrak{f}(\beta), \mathfrak{f}(\gamma)) \mid \mathfrak{f} \in [\![\alpha \equiv \text{Cons } (\beta, \gamma)]\!]\}$$

where we use conventional semantic brackets "$[\![\bullet]\!]$" to denote the semantics. For the top-level goal, we need to substitute its free syntactic variables with distinct semantic ones, calculate the semantics, and build the explicit representation for the relation as shown above. The relation, obviously, does not depend on the concrete choice of semantic variables but depends on the order in which the values of representing functions are tupled. This order can be conventionalized, which gives us a completely deterministic semantics.

Now we implement this idea. First, for a representing function

$$\mathfrak{f} : \mathcal{A} \to \mathcal{D}$$

we introduce its homomorphic extension

$$\bar{\mathfrak{f}} : \mathcal{T}_{\mathcal{A}} \to \mathcal{D}$$

which maps terms to terms:

$$\bar{\mathfrak{f}}(\alpha) = \mathfrak{f}(\alpha)$$
$$\bar{\mathfrak{f}}(C_i^{k_i}(t_1, \ldots, t_{k_i})) = C_i^{k_i}(\bar{\mathfrak{f}}(t_1), \ldots \bar{\mathfrak{f}}(t_{k_i}))$$

Let us have two terms $t_1, t_2 \in \mathcal{T}_{\mathcal{A}}$. If there is a unifier for t_1 and t_2 then, clearly, there is a substitution θ which turns both t_1 and t_2 into the same *ground* term (we do not require θ to be the most general). Thus, θ maps (some) variables into ground terms, and its application to $t_{1(2)}$ is exactly $\bar{\theta}(t_{1(2)})$. This reasoning can be performed in the opposite direction: a unification $t_1 \equiv t_2$ defines the set of all representing functions $\mathfrak{f}$ for which $\bar{\mathfrak{f}}(t_1) = \bar{\mathfrak{f}}(t_2)$.

We will use the conventional notions of pointwise modification of a function $f[x \leftarrow v]$ and substitution $g[t/x]$ of a free variable x with a term t in a goal (or a term) g.

For a representing function $\mathfrak{f} : \mathcal{A} \to \mathcal{D}$ and a semantic variable α we define the following *generalization* operation:

$$\mathfrak{f} \uparrow \alpha = \{\mathfrak{f}[\alpha \leftarrow d] \mid d \in \mathcal{D}\}$$

Informally, this operation generalizes a representing function into a set of representing functions in such a way that the values of these functions for a given variable cover the whole $\mathcal{D}$. We extend the generalization operation for sets of representing functions $\mathfrak{F} \subseteq \mathcal{A} \to \mathcal{D}$:

$$\mathfrak{F} \uparrow \alpha = \bigcup_{\mathfrak{f} \in \mathfrak{F}} (\mathfrak{f} \uparrow \alpha)$$

Now we are ready to specify the semantics for goals (see Fig. 2). We've already given the motivation for the semantics of unification: the condition $\bar{\mathfrak{f}}(t_1) = \bar{\mathfrak{f}}(t_2)$ gives us the set of all (otherwise unrestricted) representing functions which "equate" terms t_1 and t_2. Set union and intersection provide a conventional interpretation for disjunction and conjunction of goals. In the case of a relational invocation we unfold the definition of the corresponding relational symbol and substitute its formal parameters with actual ones.

The only non-trivial case is that of "**fresh** x . g". First, we take an arbitrary semantic variable α, not free in g, and substitute x with α. Then we calculate the semantics of $g[\alpha/x]$. The interesting part is the next step: as x can not be free in "**fresh** x . g", we need to generalize the result over α since in our model the semantics of a goal specifies a relation over its free variables. We introduce some nondeterminism by choosing arbitrary α, but we can prove that with different choices of free variable the semantics of a goal does not change.

$$\begin{array}{llr}
[\![t_1 \equiv t_2]\!] & = \{\mathfrak{f} : \mathcal{A} \to \mathcal{D} \mid \bar{\mathfrak{f}}(t_1) = \bar{\mathfrak{f}}(t_2)\} & [\text{UNIFY}_D] \\
[\![g_1 \wedge g_2]\!] & = [\![g_1]\!] \cap [\![g_2]\!] & [\text{CONJ}_D] \\
[\![g_1 \vee g_2]\!] & = [\![g_1]\!] \cup [\![g_2]\!] & [\text{DISJ}_D] \\
[\![\mathbf{fresh}\ x\,.\,g]\!] & = ([\![g\,[\alpha/x]]\!]) \uparrow \alpha,\ \alpha \notin FV(g) & [\text{FRESH}_D] \\
[\![R\,(t_1,\dots,t_k)]\!] & = [\![g\,[t_1/x_1,\dots,t_k/x_k]]\!],\ \text{where } R = \lambda\,x_1\dots x_k\,.\,g & [\text{INVOKE}_D]
\end{array}$$

Fig. 2. Denotational semantics of goals

Lemma 1. *For any goal* **fresh** *x . g, for any two variables α and β which are not free in this goal, if $\mathfrak{f} \in [\![g\,[\alpha/x]]\!]$, then for any representing function $\mathfrak{f}'$, such that*

1. $\mathfrak{f}'(\beta) = \mathfrak{f}(\alpha)$
2. $\forall \gamma : \gamma \neq \alpha \wedge \gamma \neq \beta,\ \mathfrak{f}'(\gamma) = \mathfrak{f}(\gamma)$

it is true that $\mathfrak{f}' \in [\![g\,[\beta/x]]\!]$.

The proof turned out to be the most cumbersome among all others in the case where g is a nested **fresh** construct. In that case, we have to constructively build two representing functions (including an intermediate one for an intermediate goal) by pointwise modification. The details of this proof can be found in the extended version of the paper.[3]

We can prove the following important *closedness condition* for the semantics of a goal g.

Lemma 2 (Closedness condition). *For any goal g and two representing functions $\mathfrak{f}$ and $\mathfrak{f}'$, such that $\mathfrak{f}|_{FV(g)} = \mathfrak{f}'|_{FV(g)}$, it is true, that $\mathfrak{f} \in [\![g]\!] \Leftrightarrow \mathfrak{f}' \in [\![g]\!]$.*

In other words, representing functions for a goal g restrict only the values of free variables of g and do not introduce any "hidden" correlations. This condition guarantees that our semantics is closed in the sense that it does not introduce artificial restrictions for the relation it defines.

4 Operational Semantics

In this section we describe the operational semantics of MINIKANREN, which corresponds to the known implementations with interleaving search. The semantics is given in the form of a labeled transition system (LTS) [17]. From now on we assume the set of semantic variables to be linearly ordered ($\mathcal{A} = \{\alpha_1, \alpha_2, \dots\}$).

We introduce the notion of substitution

$$\sigma : \mathcal{A} \to \mathcal{T}_\mathcal{A}$$

as a (partial) mapping from semantic variables to terms over the set of semantic variables. We denote Σ the set of all substitutions, $\mathcal{D}om\,(\sigma)$—the domain for a substitution σ, $\mathcal{V}\mathcal{R}an\,(\sigma) = \bigcup_{\alpha \in \mathcal{D}om\,(\sigma)} \mathcal{F}\mathcal{V}\,(\sigma\,(\alpha))$—its range (the set of all free variables in the image).

---

[3] The extended version of this paper is available at https://arxiv.org/abs/2005.01018.

The *non-terminal states* in the transition system have the following shape:

$$S = \mathcal{G} \times \Sigma \times \mathbb{N} \mid S \oplus S \mid S \otimes \mathcal{G}$$

As we will see later, an evaluation of a goal is separated into elementary steps, and these steps are performed interchangeably for different subgoals. Thus, a state has a tree-like structure with intermediate nodes corresponding to partially-evaluated conjunctions ("$\otimes$") or disjunctions ("$\oplus$"). A leaf in the form $\langle g, \sigma, n \rangle$ determines a goal in a context, where g is a goal, σ is a substitution accumulated so far, and n is a natural number, which corresponds to a number of semantic variables used to this point. For a conjunction node, its right child is always a goal since it cannot be evaluated unless some result is provided by the left conjunct.

The full set of states also include one separate terminal state (denoted by $\diamond$), which symbolizes the end of the evaluation.

$$\hat{S} = \diamond \mid S$$

We will operate with the well-formed states only, which are defined as follows.

Definition 1. *Well-formedness condition for extended states:*
- $\diamond$ *is well-formed;*
- $\langle g, \sigma, n \rangle$ *is well-formed iff* $\mathcal{FV}(g) \cup \mathcal{D}om(\sigma) \cup \mathcal{VR}an(\sigma) \subseteq \{\alpha_1, \ldots, \alpha_n\}$;
- $s_1 \oplus s_2$ *is well-formed iff* s_1 *and* s_2 *are well-formed;*
- $s \otimes g$ *is well-formed iff* s *is well-formed and for all leaf triplets* $\langle \_, \_, n \rangle$ *in* s *it is true that* $\mathcal{FV}(g) \subseteq \{\alpha_1, \ldots, \alpha_n\}$.

Informally the well-formedness restricts the set of states to those in which all goals use only allocated variables.

Finally, we define the set of labels:

$$L = \circ \mid \Sigma \times \mathbb{N}$$

The label "$\circ$" is used to mark those steps which do not provide an answer; otherwise, a transition is labeled by a pair of a substitution and a number of allocated variables. The substitution is one of the answers, and the number is threaded through the derivation to keep track of allocated variables.

The transition rules are shown in Fig. 3. The first two rules specify the semantics of unification. If two terms are not unifiable under the current substitution σ then the evaluation stops with no answer; otherwise, it stops with the most general unifier applied to a current substitution as an answer.

The next two rules describe the steps performed when disjunction or conjunction is encountered on the top level of the current goal. For disjunction, it schedules both goals (using "$\oplus$") for evaluating in the same context as the parent state, for conjunction—schedules the left goal and postpones the right one (using "$\otimes$").

The rule for "**fresh**" substitutes bound syntactic variable with a newly allocated semantic one and proceeds with the goal.

The rule for relation invocation finds a corresponding definition, substitutes its formal parameters with the actual ones, and proceeds with the body.

The rest of the rules specify the steps performed during the evaluation of two remaining types of the states—conjunction and disjunction. In all cases, the left state is evaluated first. If its evaluation stops, the disjunction evaluation proceeds with the right state, propagating the label (SUMSTOP and SUMSTEP), and the conjunction schedules the right goal for evaluation in the context of the returned answer (PRODSTOPANS) or stops if there is no answer (PRODSTOP).

$$\langle t_1 \equiv t_2, \sigma, n \rangle \xrightarrow{\circ} \Diamond, \; \nexists \, mgu \, (t_1\sigma, t_2\sigma) \qquad \text{[UNIFYFAIL]}$$

$$\langle t_1 \equiv t_2, \sigma, n \rangle \xrightarrow{(mgu\,(t_1\sigma,t_2\sigma)\circ\sigma,\,n)} \Diamond \qquad \text{[UNIFYSUCCESS]}$$

$$\langle g_1 \vee g_2, \sigma, n \rangle \xrightarrow{\circ} \langle g_1, \sigma, n \rangle \oplus \langle g_2, \sigma, n \rangle \qquad \text{[DISJ]}$$

$$\langle g_1 \wedge g_2, \sigma, n \rangle \xrightarrow{\circ} \langle g_1, \sigma, n \rangle \otimes g_2 \qquad \text{[CONJ]}$$

$$\langle \mathbf{fresh} \; x\,.\,g, \sigma, n \rangle \xrightarrow{\circ} \langle g \, [\alpha_{n+1} / x], \sigma, n+1 \rangle \qquad \text{[FRESH]}$$

$$\frac{R_i^{k_i} = \lambda x_1 \ldots x_{k_i}\,.\,g}{\left\langle R_i^{k_i}\,(t_1, \ldots, t_{k_i}), \sigma, n \right\rangle \xrightarrow{\circ} \left\langle g\,[t_1 / x_1 \ldots t_{k_i} / x_{k_i}], \sigma, n \right\rangle} \qquad \text{[INVOKE]}$$

$$\frac{s_1 \xrightarrow{\circ} \Diamond}{(s_1 \oplus s_2) \xrightarrow{\circ} s_2} \qquad \text{[SUMSTOP]}$$

$$\frac{s_1 \xrightarrow{r} \Diamond}{(s_1 \oplus s_2) \xrightarrow{r} s_2} \qquad \text{[SUMSTOPANS]}$$

$$\frac{s \xrightarrow{\circ} \Diamond}{(s \otimes g) \xrightarrow{\circ} \Diamond} \qquad \text{[PRODSTOP]}$$

$$\frac{s \xrightarrow{(\sigma,n)} \Diamond}{(s \otimes g) \xrightarrow{\circ} \langle g, \sigma, n \rangle} \qquad \text{[PRODSTOPANS]}$$

$$\frac{s_1 \xrightarrow{\circ} s_1'}{(s_1 \oplus s_2) \xrightarrow{\circ} (s_2 \oplus s_1')} \qquad \text{[SUMSTEP]}$$

$$\frac{s_1 \xrightarrow{r} s_1'}{(s_1 \oplus s_2) \xrightarrow{r} (s_2 \oplus s_1')} \qquad \text{[SUMSTEPANS]}$$

$$\frac{s \xrightarrow{\circ} s'}{(s \otimes g) \xrightarrow{\circ} (s' \otimes g)} \qquad \text{[PRODSTEP]}$$

$$\frac{s \xrightarrow{(\sigma,n)} s'}{(s \otimes g) \xrightarrow{\circ} (\langle g, \sigma, n \rangle \oplus (s' \otimes g))} \qquad \text{[PRODSTEPANS]}$$

Fig. 3. Operational semantics of interleaving search

The last four rules describe *interleaving*, which occurs when the evaluation of the left state suspends with some residual state (with or without an answer). In the case of disjunction the answer (if any) is propagated, and the constituents of the disjunction are swapped (SUMSTEP, SUMSTEPANS). In the case of conjunction, if the evaluation step in the left conjunct did not provide any answer, the evaluation is continued in the same order since there is still no information to proceed with the evaluation of the right conjunct (PRODSTEP); if there is some answer, then the disjunction of the right conjunct in the context of the answer and the remaining conjunction is scheduled for evaluation (PRODSTEPANS).

The introduced transition system is completely deterministic: there is exactly one transition from any non-terminal state. There is, however, some freedom in choosing the order of evaluation for conjunction and disjunction states. For example, instead of evaluating the left substate first, we could choose to evaluate the right one, etc. This choice reflects the inherent non-deterministic nature of search in relational (and, more generally, logical) programming. Although we could introduce this ambiguity into the semantics (by replacing specific rules for disjunctions and conjunctions evaluation with some conditions on it), we want an operational semantics that would be easy to present and easy to employ to describe existing language extensions (already described for a specific implementation of interleaving search), so we instead base the semantics on one canonical search strategy. At the same time, as long as deterministic search procedures are sound and complete, we can consider them "equivalent".[4]

It is easy to prove that transitions preserve well-formedness of states.

Lemma 3. *(Well-formedness preservation) For any transition* $s \xrightarrow{l} \hat{s}$, *if* s *is well-formed then* $\hat{s}$ *is also well-formed.*

A derivation sequence for a certain state determines a *trace*—a finite or infinite sequence of answers. The trace corresponds to the stream of answers in the reference MINIKANREN implementations. We denote a set of answers in the trace for state $\hat{s}$ by $\mathcal{T}r_{\hat{s}}$.

We can relate sets of answers for the partially evaluated conjunction and disjunction with sets of answers for their constituents by the two following lemmas.

Lemma 4. *For any non-terminal states* s_1 *and* s_2, $\mathcal{T}r_{s_1 \oplus s_2} = \mathcal{T}r_{s_1} \cup \mathcal{T}r_{s_2}$.

Lemma 5. *For any non-terminal state* s *and goal* g, $\mathcal{T}r_{s \otimes g} \supseteq \bigcup_{(\sigma,n) \in \mathcal{T}r_s} \mathcal{T}r_{\langle g, \sigma, n \rangle}$.

These two lemmas constitute the exact conditions on definition of these operators that we will use to prove the completeness of an operational semantics.

We also can easily describe the criterion of termination for disjunctions.

Lemma 6. *For any goals* g_1 *and* g_2, *substitution* σ, *and number* n, *the trace from the state* $\langle g_1 \vee g_2, \sigma, n \rangle$ *is finite iff the traces from both* $\langle g_1, \sigma, n \rangle$ *and* $\langle g_2, \sigma, n \rangle$ *are finite.*

These simple statements already allow us to prove two important properties of interleaving search as corollaries: the "fairness" of disjunction—the fact that the trace for disjunction contains all the answers from both streams for disjuncts—and the "commutativity" of disjunctions—the fact that swapping two disjuncts (at the top level) does not change the termination of the goal evaluation.

---

[4] There still can be differences in observable behavior of concrete goals under different sound and complete search strategies. For example, a goal can be refutationally complete [6] under one strategy and non-complete under another.

5   Equivalence of Semantics

Now we can relate two different kinds of semantics for MINIKANREN described in the previous sections and show that the results given by these two semantics are the same for any specification. This will actually say something important about the search in the language: since operational semantics describes precisely the behavior of the search and denotational semantics ignores the search and describes what we *should* get from a mathematical point of view, by proving their equivalence we establish the *completeness* of the search, which means that the search will get all answers satisfying the described specification and only those.

$$
\begin{aligned}
\llbracket \langle \rangle \rrbracket &= \varnothing \\
\llbracket \langle g, \sigma, n \rangle \rrbracket &= \llbracket g \rrbracket \cap \llbracket \sigma \rrbracket \\
\llbracket s_1 \oplus s_2 \rrbracket &= \llbracket s_1 \rrbracket \cup \llbracket s_2 \rrbracket \\
\llbracket s \otimes g \rrbracket &= \llbracket s \rrbracket \cap \llbracket g \rrbracket
\end{aligned}
$$

Fig. 4. Denotational semantics of states

But first, we need to relate the answers produced by these two semantics as they have different forms: a trace of substitutions (along with the numbers of allocated variables) for the operational one and a set of representing functions for the denotational one. We can notice that the notion of a representing function is close to substitution, with only two differences:

- representing functions are total;
- terms in the domain of representing functions are ground.

Therefore we can easily extend (perhaps ambiguously) any substitution to a representing function by composing it with an arbitrary representing function preserving all variable dependencies in the substitution. So we can define a set of representing functions that correspond to a substitution as follows:

$$
\llbracket \sigma \rrbracket = \{ \bar{\mathfrak{f}} \circ \sigma \mid \mathfrak{f} : \mathcal{A} \mapsto \mathcal{D} \}
$$

And the *denotational analog* of operational semantics (a set of representing functions corresponding to the answers in the trace) for a given state $\hat{s}$ is then defined as the union of sets for all substitutions in the trace:

$$
\llbracket \hat{s} \rrbracket_{op} = \cup_{(\sigma, n) \in \mathcal{T}r_{\hat{s}}} \llbracket \sigma \rrbracket
$$

This allows us to state theorems relating the two semantics.

Theorem 1 (Operational semantics soundness). *If indices of all free variables in a goal g are limited by some number n, then $\llbracket \langle g, \epsilon, n \rangle \rrbracket_{op} \subseteq \llbracket g \rrbracket$.*

It can be proven by nested induction, but first, we need to generalize the statement so that the inductive hypothesis is strong enough for the inductive step.

To do so, we define denotational semantics not only for goals but for arbitrary states. Note that this definition does not need to have any intuitive interpretation, it is introduced only for the proof to go smoothly. The definition of the denotational semantics for extended states is shown on Fig. 4. The generalized version of the theorem uses it.

Lemma 7 (Generalized soundness). *For any well-formed state $\hat{s}$*

$$\llbracket \hat{s} \rrbracket_{op} \subseteq \llbracket \hat{s} \rrbracket.$$

It can be proven by the induction on the number of steps in which a given answer (more accurately, the substitution that contains it) occurs in the trace. We break the proof in two parts and separately prove by induction on evidence that for every transition in our system the semantics of both the label (if there is one) and the next state are subsets of the denotational semantics for the initial state.

Lemma 8 (Soundness of the answer). *For any transition $s \xrightarrow{(\sigma, n)} \hat{s}$,* $\llbracket \sigma \rrbracket \subseteq \llbracket s \rrbracket.$

Lemma 9 (Soundness of the next state). *For any transition $s \xrightarrow{l} \hat{s}$,* $\llbracket \hat{s} \rrbracket \subseteq \llbracket s \rrbracket.$

It would be tempting to formulate the completeness of operational semantics as soundness with the inverted inclusion, but it does not hold in such generality. The reason for this is that the denotational semantics encodes only the dependencies between free variables of a goal, which is reflected by the closedness condition, while the operational semantics may also contain dependencies between semantic variables allocated in **fresh** constructs. Therefore we formulate completeness with representing functions restricted on the semantic variables allocated in the beginning (which includes all free variables of a goal). This does not compromise our promise to prove the completeness of the search as MINIKANREN returns substitutions only for queried variables, which are allocated in the beginning.

Theorem 2 (Operational semantics completeness). *If the indices of all free variables in a goal g are limited by some number n, then*

$$\{ \mathfrak{f}|_{\{\alpha_1, \ldots, \alpha_n\}} \mid \mathfrak{f} \in \llbracket g \rrbracket \} \subseteq \{ \mathfrak{f}|_{\{\alpha_1, \ldots, \alpha_n\}} \mid \mathfrak{f} \in \llbracket \langle g, \epsilon, n \rangle \rrbracket_{op} \}.$$

Similarly to the soundness, this can be proven by nested induction, but the generalization is required. This time it is enough to generalize it from goals to states of the shape $\langle g, \sigma, n \rangle$. We also need to introduce one more auxiliary semantics—*step-indexed denotational semantics* (denoted by $\llbracket \bullet \rrbracket^i$). It is an implementation of the well-known approach [2] of indexing typing or semantic logical relations by a number of permitted evaluation steps to allow inductive reasoning on it. In our case, $[\![g]\!]^i$ includes only those representing functions that one can get after no more than i unfoldings of relational calls.

The step-indexed denotational semantics is an approximation of the conventional denotational semantics; it is clear that any answer in conventional denotational semantics will also be in step-indexed denotational semantics for some number of steps.

Lemma 10. $[\![g]\!] \subseteq \cup_i [\![g]\!]^i$

Now the generalized version of the completeness theorem is as follows.

Lemma 11 (Generalized completeness). *For any set of relational definitions, for any number of unfoldings i, for any well-formed state $\langle g, \sigma, n \rangle$,*

$$\{f|_{\{\alpha_1,...,\alpha_n\}} \mid f \in [\![g]\!]^i \cap [\![\sigma]\!]\} \subseteq \{f|_{\{\alpha_1,...,\alpha_n\}} \mid f \in [\![\langle g, \sigma, n \rangle]\!]_{op}\}.$$

The proof is by the induction on number of unfoldings i. The induction step is proven by structural induction on goal g. We use Lemmas 4 and 5 for evaluation of a disjunction and a conjunction respectively, and Lemma 1 in the case of fresh variable introduction to move from an arbitrary semantic variable in denotational semantics to the next allocated fresh variable. The details of this proof may be found in the extended version of the paper.

6 Specification in Coq

We certified all the definitions and propositions from the previous sections using the Coq proof assistant.[5] The Coq specification for the most part closely follows the formal descriptions we gave by means of inductive definitions (and inductively defined propositions in particular) and structural induction in proofs. The detailed description of the specification, including code snippets, is provided in the extended version of the paper, and in this section we address only some non-trivial parts of it and some design choices.

The language formalized in Coq has a few non-essential simplifications for the sake of convenience. Specifically, we restrict the arities of all constructors to be either zero or two and require all relations to have exactly one argument. These restrictions do not make the language less expressive in any way since we can always represent a sequence of terms as a list using constructors Nil^0 and Cons^2.

In our formalization of the language we use higher-order abstract syntax [27] for variable binding, therefore we work explicitly only with semantic variables. We preferred it to the first-order syntax because it gives us the ability to use substitution and the induction principle provided by Coq. On the other hand, we need to explicitly specify a requirement on the syntax representation, which is trivially fulfilled in the first-order case: all bindings have to be "consistent", i.e. if

---

[5] The specification is available at https://github.com/dboulytchev/miniKanren-coq.

we instantiate a higher-order **fresh** construct with different semantic variables the results will be the same up to some renaming (provided that both those variables are not free in the body of the binder). Another requirement we have to specify explicitly (independent of HOAS/FOAS dichotomy) is a requirement that the definitions of relations do not contain unbound semantic variables.

To formalize the operational semantics in COQ we first need to define all preliminary notions from unification theory [3] which our semantics uses. In particular, we need to implement the notion of the most general unifier (MGU). As it is well-known [25] all standard recursive algorithms for calculating MGU are not decreasing on argument terms, so we can't define them as simple recursive functions in COQ due to the termination check failure. The standard approach to tackle this problem is to define the function through well-founded recursion. We use a distinctive version of this approach, which is more convenient for our purposes: we define MGU as a proposition (for which there is no termination requirement in COQ) with a dedicated structurally-recursive function for one step of unification, and then we use a well-founded induction to prove the existence of a corresponding result for any arguments and defining properties of MGU. For this well-founded induction, we use the number of distinct free variables in argument terms as a well-founded order on pairs of terms.

In the operational semantics, to define traces as (possibly) infinite sequences of transitions we use the standard approach in COQ—coinductively defined streams. Operating with them requires a number of well-known tricks, described by Chlipala [9], to be applied, such as the use of a separate coinductive definition of equality on streams.

The final proofs of soundness and completeness of operational semantics are relatively small, but the large amount of work is hidden in the proofs of auxiliary facts that they use (including lemmas from the previous sections and some technical machinery for handling representing functions).

7   Applications

In this section, we consider some applications of the framework and results, described in the previous sections.

7.1   Correctness of Transformations

One important immediate corollary of the equivalence theorems we have proven is the justification of correctness for certain program transformations. The completeness of interleaving search guarantees the correctness of any transformation that preserves the denotational semantics, for example:

- changing the order of constituents in conjunctions and disjunctions;
- distributing conjunctions over disjunctions and vice versa, for example, normalizing goals info CNF or DNF;
- moving fresh variable introduction upwards/downwards, for example, transforming any relation into a top-level fresh construct with a freshless body.

Note that this way we can guarantee only the preservation of results as *sets of ground terms*; the other aspects of program behavior, such as termination, may be affected by some of these transformations.[6]

One of the applications for these transformations is a conversion from/to PROLOG. As both languages use essentially the same fragment of first-order logic, their programs are mutually convertible. The conversion from PROLOG to MINIKANREN is simpler as the latter admits a richer syntax of goals. The inverse conversion involves the transformation into a DNF and splitting the disjunction into a number of separate clauses. This transformation, in particular, makes it possible to reuse our approach to describe the semantics of PROLOG as well. In the following sections we briefly address this problem.

7.2   SLD Semantics

The conventional PROLOG SLD search differs from the interleaving one in just one aspect—it does not perform interleaving. Thus, changing just two rules in the operational semantics converts interleaving search into the depth-first one:

$$\frac{s_1 \xrightarrow{\circ} s_1'}{(s_1 \oplus s_2) \xrightarrow{\circ} (s_1' \oplus s_2)} \text{ [DisjStep]} \quad \frac{s_1 \xrightarrow{r} s_1'}{(s_1 \oplus s_2) \xrightarrow{r} (s_1' \oplus s_2)} \text{ [DisjStepAns]}$$

With this definition we can almost completely reuse the mechanized proof of soundness (with minor changes); the completeness, however, can no longer be proven (as it does not hold anymore).

7.3   Cut

Dealing with the "cut" construct is known to be a cornerstone feature in the study of operational semantics for PROLOG. It turned out that in our case the semantics of "cut" can be expressed naturally (but a bit verbosely). Unlike SLD-resolution, it does not amount to an incremental change in semantics description. It also would work only for programs directly converted from PROLOG specifications.

The key observation in dealing with the "cut" in our setting is that a state in our semantics, in fact, encodes the whole current search tree (including all backtracking possibilities). This opens the opportunity to organize proper "navigation" through the tree to reflect the effect of "cut". The details of the semantic description can be found in the extended version of the paper.

For this semantics, we can repeat the proof of soundness w.r.t. to the denotational semantics. There is, however, a little subtlety with our construction: we cannot formally prove that our semantics indeed encodes the conventional meaning of "cut" (since we do not have other semantics of "cut" to compare with).

---

[6] Possible slowdown and loss of termination after reorderings in conjunction is a famous example of this phenomenon in MINIKANREN, known as conjunction non-commutativity [6].

Nevertheless, we can demonstrate a plausible behavior using the extracted reference interpreter.

7.4 Reference Interpreters

Using the COQ extraction mechanism, we extracted two reference interpreters from our definitions and theorems: one for conventional MINIKANREN with interleaving search and another one for SLD search with cut. These interpreters can be used to practically investigate the behavior of specifications in unclear, complex, or corner cases. Our experience has shown that these interpreters demonstrate the expected behavior in all cases.

8 Related Work

The study of formal semantics for logic programming languages, particularly PROLOG, is a well-established research domain. Early works [10,16] addressed the computational aspects of both pure PROLOG and its extension with the cut construct. Recently, the application of certified/mechanized approaches came into focus as well. In particular, in one work [21] the equivalence of a few differently defined semantics for pure PROLOG is proven, and in another work [20] a denotational semantics for PROLOG with cut is presented; both works provide COQ-mechanized proofs. It is interesting that the former one also advocates the use of higher-order abstract syntax. We are not aware of any prior work on certified semantics for PROLOG which contributed a correct-by-construction interpreter. Our certified description of SLD resolution with cut can be considered as a certified semantics for PROLOG modulo occurs check in unification (which PROLOG does not have by default).

The implementation of first-order unification in dependently typed languages constitutes a well-known challenge with a number of known solutions. The major difficulty comes from the non-structural recursivity of conventional unification algorithms, which requires to provide a witness for convergence. The standard approach is to define a generally-recursive function and a well-founded order for its arguments. This route is taken in a number of works [5,19,26,28], where the descriptions of unification algorithms are given in COQ, LCF and ALF. The well-founded used there is lexicographically ordered tuples, containing the information about the number of different free variables and the sizes of the arguments. We implement a similar approach, but we separate the test for the non-matching case into a dedicated function. Thus, we make a recursive call only when the current substitution extension is guaranteed, which allows us to use the number of different free variables as the well-founded order. An alternative approach suggested by McBride [25] gives a structurally recursive definition of the unification algorithm; this is achieved by indexing the arguments with the numbers of their free variables.

The use of higher-order abstract syntax (HOAS) for dealing with language constructs in COQ was addressed in early work [11], where it was employed to describe the lambda calculus. The inconsistency phenomenon of HOAS representation, mentioned in Sect. 6, is called there "exotic terms" there and is handled using a dedicated inductive predicate "Valid_v". The predicate has a non-trivial implementation based on subtle observations on the behavior of bindings. Our case, however, is much simpler: there is not much variety in "exotic terms" (for example, we do not have reductions in terms), and our consistency predicate can be considered as a limited version of "Valid_v" for a more limited language.

The study of formal semantics for MINIKANREN is not a completely novel venture. Previously, a nondeterministic small-step semantics was described [24], as well as a big-step semantics for a finite number of answers [29]; neither uses proof mechanization and in both works the interleaving is not addressed.

The work of Kumar [22] can be considered as our direct predecessor. It also introduces both denotational and operational semantics and presents a HOL-certified proof for the soundness of the latter w.r.t. the former. The denotational semantics resembles ours but considers only queries with a single free variable (we do not see this restriction as important). On the other hand, the operational semantics is non-deterministic, which makes it impossible to express interleaving and extract the interpreter in a direct way. In addition, a specific form of "executable semantics" is introduced, but its connection to the other two is not established. Finally, no completeness result is presented. We consider our completeness proof as an essential improvement.

The most important property of interleaving search—completeness—was postulated in the introductory paper [18], and is delivered by all major implementations. Hemann et al. [15] give a proof of completeness for a specific implementation of MINIKANREN; however, the completeness is understood there as preservation of all answers during the interleaving of answer streams, i.e. in a more narrow sense than in our work since no relation to denotational semantics is established.

9   Conclusion and Future Work

In this paper, we presented a certified formal semantics for core MINIKANREN and proved some of its basic properties (including interleaving search completeness, disjunction fairness and commutativity), which are believed to hold in existing implementations. We also derived a semantics for conventional SLD resolution with cut and extracted two certified reference interpreters. We consider our work as the initial setup for the future development of MINIKANREN semantics.

The language we considered here lacks many important features, which are already introduced and employed in many implementations. Integrating these extensions—in the first hand, disequality constraints,—into the semantics looks a natural direction for future work. We are also going to address the problems of proving some properties of relational programs (equivalence, refutational completeness, etc.).

References

1. Alvis, C.E., Willcock, J.J., Carter, K.M., Byrd, W.E., Friedman, D.P.: cKanren: miniKanren with constraints. In: Proceedings of the 2011 Annual Workshop on Scheme and Functional Programming (2011)
2. Appel, A.W., McAllester, D.A.: An indexed model of recursive types for foundational proof-carrying code. ACM Trans. Program. Lang. Syst. **23**(5), 657–683 (2001)
3. Baader, F., Snyder, W.: Handbook of automated reasoning. In: Unification Theory. Elsevier Science Publishers B. V., Amsterdam, The Netherlands (2001)
4. Bertot, Y., Castéran, P.: Interactive Theorem Proving and Program Development - Coq'Art: The Calculus of Inductive Constructions. Texts in Theoretical Computer Science. An EATCS Series. Springer (2004)
5. Bove, A.: Programming in martin-löf type theory: Unification - a non-trivial example, pp. 22–42, Department of Computer Science, Chalmers University of Technology (1999)
6. Byrd, W.E.: Relational Programming in miniKanren: Techniques, Applications, and Implementations. PhD thesis, Indiana University (2009)
7. Byrd, W.E., Friedman, D.P.: αkanren: a fresh name in nominal logic programming. In: Proceedings of the 2007 Annual Workshop on Scheme and Functional Programming, pp. 79–90 (2007)
8. Byrd, W.E., Friedman, D.P., Kumar, R., Near, J.P.: A shallow Scheme embedding of bottom-avoiding streams. In: To appear in a special issue of Higher-Order and Symbolic Computation, in honor of Mitchell Wand's 60th birthday
9. Chlipala, A.: Certified Programming with Dependent Types - A Pragmatic Introduction to the Coq Proof Assistant. MIT Press, Cambridge (2013)
10. Debray, S.K., Mishra, P.: Denotational and operational semantics for PROLOG. In: Formal Description of Programming Concepts - III: Proceedings of the IFIP TC 2/WG 2.2 Working Conference on Formal Description of Programming Concepts - III, Ebberup, Denmark, 25–28 August 1986, pp. 245–274 (1987)
11. Despeyroux, J., Felty, A., Hirschowitz, A.: Higher-order abstract syntax in Coq. In: Dezani-Ciancaglini, M., Plotkin, G. (eds.) TLCA 1995. LNCS, vol. 902, pp. 124–138. Springer, Heidelberg (1995). https://doi.org/10.1007/BFb0014049
12. Friedman, D.P., Byrd, W.E., Kiselyov, O.: The Reasoned Schemer. MIT Press, Cambridge (2005)
13. Hemann, J., Friedman, D.P.: μKanren: a minimal functional core for relational programming. In: Proceedings of the 2013 Annual Workshop on Scheme and Functional Programming (2013)
14. Hemann, J., Friedman, D.P.: A framework for extending microKanren with constraints. In Proceedings 29th and 30th Workshops on (Constraint) Logic Programming and 24th International Workshop on Functional and (Constraint) Logic Programming, WLP 2015 / WLP 2016 / WFLP 2016, Dresden and Leipzig, Germany, 22nd September 2015 and 12–14th September 2016, pp. 135–149 (2017)
15. Hemann, J., Friedman, D.P., Byrd, W.E., Might, M.: A small embedding of logic programming with a simple complete search. In: Proceedings of the 12th Symposium on Dynamic Languages, DLS 2016, Amsterdam, The Netherlands, 1 Nov 2016, pp. 96–107 (2016)
16. Jones, N.D., Mycroft, A.: Stepwise development of operational and denotational semantics for Prolog. In: Proceedings of the 1984 International Symposium on Logic Programming, Atlantic City, New Jersey, USA, 6–9 Feb 1984, pp. 281–288 (1984)

17. Keller, R.M.: Formal verification of parallel programs. Commun. ACM **19**(7), 371–384 (1976)
18. Kiselyov, O., Shan, C., Friedman, D.P., Sabry, A.: Backtracking, interleaving, and terminating monad transformers: (functional pearl), pp. 192–203 (2005)
19. Kothari, S., Caldwell, J.: A machine checked model of idempotent MGU axioms for lists of equational constraints. In: Proceedings 24th International Workshop on Unification, UNIF 2010, Edinburgh, United Kingdom, 14th July 2010, pp. 24–38 (2010)
20. Kriener, J., King, A.: Semantics for Prolog with cut - revisited. In: Functional and Logic Programming - 12th International Symposium, FLOPS 2014, Kanazawa, Japan, 4–6 June 2014, Proceedings, pp. 270–284 (2014)
21. Kriener, J., King, A., Blazy, S.: Proofs you can believe. In: proving equivalences between Prolog semantics in Coq. In: 15th International Symposium on Principles and Practice of Declarative Programming, PPDP '13, Madrid, Spain, 16–18 Sept 2013, pp. 37–48 (2013)
22. Kumar, R.: Mechanising aspects of miniKanren in HOL. Bachelor Thesis, The Australian National University (2010)
23. Lloyd, J.W.: Foundations of Logic Programming, 1st edn. Springer (1984)
24. Lozov, P., Vyatkin, A., Boulytchev, D.: Typed relational conversion. In: Wang, M., Owens, S. (eds.) TFP 2017. LNCS, vol. 10788, pp. 39–58. Springer, Cham (2018). https://doi.org/10.1007/978-3-319-89719-6_3
25. McBride, C.: First-order unification by structural recursion. J. Funct. Program. **13**(6), 1061–1075 (2003)
26. Paulson, L.C.: Verifying the unification algorithm in LCF. Sci. Comput. Program. **5**(2), 143–169 (1985)
27. Pfenning, F., Elliott, C.: Higher-Order Abstract Syntax, pp. 199–208 (1988)
28. Ribeiro, R., Camarão, C.: A mechanized textbook proof of a type unification algorithm. In: Cornélio, M., Roscoe, B. (eds.) SBMF 2015. LNCS, vol. 9526, pp. 127–141. Springer, Cham (2016). https://doi.org/10.1007/978-3-319-29473-5_8
29. Rozplokhas, D., Boulytchev, D.: Improving refutational completeness of relational search via divergence test. In: Proceedings of the 20th International Symposium on Principles and Practice of Declarative Programming, PPDP 2018, Frankfurt am Main, Germany, 03–05 Sept 2018, pp. 18:1–18:13 (2018)
30. Swords, C., Friedman, D.P.: rKanren: guided search in miniKanren. In: Proceedings of the 2013 Annual Workshop on Scheme and Functional Programming (2013)
31. Tarski, A.: A lattice-theoretical fixpoint theorem and its applications. Pac. J. Math. **5**, 06 (1955)
32. Wadler, P.: Monads for functional programming. In: Advanced Functional Programming, First International Spring School on Advanced Functional Programming Techniques, Båstad, Sweden, 24–30 May 1995, Tutorial Text, pp. 24–52 (1995)

Algebraic and Coalgebraic Perspectives on Interaction Laws

Tarmo Uustalu[1,2] and Niels Voorneveld[2(✉)]

[1] Department of Computer Science, Reykjavik University, Reykjavik, Iceland
`tarmo@ru.is`
[2] Department of Software Science, Tallinn University of Technology, Tallinn, Estonia
`niels.voorneveld@taltech.ee`

Abstract. *Monad algebras*, turning computations over return values into values, are used to handle algebraic effects invoked by programs, whereas *comonad coalgebras*, turning initial states into environments ("cocomputations") over states, describe production of coalgebraic coeffects that can respond to effects. *(Monad-comonad) interaction laws* by Katsumata et al. describe interaction protocols between a computation and an environment. We show that any triple of those devices can be combined into a single algebra handling computations over state predicates. This method yields an isomorphism between the category of interaction laws, and the category of so-called *merge functors* which merge algebras and coalgebras to form combined algebras. In a similar vein, we can combine interaction laws with coalgebras only, retrieving Uustalu's stateful runners. If instead we combine interaction laws with algebras only, we get a novel concept of continuation-based runners that lift an environment of value predicates to a single predicate on computations of values. We use these notions to study different running examples of interactions of computations and environments.

Keywords: Monad algebras · Comonad coalgebras · Interaction laws · Runners · Monad morphisms · Effects · Coeffects

1 Introduction

Programs can exhibit effects which impact how they are run. Such effects (requests to the environment) may communicate with, invoke changes in, and otherwise influence the environment, producing coeffects (responses to the computation). How does one describe the protocols of such interactions?

Katsumata et al. [7] proposed to use *(monad-comonad) interaction laws*. We model the notion of effect using a monad T following Moggi [10], and the notion of coeffect using a comonad D, as pioneered by Power and Shkaravska [18]. The environment interacts with the effects, resolving some, ignoring others, and potentially producing new effects. A residual monad R is specified to capture these ignored and newly produced effects. This process of interaction is formalised using an R-residual interaction law between T and D.

© Springer Nature Switzerland AG 2020
B. C. d. S. Oliveira (Ed.): APLAS 2020, LNCS 12470, pp. 186–205, 2020.
https://doi.org/10.1007/978-3-030-64437-6_10

But there is more to say about running computations in interaction with environments from the "pragmatic" point of view: namely, how information is extracted from completed runs and how environments are prepared for runs.

We use algebras to interpret outcomes of completed runs, i.e., residual computations. Under favourable circumstances, algebras $\xi : RX \to X$ for a set of values X can be used to extract a single value from a computation over values; in this situation one often talks of them as *handlers* [16]. More generally, algebras can be used to observe or test computations, in terms of a set Z of observables (generalized truth values), as done, e.g., by Hasuo [5]. Algebras $\zeta : RZ \to Z$ lift value predicates $P : X \to Z$ to computation predicates $\zeta \circ RP : RX \to Z$.

Coalgebras $\chi : Y \to DY$, on the other hand, can be used to specify the environment that any initial state yields; an environment itself describing the response and state-change behaviour of a world a computation may be placed in. The carrier of such a coalgebra is the state set of the environment.

In this paper, we show that, given an algebra of R with carrier Z describing the handling of computations over observables, and a coalgebra of D with carrier Y describing the production of environments over states, we can turn an R-residual interaction law between T and D into a single algebra on T. This resulting algebra with carrier $Y \Rightarrow Z$ handles computations over state predicates, and can be used to describe, in one go, the behaviour of the whole system. This combination of tools gives rise to an isomorphism between the category of R-residual interaction laws between T and D and the category of *merge functors*, which merge coalgebras of D into algebras of R to form algebras of T.

We look at three running examples. One example is a computation which requests probabilistic weights from the environment for resolving nondeterministic choices. These weights are stored in the residual computation of weighted probabilistic choices. The second example incorporates an uncertain data reader, in which repeated state readings may be necessary before an effect is resolved, and each reading has an associated cost. We see this cost as an emergent effect resulting from the interaction, which we put in the residual computation. The last example combines probability with a comonadic model of global store.

There are many applications for this result on combining algebras, coalgebras and interaction laws. Firstly, it allows us to add program-environment interaction on top of pre-existing effect descriptions. For instance, if we have an algebra for an effect, e.g. a handler or some predicate lifting, it can be completed with an interaction law in order to add environments to the picture. This can, for instance, be seen in the last example, where we add global store to probability. Secondly, using algebras also enables us to describe more fully situations of program-environment interaction that cannot be analyzed in terms of an interaction law alone, as seen in the other two running examples. We thus obtain a flexible framework for describing, and potentially implementing, program-environment interactions.

The running examples are implemented using algebraic effects in the sense of Plotkin and Power [14,15] (see also Bauer [3]), which use effect operations from a signature that can be encoded by a functor F. To easily construct interaction laws, we use *functor-comonad interaction laws*. Such a law between F and D can be extended to an interaction law between the free monad on F and comonad D via an isomorphism.

Two additional descriptions lie between interaction laws and merge functors. Combining interaction laws only with coalgebras yields *stateful runners* [7,20], and combining them only with algebras yields a novel concept of *continuation-based* runners, lifting an environment over value predicates to a single predicate on computations over values. Both types of runners can also be described as monad morphisms.

The next two sections give some preliminaries, where Sect. 2 focusses on formulating handler algebras and producer coalgebras, and Sect. 3 studies interaction laws. Section 4 introduces merge functors, and Sect. 5 establishes their isomorphism with interaction laws. Section 6 presents a way to formulate interaction laws locally on effect operations, and lastly, Sect. 7 talks about stateful and continuation-based runners.

We introduce the categorical concepts necessary for following the main story of the paper, but side remarks use more advanced category theory. Throughout the paper, we work with one Cartesian closed base category $\mathcal{C}$. The examples are all for **Set**. We write $Y \Rightarrow Z$ and occasionally Z^Y for exponents.

2 Effect Handling and Coeffect Production

2.1 Effect Handling

Effectful programs may produce multiple return values, no return values, or different return values in different situations, and they may communicate information to the environment. Following Moggi [10], the behaviours of such programs are abstracted into effectful computations. Effectful computations over a set of return values X are elements of the set TX for T some monad. A computation represents the behaviours of the program in terms of the requests it makes to the world (effects) it is run in and values it eventually can return depending on how the requests are responded.

Given a computation $t \in TX$ over the set of return values X, we may want to retrieve a single return value. To this end, we can use a monad algebra of T.

Definition 1. *An algebra $\xi : TX \to X$ of the underlying functor of a monad $T = (T, \eta^T, \mu^T)$ is said to be a* monad algebra *if it satisfies the following equations:*

$$
\begin{array}{ccc}
X & & TTX \xrightarrow{\;T\xi\;} TX \\
\eta^T_X \downarrow \;\diagdown & & \mu^T_X \downarrow \qquad\quad \downarrow \xi \\
TX \xrightarrow[\;\xi\;]{} X & & TX \xrightarrow[\;\xi\;]{} X
\end{array}
$$

We denote the category of monad algebras of T by $\mathbf{Alg}(T)$. The Kleisli category $\mathbf{Kl}(T)$ is isomorphic to the full subcategory of $\mathbf{Alg}(T)$ given by monad algebras $\mu^T_X : T(TX) \to TX$ (the free algebras).

Besides directly extracting a return value from a computation, we can also use algebras to make observations about computations. Suppose that X is some set of values, Z is a set of observables, perhaps (generalized) truth values, and that RX for R some monad is the set of effectful computations over these values. Given a morphism $P : X \to Z$ that assigns observables to values (is a value predicate), an algebra $\zeta : RZ \to Z$ associates an observable to any given effectful computation via $\zeta \circ RP : RX \to Z$ (is a computation predicate).

Consider, for instance, the distributions monad $\mathcal{D}$. A randomized computation is represented by an element $t \in \mathcal{D}X$ for some value set X. Not every set X can be (meaningfully) endowed with an algebra structure $\xi : \mathcal{D}X \to X$: there may be no way of combining the many possible return values $x \in X$ appearing in a computation $t \in \mathcal{D}X$ into a single value.

A solution to this issue is to work with observations. We use a set of observables Z, which in this case we can take to be probabilities, the real number interval from 0 to 1 denoted by $[0, 1]$. Given some predicate on return values $P : X \to Z$ (assigning a probability to each $x \in X$), we can transform $t \in \mathcal{D}X$ into $(\mathcal{D}P)(t) \in \mathcal{D}[0, 1]$. We then use an algebra $\mathsf{E} : \mathcal{D}[0, 1] \to [0, 1]$ for calculating *expectations* to compute an observed probability for t.

We can take a more syntactical approach, describing effects using algebraic effect operations [15]. We consider a signature of effect operations Σ, each operation op having arity given by an object of the category $ar(\mathsf{op}) \in \mathcal{C}$. This arity tells us how many possible continuations there are for a program when this effect is encountered. For instance, a binary choice operation would have arity 2, meaning there are two continuations.

Given such a signature Σ, we generate the free monad $T_\Sigma X := \mu V. X + \sum_{\mathsf{op} \in \Sigma}(ar(\mathsf{op}) \Rightarrow V)$. Given $f : ar(\mathsf{op}) \Rightarrow T_\Sigma X$, we write $\mathsf{op}(f) \in T_\Sigma X$ for the appropriate element in $T_\Sigma X$. If $ar(\mathsf{op}) = n = \{0, \dots, n-1\}$ and $t_0, \dots, t_{n-1} \in T_\Sigma X$, we may alternatively write $\mathsf{op}(t_0, \dots, t_{n-1})$.

Example 1 (Probabilistic weights). Consider computations which can, for each $q \in [0, 1]$, have a q-weighted probabilistic binary choice or_q with $ar(\mathsf{or}_q) = \mathbf{2}$. Let $\Sigma := \{\mathsf{or}_q \mid q \in [0, 1]\}$, with computations over Z living in the free monad $RZ := T_\Sigma Z$ of binary leaf trees with nodes labelled with weights. As observables, we take expectations of truth $[0, 1]$, and we inductively define our algebra $\mathsf{Exp} : R[0, 1] \to [0, 1]$ by $\mathsf{Exp}(\mathsf{or}_q(x, y)) := (1 - q)\mathsf{Exp}(x) + q\mathsf{Exp}(y)$.

Example 2 (Cost of computations). We consider a simpler example where we associate a *cost* to certain computation steps. This can for instance represent time investment, or expenditure of some other resource like memory or energy. We consider a single tick operation $\Sigma := \{\mathsf{tick}\}$ with arity 1, and allow computation to continue forever: $RZ := \nu W. Z + W$. This monad is given by final coalgebras, not initial algebras, i.e., is not the free monad on the identity functor, but the free completely iterative monad in the sense of Aczel et al. [1], informally, the smallest monad that supports both the tick operation and (guarded) iteration. As an algebra, we take the cost tallying device $\mathsf{Tal} : R(\mathbb{N}_\infty) \to \mathbb{N}_\infty$ given by $\mathsf{Tal}(\mathsf{tick}(t)) = 1 + \mathsf{Tal}(t)$ for finite sequences of ticks and $\mathsf{Tal}(t) = \infty$ for t the infinite sequence of ticks.

2.2   Coeffect Production

On the other side of the story, we consider environments. They react to requests of the computation, but are otherwise passive. An environment reacts to requests by responding, and it also has a state that it changes as it responds. Such a process is called coeffectful. Notions of coeffect can be modelled with a comonad D. Environments over a state set Y are elements of DY; an environment is a description of the response and state-change behaviour of the world, including an initial state, which can be extracted using the counit ε_Y.

Most of the work on coeffects modelled by comonads has concentrated on scenarios where a notion of computation is coeffectful by primarily relying on coeffect *consumption* (coeffect *cooperations*); computations are modelled by co-Kleisli arrows, e.g., [12,22]. Typical examples of this are computations with causal stream functions (dataflow computation) and stencil computations (a.k.a. cellular automata) [4,21]. Here, in contrast, we are interested not in coeffectful computations, but in coeffectful environments. Central for us in this endeavour are coeffect *producers*, which are coalgebras of the comonad. They assign to every initial state drawn from a fixed state set an environment in a consistent way: given an environment assigned to some initial state by a coeffect producer, its continuation from any point must be obtainable by applying the coeffect producer to the state reached by that point as the new initial state. See, e.g., [13,18,20] for examples.

Definition 2. *An coalgebra* $\chi : Y \to DY$ *of the underlying functor of a comonad* $D = (D, \varepsilon, \delta)$ *is called a* comonad coalgebra *if it satisfies the following equations:*

$$
\begin{array}{cc}
\begin{array}{c}
Y \\
{\scriptstyle \varepsilon_Y} \uparrow \quad \diagdown \\
DY \xleftarrow{\quad} Y \\
\qquad \chi
\end{array}
&
\begin{array}{ccc}
DDY & \xleftarrow{D\chi} & DY \\
{\scriptstyle \delta_Y} \uparrow & & \uparrow {\scriptstyle \chi} \\
DY & \xleftarrow{\quad \chi \quad} & Y
\end{array}
\end{array}
$$

Let **Coalg**(D) be the category of comonad coalgebras on D. The coKleisli category **CoKl**(D) is isomorphic to the full subcategory of **Coalg**(D) given by comonad coalgebras $\delta_Y : DY \to D(DY)$ (the cofree coalgebras).

To facilitate the description of examples, we can again take a more syntactical approach. Typically, a coeffect is described using coalgebraic cooperations. We consider a signature Π of such cooperations, each $\mathsf{cop} \in \Pi$ having an arity $ar(\mathsf{cop}) \in \mathcal{C}$. The arity gives the range of responses the environment can give.

The state of the environment contains for each cooperation a particular response and a new environment. Given a signature Π, we consider the cofree comonad $D_\Pi Y := \nu W. Y \times \Pi_{\mathsf{cop} \in \Pi}(ar(\mathsf{cop}) \times W)$. Supposing $e \in D_\Pi Y$ and $\mathsf{cop} \in \Pi$, we have that $\mathsf{cop}(e) \in ar(\mathsf{cop}) \times D_\Pi Y$ is a pair (c, e') consisting of a piece of data c provided by the environment and the continuation of the environment e'.

Example 3 (Stream of data). Given some object of data C, we consider an environment which can supply a *stream* of datapoints from C. We take one cooperation $\Pi := \{\mathsf{give}\}$ of arity C, and consider the comonad $DY := D_\Pi Y \cong$

$\nu W.Y \times (C \times W) \cong (Y \times C)^{\mathbb{N}}$ of streams over $Y \times C$. As environment we take $E := C^{\mathbb{N}} \cong D1$. The *producer* is the cofree coalgebra $\delta_1 : E \to DE$, which sends a stream σ to $\delta_1(\sigma)$ where $\mathsf{give}(\delta_1(\sigma)) := (\sigma(0), \delta_1(\lambda n.\, \sigma(n+1)))$.

Example 4 (Global store). We consider a set of data C, and an environment which has one datapoint from C stored in its memory. We have $\Pi := \{\mathsf{give}\} \cup \{\mathsf{change}_c \mid c \in C\}$, where $ar(\mathsf{give}) := C$ and $ar(\mathsf{change}_c) := 1$. We can take $DY := D_\Pi Y \cong \nu W.Y \times (C \times W) \times (1 \times W)^C$ to be the cofree comonad, which allows for giving and receiving data C. A producer for a *global store* environment generates from a global state the appropriate environment which acts in the following way: (1) when data is provided on request, the internal state does not change, and (2) when data is received, the environment changes its internal state accordingly. We formulate the producer $\mathsf{GS} : Y \to DY$ with $Y := C$ where $\mathsf{give}(\mathsf{GS}(c)) := (c, \mathsf{GS}(c))$ and $\mathsf{change}_d(\mathsf{GS}(c)) := (*, \mathsf{GS}(d))$. A smaller comonad defined by $D'Y := C \times (C \Rightarrow Y)$ allows only producers that obey the coequations of global store; these amount to arrays, a.k.a. lenses. The set $D'Y$ consists of the elements of DY satisfying the coequations; as seen in the literature [13,18].

3   Interaction Laws

We now formulate how computations can interact with environments, with coeffects reacting to effects. Supposing we have the effects of interest described by some monad T, and the coeffects by a comonad D, an *interaction law* between T and D tells us how coeffects can be used to resolve effects.

In general, not all effects of a computation may be resolved by the environment it is run against. Moreover, the interaction between effects and coeffects may produce new effects. We therefore use another monad $R = (R, \eta, \mu)$ for residual effects. We study R-residual interaction laws of T and D by Katsumata et al. [7]. They are an elaboration of ideas and abstraction of concepts by Plotkin and Power [13] and Møgelberg and Staton [9].

Definition 3. *An R-residual interaction law of $T = (T, \eta^T, \mu^T)$ and $D = (D, \varepsilon, \delta)$ is given by a natural transformation typed $\psi^{(1)}_{X,Y} : TX \times DY \to R(X \times Y)$ satisfying the (co)unit and (co)multiplication agreement equations*

By the Yoneda lemma, a natural transformation $\psi^{(1)}$ above can be alternatively given as a natural transformation typed [1]

$$\psi^{(0)}_{X,Y,Z} : \mathcal{C}(X \times Y, Z) \to \mathcal{C}(TX \times DY, RZ)$$

---

[1] Note that this is not the same in general as to have a natural transformation typed $X \times Y \Rightarrow Z \to TX \times DY \Rightarrow RZ$.

and therefore by Currying and symmetry also by natural transformations

$$\psi^{(2)}_{X,Z} : D(X \Rightarrow Z) \to TX \Rightarrow RZ, \qquad \psi^{(3)}_{Y,Z} : T(Y \Rightarrow Z) \to DY \Rightarrow RZ.$$

In this paper, we use all these formats, especially the 3rd in the next few sections. Translating the equations of interaction laws into the 3rd format, we get:

$$
Y \Rightarrow Z \xrightarrow{\eta^T_{Y \Rightarrow Z}} T(Y \Rightarrow Z) \qquad TT(Y \Rightarrow Z) \xrightarrow{T\psi_{Y,Z}} T(DY \Rightarrow RZ) \xrightarrow{\psi_{DY,RZ}} DDY \Rightarrow RRZ
$$
$$
\varepsilon_Y \Rightarrow \eta_Z \searrow \quad \downarrow \psi_{Y,Z} \qquad \mu^T_{Y \Rightarrow Z} \downarrow \qquad\qquad\qquad\qquad\qquad \downarrow \delta_Y \Rightarrow \mu_Z
$$
$$
DY \Rightarrow RZ \qquad\qquad T(Y \Rightarrow Z) \xrightarrow{\qquad\qquad \psi_{Y,Z} \qquad\qquad} DY \Rightarrow RZ
$$

We will write $\mathbf{MCIL}_R(T, D)$ for the set of R-residual interaction laws between T and D (ignoring the exact format chosen).

The intuition for interaction laws is as follows. In the 0th format, X is the set of return values of computations, Y is the state set of environments and Z is the set of observables (or truth values). An interaction law ψ says that, as soon as we know how to observe a value-state pair, a computation over values and an environment can be combined to yield a computation over observables. It must be natural in X, Y, Z to reflect that interactions only pass values, states and observables around, but do not inspect them. In the 1st format, the observables are $X \times Y$, i.e., value-state pairs are directly observable. In the 2nd format, the states of environments are $X \Rightarrow Z$, i.e., value predicates. In the 3rd format, the values that given computations return are $Y \Rightarrow Z$, i.e., state predicates.

Later in the paper, we will use algebras and coalgebras to explain what interaction laws do in different terms.

Example 5 (Probabilistic weight requester). In this example, computations may have to make certain binary choices. They are represented by binary trees $TX := T_{\Sigma'}X$ where Σ' has one operation or of arity $\mathbf{2}$. To make a nondeterministic choice, a computation requests a probabilistic weight from its environment. This environment is given by a stream DY of such weights as in Example 3, using as data object $C := [0, 1]$. Having received a weight for each choice, it generates a tree of probabilistic choices: $RZ := T_\Sigma Z$ as in Example 1. This is done using an *interaction law* $\psi_{Y,Z} : T(Y \Rightarrow Z) \to DY \Rightarrow RZ$ where:

$-\ \psi_{Y,Z}(\mathsf{or}(a, b))(e) := \mathsf{or}_q(\psi_{Y,Z}(a)(e'), \psi_{Y,Z}(b)(e')), \quad \text{if } (q, e') = \mathsf{give}(e).$

Example 6 (Uncertain stream reader). We use DY as in Example 3, and consider a computation which can request datapoints (elements of a set C) from its environment. Programs use one effect operation $\Sigma' := \{\mathsf{get}\}$ with $ar(\mathsf{get}) := C$ and $TX := T_{\Sigma'}X$. Upon a request, the environment will keep giving datapoints until it gives the same datapoint twice in a row. We associate to each give a cost, which we store with a tick in the residual computation in $RZ := \nu W. Z + W$, as given in Example 2. We describe this multistep protocol with the interaction law $\psi_{Y,Z}$ as follows: given $e \in DY$, with $(c_0, e_0) := \mathsf{give}(e)$, and $(c_1, e_1) := \mathsf{give}(e_0)$:

$$
-\ \psi_{Y,Z}(\mathsf{get}(f))(e) := \begin{cases} \mathsf{tick}(\mathsf{tick}(\psi_{Y,Z}(f(c_0))(e_1))) & \text{if } c_0 = c_1, \\ \mathsf{tick}(\psi_{Y,Z}(\mathsf{get}(f))(e_0)) & \text{if } c_0 \neq c_1 \ . \end{cases}
$$

Example 7 (Combining global store with probability). Lastly, we consider a more traditional example, where some but not all effects are resolved, and no new effects are generated. Take Σ and Π from Examples 1 and 4 respectively, and let $\Sigma' := \Sigma + \{\mathsf{lookup}, \mathsf{update}_c \mid c \in C\}$ where $ar(\mathsf{lookup}) := C$ and $ar(\mathsf{update}_c) := 1$. We take computations which can request and update a global store, and make probabilistic choices, denoted by $TX := T_{\Sigma'}X$. As comonad we use the environment $DY := D_\Pi Y$, and as residual monad $RZ := R_\Sigma Z$ the weighted choice trees. The interaction law $\psi_{Y,Z}$ resolves only the global store requests. For $e \in DY$, let $(c, e') := \mathsf{give}(e)$, and for each $d \in C$ let $(*, e_d) := \mathsf{change}_d(e)$, then

- $\psi_{Y,Z}(\mathsf{lookup}(f))(e) := \psi_{Y,Z}(f(c))(e')$,
- $\psi_{Y,Z}(\mathsf{update}_d(t))(e) := \psi_{Y,Z}(t)(e_d)$,
- $\psi_{Y,Z}(\mathsf{or}_q(a, b))(e) := \mathsf{or}_q(\psi_{Y,Z}(a)(e), \psi_{Y,Z}(b)(e))$.

In Sect. 6, we discuss a method for showing that the above constructions satisfy the unit and multiplication equations for interaction laws.

Katsumata et al. [7] proved that R-residual interaction laws of T, D are in a bijection with monad morphisms from T to the monad $D \twoheadrightarrow R$ where $D \twoheadrightarrow -$ is the right adjoint of $- \star D$ and $\star$ is the Day convolution. This monad is explicitly given by $(D \twoheadrightarrow R)X = \int_Y DY \Rightarrow R(X \times Y) \cong \int_{Y,Z} C(X \times Y, Z) \pitchfork (DY \Rightarrow RZ) \cong \int_Z D(X \Rightarrow Z) \Rightarrow RZ$ (with $\int$ with subscript for ends and $\pitchfork$ for powers).

A *morphism* between two interaction laws (T, D, R, ψ) and (T', D', R', ψ') is given by (co)monad morphisms $t : T \to T'$, $d : D' \to D$ and $r : R \to R'$ satisfying the left equation below for the 1st format and the right equation for the 3rd format:

$$
\begin{array}{ccc}
TX \times DY \xrightarrow{\psi_{X,Y}} R(X \times Y) & \qquad & T(Y \Rightarrow Z) \xrightarrow{\psi_{X,Y}} DY \Rightarrow RZ \\
\big\downarrow{\scriptstyle TX \times d_Y} \qquad \big\downarrow{\scriptstyle r_{X \times Y}} & & \big\downarrow{\scriptstyle t_{Y \Rightarrow Z}} \qquad \big\downarrow{\scriptstyle d_Y \Rightarrow r_Z} \\
T'X \times D'Y \xrightarrow{\psi'_{X,Y}} R'(X \times Y) & & T'(Y \Rightarrow Z) \xrightarrow{\psi'_{X,Y}} D'Y \Rightarrow R'Z \\
{\scriptstyle t_X \times D'Y} & &
\end{array}
$$

(Note the direction of d.) Interaction laws form a category. The bijection with monad morphisms extends to an isomorphism of categories, see [7].

4   Merge Functors

We are interested in how interaction laws can be combined with algebras for handling residual effects and coalgebras for producing coeffects. In general, we get what we call a merge functor. This merges a coalgebra into an algebra creating a new algebra.

Definition 4. *A merge functor for T, D, R is given by a functor $M :$ $(\mathbf{Coalg}(D))^{\mathrm{op}} \times \mathbf{Alg}(R) \to \mathbf{Alg}(T)$ which is carrier-exponentiating:*

$$
\begin{array}{ccc}
(\mathbf{Coalg}(D))^{\mathrm{op}} \times \mathbf{Alg}(R) & \xrightarrow{\;M\;} & \mathbf{Alg}(T) \\
\big\downarrow{\scriptstyle U^{\mathrm{op}} \times U} & & \big\downarrow{\scriptstyle U} \\
\mathcal{C}^{\mathrm{op}} \times \mathcal{C} & \xrightarrow[\;\Rightarrow\;]{} & \mathcal{C}
\end{array}
$$

U are the relevant forgetful functors, which are the left (resp. right) adjoints of the co-Eilenberg-Moore (resp. Eilenberg-Moore) adjunctions of D (resp. R, T).

Note in particular the three conditions which need to hold for M to be a merge functor:

- Every functor algebra in the image of M needs to be a monad algebra;
- M needs to be functorial in its comonad coalgebra and monad algebra arguments, sending coalgebra and algebra morphisms to an algebra morphism;
- On the level of carriers, M needs to be the exponentiation function.

Here is a variation of merge functors. A *Kleisli merge functor* for T, D, R is a functor $N : (\mathbf{CoKl}(D))^{\mathrm{op}} \times \mathbf{Kl}(R) \to \mathbf{Alg}(T)$ which is carrier-exponentiating in the sense that

$$
\begin{array}{ccc}
(\mathbf{CoKl}(D))^{\mathrm{op}} \times \mathbf{Kl}(R) & \xrightarrow{\ N\ } & \mathbf{Alg}(T) \\
\downarrow{\scriptstyle F^{\mathrm{op}} \times F} & \Rightarrow & \downarrow{\scriptstyle U} \\
\mathcal{C}^{\mathrm{op}} \times \mathcal{C} & \longrightarrow & \mathcal{C}
\end{array}
$$

where $F : \mathbf{CoKl}(D) \to \mathcal{C}$ is the left adjoint of the coKleisli adjunction of D and $F : \mathbf{Kl}(R) \to \mathcal{C}$ is the right adjoint of the Kleisli adjunction of R.

Here and in the rest of this paper, when we refer to $\mathbf{CoKl}(D)$, we mean the full subcategory of $\mathbf{Coalg}(D)$ given by the cofree coalgebras, which is isomorphic, and similarly for $\mathbf{Kl}(R)$ and the full subcategory of $\mathbf{Alg}(R)$ given by the free algebras. Under this view, the two functors F are still forgetful functors.[2]

Proposition 1. *Any Kleisli merge functor has a unique extension to merge functors. This gives us a bijection between the sets of merge functors and Kleisli merge functors for T, D, R:*

$$
\frac{(\mathbf{CoKl}(D))^{\mathrm{op}} \times \mathbf{Kl}(R) \to_{\mathrm{ce.}} \mathbf{Alg}(T)}{(\mathbf{Coalg}(D))^{\mathrm{op}} \times \mathbf{Alg}(R) \to_{\mathrm{ce.}} \mathbf{Alg}(T)}
$$

(where 'ce.' stands for carrier-exponentiating).

To see why this is, let us observe the following. Suppose we have a merge functor $M : \mathbf{Coalg}(D)^{\mathrm{op}} \times \mathbf{Alg}(R) \to \mathbf{Alg}(T)$. For any comonad coalgebra $\chi : Y \to DY$ and any monad algebra $\zeta : RZ \to Z$, by functoriality of M and the counit and unit equations of χ and ζ, we have

$$
\begin{array}{ccccc}
T(Y \Rightarrow Z) & \xrightarrow{T(\varepsilon_Y \Rightarrow \eta_Z)} & T(DY \Rightarrow RZ) & \xrightarrow{M(\delta_Y, \mu_Z)} & DY \Rightarrow RZ \\
 & \underset{T(\chi \Rightarrow \zeta)}{\searrow} & \downarrow & & \downarrow{\scriptstyle \chi \Rightarrow \zeta} \\
 & & T(Y \Rightarrow Z) & \xrightarrow{M(\chi, \zeta)} & Y \Rightarrow Z
\end{array}
$$

This uses functoriality of M on the facts that χ is a coalgebra morphism from χ to δ_Y and that ζ is an algebra morphism from μ_Z to ζ, which are consequences of the comultiplication and multiplication equations of χ and ζ.

---

[2] Namely, they send δ_Y^D and μ_Z^R to DY and RZ respectively.

So any merge functor is determined by its Kleisli merge sub-functor. We therefore have but one candidate for extending a given Kleisli merge functor N : $(\mathbf{CoKl}(D))^{\mathrm{op}} \times \mathbf{Kl}(R) \to \mathbf{Alg}(T)$ into a merge functor $\widehat{N}$, which is: $\widehat{N}(\chi, \zeta) = (\chi \Rightarrow \zeta) \circ N(\delta_Y, \mu_Z) \circ T(\varepsilon_Y \Rightarrow \eta_Z)$. It is easy to show that $\widehat{N}$ is functorial and that the functor algebras it delivers are monad algebras.

5   The Interaction Law, Merge Functor Isomorphism

Given an interaction law ψ, we define a Kleisli merge functor M_ψ as follows. For a cofree coalgebra $\delta_Y : DY \to DDY$ and a free algebra $\mu_Z : RRZ \to RZ$, we construct an algebra

$$M_\psi(\delta_Y, \mu_Z) := T(DY \Rightarrow RZ) \xrightarrow{\psi_{DY,RZ}} DDY \Rightarrow RRZ \xrightarrow{\delta_Y \Rightarrow \mu_Z} DY \Rightarrow RZ.$$

M_ψ is easily seen to be functorial and delivering monad algebras.

The construction $M_{(-)}$ gives rise to the following coincidence.

Proposition 2. *There is a bijection between R-residual interaction laws of T and D, and Kleisli merge functors for T, D, R:*

$$\frac{\mathbf{MCIL}_R(T, D)}{(\mathbf{CoKl}(D))^{\mathrm{op}} \times \mathbf{Kl}(R) \to_{\mathrm{ce.}} \mathbf{Alg}(T)}$$

We need to show that the construction $M_{(-)}$ gives a bijection. We do this by explicitly defining the inverse. Given a Kleisli merge functor $M : (\mathbf{CoKl}(D))^{\mathrm{op}} \times \mathbf{Kl}(R) \to \mathbf{Alg}(T)$, we construct a natural transformation

$$\psi^M_{Y,Z} :- T(Y \Rightarrow Z) \xrightarrow{T(\varepsilon_Y \Rightarrow \eta_Z)} T(DY \Rightarrow RZ) \xrightarrow{M(\delta_Y, \mu_Z)} DY \Rightarrow RZ$$

It is easy to verify that ψ^M fulfills the conditions of an interaction law.

Lemma 1. *The construction $\psi^{(-)}$ is an inverse to the construction $M_{(-)}$.*

Proof. We show that $\psi^{M_\psi} = \psi$.

The diagram commutes by the definition of M_ψ, the (co)unit and (co)multiplication equations of ψ, and right unitality of T. As the path at the top is the constructed interaction law ψ^{M_ψ}, and that at the bottom is the given interaction law ψ, the two coincide.

We show that $M^{\psi_M} = M$:

$$T(DY \Rightarrow RZ) \xrightarrow[]{\;\; T(\varepsilon_{DY} \Rightarrow \eta_{RZ})\;\;} T(DDY \Rightarrow RRZ) \xrightarrow{M(\delta_{DY}, \mu_{RZ})} DDY \Rightarrow RRZ$$

(with the curved top arrow labelled $\psi^M_{DY,RZ}$)

$$\downarrow T(\delta_Y \Rightarrow \mu_Z) \qquad\qquad \downarrow \delta_Y \Rightarrow \mu_Z$$

$$T(DY \Rightarrow RZ) \xrightarrow{M(\delta_Y, \mu_Z)} DY \Rightarrow RZ$$

The diagram commutes by the definition of ψ^M, left unitality of D and R and functoriality of M applied to the facts that δ_Y and μ_Z are (co)algebra morphisms. Following the top path, we get the constructed merge function M_{ψ^M}, whereas following the bottom path yields the given merge function M. We conclude that the two coincide. □

This finishes the proof of Proposition 2. Combining this with Proposition 1, we have proved the following.

Corollary 1. *There is a bijection between R-residual interaction laws of T, D and merge functors for T, D, R.*

Explicitly, the bijection of Corollary 1 sends an interaction law ψ to M_ψ : $(\mathbf{Coalg}(D))^{\mathrm{op}} \times \mathbf{Alg}(R) \to \mathbf{Alg}(T)$ which does:

$$M_\psi(\chi : Y \to DY, \zeta : RZ \to Z) := T(Y \Rightarrow Z) \xrightarrow{\psi_{Y,Z}} DY \Rightarrow RZ \xrightarrow{\chi \Rightarrow \zeta} Y \Rightarrow Z \ .$$

Example 8 (Probabilistic weight requester). We use the interaction law ψ from Example 5 to merge the coalgebra δ_1 from Example 3 into the algebra Exp from Example 1. We get $M_\psi(\delta_1, \mathsf{Exp}) : T(E \Rightarrow [0,1]) \to E \Rightarrow [0,1]$, with as carrier set the $[0,1]$-valued predicates on streams $E = [0,1]^{\mathbb{N}}$. Suppose we have some predicate $P : X \to E \Rightarrow [0,1]$ giving some expectation to each return value and final state. Then, given some computation $t \in TX$, we can find the weakest precondition $M_\psi(\delta_1, \mathsf{Exp})(TP(t)) \in E \Rightarrow [0,1]$, which gives, for each initial state e of the environment, the expectation of the computation, determined by the postcondition P on the return value and the final states yielded.

Example 9 (Uncertain stream reader). We use the interaction law ψ from Example 6 to merge the coalgebra δ_1 from Example 3 into the algebra Tal from Example 2. We get $M_\psi(\delta_1, \mathsf{Tal}) : T(E \Rightarrow \mathbb{N}_\infty) \to E \Rightarrow \mathbb{N}_\infty$, with as carrier set $\mathbb{N}_\infty$-valued predicates on streams $E = C^{\mathbb{N}}$. This merged algebra computes, for each initial state of the environment, how many responses the environment gives during the interaction, and adds it to the perceived value of the final state. Streams which behave unreliably will naturally give more datapoints, as they create more uncertainty. For instance, the stream $10000\ldots$ will make a program return the same values as the stream $0000\ldots$, but it may invoke more ticks (one more tick) than the latter. So, for each $t \in T(E \Rightarrow \mathbb{N}_\infty)$, $M_\psi(\delta_1, \mathsf{Tal})(t)(10000\ldots) \geq M_\psi(\delta_1, \mathsf{Tal})(t)(0000\ldots)$.

Example 10 (Combining global store with probability). Lastly, we use the interaction law ψ from Example 7 to merge GS from Example 4 into Exp from Example 1. We retrieve the algebra $M_\psi(\mathsf{GS}, \mathsf{Exp}) : T(C \Rightarrow [0,1]) \to C \Rightarrow [0,1]$ from previous work [23], whose carrier set is given by $[0,1]$-valued store predicates.

We have not yet specified what a morphism between merge functors is. We define them so that they will coincide with morphisms between interaction laws. We say that a morphism between two merge functors (T, D, R, M) and (T', D', R', M') is a triple of (co)monad morphisms $t : T \to T'$, $d : D' \to D$ and $r : R \to R'$ such that, for any comonad coalgebra $\chi : Y \to D'Y$ and any monad algebra $\zeta : R'Z \to Z$, $M'(\chi, \zeta) \circ t_{Y \Rightarrow Z} = M(d_Y \circ \chi, \zeta \circ r_Z)$.

Proposition 3. *A triple (t, d, r) of (co)monad morphisms forms a morphism between interaction laws ψ and ψ' if and only if it is a morphism between merge functors M_ψ and $M_{\psi'}$.*

Corollary 2. *The category of residual interaction laws is isomorphic to the category of merge functors, thus preserving the underlying (co)monads.*

Since the isomorphism preserves the underlying (co)monads of its objects, we can also fix some of T, D, and R, and the isomorphism still holds. For instance, we get an isomorphism between R-residual interaction laws for some fixed R, and the category of merge functors for the same fixed R, with D and T varying.

6   Interaction Laws for Free Monads

One thing we have not yet done is show that the interaction laws of the examples satisfy the unit and multiplication equations. This is often tedious to do in practice. In this section, we discuss a recipe for generating interaction laws when T is a free monad. This recipe is exhaustive and without redundancy: it generates all interaction laws exactly once. We start with a general Cartesian closed category $\mathcal{C}$ first, and do some further simplifications for **Set** later on.

Given a functor F, the underlying functor T of the free monad on F is given by initial algebra carriers: $TX := \mu V. X + FV$. The structure maps $X + FTX \to TX$ split into $\eta_X^T : X \to TX$ and $\sigma_X : FTX \to TX$. The unit is η_X^T and the multiplication μ_X^T is the unique solution to the initial algebra diagram:

$$
\begin{array}{ccccc}
TX & \xrightarrow{\eta_{TX}^T} & TTX & \xleftarrow{\sigma_{TX}} & FTTX \\
 & \searrow & \downarrow{\mu_X^T} & & \downarrow{F\mu_X^T} \\
 & & TX & \xleftarrow{\sigma_X} & FTX
\end{array}
$$

Now R-residual interaction laws between D and T can be defined in "small steps", in terms of F, giving rise to the following result.

Proposition 4. *If T is the free monad on F, then there is a bijection between R-residual interaction laws of T, D and natural transformations typed $\phi_{Y,Z} : F(Y \Rightarrow Z) \to DY \Rightarrow RZ$ (subject to no equations!).*

The natural transformation $\phi_{Y,Z}$ given above can also be seen as a *functor-comonad interaction law*; an intermediate between functor-functor and monad-comonad interaction laws of Katsumata et al. [7].

Given a functor-comonad interaction law $\phi_{Y,Z}$, we construct a natural transformation $\psi_{Y,Z}$ as the unique solution of the following initial algebra diagram:

$$
\begin{array}{ccc}
Y \Rightarrow Z \xrightarrow{\eta^T_{Y \Rightarrow Z}} T(Y \Rightarrow Z) & \xleftarrow{\quad\sigma_{Y \Rightarrow Z}\quad} & FT(Y \Rightarrow Z) \\
{\scriptstyle \varepsilon_Y \Rightarrow \eta_Z} \searrow \quad \downarrow{\scriptstyle \psi_{Y,Z}} & & \downarrow{\scriptstyle F\psi_{Y,Z}} \\
DY \Rightarrow RZ \xleftarrow{\delta_Y \Rightarrow \mu_Z} DDY \Rightarrow RRZ & \xleftarrow{\phi_{DY,RZ}} & F(DY \Rightarrow RZ)
\end{array}
$$

The natural transformation ψ satisfies the equations of a monad-comonad interaction law. In the reverse direction, we extract from a given monad-comonad interaction law ψ a natural transformation ϕ as follows:

$$
\phi_{Y,Z} := F(Y \Rightarrow Z) \xrightarrow{F\eta^T_{Y \Rightarrow Z}} FT(Y \Rightarrow Z) \xrightarrow{\sigma_{Y \Rightarrow Z}} T(Y \Rightarrow Z) \xrightarrow{\psi_{Y,Z}} DY \Rightarrow RZ
$$

Combining the proposition with Corollary 1, we get a corollary exploiting that the category $\mathbf{Alg}(T)$ is isomorphic to $\mathbf{alg}(F)$.

Corollary 3. *There is a bijection between R-residual functor-comonad interaction laws of F and D and functors $(\mathbf{Coalg}(D))^{\mathrm{op}} \times \mathbf{Alg}(R) \to \mathbf{alg}(F)$ that are exponentiation on the level of carriers.*

In the particular case of our examples, where $FX := \sum_{\mathsf{op} \in \Sigma}(ar(\mathsf{op}) \Rightarrow X)$, the functor-comonnad interaction law ϕ required for specifying the monad-comonad interaction law ψ decomposes, for each effect operation $\mathsf{op} \in \Sigma$, into a transformation $ar(\mathsf{op}) \Rightarrow (Y \Rightarrow Z) \to DY \Rightarrow RZ$ natural in Y and Z, an *operation-wise interaction law*. If R is strong and these natural transformations are strong in Z, which holds for our examples since they are in the category of sets, these natural transformations amount to transformations $\phi_Y^{\mathsf{op}} : DY \to R(ar(\mathsf{op}) \times Y)$ natural in Y for each operation op.

The transformation ϕ_Y^{op} specifies what happens when the operation op is encountered in the evaluation of some program. It tells us, given an environment, which effects are encountered, which continuation is chosen for the program, and what the new state is. The resulting interaction law ψ induced by our ϕ's given Proposition 4 will satisfy the following equation:

$$
\psi_{Y,Z}(\mathsf{op}(t_1, \ldots, t_n))(e) = \mu_Z(R(\lambda(i, e').\psi_{Y,Z}(t_i)(e')) (\phi_{DY}^{\mathsf{op}}(\delta_Y(e)))) \tag{1}
$$

We show that the interaction laws for the examples satisfy the desired equations. This is done by specifying the natural transformations in such a way that the induced Eq. 1 coincides with the specification required in the examples.

For Example 5, where we have one operation or of arity $2 = \{0, 1\}$, we define: $\phi_Y^{\mathsf{or}}(e) := \mathsf{or}_q(\eta_Z(0, y), \eta_Z(1, y))$, where $(q, e') := \mathsf{give}(e)$ and $y := \varepsilon_Y(e')$. The transformation ϕ^{or}, which is obviously natural, tells us to allocate a probability of q to continue with 0, and $1 - q$ probability to continue with 1, and to finish in both cases in the next state, which is y.

The local transformation for Example 6 is slightly more involved. Here we have an effect operation get of arity C. The transformation $\phi_Y^{\text{get}} : DY \to R(C \times Y)$ keeps applying give until the same data point comes out twice in a row (which may never happen) and returns the corresponding number of ticks and that data point and the final state (or an infinite sequence of ticks).

It is possible to design methods for defining interaction laws, using the above ideas. We would specify how to naturally generate three things from the environment: (1) which residual effects we get, (2) what piece of data is communicated to the program (the continuation), and (3) what is the state afterwards.

7   Runners

We have seen how an interaction law can be combined with a coalgebra of D and an algebra of R to yield an algebra of T. There are also intermediate constructions, combining the interaction law with only a coalgebra or an algebra. Depending on the choice, we get different results. Since they amount to monad morphisms from T to other monads, it is justified to call them runners.

7.1   Stateful Runners

Combining interaction laws with just coalgebras (rather than coalgebras and algebras) yields stateful runners in the sense of Uustalu [20].

An R-residual *stateful runner* of T for an object $Y \in \mathcal{C}$ is a natural transformation typed $\theta_X : TX \times Y \to R(X \times Y)$ subject to appropriate equations. With the appropriate concept of map, stateful runners make a category $\mathbf{Run}_R(T)$.

The following result gives alternative characterizations of stateful runners.

Proposition 5. *For any object $Y \in \mathcal{C}$, the following sets are in bijection:*

1. *R-residual stateful runners of T with carrier Y,*
2. *monad morphisms from T to St_Y^R, the R-transformed state monad for state set Y, defined by $\mathsf{St}_Y^R X := Y \Rightarrow R(X \times Y)$,*
3. *functors $\Theta : \mathbf{Alg}(R) \to \mathbf{Alg}(T)$ such that*

$$
\begin{array}{ccc}
\mathbf{Alg}(R) & \xrightarrow{\;\Theta\;} & \mathbf{Alg}(T) \\
{\scriptstyle U}\downarrow & & \downarrow{\scriptstyle U} \\
\mathcal{C} & \xrightarrow[\;Y\Rightarrow-\;]{} & \mathcal{C}
\end{array}
$$

The bijection between the first two items was pointed out in previous work [7, 20]. These bijections extend to isomorphisms of the relevant total categories such as $\mathbf{Run}_R(T)$.

From the bijection between the 1st and 3rd item, by Corollary 1, we can conclude that interaction laws are in bijection with D-*coalgebraic specifications* of runners, which we define to be carrier-preserving functors $\Psi : \mathbf{Coalg}(D) \to \mathbf{Run}_R(T)$. Katsumata et al. [7] proved this bijection directly, rather than from Corollary 1 and Proposition 5, circumventing functors $\mathbf{Alg}(R) \to \mathbf{Alg}(T)$.

Explicitly, given an interaction law ψ (in the 1st format), the runner spec Ψ for comonad coalgebras $\chi : Y \to DY$ is given by

$$(\Psi \chi)_X := TX \times Y \xrightarrow{\;TX \times \chi\;} TX \times DY \xrightarrow{\;\psi_{X,Y}\;} R(X \times Y) \; .$$

Given a runner spec Ψ, the interaction law is defined by

$$\psi_{X,Y} := TX \times DY \xrightarrow{\;(\Psi \delta_Y)_X\;} R(X \times DY) \xrightarrow{\;R(X \times \varepsilon_Y)\;} R(X \times Y) \; .$$

Ahman and Bauer [2] defined runners of T as coalgebras of a specific comonad, namely the Sweedler dual of T with respect to R, studied in detail by Katsumata et al. [7]. That comonad is the greatest comonad that T interacts with R-residually. For that comonad, one has $\mathbf{Coalg}(D) \cong \mathbf{Run}_R(T)$, justifying this alternative definition. Runners of T for $R := \mathsf{Id}$ have also been called *coalgebras* of the monad T (notice: coalgebras, not algebras) [17].

Example 11 (Probabilistic weight requester). We look at Example 8 under the lens of stateful runners. Let Ψ be the coalgebraic specification of runners associated to ψ, and consider the runner $\Psi(\delta_1) : TX \times E \to R(X \times E)$. Given some computation $t \in TX$ and some state of the environment given by a stream of data $\sigma \in C^{\mathbb{N}}$, the runner produces some weighted choice tree $\Psi(\delta_1)(t, \sigma) \in T_{\Sigma}(X \times E)$. In this example, σ is used to label all the nodes of the initial tree t with the values of the stream σ. If the node has height n in the tree, it will be given label $\sigma(n)$. Each leaf of t will be joined with the remainder of the σ leftover after labelling. For instance, $\Psi(\delta_1)$ given stream $qpqpqpqp\ldots$ will send the following tree of TX to the given tree in $R(X \times E)$:

7.2 Continuation-Based Runners

If we combine interaction laws with algebras only, we get a novel concept of continuation-based runners.

We define a D-fuelled *continuation-based runner* of T for an object $Z \in \mathcal{C}$ to be a natural transformation typed $\theta_X : D(X \Rightarrow Z) \to TX \Rightarrow Z$ satisfying

With the appropriate concept of map, D-fuelled continuation-based runners form a category $\mathbf{CRun}_D(T)$.

We make the following observation that also extends to isomorphisms of categories.

Proposition 6. *For any object $Z \in \mathcal{C}$, the following sets are in bijection:*

1. *D-fuelled continuation-based runners of T with carrier Z,*
2. *monad morphisms from T to Cnt_Z^D, the D-transformed continuation monad for answer set Z, defined by $\mathsf{Cnt}_Z^D X := D(X \Rightarrow Z) \Rightarrow Z$,*
3. *functors $\Theta : (\mathbf{Coalg}(D))^{\mathrm{op}} \to \mathbf{Alg}(T)$ such that*

$$
\begin{array}{ccc}
(\mathbf{Coalg}(D))^{\mathrm{op}} & \xrightarrow{\ \Theta\ } & \mathbf{Alg}(T) \\
{\scriptstyle U^{\mathrm{op}}}\downarrow & & \downarrow{\scriptstyle U} \\
\mathcal{C}^{\mathrm{op}} & \xrightarrow[{\ -\Rightarrow Z\ }]{} & \mathcal{C}
\end{array}
$$

It follows from Corollary 1 that R-residual T, D-interaction laws are in a bijection with R-*algebraic specifications* of D-fuelled continuation-based T-runners, by which we mean carrier-preserving functors $\Psi : \mathbf{Alg}(R) \to \mathbf{CRun}_D(T)$.

Explicitly, given an interaction law ψ in the 2nd format, the corresponding runner spec Ψ is defined by

$$
(\Psi\zeta)_X := D(X \Rightarrow Z) \xrightarrow{\psi_{X,Z}} TX \Rightarrow RZ \xrightarrow{TX \Rightarrow \zeta} TX \Rightarrow Z
$$

for monad algebras $\zeta : RZ \to Z$. In the reverse direction, given a runner spec Ψ, the interaction law ψ is

$$
\psi_{X,Z} := D(X \Rightarrow Z) \xrightarrow{D(X \Rightarrow \eta_Z)} D(X \Rightarrow RZ) \xrightarrow{(\Psi\mu_Z)_X} TX \Rightarrow RZ .
$$

Continuation-based runners can be understood as a predicate-lifting device: they lift an environment that has as states Z-valued predicates on values X to a Z-valued predicate on computations TX.

Example 12 (Uncertain stream reader). We look at Example 9 under the lens of continuation-based runners. Let Ψ be the algebraic specification of runners associated to ψ, and consider the runner $\Psi(\mathsf{Tal}) : D(X \Rightarrow \mathbb{N}_\infty) \to TX \Rightarrow \mathbb{N}_\infty$. Take $P \in D(X \Rightarrow \mathbb{N}_\infty)$ to be some environment over value predicates as states, which can be expressed as an element of $((X \Rightarrow \mathbb{N}_\infty) \times C)^{\mathbb{N}}$ given by a stream of data $\sigma \in C^{\mathbb{N}}$ and, for any $n \in \mathbb{N}$, a value predicate $P_n \in X \Rightarrow \mathbb{N}_\infty$, determining what the cost of any return value would be if it were yielded after n gives.

Given a computation $t \in TX$, the predicate $\Psi(\mathsf{Tal})(t)$ delivered by the runner computes (1) the number n of gives necessary for reaching its return value $x \in X$ (some number of give responses for each get request made), and (2) the cost associated to x at that point, which is $P_n(x)$. This predicate then yields the sum $n + P_n(x)$ as the total cost of the computation.

7.3 Running with Both a Coalgebra and an Algebra Given

A running perspective is possible also in the situation of merge functors where both a coalgebra and an algebra are given, but nothing too exciting happens. In this case, we concern ourselves only with the final merged algebra as produced by the merge functor. Here are some equivalent definitions of monad algebras.

Proposition 7. *For any object $W \in \mathcal{C}$, the following sets are in bijection:*

1. *transformations $\mathcal{C}(X, W) \to \mathcal{C}(TX, W)$ natural in X subject to appropriate equations,[3]*
2. *monad morphisms from T to the "external continuation" monad XCnt_W for answer set W,[4] defined by $\mathsf{XCnt}_W X := \mathcal{C}(X, W) \pitchfork W$,*
3. *monad algebras of T with carrier W.*

A bijection like that between 2 and 3 holds for T a strong monad when one replaces the external continuation monad XCnt_W with the ordinary continuation monad $\mathsf{Cnt}_W^{\mathsf{Id}}$[5] and monad morphisms with strong monad morphisms [8]. In **Set**, the two continuation monads are isomorphic, every functor is uniquely strong and every natural transformation is strong; therefore, the two bijections become the same.

By Corollary 1, R-residual interaction laws of T, D are in a bijection with functors sending a comonad coalgebra of D with carrier Y and a monad algebra of R with carrier Z to a monad algebra of T with carrier $Y \Rightarrow Z$. By Proposition 7, such algebras are in a bijection with $\mathcal{C}(X \times Y, Z) \to \mathcal{C}(TX \times Y, Z)$ natural in X subject to two equations ("state and continuation based runners"), which amount to natural transformations $TX \times Y \to \mathsf{XCnt}_Z(X \times Y)$ (XCnt_Z-residual state-based runners) or $\mathsf{XCost}_Y(X \Rightarrow Z) \to TX \Rightarrow Z$ (XCost_Y-fuelled continuation-based runners) where $\mathsf{XCost}_Y W = \mathcal{C}(Y, W) \bullet Y$ is the "external costate" monad, with $\bullet$ denoting tensor. They are also in a bijection with monad morphisms to the monad $\mathsf{XCnt}_{Y \Rightarrow Z}$. This monad is isomorphic both to the external-continuation-transformed state monad defined by $\mathsf{XCntSt}_{Y,Z} X := Y \Rightarrow \mathsf{XCnt}_Z(X \times Y)$ and the external-costate-transformed continuation monad defined by $\mathsf{XCostCnt}_{Y,Z} X := \mathsf{XCost}_Y(X \Rightarrow Z) \Rightarrow Z$.

8   Conclusion

We have seen isomorphisms between, among others, the following four descriptions of interactions between a computation and an environment.

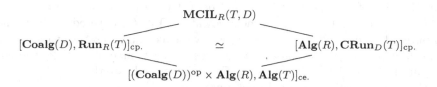

$$\mathbf{MCIL}_R(T, D)$$

$$[\mathbf{Coalg}(D), \mathbf{Run}_R(T)]_{\mathrm{cp.}} \qquad \simeq \qquad [\mathbf{Alg}(R), \mathbf{CRun}_D(T)]_{\mathrm{cp.}}$$

$$[(\mathbf{Coalg}(D))^{\mathrm{op}} \times \mathbf{Alg}(R), \mathbf{Alg}(T)]_{\mathrm{ce.}}$$

where 'cp.' means "carrier-preserving" and 'ce.' means "carrier-exponentiating". The right and bottom corners of the diamond are new. Moreover, just as interaction laws are the same as monad morphisms from T to $D \rightarrowtail R$, for each of the

---

[3] Also known as monad algebras of T with carrier W in "no-iteration" form.

[4] Also called the endomorphism monad.

[5] Also called the double dualization monad.

three types of specializations of interaction laws (based on a coalgebra or/and an algebra), runners of the corresponding type also amount to monad morphisms from T to specific monads. This is also new for the right and bottom corners.

Algebras $\xi : T(Y \Rightarrow Z) \rightarrow Y \Rightarrow Z$ delivered by a merge functor do not mention interaction laws or comonads. As such, they are suitable for developments purely in terms of monads and their algebras. If an algebra is a continuous morphism in the category of ω-cpos, and its carrier set forms a complete lattice, then it gives rise to a congruent notion of program equivalence (as seen in previous work [19,23]). It should be relatively easy to extend developed theory to the algebraically compact setting of ω-cpos, using a construction like the one from Sect. 6 to specify R-residual interaction laws between D and T for $TX := \mu V. (X + FV)_\perp$. We want to investigate what such a notion of program-environment equivalence would look like.

On the other hand, the merged algebra created using the tools of this paper can be used as a basis for defining and verifying properties of programs. In particular, the emphasis on state predicates makes it perfectly suitable for formulating Hoare logic judgments [6]. Consider a postcondition given by $Q : X \times Y \rightarrow Z$, which gives for each possible return value from X and final state from Y a quantitative degree of truth from X. Then, a computation over X, which is an element t of TX, can be transformed using Q into an element of $T(Y \Rightarrow Z)$. Using the merged algebra, we can compute the weakest precondition $\mathsf{wp}(t, Q) : Y \rightarrow Z$, associating to each possible initial state the corresponding final degree of truth. In Hoare logic style, we can then formulate that, given a precondition $P : Y \rightarrow Z$, $\{P\} t \{Q\}$ holds if, for all $y \in Y$, $P(y) \leq \mathsf{wp}(t, Q)(y)$ (assuming a partial order on Z). If this is applied to the example of probability with global store, we retrieve the usual notion of probabilistic Hoare logic [11]. More generally, we see this as a potential framework for a flexible Hoare-style logic on (quantitative) state predicates.

Another subject for future research is the *cascading* of interaction laws. If we have two interaction laws, each with their own notion of environment, and the second interacts with the residual effects of the first, we can combine them into one. This way, computations interact with two layers of environment simultaneously. Using the Day convolution to parallel-compose the comonads representing the two notions of environment, we can cascade the interaction laws into a single law. A similar construction can be done on merge functors so that the two constructions correspond.

Acknowledgements. Exequiel Rivas found out and told us that stateful runners have been studied under the name of monad coalgebras.

T.U. was supported by the Icelandic Research Fund project grant no. 196323-052 and by the Estonian Ministry of Education and Research institutional research grant no. IUT33-13. N.V. was supported by the Estonian IT Academy research measure (the European Social Fund project no. 2014-2020.4.05.19-0001).

References

1. Aczel, P., Adámek, J., Milius, S., Velebil, J.: Infinite trees and completely iterative theories: a coalgebraic view. Theor. Comput. Sci. **300**(1–3), 1–45 (2003)
2. Ahman, D., Bauer, A.: Runners in action. In: Müller, P. (ed.) ESOP 2020. LNCS, vol. 12075, pp. 29–55. Springer, Cham (2020). https://doi.org/10.1007/978-3-030-44914-8_2
3. Bauer, A.: What is algebraic about algebraic effects and handlers? arXiv eprint 1807.05923 [cs.LO] (2018). https://arxiv.org/abs/1807.05923
4. Capobianco, S., Uustalu, T.: A categorical outlook on cellular automata. In: Kari, J. (ed.) Proceedings of 2nd Symposium on Cellular Automata, JAC 2010. TUCS Lecture Notes, vol. 13, pp. 88–89. University of Turku, Turku (2010)
5. Hasuo, I.: Generic weakest precondition semantics from monads enriched with order. Theor. Comput. Sci. **604**, 2–29 (2015). https://doi.org/10.1016/j.tcs.2015.03.047
6. Hoare, C.A.R.: An axiomatic basis for computer programming. Commun. ACM **26**(1), 53–56 (1983). https://doi.org/10.1145/357980.358001
7. Katsumata, S., Rivas, E., Uustalu, T.: Interaction laws of monads and comonads. In: Proceedings of 35th Annual ACM/IEEE Symposium on Logic in Computer Science, LICS 2020, pp. 604–618. ACM, New York (2020). https://doi.org/10.1145/3373718.3394808
8. Kock, J.: On the double dualization monads. Math. Scand. **27**, 151–165 (1970). https://doi.org/10.7146/math.scand.a-10995
9. Møgelberg, R.E., Staton, S.: Linear usage of state. Log. Meth. Comput. Sci. **10**(1), 1–52 (2014). https://doi.org/10.2168/lmcs-10(1:17)2014
10. Moggi, E.: Notions of computation and monads. Inf. Comput. **93**(1), 55–92 (1991). https://doi.org/10.1016/0890-5401(91)90052-4. Article 17
11. Morgan, C., McIver, A., Seidel, K.: Probabilistic predicate transformers. ACM Trans. Program. Lang. Syst. **18**(3), 325–353 (1996). https://doi.org/10.1145/229542.229547
12. Petricek, T., Orchard, D., Mycroft, A.: Coeffects: a calculus of context-dependent computation. SIGPLAN Not. **49**(9), 123–135 (2014). https://doi.org/10.1145/2692915.2628160
13. Plotkin, G., Power, J.: Tensors of comodels and models for operational semantics. Electron. Notes Theor. Comput. Sci. **218**, 295–311 (2008). https://doi.org/10.1016/j.entcs.2008.10.018
14. Plotkin, G., Power, J.: Notions of computation determine monads. In: Nielsen, M., Engberg, U. (eds.) FoSSaCS 2002. LNCS, vol. 2303, pp. 342–356. Springer, Heidelberg (2002). https://doi.org/10.1007/3-540-45931-6_24
15. Plotkin, G.D., Power, J.: Algebraic operations and generic effects. Appl. Categ. Struct. **11**, 69–94 (2003). https://doi.org/10.1023/a:1023064908962
16. Plotkin, G.D., Pretnar, M.: Handling algebraic effects. Log. Meth. Comput. Sci. **9**(4), 1–36 (2013). https://doi.org/10.2168/lmcs-9(4:23)2013. Article 23
17. Poinsot, L., Porst, H.E.: Internal coalgebras in cocomplete categories: generalizing the Eilenberg-Watts theorem. J. Algebra Appl. (to appear). https://doi.org/10.1142/s0219498821501656
18. Power, J., Shkaravska, O.: From comodels to coalgebras: state and arrays. Electron. Notes Theor. Comput. Sci. **106**, 297–314 (2004). https://doi.org/10.1016/j.entcs.2004.02.041

19. Simpson, A., Voorneveld, N.: Behavioural equivalence via modalities for algebraic effects. ACM Trans. Program. Lang. Syst. **42**(1), 1–45 (2020). https://doi.org/10.1145/3363518. Article 4

20. Uustalu, T.: Stateful runners of effectful computations. Electron. Notes Theor. Comput. Sci. **319**, 403–421 (2015). https://doi.org/10.1016/j.entcs.2015.12.024

21. Uustalu, T., Vene, V.: The essence of dataflow programming. In: Horváth, Z. (ed.) CEFP 2005. LNCS, vol. 4164. Springer, Heidelberg (2006). https://doi.org/10.1007/11894100_5

22. Uustalu, T., Vene, V.: Comonadic notions of computation. Electron. Notes Theor. Comput. Sci. **203**(5), 263–284 (2008). https://doi.org/10.1016/j.entcs.2008.05.029

23. Voorneveld, N.: Quantitative logics for equivalence of effectful programs. Electron. Notes Theor. Comput. Sci. **347**, 281–301 (2019). https://doi.org/10.1016/j.entcs.2019.09.015

Program Generation, Transactions and Automation

Stack-Driven Program Generation
of WebAssembly

Árpád Perényi and Jan Midtgaard[✉] [iD]

The Maersk Mc-Kinney Moller Institute, University of Southern Denmark,
Campusvej 55, 5230 Odense M, Denmark
arpad.perenyi@gmail.com, mail@janmidtgaard.dk

Abstract. WebAssembly (Wasm) is a popular portable assembly-like language. Besides browser support in the four most common browsers (Chrome, Firefox, Safari, Edge) a number of standalone Wasm engines are available. With several such independent implementations naturally follows a risk of disagreement between the individual implementations.

To help ensure agreement between Wasm implementations, we develop a stack-directed program generator to drive differential testing of the four browsers' Wasm engines. We describe our experimental setup, our development of a stack-directed shrinker for reducing a generated counterexample program, and finally report on a number of disagreements and bugs found. Surprisingly our black-box generator found 2 crashing bugs, despite browser vendor efforts to fuzz test their Wasm engines using a state-of-the-art fuzzer.

1 Introduction

WebAssembly (Wasm) is a new open web standard [26] for executing low-level code in web pages. In order to succeed, Wasm programs should be interpreted consistently by the four major browsers implementations (Chrome, Firefox, Safari, Edge). To ensure such consistency both a reference interpreter and an extensive test suite is available. Given the incompleteness of testing, one may wonder whether these efforts are sufficient to guarantee consistency. In this paper we present a generator of arbitrary Wasm programs and report on testing for this consistency. Furthermore we present a *shrinker* to automatically reduce a machine-generated counterexample illustrating inconsistency.

For example, a Wasm program produced by our generator was able to crash SpiderMonkey, the JavaScript engine inside the Firefox web browser. Figure 1 illustrates a reduced version of the test case and Firefox's behavior upon attempting to run it.

Overall the contributions of this paper are:

- We suggest the ideas of (backwards) stack-directed program generation and stack-directed shrinking.
- We illustrate the approach with an application to WebAssembly.

© Springer Nature Switzerland AG 2020
B. C. d. S. Oliveira (Ed.): APLAS 2020, LNCS 12470, pp. 209–230, 2020.
https://doi.org/10.1007/978-3-030-64437-6_11

```
(module
  (func)
  (start 0)
  (table $0 1 anyfunc)
  (elem 0
    (offset (i32.const 0)) 0))
```

Fig. 1. Wasm program crashing SpiderMonkey

```
(module
  (func (param i32) (param i32) (result i32)
    (get_local 0)
    (get_local 1)
    (i32.add))
  (export "add" (func 0)))
```

Listing 1. A Wasm module in text format with a simple addition function

- We demonstrate that the approach is both viable and useful as illustrated by a number of real-world Wasm engine bugs found (including crashing bugs).
- We discuss ours findings, documenting real-world bugs that escaped a coverage-guided "gray-box" fuzzer thus questioning the current focus on such generators.

2   Background

We first present background material on Wasm and property-based testing.

2.1   WebAssembly

The Wasm standard defines a low-level programming language for a stack-based virtual machine [12]. For example, Listing 1 shows a simple Wasm module with a function that takes two arguments and returns their sum. The function loads each of the numbered parameters onto the operand stack, adds them, and leaves the result on the stack. Wasm is designed for embedding. This is expressed as *exporting* functions for the surrounding context to call and *importing* functions from the surrounding context for Wasm to call. For example, Listing 1 exports the module's function under the name "add". In a web-embedding context, this means Wasm modules can call imported JavaScript functions and that JavaScript can call the exported Wasm functions. Similarly a Wasm module can import and export functions from other Wasm modules.

Wasm programs can be expressed in both a textual assembly-like format (.wat) as in Listing 1 and in a corresponding binary format (.wasm). Translators are available to translate between the two. In a web-embedding context a Wasm-module can be loaded from an untrusted source into a browser. A module then has to be validated to ensure that it is well formed and safe to run. The validator is phrased as a type system centered around four *value types*: i32, i64, f32 and f64, denoting 32-bit and 64-bit integers and 32-bit and 64-bit floating-point numbers, respectively. For the example in Listing 1 the validator checks that the two arguments on the stack when performing i32.add are indeed i32s and that the i32 result agrees with the function's declared result type.

```
(module
  (table 10 funcref)
  (func $f)
  (func $f2 (call_indirect 3))
  (elem (i32.const 0) $f)
  (elem (i32.const 3) $f))
```

Listing 2. Wasm table initialization

A Wasm program consists of one or more modules. Besides functions, a module can contain a combination of elements which we now cover.

Global Variables. A Wasm module can contain global variables. A global variable can be accessed throughout the module using the **get_global** instruction. Each global is declared with a value type and optionally marked as *mutable*. Mutable global variables can be updated using the **set_global** instruction. Global variables can both be imported and exported.

Memories and Data Segments. A Wasm module can also contain a memory which is a mutable array of raw bytes. By default the memory is initialized with zeroes. A module can contain a separate section of *data segments* that each specify the initial memory contents at a specific *offset* and *length*. When a Wasm module is loaded and *instantiated*, the allocated memory is initialized accordingly before Wasm code is run.

Functions. A module can contain multiple functions. Each function's parameters are defined as locals and can only be accessed by the defining function. Locals are mutable. They can be read and updated with the **get_local** and **set_local** instructions, which push and pop values to and from the stack. A function can optionally declare a return value type. In the current version of Wasm, a function can return at most one value. A function's body is a possibly empty instruction sequence. The instructions may interact with the stack, locals, globals, memories, or tables. A module can also contain a dedicated *start function*. The start function is executed automatically after the memories and tables have been initialized. The start function cannot take any arguments or return any value. For example, the Wasm module in Fig. 1 designates function 0, the module's only (empty) function as the start function.

Tables. A Wasm module may contain a table of functions. In the current version of Wasm, a module can only contain a single table instance. A table instance can be defined by the module itself or imported from another module, hence a table can also be exported. Tables require a minimum size and can optionally declare a maximum size. A table can also be initialized through *element segments*. The `call_indirect` instruction calls a function through a table. Listing 2 shows an example of a table initialization via element segments. The table is declared to contain 10 elements, with `funcref` (function reference) type.[1] The named function `$f` is then added to the table at indices 0 and 3. The named function `$f2` calls the function `$f` indirectly through the table.

(value types)	$t ::= $ i32 $\mid$ i64 $\mid$ f32 $\mid$ f64	
(packed types)	$tp ::= $ i8 $\mid$ i16 $\mid$ i32	
(function types)	$tf ::= t^* \rightarrow t^*$	
(global types)	$tg ::= $ mut$^?$ t	
(functions)	$f ::= ex^*$ func tf local t^* e^*	
	$\mid ex^*$ func tf e^* im	
(globals)	$glob ::= ex^*$ global tg e^*	
	$\mid ex^*$ global tg im	
(tables)	$tab ::= ex^*$ table n i^*	
	$\mid ex^*$ table n im	
(memories)	$mem ::= ex^*$ memory n	
	$\mid ex^*$ memory n im	
(imports)	$im ::= $ import "*name*" "*name*"	
(exports)	$ex ::= $ export "*name*"	
(modules)	$m ::= $ module f^* $glob^*$ $tab^?$ $mem^?$	

$unop_{iN} ::= $ clz $\mid$ ctz $\mid$ popcnt
$unop_{fN} ::= $ neg $\mid$ abs $\mid$ ceil
  $\mid$ floor $\mid$ trunc
  $\mid$ nearest $\mid$ sqrt
$binop_{iN} ::= $ add $\mid$ sub $\mid$ mul
  $\mid$ div$_{sx}$ $\mid$ rem$_{sx}$ $\mid$ and
  $\mid$ or $\mid$ xor $\mid$ shl
  $\mid$ shr$_{sx}$ $\mid$ rotl $\mid$ rotr
$binop_{fN} ::= $ add $\mid$ sub $\mid$ mul $\mid$ div
  $\mid$ min $\mid$ max $\mid$ copysign
$testop_{iN} ::= $ eqz
$relop_{iN} ::= $ eq $\mid$ ne $\mid$ lt$_{sx}$
  $\mid$ gt$_{sx}$ $\mid$ le$_{sx}$ $\mid$ ge$_{sx}$
$relop_{fN} ::= $ eq $\mid$ ne $\mid$ lt
  $\mid$ gt $\mid$ le $\mid$ ge
$cvtop ::= $ convert $\mid$ reinterpret
$sx ::= $ s $\mid$ u

(instructions) $e ::= $ unreachable $\mid$ nop $\mid$ drop $\mid$ select $\mid$ block tf e^* end $\mid$ loop tf e^* end
  $\mid$ if tf e^* else e^* end $\mid$ br i $\mid$ br_if i $\mid$ br_table i^+ $\mid$ return
  $\mid$ call i $\mid$ call_indirect tf $\mid$ get_local i $\mid$ set_local i $\mid$ tee_local i
  $\mid$ get_global i $\mid$ set_global i $\mid$ t.load $(tp\_sx)^?$ a o $\mid$ t.store $tp^?$ a o
  $\mid$ current_memory $\mid$ grow_memory $\mid$ t.const c
  $\mid$ $t.unop_t$ $\mid$ $t.binop_t$ $\mid$ $t.testop_t$ $\mid$ $t.relop_t$ $\mid$ $t.cvtop_t$ $t\_sx^?$

(context) $C ::= \{$ func tf^*, table $n^?$, memory $n^?$, global tg^*,
  local t^*, label $(t^*)^*$, return $(t^*)^? \}$

Fig. 2. Abstract syntax of modules and contexts

Instructions. We summarize the abstract syntax of Wasm instructions and modules in Fig. 2. Instructions can consume multiple arguments and produce a result value by popping and pushing the stack. In the current version of Wasm, instructions can push at most one value to the stack. *Numeric instructions* perform basic operations over numeric values of a specific type, e.g., `i32.add` in Listing 1. *Parametric instructions* operate on operands of any type, e.g., the `select` instruction selects one of its first two operands based on whether its

---

[1] In revised text format https://github.com/WebAssembly/spec/issues/884.

third operand is zero or not. *Variable instructions* get or set the values of local and global variables, e.g., get_local in Listing 1. *Memory instructions* query or mutate the memory, e.g., the memory.grow instruction extends the size of a module's memory. *Control instructions* affect the flow of control, e.g., the return instruction breaks from the current instruction block and returns the current value from the top of the stack.

Module Validation. A Wasm module is executed in a web browser after validation and instantiation. While validation ensures internal consistency and memory safety of a module, instantiation ensures that the imports and exports are correctly formulated. The validator is phrased as a syntax-directed type system [7] over the abstract syntax of a module. Typing is relative to a context C holding information about the surrounding functions, tables, memories, globals, locals, labels, and return type for a given program point. Figure 2 recalls the abstract syntax of Wasm modules and contexts, utilizing *extended BNF* grammars for succinctness. We furthermore let t range over value type, tf range over function types, tg range over global types, and n range over numbers.

$$\text{(EMPTY)} \frac{}{C \vdash \epsilon : [t^*] \to [t^*]} \qquad \boxed{C \vdash e^* : [t^*] \to [t^*]}$$

$$\text{(NON-EMPTY)} \frac{C \vdash e^* : [t_1^*] \to [t_0^* \, t^*] \quad C \vdash e : [t^*] \to [t_3^*]}{C \vdash e^* \, e : [t_1^*] \to [t_0^* \, t_3^*]}$$

$$\text{(CONG)} \frac{C \vdash e^* : [t_1^*] \to [t_2^*]}{C \vdash e^* : [t^* \, t_1^*] \to [t^* \, t_2^*]}$$

$$\boxed{C \vdash e : [t^*] \to [t^*]}$$

$$\text{(CONST)} \frac{}{C \vdash t.\textbf{const} \, c : \epsilon \to [t]} \qquad \text{(BINOP)} \frac{}{C \vdash t.binop : [t \, t] \to [t]}$$

$$\text{(DROP)} \frac{}{C \vdash \textbf{drop} : [t] \to \epsilon} \qquad \text{(CALL)} \frac{C_{\text{func}}(i) = tf}{C \vdash \textbf{call} \, i : tf}$$

$$\text{(CALLINDIR)} \frac{tf = [t_1^*] \to [t_2^*] \quad C_{\text{table}} = n}{C \vdash \textbf{call\_indirect} \, tf : [t_1^* \, i32] \to [t_2^*]}$$

$$\text{(LOOP)} \frac{tf = [t_1^n] \to [t_2^m] \quad C, \text{label}(t_1^n) \vdash e^* : tf}{C \vdash \textbf{loop} \, tf \, e^* \, \textbf{end} : tf} \qquad \text{(BR)} \frac{C_{\text{label}}(i) = [t^*]}{C \vdash \textbf{br} \, i : [t_1^* \, t^*] \to [t_2^*]}$$

Fig. 3. Typing rules for instructions and instruction sequences

Figure 3 displays a selection of the typing rules. The two judgements are of the form $C \vdash e : [t^*] \to [t^*]$, where e is a single instruction (or an instruction sequence e^*) and $[t^*]$ is a stacktype. The stacktype expresses e's requirement to elements on the stack prior to its execution (a precondition) and the elements on the stack as a result of e (a postcondition). Arrow types $tf = [t^*] \rightarrow [t^*]$ double as *function types*, as functions receive parameters and leave their results on the stack.

The rule (EMPTY) says that an empty instruction sequence is valid in any context C and that any value types t^* on the stack will remain unchanged. The rule (NON-EMPTY) for a non-empty instruction sequence e^*e ensures that (parts of) the resulting stack from executing e^* agrees with the stack input expected by e. The congruence rule (CONG) allows one to disregard untouched elements on the stack and thereby apply the instructions rule in an arbitrary context.

The rule (CONST) says that a `const` instruction requires no input from the stack and leaves type t on top of the stack. Similarly the rule (BINOP) for a binary operation requires two elements with type t on top of the stack, and leaves a single element with type t. The rule (DROP) says that a `drop` instruction is valid in any context C with a one-element stack and results in an empty stack ϵ. The rule (CALL) for a function `call` instruction expects the function to have some index i and function type $tf = [t_1^*] \rightarrow [t_2^*]$ and requires the parameters to be present on the stack at entry and leaves the (optional) result type on the stack. The rule (CALLINDIR) for a `call_indirect` instruction additionally ensures that a function table is present and that the function's index is available as an `i32` on top on the stack. The rule (LOOP) checks a `loop` instruction's body recursively in a context that records the loop head's label and expected input type. Finally the rule (BR) for a branch instruction `br` i checks agreement between the stack's input types and the expected stack types $[t^*]$ at the target label i.

2.2 Property-Based Testing

Property-based testing (also known as QuickCheck) is a randomized testing approach introduced by Claessen and Hughes [8]. Originally QuickCheck was phrased as a Haskell library, but the approach has since been ported to over 30 other programming languages. In this paper we will use the QCheck property-based testing library [9] for OCaml. In property-based testing, a test is described by a *generator* and a *property*. The generator delivers randomized test input whereas the property expresses a test specification for each such generated input.[2] As an example, consider the following QCheck test:

```
open QCheck
let t = Test.make (pair pos_int pos_int)
          (fun (a, b) -> a + b >= 0)
```

Here the generator produces pairs of positive integers (including zero). It is phrased by composing QCheck's built-in `pos_int` and `pair` generator combinators. For each such pair (a, b) we wish to test the property $a+b \geq 0$. The generator

---

[2] Other generation approaches exist, e.g., SmallCheck's enumeration up to some bound [24].

and the property are passed as arguments to `Test.make` and the resulting test is bound to the name `t`.

We can now provide QCheck with a (singleton) list of tests to run:

```
QCheck_runner.run_tests ~verbose:true [t]
```

This runs a loop for 100 iterations (a configurable number) checking that each generated pair satisfies the specified property. The framework reports a *counterexample* if it finds one, i.e., a generated test input that fails to satisfy the specified property. QCheck quickly finds a counterexample for our example property:

```
generated error fail pass / total     time test name
[✗]    4    0    1    3 / 100     0.0s anon_test_1

--- Failure ---------------------------------------------

Test anon_test_1 failed (22 shrink steps):

(829922565348744309, 3781763453078643595)
```

In this case, the 4th generated pair failed the property. We confirm that the reported pair represents a counterexample, due to integer overflow:

```
# 829922565348744309 + 3781763453078643595;;
- : int = -4611686018427387904
```

Note how this sum coincides with OCaml's `min_int`, the least representable integer within OCaml's 63-bit integer type. In general, a counterexample triggers a second *shrinking* loop, that repeatedly tries to reduce the test input and checks whether the reduced input still fails the property. In the above case, using QCheck's built-in shrinkers for integers and pairs it took 22 shrink steps to reduce the counterexample.

To test more complex systems, custom generators and shrinkers can be developed. Such generators and shrinkers can be used for testing multiple different properties. Since its inception, property-based testing has found bugs missed by hand-written tests across a range of domains, such as telecom protocols [2], data structures [1,18], election software [15], automotive software [14], and compilers [19,20].

3   Generating WebAssembly

Generating Wasm programs from a more high-level language, such as C, is a viable solution. In the process of mechanising and verifying the WebAssembly specification, Watt [25] opted for this approach to verify his model. Although this approach produces valid Wasm programs that pass the type-checker, it is not an ideal solution, since the produced programs are confined to the subset of Wasm utilized by the compiler.

To achieve the highest possible coverage of the Wasm language, we instead chose to directly generate Wasm text format programs that can be translated to the binary format and executed in a browser. To ensure this, the generated programs must both be syntactically correct to pass the parser, as well as type-correct to pass the validator. Structuring a generator according to the productions of the grammar ensures the former. To ensure the generated program also passes validation, the generation should follow the typing rules of the language. Pałka et al. [20] suggested to structure such a *type-directed program generator* according to the typing rules. For a functional language with roots in a typed λ-calculus, this means that a typing relation of the form $\Gamma \vdash e : \tau$, is interpreted as a generation procedure with two inputs: the surrounding type environment Γ and the goal type τ. In this way, the generator proceeds to build a term recursively, in each step randomly choosing among the typing rules able to satisfy (unifying with) the goal type.

With Wasm's typing rules tracking value types on the stack, we propose to phrase a *stack-directed program generator*. In the rest of this paper we show that such a generator is both viable and useful, as it has helped locate subtle bugs in major Wasm engines.

3.1   A Stack-Directed Generator

Our generator can generate modules with an arbitrary number of globals and functions and with an optional memory and an optional table, both of arbitrary size. In order for the context to have the right entries in scope, this mandates a certain structure for the generator. Overall our module generator is structured in the following order:

- generate context with an optional memory and an optional table
- generate global types and constant initializers, function signatures, and optional data segments for the memory
- generate optional element segments for the table
- generate function bodies

By generating the function signatures before the function bodies, we can add them to the context, thus enabling us to generate both recursive and mutually recursive functions. With this order the globals and the optional memory and table are similarly in scope for function bodies. Our generator of function bodies follows the typing rule specification:

$$\frac{tf = [t_1^*] \rightarrow [t_2^*] C, \texttt{local } t_1^*, \texttt{label } (t_2^*), \texttt{return } (t_2^*) \vdash e^* : [] \rightarrow [t_2^*]}{C \vdash ex^* \texttt{ func } tf \, e^*}$$

Upon entry to a function, the stack is empty and the actual parameters are available as locals. To generate a body we extend the context accordingly and seek to generate a body with the desired result type $[t_2^*]$. This way we generate Wasm programs backwards in a goal-directed manner.

Our instruction generator performs a back-tracking randomized search. We use option types to distinguish a successful generation attempt from a failed one. The algorithm for generating instructions is phrased as two mutually recursive

```
(** instrs_rule : context_ -> value_type list -> int -> (instr list) option Gen.t **)
let rec instrs_rule context output_ts size =
  let recgen con t_opt tr = Gen.(instr_rule con t_opt (size/4) >>= function
    | None                     -> return None
    | Some (con', instr', ts') ->
      instrs_rule con' (ts'@tr) (3*size/4) >>= (function
          | None                -> return None
          | Some instrs -> return (Some (instr'::instrs)))) in
  match output_ts with
  | [] ->
    let empty_gen = recgen context None [] in
    Gen.(oneof [ empty_gen; return (Some []) ])
  | t1::trst  ->
    let empty_gen = recgen context None output_ts in
    let non_empty_gen = recgen context (Some t1) trst in
    Gen.frequency [ 1, empty_gen; 4, non_empty_gen; ]
```

Listing 3. The implementation of `instrs_rule`

function `instrs_rule` and `instr_rule` for generating instruction sequences and single instructions, respectively, thereby reflecting the two forms of typing judgments in Fig. 3. The two search functions are both parameterized by the context (modeling C) and a *"gas parameter"* to bound the search depth. In addition `instrs_rule` expects a goal stack type matching the resulting stack type in the corresponding typing judgments. Similarly `instr_rule` expects an optional goal type matching the potentially absent type result in the corresponding typing judgments.

Listing 3 contains the implementation of `instrs_rule` which heavily utilizes the monadic interface (`return`, `>>=`) of QCheck generators. It depends on a local function `recgen` that generates the last instruction `instr'` and an instruction list preceding it and then gluing them together. We dedicate $\frac{3}{4}$ of the gas parameter `size` to generating the instruction list, thinking that more gas should be dedicated to generating a sequence than an individual instruction. The `instr_rule` generator performs a weighted shuffle of the compatible instruction rules and then tries them one at a time in the resulting order. When no rules are left to try it returns `None` to signal failure and backtrack.

Our generator produces a single module with three hard-coded export and import functions. The three exported functions return an `i32`, an `f32`, and an `f64` for the surrounding engine to invoke. We omit `i64` as a surrounding JavaScript engine currently has no way to represent these precisely. We import three printing functions for printing `i32`, `f32`, and `f64` values to increase the chance of some observable program output. Currently our generator does not produce modules that export or import globals, tables, and memories.

Our implementation builds on the reference interpreter for Wasm [23]. This saved us from reimplementing a representation of Wasm modules. On the other hand, the representation is not custom fit for program generation, e.g., with positional information surrounding all internal AST nodes and functions referenced by list index which complicates shrinking (described in Sect. 4).

4   A Stack-Directed Shrinker

As illustrated in Sect. 2.2, a shrinker is useful to automatically reduce a counterexample to help narrow down a potential bug. This is vital as our generator sometimes produces modules with several large data segments and many functions with long and complex bodies. We have therefore implemented a shrinker. Since the generator was carefully engineered to produce modules that pass validation, our shrinker's reductions should preserve this property. We achieve this by stack-type preserving simplifications.

Our shrinker is composed of a number of overall heuristics which attempt the reductions with most impact first. The surrounding QCheck library (like its Haskell ancestor) wraps this shrinker in a loop that repeatedly applies simplifications while still leading to a false property. This way, the individual shrink heuristics complement each other and work together to reduce a counterexample module. To shrink a given Wasm module, the shrinker attempts the following, in order:

- shrink functions and function types simultaneously
- shrink imports and import types simultaneously
- shrink function bodies
- remove unneeded functions
- remove the start function
- reduce the exported functions
- reduce the globals
- reduce the declared types
- remove the table
- shrink the element segment
- remove the memory
- shrink the data segment

Few of these rewrite steps are semantics preserving. Functions are shrunk by first attempting to aggressively remove their body or replace it with a constant 0 of the appropriate return type. If this fails, a more complex instruction list shrinker is invoked. The instruction list shrinker pattern matches on either 1, 2, or 3 consecutive instructions and attempts stack-preserving rewrites for each of them. Below we give examples from each category.

One Instruction. Removing `nop` instructions is the most simple as it has no effect on the stack. Similarly we can remove `tee_local` and unary operations

Fig. 4. Experimental setup

as they leave the same value type on the stack as they consume. Additionally we rewrite global references to a lower index of the same type, e.g., get_global 321 to get_global 3 of the same type. Although it hardly represents a reduction in itself, it typically triggers further reductions in the module's list (tail) of global variables. As a final example we rewrite a call instruction into a drop instruction for each argument, finishing with an optional const 0 of the appropriate type for non-void functions. Again, locally this may not constitute a reduction. However it may trigger removal of the target function or further reductions involving the drop instructions.

Two Instructions. Motivated by the above we remove consecutive sequences of const c drop, get_local i drop, and get_global i drop. Similarly we remove subsequences of const c br_if i and of get_local i set_local j and its variations and combinations involving globals. Sequences const c $testop_{iN}$ that perform a test on c are replaced with const 0 and sequences const c **if** _ is_1 **else** is_2 is with a two-armed conditional we attempt to rewrite into either is_1@is or is_2@is. Finally, we rewrite two consecutive unreachable instructions into a single one. Combined with another heuristic that swaps two instructions if the first is unreachable, this has the effect of bubbling unreachable instructions last and eliminating duplicates.

Three Instructions. We rewrite a sub-sequence const c const c' compare into a const 0 thus removing two instructions. Similarly to the 2 instruction-case, we omit a sequence consisting of const c const c' select. Since select expects three value types [t t i32] on the stack and leaves either the second or the third, the reduction has the effect of leaving a t and thus preserving the types.

The heuristics were inspired by actual counterexample programs. Generally, we found that the shrinker got faster as we added more aggressive heuristics, e.g., removing unused functions saved shrinker time over repeatedly reducing function bodies. We confirmed this observation by rerunning such tests with the same randomization seed with and without the added heuristic. Overall the shrinker fills 535 lines of OCaml code.

5   Testing Experiments

We first describe our experimental setup before discussing our findings.

5.1   Experimental Setup

We use our generator and accompanying shrinker to test four Wasm engines against the reference interpreter. Concretely we use JSVU [11] to install pre-built command-line versions of Chakra (ch) from Edge, JavaScriptCore (jsc) from Safari, SpiderMonkey (sm) from Firefox, and V8 (v8) from Chrome. This installs nightly builds of each of the four engines. Each JavaScript (JS) engine contains a WebAssembly module to test.

The pre-built engines support pure JS and Wasm. As such we cannot run them on a JS-file that requires file-reading or network to load a generated Wasm module. As a workaround we have written a conversion script, `convert.js`, in Node.js which supports file-reading. The script converts a `.wasm`-file into a self-contained JS-file with an embedded `Uint8Array` containing the Wasm module, thus suitable for running in each engine (see Fig. 4). The self-contained JS-file sorts the Wasm-module's exported functions, calls them in sorted order, prints the return value from each, and redirects any output to a temporary file. As we may generate an infinite loop we run each engine with a `timeout` of 10 s akin to CSmith [27]. Finally we use the `cmp` command to compare the resulting output files. Overall, our agreement property ensures that the conversions succeed, that the `timeout`s return identical return codes, and that their redirected outputs agree. To further compare the four engines with the reference interpreter, we `fork` a separate process that interprets the module's AST directly, using a `Unix.alarm` to time out. There are more complications however:

Printing Across Engines. Pure JS does not support `console.log`, but 3 out of 4 engines support it. As a further complication we experienced that V8 would buffer output when this was redirected to a file. This would show up as a difference in behavior, e.g., when a generated program `console.log`s one line and then enters an infinite loop: after a 10 s timeout the other three engines would have output, whereas V8 would not. We eventually settled on using `print` which happens to be supported by all four JS engines, despite not being part of the ECMAScript standard.

Host Error Messages. When invoking a generated Wasm module from JS throws an exception, the attached error message varies across the different JS engines. We solved this issue by formulating regular expressions for each engine to catch and normalize engine-specific error messages into comparable ones.

Printing Floating Point Numbers. The different JS engines apply different algorithms for printing floating point numbers. For example, one generated Wasm program returned the floating point number `6.980439946950613e+234` to the hosting JS engine. However when invoked as `print(6.980439946950613e+234)` the constant prints as `6.980439946950614e+234` in all 3 engines except Chakra where it prints as `6.980439946950613e+234`. This is a known issue and Chakra's engineers have already adjusted their printer to agree more with the other JS engines.[3] Since we are concerned with testing Wasm engines we did not want such differences to raise any flags. As a first attempt we added logic to only print a certain amount of significant digits, thus checking agreement up to this bound. This left the difficulty of deciding how many significant digits to leave. Eventually we settled on a simpler approach: `(6.980439946950613e+234).toString(2)` instead prints the number in base 2 which agrees across all engines. To compare these outputs with the reference interpreter's output, we then had to implement a compatible base 2 printing for it.

---

[3] https://github.com/microsoft/ChakraCore/issues/149.

Stack Size. Our generator has a chance of generating programs that require increasing amounts of stack space and ultimately stack overflow due to excessive (sometimes indirect) recursive calls. When such programs have output, the number of written characters may differ across implementations. We solved this problem by comparing only the 5000 first output characters of each JS-embedded implementation. For the reference interpreter with a significantly smaller stack, we compare only its first 300 output characters. Even so, the test setup found a counterexample program where each of the 4 JS engines blew the stack before the 10 s timeout, whereas the reference interpreter did not. For this example, JavaScriptCore would blow the stack after 0.241 s, V8 after 6.148 s, SpiderMonkey after 0.164 s, Chakra after 1.861 s, and the OCaml interpreter after 19.664 s (all measured with the time command), which may indicate either a significantly slower reference interpreter or some tail-call optimization.

Maximum Table Size. The official specification declares the maximum table size to be $2^{32} = 4.294.967.296$ however none of the four JS engines support that value. At first glance all of the four engines allow the maximum table size to be 10.000.000. Analyzing further, we determined that JavaScriptCore supports a table with a maximum size of 9.999.999. For a table size set to 10.000.000 precisely, jsc throws the error message couldn't create Table. All four engines accepted tables less than 10.000.000 entries, hence we adjusted the generator accordingly.

Maximum Number of Parameters. During testing, we came across a Wasm module that caused all of the four tested JS engines to err. This happened because the number of function parameters exceeded 1.000. Examining the specification, we did not find any mention of a limitation on the maximum number of function parameters. Subsequently we adjusted the generator to stay below this bound.

Square Root Non-determinism. Our generator found a counterexample calculating the square root of a negative number thus resulting in a NaN floating-point value, which would later be reinterpreted as an integer value and eventually printed. Because NaNs can carry additional underspecified bits, this also showed up as observable output differences. This constitutes one of the few known sources of Wasm non-determinism [26].

5.2   Testing the Generator

The generator is a non-trivial piece of software with a risk of itself containing errors. To reduce these errors and to "take our own medicine" we test the generator using property-based testing. Specifically the generator is engineered to output valid Wasm modules. As there further exists many implementations of the validation algorithm in the reference interpreter and in each of the JS engines, these lend themselves to test the property *each generated Wasm module passes validation*. By testing this property for each of the validation implementations, we effectively test both our own generator as well as each of the validation implementations.

5.3   Testing the Shrinker

The shrinker also represents a non-trivial piece of code. To develop and debug it we again property-based tested it. Initially we tested whether the first shrinking candidate would pass validation. This did not find much. Eventually we arrived at a relatively simple property: *for all generated modules m and small natural numbers n, the first n shrink candidates of m should all be valid*, meaning shrinking should not accidentally turn a valid module into an invalid one while attempting to reduce it in up to n steps.

The refined strategy found multiple bugs as we continued to expand and improve the shrinker: It found problems lifting If branches and Loop body out which both caused labels to be off. It found another shrinker bug related to reducing functions, types, and imports: These are represented as 3 lists, each containing numbered types and functions. Any reduction in either list therefore means that potentially all function or type indices need to be updated. However the representation has catches we did not anticipate: The imports are present in the type list but not in functions, meaning function indices needed adjusting with ±3 with 3 hard-coded imports, unless a called function was itself an import.

5.4   Statistics

To ensure that our generator has a reasonable distribution, we have computed statistics across 1000 generated modules. Our statistics covers the number of functions (min: 4, avg: 8.93, max: 14), the total function length (min: 6, avg: 153.18, max: 648), element segment length (min: 0, avg: 1.81, max: 94), number of globals (min: 0, avg: 333.74, max: 9959), data segment length (min: 0, avg: 2.54, max: 87), number of print calls (min 0, avg: 0.96, max 7), as well as percentages of the different instructions. Across the latter, nop occurs most often with an average of 12.24% and callindir is the most rare occurring with an average of 0.24%. We have added weights to the different instructions in an attempt to even these.

5.5   Bugs Found

At the time of writing we have found five bugs of which two were already known. Out of the five bugs three led to a crash of SpiderMonkey and JavaScriptCore. Below we describe the found counterexamples in more detail.

SpiderMonkey Crash. Our generator found a module which would crash SpiderMonkey with a null pointer de-reference. The hand-shrunk test program is illustrated in Fig. 1.[4] We then created a minimal HTML document encapsulating the test program to investigate how a full Firefox browser would react to it. Upon running the encapsulated counterexample, the released Firefox version

---

[4] This was found, hand-shrunk, and reported before we developed the automatic shrinker.

crashed the tab as illustrated in Fig. 1. We reported the bug in BugZilla and the error was quickly confirmed and fixed.[5]

Internally, SpiderMonkey's Wasm-engine creates a vector of "exported function" objects, each with a (bit-packed) Boolean, indicating whether a function is marked explicitly as exported. In the test program the same function occurs both as a start function and in a table, causing it to occur twice in the vector, with only one occurrence being marked explicitly. A subsequent removal of duplicates would however eliminate the marked function entry, leaving only an unmarked one. At run-time the JIT-compiler would then expect all explicitly exported functions to have an 'eager stub', which would be `null` in this case and thus cause a crash.

```
(module
  (type $0 (func))
  (type $1 (func (result f64)))
  (func $0 (type 0))
  (func $1
    (type 1)
    (loop (result f64)
      (f64.const 0.0) (i32.const 0) (br_table 1) (call 0))
    (br 0)
    (unreachable))
  (export "runf64" (func 1)))
```

Listing 4. Shrunk Wasm module causing JavaScriptCore to loop

The bug is particularly interesting, because SpiderMonkey already employs a fuzzer based on libFuzzer to detect such issues. However the above issue had escaped it. We believe this is due to the nature of the bug, being a "logical bug". As such, a coverage-driven fuzzer can visit all branches of the described code to achieve 100% coverage yet still miss the bug. While anecdotal, this represents a real-world bug escaping a state-of-the-art gray-box fuzzer yet being caught by a black-box QuickCheck generator.

JavaScriptCore `br_table` Difference. Our generator and shrinker automatically found the module in Listing 4 to exhibit different behavior on JavaScript-Core. The other three engines would print 0 when running and printing the result of the exported function, whereas JavaScriptCore would loop. The cause for the difference is the `br_table 1` instruction, which takes a (in this case empty) table of labels and does one of two things: (1) if the value on the stack is a valid index into the table it jumps to that, otherwise (2) it jumps to the provided "fallback" label (1 above). With label 1 representing the outermost control-context (the surrounding function) this effectively represents a return. JavaScriptCore would instead jump to label 0, effectively restarting the surrounding `loop`. This was due to a bug in an underlying jump optimizer.

---

[5] https://bugzilla.mozilla.org/show_bug.cgi?id=1545086.

This was reported and quickly acknowledged and fixed.[6] The reported test case was additionally added to the suite of stress tests. Interestingly, multiple Safari users reported this bug as websites using Wasm for font rendering were mis-rendered. While also anecdotal, the example illustrates real-world benefit of our generator: The minimal counterexample enabled developers to quickly identify and fix a real-world problem hitting end users.

JavaScriptCore Crash 1. Listing 5 shows another counterexample program we found triggering a segmentation fault in JavaScriptCore. Upon further inspection, this crash was only triggered in the nightly builds and thus the error had not made its way into production. Again we reported the bug along with a sequence of repeatedly smaller counterexamples, also establishing that the error was introduced by a commit between versions 249479 and 250961 of the nightly builds.[7] The error was never confirmed though, and eventually the error was discovered and fixed by other means. We speculate that our ability to file and report bugs has improved since this early bug report.

```
(module
  (type $0 (func (result f32)))
  (global $0 i32 (i32.const 1))
  (func $0
    (type 0)
    (f32.const 0.0)
    (f32.const 0.0)
    (i32.const 0)
    (select)
    (loop (result f32)
      (f32.const 0.0) (global.get 0) (br_if 0))
    (drop))
  (export "runf32" (func 0)))
```

Listing 5. Module causing JavaScriptCore to crash

```
(module
  (func (export "run")
    (param i32)
    (unreachable)
    (tee_local 0)
    (drop)))
```

Listing 6. Module erroneously rejected at compile-time by Chakra

---

[6] https://bugs.webkit.org/show_bug.cgi?id=209333.
[7] https://bugs.webkit.org/show_bug.cgi?id=202786.

JavaScriptCore Crash 2 (Known). We found another example that would crash JavaScriptCore with the error `FATAL: No color for %ftmp0`, indicating an error in `jsc`'s underlying graph-coloring register allocator. In contrast, the other three engines would all fail with a stack overflow. Again this was reported and acknowledged.[8] This issue was limited to an earlier revision and had since then been resolved.

Chakra Compile-Time Rejection (Known). A different mismatch our test setup located involved an `unreachable` and a `tee_local` instruction as illustrated in Listing 6. The module is erroneously rejected at compile-time by Chakra's validator with an error `Can't tee_local unreachable values`, whereas the three other engines throw a run-time error when trying to execute the `unreachable` instruction. Again this was reported[9] but the issue was already known.[10] A fix was merged in Feb. 2019 but still has not made its way into a release.

5.6 Inconsistencies in Web-Embedding

Imports aside, Wasm programs can only be observed for errors or non-termination. We found three issues related to the web-embedding of Wasm.

Different Stack Overflow Exceptions. Our generator found a counterexample program that would blow the call stack by indirectly calling itself. On V8 and JavaScriptCore this would result in an exception instance of `RangeError`, on SpiderMonkey an instance of `InternalError`, and on Chakra an instance of `Error`.

Different Data Segment Exceptions. Similarly our generator produced an example module with out-of-bounds data segment initializers, which would cause different errors across engines: V8 and SpiderMonkey would throw a `RuntimeError` exception, whereas Chakra and JavaScriptCore would throw a `LinkError` exception.

Different Exception Name Properties. JavaScriptCore has inconsistent name properties for JavaScript exceptions, which showed up when printing a detailed error for comparison. Consider the following JavaScript program:

```
let e1 = new WebAssembly.CompileError("a compile error")
let e2 = new WebAssembly.LinkError("a link error")
let e3 = new WebAssembly.RuntimeError("a runtime error")
print(e1.name, e1);
print(e2.name, e2);
print(e3.name, e3);
```

---

[8] https://bugs.webkit.org/show_bug.cgi?id=209294.

[9] https://github.com/microsoft/ChakraCore/issues/6185.

[10] https://github.com/microsoft/ChakraCore/pull/5889.

On V8, SpiderMonkey, and Chakra this yields:

```
CompileError CompileError: a compile error
LinkError LinkError: a link error
RuntimeError RuntimeError: a runtime error
```

but on JavaScriptCore it yielded:

```
Error Error: a compile error (evaluating 'new [...]')
Error Error: a link error (evaluating 'new [...]')
Error Error: a runtime error (evaluating 'new [...]')
```

The difference was reported but no acknowledgment has been received yet.[11]

5.7   Testing Buggy Behavior

Chakra's different behavior on an unreachable tee_local is relatively often tested, causing our tester to repeatedly rediscover and report it. Despite having its fix merged into the master branch over a year ago, the fix has still not made it into a released version. For this reason, we follow the approach of Hughes in the AUTOSAR project [14] and adjust the test to the documented buggy behavior. We thus consider a Chakra error about unreachable tee_local acceptable, despite differing from the other engines.

5.8   A Performance Experiment

We conducted a small experiment to measure the performance of the generator. The experiment was conducted on a normally loaded MacBook Pro laptop. We invoked the tester 6 times, each generating and comparing the output of 100 Wasm programs. Out of the 6 invocations, 1 exhibited different behavior on the 9th generated program. After 19 shrinking steps and 78.6 s a counterexample of 'different data segment exceptions' was reported. For the 5 successful invocations we counted 0–3 timeouts with each invocation taking from 87.8 to 257.1 s (avg: 158.7). We then reran the experiment with the same randomization seeds, this time excluding a reference interpreter comparison. We observed the same timeouts and the same counterexample, this time taking 79.9 s. The 5 successful invocations now took from 82.3 to 200.0 s (avg: 131.7).

6   Related Work

The research literature is rich with contributions within program generation for testing language processors. Purdom [21] originally suggested an algorithm for generating a set of sentences to test parsers and context-free grammars. McKeeman [17] coined the phrase *differential testing* (for software), to characterize his C compiler testing approach. This involved both a *stochastic grammar*

---

[11] https://bugs.webkit.org/show_bug.cgi?id=204054.

associating weights to each production, as well as a test-case reducer repeatedly applying simplifying heuristics.

Our work builds on Palka et al. [20], who tested the GHC Haskell compiler's strictness analyzer by generating random lambda terms. Their generator was structured as a bottom-up reading of the typing rules, thus introducing the idea of using the typing rules as a specification for a generation procedure of well-typed terms. Like our Wasm generator, their generator used backtracking to enable a higher success rate for term generation. Midtgaard et al. [19] also built on Palka et al. [20] in their OCaml program generation approach. To prevent generating programs with evaluation order dependence, they suggest to structure a generator according to a *type and effects system* with dedicated effect indicators. Reading the type and effects system bottom-up, their generator was able to generate evaluation order independent programs and thus find multiple bugs in OCaml compilers. Like us, they also developed a dedicated type-preserving shrinker to shorten counterexample programs.

Alternatives to a randomized recursive generator exist, such as enumeration-based program generation in the style of SmallCheck [22] and Bolzmann samplers to generate typed lambda terms of an approximate size [5]. Both these approaches have currently only been attempted on languages with relatively few language constructs.

Multiple C compilers have been tested by means of randomized testing. Yang et al. introduced CSmith [27], a randomized test-case generator of C program inputs. They used the generator to differentially test each produced program across various C compilers to find differences in their outputs. CSmith generates C programs via a grammar that describes a subset of the C language. It generates a C program with a top-level main function that returns the result of the program via a checksum. The rest of the program is randomly generated. CSmith compares the checksum output across the various compilers. Yang et al. also had to work around the non-deterministic parts of the C language when calculating the checksum. Like our generator, a program from CSmith can loop infinitely and therefore Yang et al. run each program with a timeout.

Barany used differential testing to find missed compiler optimizations in C programs [4]. To do so, he generated random C programs and compared the optimised program code generated by GCC, Clang, and CompCert. For the C program generation he used both CSmith [27] and *ldrgen* [3], a newly developed generator. The ldrgen generator addresses CSmith's tendency to generate dead code by introducing liveness triples in the generation inference rules in addition to the typing context. At each generation step, the liveness of the instruction influences the result. Using this approach, Barany identified multiple missed optimizations in all three tested compilers.

Le et al. [16] introduced *equivalence modulo inputs* (EMI) as an alternative compiler testing approach to differential testing. EMI defines the concept of equivalence of programs on the same input. As a proof of concept they developed Orion to target C compilers. Orion takes a test program as an input. First it extracts coverage information from the given program, and secondly it then generates EMI variants of the program. Le et al. used the generated EMI variants to test GCC, LLVM and ICC. As a result of their work, Le et al. have found and reported 147 unique bugs in GCC and LLVM.

Donaldson et al. [10] developed GLFuzz, thus using the concept of EMI to test graphics shader compilers in graphics cards. For a given shader input to GLFuzz, GLFuzz repeatedly applies a set of semantics-preserving transformations to the shader. The resulting shader renders a similar image to the original, thereby allowing a comparison between the original and the transformed shader's result. When a significantly different image is rendered, GLFuzz performs reduction (shrinking) to find a minimal set of transformations that lead to a significant difference after rendering. With this approach, Donaldson et al. found defects in all the GPU and driver configurations they tested.

Holler et al. [13] developed LangFuzz, a language-independent program generator. LangFuzz requires a language grammar, sample source code of language implementations, and a test suite. In contrast to CSmith and our own generator which take a generative approach, LangFuzz also utilizes a mutative approach to learn from the provided code samples and produce similar programs. LangFuzz first parses the supplied code samples and builds up code fragments. Afterwards random code fragments are selected and mutated. Finally the mutated program is run against the test suite. As a result of the mutation process, there is a higher chance of finding bugs if the sample source code base contains source code of known bugs. Holler et al. used LangFuzz to generate both JavaScript and PHP programs and found multiple implementation bugs for both.

Watt formalized and verified the Wasm specification within Isabelle [25]. As part of testing his formal model against Wasm engines, he conducted fuzz tests (property-based tests). He used CSmith to generate C programs and then compiled them to Wasm using the Binaryen toolchain [6]. As mentioned, this approach confines tests to the subset of the Wasm language utilized by the Binaryen backend. In contrast, our generator is not limited to such a subset. Consequently we have been able to find errors that span the entire language specification. On the other hand, our generator benefits from both the Wasm specification and Watt's formalization of it to generate valid programs.

7   Conclusion

We have presented a stack-driven generator of WebAssembly programs. For each generated Wasm program we compare the reference interpreter's output against each of the four major browsers WebAssembly engines. In doing so, we have been able to find both major and minor differences, including crashing bugs. To reduce the produced programs, we have developed a stack-driven shrinker. The resulting, minimal counterexample programs allow our bug reports to be short and to the point. With WebAssembly moving beyond client-side web development to new domains such as smart contracts and blockchain, we believe our generator can be a useful tool to ensure agreement across Wasm engines. We have released the source code of the generator under a BSD-license: https://github.com/jmid/wasm-prop-tester.

Acknowledgments. We are grateful to Andreas Rossberg for suggesting to build a Wasm generator, following a presentation of our OCaml generator [19]. We also thank the APLAS reviewers for their constructive comments.

References

1. Arts, T., Castro, L.M., Hughes, J.: Testing Erlang data types with Quviq QuickCheck. In: Proceedings of the of ERLANG 2008, pp. 1–8 (2008)
2. Arts, T., Hughes, J., Johansson, J., Wiger, U.: Testing telecoms software with Quviq QuickCheck. In: Proceedings of ERLANG 2006 (2006)
3. Barany, G.: Liveness-driven random program generation. In: Proceedings of LOP-STR 2017, pp. 112–127 (2017)
4. Barany, G.: Finding missed compiler optimizations by differential testing. In: Proceedings of CC 2018, pp. 82–92 (2018)
5. Bendkowski, M., Grygiel, K., Tarau, P.: Boltzmann samplers for closed simply-typed lambda terms. In: Lierler, Y., Taha, W. (eds.) PADL 2017. LNCS, vol. 10137, pp. 120–135. Springer, Cham (2017). https://doi.org/10.1007/978-3-319-51676-9_8
6. Binaryen: Compiler infrastructure and toolchain library for WebAssembly. https://github.com/WebAssembly/binaryen. Accessed 02 July 2020
7. Cardelli, L.: Type systems. ACM Comput. Surv. **28**(1), 263–264 (1996)
8. Claessen, K., Hughes, J.: QuickCheck: a lightweight tool for random testing of Haskell programs. In: Proceedings of ICFP 2000, pp. 53–64 (2000)
9. Cruanes, S.: QCheck: QuickCheck inspired property-based testing for OCaml. https://github.com/c-cube/qcheck. Accessed 02 July 2020
10. Donaldson, A.F., Evrard, H., Lascu, A., Thomson, P.: Automated testing of graphics shader compilers. PACMPL **1**(OOPSLA), 93:1–93:29 (2017)
11. GoogleChromeLabs: JSVU, JavaScript (engine) version updater. https://github.com/GoogleChromeLabs/jsvu. Accessed 04 July 2020
12. Haas, A., et al.: Bringing the web up to speed with WebAssembly. In: Proceedings of PLDI 2017, pp. 185–200 (2017)
13. Holler, C., Herzig, K., Zeller, A.: Fuzzing with code fragments. In: Proceedings of the 21st USENIX Security Symposium (2012)
14. Hughes, J.: Experiences with QuickCheck: testing the hard stuff and staying sane. In: Lindley, S., McBride, C., Trinder, P., Sannella, D. (eds.) A List of Successes That Can Change the World. LNCS, vol. 9600, pp. 169–186. Springer, Cham (2016). https://doi.org/10.1007/978-3-319-30936-1_9
15. Koopman, P., Plasmeijer, R.: Testing with functional reference implementations. In: Page, R., Horváth, Z., Zsók, V. (eds.) TFP 2010. LNCS, vol. 6546, pp. 134–149. Springer, Heidelberg (2011). https://doi.org/10.1007/978-3-642-22941-1_9
16. Le, V., Afshari, M., Su, Z.: Compiler validation via equivalence modulo inputs. In: Proceedings of PLDI 2014, pp. 216–226 (2014)
17. McKeeman, W.M.: Differential testing for software. Digit. Tech. J. **10**(1), 100–107 (1998)
18. Midtgaard, J.: QuickChecking patricia trees. In: Wang, M., Owens, S. (eds.) TFP 2017. LNCS, vol. 10788, pp. 59–78. Springer, Cham (2018). https://doi.org/10.1007/978-3-319-89719-6_4
19. Midtgaard, J., Justesen, M.N., Kasting, P., Nielson, F., Nielson, H.R.: Effect-driven QuickChecking of compilers. PACMPL **1**(ICFP), 15:1–15:23 (2017)

20. Pałka, M.H., Claessen, K., Russo, A., Hughes, J.: Testing an optimising compiler by generating random lambda terms. In: Proceedings of AST 2011, pp. 91–97 (2011)
21. Purdom, P.: A sentence generator for testing parsers. BIT **12**(3), 366–375 (1972)
22. Reich, J.S., Naylor, M., Runciman, C.: Lazy generation of canonical test programs. In: Gill, A., Hage, J. (eds.) IFL 2011. LNCS, vol. 7257, pp. 69–84. Springer, Heidelberg (2012). https://doi.org/10.1007/978-3-642-34407-7_5
23. Rossberg, A.: WebAssembly reference interpreter. https://github.com/WebAssembly/spec/tree/master/interpreter. Accessed 02 July 2020
24. Runciman, C., Naylor, M., Lindblad, F.: SmallCheck and lazy SmallCheck: automatic exhaustive testing for small values. In: Proceedings of Haskell 2008, pp. 37–48 (2008)
25. Watt, C.: Mechanising and verifying the WebAssembly specification. In: Proceedings of CPP 2018, pp. 53–65 (2018)
26. WebAssembly: Official website. https://webassembly.org/. Accessed 02 July 2020
27. Yang, X., Chen, Y., Eide, E., Regehr, J.: Finding and understanding bugs in C compilers. In: Proceedings of PLDI 2011, pp. 283–294 (2011)

Banyan: Coordination-Free Distributed Transactions over Mergeable Types

Shashank Shekhar Dubey[1(✉)], K. C. Sivaramakrishnan[1], Thomas Gazagnaire[2], and Anil Madhavapeddy[3]

[1] Indian Institute of Technology, Madras, India
ssdubey@cse.iitm.ac.in
[2] Tarides, Paris, France
[3] University of Cambridge Computer Laboratory, Cambridge, UK

Abstract. Programming loosely connected distributed applications is a challenging endeavour. Loosely connected distributed applications such as geo-distributed stores and intermittently reachable IoT devices cannot afford to coordinate among all of the replicas in order to ensure data consistency due to prohibitive latency costs and the impossibility of coordination if availability is to be ensured. Thus, the state of the replicas evolves independently, making it difficult to develop correct applications. Existing solutions to this problem limit the data types that can be used in these applications, which neither offer the ability to compose them to construct more complex data types nor offer transactions.

In this paper, we describe Banyan, a distributed programming model for developing loosely connected distributed applications. Data types in Banyan are equipped with a three-way merge function à la Git to handle conflicts. Banyan provides isolated transactions for grouping together individual operations which do not require coordination among different replicas. We instantiate Banyan over Cassandra, an off-the-shelf industrial-strength distributed store. Several benchmarks, including a distributed build-cache, illustrates the effectiveness of the approach.

1 Introduction

When applications replicate data across different sites, they need to make a fundamental choice regarding the consistency of data. Strong consistency properties such as Linearizability [20] and Serializability [9] makes it easier to design correct applications. However, strong consistency is often at odds with high performance. Strong consistency necessitates that all the replicas coordinate to agree on a global order in which any conflicting operations are resolved. The CAP theorem [17] and PACELC theorem [1] state that strongly consistent applications exhibit higher latencies when all the replicas are reachable, and they are unavailable when some of the replicas are unreachable. This limitation has spurred the development of commercial weakly consistent distributed databases for wide-area applications such as DynamoDB [2], Cassandra [3], CosmosDB [4] and Riak [32]. However, developing correct applications under weak consistency

© Springer Nature Switzerland AG 2020
B. C. d. S. Oliveira (Ed.): APLAS 2020, LNCS 12470, pp. 231–250, 2020.
https://doi.org/10.1007/978-3-030-64437-6_12

is challenging due to the fact that the operations may be reordered in complex ways even if issued by the same session [11]. Moreover, these databases only offer a limited set of sequential data types with a built-in conflict resolution strategies such as last-write-wins and multi-valued objects. Such built-in conflict resolution leads to anomalies such as write-skew [8] which makes it difficult (and often impossible) to develop complex applications with rich behaviours.

Rather than programming with sequential data types while reasoning about their semantics in a weakly consistent setting, an alternative strategy is to equip the data types with the ability to reconcile conflicts. Kaki et al. [23] recently proposed Mergeable Replicated Data Types (MRDTs) as a way to automatically derive correct distributed variants of ordinary data types. The inductively defined data types are equipped with an invertible relational specification which is used to derive a three-way merge function à la Git [18], a distributed version control system.

What does it take to make MRDTs a practical alternative to implementing high-throughput, low-latency distributed applications such as the ones that would be implemented over industrial-strength distributed databases? There are several key challenges to getting there.

Firstly, while MRDTs define merge semantics for operations on individual objects, Kaki et al. do not describe the semantics of composition of operations on multiple objects – i.e. transactions. Transactions are indispensable for building complex applications. Strongly consistent distributed transactions suffer from unavailability [1], whereas highly-available transactions [5] combined with weakly consistent operations often lead to incomprehensible behaviours [36].

Secondly, MRDTs impose significant burden on the storage and network layer to be able to support three-way merges to reconcile conflicts. Kaki et al. implement MRDTs over Irmin [21], a Git-like store for arbitrary objects, not just files. As with Git, in order to reconcile conflicts, three-way merges in MRDTs require the storage layer to record enough history to be able to retrieve the *lowest common ancestor* (LCA) state. For a distributed database, performance of the network layer is quite important for throughput and latency. Industrial-strength distributed databases use gossip protocols [24] to quickly disseminate updates in order to ensure fast convergence between the replicas. Git comes equipped with a remote protocol for transferring objects between remote sites using *push* and *pull* mechanisms. Unfortunately, directly using the Git remote protocols would mean that the client will have to name branches explicitly, complicating the programming model. The onus is on the client to ensure that all the branches that have updates are merged in order to ensure that there is convergence. This is undesirable.

Contributions. In this paper, we present Banyan, a programming model for building loosely connected distributed applications that provides coordination-free transactions over MRDTs. Banyan provides per-object causal consistency, and the transaction model is built on the principles of Git-like branches. Rather than relying on Git remote protocol for dissemination across replicas, we instantiate Banyan on top of Cassandra, an industrial-strength, off-the-shelf distributed store [26]. Unlike Git, Banyan does not expose named branches explicitly, and ensures eventual convergence. Importantly, Banyan only relies on eventual consistency, and Banyan can be instantiated on any eventually consistent key-value store. Extensive evaluation shows that Banyan makes it easy to build complex high-performance distributed applications.

The rest of the paper is organised as follows. We motivate the Banyan model by designing a distributed build cache in the next section. Section 3 describes the Banyan programming model. Section 4 describes the instantiation of Banyan on Cassandra. We evaluate the instantiation of Banyan on top of Cassandra in Sect. 5. Sections 6 and 8 present the related work and conclusions, respectively.

2   Motivation: A Distributed Build Cache

A distributed build cache enables a team of developers and/or a continuous integration (CI) system to reuse the build artefacts between several builds. Such a facility is provided by modern build tools such as Gradle [19] and Bazel [7], which can store and retrieve build artefacts from cloud storage services such as Amazon S3 or Google Cloud Storage. Consider the challenge of building a distributed build cache for OCaml packages. Let us assume that the builds are reproducible – that is, independent builds of the same source files yield the same artefact. In addition to storing the artefacts, it would be useful to gather statistics about the artefacts such as creation time, last accessed time and number of cache hits. Such information may be used in the cache eviction policy or replicating artefacts across several sites for increased availability. While an artefact itself is reproducible, care must be taken to ensure that the statistics are consistent. For the sake of exposition, we will assume that all the build hosts use the same operating system and compiler version.

2.1   Mergeable Types

Let us build this distributed cache using Banyan, implementing it in OCaml. At its heart, Banyan is a distributed key-value store. The keys in Banyan are *paths*, represented as list of strings. The values are algebraic data types equipped a merge function that reconciles conflicting updates. In this example, we will use the following schema: [<pkg_name>; <version>; <kind>; <filename>] for the keys, where <kind> is either lib indicating binary artefact or stats indicating statistics about the artefact. The value type is given below:

```
type timestamp = float
type value =
  | B of bigarray  (*binary artefact*)
  | S of timestamp (*created*) * timestamp (*last accessed*)
      * int (*hits*)
```

The value is either a binary artefact or a statistics triple. Figure 1 shows the slice of the build cache key-value store. The cache stores the artefacts (cmx and cmi files) produced as a result of compiling the source file lwt_mutex.ml from the package lwt version 5.3.0. The build cache also stores the statistics for every artefact. The example shows that the lwt_mutex.cmx was accessed 25 times. When several developers and/or CI pipelines are running concurrently on different hosts, they may attempt to add the same artefact to the store, or, if the artefact is already present, retrieve it from the cache and update the corresponding artefact statistics. It would be unwise to synchronize across all of the hosts for updating the store, and suffer the latency hit and potential unavailability. Hence, Banyan only writes an update to one of the replicas. The replicas asynchronously share the

Key	Value
/lwt/5.3.0/lib/ lwt_mutex.cmx	B(0x…)
/lwt/5.3.0/lib/ lwt_mutex.cmi	B(0x…)
/lwt/5.3.0/stats/ lwt_mutex.cmx	S(1593518762.20, 1593518822.36, 25)

Fig. 1. A slice of the build cache key-value store.

updates between each other, and resolve conflicting updates using user-defined three-way merge function. The merge function for the build cache is given below.

```
1  let merge (lca: value option) (v1: value) (v2: value) : value =
2    match lca, v1, v2 with
3    | None, B a1, B a2 (* no lca *)
4    | Some (B _), B a1, B a2 -> assert (a1 = a2); B a1
5    | None, S(c1,la1,h1), S(c2,la2,h2) -> (* no lca *)
6        S(min c1 c2, max la1 la2, h1 + h2)
7    | Some(S(_,_,h0)), S(c1,la1,h1), S(c2,la2,h2)->
8        S(min c1 c2, max la1 la2, h1 + h2 - h0)
9    | _ -> failwith "impossible"
```

The key idea here is that Banyan tracks the *causal history* of the state updates such that it is always known what the *lowest common ancestor* (LCA) state is, if one exists. This idea is analogous to how Git tracks history with the notion of *branches*. The merge function is applied to the LCA and the two conflicting versions to determine the new state. In the case of build cache, since the builds are reproducible, the binary artefacts will be the same (line 4). The only interesting conflicts are in the statistics. The merge

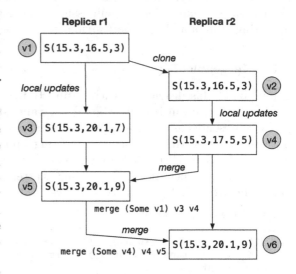

Fig. 2. Merging conflicting statistics updates.

function picks the earliest creation timestamp, latest last accessed timestamp, and the sum of the new cache hits since the LCA in the two branches and the original value at the LCA, if present (lines 5–8).

Figure 2 shows how the merge function helps reconcile conflicts. The arrows capture the happens-before relationship between the states. Assume that replica r2 starts off by cloning the branch corresponding to replica r1. Subsequently both r1 and r2 performed local updates. The remote updates are reconciled by calling the merge function on each of the conflicting values. The value v5 is obtained with merging the values v3 and v4 with v1 as LCA. Importantly, observe that the cache hit count is 9 in v5 which corresponds to the sum of 3 hits in the initial state, 4 additional hits in r1 and 2 additional hits in r2. At this point, r1 has all the changes from r2, but the vice-versa is not true. Subsequently, when r1 is merged into r2, both the replicas have converged.

```
let compile s (* session *) =
  let ts = Unix.gettimeofday () in
  let lib = ["lwt";"5.3.0";"lib"] in
  let stats = ["lwt";"5.3.0";"stats"] in
  refresh s >>= fun () ->
  read s (lib @ ["lwt_mutex.cmx"]) >>= fun v ->
  match v with
  | None ->
      let (cmx, cmi, o) = ocamlopt "lwt_mutex.ml" in
      write s (lib @ ["lwt_mtex.cmx"]) (B cmx) >>= fun _ ->
      write s (stats @ ["lwt_mutex.cmx"]) (S (ts,ts,0))
                                          >>= fun _ ->
      ... (* similarly for cmi and o files *)
      publish s >>= fun _ ->
      return (cmx, cmi, o)
  | Some cmx ->
      read s (stats @ ["lwt_mutex.cmx"])
                          >>= fun (Some M(c,la,h)) ->
      write s (stats @ ["lwt_mutex.cmx"]) (S (c,ts,h+1))
                          >>= fun _ ->
      read s (lib @ ["lwt_mutex.cmi"]) >>= fun (Some cmi) ->
      read s (lib @ ["lwt_mutex.o"]) >>= fun (Some o) ->
      ... (* update stats for cmi and o file *)
      publish s >>= fun _ ->
      return (cmx, cmi, o)
```

Fig. 3. Compiling lwt_mutex.ml.

2.2 Transactions

Now that we the mergeable value type for the build cache, let us see how we can compile lwt_mutex.ml using Banyan. Figure 3 shows the code for compiling lwt_mutex.ml. In Banyan, the clients interact with the store in *isolated* sessions. A session can fetch recent updates using the **refresh** primitive and make *all* the local updates visible to other sessions using the **publish** primitive. During **refresh**, any conflicting updates are resolved using the three-way merge function associated with the value type.

In order to compile lwt_mutex.ml, we first refresh the session to get any recent updates. Then, we check whether the lwt_mutex.cmx file is in the build cache. If not, the source file is compiled, and the resultant artefacts (cmx, cmi, o files) and the corresponding entries for updated statistics are written to the store. Finally, the all the local updates are published.

The all or nothing property of **refresh** and **publish** is critical for the correctness of this code. Observe that when the artefact is locally compiled, all the artefacts and their statistics are published atomically. This ensures that if a session sees the cmx file, then other artefacts and their statistics will also be visible. Thus, Banyan makes it easy to write highly-available, complex distributed applications in an idiomatic fashion.

3   Programming Model

In this section, we shall describe the system and programming model of Banyan from the developers point-of-view. The Banyan store consists of several replicas, which are fully or partially replicated [13]. The replicas asynchronously distribute updates amongst themselves until they converge. The key property that enables Banyan to support mergeable types and isolated transactions is that Banyan tracks the history of the store in the same way that Git tracks the history of a repository.

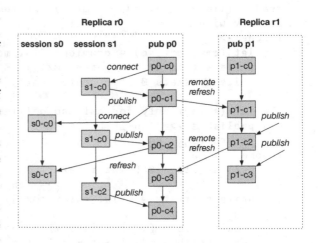

Fig. 4. Banyan system and programming model.

Figure 4 presents the schematic diagram of the system and programming model. Each replica has a distinguished public branch pub, which records the history of the changing state at that replica. Each node in this connected history graph represents a *commit*. Whenever a new client connection is established, a new branch is forked off the latest commit in the public branch. Any reads or writes in this session are only committed to this branch unless explicitly published. This ensures the isolation property of each session. The figure shows the creation of two sessions in the replica r0.

The simplified Banyan API is given below:

```
type config  (* Store configuration *)
type session
```

```
type key = string list
type value    (* Type of mergeable values in the store *)

val connect : config -> session Lwt.t
val close   : session -> unit Lwt.t
val read    : session -> key -> value option Lwt.t
val write   : session -> key -> value -> unit Lwt.t
val publish : session -> unit Lwt.t
val refresh : session -> unit Lwt.t
```

When a client connects to a Banyan store, a new session is created, which is rooted to one of the replicas in the store. Every write creates a commit in the session performing the write. As previously explained, Banyan permits the sessions to atomically **publish** their updates and **refresh** to obtain latest updates. The **publish** operation squashes all the local commits since the previous **refresh** or **publish** to a single commit, and then *pushes* the changes to the public branch on the replica to which the session is rooted. The **refresh** operation *pulls* updates from the public branch into the current sessions branch. Both **publish** and **refresh** may invoke the merge function on the value type if there are conflicts. The objects that written to each replica are asynchronously replicated to other replicas. Banyan offers causal consistency for operations on each key.

Periodically, the changes from other public branches are *pulled* into a replica's public branch (remote refresh). This operation happens *implicitly* and asynchronously, and does not block the client on that replica. When a session is closed, the outstanding writes are implicitly published. Similarly, when a session is connected, there is an implicit refresh operation.

Observe that both the local and the remote refresh operations are non-blocking – it is always safe for **refresh** to return with updates only from a subset of public branches. The only push operation is due to **publish**. When pushing to a branch, it is necessary to atomically update the target branch to avoid concurrency errors. The key observation is that only the session that belongs to a replica can push to the public branch on that replica. This can be achieved with replica-local concurrency control and does not require coordination among the replicas. Hence, Banyan transactions do not need inter-replica coordination, and hence, are available.

When a particular replica goes down, the sessions that are rooted to that replica may not have enough history to be able to **refresh** and **publish** to other replicas. In particular, **refresh** and **publish** will need to discover the LCA in the case of conflicting updates. Since the objects are asynchronously replicated across the replicas, the recent writes to the replica that went down may not have been replicated to other replicas. Hence, Banyan requires sticky availability [5] – the sessions need to reach the logical replica to which it originally connected. In practice, with partial replication, a logical replica may be represented by a set of physical servers. As long as one of these physical servers is reachable, the system remains available for that session.

Compared to traditional transactions usually executed at a particular isolation level, **refresh** and **publish** permits more fine-grained, explicit control of visibility. In Banyan, transactions are delimited by `publish` operations, begin and end of sessions. For example, the set of writes performed between consecutive `publish` operations are made visible atomically outside the session. The transaction may abort if the three-way merge function throws an exception. However, in practice, the useful MRDTs are designed in such a way that a merge is always possible, and the failure of the merge function represents a bug. This idea of merge always being possible ensures *strong eventual consistency*, espoused by convergent replicated data types [33]. Banyan adds transactional support over strong eventual consistency.

The `publish` and `refresh` can be used to achieve well-known isolation levels. For example, consider parallel snapshot isolation (PSI) [35], which is an extension of snapshot isolation (SI) [8] for geo-replicated systems. Like SI, the transactions in PSI operate on a snapshot of the state at a replica. While SI precludes write-write conflicts, PSI admits them on mergeable types. Since all the data types in Banyan are mergeable types, every write-write conflict can be resolved. We can achieve PSI by `refresh`ing at that beginning of the transaction and `publish`ing at the end of the transaction with no intervening `refresh`es.

Similarly, we get monotonic atomic view (MAV) [5] isolation level if two consecutive `publish` operations are interspersed with `refresh`es. Since the `refresh`es may bring in new updates from committed transactions, the state of the transaction grows monotonically.

4   Implementation

In this section, we describe the instantiation of Banyan on Cassandra [3], a popular, industrial-strength, column-oriented, distributed database. Cassandra offers eventual consistency with a last-write-wins conflict resolution policy. Cassandra also offers complex data types such as `list`, `set` and `map` with baked-in conflict resolution policies. Given the richness of replicated data types, the available complex data types are quite limiting. Cassandra also offers lightweight transactions (distributed compare-and-update) implemented using the Paxos consensus protocol [27]. Lightweight transactions are limited to operate on only one object. Banyan does not use lightweight transactions since their cost is prohibitively high due to consensus. As mentioned previously Banyan only requires sticky availability, and so uses a replica-local lock for ensuring mutual exclusion when multiple sessions try to update the public branch on a replica concurrently.

By instantiating Banyan on Cassandra, we offload the concerns of replication, fault tolerance, availability and convergence to the backing store. On top of Cassandra, Banyan uses Irmin [21], an OCaml library for persistent stores with built-in branching, merging and reverting facilities. Irmin can be configured to use different storage backends, and in our case, the storage is Cassandra. Importantly, Cassandra being a distributed database serves the purpose of the networking layer in addition to persistent storage. While Irmin permits arbitrary branching and merging, Banyan is a specific workflow on top of Irmin which retains high availability.

4.1 Irmin Data Model

The expressivity of Irmin imposes significant burden on the underlying storage. For efficiently storing different versions of the state as the store evolves, Irmin uses the Git object model. Figure 5 shows a snapshot of the state of the Irmin store. There are two kinds of stores: a mutable tag store and an immutable, content-addressed block store. The tag store records the branches

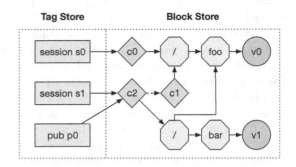

Fig. 5. A sample Irmin store. The rectangles are tags, diamonds are commit objects, octagons are tree object, and circles are blob objects.

and the commit that corresponds to this branch. In this example, we have three branches, session s0, session s1 and pub p0.

The block store is content-addressed and has three different kinds of objects: commits, tree and blobs. A commit object represents a commit, and it may have several parent commits and a single reference to a tree node. For example, the commit c2's parent is c1, and c0 and c1 do not have any parent commits. The tree object corresponds to directory entries in a filesystem, and recursively refer to other tree objects or a blob object. Unlike Git, Irmin allows blob objects to be arbitrary values, not just files. The blob objects may refer to other blob objects. In the session s1, reading the keys ["foo"] and ["bar"] would yield Some v0 and Some v1, respectively.

Observe that all the commits share the tree object foo and its descendents, thanks to the block store being content addressed. Content addressibility of the block store means that as the store evolves, the contents of the store are shared between multiple commits, if possible. On the other hand, updating a value in a deep hierarchy of tree objects would necessitate allocating a new spine in order to maintain both the old and the new versions. Thus, each write in Banyan will turn into several writes to the underlying storage.

4.2 Cassandra Instantiation

For instantiating Banyan on Cassandra, we use two tables, one for the tag store and another for the block store. For the tag store, the key is a string (tag) and the value is a blob (hash of the commit node). For the block store, the key is a blob (hash of the content), and the value is a blob (content). Irmin handles the logic necessary to serialize and deserialize the various Git objects into binary blobs and back.

Cassandra replicates the writes to the tag and block tables asynchronously amongst the replicas. Each replica periodically merges the public branches of other replicas into its public branch to fetch remote updates. Due to eventual consistency of Cassandra, it may be the case that not all the objects from a remote replica are available locally. For example, the merge function may find a new commit from a remote replica, but the tree object referenced by a commit object may not available locally. In this situation, Banyan simply skips merging this branch in this round. Cassandra ensures that eventually the remote tree object will arrive at this replica and will be merged in a subsequent remote refresh operation. Thus, fetching remote updates is a non-blocking operation.

In Irmin, the tag store is updated with a compare-and-swap to ensure that concurrent updates to the same tag should be disallowed. Naively implementing this in Cassandra would necessitate the use of lightweight transactions and suffer prohibitive costs. By restricting the Banyan programming model (Sect. 3) such that entries in the tag store (in particular, the tag corresponding to the public branch of the replica) is only updated on that replica, we remove the necessity for lightweight transactions. Thus, we do not depend on any special features of Cassandra to realise the Banyan model, and Banyan can be instantiated on any eventually consistent key-value store.

4.3 Recursive Merges

A particular challenge in making Banyan scalable is the problem of recursive merges. Consider a simple mergeable counter MRDT, whose implementation is:

```
let merge lca v1 v2 =
  let old = match lca with None -> 0 | Some v -> v in
  v1 + v2 - old
```

Consider the execution history presented in Fig. 6 which shows the evolution of a single counter. The history only shows the interaction between two replicas, and does not show any sessions. Each node in the history is a commit. Since we want to focus on a single counter, for simplicity, we ignore the tree nodes and the node labels show the counter value.

Initially the counters are 0, and each replica concurrently increments the counter by 4 and 5. When the replicas perform remote refreshes, they invoke merge None 4 5 to resolve the conflict updates yielding 9. The LCA is None since there is no common ancestor.

Subsequently, the replicas increment the counters by 3 and 5. Now, consider that the replicas merge each other's branches. When merging 12 and 14, there are two equally valid LCAs 4 and 5. Picking either one of them leads to incorrect result. At this point, Irmin merges the two LCAs using merge None 4 5 to yield 9, which is used as the LCA for merging 12 and 14. This yields the value 17. The result of merging the LCAs is represented as a rounded rectangle. Importantly, the result of the recursive merge 9 is not a parent commit of 12 and 14 (distinguished by the use of dotted arrows). This is because the commit nodes are stored in the content-addressed store, and adding a new parent to the commit node would create a distinct node, whose hash is different from the original node. Any other nodes that referenced the original commit node will continue to reference the old node. As a result, the recursive merges will need to be performed again for subsequent requests!

Consider that the replicas further evolve by incrementing 1 and 2, yielding 18 and 19. When these commits are merged on remote refresh, there are two LCAs 12 and 14, which need to be merged. This in turn has two LCAs 4 and 5, which need to be merged. Thus, every subsequent recursive merge, which is very likely since the replicas merge each other's branches, requires repeating all the previous recursive merges. This does not scale.

We solve this problem by having a separate table in Cassandra that acts as a cache, recording the result of LCA merges. Whenever Banyan encounters a recursive merge, the cache is first consulted before performing the merge. In this example, when 18

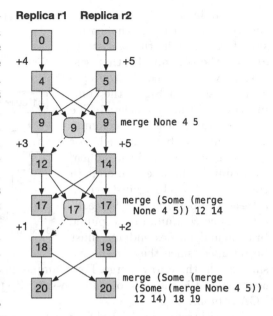

Fig. 6. Recursive merge. Rounded rectangles are the results of recursive merges.

and 19 are being merged, Banyan first checks whether the two LCAs 12 and 14 are in the cache. They would not be. This triggers a recursive merge of LCAs 4 and 5, whose result is in the cache, and is reused. The cache is also updated with an entry that records that the merge of the LCAs 12 and 14 is the commit corresponding to 17.

4.4   Garbage Collection

While traditional database systems only store the most recent version of the data, Banyan necessitates that previous versions of the data must also be kept around for three-way merges. While persistence of prior versions [15,16] is a useful property for audit and tamper evidence, the Banyan API presented here does not provide a way to access earlier versions. The question then is: when can those prior versions be garbage collected?

We have not yet implemented the garbage collector for Banyan on Cassandra, but we sketch the design here. Git is equipped with a garbage collector that considers that any object in the block store that is reachable from the tag store is alive. Unreachable objects are deleted. Our aim is to assist the Git-like garbage collector by pruning the history graph of nodes which will no longer be used. The key idea is that if a commit node will not be used for LCA computation, then that commit node may be deleted. Deleting commit nodes will leave dangling references from its referees, but Irmin can be extended to ignore dangling references to commit nodes.

For individual sessions, once the session is closed, the corresponding entry in the tag store, and all the commits by that session may be deleted. In the execution history in Fig. 7, the commit node s0-c0 may be deleted. The next question is when can commits on public branch be deleted. For each ongoing session in a replica, we maintain the latest commit in the public branch against which refresh was performed. The earliest of such commits in the public branch and its descendants must be retained, since they are neces-

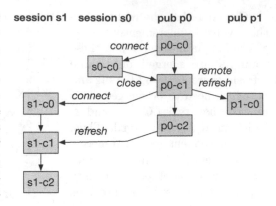

Fig. 7. Garbage collection. Here, the commits p0-c0 and s0-c0 may be deleted.

sary for the three-way merge. For example, in Fig. 7, session s1 refreshed against p0-c2, and s1 is the only ongoing session. If s1 publishes, then p0-c2 will be the LCA commit.

A similar reasoning is used for remote refreshes. When a commit in the public branch of a replica has been merged into the public branches of all the other replicas, then the ancestors of such commits will not be accessed and can be deleted. In Fig. 7, assume that we only have two replicas. Since p0-c1 was merged by the public branch p1, p0-c1 will be the LCA commit for subsequent remote refreshes by p1. Given that p0-c0 is neither necessary for remote refreshes nor for ongoing sessions, p0-c0 can be deleted.

5   Evaluation

In this section, we evaluate the performance of Banyan's instantiation on Cassandra. Our goal is to assess the suitability of Banyan for programming loosely connected distributed applications. To this end, we first quantify the overheads of implementing Banyan over Cassandra. Subsequently, we assess the performance of MRDTs implemented using Banyan. And finally, we study the performance of distributed build cache (Sect. 2).

5.1   Experimental Setup

For the experiments, we use a Cassandra cluster with 4 nodes within the same data center. Each Cassandra node runs on a baremetal Intel®Xeon®E3-1240 CPU, with 4 physical cores, and 2 hardware threads per core. Each core runs at 3.70 GHz and has 128 KB of L1 data cache, 128 KB of L1 instruction cache, 1 MB L2 cache and 8 MB of L3 cache. Each machine has 32 GB of main memory. The machines are unloaded except for the Cassandra node. The ping latency between the machines is 0.5 ms on average. The clients are run on a machine with the same configuration in the same data center.

For the experiments, Cassandra cluster is configured with a replication factor of 1, read and write consistency levels of ONE. Hence, the cluster maintains a single copy of each data item, and only waits for one of the servers to respond to return the result of read and write to the client. These choices lead to eventual consistency where the reads may not return the latest write. The cluster may be configured with larger replication factor for better fault tolerance. However, stronger consistency levels are not useful since Banyan enforces per-key causal consistency over the underlying eventual consistency offered by Cassandra. In fact, choosing strong consistency for reads and writes in Cassandra does not offer strong consistency in Banyan since the visibility of updates in Banyan is explicitly controlled with the use of refresh and publish.

5.2   Baseline Overheads

Given that Banyan has to persist every version of the store, what is the impact of Banyan when compared to using Cassandra in a scenario where Cassandra would be sufficient? We measure the throughput of performing 32k operations, with 80% reads and 20% writes with different numbers of clients. The keys and values are 8 and 128 byte strings, respectively. For Banyan, we use last-writer-wins resolution policy, which is the policy used by Cassandra. The results are presented in Fig. 8.

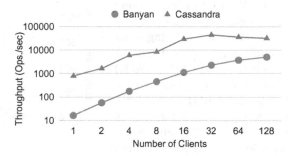

Fig. 8. Performance comparison between Banyan and Cassandra on LWW string value.

With 1 client, Banyan performs 16 operations per second, while Cassandra performs 795 operations per second. Cassandra offers 50× more throughput than Banyan with 1 client. This is due to the fact that every read (write) performs 4 reads (3 reads and 4 writes) to the underlying store to create and access the tag, commit and tree nodes. Banyan additionally includes marshalling and hashing overheads for accessing the content-addressed block store. Cassandra does not include any of these overheads. Luckily, Banyan overheads are local to a client, and hence, can be easily parallelized. With 1 client, the cluster is severely under utilized, and the client overheads dominate. With increasing number of clients, the cluster is better utilized. At 128 clients, Cassandra performs 31274 operations per second where as Banyan performs 5131 operations per second, which is a slowdown of 6.2×. We believe that these are reasonable overheads given the stronger consistency and isolation guarantees, and better programming model offered by Banyan.

At the end of 32k operations, Cassandra uses 4.9 MB of disk space, while Banyan uses 1.8 GB of disk space. As mentioned earlier (Sect. 4.4), we have yet to implement garbage collection for Banyan– once implemented, we expect this space usage will come down significantly.

5.3   Mergeable Types

Counter. We begin with the counter data type discussed in Sect. 4.3. How does a Banyan counter perform on when concurrently updated by multiple clients? For the experiment, the value type is a counter that supports increment, decrement and read operations. The clients perform 32k increment or decrement operations on a key randomly selected from a small key space. Each client refreshes and publishes after every 100 operations. By choosing a small key space, we aim to study the scalability of the system with large number of conflicts.

Figure 9 shows the performance result for two key spaces of size 1024 and 4096 keys. With 1 client, there are no conflicts. The conflicts increases with increasing number of clients. We get a peak throughput of 1814 (2027) operations per second with a key space of 1024 (4096) keys. Observe that the number of conflicts is considerably lower with 4096 keys when compared to 1024 keys. As a result, the throughput is higher with 4096

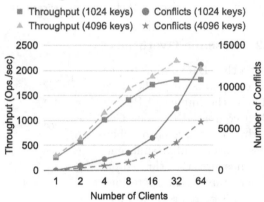

Fig. 9. Performance of counter MRDT.

keys. The result shows that the throughput of the system is proportional to the number of conflicting operations.

Blob Log. Another useful class of MRDTs are *mergeable logs*, where each log message is a string. Such a distributed log is useful for collecting logs in a distributed system, and examining the logs in their global time order. To this end, each log entry is a pair of timestamp and message, and the log itself is a list of such entries in reverse chronological order. The merge function for the mergeable log extracts the newer log entries from both the versions, sorts the newer entries in reverse chronological order and returns the list obtained by appending the sorted newer entries to the front of the log at the LCA.

While this implementation is simple, it does not scale well. In particular, each commit stores the entire log as a single serialized blob. This does not take advantage of the fact that every commit can share the tail of the log with its predecessor. Moreover, every append to the log needs to deserialize the entire log, append the new entry and serialize the log again. Hence, append is an $O(n)$ operation, where n is the size of the log. Merges are also worst case $O(n)$. This is undesirable. We call this implementation a *blob log*.

Linked Log. We can implement an efficient log by taking advantage of the fact that every commit shares the tail of the log with its predecessor. The value type in this log is:

```
type value =
  | L of float (* timestamp *) * string (* message *)
         * blob (* hash of prev value *)
  | M of blob list (* hashes of the values being merged *)
```

The value is either a log entry `L(t,m,h)` with timestamp t, message m and a hash of the previous value h, or `M hs` where hs is the list of hashes of the values being merged. Appending to the log only needs to add a new object that refers to the previous log value. Hence, append is $O(1)$. Figure 10 shows a snapshot of the log assuming a single key x. The log at x in the public branch `p0` (session `s0`) is `[a;b;c]` (`[a;b;d]`). The merge operation

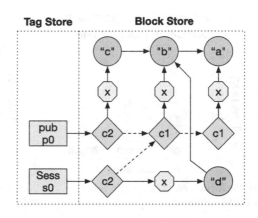

Fig. 10. A snapshot of linked log storage.

simply adds a new value `M [h1;h2]`, which refers to the hashes of the two log values being merged. This operation is also $O(1)$. The read function for the log does the heavy-lifting of reading the log in reverse chronological order.

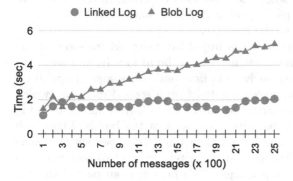

Fig. 11. Performance of mergeable logs.

Observe that unlike the examples seen so far where the values do not refer to other values, this *linked log* implementation refers to other values as heap data structures would do. Figure 11 shows the time taken to add 100 additional messages to the log with 4 clients. Observe that the time stays constant with linked log but increases linearly with blob log. By being able to share objects across different commits (versions), Banyan leads to efficient implementations of useful data structures.

5.4   Distributed Build Cache

In this section, we evaluate the performance of distributed build cache described in Sect. 2. We have chosen three OCaml packages: `git`, `irmin` and `httpaf` with common dependent packages. In the first experiment, we measure the benefit of building a package that has already been built in another workspace. Hence, the package artefacts will already be in the build cache.

For each library, we measure the baseline build time (1) without using the build cache, (2) using an empty build cache, and (3) building the same package on a machine with the same package having built earlier on a different machine.

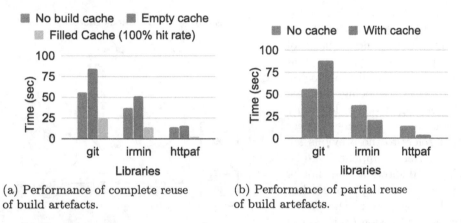

(a) Performance of complete reuse of build artefacts.

(b) Performance of partial reuse of build artefacts.

Fig. 12. Performance of complete and partial reuse of build artefacts.

Figure 12a shows the results. We see that case using an empty build cache is slower than not using the cache since the artefacts are stored in the cache. We also see that building the same package on a different machine is faster due to the build cache when compared to the baseline.

A more realistic scenario is partial sharing of artefacts, where some of the dependencies are in the cache and other need to be build locally, and added to the cache. In this experiment, git package is first built on a machine with an empty cache. Subsequently, irmin package is built on a second machine (which will now benefit from the common artefacts in the cache). And finally, building httpaf on a third machine, which benefits from both of the builds. Figure 12b shows the results. As expected, the git package build is slower with a cache than without since the cache is empty and the artefacts need to be written to the cache additionally. Subsequent package builds benefit from partial sharing of build artefacts. The results illustrate that Banyan not only makes it easy to build complex applications like distributed build caches, but the implementation also performs well under realistic workloads.

6   Related Work

Several prior works have addressed the challenge of balancing the programmability and performance under eventual consistency. RedBlue consistency [28] offers causal consistency by default (blue), but operations that require strong consistency (red) are executed in single total order. Quelea [34] and MixT [31] offer automated analysis for classifying and executing operations at different consistency levels embedded in weakly isolated transactions, paying the cost of proportional to the consistency level. Indeed, mixing weaker consistency and transactions has been well-studied [4,10,25].

Banyan only supports causal consistency, but it is known to be the strongest consistency level that remains available [29]. While prior works attempt to reconcile traditional isolation levels with weak consistency, Banyan leaves the choice of reading and writing updates to and from other transactions to the client through the use of publish and refresh. We believe that traditional database isolation levels are already quite difficult to get right [22], and attempting to provide a fixed set of poorly understood isolation levels under weak consistency will lead to proliferation of bugs.

Banyan is distinguished by the equipping data types with the ability to handle conflicts (three-way merge functions). Banyan builds on top of Irmin [21]. Irmin allows arbitrary branching and merging between different branches at the cost of having to expose the branch name. Banyan refreshes and publishes implicitly to the public branch at a repository, which obviates the need for naming branches explicitly. Irmin does not include a distribution and convergence layer; Banyan uses Cassandra for this purpose. Banyan provides causal consistency and coordination free transactions over weakly consistent Cassandra. Several prior work have similarly obtained stronger guarantees on top of weaker stores [6,34].

TARDiS [14] supports user-defined data types, and a transaction model similar to Banyan. TARDiS is however a machine model that exposes the details of explicit branches and merges to the developer, whereas Banyan is a programming model that can be instantiated on any eventually consistent key-value store. For instance, in TARDiS programmers need to invoke a separate merge transaction that does an n-way merge. Banyan transaction model is more flexible than TARDiS. For example, Banyan can support monotonic atomic view, which TARDiS cannot – TARDiS transactions do not have a way of allowing more recent updates since the transaction began. TARDiS does not discuss merges without LCAs or the issue with recursive merges. We found recursive merges to be a very common occurrence in practice.

Concurrent revisions [12] describe a programming model with branch and merge workflow with explicit branches and restrictions on the shape of history graphs. Banyan makes the choice of branches to publish and refresh implicit leading to a simpler model. Concurrent revisions does not include an implementation. Antidote SQL [30] is a database system for geo-distributed applications that provides the user the ability to relax SQL consistency when possible, but remain strict when necessary. Similar to Banyan, Antidote SQL transactions are executed over replicated data types. While Antidote SQL only permits parallel snapshot isolation level [35], by making refresh and publish explicit, Banyan permits weaker isolation levels such as monotonic atomic view [5].

7   Limitations and Future Work

Many eventually consistent databases such as CosmosDB [4], DynamoDB [2] and Cassandra provide tunable consistency levels for operations ranging from eventual consistency to strong consistency. Banyan only provides causal consistency, which is known to be the strongest available consistency level, but does not provide weaker or strong consistency levels. As such applications that require strong consistency, such as bank accounts with a minimum balance requirement, cannot be expressed in Banyan. We believe that we can extend Banyan with strongly consistent operations. However, operations with weaker consistency (and presumably better performance) cannot be incorporated in Banyan due to the underlying expectation about the *causal history* for each operation.

We have yet to implement the garbage collector for Banyan based on the design sketched in Sect. 4.4. In the absence of a garbage collector, the storage requirements are quite significant compared to traditional databases which only store the most recent version of the data (Sect. 5.2). We leave the implementation of the garbage collector for future work.

8   Conclusions

We present Banyan, a novel programming model for developing loosely connected distributed applications based on the principles of Git. We illustrate the practicality of this approach by instantiating Banyan on Cassandra, an off-the-shelf eventually consistent distributed store. Our experimental results suggests that Banyan makes it easy to build complex distributed applications without compromising performance.

Acknowledgements. Parts of this research were funded by grants from the Tezos Foundation.

References

1. Abadi, D.: Consistency tradeoffs in modern distributed database system design: CAP is only part of the story. Computer **45**(2), 37–42 (2012). https://doi.org/10.1109/MC.2012.33
2. Amazon DynamoDB: Fast and flexible NoSQL database service for any scale (2020). https://aws.amazon.com/dynamodb/
3. Apache Cassandra: The right choice when you need scalability and high availability without compromising performance (2020). https://cassandra.apache.org/
4. Azure CosmosDB: Build or modernise scalable, high-performance apps (2020). https://azure.microsoft.com/en-in/services/cosmos-db/
5. Bailis, P., Davidson, A., Fekete, A., Ghodsi, A., Hellerstein, J.M., Stoica, I.: Highly available transactions: virtues and limitations. Proc. VLDB Endow. **7**(3), 181–192 (2013). https://doi.org/10.14778/2732232.2732237

6. Bailis, P., Ghodsi, A., Hellerstein, J.M., Stoica, I.: Bolt-on causal consistency. In: Proceedings of the 2013 ACM SIGMOD International Conference on Management of Data, SIGMOD 2013, pp. 761–772 (2013). https://doi.org/10.1145/2463676. 2465279

7. Bazel: A fast, scalable, multi-language build system (2020). https://bazel.build/

8. Berenson, H., Bernstein, P., Gray, J., Melton, J., O'Neil, E., O'Neil, P.: A critique of ANSI SQL isolation levels. SIGMOD Rec. **24**(2), 1–10 (1995). https://doi.org/10.1145/568271.223785

9. Bernstein, P.A., Shipman, D.W., Wong, W.S.: Formal aspects of serializability in database concurrency control. IEEE Trans. Softw. Eng. **5**(3), 203–216 (1979). https://doi.org/10.1109/TSE.1979.234182

10. Brutschy, L., Dimitrov, D., Müller, P., Vechev, M.: Serializability for eventual consistency: criterion, analysis, and applications. In: Proceedings of the 44th ACM SIGPLAN Symposium on POPL, POPL 2017, pp. 458–472. (2017). https://doi.org/10.1145/3009837.3009895

11. Burckhardt, S., Gotsman, A., Yang, H., Zawirski, M.: Replicated data types: specification, verification. Optimality. SIGPLAN Not. **49**(1), 271–284 (2014). https://doi.org/10.1145/2578855.2535848

12. Burckhardt, S., Leijen, D., Fähndrich, M., Sagiv, M.: Eventually consistent transactions. In: Seidl, H. (ed.) ESOP 2012. LNCS, vol. 7211, pp. 67–86. Springer, Heidelberg (2012). https://doi.org/10.1007/978-3-642-28869-2_4

13. Crain, T., Shapiro, M.: Designing a causally consistent protocol for geo-distributed partial replication. In: Proceedings of the First Workshop on Principles and Practice of Consistency for Distributed Data, PaPoC 2015 (2015). https://doi.org/10.1145/2745947.2745953

14. Crooks, N., Pu, Y., Estrada, N., Gupta, T., Alvisi, L., Clement, A.: TARDiS: a branch-and-merge approach to weak consistency. In: Proceedings of the 2016 International Conference on Management of Data, SIGMOD 2016, pp. 1615–1628 (2016). https://doi.org/10.1145/2882903.2882951

15. Driscoll, J.R., Sarnak, N., Sleator, D.D., Tarjan, R.E.: Making data structures persistent. In: Proceedings of the Eighteenth Annual ACM Symposium on Theory of Computing, STOC 1986, pp. 109–121 (1986). https://doi.org/10.1145/12130.12142

16. Farinier, B., Gazagnaire, T., Madhavapeddy, A.: Mergeable persistent data structures. In: Vingt-sixièmes Journées Francophones des Langages Applicatifs (JFLA 2015) (2015)

17. Gilbert, S., Lynch, N.: Brewer's conjecture and the feasibility of consistent, available, partition-tolerant web services. SIGACT News **33**(2), 51–59 (2002). https://doi.org/10.1145/564585.564601

18. Git: A distributed version control system (2020). https://git-scm.com/

19. Gradle: An open-source build automation tool (2020). https://gradle.org/

20. Herlihy, M.P., Wing, J.M.: Linearizability: a correctness condition for concurrent objects. ACM Trans. Program. Lang. Syst. **12**(3), 463–492 (1990). https://doi.org/10.1145/78969.78972

21. Irmin: A distributed database built on the principles of Git (2020). https://irmin.org/

22. Kaki, G., Nagar, K., Najafzadeh, M., Jagannathan, S.: Alone together: compositional reasoning and inference for weak isolation. Proc. ACM Program. Lang. **2**(POPL) (2017). https://doi.org/10.1145/3158115

23. Kaki, G., Priya, S., Sivaramakrishnan, K., Jagannathan, S.: Mergeable replicated data types. Proc. ACM Program. Lang. **3**(OOPSLA) (2019). https://doi.org/10.1145/3360580

24. Kermarrec, A.M., van Steen, M.: Gossiping in distributed systems. SIGOPS Oper. Syst. Rev. **41**(5), 2–7 (2007). https://doi.org/10.1145/1317379.1317381

25. Kraska, T., Pang, G., Franklin, M.J., Madden, S., Fekete, A.: MDCC: multi-data center consistency. In: Proceedings of the 8th ACM European Conference on Computer Systems, EuroSys 2013, pp. 113–126 (2013). https://doi.org/10.1145/2465351.2465363

26. Lakshman, A., Malik, P.: Cassandra: a decentralized structured storage system. SIGOPS Oper. Syst. Rev. **44**(2), 35–40 (2010). https://doi.org/10.1145/1773912.1773922

27. Lamport, L.: Paxos made simple. ACM SIGACT News (Distrib. Comput. Column) **32**(4), 51–58 (2001). https://www.microsoft.com/en-us/research/publication/paxos-made-simple/. (Whole Number 121, December 2001)

28. Li, C., Porto, D., Clement, A., Gehrke, J., Preguiça, N., Rodrigues, R.: Making geo-replicated systems fast as possible, consistent when necessary. In: Proceedings of the 10th USENIX Conference on Operating Systems Design and Implementation, OSDI 2012, pp. 265–278 (2012)

29. Lloyd, W., Freedman, M.J., Kaminsky, M., Andersen, D.G.: Don't settle for eventual: scalable causal consistency for wide-area storage with COPS. In: Proceedings of the Twenty-Third ACM Symposium on Operating Systems Principles, SOSP 2011, pp. 401–416 (2011). https://doi.org/10.1145/2043556.2043593

30. Lopes, P., et al.: Antidote SQL: relaxed when possible, strict when necessary. CoRR abs/1902.03576 (2019). http://arxiv.org/abs/1902.03576

31. Milano, M., Myers, A.C.: MixT: a language for mixing consistency in geodistributed transactions. In: Proceedings of the 39th ACM SIGPLAN Conference on PLDI, pp. 226–241 (2018). https://doi.org/10.1145/3192366.3192375

32. Riak: Enterprise NoSQL Database (2020). https://riak.com/

33. Shapiro, M., Preguiça, N., Baquero, C., Zawirski, M.: Conflict-free replicated data types. In: Défago, X., Petit, F., Villain, V. (eds.) SSS 2011. LNCS, vol. 6976, pp. 386–400. Springer, Heidelberg (2011). https://doi.org/10.1007/978-3-642-24550-3_29

34. Sivaramakrishnan, K., Kaki, G., Jagannathan, S.: Declarative programming over eventually consistent data stores. In: Proceedings of the 36th ACM SIGPLAN Conference on PLDI, pp. 413–424 (2015). https://doi.org/10.1145/2737924.2737981

35. Sovran, Y., Power, R., Aguilera, M.K., Li, J.: Transactional storage for geo-replicated systems. In: Proceedings of the Twenty-Third ACM Symposium on Operating Systems Principles, SOSP 2011, pp. 385–400 (2011). https://doi.org/10.1145/2043556.2043592

36. Viotti, P., Vukolić, M.: Consistency in non-transactional distributed storage systems. ACM Comput. Surv. **49**(1) (2016). https://doi.org/10.1145/2926965

Automatically Generating Descriptive Texts in Logging Statements: How Far Are We?

Xiaotong Liu[1], Tong Jia[1], Ying Li[1(✉)], Hao Yu[1], Yang Yue[2], and Chuanjia Hou[1]

[1] Peking University, Beijing, China
li.ying@pku.edu.cn
[2] University of California Irvine, Irvine, CA 92697, USA

Abstract. In most cases, logs are the only accurate information available for administrators to understand system behavior and diagnose failure root causes. However, due to the lack of well-defined logging guidance, it is challenging for developers to decide what to log, especially logging statements that contain descriptive texts and variables. In this paper, we explore automatically generation of descriptive texts in logging statements and evaluate the effectiveness of various automatic generation methods. We propose that to generate descriptive texts in logging statements can be transferred as a retrieval-based Q&A task. According to the roles of query and answer, we design two retrieval strategies including Code&Code and Code&Log. To measure the similarity between the query and answer, we utilize two types of retrieval algorithms including Information retrieval-based and neural networks-based algorithms. We conduct a systematic analysis of various retrieval algorithms under different retrieval strategies in terms of their effectiveness, and assess their accuracy using the automatic metrics and human evaluation during which 5 instructive findings are presented. We believe that these findings can provide potential implications for both researchers and practitioners for relevant research. Moreover, we construct and release a log text dataset containing over 138K valid log texts from 85 Java projects in Apache ecosystem for future logging statement analysis and generation.

Keywords: Logging · Log text · Automatic generation · Experimental analysis

1 Introduction

Logging is a common and important programming practice to record system runtime behavior. In most cases, logs are the only accurate information available for administrators to understand system behavior and diagnose failure root causes. Therefore, logging quality is of great importance for various software maintenance tasks.

However, logging quality of today's large-scale software systems is unsatisfying. First, logging decision is not easy for developers. Insufficient logging provides limited or unclear system runtime information that may slow down the log analysis process. Conversely, excessive and intensive logging brings non-negligible overhead and may produce numerous trivial and useless logs that may mislead the developers. Second, there is currently a lack of rigorous logging guidance and domain-specific knowledge on logging practice. Industry practice study [29] shows that there is no

© Springer Nature Switzerland AG 2020
B. C. d. S. Oliveira (Ed.): APLAS 2020, LNCS 12470, pp. 251–269, 2020.
https://doi.org/10.1007/978-3-030-64437-6_13

Example1: log.info("Creating user. User Id : " + userId);
Example2: log.warn("Could not obtain value for variable " + var);
Example3: log.info("Could not find SSH credentials for token - " +
          tokenId + " and "+ "gateway id - "+ gatewayId);

Fig. 1. Examples of real-world logging statements. Log texts are marked in red and variables are in green. (Color figure online)

well-defined guideline to perform strategic logging. Developers usually need to rely on their common sense or personal knowledge to make logging decisions. This makes logging decisions hard for developers, as a user study of Microsoft shows that 68% of the participants have logging difficulties [2]. Third, software consists of components written by multiple developers, it is hard for developers to align with the project logging style during system update. Thus, developing appropriate logging statements have become a crucial but challenging problem.

A logging statement contains descriptive texts (i.e., log texts) and variables. Log texts usually describe the system status or behaviors in natural language while variables record runtime values of specific intermediate results in memory. Figure 1 shows a few real-world examples of logging statements including log texts and variables. Elaborate but concise log texts can accelerate log-based analysis process by providing better understanding of the system runtime information. On the contrary, immature log texts may confuse and mislead system developers or operators [1]. Similarly, the variables directly reflect the running status of systems and are straightforward information for system fault diagnosis. Therefore, developing appropriate logging statements means developing appropriate log texts and choosing key variables to print.

In recent years, lots of researchers have been made in developing logging statements efficiently and effectively. For instance, Log Enhancer [3] automatically adds variables into logging statements to provide abundant information for failure diagnosis. However, few research works start to study the problem of developing log texts, because generating natural language log texts is much more difficult than other problems in developing logging statements such as variable choosing. He et al. [4] conduct an empirical study on log texts. Statistical analysis results show that compared with common English, the repetitiveness in logging descriptions is more predictable.

Motived by the predictability of log texts, in this paper, we make step forward on exploring automatically generation of log texts and evaluating the effectiveness of different methods in automatic log text generation. We view automatic log text generation as a retrieval-based Question and Answer (Q&A) task, considering that code context represents the query and the appreciate log text to be inserted as the answer. Correspondingly, according to the roles of query and answer, we design two retrieval strategies including Code&Code and Code&Log. To measure the similarity between query and answer, we utilize two types of retrieval algorithms including Information retrieval-based and neural networks-based algorithms. Then, we construct a dataset with over 138 K valid log texts from 85 Java projects in Apache ecosystem. Finally, we further perform a systematic evaluation of various retrieval algorithms under different retrieval strategies in terms of their effectiveness on the dataset, during which obtain five instructive findings. Evaluation results show that different scenarios require different composition of strategies and algorithms. In most cases, CC retrieval strategy performs better than CL retrieval strategy, while IR-based algorithm performs better than NNs-based algorithms. And we demonstrate that there is still a long way to go in automatic log texts generation, and in particular, the cross-project log text generation is a major challenge. Furthermore, we find it an effective way to use the combination of the API and Variable information to generate log texts while trading off the accuracy and efficiency. At last, we also present a human evaluation to provide real practical quality of generated log texts from human view. In summary, our contributions include:

- We transfer the log text generation task as a retrieval-based Q&A task, design two log retrieval strategies CC and CL, and utilize two retrieval algorithms IR-based and NNs-based algorithms on this task.
- We analyze how different parts of code contexts influence the content of log texts as well as the effectiveness of various algorithms under different strategies, and obtain five instructive findings. These evaluation results and the corresponding findings, can provide guidelines for this problem and serve as a basis for relevant research.
- We provide a log text dataset with over 138K valid log texts and their code contexts from Apache ecosystem, which can be used for researchers to explore logging statement analysis and generation.[1]

2 Problem Specification

2.1 Problem Definition

Log texts are pieces of natural languages that describe the activity of current programs. Therefore, the content of log texts is mainly determined by the code around the logging statement called code context. As proved in prior studies [2, 4, 20], logging statements are often associated with their code contexts. In particular, a recent study [30] highlighted that the association between code context and log text is especially close. Therefore, we propose a logical assumption that similar code context should have similar log text for concise description. For instance, Fig. 2 shows two logged code snippets with similar code contexts from a real-world project. The corresponding log texts both describe the interruption activity of the code context which makes them almost the same.

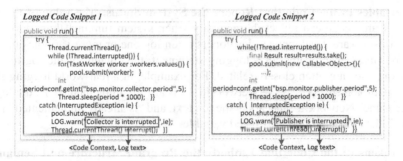

Fig. 2. An example of two similar logged code snippets.

---

[1] https://github.com/liuxiaotong0302/LogSearch.

With this assumption, we can model the log text generation problem as a retrieval-based Q&A problem [27, 28]. The purpose of retrieval-based Q&A problem is to search the most possible answer for a new query from existing Q&A knowledges. To achieve this, researchers first maintain a Q&A base with huge existing knowledge, and then utilize the new query text to search for the most possible answer from the Q&A base. Correspondingly, we model the code context as query and log text as answer. The problem is formulated as follows.

A large amount of logged code snippets form a logged code base $D = \{S_i\}_{i=1}^{M}$, $\forall i, S_i$ is a logged code snippet including (C_i, L_i), where L_i is a log text and C_i is the code context corresponding to L_i. Given a query context C^Q, our goal is to retrieve a list of top K code context and log text pair $R = [(C_k, L_k)]_{k=1}^{K}$ $\forall k, (C_k, L_k) \in D$ after ranking by the matching score of C_i or L_i, then return $[L_1, L_2, ..., L_K]$ for C^Q.

2.2 Code Context Information

Code context contains wealth of different information such as program functionality, system status, program structure and semantics, etc. This information buries in different parts of code contexts and should be carefully considered during log text generation. However, different parts of code contexts may affect the content of log text differently, thus there exists an important confusion: how do different parts of code contexts affect the content of log text? To answer this question, we test and verify three typical and major parts of code contexts in their effectiveness to the log text generation problem. Exploring the effectiveness of these parts can guide future works to select appropriate code context information, thus has a profound impact on both developers and researchers. The three parts of code contexts are described as follows.

The API Calls in the Code that Reflect the Program Functionality. Source code contains functional abstractions in a form of API calls [26]. For example, to read the content of a file, API "File.Readlines()" is called. API information has been widely used to improve code search tasks [5–7], but it has not been discussed in log text generation task. Intuitively, developers often record the functional activity of the code context in the log text, thus the API calls may greatly affect the content of log texts.

The Variables in the Code that Report the System Status. The value of the variables in source code can reflect the anomaly when system running, thus, during the process of software development, developers often log one or more variables in order to record vital system status. In a logging statement, the content of the log text and logged variables are often closely related. For example, in a real-world logging statement "log.info('Networkid = ' + NetworkId + 'is already implemented')", the logged variable name "NetworkId" appears in the log text, and "is already implemented" in the log text is developed around the logged variable.

Other Tokens in the Code that Embody the Program Structure and Semantics. In addition to the API calls and the variables mentioned above, the remaining tokens in the code context usually express the program structure and semantics. The program structure and semantics may also affect the content of the log text. For example, according to our analysis on 85 projects from Apache ecosystem, 65.8% of the log texts for error messages, which contain keywords of "error", "failed" and "exception", are printed in the catch-blocks.

2.3 Retrieval Models

There are many retrieval strategies and algorithms in the retrieval Q&A problem [11, 41]. However, these methods have never been applied and discussed in the log text generation problem. Understanding the applicable scenarios of these strategies and algorithms in the log text generation can help researchers to apply them in subsequent practice. Therefore, combined with different retrieval strategies and algorithms, we build many retrieval models for the log text generation problem, and conduct experimental analysis to explore their performance in different scenarios.

3 Workflow

Figure 3 illustrates the overall workflow for log text generation, which involves three steps: code information extraction, retrieval and ranking. In this section, we give a detailed description for two main steps: code information extraction and retrieval.

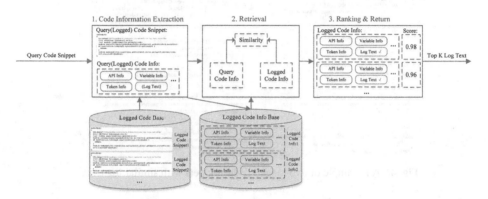

Fig. 3. The workflow of log text generation.

3.1 Code Information Extraction

As discussed before, we test and verify three typical and major parts of code contexts in their effectiveness to the log text generation problem including API calls, variables and other tokens. The logged/query code information can be extracted from logged/query code snippets and formalized as:

$$C = (A, V, T) \tag{1}$$

where C generally refers to the logged/query code snippet C_i/C^Q, A, V and T are the API, Variable and Token information.

Taking a logged/query code snippet as input, we extract API information, Variable information and Token information as follows: First, we use the Eclipse JDT compiler [8] to parse the code snippet into an AST tree. Then, we extract the API sequence and the logged variables from it. At last, to extract the Token information, we tokenize the code snippet except for the logging statement, remove the tokens that appeared in the API and Variable information, and split each token according to camel case [9]. The extracted API, Variable and Token information can be formalized as:

$$A = \left(a_1, \ldots, a_j \ldots a_{|A|}\right)$$
$$V = \left(v_1, \ldots, v_j \ldots v_{|V|}\right)$$
$$\Gamma = \left(\tau_1, \ldots, \tau_j \ldots \tau_{|\Gamma|}\right) \tag{2}$$

where $|\cdot|$ is the number of elements in a set, a_j is the j-th API in A, v_j is the j-th variable in V and τ_j is the j-th token in Γ. Figure 4 shows examples of the code information extraction of logged code snippets.

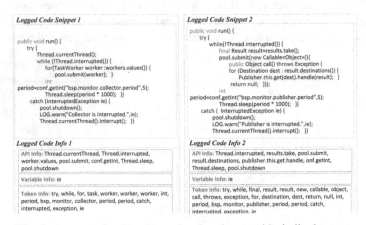

Fig. 4. An example of two logged code snippets with similar log texts.

3.2 Retrieval

The main purpose of this step is to calculate matching scores between C^Q and C_i or L_i. According to the roles of query and answer, we design two retrieval strategies including Code&Code and Code&Log. To measure the similarity between query and answer, we utilize two types of retrieval algorithms including Information retrieval-based and neural networks-based algorithms. By pairwise covering, there are four retrieval models we mainly discuss.

Retrieval Strategies. In the field of retrieval-based Q&A, there are two choices to find potentially suitable answers: constructing matching between two questions [27] or between questions and answers [28]. Similarly, we introduce two types of retrieval strategies: Code&Code (CC) strategy and Code&Log (CL) strategy.

CC Strategy. In this strategy, we score the matching degree between the query and logged code snippet as the matching score, and return the log texts whose code context gets high matching scores. The matching score can be formulated as:

$$Score = Sim(C^Q, C_i) \tag{3}$$

CL Strategy. Considering that log texts are directly affected by their code contexts [30], a code context should be the most relevant with its most appropriate log text. Thus, we design another retrieval strategy, directly scoring the matching degree between the query code context and log text as a matching score, and return the log texts with high matching score. The matching score can be formulated as:

$$Score = Sim(C^Q, L_i) \tag{4}$$

Retrieval Algorithms. To measure the similarity between query and answer, there are two types of existing mainstream retrieval algorithms: Information retrieval (IR)-based algorithms and neural networks (NNs)-based algorithms.

IR-Based Retrieval Algorithm. Code contexts and log texts are actually text sequences. Therefore, it is intuitive to calculate the text similarity directly. We choose two classic IR-based algorithms to calculate text similarity: Jaccard index [11] and Levenshtein distance [10], which are widely used to calculate text similarity [16, 24]. Among them, the mathematical principle behind Jaccard index is set theory, which is order independent; while the Levenshtein distance is based on string, which is order sensitive.

The Jaccard index measures text similarity based on the bag-of-words (BoW) model to calculate the number of common keywords in two bags of words:

$$J(X, Y) = (|X \cap Y|)/(|X \cup Y|) \tag{5}$$

The Levenshtein distance regards X and Y as strings and calculates the character-based distance, the similarity is calculated as:

$$E(X, Y) = (Max(|X|, |Y|) - d[|X|][|Y|]) / (Max(|X|, |Y|)) \tag{6}$$

where $d[|X|][|Y|]$ is the minimum number of delete, insert and replace operations to convert string X to string Y.

NNs-Based Retrieval Algorithm. In recent years, neural networks are widely used in code search tasks [6, 7], but never discussed in log text generation task. The basic principle is to map the hidden information of the inputs to the vectors, and then calculate the matching scores in the vector space. Given two data sets X and Y, we embed them into a unified vector space by neural networks so that similar concepts across the two modalities occupy nearby regions of the space:

$$N(X, Y) = S(\varphi(X), \phi(Y)) \tag{7}$$

where φ and ϕ are embedding functions to map X and Y to vectors, and $S(\cdot, \cdot)$ is a vector similarity measure, for instance, cosine similarity.

Retrieval Models. By combining two retrieval strategies and two retrieval algorithms, four retrieval models are built.

CC-IR Model. After a statistical analysis of the dataset, we find that the if code snippets print similar log texts, their API information, Variable information and Token information are also similar respectively (see Fig. 4). Based on this, by adopting the CC strategy and using the IR-based algorithm, we build the CC-IR model. In this model, we utilize the IR-based algorithm to calculate the API, Variable and Token information matching scores respectively, then take the sum of the scores as the final matching score, which can be formulated as:

$$Sim\left(C^Q, C_i\right) = J/E\left(A^Q, A_i^C\right) + J/E\left(V^Q, V_i^C\right) + J/E\left(\Gamma^Q, \Gamma_i^C\right) \quad (8)$$

where J/E refers to Jaccard index/Levenshtein distance.

CL-IR Model. By adopting the CL strategy and using the IR-based algorithm, we build the CL-IR model. In this model, we utilize the IR-based algorithm to calculate the matching scores between three types of key information of query code snippet and each log text respectively, and finally sum up three matching scores:

$$Sim\left(C^Q, L_i\right) = J/E\left(A^Q, L_i\right) + J/E\left(V^Q, L_i\right) + J/E\left(\Gamma^Q, L_i\right) \quad (9)$$

CC-NNs Model. By adopting the CC strategy and using NNs-based algorithm, we build the CC-NNs model (see Fig. 5). Deriving from the model proposed in [7], we embed the query and logged code information into vectors through a code embedding component and then calculate the matching score with cosine similarity. The code embedding component consist of three sub-modules and a fusion layer as follows.

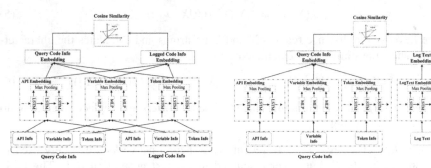

Fig. 5. The structure of the CC-NNs model.   **Fig. 6.** The structure of the CL-NNs model.

The *API Embedding sub-module* and the *Token Embedding sub-module* embed the API information and Token information using LSTM with maxpooling. They take the embedding vector of API a_t and token τ_t as input at each time step, and output the information embedding vector $Vec(A)$ and $Vec(\Gamma)$:

$$h_t = tanh\left(W^X\left[h_{t-1}; x_t\right]\right), \forall t = 1, 2, \ldots, |X|$$

$$Vec(X) = maxpooling\big([h_1, h_2, \ldots, h_{|X|}]\big) \tag{10}$$

where X is A and T, x_t is a_t and τ_t, W^X is the parameter matrix in the LSTM.

The *Variable Embedding sub-module* embeds Variable information into vector $Vec(V)$ using an MLP with an attached maxpooling:

$$h_t = tanh\big(W^V v_t\big), \forall t = 1, 2, \ldots, |V|$$
$$Vec(V) = maxpooling\big([h_1, h_2, \ldots, h_{|V|}]\big) \tag{11}$$

where W^V is the parameter matrix in the MLP.

The fully connected layer fuses the outputs of three sub-modules into one vector:

$$Vec(C) = tanh\big(W^C[Vec(A); Vec(V); Vec(\Gamma)]\big) \tag{12}$$

where $[x;y;z]$ is the concatenation of x, y, z, W^C is the matrix of parameters in the MLP.

By feeding C^Q and C_i into the code embedding component, we obtain the query code information embedding $Vec(C^Q)$ and the logged code information embedding $Vec(C_i)$. Finally, the matching score is calculated with cosine similarity:

$$Sim\big(C^Q, C_i\big) = \frac{Vec(C^Q) \cdot Vec(C_i)}{||Vec(C^Q)||\ ||Vec(C_i)||} \tag{13}$$

CL-NNs Model. By adopting the CL strategy and using the NNs-based algorithm, we construct the CC-NNs model (see Fig. 6). We embed the query code information and log text into vectors through a code embedding component and a log embedding component respectively, then apply cosine similarity to calculate matching score.

The code embedding component in CL-NNs model is the same as that in CC-NNs. As for the log embedding component, we use LSTM to embed the log text into a vector:

$$h_t = tanh\big(W^L[h_{t-1}; w_t]\big), \forall t = 1, 2, \ldots, |L|$$
$$Vec(L) = maxpooling\big([h_1, h_2, \ldots, h_{|L|}]\big) \tag{14}$$

where W^L is parameter matrix in the LSTM.

The code embedding component takes API, Variable and Token information of query code snippet as input, then we get the embedding vector $Vec(C^Q)$. The log embedding component takes the i-th log text as input and we get the embedding vector $Vec(L_i)$. Finally, the matching score is calculated with cosine similarity:

$$Sim\big(C^Q, L_i\big) = \frac{Vec(C^Q) \cdot Vec(L_i)}{||Vec(C^Q)||\ ||Vec(L_i)||} \tag{15}$$

4   Evaluation Study

4.1   Dataset

In this paper, we select projects from Apache ecosystem [25] to construct our dataset. Apache ecosystem develops and incubates hundreds of freely-available, enterprise-grade projects that serve as the backbone for some of the most visible and widely used applications in computing today. The projects in Apache ecosystem are not lapped up, but are selected based on their project status, contribution model and data availability. They must be active projects using the pull-request model to solicit contributions, and also need to have a sufficient number of activities from 2016 to 2018. Therefore, we require all selected projects to have at least 100 issues, 50 pull requests and 100 commits. Such criteria guarantee that we can get a sufficient amount of elite members' activities for analysis and logging statements in our dataset can be considered to have relatively good specifications. At last, we keep 85 projects from Apache ecosystem.

These projects contain 164,996 method bodies that contain at least one logging statement, from which we extract 194,771 logging statements. After filtering out logging statements which only print non-alphanumeric characters, we obtain 159266 log statements. To have a clearer understanding of our datasets and make it easier to use, we make a statistical analysis on these logging statements. The analysis results show that majority (70.96%) of logging statements contain log texts and variables concurrently, reflecting the strong correlation between log texts and log variables. In addition to 12.74% of logging statements print variables only, 87.26% contain log texts, which embodies the significance of log texts in the log printing process of software system development. Finally, the 138,974 (87.26%) logging statements containing log texts are regarded as valid logging statements and the log texts of them are regarded as valid log text. After extracting the code contexts of the log texts and extracting the code information, we obtain 138,974 quadruples of log texts, API, Variable and Token information retained in our dataset.

4.2   Experimental Setup

Dataset Partition. After obtaining the dataset consisting of 138,974 pairs of code context and log text, we split the dataset into a logged code base and a query code set to evaluate the effectiveness of various automatic generation methods. We use 10-fold cross validation, where 90% of the dataset (125024 pairs) are the logged code base and the training corpus, the remaining 10% (13950 pairs) are the query set after shuffling.

Evaluation Metrics. We use BLEU [12] and ROUGE [13] as evaluation metrics to evaluate the effectiveness of models in our experiment, which are popular evaluation metrics widely used in machine translation and text summarization tasks [14, 15]. In our experiments, the log text generated by retrieval models is regarded as candidate and the real log text is regarded as reference. The ranges of both BLEU and ROUGE are [0,1], which are often presented as a percentage value range in [0,100]. In our experiment, we take BLEU-1, BLEU-4, ROUGE-1 and ROUGE-L into account.

Considering that our models return a log text list instead of a single one, we designed some derived final evaluation metrics based on BLEU and ROUGE. Specifically, *-MAX refers to the highest score achieved in the list, and *-TOP refers to the score of the first result. We obtain 8 accuracy evaluation metrics: BLEU-1-MAX(B1M), BLEU-1-TOP(B1T), BLEU-4-MAX(B4M), BLEU-4-TOP(B4T), ROUGE-1-MAX(R1M), ROUGE-1-TOP(R1T), ROUGE-L-MAX(RLM) and ROUGE-L-TOP(RLT).

Parameter Setting. The number of returned log text K is set to 5. For NNs-based models, the dictionary sizes of API information, Variable information, Token information and log text are set to 10000, 8000, 8000 and 8000 respectively. Besides, the batch size is set to 128 and we train the models with 200 epochs. For a log text, we define 10 lines of code preceding and 5 lines of code succeeding of it in a method body as its code context. A large number of experiments demonstrate that the setting of the number of code preceding and succeeding have little effect on the final results, and the setting of 10 and 5 is especially telling without large efficiency burden.

Parameter Setting. The number of returned log text K is set to 5. For NNs-based models, the dictionary sizes of API information, Variable information, Token information and log text are set to 10000, 8000, 8000 and 8000 respectively. Besides, the batch size is set to 128 and we train the models with 200 epochs. For a log text, we define 10 lines of code preceding and 5 lines of code succeeding of it in a method body as its code context. A large number of experiments demonstrate that the setting of the number of code preceding and succeeding have little effect on the final results, and the setting of 10 and 5 is especially telling without large efficiency burden.

4.3 Evaluation Results

RQ1: What Is the Effectiveness of Two Retrieval Strategies and Two Algorithms?
We apply the four groups of models from the combination of two strategies and two algorithms on our dataset. The retrieval results are presented in Table 1.

Table 1. Retrieval results of four constructed models

		B1M	B1T	B4M	B4T	R1M	R1T	RLM	RLT
CC-IR	Le	56.68	48.79	28.29	24.50	59.72	51.16	58.14	49.99
	Ja	**58.90**	**50.25**	**29.21**	**24.70**	**62.05**	**52.93**	**60.38**	**51.59**
CL-IR	Le	11.63	6.14	3.33	1.77	15.97	8.85	13.62	7.54
	Ja	11.90	6.94	4.24	2.33	16.24	10.19	14.01	8.65
CC-NNs		52.82	35.29	26.45	17.03	55.73	37.46	54.13	36.34
CL-NNs		28.28	19.44	10.78	7.60	32.17	22.26	29.72	20.66

Overall, the CC-IR model with Jaccard index achieves the highest accuracy scores of all models. However, there is no considerable disparity between the results of the CC-IR model with Jaccard index and Levenshtein distance, and they both achieve higher accuracy scores than other models. In addition, results show that the relative trend of these scores among models is consistent. For instance, if the B1M score of the CC-NNs model is higher than the CL-NNs model, the B4M score and other accuracy scores of CC- NNs model is also higher than that of the CL-NNs model.

By comparing the CC and CL retrieval strategies, we can observe that the accuracy scores of the CC-IR model are all higher than the CL-IR model, and the CC-NNs model is better than the CL-NNs model. However, in the experiment, we find that the retrieval efficiency of the CL strategy is higher than that of the CL strategy because the length of log texts is far less than code contexts. The B1M and R1M scores of models adopting the CC strategy are all greater than 52.82 and 55.73 respectively, which is higher than 28.28 and 32.17, the highest scores when adopting the CL strategy. It is a rational explanation that the data structure of code context and log text is heterogeneous, and there is difference between high-level intent reflected in the natural language log text and low-level implementation details in the code context. Thus, the difficulty in matching code context and log text is more highlighted than matching between code contexts.

Finding 1: Because of the difference between high-level intent reflected in the natural language log text and low-level implementation details in the code context, the CL strategy is less applicable to retrieve log texts than the CC strategy.

The relative effectiveness of the IR-based and NNs-based algorithms exhibit diversity when adopting different strategies. In the CC strategy, the CC-NNs model achieves inferior performance against the CC-IR model in terms of accuracy while it reverses in the CL strategy. Previously we expect to obtain higher accuracy scores with the NNs-based algorithm than the simple IR-based algorithm, since we consider the NNs-based algorithm captures deeper information of code contexts and log texts. However, it is not quite in line with expectations when adopting the CC strategy.

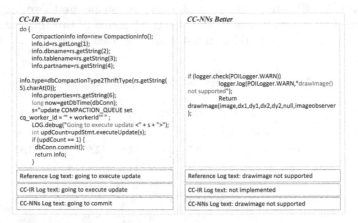

Fig. 7. Two result examples when the CC-IR model performs better and the CC-NNs model performs better.

The identifiers in the source code are not limited and substantial numbers identifiers in the training set appear only a few times. In this condition, the training set and test set usually contains a large amount of words out of vocabulary (OOV), which leads to the inevitable information loss for the NNs-based algorithm. That is the main reason of the worse performance of the NNs-based algorithm. Figure 7 shows two retrieval result examples when the CC-IR model performs better and the CC-NNs model performs better. When the CC-IR performs better, the length of code contexts is often longer and contains more OOV words. And when the CC-NNs model performs better, the length of code contexts is often shorter and contains less OOV words. However, the exception is met when adopting the CL strategy. After manual analysis of the dataset, we find that even if the information of code contexts and log texts is indeed correlated, the keywords are rarely shared between them. Therefore, the IR-based algorithm which relies heavily on coexisting keywords or characters on code contexts and log texts suffers from greater loss of information than that caused by OOV.

> *Finding 2:* The NNs-based algorithm performs worse than the IR-based algorithm when adopting the CC strategy due to OOV, and vice versa in the CL strategy since the IR-based one relies heavier on the rarely shared keywords.

RQ2: What Is the Effectiveness of Cross-Project Retrieval?
When a completely new project is developed, we need to generate log texts from some other existing relatively mature software systems for developers. That is what we call a cross-project log text generation scenario. It is essential to evaluate the effectiveness of different retrieval strategies and algorithms in the cross-project scenario.

Table 2. Retrieval results in cross-project scenario

		B1M	B1T	B4M	B4T	R1M	R1T	RLM	RLT
CC-IR	Le	14.20	8.37	4.54	3.13	17.33	9.94	15.55	9.10
	Ja	**14.41**	**8.40**	**4.66**	**3.18**	**17.62**	**10.09**	**15.74**	**9.19**
CL-IR	Le	8.09	4.10	1.59	0.77	12.12	6.81	9.97	5.57
	Ja	7.57	4.34	1.59	0.84	12.16	8.25	9.77	6.44
CC-NNs		13.67	6.43	4.37	2.28	16.70	7.78	14.96	7.06
CL-NNs		13.11	7.47	3.15	1.86	16.52	9.68	14.35	8.41

The general dataset partitioning strategy described in Sect. 4.2 simulates the general scenario, where we can retrieve log texts from the current or other projects. To simulate a strict cross-project scenario, we design a cross-project partitioning strategy to repartition the dataset into a new logged code base and query set. First, we sort all the projects by the number of log texts contained. Second, we extract the log texts and their code contexts from the first 35 projects to construct a new logged code base, which contains 125807 pairs of code context and log text, and 13167 pairs in the remaining 50 projects make up a new query set. This not only ensures that the log texts in the new logged code base and query set come from different projects, but ensures the log texts in the logged code base are more mature than the query set, which is in line with the actual application scenario. We apply the four groups of retrieval models on the repartitioned dataset and the results are presented in Table 2.

According to the experiment results, the CC strategy still outperforms the CL strategy. Besides, when the CC strategy is adopted, the IR-based algorithm is better than the NNs-based algorithm, and vice versa in the CL strategy. The above findings are consistent with that in RQ1, which shows that the findings of RQ1 is also applicable in the cross-project scenario. However, results show that compared with the generic scenario, the accuracy scores are lower overall in the cross-project scenario. The highest B1M score of all models obtained by the CC-IR model is 14.41, which is only better than that of the worst CL-IR model in the generic scenario. The above experimental results provide us a **negative empirical result**: The retrieval models do not perform well in the cross-project scenario.

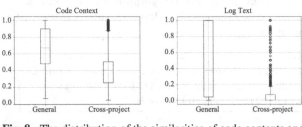

Fig. 8. The distribution of the similarities of code contexts and log texts in the generic and cross-project scenario.

To address the problem of poor performance in the cross-project scenario, we conduct a statistic analysis over similarities between code contexts in different projects, as well as log texts. For code contexts, we study the highest similarity between code contexts in query code snippets and logged code base by the CC-IR model with Jaccard index. For log texts, the similarities refer to similarities between reference log texts and the first retrieved log text by the CC-IR model with Jaccard index. The statistic results of the generic and cross-project scenario are shown in Fig. 8 as boxplots. We can observe that in the cross-project scenario, the similarities between code contexts and log texts in query code snippets and the logged code base are generally lower than the generic scenario, which means that the code context and their corresponding log texts vary dramatically in different projects. After getting these results, an intuitive understanding is obtained that the functions implemented by different projects and the coding habits of developers are different, which leads to great differences in the source code itself, so their corresponding log texts are also quite different.

> *Finding 3:* Log texts in different projects differ greatly, so it is still challenging to apply the existing log text retrieval methods to the cross-project scenario.

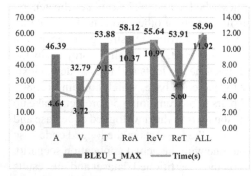

Fig. 9. The comparison results of retrieval time for and B1M of each information combination.

RQ3: What Is the Impact of Different Types of Information in Code Contexts on Log Texts? We know that a variety of key information in code contexts affect the content of log texts, so do different types of information perform different degrees of impact on log texts? This is what we want to explore in this section. We utilize the CC-IR model with Jaccard index which performs best in previous experiments on the dataset partitioned in the general way. On this basis, we first use API, Variable and Token information to retrieve log texts separately, and then remove one of them from all information to retrieve log texts. Figure 9 shows the retrieval results, where Re* means Remove *.

Overall, the retrieval results using one or two types of information are diverse and worse than using all three types. Comparing the results of using three types of information respectively, the accuracy scores of using Token information only are the highest, whose B1M score reaches 53.88 which is close to using all. Besides, when Token information is removed from all three types of information, the B1M score decreases from 58.90 to 53.91, which is the most significant decline of the removal of API and variable information. That is to say, the Token information affect the content of log texts to the greatest extent among three types of information.

> *Finding 4:* The API, Variable and Token information perform different degrees of impact on log texts, among which the Token information is the most important.

We can observe when using the combination of the API and Variable information, the accuracy is almost the same as using the Token information only, and both of their B1M scores are close to 54. We also find that when using the combination of API and Variable information, the retrieval time is 5.60 s, which is almost half of using Token information 9.13 s. After a statistical analysis, we find the average length of log texts, API information, Variable information and Token information are 5, 7, 2 and 38 respectively. The average length of API and Variable information is much shorter than Token, which is the main reason why retrieval efficiency of using the combination of the API and Variable information is significantly higher than using the Token information. Therefore, using the combination of API and Variable information is a recommended choice when a trade-off between accuracy and efficiency is needed.

> *Finding 5:* It is an effective way to use the combination of the API and Variable information to generate log texts while trading off accuracy and efficiency.

5 Human Evaluation

In this section, we perform a manual verification to evaluate the quality of the automatically generated log texts by the CC-IR(Ja), CL-IR(Ja), CC-NNs and CL-NNs models compared with the ground truth so as to provide real practical quality of generated log texts from human view.

5.1 Procedure

We first randomly select 100 log texts generated by the CC-IR, CL-IR, CC-NNs and CL-NNs models separately. Then we mix these 400 log texts together and divide them into eight groups. At last, we invite eight participants with rich programming experience to give score between 0 to 4 to measure the similarities between the generated log texts and ground truth log texts. Each group is evaluated by 2 participants and the participants do not know which model generates the log texts. We follow the score criterion defined by [31], which score 0 means there is no similarity between the two messages, and score 4 means two messages are identical in meaning.

5.2 Evaluation Results

Same as [31], we regard 0 and 1 scores as low quality level, score 2 as medium quality level, and score 3 and 4 as high quality level. Table 3 illustrates the proportions of log texts that are evaluated as different quality levels and the mean scores of log texts generated by each model, which shows that: (1) The mean score and the proportion of high-quality CC-IR log texts is much higher than that of CC-NNs, and the proportion of low-quality CC-IR log texts is significantly lower than that of CC-NNs. Therefore, the IR-based algorithm outperforms the NNs-based one in the CC strategy. (2) The mean score and proportion of high-quality CL-NNs log texts is higher than that of CL-IR, and the proportion of low-quality CL-NNs log texts is lower than that of CL-IR. So the NNs-based algorithm outperforms the IR-based one in the CL strategy. (3) CC-IR performs best and more than half of the generated log texts can be actually useful in practice. The above conclusions are consistent with the evaluation results of automatic metrics.

Table 3. Proportions of log text quality results from human evaluation

	Low	Medium	High	Mean score
CC-IR (Ja)	19.0%	29.0%	52.0%	2.53
CL-IR (Ja)	52.0%	43.0%	5.0%	0.75
CC-NNs	37.0%	23.0%	40.0%	1.81
CL-NNs	40.0%	43.0%	17.0%	1.28

6 Threats to Validity

First, the complete research work is examined only on Java projects. However, methods in our research does not have strict specific to Java language, and can easily be extended to other languages. Therefore, the findings of this paper can still serve as a good basis for follow-up work.

Second, we explore the effectiveness of three key parts of code contexts including API calls, variables and other tokens in log text generation task. Besides the three parts, there is also some other information that requires further study. For example, program syntax tree may influence the functional call orders and structures of different methods, which may also affect the content of the log text. We will further explore other parts of code contexts and different weights of different parts in future work.

Third, there are other modeling methods for log text generation task besides retrieval-based Q&A modeling. For instance, we also model the problem as a context-aware editing task [19]. We built a retrieval sub-module to obtain retrieved log texts, then built a generative sub-module to rewrote the log texts. However, the generative sub-module generates worse log texts than the retrieved ones. Thus compared with retrieval-based Q&A modeling, this modeling method is less effective at this stage. However, the automatic generation methods explored in this paper are limited, in the future, more attempts on other retrieval, generative or rewriting methods are still worth exploring.

7 Related Work

Proper logging is important yet tough in practice, so it is necessary to research log enhancement technology, which is used to improve logging quality. The log enhancement involves three main issues: *where to log, what to log* and *how to log*.

Some *where to log* research work [2, 17–19] was designed to provide for developers the suitable logging points. Specifically, ErrLog [17] summarizes various generic exception patterns associated with system faults to predict Error or Warn logging points. LogAdvisor [2] makes informed decisions for developers whether a code snippet should be placed a logging statement. They focused on exception snippet and return-value-check code snippet while LogOptPlus [18] works on catch-blocks and if-blocks. Jia et al. [19] automatically identified the log points reflecting the abnormal behavior of the system in case of failure.

What to log research work [1, 3, 4, 21, 30] focused on the content of logging statements instead of logging points. LogEnhancer [3] adds variables containing useful information to logging statements to distinguish different execution paths. Cinque et al. [21] customed four types of errors and marked them everywhere the errors may occur in the source code. Yuan et al. [1] gave some guidelines on which variables to log by summarizing the human logs. As far as we know, only [4, 30] focused on the log text so far. He et al. [4] conducted an empirical study on log texts in mature software projects and statistical analysis results showed that the repetitiveness in log texts is more predictable than common English. Li et al. [30] uncovered patterns of duplicate logging code smells and highlighted the importance of code contexts of log texts.

How to log research work [22, 23] aimed to develop and maintain high-quality logging statement. Chen et al. [22] analyze the modification history of log statements manually, and summarizes a series of anti-patterns, and Li et al. [23] predict an appropriate log level for developers when they add a new logging statement.

8 Conclusion

In order to ensure the smooth development of the system and accelerate the software maintenance, developers are expected to design elaborate but concise descriptive texts in logging statements. However, there is a lack of well-defined logging guidance and domain-specific knowledge, it is a challenge for developers to make appropriate decisions about log text. In this paper, we transform log text generation as a retrieval-based Q&A task and perform an experimental analysis on it. We present several retrieval strategies and retrieval algorithms to solve this problem. We further perform a systematic evaluation of the presented methods and different parts of code contexts on our dataset which contains over 138 K valid log texts from 85 Java projects in Apache ecosystem. Finally, a few instructive findings are proposed for future researches of automatic log text generation. We believe that our dataset released and instructive findings will accelerate the development of this field.

References

1. Chen, B., Jiang, Z.M.J.: Characterizing logging practices in Java-based open source software projects–a replication study in Apache Software Foundation. Empirical Softw. Eng. **22**, 330–374 (2017)
2. Zhu, J., He, P., Fu, Q., Zhang, H., Lyu, M.R., Zhang, D.: Learning to log: helping developers make informed logging decisions. In: Proceedings of the 37th International Conference on Software Engineering, vol. 1, pp. 415–425. IEEE Press (2015)
3. Yuan, D., Zheng, J., Park, S., Zhou, Y., Savage, S.: Improving software diagnosability via log enhancement. ACM Trans. Comput. Syst. (TOCS) **30**, 4 (2012)
4. He, P., Chen, Z., He, S., Lyu, M.R.: Characterizing the natural language descriptions in software logging statements. In: Proceedings of the 33rd ACM/IEEE International Conference on Automated Software Engineering, pp. 178–189. ACM (2018)
5. Lv, F., Zhang, H., Lou, J.-g., Wang, S., Zhang, D., Zhao, J.: Codehow: effective code search based on API understanding and extended boolean model (e). In: 30th IEEE/ACM International Conference on Automated Software Engineering (ASE), pp. 260–270. IEEE (2015)
6. Gu, X., Zhang, H., Zhang, D., Kim, S.: Deep API learning. In: Proceedings of the 24th ACM SIGSOFT International Symposium on Foundations of Software Engineering, pp. 631–642
7. Gu, X., Zhang, H., Kim, S.: Deep code search. In: IEEE/ACM 40th International Conference on Software Engineering (ICSE), pp. 933–944. IEEE (2018)
8. Eclipse JDT. http://www.eclipse.org/jdt/
9. Camel Case. https://en.wikipedia.org/wiki/camelcase
10. Levenshtein Distance. https://en.wikipedia.org/wiki/Levenshtein_distance
11. Jaccard Index. https://en.wikipedia.org/wiki/Jaccard_index
12. Papineni, K., Roukos, S., Ward, T., Zhu, W.-J.: BLEU: a method for automatic evaluation of machine translation. In: Proceedings of the 40th annual meeting on association for computational linguistics, pp. 311–318. Association for Computational Linguistics (2002)
13. Lin, C.-Y.: Rouge: a package for automatic evaluation of summaries. In: Text Summarization Branches Out, pp. 74–81 (2004)
14. Luong, M.-T., Pham, H., Manning, C.D.: Effective approaches to attention-based neural machine translation. arXiv preprint arXiv:1508.04025 (2015)
15. See, A., Liu, P.J., Manning, C.D.: Get to the point: summarization with pointer-generator networks. arXiv preprint arXiv:1704.04368 (2017)
16. Wu, Y., Wei, F., Huang, S., Wang, Y., Li, Z., Zhou, M.: Response generation by context-aware prototype editing. In: Proceedings of the AAAI Conference on Artificial Intelligence, pp. 7281–7288 (2019)
17. Yuan, D., et al.: Be conservative: enhancing failure diagnosis with proactive logging. In: Presented as part of the 10th {USENIX} Symposium on Operating Systems Design and Implementation ({OSDI} 2012), pp. 293–306 (2012)
18. Lal, S., Sardana, N., Sureka, A.: LogOptPlus: learning to optimize logging in catch and if programming constructs. In: IEEE 40th Annual Computer Software and Applications Conference (COMPSAC), pp. 215–220. IEEE (2016)

19. Jia, T., Li, Y., Zhang, C., Xia, W., Jiang, J., Liu, Y.: Machine deserves better logging: a log enhancement approach for automatic fault diagnosis. In: IEEE International Symposium on Software Reliability Engineering Workshops (ISSREW), pp. 106–111. IEEE (2018)
20. Zhao, X., Rodrigues, K., Luo, Y., Stumm, M., Yuan, D., Zhou, Y.: The game of twenty questions: do you know where to log? In: Proceedings of the 16th Workshop on Hot Topics in Operating Systems, pp. 125–131. ACM (2017)
21. Cinque, M., Cotroneo, D., Pecchia, A.: Event logs for the analysis of software failures: a rule-based approach. IEEE Trans. Software Eng. **39**, 806–821 (2012)
22. Chen, B., Jiang, Z.M.J.: Characterizing and detecting anti-patterns in the logging code. In: Proceedings of the 39th International Conference on Software Engineering, pp. 71–81. IEEE Press (2017)
23. Li, H., Shang, W., Hassan, A.E.: Which log level should developers choose for a new logging statement? Empirical Softw. Eng. **22**(4), 1684–1716 (2016). https://doi.org/10.1007/s10664-016-9456-2
24. Su, Z., Ahn, B.-R., Eom, K.-Y., Kang, M.-K., Kim, J.-P., Kim, M.-K.: Plagiarism detection using the Levenshtein distance and Smith-Waterman algorithm. In: 3rd International Conference on Innovative Computing Information and Control, pp. 569–569. IEEE (2008)
25. Apache Ecosystem. https://www.apache.org/
26. McMillan, C., Grechanik, M., Poshyvanyk, D., Fu, C., Xie, Q.: Exemplar: a source code search engine for finding highly relevant applications. IEEE Trans. Softw. Eng. **38**, 1069–1087 (2011)
27. Wang, K., Ming, Z., Chua, T.-S.: A syntactic tree matching approach to finding similar questions in community-based QA services. In: Proceedings of the 32nd ACM SIGIR conference on Research and development in information retrieval, pp. 187–194. ACM (2019)
28. Shen, Y., Rong, W., Sun, Z., Ouyang, Y., Xiong, Z.: Question/answer matching for CQA system via combining lexical and sequential information. In: Twenty-Ninth AAAI Conference on Artificial Intelligence (2015)
29. Pecchia, A., Cinque, M., Carrozza, G., Cotroneo, D.: Industry practices and event logging: assessment of a critical software development process. In: Proceedings of the 37th International Conference on Software Engineering, vol. 2, pp. 169–178. IEEE Press (2015)
30. Li, Z., Chen, T.-H., Yang, J., Shang, W.: DLFinder: characterizing and detecting duplicate logging code smells. In: IEEE/ACM 41st International Conference on Software Engineering (ICSE), pp. 152–163. IEEE (2019)
31. Liu, Z., Xia, X., Hassan, A.E., Lo, D., Xing, Z., Wang, X.: Neural-machine-translation-based commit message generation: how far are we? In: IEEE/ACM 33rd International Conference on Automated Software Engineering (ASE), pp. 373–384. IEEE (2018)

Synthesis and Program Transformation

Parameterized Synthesis with Safety Properties

Oliver Markgraf[1]($\boxtimes$), Chih-Duo Hong[3], Anthony W. Lin[1,2],
Muhammad Najib[1], and Daniel Neider[2]

[1] Technical University of Kaiserslautern, Kaiserslautern, Germany
`markgraf@cs.uni-kl.de`
[2] Max Planck Institute for Software Systems, Kaiserslautern, Germany
[3] University of Oxford, Oxford, England

Abstract. Parameterized synthesis offers a solution to the problem of constructing correct and verified controllers for parameterized systems. Such systems occur naturally in practice (e.g., in the form of distributed protocols where the amount of processes is often unknown at design time and the protocol must work regardless of the number of processes). In this paper, we present a novel learning-based approach to the synthesis of reactive controllers for parameterized systems from safety specifications. We use the framework of regular model checking to model the synthesis problem as an infinite-duration two-player game and show how one can utilize Angluin's well-known L^* algorithm to learn correct-by-design controllers. This approach results in a synthesis procedure that is conceptually simpler than existing synthesis methods with a completeness guarantee, whenever a winning strategy can be expressed by a regular set. We have implemented our algorithm in a tool called L^*-PSynth and have demonstrated its performance on a range of benchmarks, including robotic motion planning and distributed protocols. Despite the simplicity of L^*-PSynth it competes well against (and in many cases even outperforms) the state-of-the-art tools for synthesizing parameterized systems.

Keywords: Parameterized systems · Reactive synthesis · Machine learning · Angluin's algorithm · Regular model checking

1 Introduction

Parameterized systems are systems with a parameterized number of components. Such systems are ubiquitous in distributed and/or reactive systems, (e.g., where the number of clients, the size of the environment, etc. can take arbitrary finite values and the correctness property must hold regardless of the assigned value). For example, in order to verify safety/liveness of a Dining Philosopher Protocol with n philosophers, we need to prove the property for *each* value of $n \geq 3$. This is known as the *parameterized verification problem*, which is undecidable even for safety properties [7].

© Springer Nature Switzerland AG 2020
B. C. d. S. Oliveira (Ed.): APLAS 2020, LNCS 12470, pp. 273–292, 2020.
https://doi.org/10.1007/978-3-030-64437-6_14

Verification of parameterized systems has been the subject of many papers spanning across four decades (e.g., see [3,9,47,49] for surveys). Many different techniques for verifying parameterized systems have been proposed including cutoff techniques [4,9], acceleration [2,3], learning [16,29,35,45,46], and abstractions [11], to name a few. The problem of verifying *safety* property (i.e., bad things will never happen) has occupied a lot of these research results, owing to its widely recognized importance.

In this paper, we are interested in automatically synthesizing correct parameterized systems with a safety guarantee. In this setting, parameterized systems are only partially specified, and the task of a synthesis algorithm is to "fill in" the missing specification in such a way that the desired property is satisfied. Synthesis algorithms aim to produce a correct-by-construction implementation of some formal properties in a fully automatic fashion, thereby saving the need for performing a further verification step. Program synthesis has been an active research area with many applications (e.g., to patch faulty parts of a system [1,22,25,43] or to fill the low-level details of a partial implementation [40–42]). However, there has not been much work on synthesis for parameterized systems with safety guarantee.

A common approach to the synthesis with a safety guarantee is by utilizing games, more specifically a type of games called *safety games*. Safety games are two-player games with *safety objectives* (i.e., the objective is to always stay inside a "safe" region). Safety games have been widely applied in the context of verification and synthesis of reactive systems. One example of their usage is for synthesis of safe controllers, such as a vacuum cleaner robot that tries to avoid bumping into humans while cleaning the room or a controller for a safety-critical system that maintains the temperature of a power plant within a certain safe level. Safety games have been extensively studied in many settings in the literature, both with finite-state arenas and infinite-state arenas, and including timed systems, hybrid systems, counter systems, and arenas generated by finite-state transducers. Some examples, among many others, can be found in [13,14,17,18,23,34,35,44]. A parameterized system can naturally be construed as an infinite-state system. Each parameter instantiation gives us a finite system, but there are infinitely many such instantiations. The corresponding infinite-state system is a disjoint union of all finite systems obtained from all possible parameter instantiations. This is an undecidable problem; in fact, verifying safety properties (i.e. one-player games) is already undecidable for parameterized systems [7]. There are a handful of generic methods and tools that have been designed in the past six years to handle safety games over general infinite-state systems [8,26,34,35]. Examples include CONSYNTH [8], DT-Synth [34], JSyn-VG [26], SAT-Synth [35], and RPNI-Synth [35], which have varying degrees of automation and expressivity. For instance, the former three synthesis tools (i.e., CONSYNTH, DT-Synth, and JSyn-VG) support safety games over arenas with infinitely many vertices that are modeled using integer or real linear arithmetic. By contrast, the latter two tools (i.e., SAT-Synth and RPNI-Synth) work in a setting similar to *regular model checking* [3,28], which encodes parameterized systems by means of regular languages and finite-state transducers. Since regular model checking is a popular and highly expressive framework for modelling and verifying parameterized systems, we follow the approach by SAT-Syth and RPNI-Synth throughout this paper.

Many of these aforementioned algorithms rely heavily on user guidance or are highly intricate. CONSYNTH, for instance, requires the user to provide templates that carry high-level information about possible solutions in order to prune the search space. SAT-Synth, on the other hand, repeatedly solves an NP-complete problem (learning of minimal finite-state machines from examples) and, hence, is computationally expensive. In this paper, we thus provide a different and *substantially simpler* solution to the synthesis problem, which does not require user guidance and is computationally efficient.

Contribution. The main contribution of this paper is to show how a simple *exact learning* algorithm for automata (e.g. Angluin's L^* algorithm [5]) can be employed effectively for solving regular safety games in regular model checking [3], while remaining competitive with existing tools for parameterized synthesis with safety properties. Furthermore, we show the efficacy of our procedure in various problem domains including path planning in a grid with adversaries, two-player zero-sum games (e.g. Nim), and distributed protocols. We elaborate below why this is a challenging problem.

We first quickly recall the framework of exact learning of regular languages [5,27]. A learner's goal is to learn an unknown regular language L (represented by minimal DFA—deterministic finite automaton) with the guide of a teacher, who can answer a *membership* query and an *equivalence* query. A membership query checks whether a given word $w \in \Sigma^*$ is in L. On the other hand, an equivalence query asks whether the language $L' := L(A)$ of a given DFA A coincides with L; if not, the teacher has to return a counterexample $w \in (L \setminus L') \cup (L' \setminus L)$ to the learner. In her seminal paper [5], she provided the so-called L^* algorithm, which learns a DFA in polynomial-time[1]. Different exact learning algorithms for automata are by now available that in practice may outperform Angluin's original algorithm, e.g., see [27].

Angluin's exact learning of regular languages is conceptually simple, but when a problem can be successfully modelled in this framework (e.g. see [15,16] for such examples in verification), one can tap into a wealth of efficient learning algorithms. When employing this for infinite-state verification, the language L to be learned typically represents a kind of correctness proof (e.g. invariants). This is problematic because this is *not unique*, which is necessary for a successful modelling in the exact learning framework. The proposed strategy in this paper is to design the so-called *strict but generous teacher*, which essentially drives the learner to learn the safe region reachable from the set of initial states (which is *unique*) but accepts a different correct proof from the learner.

---

[1] The running time by definition accounts for the amount of time taken by the learner plus the maximum size of the counterexamples provided by the teacher. We assume the teacher is an oracle that can return an answer in constant time.

For this idea to work, a membership query (asking whether a given configuration is reachable and in a safe region) should not be an undecidable problem. To this end, we propose to consider length-preserving transducers, which is known to be sufficiently general [3]. With this restriction, we obtain a framework where membership queries become decidable, and can in fact be checked using fast finite-state model checkers.

We have implemented our approach in a tool called L^*-*PSynth*. We also provide some case studies as benchmarks in order to evaluate our implementation. Some of the case studies are taken from [35], while the rest are known games, or inspired by some real world applications. Furthermore, we compare the performance of our tool (using the provided benchmarks) against three existing sate-of-the-art tools: *SAT-Synth*, *RPNI-Synth* [35] and *DT-Synth* [34]. Despite its simplicity, the tool competes well in practice against the other three tools, and even in many cases, outperforms them.

Organization. We start with a couple of motivating examples in the next section. Section 3 contains preliminaries. We describe the algorithm of our proposed approach in Sect. 4. In Sect. 5, we provide some case studies and report the experiments to measure the performance of our implementation against two existing tools. We conclude in Sect. 7.

2   Motivating Examples

Robotic Motion Planning Example. Consider two robots inhabiting a bounded two-dimensional grid world, one controlled by a controller/system that we wish to synthesize, and the other controlled by the environment (which we do not control.) We call this game "follow game", which, later in Sect. 5, is also used as one of the benchmarks. In this game, both robots move in alternating turns, and by one grid on each turn. The goal of the game is to find (and synthesize) a strategy such that the robot controlled by the system stays within a certain distance to the environment's robot. We can consider this game as an abstraction of some system in which some drones need to be in close proximity to some moving targets. Such a strategy thus can be synthesized as a controller for the drones.

In order to abstract away from the details, we turn the area in which a drone operates into a bounded two-dimensional grid world, where a number of parameters (e.g., width, height, obstacle coordinates, etc.) can be taken into account. Every possible configuration of a specific grid world, including the positions of the robots, is modeled by a vertex in the game graph of a regular safety game. One snippet of such a graph for a variation of the follow game is shown in Fig. 1. Obstacles, i.e., inaccessible grids, are marked black; the system's robot (represented by Player 0) is depicted by a triangle. and the environment's robot (represented by Player 1) by a circle. A directed edge between two grid worlds indicates that there is a possible action from current configuration to reach the target configuration. Furthermore, all parameterizations are fixed at runtime, and thus, there are no edges from a configuration into another configuration with different parameters.

Notice that each of the configuration in a runtime can either be "safe", i.e., the drone is within an acceptable proximity to the target, or "unsafe", i.e., beyond the proximity. Figure 2 shows an automaton that parameterizes the grid world of the follow game by encoding the positions of both robots as bit vectors. The first symbol indicates which player is allowed to move their robot: $\begin{bmatrix} 1 \\ 1 \end{bmatrix}$ means Player 1 can move their robot, whereas $\begin{bmatrix} 0 \\ 0 \end{bmatrix}$ indicates Player 0's turn. The subsequent vector $\begin{bmatrix} x_1 \\ x_2 \end{bmatrix}$ encodes the x-coordinates of Player 0's and Player 1's robots in the unary numeral system number, respectively, followed by a separating symbol S and $\begin{bmatrix} y_1 \\ y_2 \end{bmatrix}$ which encodes the y-coordinates. The symbol 0 is used as padding symbol to keep the length of each word encoding a grid world to be the same.

An automaton representing one winning strategy for the follow game with the robots start at the same position, and where the grid world does not contain any obstacles, is shown in Fig. 3. The intuition behind this automaton is that whenever Player 1 takes a turn, the robots are on top of each other, and once Player 0 takes a turn, the x and y-coordinates differ by at most one, which translates into a simple strategy for Player 0: always move the robot on top of Player 1's robot. Given such a setting, the objective of the synthesis is to find a strategy that takes into account the parameters, and, regardless of the value of the parameters, works for every possible grid world.

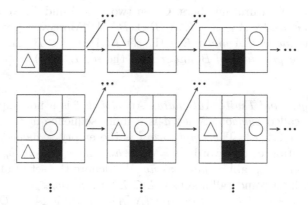

Fig. 1. One segment of the safety game graph of one version of the follow game.

Distributed Protocol Example. Consider a distributed system which operates on n processes that may enter critical section. Additionally, there is a single token in the system. A process can only enter the critical section if it is in possession of the token. We are interested in a controller which guarantees that at most one process is in the critical section at a given time. The controller handles the

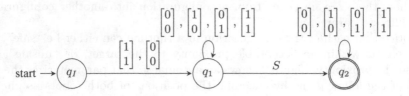

Fig. 2. Automaton representing the grid world.

resource allocation, i.e., decides which process gets the token and how long the process keeps it. However, similar to the ring token protocol, it can only move the token to the right. The processes can be *idle* (e.g., doing computations in non-critical sections), *requesting* a token, or *in the critical section*. The controller has to give a process the token if the process is in requesting state and the token passes the process. The obvious parameter for this protocol is the amount of processes which are dependent on the system. With parameterization synthesis, it is enough to only synthesize one controller which can function regardless of the number of processes. Indeed, later in Sect. 5, we use this motivating example as one of the benchmarks—we call it "resource allocation game"—and synthesize the controller.

3   Preliminaries

Let $\mathbb{N}$ be the set of natural numbers. Given two sets A and B, we denote their *symmetric difference* by $A \ominus B = (A \setminus B) \cup (B \setminus A)$. Moreover, given a relation $E \subseteq A \times B$, the *image of A under E* is the set $E(A) = \{b \in B \mid \exists a \in A \colon (a, b) \in E\}$; similarly, the *preimage of B under E* is the set $E^{-1}(B) = \{a \in A \mid \exists b \in B \colon (a, b) \in E\}$.

Word, Languages, and Finite Automata. An *alphabet* is a nonempty finite set Σ of elements, called *symbols*. A *word* is a finite sequence $w = a_1 \ldots a_n$ with $a_i \in \Sigma$ for $i \in \{1, \ldots, n\}$. The *empty word* is the empty sequence, denoted by ϵ. The concatenation of two words $u = a_1 \ldots a_m$ and $v = b_1 \ldots b_n$ is the word $u \cdot v = a_1 \ldots a_m b_1 \ldots b_n$, abbreviated as uv. We denote the set of all words over the alphabet Σ by Σ^* and call a subset $L \subseteq \Sigma^*$ a *language*.

A *nondeterministic finite automaton (NFA)* is a tuple $\mathcal{A} = (Q, \Sigma, q_I, \delta, F)$ consisting of a nonempty finite set Q of states, an input alphabet Σ, an initial state $q_I \in Q$, a transition relation $\delta \subseteq Q \times \Sigma \times Q$, and a set $F \subseteq Q$ of final states. A *run* of an NFA $\mathcal{A}$ on a word $w = a_1 \ldots a_n$ is a sequence $q_0 q_1 \ldots q_n$ of states such that $q_0 = q_I$ and $(q_{i-1}, a_i, q_i) \in \delta$ for $i \in \{1, \ldots, n\}$. We call a run $q_0 \ldots q_n$ accepting if $q_n \in F$. The language of an NFA $\mathcal{A}$, denoted by $L(\mathcal{A})$, is the set of all words $w \in \Sigma^*$ for which an accepting run of $\mathcal{A}$ on w exists. A language $L \subseteq \Sigma^*$ is called *regular* if there exists an NFA $\mathcal{A}$ with $L(\mathcal{A}) = L$. A *deterministic finite automaton (DFA)* is an NFA where the transition relation is effectively a function $\delta \colon Q \times \Sigma \to Q$.

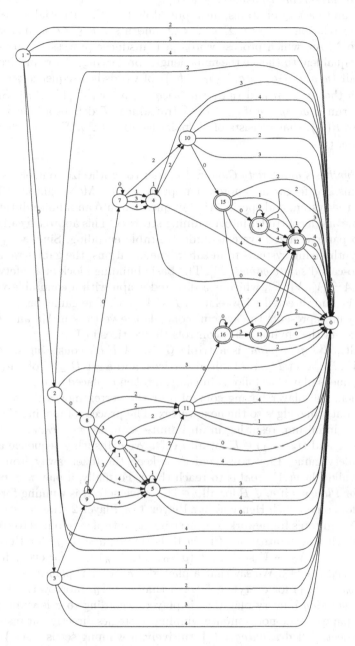

Fig. 3. Automaton representing one winning strategy for a simplified version of the follow game. The legend for the symbols is as follows: $0 \mapsto \left[\begin{smallmatrix}1\\1\end{smallmatrix}\right]$, $1 \mapsto \left[\begin{smallmatrix}0\\0\end{smallmatrix}\right]$, $2 \mapsto S$, $3 \mapsto \left[\begin{smallmatrix}0\\1\end{smallmatrix}\right]$, $4 \mapsto \left[\begin{smallmatrix}1\\0\end{smallmatrix}\right]$.

A *length-preserving transducer* is a tuple $\mathcal{T} = (Q, \Sigma, q_I, \delta, F)$ consisting of a nonempty finite set Q of states, an input alphabet Σ, an initial state $q_I \in Q$, a transition relation $\delta \subseteq Q \times \Sigma \times \Sigma \times Q$, and a set $F \subseteq Q$ of final states. In contrast to NFAs, which process words, a transducer processes pairs of words that have equal length (hence the name length-preserving). More precisely, a *run* of $\mathcal{T}$ on pair $(u, v) = \big((a_1 \ldots a_n), (b_1 \ldots b_n)\big)$ of words is a sequence $q_0 q_1 \ldots q_n$ of states such that $q_0 = q_I$ and $\big(q_{i-1}, (a_i, b_i), q_i\big) \in \delta$ for $i \in \{1, \ldots, n\}$. Similar to NFAs, the run is *accepting* if $q_n \in F$. A transducer $\mathcal{T}$ defines a binary relation, denoted by $R(\mathcal{T})$, that consists of all pairs $(u, v) \in (\Sigma \times \Sigma)^*$ for which $\mathcal{T}$ has an accepting run.

Reactive Synthesis and Safety Games. In order to synthesize controllers for reactive systems, we follow an approach popularized by McNaughton [30], which translates the system and specification in question into an infinite-duration two-player game and a controller into a winning strategy. This approach can be easily applied to parameterized systems under suitable encoding. Since we are interested in synthesizing systems from safety specifications, the games we are faced with are so-called *safety games* [23]. The basic building block of a safety game is an *arena* $\mathcal{A} = (V_0, V_1, E)$, which is a directed graph with a countable vertex set $V = V_0 \uplus V_1$ and directed edge relation $E \subseteq V \times V$. The game has two players: *Player 0*, who represents the system, controls the vertices in V_0, and *Player 1*, who represents the environment, controls the vertices in V_1.

Formally, a *safety game* is a triple $\mathcal{G} = (\mathcal{A}, I, B)$ consisting of an arena $\mathcal{A} = (V_0, V_1, E)$, a set $I \subseteq V$ of initial vertices, and a set $B \subseteq V$ of bad vertices. A safety game is played as follows: initially, a token is placed on one initial vertex $v_0 \in I$; then, the player having control over the vertex moves the token along one of the outgoing edges to the next vertex. The process of moving the token is repeated ad infinitum, resulting in an infinite sequence $\pi = v_0 v_1 \ldots$ of vertices where $v_0 \in I$ and $(v_i, v_{i+1}) \in E$ for all $i \in \mathbb{N}$. We call such a sequence a *play*.

In a safety game, Player 0's goal is to keep the token away from the bad vertices, while Player 1's goal is to reach them. Formally, a play $\pi = v_0 v_1 \ldots$ is *winning for Player 0* if $v_i \notin B$ for all $i \in \mathbb{N}$. Conversely, it is winning for Player 1 if $v_i \in B$ for some $i \in \mathbb{N}$. Hence either Player 1 or Player 2 wins for each play.

In McNaughton's framework, synthesizing a controller amounts to computing a so-called winning strategy for Player 0. Formally, a *strategy* for Player 0 is a mapping $\sigma \colon V^* \times V_0 \to V$ such that $\big(\sigma(v_0 \ldots v_n), v_n\big) \in E$ for every finite play prefix $v_0 \ldots v_n \in V^* V_0$. We say that a play $\pi = v_0 v_1 \ldots$ is *played according to σ* if $v_i = \sigma(v_0 \ldots v_{i-1})$ for every $i \in \mathbb{N}$ such that $v_i \in V_0$. Moreover, a strategy is said to be *winning* if every play that is played according to σ is winning.

In this paper, we do not compute winning strategies directly but instead learn a proxy object, called *winning set*. Intuitively, a winning set is a set $W \subseteq V$ of vertices that contains all initial vertices, contains no bad vertex, and is a "trap" for Player 1 in the sense that Player 1 cannot force the play to a vertex outside the winning set. Formally, winning sets are defined as follows.

Definition 1 (Winning set). *Let $\mathcal{G} = (\mathcal{A}, I, B)$ be a safety game over the arena $\mathcal{A} = (V_0, V_1, E)$. A winning set is a set $W \subseteq V$ of vertices satisfying the following four properties:*

1. *$I \subseteq W$: all initial vertices are subsumed by the winning set (initial condition).*
2. *$B \cap W = \emptyset$: no bad vertex is contained in the winning set (bad condition).*
3. *$E(\{v\}) \cap W \neq \emptyset$ for all $v \in W \cap V_0$: every vertex of Player 0 inside the winning set has at least one outgoing edge connected to another vertex inside the winning set (existential closedness).*
4. *$E(\{v\}) \subseteq W$ for all $v \in W \cap V_1$: the successors of every Player 1 vertex inside the winning set is also inside the winning set (universal closedness).*

A winning strategy for Player 0 can be derived from a winning set W in a straightforward manner: starting with a vertex $v \in I$ (and, hence, $v \in W$), every time Player 0 is in control of the token, the strategy is to move the token to a successor vertex which is also inside the winning set W. It is not hard to verify that this strategy is in fact winning for Player 0 from every vertex in W: first, all initial vertices are contained in the winning set, and every Player 0 vertex has a successor which is inside the winning set; second, since Player 1 can never leave the winning set (due to universal closedness) and since no vertex inside the winning set is bad, it is guaranteed that following the strategy results in a winning play regardless of the moves of Player 1.

Regular Safety Games. We represent safety games using finite automata and transducers. A *regular arena* is an arena $\mathcal{A_R} = (L(\mathcal{A}_{V_0}), L(\mathcal{A}_{V_1}), R(\mathcal{T}_E))$ where $\mathcal{A}_{V_0}$ and $\mathcal{A}_{V_1}$ are NFAs and $\mathcal{T}_E$ is a length-preserving transducer. A *regular safety game* is a safety game $\mathcal{G_R} = (\mathcal{A_R}, L(\mathcal{A}_I), L(\mathcal{A}_B))$ where $\mathcal{A}_I$ and $\mathcal{A}_B$ are given as NFAs.

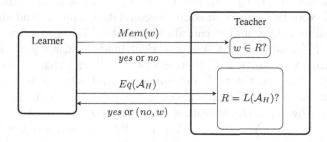

Fig. 4. General active automata learning framework. The teacher must be able to answer $w \in R$? and must have some way to determine whether $R = L(\mathcal{A}_H)$.

4 Algorithm

An Active Automata Learning Algorithm. Suppose R is a regular language whose definition is not directly accessible. *Automata learning* algorithms [5,10, 27,39] automatically infer a DFA $\mathcal{A}_H$ recognising R. The setting of an active learning algorithm is shown in Fig. 4 assumes a *teacher* who has access to R and can answer the following two queries: (1) Membership query $Mem(w)$: is the word w a member of R, i.e., $w \in R$? (2) Equivalence query $Eq(\mathcal{A}_H)$: is the language of $\mathcal{A}_H$ equal to R, i.e., $L(\mathcal{A}_H) = R$? If not, it returns a counterexample $w \in L(\mathcal{A}_H) \ominus R$. The learning algorithm will then construct an DFA $\mathcal{A}_H$ such that $L(\mathcal{A}_H) = R$ by interacting with the teacher. Such an algorithm works iteratively: in each iteration, it performs membership queries to get from the teacher information about R. Using the results of the queries, it proceeds by constructing a hypothesis DFA $\mathcal{A}_H$ and makes an equivalence query $Eq(\mathcal{A}_H)$. If $L(\mathcal{A}_H) = R$, the learning algorithm terminates and outputs $\mathcal{A}_H$. Otherwise, the algorithm uses the counterexample w returned by the teacher to refine the hypothesis DFA in the next iteration.

For completeness, we briefly describe how the learning algorithm computes hypothesis automata. The foundation of the algorithm is the Myhill-Nerode theorem [36], which states that the minimal DFA recognizing R is isomorphic to the set of equivalence classes defined by the following relation: $x \equiv_R y$ iff it holds that $\forall z \in \Sigma^* : xz \in R \leftrightarrow yz \in R$. Informally, two words x and y belong to the same state of the minimal DFA recognising R iff they cannot be distinguished by any suffix z. In other words, if one can find a suffix z' such that $xz' \in R$ and $yz' \notin R$ or vice versa, then x and y belong to different states of the minimal DFA.

The learning algorithm maintains a Boolean table where the rows are indexed by $X \subseteq \Sigma^*$ and the columns indexed by $Y \subseteq \Sigma^*$. Each cell (x, y) of the table indicates whether or not $xy \in R$. For $x, x' \in X$, we write $x \sim_Y x'$ iff $xy \equiv_R x'y$ for all $y \in Y$. Note that $\sim_Y$ is an equivalence relation over X, and that $x \sim_Y x'$ iff the rows indexed by x and x' contain the identical Boolean values. The table is *consistent* iff for all $x, x' \in X$ and $x \neq x'$, it holds that $x \not\sim_Y x'$. The table is *closed* iff for all $x \in X$ and $a \in \Sigma$, there exists $x' \in X$ such that $xa \sim_Y x'$. By the Myhill-Nerode theorem, the table determines a DFA when it is consistent and closed: the states of the DFA are $\{[x]_Y : x \in X\}$ (where $[\cdot]_Y$ is the equivalence classes induced by $\sim_Y$), the accepting states are $\{[x]_Y : x \in X \cap R\}$, and the transition function $\delta : [X]_Y \times \Sigma \to [X]_Y$ is defined by $\delta([x]_Y, a) = [xa]_Y$. Note that this DFA is minimal as every two states of it can be distinguished by some word in Y by the definition of consistency.

During the learning process, the algorithm fills and extends the table through membership queries until the table is consistent and closed. The algorithm then determines a hypothesis automaton $\mathcal{A}_H$ from the table and makes an equivalence query $Eq(\mathcal{A}_H)$. If the teacher returns a counterexample w, the algorithm will perform a binary search over w using membership queries to find a suffix y of w and extend Y to $Y \cup \{y\}$, which will identify at least one more state for R by the Myhill-Nerode theorem.

Proposition 1 ([39]). *The learning algorithm in Fig. 4 finds the minimal DFA $\mathcal{A}_H$ for the target regular language R using at most n equivalence queries and $n(n + n|\Sigma|) + n \log m$ membership queries, where n is the number of state of H and m is the length of the longest counterexample returned from the teacher.*

A Teacher for Learning Winning Set. Let $\mathcal{G}_\mathcal{R} = (\mathcal{A}_\mathcal{R}, L(\mathcal{A}_I), L(\mathcal{A}_B))$ be a regular safety game with regular arena $\mathcal{A}_\mathcal{R} = (L(\mathcal{A}_{V_0}), L(\mathcal{A}_{V_1}), R(\mathcal{T}_E))$. We describe below a teacher to learn a regular winning set for $\mathcal{G}_\mathcal{R}$. Since $\mathcal{G}_\mathcal{R}$ can have multiple winning sets, we aim to learn the *maximal* winning set, which, if exists, is unique as winning sets are closed under union.

Theorem 1. *The target object in Fig. 4, the maximal winning set, is unique.*

Membership Query. To answer a membership query $Mem(w)$, the teacher needs to check whether Player 1 can force Player 0 to visit a bad vertex from vertex w. Since the transition relation is length-preserving, only a finite number of vertices (i.e. at most $|\Sigma|^{|w|}$ vertices) can be reached from vertex w. Therefore, this check can be done by solving an induced *finite* safety game with $I_w = \{w\}$ as the set of initial vertices and $B_w = \{w' \in L(\mathcal{A}_B) : |w'| = |w|\}$ as the set of bad vertices. Safety games over finite graphs are known to be decidable [23], thus making our membership query decidable.

Equivalence Query. To answer an equivalence query $Eq(\mathcal{A}_H)$, the teacher simply checks that all conditions in Definition 1 are fulfilled by the hypothesis DFA $\mathcal{A}_H$. Note that a DFA satisfying these conditions serves as a proof for safety even if it does not recognize the maximal winning set. The pseudo code of the equivalence check can be found in Algorithm 1. Given an equivalence query $Eq(\mathcal{A}_H)$ by the learner, the teacher first checks if $L(\mathcal{A}_I) \not\subseteq L(\mathcal{A}_H)$ and if there is $v \in L(\mathcal{A}_I) \setminus L(\mathcal{A}_H)$, the teacher returns v as a counterexample.

Secondly, the teacher checks whether $L(\mathcal{A}_B) \cap L(\mathcal{A}_H) \neq \emptyset$. If there is a $v \in L(\mathcal{A}_B) \cap L(\mathcal{A}_H)$, then the teacher returns v as a counterexample.

According to the third part of Definition 1, the teacher checks if there exists $v \in L(\mathcal{A}_H) \cap L(\mathcal{A}_{V_0})$ and $R(\mathcal{T}_E)(\{v\}) \cap L(\mathcal{A}_H) = \emptyset$. Here either v should be excluded from the hypothesis or one of its successors should be included. The teacher then makes membership queries to check if v should be excluded: if $Mem(v)$ returns "no", the teacher returns v as counterexample. Otherwise, the teachers returns some $u \in R(\mathcal{T}_E)(\{v\})$ as a counterexample such that $Mem(u)$ is "yes".

Lastly, the teacher checks if there exists $v \in L(\mathcal{A}_H) \cap L(\mathcal{A}_{V_1})$ and $R(\mathcal{T}_E)(\{v\}) \not\subseteq L(\mathcal{A}_H)$. Again, either v should be excluded or one of its successors should be included. If $Mem(v)$ returns "no", the teacher returns v as a counterexample. Otherwise, the teacher returns some $u \in R(\mathcal{T}_E)(\{v\}) \setminus L(\mathcal{A}_H)$ as a counterexample.

Since the teacher checks all conditions in Definition 1 for an equivalence query, if the teacher replies "yes" then the hypothesis DFA indeed recognizes a winning set. Otherwise, the teacher will pinpoint a counterexample violating

---

Algorithm 1: Resolving an equivalence query for regular safety games

---

Input: $\mathcal{G}_\mathcal{R} = (\mathcal{A}_\mathcal{R}, L(\mathcal{A}_I), L(\mathcal{A}_B))$ over the regular arena
$\mathcal{A}_\mathcal{R} = (L(\mathcal{A}_{V_0}), L(\mathcal{A}_{V_1}), R(\mathcal{T}_E))$ and an hypothesis DFA $\mathcal{A}_H$.

1   **if** $L(\mathcal{A}_I) \setminus L(\mathcal{A}_H) \neq \emptyset$ **then**
2 | Find some $v \in L(\mathcal{A}_I) \setminus L(\mathcal{A}_H)$ and **return** ("no", v)

3   **if** $L(\mathcal{A}_H) \cap L(\mathcal{A}_B) \neq \emptyset$ **then**
4 | Find some $v \in L(\mathcal{A}_H) \cap L(\mathcal{A}_B)$ and **return** ("no", v)

5   **if** *there is* $v \in L(\mathcal{A}_{V_0}) \cap L(\mathcal{A}_H)$ *such that* $R(\mathcal{T}_E)(\{v\}) \cap L(\mathcal{A}_H) = \emptyset$ **then**
6 | **if** $Mem(v)$ *is* "yes" **then**
7 | | Find some $u \in R(\mathcal{T}_E)(\{v\})$ such that $Mem(u)$ is "yes"
8 | | **return** ("no", u)
9 | **else**
10 | | **return** ("no", v)

11   **if** *there is* v *such that* $v \in L(\mathcal{A}_{V_1}) \cap L(\mathcal{A}_H)$ *and* $R(\mathcal{T}_E)(\{v\}) \nsubseteq L(\mathcal{A}_H)$ **then**
12 | **if** $Mem(v)$ *is* "yes" **then**
13 | | Find some $u \in R(\mathcal{T}_E)(\{v\}) \setminus L(\mathcal{A}_H)$ and **return** ("no", u)
14 | **else**
15 | | **return** ("no", v)

16 **return** "yes"

---

the definition. Furthermore, observe that the counterexamples pinpointed by the teacher are located in the symmetric difference of the candidate language and the maximal winning set. Therefore, if the maximal winning set can be recognized by a DFA of n states, the learning algorithm will terminate in n iterations by Proposition 1. We summarize the soundness and completeness of our learning method in the following theorem.

Theorem 2. *Given a regular safety game* $\mathcal{G}_\mathcal{R} = (\mathcal{A}_\mathcal{R}, L(\mathcal{A}_I), L(\mathcal{A}_B))$, *the learning algorithm in Fig. 4 computes a winning set on termination. Furthermore, when the maximal winning set* W *is regular, the algorithm will terminate in at most* n *iterations where* n *is the size of the minimal DFA of* W.

5   Case Studies and Experiments

In this section, we provide some case studies as benchmarks and report the results of the experiments based on given benchmarks. In order to asses the performance of our tool, *L**-*PSynth*, we compare it with three existing tools that are able to solve safety games over infinite graphs: *SAT-Synth*, *RPNI-Synth* [35] and *DT-Synth* [34]

Tools. The tools *SAT-Synth* and *RPNI-Synth* both compute a winning set based on learning finite automata with a teacher that answers to equivalence queries. In contrast to *L**-*PSynth*—which solves regular safety games—these tools are able to solve *rational safety games*, which is a more general type of safety games, since in these games, edge relations may be represented by non length-preserving transducers. Furthermore, the learner of *SAT-Synth* uses a SAT solver to learn automata, while *RPNI-Synth* is based on the popular RPNI learning algorithm [37].

The tool *DT-Synth* uses formulas in the first-order theory of linear integer arithmetic to encode safety games. It uses a learning algorithm that learns from data in the form of Horn clauses. The teacher in this tool was built on top of the constraint solver Z3 [31].

L*-PSynth is implemented with the use of automata libraries and an existing implementation of an L* learner[16]. The teacher is implemented in Java and uses existing automata methods to implement the algorithms from Sect. 4. The input format is a text file which encodes a regular safety game $\mathcal{G_R} = (\mathcal{A_R}, L(\mathcal{A_I}), L(\mathcal{A_B}))$.[2]

The teacher for *L*-PSynth* is an extension of the one used by *SAT-Synth*, *RPNI-Synth*, and *DT-Synth*: it also answers to membership queries in order to accommodate for the additional queries the learner might ask, since, beside equivalence queries, our learner also asks membership queries.

Benchmarks. Some of the benchmarks are taken from [35] with some modification to fit the framework of regular safety games. In particular, we adjust the arenas of the game, from infinite arenas into arenas with arbitrary but bounded size. The other benchmarks are either known games which are translated to a regular safety game, e.g., the Nim game [12], or inspired by some processes that happen in real world, such as resource allocation protocols or the movement of an autonomous robotic vacuum cleaner. The list of benchmarks is as follows:

Box game: A robot moves in an two-dimensional grid world of size $n \times m$ with $n, m \geq 3$.[3] Player 0 controls the vertical movement of the robot while Player 1 controls the horizontal movement. Player 0 wins if the robot stays within a horizontal stripe of width 3 around the middle of the arena. We can consider this kind of game as an abstraction of some autonomous control system, e.g., a controller that ensures a drone stay in some range of altitude.

Control unit game: Consider a system that controls the temperature of n power plants within a certain safe level. We can model this as a game between two players, 0 and 1. Player 0 acts as the controller who can decrease the temperature of some plant (e.g., by reducing the boiler temperature). Player 1 acts as the environment who may increase the temperature of some plant (e.g., weather changes, cooling system malfunction). The game is played in a sequential fashion, i.e., Player 0 and Player 1 can alternately increase or decrease the temperature of a plant. Player 0 wins if none of the plants reach critical temperature.

---

[2] Code and benchmarks are available at https://github.com/lstarsynth/lstar-psynth.
[3] The encoding in the benchmarks use a grid world of size $2^n \times 2^n$ which can be easily reduced to $n \times m$.

Diagonal game: A variation of the Box game where Player 0 again controls the vertical movement and Player 1 controls the horizontal movement of a robot in a bounded two-dimensional grid world. Player 0 wins if the robot stays within a two cells of the diagonal in the arena.

Evasion game: Two robots are moving in an bounded discrete two-dimensional grid world of size $n \times m$ with $n, m \geq 3$. Each Player is in control of one robot and they can move their respective robot at most one cell in any direction (either vertically or diagonally.) If the system moves its robot outside of a bound it automatically wins[4]. Player 0 wins if Player 1 never moves its robot on top of Player 0's robot.

Follow game: A variation of the evasion game where Player 0 wins if it manages to keep its robot within a Manhattan distance of two cells to Player 1's robot.

Nim game: The standard Nim game consists of three piles of chips and two players taking alternating turns. On each turn, each player must remove one chip, and may remove any number of chips so long as they all come from the same pile. The player who removes the last chip wins the game[5]. The game is modified to be an infinite duration game by adding an infinite loop at the end of the game. A winning strategy is computed for all winning starting positions which are determined by the *Nim sum*. More information on the Nim game and its winning strategy can be found in [21].

Resource allocation game: This game involves a single token and n processes. Each process has three states: *idle, requesting,* and *in critical section.* A process can move from a requesting state to the critical section if and only if it has the token. If a process is in a requesting state, it is guaranteed by design of the game, that it will eventually get the token. Player 0 controls the token and can either: (i) move the token from one process to another, or (ii) keep it in the same place if the process is in the critical section, or if there are only idle processes. Player 1 can change the state of a process from idle to requesting or vice versa. Additionally, Player 1 can move a process to the critical section if the process is in control of the token. Once a process enters the critical section, it may stay in the critical section even without the token. Player 0 wins if at all times, there is no process in the critical section without the token.

Robot vacuum cleaner game: A vacuum cleaner robot and a human move in an two-dimensional grid world of size $2^n \times 2^n$ with $n \geq 2$. Player 0 controls the movement of the robot and Player 1 controls the movement of the human. Player 0 wins if the robot never bumps into the human, and if the human tries to step on the robot, it moves away.

Solitary box: Another variation of the Box game where only Player 0 controls the vertical and horizontal movement of the robot.

---

[4] The original version of the evasion game is played in an infinite grid world, thus, making one valid strategy to always move into one direction, which resembles Player 0 moving out of bound.

[5] This version of winning condition is called "misère play condition", in which the last player making a move loses. Nim can also be played with "normal play condition", i.e., the last player making a move wins.

Table 1. Results on the benchmarks on L^*-*PSynth*, *SAT-Synth* and *RPNI-Synth*. "Size" measures the size of the final automata synthesized by the algorithms. "—" indicates a timeout after 300s. "N/A" corresponds to not supported by the tool.

Game	L^*-*PSynth*		*SAT-Synth*		*RPNI-Synth*		*DT-Synth*
	Time in s	Size	Time in s	Size	Time in s	Size	Time in s
Box	1.62	5	6.83	4	1.92	7	5.76
Control unit	0.40	3	185.50	5	1.13	5	N/A
Diagonal	0.68	3	113.52	7	1.62	7	139.36
Evasion	4.77	11	122.41	7	2.52	11	10.83
Follow	6.71	16	207.12	16	18.53	16	31.67
Nim	3.64	4	—	—	7.12	5	N/A
Resource allocation	0.65	4	24.00	3	3.77	4	N/A
Robot vacuum cleaner	1.21	3	—	—	—	—	—
Solitary box	1.14	4	5.71	4	0.30	4	1.89

Results. The result of the benchmarks on L^*-*PSynth*, *SAT-Synth*, *RPNI-Synth* and *DT-Synth* is shown in Table 1. In this table, we report the time each tool took to synthesize an automaton that encodes a winning set, as well as the size of the respective automaton[6]. We conducted the experiments on an Intel Xeon E7-8857 v2 CPU with 4 GB of RAM running a 64-bit Debian operating system. From the results, we can see that L^*-*PSynth* was able to solve all games, whereas *RPNI-Synth* and *DT-Synth* were not able to solve the robot vacuum cleaner game, and *SAT-Synth* did not solve the robot vacuum cleaner game and the Nim game. Moreover, the aggregated runtime to solve all 9 games for L^*-*PSynth* is 20.82 s compared to *RPNI-Synth* which took 36.91 s to solve 8 games in total. *SAT-Synth* was able to solve 7 games taking 665.09 s. Finally, *DT-Synth* was only able to solve 5 games within 189.51 s —this is partly due to the inability of *DT-Synth* encoding to represent three benchmarks: control unit, Nim, and resource allocation. Given the results, it is not surprising that L^*-*PSynth* was able to outperform the other tools, since the benchmarks are more well suited for regular safety game framework. On the other hand, if we consider the size of the solutions, *RPNI-Synth* performed worst, with only 2 out of 9 solutions that are at least as small as those produced by other tools, followed by *SAT-Synth* 5 out of 9 games. L^*-*PSynth* performed best with 6 out of 9 solutions that are at least as small as others[7]. Again, this is not a surprising result with respect to *RPNI-Synth* performance, since it was not tailored to find small solutions, whereas *SAT-Synth* was designed to find such solutions. However, although L^*-*PSynth* was also not tailored to optimize the solution size[8], it produced better solutions compared

---

[6] Apart from *DT-Synth*, since instead of automata, it produces witnesses as decision trees.

[7] Including one case (robot vacuum cleaner) in which the other two tools timed out.

[8] In spite of the fact that Angluin's algorithm computes the minimal DFA for a given target language, it is not necessarily encoded by a small automaton.

to *SAT-Synth*. From the experiments, it appears that L^*-*PSynth* performs well on benchmarks where a winning strategy can be synthesized by only looking at small n in the parameterization. If larger n is needed in order to find a winning strategy, the runtime significantly increases (up to 5–10 times as much time needed) as in the case for the evasion, follow and Nim game. We believe this correlates to the runtime of Angluin's algorithm which is strongly dependent on the length of words and counterexamples considered in a given run, which increases as n increases.

Parameterization in DT-Synth. Encoding the benchmarks as safety games in *DT-Synth* is not straightforward, and, in some cases, not possible (i.e., with control unit, Nim, and resource allocation.) This is because, in those corresponding cases, either the games specifically parameterize the amount of processes, or perform bit-sensitive operations. For the rest of the games that are played on arenas of the size $n \times m$, this can be represented in *DT-Synth* by letting the environment pick two additional variables, n and m. These variables further constrain the initial states and modify the transition system accordingly, i.e., enable/disable transitions, based on their value.

6 Related Work

In the context of safety games, a constraint-based approach for solving safety games over infinite graphs [8,26] and various learning approaches for finite graphs and infinite graphs have been proposed [32,34,35]. Similar to the framework of Neider et al. [35] we encode safety games symbolically using the idea of regular model checking. Their work considers rational safety games which differ with our regular safety games in the definition of the edge relation. The edge relation in our framework is encoded by length-preserving transducers while rational safety games allow a more general type of transducer. The framework for solving rational safety games is implemented in two tools, *SAT-Synth* and *RPNI-Synth*. On the other hand, the framework in another learning-based approach, which is implemented in the tool *DT-Synth*, does not fix the representation of safety games and uses formulas in the first-order theory of linear integer arithmetic to encode them [34]. This leads to some encoding difficulties with parameterized systems as discussed in Sect. 5. The learner in both frameworks learns passively from a sample and can only ask the teacher equivalence queries while the algorithm we design is able to employ a learner which is allowed to ask membership queries in addition to equivalence queries. All frameworks mentioned above operate on safety games over infinite-state arenas, whereas we consider infinitely many finite graphs due to the nature of length-preserving transducers. However, this is not a restriction as we can parameterize the value that goes towards infinity and finding a strategy which works for every n also gives us a strategy for every specific place in the infinite-state arena for an appropriately chosen n. There might be games which will not have a strategy for finite graphs (see evasion game in Sect. 5) where we extend transitions to go "out of bound" of the parameter and always stay safe. This works because there is a way for one robot to catch the other then there is going to be a finite example on grid world with a specific size.

The framework of regular model checking is used in many different areas of research to verify different properties such as safety [16,24,33,35] or liveness [29, 38,48]. In particular, for verification of those properties in parameterized systems regular model checking has seen successful application [16,29]. Furthermore, the approaches in [16,29] also employ Angluin-style L*-learning to verify properties of parameterized systems.

7   Conclusion

In this paper, we have developed a learning-based methodology for synthesizing parameterized systems from safety specifications. Our approach reduces this synthesis problem to a two-player safety game in an infinite arena, where synthesizing a controller amounts to computing a winning strategy (a winning set) for the player embodying the system. Inspired by Regular Model Checking and the work by Neider and Topcu, we encode sets of vertices by means of finite automata and edges using length-preserving transducers. This encoding allows us to utilize Angluin's popular automata learning algorithm, which significantly reduces the complexity of the underlying learning problem as compared to the earlier work by Neider and Topcu (the former being polynomial while the latter being NP-complete). In fact, our experimental evaluation shows that a prototype of our approach is very effective in synthesizing various types of parameterized systems, including process resource allocation and robotic motion planning.

There exist various interesting directions for future work. First, we plan to extend our framework to liveness properties, for example, by learning *ranking functions* rather than winning sets [19,20]. Second, we would like to consider game arenas with uncountably many vertices, which often arise in the context of cyber-physical systems. One possible approach to this problem would be to encode such arenas by means of ω-regular languages and ω-transducers, and then use existing learning algorithms for ω-automata (e.g., Büchi automata) to learn winning sets [6]. Finally, we want to modify our approach such that it learn a strategy directly rather than a proxy object (i.e., a winning set). This would allow us to also optimize for other criteria such as size or number of operations required to compute the next move.

Acknowledgement. This work was partially funded by the ERC Starting Grant AV-SMP (grant agreement no. 759969) and MPI-Fellowship as well as the DFG grant no. 434592664.

References

1. Griesmayer, A., Staber, S., Bloem, R.: Automated fault localization for C programs. Electron. Notes Theoret. Comput. Sci. **174**(4), 95–111 (2007)

2. Abdulla, P.A., Jonsson, B., Mahata, P., d'Orso, J.: Regular tree model checking. In: Brinksma, E., Larsen, K.G. (eds.) CAV 2002. LNCS, vol. 2404, pp. 555–568. Springer, Heidelberg (2002). https://doi.org/10.1007/3-540-45657-0_47

3. Abdulla, P.A.: Regular model checking. STTT **14**(2), 109–118 (2012). https://doi.org/10.1007/s10009-011-0216-8

4. Abdulla, P.A., Haziza, F., Holík, L.: Parameterized verification through view abstraction. STTT **18**(5), 495–516 (2016). https://doi.org/10.1007/s10009-015-0406-x

5. Angluin, D.: Learning regular sets from queries and counterexamples. Inf. Comput. **75**(2), 87–106 (1987)

6. Angluin, D., Fisman, D.: Learning regular omega languages. Theor. Comput. Sci. **650**, 57–72 (2016)

7. Apt, K.R., Kozen, D.: Limits for automatic verification of finite-state concurrent systems. Inf. Process. Lett. **22**(6), 307–309 (1986)

8. Beyene, T.A., Chaudhuri, S., Popeea, C., Rybalchenko, A.: A constraint-based approach to solving games on infinite graphs. In: Jagannathan, S., Sewell, P. (eds.) The 41st Annual ACM SIGPLAN-SIGACT Symposium on Principles of Programming Languages, POPL 2014, San Diego, CA, USA, 20–21 January 2014 (2014)

9. Bloem, R., et al.: Decidability of Parameterized Verification. Synthesis Lectures on Distributed Computing Theory. Morgan & Claypool Publishers, San Rafael (2015)

10. Bollig, B., Habermehl, P., Kern, C., Leucker, M.: Angluin-style learning of NFA. In: IJCAI, pp. 1004–1009

11. Bouajjani, A., Habermehl, P., Rogalewicz, A., Vojnar, T.: Abstract regular (tree) model checking. STTT **14**(2), 167–191 (2012). https://doi.org/10.1007/s10009-011-0205-y

12. Bouton, C.L.: Nim, a game with a complete mathematical theory. Ann. Math. **3**(1/4), 35–39 (1901). http://www.jstor.org/stable/1967631

13. Camacho, A., Muise, C.J., Baier, J.A., McIlraith, S.A.: LTL realizability via safety and reachability games. In: Proceedings of the Twenty-Seventh International Joint Conference on Artificial Intelligence, IJCAI 2018, Stockholm, Sweden, 13–19 July 2018, pp. 4683–4691 (2018)

14. Chatain, T., David, A., Larsen, K.G.: Playing games with timed games. In: 3rd IFAC Conference on Analysis and Design of Hybrid Systems, ADHS 2009, Zaragoza, Spain, 16–18 September 2009, pp. 238–243 (2009)

15. Chen, Y.-F., Clarke, E.M., Farzan, A., Tsai, M.-H., Tsay, Y.-K., Wang, B.-Y.: Automated assume-guarantee reasoning through implicit learning. In: Touili, T., Cook, B., Jackson, P. (eds.) CAV 2010. LNCS, vol. 6174, pp. 511–526. Springer, Heidelberg (2010). https://doi.org/10.1007/978-3-642-14295-6_44

16. Chen, Y., Hong, C., Lin, A.W., Rümmer, P.: Learning to prove safety over parameterised concurrent systems. In: Formal Methods in Computer Aided Design, FMCAD 2017, Vienna, Austria, 2–6 October 2017, pp. 76–83 (2017)

17. Doyen, L.: Games and automata: from boolean to quantitative verification. habilitation, ENS de Cachan, LSV (2011)

18. Ehlers, R., Seshia, S.A., Kress-Gazit, H.: Synthesis with identifiers. In: McMillan, K.L., Rival, X. (eds.) VMCAI 2014. LNCS, vol. 8318, pp. 415–433. Springer, Heidelberg (2014). https://doi.org/10.1007/978-3-642-54013-4_23

19. Fang, Y., Piterman, N., Pnueli, A., Zuck, L.: Liveness with incomprehensible ranking. In: Jensen, K., Podelski, A. (eds.) TACAS 2004. LNCS, vol. 2988, pp. 482–496. Springer, Heidelberg (2004). https://doi.org/10.1007/978-3-540-24730-2_36

20. Fang, Y., Piterman, N., Pnueli, A., Zuck, L.: Liveness with invisible ranking. In: Steffen, B., Levi, G. (eds.) VMCAI 2004. LNCS, vol. 2937, pp. 223–238. Springer, Heidelberg (2004). https://doi.org/10.1007/978-3-540-24622-0_19
21. Ferguson, T.S.: Game theory (2014). https://www.math.ucla.edu/~tom/Game_Theory/Contents.html
22. Fey, G., Staber, S., Bloem, R., Drechsler, R.: Automatic fault localization for property checking. IEEE Trans. Comput. Aided Des. Integr. Circ. Syst. **27**, 1138–1149 (2008)
23. Grädel, E., Thomas, W., Wilke, T. (eds.): Automata Logics, and Infinite Games. LNCS, vol. 2500. Springer, Heidelberg (2002). https://doi.org/10.1007/3-540-36387-4
24. Habermehl, P., Vojnar, T.: Regular model checking using inference of regular languages. In: Bradfield, J.C., Moller, F. (eds.) Proceedings of the 6th International Workshop on Verification of Infinite-State Systems, INFINITY 2004 (2004)
25. Jobstmann, B., Griesmayer, A., Bloem, R.: Program repair as a game. In: Etessami, K., Rajamani, S.K. (eds.) CAV 2005. LNCS, vol. 3576, pp. 226–238. Springer, Heidelberg (2005). https://doi.org/10.1007/11513988_23
26. Katis, A., et al.: Validity-guided synthesis of reactive systems from assume-guarantee contracts. In: Beyer, D., Huisman, M. (eds.) TACAS 2018. LNCS, vol. 10806, pp. 176–193. Springer, Cham (2018). https://doi.org/10.1007/978-3-319-89963-3_10
27. Kearns, M.J., Vazirani, U.: An Introduction to Computational Learning Theory. MIT Press, Cambridge (2014)
28. Kesten, Y., Maler, O., Marcus, M., Pnueli, A., Shahar, E.: Symbolic model checking with rich assertional languages. TCS **256**(1–2), 93–112 (2001)
29. Lin, A.W., Rümmer, P.: Liveness of randomised parameterised systems under arbitrary schedulers. In: Chaudhuri, S., Farzan, A. (eds.) CAV 2016. LNCS, vol. 9780, pp. 112–133. Springer, Cham (2016). https://doi.org/10.1007/978-3-319-41540-6_7
30. McNaughton, R.: Infinite games played on finite graphs. Ann. Pure Appl. Logic **65**(2), 149–184 (1993)
31. de Moura, L., Bjørner, N.: Z3: an efficient SMT solver. In: Ramakrishnan, C.R., Rehof, J. (eds.) TACAS 2008. LNCS, vol. 4963, pp. 337–340. Springer, Heidelberg (2008). https://doi.org/10.1007/978-3-540-78800-3_24
32. Neider, D.: Small strategies for safety games. In: Bultan, T., Hsiung, P.-A. (eds.) ATVA 2011. LNCS, vol. 6996, pp. 306–320. Springer, Heidelberg (2011). https://doi.org/10.1007/978-3-642-24372-1_22
33. Neider, D., Jansen, N.: Regular model checking using solver technologies and automata learning. In: Brat, G., Rungta, N., Venet, A. (eds.) NFM 2013. LNCS, vol. 7871, pp. 16–31. Springer, Heidelberg (2013). https://doi.org/10.1007/978-3-642-38088-4_2
34. Neider, D., Markgraf, O.: Learning-based synthesis of safety controllers. In: Formal Methods in Computer Aided Design, FMCAD 2019, San Jose, CA, USA, 22–25 October 2019. pp. 120–128 (2019)
35. Neider, D., Topcu, U.: An automaton learning approach to solving safety games over infinite graphs. In: Chechik, M., Raskin, J.-F. (eds.) TACAS 2016. LNCS, vol. 9636, pp. 204–221. Springer, Heidelberg (2016). https://doi.org/10.1007/978-3-662-49674-9_12
36. Nerode, A.: Linear automaton transformations. Proc. Am. Math. Soc. **9**(4), 541–544 (1958)

37. Oncina, J., Garcia, P.: Inferring regular languages in polynomial updated time. In: Pattern Recognition and Image Analysis: Selected Papers from the IVth Spanish Symposium, pp. 49–61. World Scientific (1992)
38. Pnueli, A., Shahar, E.: Liveness and acceleration in parameterized verification. In: Emerson, E.A., Sistla, A.P. (eds.) CAV 2000. LNCS, vol. 1855, pp. 328–343. Springer, Heidelberg (2000). https://doi.org/10.1007/10722167_26
39. Rivest, R.L., Schapire, R.E.: Inference of finite automata using homing sequences. Inf. Comput. **103**(2), 299–347 (1993)
40. Solar-Lezama, A.: The sketching approach to program synthesis. In: Hu, Z. (ed.) APLAS 2009. LNCS, vol. 5904, pp. 4–13. Springer, Heidelberg (2009). https://doi.org/10.1007/978-3-642-10672-9_3
41. Solar-Lezama, A., Arnold, G., Tancau, L., Bodík, R., Saraswat, V.A., Seshia, S.A.: Sketching stencils. ACM (2007)
42. Solar-Lezama, A., Tancau, L., Bodík, R., Seshia, S.A., Saraswat, V.A.: Combinatorial sketching for finite programs (2006)
43. Staber, S., Bloem, R.: Fault localization and correction with QBF. In: Marques-Silva, J., Sakallah, K.A. (eds.) SAT 2007. LNCS, vol. 4501, pp. 355–368. Springer, Heidelberg (2007). https://doi.org/10.1007/978-3-540-72788-0_34
44. Tomlin, C.J., Lygeros, J., Sastry, S.S.: A game theoretic approach to controller design for hybrid systems. Proc. IEEE **88**, 949–970 (2000)
45. Vardhan, A., Sen, K., Viswanathan, M., Agha, G.: Using language inference to verify omega-regular properties. In: Halbwachs, N., Zuck, L.D. (eds.) TACAS 2005. LNCS, vol. 3440, pp. 45–60. Springer, Heidelberg (2005). https://doi.org/10.1007/978-3-540-31980-1_4
46. Vardhan, A., Viswanathan, M.: LEVER: a tool for learning based verification. In: Ball, T., Jones, R.B. (eds.) CAV 2006. LNCS, vol. 4144, pp. 471–474. Springer, Heidelberg (2006). https://doi.org/10.1007/11817963_43
47. Vojnar, T.: Cut-offs and automata in formal verification of infinite-state systems, : habilitation Thesis. Brno University of Technology, Faculty of Information Technology (2007)
48. Vojnar, T.: Cut-offs and Automata in Formal Verification of Infinite-State Systems. FIT Monograph 1, Faculty of Information Technology BUT (2007)
49. Zuck, L.D., Pnueli, A.: Model checking and abstraction to the aid of parameterized systems (a survey). Comput. Lang. Syst. Struct. **30**, 139–169 (2004)

Relational Synthesis for Pattern Matching

Dmitry Kosarev[1,2]($\boxtimes$) (iD), Petr Lozov[1,2] (iD), and Dmitry Boulytchev[1,2] (iD)

[1] Saint Petersburg State University, Saint Petersburg, Russia
Dmitrii.Kosarev@pm.me, lozov.peter@gmail.com, dboulytchev@math.spbu.ru
[2] JetBrains Research, Saint Petersburg, Russia

Abstract. We present a completely declarative approach to synthesizing pattern matching construct implementations based on application of relational programming, a specific form of constraint logic programming. Our approach is based on relational representations of both the high-level semantics of pattern matching and the semantics of an intermediate-level implementation language. This choice makes our approach, in principle, very scalable as we only need to modify the high-level semantics in order to synthesize the implementation of a pattern matching new feature. Our evaluation on a set of small samples, partially taken from existing literature shows, that our framework is capable of synthesizing optimal implementations quickly. Our in-depth stress evaluation on a number of artificial benchmarks, however, has shown the need for future improvements.

Keywords: Relational programming · Relational interpreters · Pattern matching

1 Introduction

Algebraic data types (ADT) are an important tool in functional programming which deliver a way to represent flexible and easy to manipulate data structures. To inspect the contents of an ADT's values a generic construct—*pattern matching*—is used. The importance of pattern matching efficient implementation stimulated the development of various advanced techniques which provide good results in practice. The objective of our work is to use these results as a baseline for a case study of relational synthesis[1]—an approach for program synthesis based on application of relational programming [6,10], and, in particular, relational interpreters [7] and relational conversion [17]. Relational programming can be considered as a specific form of constraint logic programming centered around MINIKANREN[2], a combinator-based DSL, implemented for a number

---

The reported study was funded by RFBR, projects number 18-01-00380 and 19-31-90053.

[1] We have to note that this term is overloaded and can be used to refer to completely different approaches than we utilize.

[2] http://minikanren.org.

© Springer Nature Switzerland AG 2020
B. C. d. S. Oliveira (Ed.): APLAS 2020, LNCS 12470, pp. 293–310, 2020.
https://doi.org/10.1007/978-3-030-64437-6_15

of host languages. Unlike PROLOG, which employs a deterministic depth-first search, MINIKANREN advocates a more declarative approach, in which a user is not allowed to rely on a concrete search discipline, which means, that the specifications, written in MINIKANREN, are understood much more symmetrically. The distinctive feature of MINIKANREN is complete *interleaving search* [12]. The basic constraint is unification with occurs check, although advanced implementations support other primitive constructs, such as disequality or finite-domain constraints [1]. Syntactically, MINIKANREN is mutually convertible to PROLOG, but, unlike latter, makes use of explicit logical connectives (conjunction and disjunction), existential quantification and unification.

A distinctive application of relational programming is implementing *relational interpreters* [9]. Unlike conventional interpreters, which for a program and input value produce output, relational interpreters can operate in various directions: for example, they are capable of computing an input value for a given program and a given output, or even synthesize a program for a given pairs of input-output values. The latter case forms a basis for program synthesis [5,7].

Our approach is based on relational representation of the source language pattern matching semantics on the one hand, and the semantics of the intermediate-level implementation language on the other. We formulate the condition necessary for a correct and complete implementation of pattern matching and use it to construct a top-level goal which represents a search procedure for all correct and complete implementations. We also present a number of techniques which make it possible to come up with an *optimal* solution as well as optimizations to improve the performance of the search. Similarly to many other prior works we use the size of the synthesized code, which can be measured statically, to distinguish better programs. Our implementation[3] makes use of OCANREN[4]—a typed implementation of MINIKANREN for OCAML [13], and NOCANREN[5]—a converter from the subset of plain OCAML into OCANREN [17]. An initial evaluation, performed for a set of benchmarks taken from other papers, showed our synthesizer performing well. However, being aware of some pitfalls of our approach, we came up with a set of counterexamples on which it did not provide any results in observable time, so we do not consider the problem completely solved. We also started to work on mechanized formalization[6], written in COQ [4], to make the justification of our approach more solid and easier to verify, but this formalization is not yet complete.

2   Related Works

Pattern matching can be considered as a generalization of conventional conditional control-flow construct " `if` .. `then` .. `else`" and in principle can be decomposed into a nested hierarchy of those; from this standpoint the problem

---

[3] https://github.com/Kakadu/pat-match/tree/aplas2020.
[4] https://github.com/JetBrains-Research/OCanren.
[5] https://github.com/Lozov-Petr/noCanren.
[6] https://github.com/dboulytchev/Coq-matching-workout.

of pattern matching implementation can be considered trivial. However, some decompositions are obviously better than others. We repeat here an example from [20] to demonstrate this difference (see Fig. 1). Here we match a triple of boolean values x, y, and z against four patterns (Fig. 1a; we use OCAML [16] as reference language). The naïve implementation of this example is shown on Fig. 1b; however if we decide to match y first the result becomes much better (Fig. 1c).

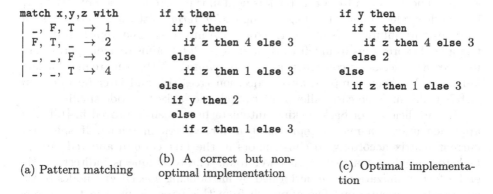

(a) Pattern matching

(b) A correct but non-optimal implementation

(c) Optimal implementation

Fig. 1. Pattern matching implementation example

The quality of a pattern matching implementation can be measured in various ways. One can either optimise the run time cost by minimizing the amount of checks performed, or the static cost by minimizing the size of the generated code. *Decision trees* are considered suitable for the first criterion as they check every subexpression no more than once. However, minimizing the size of a decision tree is known to be NP-hard [3], and as a rule various heuristics, using, for example, the number of nodes, the length of the longest path and the average length of all paths are applied during compilation. In [28] the results of experimental evaluation of nine heuristics for Standard ML of New Jersey are reported.

For minimizing the static cost *backtracking automata* can be used since they admit a compact representation but in some cases can perform repeated checks.

There is a certain difference in dealing with pattern matching in strict and non-strict languages. For strict languages checking sub-expressions of the scrutinee in any order is allowed. The pattern matching implementation for strict languages can operate in *direct* or *indirect* styles. In the direct style the construction of an implementation is done explicitly. In indirect the construction of implementation requires some post-processing, which can vary from easy simplifications to complicated supercompilation techniques [29]. The main drawback of indirect approach is that the size of intermediate data structures can be exponentially large.

For non-strict languages pattern matching should evaluate only those sub-expressions which are necessary for performing pattern matching. If not done carefully pattern matching can change the termination behavior of the program. In general non-strict languages put more constraints on pattern matching and thus admit a smaller set of heuristics. A few approaches for checking subexpressions in lazy languages have been proposed. In [2] a simple left-to-right order of subexpression checking was proposed with a proof that this particular order doesn't affect termination. The backtracking automaton being built takes a form of a DAG to reduce the code size. A few refinements have been added in [32] as a part of textbook [24] on the implementation of lazy functional languages. The approach from this book is used in the current version of GHC [21]. [14] models values in lazy languages using *partial terms*, although it doesn't scale to types with infinite sets of constructors (like integers). The approach doesn't test all subexpressions from left to right as does [2] but aims to avoid performing unnecessary checks by constructing *lazy automaton*. Pattern matching for lazy languages has been compiled also to decision trees [18] and later into *decision DAGs* which in some cases allows the compiler to make the code smaller [19].

The inefficiency of backtracking automata have been improved in [15]. The approach utilizes a matrix representation for pattern matching. It splits the current matrix according to constructors in the first column and reduces the task to compiling matrices with fewer rows. The technique is indirect; in the end a few optimizations are performed by introducing special *exit* nodes to the compiled representation. The approach from this paper is used in the current implementation of the OCAML compiler.

The previous approach uses the first column to split the matrix. In [20] the *necessity* heuristic has been introduced which recommends which column should be used to perform the split. Good decision trees which are constructed in this work can perform better in corner cases than [15], but for practical use the difference is insignificant.

While existing approaches deliver appropriate solutions for certain forms of pattern matching constructs, they have to be extended in an *ad hoc* manner each time the syntax and semantics of pattern matching construct changes. For example, besides a simple conventional form of pattern matching there are a number of extensions: guards (first appeared in KRC language [31]), disjunctive patterns [16], non-linear patterns [22], active patterns [30] and pattern matching for polymorphic variants [11] which require a separate customized algorithms to be developed.

3   The Pattern Matching Synthesis Problem

We describe here a simplified view on pattern matching which does not incorporate some practically important aspects of the construct such as name bindings in patterns, guards or even semantic actions in branches. In a purified form, however, it represents the essence of pattern matching as an "inspect-and-branch" procedure. Other features can be easily added later once a solution for the essential part of the problem is found.

$$\langle v; \_ \rangle \qquad\qquad\qquad \text{[WILDCARD]}$$

$$\frac{\forall i \ \langle v_i; p_i \rangle}{\langle C^k v_1 \ldots v_k; \ C^k p_1 \ldots p_k \rangle}, \ k \geq 0 \ \text{[CONSTRUCTOR]}$$

Fig. 2. Matching against a single pattern

First, we introduce a finite set of *constructors* $\mathcal{C}$, equipped with arities, a set of values $\mathcal{V}$ and a set of patterns $\mathcal{P}$:

$$\mathcal{C} = \{C_1^{k_1}, \ldots, C_n^{k_n}\}$$
$$\mathcal{V} = \mathcal{C}\,\mathcal{V}^*$$
$$\mathcal{P} = \_ \mid \mathcal{C}\,\mathcal{P}^*$$

We define a matching of a value v (*scrutinee*) against an ordered non-empty sequence of patterns $p_1, \ldots, p_k$ by means of the following relation

$$\langle v; p_1, \ldots, p_k \rangle \longrightarrow i, \ 1 \leqslant i \leqslant k + 1$$

which gives us the index of the leftmost matched pattern or $k + 1$ if no such pattern exists. We use an auxiliary relation $\langle ; \rangle \subseteq \mathcal{V} \times \mathcal{P}$ to specify the notion of a value matched by an individual pattern (see Fig. 2). The rule [WILDCARD] says that a wildcard pattern "_" matches any value, and [CONSTRUCTOR] specifies that a constructor pattern matches exactly those values which have the same constructor at the top level and all subvalues matched by corresponding sub-patterns. The definition of "$\rightarrow$" is shown on Fig. 3. An auxiliary relation "$\rightarrow_*$" is introduced to specify the left-to-right matching strategy, and we use current index as an environment. An important rule, [MATCHOTHERWISE] specifies that if we exhausted all the patterns with no matching we stop with the current index (which in this case is equal to the number of patterns plus one).

The relation "$\rightarrow$" gives us a *declarative* semantics of pattern matching. Since we are interested in synthesizing implementations, we need a *programmatical* view on the same problem. Thus, we introduce a language $\mathcal{S}$ (the "switch" language) of test-and-branch constructs:

$$\mathcal{M} = \ \bullet$$
$$\mid \mathcal{M}\,[\mathbb{N}]$$
$$\mathcal{S} = \ \mathbf{return}\,\mathbb{N}$$
$$\mid \mathbf{switch}\ \mathcal{M}\ \mathbf{with}\ [\mathcal{C} \rightarrow \mathcal{S}]^*\ \mathbf{otherwise}\ \mathcal{S}$$

Here $\mathcal{M}$ stands for a *matching expression*, which is either a reference to a scrutinee "$\bullet$" or a (multiply) indexed subexpression of a scrutinee. Programs in the switch language can discriminate on the structure of matching expressions, testing their top-level constructors and eventually returning natural numbers as results. The switch language is similar to the intermediate representations for pattern matching code used in previous works on pattern matching implementation [15,20], and switch programs are analogous to *decision trees*.

$$\frac{\langle v; p_1 \rangle}{i \vdash \langle v; p_1, \ldots, p_k \rangle \longrightarrow_* i} \qquad \text{[MATCHHEAD]}$$

$$\frac{\neg \langle v; p_1 \rangle \qquad i+1 \vdash \langle v; p_2, \ldots, p_k \rangle \longrightarrow_* j}{i \vdash \langle v; p_1, \ldots, p_k \rangle \longrightarrow_* j} \qquad \text{[MATCHTAIL]}$$

$$i \vdash \langle v; \varepsilon \rangle \longrightarrow_* i \qquad \text{[MATCHOTHERWISE]}$$

$$\frac{1 \vdash \langle v; p_1, \ldots, p_k \rangle \longrightarrow_* i}{\langle v; p_1, \ldots, p_k \rangle \longrightarrow i} \qquad \text{[MATCH]}$$

Fig. 3. Matching against an ordered sequence of patterns

$$v \vdash \bullet \longrightarrow_{\mathcal{M}} v \qquad \text{[SCRUTINEE]}$$

$$\frac{v \vdash m \longrightarrow_{\mathcal{M}} C^k v_1 \ldots v_k}{v \vdash m[i] \longrightarrow_{\mathcal{M}} v_i} \qquad \text{[SUBMATCH]}$$

Fig. 4. Semantics of matching expression

The semantics of the switch language is given by mean of relations "$\longrightarrow_{\mathcal{M}}$" and "$\longrightarrow_{\mathcal{S}}$" (see Fig. 4 and 5). The first one describes the semantics of matching expression, while the second describes the semantics of the switch language itself. In both cases the scrutinee v is used as an environment ($v \vdash$).

The following observations can be easily proven by structural induction.

Observation 1. *For arbitrary pattern the set of matching values is non-empty:*

$$\forall p \in \mathcal{P} : \{v \in \mathcal{V} \mid \langle v; p \rangle\} \neq \varnothing$$

Observation 2. *Relations "$\longrightarrow$" and "$\longrightarrow_{\mathcal{S}}$" are functional and deterministic respectively:*

$$\forall p_1, \ldots, p_k \in \mathcal{P}, \forall v \in \mathcal{V}, \forall \pi \in \mathcal{S} : |\{i \in \mathbb{N} \mid \langle v; p_1, \ldots, p_k \rangle \longrightarrow i\}| = 1$$
$$|\{i \in \mathbb{N} \mid v \vdash \pi \longrightarrow_{\mathcal{S}} i\}| \leqslant 1$$

With these definitions, we can formulate the *pattern matching synthesis problem* as follows: for a given ordered sequence of patterns $p_1, \ldots, p_k$ find a switch program π, such that

$$v \vdash \mathbf{return}\ i \longrightarrow_{\mathcal{S}} i \qquad\qquad\qquad [\textsc{Return}]$$

$$\frac{\begin{array}{c} v \vdash m \longrightarrow_{\mathcal{M}} C^k\ v_1 \dots v_k \\ v \vdash s \longrightarrow_{\mathcal{S}} i \end{array}}{v \vdash \mathbf{switch}\ m\ \mathbf{with}\ [C^k \to s]s^*\ \mathbf{otherwise}\ s' \longrightarrow_{\mathcal{S}} i} \qquad [\textsc{SwitchMatched}]$$

$$\frac{\begin{array}{c} v \vdash m \longrightarrow_{\mathcal{M}} D^n\ v_1 \dots v_n \\ C^k \neq D^n \\ v \vdash \mathbf{switch}\ m\ \mathbf{with}\ s^*\ \mathbf{otherwise}\ s' \longrightarrow_{\mathcal{S}} i \end{array}}{v \vdash \mathbf{switch}\ m\ \mathbf{with}\ [C^k \to s]s^*\ \mathbf{otherwise}\ s' \longrightarrow_{\mathcal{S}} i} \quad [\textsc{SwitchNotMatched}]$$

$$\frac{v \vdash s \longrightarrow_{\mathcal{S}} i}{v \vdash \mathbf{switch}\ m\ \mathbf{with}\ \varepsilon\ \mathbf{otherwise}\ s \longrightarrow_{\mathcal{S}} i} \qquad [\textsc{SwitchOtherwise}]$$

Fig. 5. Semantics of switch programs

$$\forall v \in \mathcal{V},\ \forall 1 \leqslant i \leqslant n+1 : \langle v;\ p_1, \dots, p_n \rangle \longrightarrow i \iff v \vdash \pi \longrightarrow_{\mathcal{S}} i \qquad (\star)$$

In other words, program π delivers a correct and complete implementation for pattern matching.

4   Pattern Matching Synthesis, Relationally

In this section we describe a relational formulation for the pattern matching synthesis problem. Practically, this amounts to constructing a goal with a free variable corresponding to the switch program to synthesize for (arbitrary) list of patterns. In order to come up with a tractable goal certain steps have to be performed. We first describe the general idea, and then consider these steps in detail.

Our idea of using relational programming for pattern matching synthesis is based on the following observations:

- For the switch language we can implement a relational interpreter[7] $eval_{\mathcal{S}}^o$ with the following property: for arbitrary $v \in \mathcal{V}$, $\pi \in \mathcal{S}$ and $i \in \mathbb{N}$

$$eval_{\mathcal{S}}^o\ v\ \pi\ i \iff v \vdash \pi \longrightarrow_{\mathcal{S}} i$$

---

[7] Conventionally for MINIKANREN, the names of relations are superscripted by "^{o}".

In other words, $eval_{S}^{o}$ interprets a program π for a scrutinee v and returns exactly the same branch (if any) which is prescribed by the semantics of the switch language.

- On the other hand, we can directly encode the declarative semantics of pattern matching as a relational program $match^{o}$ such that for arbitrary $v \in \mathcal{V}$, $p_i \in \mathcal{P}$ and $i \in \mathbb{N}$

$$match^{o} \, v \, p_1, \ldots, p_k \, i \iff \langle v; \, p_1, \ldots, p_k \rangle \longrightarrow i$$

Again, $match^{o}$ succeeds with $1 \leqslant i \leqslant k$ iff p_i is the leftmost pattern, matching v; otherwise it succeeds with $i = k + 1$.

We address the construction of relational interpreters for both semantics in Sect. 4.1.

Being relational, both $eval_{S}^{o}$ and $match^{o}$ do not just succeed or fail for ground arguments, but also can be *queried* for arguments with free logical variables, thus performing a search for all substitutions for these variables which make the relation hold. This observation leads us to the idea of utilizing the definition of the pattern matching synthesis problem, replacing "$\rightarrow$" with $match^{o}$, "$\rightarrow_{S}$" with $eval^{o}$, and π with a free logical variable $\textcircled{?}$, which gives us the goal

$$\forall v \in \mathcal{V}, \, \forall 1 \leqslant i \leqslant n+1 : match^{o} \, v \, p_1, \ldots, p_n \, i \iff eval^{o} \, v \, \textcircled{?} \, i$$

This goal, however, is problematic from relational point of view for a number of reasons.

First, MINIKANREN provides rather a limited support for universal quantification. Apart from being inefficient from a performance standpoint, existing implementations either do not coexist with disequality constraints [5] or do not support quantified goals with an infinite number of answers [23]. As we will see below, both restrictions are violated in our case. Second, there is no direct support for the equivalence of goals ("$\Leftrightarrow$"). Thus, reducing the original synthesis problem to a viable relational goal involves some "massaging".

We eliminate the universal quantification over the infinite set of scrutinees, replacing it by a *finite* conjunction over a *complete set of samples*. For a sequence of patterns $p_1, \ldots, p_k$ a complete set of samples is a finite set of values $\mathcal{E}(p_1, \ldots, p_k) \subseteq \mathcal{V}$ with the following property:

$$\forall \pi \in \mathcal{S} : [\forall v \in \mathcal{E}(p_1, \ldots, p_k), \, \forall i \in \mathbb{N} : \langle v; \, p_1, \ldots, p_k \rangle \longrightarrow i \iff v \vdash \pi \longrightarrow_{S} i] \Rightarrow$$
$$[\forall v \in \mathcal{V}, \, \forall i \in \mathbb{N} : \langle v; \, p_1, \ldots, p_k \rangle \longrightarrow i \iff v \vdash \pi \longrightarrow_{S} i]$$

In other words, if a program implements a correct and complete pattern matching for all values in a complete set of samples, then this program implements a correct and complete pattern matching for all values. The idea of using a complete set of samples originates from the following observation: each pattern describes a (potentially infinite) set of values, and pattern matching splits the set of all values into equivalence classes, each corresponding to a certain matching pattern. Moreover, the values of different classes can be distinguished only by looking down to a *finite* depth (as different patterns can be distinguished in this way). The generation of a complete sample set will be addressed below (see Sect. 4.2). Example-based program synthesis is not a completely new technique in relational programming [7]; in our case, however, we can ensure the correctness of the synthesis result, while in previous reports it had to be established externally.

To eliminate the universal quantification over the set of answers we rely on the functionality of declarative pattern matching semantics. Indeed, given a fixed sequence $p_1, \ldots, p_k$ of patterns, for every value v there is exactly one answer value i, such that $\langle v; p_1, \ldots, p_k \rangle \longrightarrow i$. We can reformulate this property as

$$\exists i : \langle v; p_1, \ldots, p_k \rangle \longrightarrow i \implies \left(\forall j : \langle v; p_1, \ldots, p_k \rangle \longrightarrow j \implies j = i \right)$$

Thus, we can replace universal quantification over the sets of answers by existential one, for which we have an efficient relational counterpart—the " **fresh**" construct.

Following the same argument, we may replace the equivalence with conjunction: indeed, if

$$\langle v; p_1, \ldots, p_k \rangle \longrightarrow i$$

for some i, then (by functionality), for any other $j \neq i$

$$\neg \left(\langle v; p_1, \ldots, p_k \rangle \longrightarrow j \right)$$

A correct pattern matching implementation π should satisfy the condition

$$v \vdash \pi \longrightarrow_{\mathcal{S}} i$$

But, by the determinism of the switch language semantics, it immediately follows, that for arbitrary $j \neq i$

$$\neg \left(v \vdash \pi \longrightarrow_{\mathcal{S}} j \right)$$

Thus, the goal we eventually came up with is

$$\bigwedge_{v \in \mathcal{E}\,(p_1, \ldots, p_k)} \mathbf{fresh}\ (i)\ \{match^o\ v\ p_1, \ldots, p_k\ i\ \wedge\ eval^o_{\mathcal{S}}\ v\ \textcircled{?}\ i] \qquad (\star\star)$$

From a relational point of view this is a pretty conventional goal which can be solved by virtually any decent MINIKANREN implementation in which the relations $eval^o_{\mathcal{S}}$ and $match^o$ can be encoded.

Finally, we can make the following important observation. Obviously, any pattern matching synthesis problem has at least one trivial solution. This, due to the completeness of relational interleaving search [12, 27], means that the goal above *can not diverge* with no results. Actually it is rather easy to see that any pattern matching synthesis problem has *infinitely many* solutions: indeed, having just one it is always possible to "pump" it with superfluous "**otherwise**" clauses; thus, the goal above is *refutationally complete* [6, 26]. These observations justify the totality of our synthesis approach. In Section 5 we show how we can make it provide optimal solution.

4.1   Constructing Relational Interpreters

In this section we address the implementation of relations $eval_S^o$ and $match^o$. In principle, it amounts to accurate encoding of relations "⇒" and "⇒$_S$" in MINIKANREN (in our case, OCANREN). We, however, make use of a relational conversion [17] tool, called NOCANREN, which automatically converts a subset of OCAML into OCANREN. Thus, both interpreters are in fact implemented in OCAML and repeat corresponding inference rules almost literally in a familiar functional style. For example, functional implementation of a declarative semantics looks like follows:

```
let rec ⟨v; p⟩ =
  match (v, p) with
  | (_, Wildcard)   → true
  | (Cᵏ v*, Cᵏ p*)  → list_all ⟨;⟩ (list_combine v* p*)
  | _               → false
```

```
let match° v p* =
  let rec inner i p* =
    match p* with
    | []        → i
    | p :: p*   → if ⟨v; p⟩ then i else inner S(i) p*
  in inner 0 p*
```

We mixed here the concrete syntax of OCAML and mathematical notation, used in the definition of the relation in question, to underline their similarity; the actual implementation only a few lines of code longer. Note, we use here natural numbers in Peano form and custom list processing functions in order to apply relational conversion later.

Using relational conversion saves a lot of efforts as OCANREN specifications tend to be much more verbose; in addition relational conversion implements some "best practices" in relational programming (for example, moves unifications forward in conjunctions and puts recursive calls last). Finally, it has to be taken into account that relational conversion of pattern matching introduces disequality constraints.

4.2   Dealing with a Complete Set of Samples

As we mentioned above, a complete set of samples plays an important role in our approach: it allows us to eliminate universal quantification over the set of all values. As we replace the universal quantifier with a finite conjunction with one conjunct per sample value reducing the size of the set is an important task. At the present time, however, we build an excessively large (worst case exponential of depth) number of samples. We discuss the issues with this choice in Sect. 6 and consider developing a more advanced approach as the main direction for improvement.

Our construction of a complete set of samples is based upon the following simple observations. We simultaneously define the *depth* measure for patterns and sequences of patterns as follows:

$$d(p_1, \ldots, p_k) = max\{d(p_i)\}$$
$$d(\_) = 0$$
$$d(C^k p_1, \ldots p_k) = 1 + d(p_1, \ldots, p_k)$$

As a sequence of patterns is the single input in our synthesis approach we will call its depth *synthesis depth*.

Similarly, we define the depth of matching expressions

$$d_{\mathcal{M}}(\bullet) = 1$$
$$d_{\mathcal{M}}(m[i]) = 1 + d_{\mathcal{M}}(m)$$

and switch programs:

$$d_{\mathcal{S}}(\textbf{return } i) = 0$$
$$d_{\mathcal{S}}(\textbf{switch } m \textbf{ of } C_1 \rightarrow s_1, \ldots, C_k \rightarrow s_k \textbf{ otherwise } s) =$$
$$max\{d_{\mathcal{M}}(m), d_{\mathcal{S}}(s_i), d_{\mathcal{S}}(s)\}$$

Informally, the depth of a switch program tells us how deep the program can look into a value.

From the definition of $\langle ; \rangle$ it immediately follows that a pattern p can only discriminate values up to its depth $d(p)$: changing a value at the depth greater or equal than $d(p)$ cannot affect the fact of matching/non matching. This means that we need only consider switch programs of depth no greater than the synthesis depth. But for these programs the set of all values with height no greater than the synthesis depth forms a complete set of samples. Indeed, if the height of a value less or equal to the synthesis depth, then this value is a member of complete set of samples and by definition the behavior of the synthesized program on this value is correct. Otherwise there exists some value s from the complete set of samples, such that given value can be obtained as an "extension" of s at the depth greater than the synthesis depth. Since neither declarative semantics nor switch programs can discriminate values at this depth, the behavior for a given value will coincide with the correct-by-definition behavior for s.

The implementation of complete set generation, again, is done using relational conversion. The enumeration of all terms up to a certain depth can be acquired from a function which calculates the depth of a term: indeed, converting it into a relation and then running with *fixed* depth and *free* term arguments delivers what we need. Thus, we add an extra conjunct which performs the enumeration of all values to the relational goal ($\star\star$), arriving at

$$depth^o\, v\, n \wedge \textbf{fresh}\ (i)\ \{match^o\, v\, p_1, \ldots, p_k\, i \wedge eval^o_{\mathcal{S}}\, v\, \textcircled{?}\, i\} \qquad (\star\star\star)$$

Here n is a precomputed synthesis depth in Peano form.

5   Implementation and Optimizations

In this section we address two aspects of our solution: a number of optimizations which make the search more efficient, and the way it ends up with the optimal solution.

The relational goal in its final form, presented in the previous section, does not demonstrate good performance. Thus, we apply a number of techniques, some of which require extending the implementation of the search. Namely, we apply the following optimizations:

- We make use of type information to restrict the subset of constructors which may appear in a certain branch of program being synthesized.
- After a complete set of samples is generated, we use it to put auxiliary constraints on matching expressions. For example, if we can detect that a matching expression points to a subexpression of scrutinee which can start with a single constructor (like tuples), we can prohibit it from being considered during the synthesis.
- We implement *structural constraints* which allow us to restrict the shape of terms during the search, and utilize them to implement pruning.

In our formalization we do not make any use of types since as a rule type information does not affect matching. In addition, utilizing the properties of a concrete type system would make our approach too coupled with this particular type system, hampering its reusability for other languages. Nevertheless we may use a certain abstraction of type system which would deliver only that part of information which is essential for our approach to function. Currently, we calculate the type of any matching expression in the program being synthesized and from this type extract the subset of constructors which can appear when branching on this expression is performed. The number of these constructors restricts the number of branches which a corresponding **switch** expression can have. In our implementation we assume the constructor set ordered, and we consider only ordered branches, which restricts branching even more.

Our approach to finding an optimal solution in fact implements branch-and-bound strategy. The birds-eye view of our plan is as follows:

- We construct a trivial solution, which gives us the first estimate.

- During the search we prune all partial solutions whose size exceeds the current estimate. We can do this due to the top-down nature of partial solution construction.
- When we come up with a better solution we remember it and update current estimate.

This strategy inevitably delivers us the optimal solution since there are only finitely many switch programs, shorter than trivial solution.

In order to implement this strategy we extended OCANREN with a new primitive called *structural constraint*, which may fail on some terms depending on some criterion specified by an end-user. Structural constraints can be seen as a generalization of some known constraints[8] like $\mathtt{absent}^o$ or $\mathtt{symbol}^o$ in existing MINIKANREN implementations [9], so they can be widely used in solving other problems as well. Note, we could implement other constraints we considered (on the depth of switch programs, on the type of scrutinee) as structural. However, our experience has shown that this leads to a less efficient implementation. Since these constraints are inherent to the problem, we kept them hardcoded.

5.1   Reducing the Complete Set of Samples

Although in general our approach requires an exponential number of samples to be generated, in some cases a complete set of examples can be reduced. For example, for the following pattern matching problem

$$(\_, \_ :: \_ :: \_)$$
$$(\_, \_ :: \_)$$

the synthesized program should not investigate the left subtree of the scrutinee since its contents can not alter the behaviour of pattern matching.

The set of admissible matching values $s^\cup$ also can be restricted using the same arguments which we described in Sect. 4.2. This set essentially describes the paths to the "interesting" subexpressions of the scrutinee, and it can be computed statically before the synthesis procedure:

$$s\left(m, C\ p_1 \ldots p_k\right) = \{m\} \cup \bigcup_{i=1}^{k} s(m[i], p_i)$$
$$s\left(m, \_\right) = \varnothing$$
$$s^\cup\left(p_1, \ldots, p_k\right) = \bigcup_{i=1}^{k} s(\bullet, p_i)$$

For the example above, the set $s^\cup$ is

$$\{\bullet, \bullet[1], \bullet[1][1]\}$$

---

[8] The constraint $\mathtt{symbol}^o$ is similar to $\mathtt{symbol?}$ function in Scheme. The constraint $\mathtt{absent}^o$ ensures that specific term is not a subterm of another term.

The complete set of samples then can be the following 3-element set:

$$([], [])$$
$$([], \underline{42} :: [])$$
$$(\underline{[]}, \underline{42} :: \underline{42} :: \underline{[]})$$

where underlined expressions are chosen arbitrarily. A straightforward algorithm from the Sect. 4.2 would generate the larger set of 2^3 examples.

Table 1. The results of synthesis evaluation

Patterns	Number of samples	First answer size	First answer time (ms)	Answers found	Optimal answer size	Optimal answer time (ms)	Total search time (ms)
A B C	3	2	1	2	1	2	2
true false	2	1	<1	1	N/A	N/A	<1
(true, _) (_, true) (false, false)	4	2	5	1	N/A	N/A	11
(_, false, true) (false, true, _) (_, _, false) (_, _, true)	8	6	~1000	3	4	~2100	~2300
(Succ _, Succ _) (Zero, _) (_, Zero)	4	2	30	1	N/A	N/A	~50
(Nil, _) (_, Nil) (Nil2, _) (_, Nil2) (Cons (_,_),Cons(_,_))	9	5	45	1	N/A	N/A	~800
(_, _, (Ldi _)::_) (_, _, (Push _)::_)	5	3	11	1	N/A	N/A	~ 30
(_, _, (Ldi _)::_) (_, _, (Push _)::_) (Int(_), _, (IOp _)::_)	20	7	~1700	3	5	~1800	~11000

The set $s^\cup$ can be used for sample enumeration in the following manner. During the enumeration we hold current matching expression which will be used to access current subtree of the sample. If that expression does not belong to $s^\cup$, we can choose an arbitrary inhabitant; if not we enumerate all possible top-level constructors for this subexpression and recurse. The correctness of this algorithm relies on the fact that if an expression does not belong to $s^\cup$, then all its extensions also do not belong to $s^\cup$.

6   Evaluation

We performed an evaluation of the pattern matching synthesizer on a number of benchmarks. The majority of benchmarks were prepared manually; we didn't use any specific benchmark sets mentioned in literature [28] yet. The evaluation was performed on a desktop computer with Intel Core i7-4790K CPU @ 4.00 GHz processor and 8 GB of memory, OCANREN was compiled with ocaml-4.07.1+fp+flambda. All benchmarks were executed in the native mode ten times, then average monotonic clock time was taken. The results of the evaluation are shown in Table 1.

The patterns used for synthesis form the input of synthesis algorithm. Outputs are: the size of generated complete samples set, the size of the first answer, the running time before receiving the first answer, the total number of programs synthesized, the size of the optimal (last) answer and the total time of the synthesis. The information about the last answer is omitted ("N/A") if the synthesizer has found only a single answer. After discovering the last answer the synthesizer could spend some time to check that no smaller answer existed. In all benchmarks structural constraints were checked every 100 unifications and all answers were requested.

We also give an example of synthesized program for the 4th benchmark, which was taken from [20]. We used this benchmark in the Sect. 2 as the first example (see Fig. 1).

Our algorithm starts the synthesis and in about 1 s discovers the first answer, which is equivalent to the solution on Fig. 1b and consists of 6 **switch** expressions. In about half a second it synthesizes a better answer with 5 **switch** expressions:

```
switch •[0] with
| true  →  (switch •[2] with
            | true  →  (switch •[1] with | true  → 4 | _  → 1)
            | _  → 3)
| _  →  (switch •[1] with
          | true  → 2
          | _  →  (switch •[2] with | true  → 1 | _  → 3))
```

And after about half a second it synthesizes the optimal answer of size 4. Then it searches for an answer which would have less than 4 switch expressions for some time, fails to find one and finishes the synthesis. The time between the start and the end of synthesis is shown in the last column of Table 1.

Our approach currently does not work fast for large benchmarks. On Fig. 7 we cite an example extracted from a bytecode machine for PCF [20, 25]. For such a complex examples (in terms of type definition complexity and the number and size of patterns) both the size of the search space and the number of samples is too large for our approach to work so far.

The last two benchmarks were constructed by reducing the number of types (Fig. 6) and clauses in PCF example.

```
type code = Push | Ldi of int | IOp of int | Int of int
type stack_item = Val of code | Env of int | Code of int
type scrutinee = code * stack_item list * code list
```

Fig. 6. Reduced types of PCF example

```
let rec run s c e =
  match s,c,e with
  | (_,_,Ldi i::_)  →  1
  | (_,_,Push::_)   →  2
  | (Int _,Val (Int _)::_,IOp _::_)  →  3
  | (Int _,_,Test (_,_)::c)  →  4
  | (Int _,_,Test (_,_)::c)  →  5
  | (_,_,Extend::_)  →  6
  | (_,_,Search _::_)  →  7
  | (_,_,Pushenv::_)  →  8
  | (_,Env e::s,Popenv::_)  →  9
  | (_,_,Mkclos cc::_)  →  10
  | (_,_,Mkclosrec _::_)  →  11
  | (Clo (_,_), Val _::_, Apply::_)  →  12
  | (_,(Code _::Env _::_),[])  →  13
  | (_,[],[])  →  14
```

Fig. 7. An example from a bytecode machine for PCF

7 Conclusion and Future Work

We presented an approach for pattern matching implementation synthesis using relational programming. Currently, it demonstrates a good performance only on very small problems. The performance can be improved by searching for new ways to prune the search space and by speeding up the implementation of relations and structural constraints. Also it could be interesting to integrate structural constraints more closely into OCANREN's core. Discovering an optimal order of samples and reducing the complete set of samples is another direction for research.

The language of intermediate representation can be altered, too. It is interesting to add to an intermediate language so-called *exit nodes* described in [15]. The straightforward implementation of them might require nominal unification, but we are not aware of any MINIKANREN implementation in which both disequality constraints and nominal unification [8] coexist nicely.

At the moment we support only simple pattern matching without any extensions. It looks technically easy to extend our approach with non-linear and disjunctive patterns. It will, however, increase the search space and might require more optimizations.

References

1. Alvis, C.E., Willcock, J.J., Carter, K.M., Byrd, W.E., Friedman, D.P.: cKanren: miniKanren with constraints. In: Proceedings of the 2011 Annual Workshop on Scheme and Functional Programming, October 2011
2. Augustsson, L.: Compiling pattern matching. In: Jouannaud, J.-P. (ed.) FPCA 1985. LNCS, vol. 201, pp. 368–381. Springer, Heidelberg (1985). https://doi.org/10.1007/3-540-15975-4_48
3. Baudinet, M., MacQueen, D.: Tree pattern matching for ML (1985)
4. Bertot, Y., Castéran, P.: Interactive Theorem Proving and Program Development - Coq'Art: The Calculus of Inductive Constructions. Texts in Theoretical Computer Science. An EATCS Series, Springer (2004). https://doi.org/10.1007/978-3-662-07964-5
5. Byrd, W.: Relational synthesis of programs. http://webyrd.net/cl/cl.pdf
6. Byrd, W.E.: Relational programming in miniKanren: techniques, applications, and implementations. Ph.D. thesis, Indiana University, September 2009
7. Byrd, W.E., Ballantyne, M., Rosenblatt, G., Might, M.: A unified approach to solving seven programming problems (functional pearl). PACMPL 1(ICFP), 81–826 (2017). https://doi.org/10.1145/3110252
8. Byrd, W.E., Friedman, D.P.: αKanren: a fresh name in nominal logic programming. In: Proceedings of the 2007 Annual Workshop on Scheme and Functional Programming, pp. 79–90 (2007)
9. Byrd, W.E., Holk, E., Friedman, D.P.: miniKanren, live and untagged: quine generation via relational interpreters (programming pearl). In: Proceedings of the 2012 Annual Workshop on Scheme and Functional Programming, Scheme 2012, Copenhagen, Denmark, 9–15 September 2012, pp. 8–29 (2012). https://doi.org/10.1145/2661103.2661105
10. Friedman, D.P., Byrd, W.E., Kiselyov, O.: The Reasoned Schemer. MIT Press, Cambridge (2005)
11. Garrigue, J.: Programming with polymorphic variants. In: ACM Workshop on ML (1998)
12. Kiselyov, O., Shan, C., Friedman, D.P., Sabry, A.: Backtracking, interleaving, and terminating monad transformers: (functional pearl), pp. 192–203 (2005). https://doi.org/10.1145/1086365.1086390
13. Kosarev, D., Boulytchev, D.: Typed embedding of a relational language in OCaml, pp. 1–22 (2016). https://doi.org/10.4204/EPTCS.285.1

14. Laville, A.: Comparison of priority rules in pattern matching and term rewriting. J. Symb. Comput. **11**, 321–347 (1991)
15. Le Fessant, F., Maranget, L.: Optimizing pattern matching. SIGPLAN Not. **36**(10), 26–37 (2001). https://doi.org/10.1145/507669.507641
16. Leroy, X., Doligez, D., Frisch, A., Garrigue, J., Rémy, D., Vouillon, J.: The OCaml system, Documentation and user's manual. Technical report, INRIA, August 2020. https://caml.inria.fr/pub/docs/manual-ocaml-4.11/
17. Lozov, P., Vyatkin, A., Boulytchev, D.: Typed relational conversion. In: TFP (2017)
18. Maranget, L.: Compiling lazy pattern matching. In: LFP 1992 (1992)
19. Maranget, L.: Two techniques for compiling lazy pattern matching (1994)
20. Maranget, L.: Compiling pattern matching to good decision trees. In: Proceedings of the 2008 ACM SIGPLAN Workshop on ML. ML 2008, pp. 35–46. Association for Computing Machinery, New York (2008). https://doi.org/10.1145/1411304. 1411311
21. Marlow, S., Peyton Jones, S.: The Glasgow Haskell Compiler. Lulu, The Architecture of Open Source Applications, vol. 2, January 2012. https://www.microsoft. com/en-us/research/publication/the-glasgow-haskell-compiler/
22. McBride, F., Morrison, D., Pengelly, R.: A symbol manipulation system. Mach. Intell. **5**, 337–347 (1969)
23. Moiseenko, E.: Constructive negation for minikanren. In: miniKanren and Relational Programming Workshop (2019)
24. Peyton Jones, S.: The Implementation of Functional Programming Languages. Prentice Hall, January 1987. https://www.microsoft.com/en-us/research/ publication/the-implementation-of-functional-programming-languages/
25. Plotkin, G.D.: Lcf considered as a programming language. Theoret. Comput. Sci. **5**, 223–255 (1977)
26. Rozplokhas, D., Boulytchev, D.: Improving refutational completeness of relational search via divergence test. In: Proceedings of the 20th International Symposium on Principles and Practice of Declarative Programming. PPDP 2018. Association for Computing Machinery, New York (2018). https://doi.org/10.1145/3236950. 3236958
27. Rozplokhas, D., Boulytchev, D.: Certified semantics for minikanren. In: miniKanren and Relational Programming Workshop (2019)
28. Scott, K.D., Ramsey, N.: When do match-compilation heuristics matter? (2000)
29. Sestoft, P.: ML pattern match compilation and partial evaluation. In: Danvy, O., Glück, R., Thiemann, P. (eds.) Partial Evaluation. LNCS, vol. 1110, pp. 446–464. Springer, Heidelberg (1996). https://doi.org/10.1007/3-540-61580-6_22
30. Syme, D., Neverov, G., Margetson, J.: Extensible pattern matching via a lightweight language extension. In: Proceedings of the 12th ACM SIGPLAN International Conference on Functional Programming, ICFP 2007, pp. 29–40. Association for Computing Machinery, New York (2007). https://doi.org/10.1145/ 1291151.1291159
31. Turner, D.A.: Some history of functional programming languages. In: Loidl, H.-W., Peña, R. (eds.) TFP 2012. LNCS, vol. 7829, pp. 1–20. Springer, Heidelberg (2013). https://doi.org/10.1007/978-3-642-40447-4_1
32. Wadler, P.: Compilation of pattern matching (1987)

REFINITY to Model and Prove Program Transformation Rules

Dominic Steinhöfel(✉) [ID]

Department of Computer Science, TU Darmstadt, Darmstadt, Germany
steinhoefel@cs.tu-darmstadt.de

Abstract. REFINITY is a workbench for modeling statement-level transformation rules on JAVA programs with the aim to formally verify their correctness. It is based on Abstract Execution, a verification framework for abstract programs with a high degree of proof automation, and interfaces with the KeY program prover. We describe the user interface and functionality of REFINITY, and illustrate its capabilities along the application to proving conditional correctness of a code refactoring rule.

1 Introduction

Systematic program transformations are ubiquitous in modern program development. Which programmer has never used a refactoring technique like method extraction, not to mention a compiler? Further, less mundane transformation-based approaches comprise optimization, incremental program development which is "correct-by-construction" [9] or program synthesis from a high-level specification. The latter two are examples for domains where correctness is built into the problem statement; yet, the question of correctness is also relevant, and has been approached, in other areas [5,10,12–14,17]. Mechanized correctness arguments about code transformations are frequently conducted in interactive environments like Isabelle or . An example is the work on verified compilers [12,17]. While this approach permits expressing a wide range of properties, substantial effort has to be invested to prove them *manually* by writing proof scripts. Existing approaches to prove transformations *automatically*, on the other hand, are tailored to *specific* applications (such as regression verification [6], "peephole" optimizations [13] or symbolic execution rules [2]) and lack expressiveness.

Proving the correctness of program transformation rules is a *second-order* property involving quantification over programs. It can be understood as a *relational verification* [3] problem over *schematic* programs. For example, the schematic programs "p q" and "q p" (where p, q represent arbitrary statements) describe a transformation swapping two statements. It is correct if we can prove, as usual under additional assumptions, that all instances of those two programs behave equivalently. Recently, *Abstract Execution (AE)* has been proposed [15,16], a technique for proving properties of *abstract* (i.e., schematic) programs by symbolic *execution*. AE bridges the gap between expressiveness

---

This work was funded by the Hessian LOEWE initiative within the Software-Factory 4.0 project.

B. C. d. S. Oliveira (Ed.): APLAS 2020, LNCS 12470, pp. 311–319, 2020.
https://doi.org/10.1007/978-3-030-64437-6_16

and automation by restricting the class of addressable problems to a (reasonably big) subset—*universal* properties of program *behavior*—while at the same time offering a versatile specification framework. Many transformations, even loop transformations, can be proven *fully automatically* using AE, including the example regarded in this paper and the complete refactoring case study of [15].[1]

AE is implemented on top of KeY [1], a deductive verification framework for JAVA programs based on symbolic execution. AE extends the JAVA language by *Abstract Statements (ASs)* "`\abstract_statement P;`", and *Abstract Expressions (AExps)* "`\abstract_expression T e;`", where P and e are the *identifiers* of the abstract statement/expression, and T is the type of the abstract expression e. Programs containing ASs or AExps are called *abstract programs*.

In this paper, we present REFINITY, a graphical tool for modeling statement-level program transformation rules based on AE. REFINITY supports the specification of abstract programs representing inputs and outputs of transformation rules and of relational pre- and postconditions defining the proof objective. It automatically generates non-trivial proof obligations for the KeY prover and initiates an automatic proof attempt. Thus, it significantly eases the workflow of specifying, proving and refining transformation models. We describe how to use REFINITY to model and prove statement-based refactoring techniques.

Related Work. REFINITY is, to our knowledge, the only existing relational verification tool for *abstract* programs, and, thus, for general source-to-source program transformations. Therefore, we can only compare our work to existing tools for verification of *concrete* programs. LLRêve [8], for instance, is a tool for automatically proving the equivalence of two C programs. SymDiff [11] is a "differential program verifier." Both operate on intermediate languages (LLVM IR and Boogie) and use advanced techniques for automatically relating loops and recursive procedures. REFINITY relies on manually specified loop invariants and method contracts, and therefore requires more interaction for concrete code. However, loop invariants in *abstract contexts* can frequently be specified *generically* [15].

Organization. Subsequently, we describe REFINITY's specification language for abstract programs along an illustrating example. Section 3 shows how to model and prove this example transformation in REFINITY. Section 4 concludes the paper.

REFINITY can be downloaded at key-project.org/REFINITY/, where we also publish continuously updated documentation material. Additional support can be obtained via email to the author of this paper, or via the channels mentioned at key-project.org/getting-started/. Furthermore, most GUI elements of the tool provide tooltips with brief help texts.

2   Specifying Abstract Programs

We explain the most relevant elements of REFINITY's specification language for abstract programs along a code refactoring rule. REFINITY is a frontend for AE

---

[1] Generally, proofs may require user interaction, especially when relying on incomplete theories like first-order arithmetic.

Listing 1: Input Program	Listing 2: Output Program

```
try {
  TryStmt // throws exc. if cond holds
} catch (Throwable t) {
  CatchStmt
}
```

```
if (!cond) {
  TryStmt
} else {
  CatchStmt
}
```

Fig. 1. The *Replace Exception with Test* Refactoring Schema

Listing 3: Input Program	Listing 4: Output Program

```
try {
  z = 42;
  y = z / x;
} catch (Throwable t) {
  y = z; // <- rollback
  flag = true;
}
```

```
if (x++ != 0) { // side effect in condition
  z = 42;
  y = z / x;
} else {
  y = z; // rollback incomplete + depends on TryStmt
  flag = true;
}
```

Fig. 2. Examples for Violated Constraints (*Replace Exception with Test*)

and uses its specification framework. Our aim here is not to provide a *complete* introduction to the AE framework, for which we refer to [15].

Refactoring is the process of changing code in a way that does not alter its external behavior, yet improves its internal structure [4]. The *Replace Exception with Test (REwT)* refactoring proposes to introduce a check for a condition causing an exception when it is reasonable to expect that the condition can be checked. A good example is a division of two numbers put into a **try–catch** block since an ArithmeticException is raised if the divisor is zero. Figure 1 visualizes this schema. *REwT* is a good example since it is generally *unsafe* due to a subtlety: If TryStmt changes relevant parts of the state before throwing an exception, the programs before and after the refactoring behave differently. Consider, e.g., an instantiation of TryStmt with "z = 42; y = z / x;": If x is 0, and the value of z is not changed by CatchStmt, the final value of z is 42 before the transformation, but equals the original value after.

One can create a provably correct model of *REwT* by demanding a statement Rollback before CatchStmt "resetting" locations changed by TryStmt. For the example, we could choose "x=0; z=0;" for Rollback. Note that the assigned rollback values must not depend on locations changed by TryStmt.

In the following, we call the locations that may be changed by abstract statements or expressions their *frame*, and the locations they may read their *footprint*. We have to encode the following constraints into the refactoring model: (1) TryStmt throws an exception if *cond* holds , (2) *cond* has no side effects, (3) Rollback *must* assign the whole frame of TryStmt, and (4) the frame of TryStmt and the footprint of Rollback must be disjoint. Figure 2 shows a "non-legal" example instantiation where Constraints (2) to (4) are violated.

Listing 5: Input Model	Listing 6: Output Model

```
1   /*@ ae_constraint \disjoint(
2   @    footprintRollback, frameTry);
3   @*/
4
5   try {
6
7
8
9
10
11
12
13
14
15      /*@ assignable frameTry;
16      @ accessible footprintTry;
17      @ exceptional_behavior requires
18      @    throwsExcTryStmt(
19      @        \value(footprintTry)); */
20      \abstract_statement TryStmt;
21   } catch (Throwable t) {
22      /*@ assignable \hasTo(frameTry);
23      @ accessible footprintRollback;
24      @*/
25      \abstract_statement Rollback;
26
27      /*@ assignable frameCatch;
28      @ accessible footprintCatch;
29      @*/
30      \abstract_statement CatchStmt;
31   }
```

```
/*@ ae_constraint \disjoint(
@    footprintRollback, frameTry);
@*/

if (
    /*@ assignable \nothing;
    @ accessible footprintTry;
    @ normal_behavior ensures \result
    @    <==> !throwsExcTryStmt(
    @            \value(footprintTry));
    @ exceptional_behavior
    @    requires false; @*/
    \abstract_expression boolean cond
) {
    /*@ assignable frameTry;
    @ accessible footprintTry;
    @ exceptional_behavior requires
    @    throwsExcTryStmt(
    @        \value(footprintTry)); */
    \abstract_statement TryStmt;
} else {
    /*@ assignable \hasTo(frameTry);
    @ accessible footprintRollback;
    @*/
    \abstract_statement Rollback;

    /*@ assignable frameCatch;
    @ accessible footprintCatch;
    @*/
    \abstract_statement CatchStmt;
}
```

Fig. 3. Abstract Program Model for *Replace Exception with Test*

To impose constraints on the frames and footprints of abstract elements, we have to define which locations ASs and AExps may write and read. However, no additional constraints than the mentioned ones should be enforced: Frames and footprints should match to *all* programs satisfying Constraints (1) to (4). We achieve this by using abstract, set-valued specification variables inspired by the theory of *dynamic frames* [7]. Concretely, we introduce constants *frameTry/footprintTry*, *footprintRollback*, and *frameCatch/footprintCatch*, each representing an unknown set of concrete program variables or heap locations.

The complete abstract program model for *Replace Exception with Test* is shown in Fig. 3. Constraints on ASs and AExps are imposed using specification comments starting with "@". In lines 6/7, 15/16, 22/23, and 27/28, we assign the newly introduced abstract location set variables to the abstract program elements, where the keyword **assignable** specifies a frame, and **accessible** a footprint of AS or an AExp. To realize constraint (3), we put a "**\hasTo**" specifier around the frame specification of Rollback. Without **\hasTo**, frame and footprint specifications are only upper bounds.

Constraint (1) is implemented by specifying a precondition on abrupt completion due to a thrown exception for TryStmt in lines 17–19. The specification language keyphrase used is "**exceptional_behavior requires**". There are two things to explain: i) The symbol *throwsExcTryStmt* is a new abstract predicate introduced for specification purposes, and ii) the term "**\value**(*footprintTry*)" represents the value of the location set *footprintTry* at this point in the program: The *locations* represented by *footprintTry* do not change during program execution, while their *values* can change. It remains to specify that *cond* evaluates according to the negated value of the predicate *throwsExcTryStmt*. In lines 8–10, we constrain the expression's value (represented by **\result**) accordingly. The specification keyphrase "**normal_behavior ensures**" is used to declare a *functional postcondition* on the normal completion behavior of *cond*.

For constraint (2) (*cond* is side effect-free), it suffices to specify that the frame of *cond* is empty ("**assignable \nothing**", line 6) and that it throws an exception iff "**false**" holds (lines 11&12)—i.e., never.

Finally, the disjointness of the frame of TryStmt and footprint of Rollback (Constraint (4)) is imposed on instantiations of the model by lines 1–3. The keyword "**ae_constraint**" initiates the declaration of a constraint. Apart from **\disjoint**, also other relations, like **\subset**, are supported.

This example covers all essential specification language features. We did not cover advanced features like abstract functions (similar to abstract predicates, but non-boolean), indexed abstract location set families (useful for involved loop transformations), and mutual exclusion of abrupt completion behavior (using the "**\mutex**" keyword in **ae_constraint**s). See [15] for a full account.

Expressiveness. REFINITY addresses *statement-level* transformation rules and is additionally limited to *universal, behavioral* properties supported by AE. Transformations *above* statement level, e.g., moving a field, cannot be expressed. The same holds for *structural* properties which cannot be written using a fixed abstract program scaffold with only "behavioral holes." An example is a property addressing all statements with *at most* three loops: This is not expressible, since any AS with non-empty semantics represents statements with an arbitrary number of loops. Statements with *at least* three loops *are* in scope, since one can write an abstract program with three loops of arbitrary guards and bodies.

In the following section, we demonstrate how REFINITY can be used to model and prove program transformation rules such as *Replace Exception with Test*.

3   REFINITY in Action

Figure 4 shows the abstract program model for *Replace Exception with Test* in the REFINITY GUI. The abstract program fragments representing input and output of the transformation are written to the two text fields at marker ①.

Field ② contains free program variables which can be referred to in the input and output model without declarations; we do not need this feature in our example. In the compartment labeled ③, we define abstract location set specification variables used in the model, i.e., *frameTry/footprintTry*, *footprintRollback*, and *frameCatch/footprintCatch*. REFINITY models include as default an additional

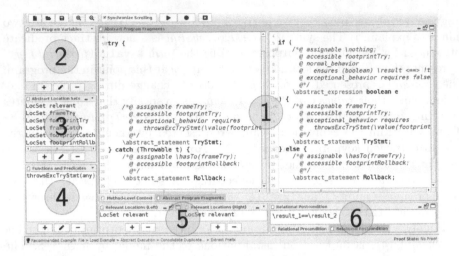

Fig. 4. The REFINITY window

location set "*relevant*" representing all relevant locations. If we do not impose further constraints, e.g., exclude some locations from *relevant*, correctness has to be proven under the assumption that all locations are in this set. The sort for abstract location sets is "LocSet". The abstract predicate *throwsExcTryStmt* is declared in input field ④. The argument sort "any" in the declaration is a super type of all types. We use "any" since we pass the value of an abstract location set to the predicate which can be instantiated to any type.

Fields ⑤ and ⑥ specify global assumptions and proof objectives for the model. The effects of the abstract program fragments specified in field ① are recorded in two *sequences* \result_1 and \result_2 for the input and output model. Their elements can be accessed using standard array syntax, e.g., \result_1[0]. If an abstract program completed due to a **return** of a value, position 0 in the sequence contains the returned value. Likewise, if it completed due to a thrown exception, the exception object is stored at position 1. Starting from position 2, the final values of "relevant locations" declared in fields ⑤ (in the order defined there) are stored. In the example, the abstract set *relevant* is the only relevant location set, which is also the REFINITY default. The standard postcondition, which we see in field ⑥, is \result_1==\result_2. Without constraints about *relevant*, this specifies that returned values, thrown exceptions, and the whole memory after termination have to be identical. More fine-grained postconditions can also be specified: e.g., when an integer variable is registered as first relevant location, "\result_1[2]>2*\result_2[2]" is admissible.

The global "Relational Precondition" (⑥) has access to the initial values of free program variables (field ②) and abstract location sets (field ③). For the example, we did not specify a global precondition.

A model can be saved in REFINITY's XML-based format using ⊟. Pressing
▶ transforms the model into a KeY proof obligation and starts the automatic
proof search. If KeY reports success, the specified model is correct. Saved proof
certificates can be validated against the loaded model using the ✿ button. Proofs
of correctly specified refactorings *without loops* usually take between 30 s and two
minutes; for loop transformations, three minutes and more are possible. During
development of a new model, KeY will usually finish unsuccessfully, leaving one
or more proof goals open. In rare cases and for highly complicated models, the
reason could be that KeY needs more time or is not able to close the proof
although the model is valid—we hit a *prover incapacity*. In the latter case, one
can try to close the proof by interacting with the prover. More likely, though,
are problems in the model. Inspecting the open goals provides information on
how to refine the model to make it sound. Possible refinements include

(1) declaring the disjointness of abstract location sets,
(2) imposing mutual exclusion on abrupt completion behavior,
(3) declaring a functional postcondition for ASs or AExps, and
(4) refining the *relational* postcondition or
(5) adding a relational *precondition*.

The proof obligation REFINITY generates for KeY consists of a JAVA class
with two methods left(...) and right(...) containing the abstract program
fragments, and of a problem description file containing proof strategy settings,
declarations of variable, function, predicate, and abstract location set symbols
and the proof goal (expressed in KeY's program logic "JAVA Dynamic Logic" [1]).
The proof goal for *Replace Exception with Test* in concrete syntax spans 36 lines.
In a condensed representation, it has the form

$$\{\_result := null \,||\, \_exc := null\}$$
$$\neg\langle\textbf{try } \{ \ \_result=obj.left()@Problem; \ \}$$
$$\textbf{catch } (Throwable\ t)\ \{\ exc=t;\ \}\rangle$$
$$\neg P(\_result, \_exc, value(relevant))$$
$$\wedge\ \{\_result := null \,||\, \_exc := null\}$$
$$\neg\langle\textbf{try } \{ \ \_result=obj.right()@Problem; \ \}$$
$$\textbf{catch } (Throwable\ t)\ \{\ exc=t;\ \}\rangle$$
$$\neg Q(\_result, \_exc, value(relevant)) \wedge Pre \wedge \cdots$$
$$\vdash \quad \exists\ Seq\ s_1, s_2;\ (P(s_1) \wedge Q(s_2) \wedge Post(s_1, s_2))$$

where obj is the object under test, *Pre* and *Post* are the global precondition and
relational postcondition, and P and Q are fresh predicates.

REFINITY spares the user from having to deal with such technicalities, simplifying the modeling process. It automatically creates the mentioned files, starts
a KeY proof with reasonable presets, and displays proof status information in its
status bar. Additionally, it supports syntactic extensions unsupported by KeY.

4   Conclusion

In this paper, we presented REFINITY, a graphical workbench for modeling and proving JAVA program transformation rules based on Abstract Execution, a verification framework for abstract programs. We demonstrated how to use REFINITY by showing how to specify and prove correct a refactoring rule with a subtle snag. This builds on previous work, where "vanilla" AE has been used to prove the correctness of several statement-based refactoring rules [16]. REFINITY significantly eases the modeling process, making AE more accessible. For the future, we plan to further increase REFINITY's usability and apply it to different types of program transformations than refactoring rules.

References

1. Beckert, B., Klebanov, V., Weiß, B.: Dynamic logic for Java. Deductive Software Verification – The KeY Book. LNCS, vol. 10001, pp. 49–106. Springer, Cham (2016). https://doi.org/10.1007/978-3-319-49812-6_3
2. Ahrendt, W., Roth, A., Sasse, R.: Automatic validation of transformation rules for Java verification against a rewriting semantics. In: Sutcliffe, G., Voronkov, A. (eds.) LPAR 2005. LNCS (LNAI), vol. 3835, pp. 412–426. Springer, Heidelberg (2005). https://doi.org/10.1007/11591191_29
3. Beckert, B., Ulbrich, M.: Trends in relational program verification. Principled Software Development, pp. 41–58. Springer, Cham (2018). https://doi.org/10.1007/978-3-319-98047-8_3
4. Fowler, M.: Refactoring: Improving the Design of Existing Code. Object Technology Series. Addison-Wesley, Boston (1999)
5. Garrido, A., Meseguer, J.: Formal specification and verification of Java refactorings. In: Proceedings of the 6th SCAM, pp. 165–174. IEEE Computer Society (2006)
6. Godlin, B., Strichman, O.: Regression verification: proving the equivalence of similar programs. Softw. Test. Verif. Reliab. 23(3), 241–258 (2013)
7. Kassios, I.T.: The dynamic frames theory. Formal Asp. Comput. 23(3), 267–288 (2011). https://doi.org/10.1007/s00165-010-0152-5
8. Kiefer, M., Klebanov, V., Ulbrich, M.: Relational program reasoning using compiler IR - combining static verification and dynamic analysis. J. Autom. Reasoning 60(3), 337–363 (2018). https://doi.org/10.1007/s10817-017-9433-5
9. Kourie, D.G., Watson, B.W.: The Correctness-by-Construction Approach to Programming. Springer, Heidelberg (2012)
10. Kundu, S., Tatlock, Z., Lerner, S.: Proving optimizations correct using parameterized program equivalence. Proc. PLDI 2009, 327–337 (2009)
11. Lahiri, S.K., Hawblitzel, C., Kawaguchi, M., Rebêlo, H.: SYMDIFF: a language-agnostic semantic diff tool for imperative programs. In: Madhusudan, P., Seshia, S.A. (eds.) CAV 2012. LNCS, vol. 7358, pp. 712–717. Springer, Heidelberg (2012). https://doi.org/10.1007/978-3-642-31424-7_54
12. Leroy, X.: Formal verification of a realistic compiler. Commun. ACM 52(7), 107–115 (2009)
13. Lopes, N.P., Menendez, D., Nagarakatte, S., Regehr, J.: Practical verification of peephole optimizations with alive. Commun. ACM 61(2), 84–91 (2018)
14. Srivastava, S., Gulwani, S., Foster, J.S.: From program verification to program synthesis. In: Proceedings of the 37th POPL, pp. 313–326 (2010)
15. Steinhöfel, D.: Abstract Execution: automatically proving infinitely many programs. Ph.D. thesis, TU Darmstadt, Department of Computer Science, Darmstadt, Germany (2020). http://tuprints.ulb.tu-darmstadt.de/8540/

16. Steinhöfel, D., Hähnle, R.: Abstract Execution. In: Proceedings of the Third World Congress on Formal Methods - The Next 30 Years, (FM), pp. 319–336 (2019). https://doi.org/10.1007/978-3-030-30942-8_20
17. Tan, Y.K., Myreen, M.O., Kumar, R., Fox, A., Owens, S., Norrish, M.: A new verified compiler backend for CakeML. In: Proceedings of the 21st ICFP. ACM (2016)

Debugging, Profiling and Constraint Solving

A Counterexample-Guided Debugger for Non-recursive Datalog

Van-Dang Tran[1,3](✉), Hiroyuki Kato[1,3], and Zhenjiang Hu[1,2]

[1] National Institute of Informatics, Tokyo, Japan
{dangtv,kato}@nii.ac.jp
[2] Peking University, Beijing, China
huzj@pku.edu.cn
[3] The Graduate University for Advanced Studies, SOKENDAI, Kanagawa, Japan

Abstract. The Datalog language is used in many potential applications including database queries, program analysis, bidirectional transformations, and so forth. In practice, such a Datalog program is expected to be well-written to meet requirements such as the round-tripping properties in bidirectional programming. Although verifying and debugging Datalog programs play an essential role to guarantee the expected properties of these programs, very few approaches have been proposed. The existing approaches require much users' effort in finding out unintended behaviors or unexpected computations of the Datalog program that neither counterexamples nor bug explanations are provided. In this paper, we propose an efficient approach to interactively debugging Datalog programs so that the user's burden is reduced. Specifically, we provide a syntax for users to specify properties of non-recursive Datalog programs, present a counterexample generator that verifies specified properties and generates counterexamples to show unexpected behaviors of user-written programs, and design a debugging engine combined with a dialog-based user interface to assist users in locating bugs in the programs with the generated counterexamples. We have implemented a prototype of our approach and demonstrated its feasibility and efficiency.

Keywords: Debugging · Datalog · Bidirectional transformation

1 Introduction

Datalog, a declarative logic programming language, has many applications in a variety of domains such as deductive databases [17], data integration [12], program analysis [4,11], bidirectional programming [21], and so forth. Verifying Datalog programs plays an essential role to guarantee the properties of those programs required by the applications. When a property is not satisfied, it is more important to reduce the user's burden in debugging the unexpected behavior of the program.

This kind of debugging problem, which arises when a property of a program is not satisfied, has not been well studied for Datalog. There are two challenges

© Springer Nature Switzerland AG 2020
B. C. d. S. Oliveira (Ed.): APLAS 2020, LNCS 12470, pp. 323–342, 2020.
https://doi.org/10.1007/978-3-030-64437-6_17

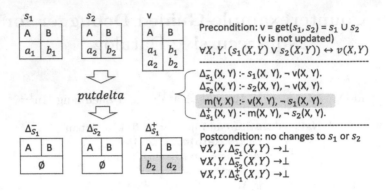

Fig. 1. Motivating example. The unexpected tuple and the buggy rule are highlighted.

in practice. The first challenge is searching for a concrete input database, i.e., a counterexample that reveals the unexpected behavior of the program. The second challenge is locating the buggy Datalog rules that break the property. By adopting the algorithmic debugging method [7], a few approaches were proposed for debugging Datalog programs [5,6,14]. However, the existing approaches neither provide users a way to specify the properties of Datalog programs nor generate counterexamples to show the incorrectness of the programs. To locate a bug, these approaches ask the users many questions about the computation correctness of the Datalog program. In other words, the users have to find out whether the Datalog program has unintended interpretations, e.g., the intention is not met by the program results. Identifying such unintended interpretations becomes costly when the input database of the program is not small.

An ideal approach to debugging would allow the user to specify the program's properties and automatically run all the checks. The properties of a program are commonly specified by a set of assertions such as equalities, domain constraints, containments, and so forth. For Datalog, which is a logic programming language in relational databases, it is intuitive for programmers to specify the assertions in the forms of relational predicates. For example, one may consider that some relations of the Datalog program must be equivalent or some relations must be empty, i.e., the corresponding predicates are always false.

We illustrate with the following example the property specifications and the debugging problem of Datalog programs.

Example 1 (Motivating Example: View Update Strategy). In this example, we consider an application of Datalog in describing view update strategies [21]. Suppose that we are given a database of two base relations $s_1(A, B)$ and $s_2(A, B)$ (Fig. 1) with a view $v(A, B)$ defined over these two relations by a union query: $v = get(s_1, s_2) = s_1 \cup s_2$. The following is a buggy Datalog program (denoted as *putdelta*) that describes a view update strategy, i.e., a description about how to update the base relations s_1 and s_2 through the view v.

$$\Delta_{s_1}^-(X, Y) :\text{-} \ s_1(X, Y), \neg v(X, Y). \tag{r1}$$

$$\Delta_{s_2}^-(X, Y) \ :\text{-} \ s_2(X, Y), \neg v(X, Y). \tag{r2}$$

$$m(Y, X) \ :\text{-} \ v(X, Y), \neg s_1(X, Y). \tag{r3}$$

$$\Delta_{s_1}^+(X, Y) \ :\text{-} \ m(X, Y), \neg s_2(X, Y). \tag{r4}$$

In *putdelta*, for a relation, Δ^+ and Δ^- denote the insertion and deletion sets on the relation, respectively. Rules (r1) and (r2) state that if a tuple $\langle X, Y \rangle$ is in s_1 or s_2 but not in v, it will be deleted from s_1 or s_2, respectively. Rule (r3) checks the tuples in v but not in s_1, and stores these tuples in a mediate relation m. The last rule states that if a tuple $\langle X, Y \rangle$ is in m but not in s_2, it will be inserted into s_1. *putdelta* takes as input the states of s_1, s_2, and v to produce the delta relations of s_1 and s_2.

Such a putback program *putdelta* is required to satisfy round-tripping properties to maintain the consistency of view updates, as formulated in the existing works [10, 21]. Here, we illustrate the problem with the property (called GET-PUT) that in the input of *putdelta*, if the view is unchanged, i.e., $v = s_1 \cup s_2$, the output of *putdelta* must be empty. We use first-order logic sentences (Fig. 1) to specify the constraints of the input (called precondition) and the constraints over the output (called postcondition).

Figure 1 shows a counterexample of GETPUT that is a collection of tuples in the source tables and the view (s_1, s_2, v). Over this counterexample, the result of *putdelta* is $\Delta_{s_1}^- = \Delta_{s_2}^- = \emptyset$ and $\Delta_{s_1}^+ = \{\langle b_2, a_2 \rangle\}$. That means tuple $\langle b_2, a_2 \rangle$ is inserted into s_1. This insertion is not expected by the postcondition. Since the input of *putdelta* satisfies the precondition but the output does not satisfy the postcondition, the GETPUT property of *putdelta* is violated.

The user may wonder why tuple $\langle b_2, a_2 \rangle$ of $\Delta_{s_1}^+$ occurs unexpectedly in the output of *putdelta*. From this unexpected tuple, the problem now is to detect which rules in the original Datalog program are the causes. Here, in the head of rule (r3), the variables X and Y are placed in the wrong positions and thereby some wrong tuples are derived. This bug must be fixed to make *putdelta* satisfy the GETPUT property.   □

We believe that for a required property of a Datalog program, the user may not only have unexpected mistakes such as typos but also have wrong intentions that do not conform to the property. Providing suggestions on how to correct the program is very useful to users but is a challenging issue. In addition, debugging is an ambiguous process that there are many possible causes for a bug. Therefore, it is essential to design an interface that lets users interact with the underlying debugging engine. For example, the user can mark suspicious rules to inspect or decide how to proceed for the bug ambiguity.

The key insight of this paper is that counterexamples play a central role in debugging Datalog programs. First, a program is buggy if and only if a counterexample exists. Second, to be useful for debugging the Datalog program, a counterexample is expected to be a realistic and simple database.

Our approach is statically generating such a counterexample rather than dynamically testing the program with randomly generated test cases as in other works such as [3]. Over the generated counterexample, bugs can be observed in the execution results of the Datalog program. Although data provenance techniques from the database literature [16] can provide useful support to explain how and why the unexpected results are derived, whether we can use this provenance information to efficiently track down the detailed source of bugs remains unclear. In this paper, we fulfill this gap by a novel method that combines the provenance information with the user interaction for resolving the ambiguity in debugging. In summary, this paper has the following contributions:

- We present a new way to use a syntactic extension of non-recursive Datalog for specifying the properties of a Datalog program.
- To explain to the user the behavior of the written Datalog program, we develop a counterexample generator that statically checks specified properties of non-recursive Datalog programs and generates counterexamples for showing why the properties are not satisfied.
- To reduce the user's effort of correcting buggy Datalog programs, we design a user interface and a provenance-based debugging engine to assist the user in locating the bugs with the counterexamples. The debugging engine provides correction hints to the user when the bugs are found.
- To demonstrate the efficiency and the usability of the proposed approach, we have implemented a prototype of the approach and evaluated it with Datalog programs in practice. The source code is available upon request.

The paper is organized as follows. Section 2 gives some background about the Datalog language with syntax extensions. In Sect. 3, we explain the design of our proposed counterexample generation method. We describe the counterexample-guided debugging approach in Sect. 4 and the experiment in Sect. 5. Section 6 presents related works. Section 7 wraps up the paper.

2   Background

A pure Datalog program is a finite set of logical rules, and each rule is an expression of the form [9]:

$$r_0(\boldsymbol{X}_0) \text{ :- } r_1(\boldsymbol{X}_1), \dots, r_n(\boldsymbol{X}_n).$$

where $r_0, r_1, \dots, r_n$ are relations, ":- " is a variant of the standard logical implication "←" from the rule body in the right-hand side to the rule head in the left-hand side. Each $\boldsymbol{X}_i$ ($i \in [0, n]$) is a tuple of variables. Each variable occurring in $\boldsymbol{X}_0$ must occur in at least one of $\boldsymbol{X}_1, \dots, \boldsymbol{X}_n$ in the body.

The relations in a Datalog program are divided into two categories:

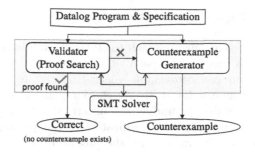

Fig. 2. Counterexample generation architecture

- *EDB relations*, which are physically stored in a relational database, called extensional database (EDB). These relations are the input of the program.
- *IDB (intensional database) relations*, which are derived from the EDB relations using the Datalog program. An IDB relation occurs in some rule heads while an EDB relation can never be in the head of a rule. An IDB relation is recursive if it appears in both the head and the body of a rule. A Datalog program is non-recursive if it has no recursive IDB relation.

We can extend Datalog by allowing negations and built-in predicates such as equality ($=$) or comparison ($<, >$) in Datalog rule bodies but in a safe way that each variable occurring in the negated atoms or the built-in predicates must also occur in some positive atoms [9]. Throughout the paper, we refer Datalog to the Datalog language with the extensions of safe negation and built-in predicates.

Let P be a Datalog program and D be the database of all the EDB and IDB relations. A tuple A in r, or a fact $r(A)$, is immediately inferred from P and D if it satisfies one of the following conditions:

- $A \in r$, where r is an EDB relation.
- $r(A) :- (\neg)r_1(A_1), \ldots, (\neg)r_n(A_n)$. is an instantiation of a rule in P, i.e., all variables in the rule are substituted with constants. Here, a negative fact $\neg r_i(A_i)$ holds if the fact $r_i(A_i)$ does not hold, i.e., A_i is not a tuple of r_i in D. This is based on the Closed World Assumption (CWA) [9].

Semantically, evaluating P is computing the minimum database D such that every tuple in D is immediately inferred from D and P. In other words, we compute the least fixpoint of the immediate inference operator. In the standard bottom-up evaluation strategy for Datalog, the least fixpoint is obtained from P and the input EDB database by deriving all IDB tuples with a finite number of immediate inferences. To deal with negations in the Datalog program, the Datalog program is stratified to ensure that all the tuples of an IDB relation are derived before using any negative facts of this IDB relation in other immediate inferences. This is because if an IDB relation is incomplete, it is not sufficient to judge a negative fact of the IDB relation. The sequence of immediate inferences used for deriving a fact is called a proof of the fact and can be represented in a proof tree with different levels of the applied rules and facts.

3   Counterexample Generation

In this section, we present our approach to statically validating and generating counterexamples for a specified property of a non-recursive Datalog program.

Figure 2 shows our counterexample generation architecture. It consists of two main parts: a validator for statically checking the specified property and a counterexample generator for finding a counterexample for the property. The Datalog program with its property specification is first passed to the validator. If the validator successfully proves that the program satisfies the property, we conclude there is no counterexample. If the validator fails, the Datalog program is passed to the counterexample generator. Since many static checks such as equivalence for Datalog programs are undecidable [19], in both the validator and generator, we transform the property of the Datalog program into logical constraints that can be solved by an SMT solver, even though the termination is not guaranteed.

3.1   Specifying Program Properties

As mentioned previously, rather than introducing a new language, our approach is to use the same language to specify properties of a non-recursive Datalog program using preconditions and postconditions. By following the syntax introduced in [8,21], we allow Datalog rules to have truth constant false (denoted as $\perp$) in the head. In this way, a precondition, as well as a postcondition, is a set of Datalog rules that have the following form:

$$\perp :- r_1(\boldsymbol{X}_1), \ldots r_n(\boldsymbol{X}_n). \tag{*}$$

That means $\forall \boldsymbol{X}, (r_1(\boldsymbol{X}_1) \wedge \ldots \wedge r_n(\boldsymbol{X}_n)) \to \perp$, where $\boldsymbol{X}$ are all the free variables.

Example 2. Consider the GETPUT property in Example 1, which says that if there is no change to the view v, there is no change to the base tables s_1 and s_2. We use non-recursive Datalog to specify the precondition as follows:

$$v^{old}(X,Y) :- s_1(X,Y).$$
$$v^{old}(X,Y) :- s_2(X,Y).$$
$$\perp :- v(X,Y), \neg v^{old}(X,Y).$$
$$\perp :- v^{old}(X,Y), \neg v(X,Y).$$

The first two rules store the union of s_1 and s_2 in a mediate relation v^{old}, and the last two rules indicate that v is the same as v^{old}, i.e., the view does not change. And we can specify the postcondition that there is no change to the base tables as follows.

$$\perp :- \Delta_{s_1}^-(X,Y).$$
$$\perp :- \Delta_{s_2}^-(X,Y).$$
$$\perp :- \Delta_{s_1}^+(X,Y).$$

3.2 Validation

We use an SMT solver to prove the specified property of the Datalog program by translating the property into a first-order logic (FO) sentence. If there is a proof such that the FO sentence is valid, the property is satisfied.

Our transformation from non-recursive Datalog to first-order logic is based on the standard transformation [2,9]. Let P be a non-recursive Datalog program, we inductively transform each relation r in P and the rules of the precondition and the postcondition into an equivalent FO formula φ_r as follows:

If r is an EDB relation, $\varphi_r = r(\boldsymbol{X_r}) = r(X_1, \ldots, X_{arity(r)})$.

If r is an IDB relation, i.e., r occurs in the head of m rules:

$$r(\boldsymbol{X_r}) \text{ :- } \alpha_{1,1}, \ldots, \alpha_{1,n_1}.$$

$$\ldots$$

$$r(\boldsymbol{X_r}) \text{ :- } \alpha_{m,1}, \ldots, \alpha_{m,n_m}.$$

The FO formula of r, if considering only the i-th rule, is $\varphi_{r,i}(\boldsymbol{X_r}) = \exists \boldsymbol{E}_i, \bigwedge\limits_{j=1}^{n_i} \beta_{i,j}$, where $\boldsymbol{E}_i$ contains the bound variables of the i-th rule, i.e., the variables not in the rule head, and

$$\beta_{i,j} = \begin{cases} \varphi_w(\boldsymbol{Z}), & \text{if } \alpha_{i,j} \text{ is an atom } w(\boldsymbol{Z}) \\ \neg\varphi_w(\boldsymbol{Z}), & \text{if } \alpha_{i,j} \text{ is a negated atom } \neg w(\boldsymbol{Z}) \\ \alpha_{i,j}, & \text{if } \alpha_{i,j} \text{ is an equality or a built-in predicate, e.g., } x < y \end{cases}$$

By combining all the rules of r, we have:

$$\varphi_r(\boldsymbol{X_r}) = \bigvee_{i=1}^{m} \varphi_{r,i}(\boldsymbol{X_r}) = \bigvee_{i=1}^{m} \left(\exists \boldsymbol{E}_i, \bigwedge_{j=1}^{n_i} \beta_{i,j} \right)$$

By having the first-order formulas of all the IDB relations, each special Datalog rule of (*), which has $\bot$ in the head in the precondition and postcondition, is transformed into a first-order sentence: $\forall \boldsymbol{X}, (\varphi_{r_1}(\boldsymbol{X}_1) \wedge \ldots \wedge \varphi_{r_n}(\boldsymbol{X}_n)) \rightarrow \bot$. The precondition, as well as the postcondition, is a conjunction of all its FO sentences transformed from the special Datalog rules.

Let φ_{pre} and φ_{post} be the first-order sentences of the precondition and the postcondition, respectively. We employ an automated theorem prover to prove whether φ_{post} holds if φ_{pre} holds. In other words, we check whether the following first-order sentence is valid: $\varphi_{pre} \rightarrow \varphi_{post}$.

3.3 Generating Counterexamples

As mentioned previously, to assist the user in debugging a specified property, we shall generate counterexamples, which are used to guide the user to the location of bugs. The simpler the counterexamples are, the easier the user can succeed in debugging the program.

To generate a counterexample, our idea is to create a symbolic database and transform the evaluation of the Datalog program over the symbolic database with the specified property into a constraint program in Rosette [20]. The Rosette symbolic execution runtime translates the program into logical constraints that are performed by an underlying SMT solver such as Z3 [1]. The result obtained by the Rosette framework is an interpretation of the symbolic input over which the specified property of the Datalog program is violated.

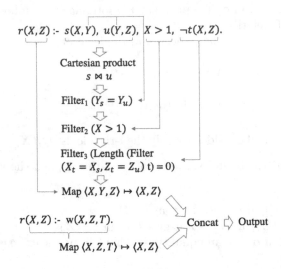

Fig. 3. Transformation from Datalog to functions

To put it more concretely, we construct a symbolic input of the source and view tables by representing each table as a list of tuples, each tuple is a list, where each element is a symbolic value. The order and the duplicates of tuples are ignored because a relation is a set of tuples rather than a list. Considering Example 1, assuming that the types of attributes A and B are integer and real, respectively, we define a symbolic table v as follows (similarly for s_1 and s_2).

```
(define-symbolic a₁ integer?)    (define-symbolic a₂ integer?)
(define-symbolic b₁ real?)       (define-symbolic b₂ real?)
(define t₁ (list a₁ b₁))         (define t₂ (list a₂ b₂))
(define v (list t₁ t₂))
```

Since string values are not supported in the underlying SMT solvers, in our transformation, we use an integer symbol for a string attribute. A value for this integer symbol will be mapped to a string value by using a predefined dictionary, where the integer value is used as an index to determine the corresponding string value. In other words, we build up a partial bijective function that maps an integer value to a string in the dictionary. Since the dictionary has finite words, we limit the values of a string attribute to be in the predefined dictionary. For example, for a relation $r(S : string)$, we define a symbolic tuple as the following:

```
(define-symbolic s₁ integer?)
(assert (and (< -1  s₁) (< s₁ dictionary_size)))
(define t₁ (list s₁))
```

The assertion in the second line ensures that the value of s_1 is in the index range of the dictionary.

We evaluate a non-recursive Datalog program over a symbolic input by using four functions: Cartesian product, Filter, Map, and Concat. Figure 3 illustrates the steps for evaluating a relation r. For each rule of r, we first take a cartesian product over all positive relations in the rule body and then apply a filter (Filter$_1$) for the join attributes, a filter (Filter$_2$) for all built-in predicates, and another filter (Filter$_3$) for the negative relations. Over the tuples resulted from these tree filters, we use a mapping function to select the attributes appearing in the rule head[1]. If r is defined by multiple rules, we evaluate r in each rule and concatenate all the resulted tuples. For a non-recursive Datalog program, which has many IDB relations, we can inductively evaluate all the IDB relations in the program.

Example 3. For the first rule in Fig. 3, we take a cartesian product of the two positive relations s and u. The result is first filtered by Filter$_2$ to select only tuples, where the second attribute of s agrees with the first attribute of u, i.e., $Y_s = Y_u$. Filter$_2$ is applied to select the tuples satisfying $X > 1$. Filter$_3$ checks whether there exists a tuple $\langle X_t, Z_t \rangle$ in t that agrees with the attributes X_s and Z_u in the tuples resulted from Filter$_2$. The mapping function takes a projection over the three-dimension tuples and results in two-dimension tuples. Function Concat gets all the tuples computed by the two rules.   □

We now turn to encode the property that is specified by the precondition and the postcondition. Recall that the precondition, as well as the postcondition, is a set of Datalog rules having constant ⊥ in the head. To encode these Datalog rules into Rosette constraints, we first replace ⊥ with a normal predicate, named $\emptyset_{pre}$ for the precondition and $\emptyset_{post}$ for the postcondition, and then encode the evaluation of the obtained Datalog rules into functions as presented previously. These two relations, $\emptyset_{pre}$ and $\emptyset_{post}$, are both expected to be empty. With the evaluation of $\emptyset_{pre}$ and $\emptyset_{post}$ over the symbolic input presented previously, we first encode the precondition into an assertion that the length of table $\emptyset_{pre}$ is equal to 0 as the following:

```
(assert (= 0 (length ∅pre)))
```

We then add another assertion that the length of table $\emptyset_{post}$ is greater than 0 to solve the constraint on the symbolic input that the precondition is satisfied but the postcondition is violated:

```
(solve (assert (< 0 (length ∅post))))
```

---

[1] It is not necessary to filter duplicates here. The duplicates will be eliminated in all the other checks and algorithms.

Algorithm 1: Counterexample generation

$n \leftarrow 0$ // The maximum size of input tables
$Success \leftarrow$ False
while *not Success* **do**
  $n \leftarrow n + 1$
  foreach *EDB relation* r_i **do** // Construct a symbolic input
  | Define r_i as a list of n symbolic tuples.
  // Encoding the property
  Replace $\perp$ in the precondition/postcondition with $\emptyset_{pre}/\emptyset_{post}$.
  Construct the evaluation of $\emptyset_{pre}$ and $\emptyset_{post}$ over the symbolic EDB relations.
  Assert the constraints for $\emptyset_{pre}$ and $\emptyset_{post}$:
    (assert (= 0 (length $\emptyset_{pre}$)))
    (solve (assert (< 0 (length $\emptyset_{post}$))))
  (A list of symbol-value pairs, *Success*) $\leftarrow$ Call the Rosette framework to resolve the constraints
  if *Success* **then**
    foreach r_i **do** // Instantiate all the EDB tables
    | Replace each symbol with the corresponding value.
    | Remove duplicates in r_i.
    return the instance of all the EDB tables.

Algorithm 1 summarizes the main steps in our proposed counterexample generation. Starting from 0, we increase the maximum size, denoted as n, of each input EDB table. With a value of n, we construct n symbolic tuples for each EDB table. We encode the specified property by constructing assertions corresponding to the precondition and the postcondition. We input these assertions to the Rosette framework [20] to find a value for each symbol in the input that the precondition is satisfied but the postcondition is not. If it succeeds, we stop the while loop, instantiate all the EDB symbolic tables, and eliminate duplicates. Otherwise, we continue the loop with an increased value of n.

4 Interactively Locating Bugs with Counterexamples

In this section, we present our method for interactively debugging a non-recursive Datalog program with counterexamples. Our approach consists of a user interface and an underlying debugging engine that assists the user in determining the location of bugs that cause the unexpected behavior of the program.

4.1 Checking Counterexamples

As presented in the previous section, a counterexample is an instance of the input database of the Datalog program such that the property, which is specified by the precondition and the postcondition, is not satisfied. Given an instance of the input database, to check whether the property is violated, we evaluate the output and check whether the input satisfies the precondition and the output does not satisfy the postcondition. Recall that both the precondition and the postcondition are written in Datalog rules with a constant $\bot$ in the head. We check these conditions by replacing $\bot$ with $\emptyset_{pre}(\boldsymbol{X})/\emptyset_{post}(\boldsymbol{X})$ for the precondition/postcondition, where $\boldsymbol{X}$ are variables in the rule body, and evaluating the obtained Datalog rules. The specified property is violated if $\emptyset_{pre}$ is empty but $\emptyset_{post}$ is not empty. Any tuple appearing in $\emptyset_{post}$ is the symptom of the unexpected behavior of the Datalog program with respect to the specified property.

Example 4. Consider the *putdelta* program with an input database in Example 1 and its GETPUT property specified in Example 2. To check GETPUT, we check the emptiness of $\emptyset_{pre}$ and $\emptyset_{post}$ in the following rules:

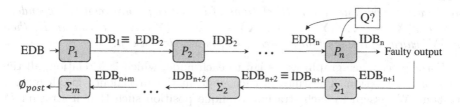

Fig. 4. Strata-based sequentialization.

$$v^{old}(X,Y) :\text{-} \ s_1(X,Y).$$
$$v^{old}(X,Y) :\text{-} \ s_2(X,Y).$$
$$\emptyset_{pre}(X,Y) :\text{-} \ v(X,Y), \neg v^{old}(X,Y).$$
$$\emptyset_{pre}(X,Y) :\text{-} \ v^{old}(X,Y), \neg v(X,Y).$$
$$\emptyset_{post}(X,Y) :\text{-} \ \Delta_{s_1}^{-}(X,Y).$$
$$\emptyset_{post}(X,Y) :\text{-} \ \Delta_{s_2}^{-}(X,Y).$$
$$\emptyset_{post}(X,Y) :\text{-} \ \Delta_{s_1}^{+}(X,Y).$$

Clearly, in the result, there is no tuple in $\emptyset_{pre}$ but there is a tuple $\langle b_2, a_2 \rangle$ in $\emptyset_{post}$. Therefore, GETPUT is violated.

4.2 Dialog-Based User Debugging Interface

Given a counterexample, the debugging problem is to locate the buggy Datalog rules that cause the symptom that the output is faulty. It is extremely ambiguous to determine the locations of bugs since there may be many possible reasons for a fault in the output. Therefore, we allow the user to be involved in the debugging process by designing a dialog-based interface that asks the user to confirm and choose relevant options to handle the ambiguity occurring in the debugging process.

Since Datalog is a declarative programming language, the computation is not explicitly described in the Datalog program. Rather than constructing the computation tree or graph from the Datalog program as in other existing works

[5,6,14], we shall sequentialize the Datalog program to construct an order of the rules for the evaluation. In other words, we partition the original Datalog program into a sequence of smaller parts, where the final output of the program is obtained by evaluating these parts one by one in the order defined by the sequence. Similarly, we also sequentialize Datalog rules of the postcondition, where the head $\perp$ is replaced by $\emptyset_{post}$.

To construct a partition $\{P_1, P_2, \ldots, P_n\}$ of a Datalog program P, we use the well-known stratification method for Datalog [9] simplified for the case that there is no recursion in the Datalog program. Specifically, we use the precedence graph defined as the following.

Definition 1. *The precedence graph G_P of a Datalog program P is a directed graph, where nodes are the IDB relations of P and edges are relation dependencies: if $r(\boldsymbol{X})$:- $\ldots r'(\boldsymbol{Y}) \ldots$ or $r(\boldsymbol{X})$:- $\ldots \neg\, r'(\boldsymbol{Y}) \ldots$ is a rule in P, then $\langle r', r \rangle$, which represents that r' precedes r, is an edge in G_P.*

For a precedence graph, we assign to each node, which is a relation, all the rules of the relation. The rules in each node in the precedence graph form a stratum. We assign to each stratum a unique position such that if stratum P_i precedes stratum P_j in the precedence graph, then $i < j$. Clearly, each stratum in the graph can be evaluated only after all its preceding stratums are evaluated.

Figure 4 shows a program P, which is partitioned into n parts $P_1, P_2, \ldots, P_n$, and postcondition rules, which are partitioned into m parts $\Sigma_1, \ldots, \Sigma_m$. The input of P, which consists of EDB relations, is the input for the first part P_1. We evaluate the output of P by evaluating each part individually that the output of P_{i-1} (IDB$_{i-1}$) becomes the input of P_i (EDB$_i$) for every part P_i. Similarly, the output of P is the input of the postcondition rules. By evaluating $\Sigma_1, \ldots, \Sigma_m$ in this order, we obtain $\emptyset_{post}$.

Any tuple unexpectedly appearing in $\emptyset_{post}$ indicates that the specified property is violated. From this fault symptom, the debugging process is to analyze how the data is changed after each stratum to detect which stratum contains the bugs. In the input/output of a stratum, there are two types of faulty tuples: *wrong tuples*, which unexpectedly appear, and *missing tuples*, which cannot be computed as expected. For example, all the tuples in $\emptyset_{post}$ are wrong. This is caused by wrong or missing tuples in the input of Σ_m, i.e., the output of Σ_{m-1}.

For each stratum P_i, if there is a wrong/missing tuple in the output of P_i (IDB$_i$), we have two possible reasons: P_i contains the buggy rules; or the input of P_i, which is the output of P_{i-1}, contains wrong/missing tuples.

Since the root cause of the property violation is in the original Datalog program P, only $P_1, P_2, \ldots, P_n$ need to be inspected. Meanwhile, the stratums of the postcondition rules, $\Sigma_1, \ldots, \Sigma_m$, do not need to be inspected. They are used to detect faulty tuples in the output of P. Our underlying debugging engine automatically predicts the possible faults in the input of each stratum Σ_i. In this way, the possible faults in the output of P are detected without user interaction.

The user interaction is allowed when the underlying debugging engine inspects the stratums from P_n to P_1. At each stratum P_i, when having a faulty tuple in the output of P_i, we let the user confirm and choose one of the two reasons for diagnosing the bugs by questioning the user about the validity of IDB_{i-1}, i.e., the input of P_i. Specifically, we evaluate all the stratums preceding P_i to obtain IDB_{i-1} and use the faulty output of P_i (IDB_i) to predict faulty tuples in IDB_{i-1}. On one hand, if the user confirms that IDB_{i-1} is valid, the underlying engine will suspect P_i to infer possible buggy rules. On the other hand, if the user finds suspiciousness in IDB_{i-1}, the underlying engine will infer possible wrong/missing tuples in IDB_{i-1} assuming P_i is correct, and then question the user to confirm the relevant faulty tuples.

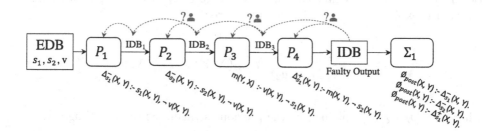

Fig. 5. Debugging interaction example.

Example 5. Figure 5 illustrates a debugging session for the *putdelta* program and its GETPUT property shown in Example 1. Here, *putdelta* is stratified into four parts, P_1, P_2, P_3, P_4, corresponding to the four rules defining the four IDB relations in the program. There is only one stratum Σ_1 for the postcondition rules.   □

4.3 Debugging Engine

We now present our underlying debugging engine that generates debugging details for the dialog-based user interaction and performs the debugging process based on the user's choices. Specifically, the debugging engine traverses all the stratums from the last one to the first one. At each stratum P_i, the debugging engine predicts possible faults in the input of the stratum that cause the faults observed in the output of the stratum and lets the user confirm and choose one fault. If the user confirms the input of P_i is correct, the engine suspects P_i. In contrast, if the user chooses one fault, the engine goes to the preceding stratum P_{i-1} for inspecting.

Assuming that the rules in the stratum are correct, and there is a faulty (wrong or missing) tuple in the output of the stratum, we predict faulty tuples in the input of the stratum based on the provenance information of the faulty tuple in the output that is how it is derived or how it is not derived.

For a wrong tuple in the output of the stratum, its provenance can be explained by constructing all the proof trees that are used by the stratum to derive the tuple. In our stratification strategy, each stratum contains only rules of an IDB relation. Therefore, the maximum height of the proof trees of wrong output tuples is 1. If a wrong tuple does not belong to the IDB relation, it is derived directly from the same wrong tuple in the input of the stratum. In contrast, if a wrong tuple belongs to the IDB relation, it is derived by an immediate inference with rules in the stratum, thus its proof trees have height 1. The proof trees can be extracted from the standard bottom-up evaluation strategy [9] of Datalog by assembling all the immediate inferences.

Example 6. Considering the *putdelta* program in Example 4 and its stratification in Fig. 5, the provenance of tuple $\langle b_2, a_2 \rangle$ of $\emptyset_{post}$ in the output of the last stratum is explained by the following proof tree:

$$\frac{\Delta_{s_1}^{+}(b_2, a_2)}{\emptyset_{post}(b_2, a_2)} \quad [\emptyset_{post}(X, Y) :- \; \Delta_{s_1}^{+}(X, Y).]$$

where $\Delta_{s_1}^{+}(b_2, a_2)$ is explained by the previous stratum as the following:

$$\frac{m(b_2, a_2) \quad \neg s_2(b_2, a_2)}{\Delta_{s_1}^{+}(b_2, a_2)} \quad [\Delta_{s_1}^{+}(X, Y) :- \; m(X, Y), \neg s_2(X, Y).]$$

$\square$

From the constructed proof trees, we detect all the faulty tuples in the input that must be changed to make the wrong tuples in the output disappear. For a wrong tuple, which is derived directly from the same tuple in the input of the stratum, we conclude this tuple in the input of the stratum is wrong. For a wrong tuple derived by the rules of the stratum, all the proof trees of this tuple must be deconstructed by changing the facts used in these proof trees.

Let w be the IDB relation defined in a stratum P_i, and $w(A_0)$ be a wrong tuple in the output of P_i. A proof tree of $w(A_0)$ has the following form:

$$\frac{(\neg)r_1(A_1) \quad \dots \quad (\neg)r_n(A_n)}{w(A_0)} \quad [w(X_0) :- \; (\neg)r_1(X_1), \dots, (\neg)r_n(X_n).]$$

Here, we apply the rule $w(X_0) :- \; (\neg)r_1(X_1), \dots, (\neg)r_n(X_n)$ with the facts $(\neg)r_1(A_1), \dots, (\neg)r_n(A_n)$ to infer $w(A_0)$. Since $w(A_0)$ is derived if all the facts $(\neg)r_1(A_1), \dots,$ and $(\neg)r_n(A_n)$ hold, changing one of $(\neg)r_1(A_1), \dots, (\neg)r_n(A_n)$ is sufficient to make $w(A_0)$ not derived, and thus correct $w(A_0)$. In other words, $w(A_0)$ is wrong because one of the facts $(\neg)r_1(A_1), \dots, (\neg)r_n(A_n)$ is wrong. We exclude facts that are from EDB relations because the EDB database is not computed by the Datalog program. We raise a question to the user interface to let the user confirm and choose one wrong tuple. This is repeatedly performed for each proof tree of each wrong tuple in the output of P_i.

Remark 1. A fact $\neg r(A)$ is wrong iff $r(A)$ is missing. This follows from the closed world assumption (CWA).

A missing tuple, which is not derived in the output of a stratum, is explained by any proof tree that fails to be constructed. The failed proof tree cannot be completed because of some facts that are required but do not hold. As presented previously, in our stratification strategy, each stratum contains only rules of an IDB relation that the proof trees of a tuple have maximum height 1. A proof tree, which has height 1, is constructed by instantiating a rule in the stratum. To avoid constructing an infinite number of proof trees that are not related to the context of the Datalog program, as other approaches [16], we restrict the Datalog program to its active domain, which is the set of all constants appearing in the EDB relations and the program. Specifically, only values in the active domain are used to instantiate a rule. In this way, we obtain a finite number of proof trees for a tuple in the output.

We detect the faulty tuples in the input that cause a missing tuple in the output as follows. If the missing tuple does not belong to the IDB relation defined by the rules in the stratum, we conclude it is missing in the input of the stratum. In contrast, we construct a proof tree of the missing tuple by instantiating a rule in the stratum and then find all the facts not holding in the rule body. Clearly, these faulty facts explain the missing tuple in the output of the stratum. In this way, by constructing all the proof trees, we enumerate all possible faults in the input and raise a question to the user for choosing the most suitable fault. To reduce the number of possible faults, we also prefer the smaller faults to the bigger ones. A fault is smaller if the number of faulty facts in the fault is smaller. The smaller a fault is, the more easily it can be fixed.

We have predicted all the faults (wrong and missing tuples) in the input of a stratum based on the assumption that the rules in the stratum are correct. At the user interface level, we have raised questions to the user to confirm the faults in the input that cause the faulty tuples in the output. Since a stratum contains only rules of an IDB relation, named r_i, changing the rules in the stratum can only correct the faulty tuples of r_i in the output. Therefore, for the faulty tuples of r_i, if in the input, there is no possible fault or the user confirms no predicted fault is suitable, we can conclude that the rules in the stratum contain the bugs and start inspecting the stratum's rules.

Given a faulty tuple in the output of a stratum and assuming that all the tuples in the input are correct, the problem is to determine which rules of r_i are wrong or whether a rule is missing. For a wrong tuple in the output, to locate the corresponding buggy rules, we use the wrong tuple's proof trees constructed before. Specifically, all the rules applied in these proof trees are wrong since they must be changed to make the wrong tuple disappear in the output. For a missing tuple in the output, the user has two ways to fix the rules for producing the missing tuple. The first option is changing one of the rules in the stratum so that it can produce the missing tuple. The second option is adding to the stratum a new rule that can be applied to derive the missing tuple.

To assist the user in correcting the buggy rules in the stratum, we give the user correction hints by showing the proof trees of the faulty tuples and showing the input and the output expected for adding/changing the rules. To be efficient, at each stratum, we show all these observations to the users for finding the cheapest way to correct all the bugs found.

Example 7. We illustrate our debugging approach by considering the *putdelta* program in Example 1 with another property, called PUTGET [21], specified as follows. There is no rule for the precondition, and the postcondition is:

$$s_1^{new}(X,Y) :\text{-}\ s_1(X,Y), \neg \Delta_{s_1}^-(X,Y) \tag{r5}$$

$$s_1^{new}(X,Y) :\text{-}\ \Delta_{s_1}^+(X,Y). \tag{r6}$$

$$s_2^{new}(X,Y) :\text{-}\ s_2(X,Y), \neg \Delta_{s_2}^-(X,Y). \tag{r7}$$

$$v^{new}(X,Y) :\text{-}\ s_1^{new}(X,Y). \tag{r8}$$

$$v^{new}(X,Y) :\text{-}\ s_2^{new}(X,Y). \tag{r9}$$

$$\bot :\text{-}\ v^{new}(X,Y), \neg v(X,Y). \tag{r10}$$

$$\bot :\text{-}\ v(X,Y), \neg v^{new}(X,Y). \tag{r11}$$

That means if we apply delta relations, $\Delta_{s_1/s_2}^{\pm}$ obtained from the *putdelta* program, to the source relations, s_1 and s_2, and calculate the view v^{new} again, we expect v^{new} to be the same as the initial view v. Let us consider a counterexample of PUTGET as the following: $s_1 = \{\langle a_1, b_1 \rangle\}$, $s_2 = \emptyset$, $v = \{\langle a_1, b_1 \rangle, \langle a_2, b_2 \rangle\}$. Over this counterexample, the result of *putdelta* is: $\Delta_{s_1}^- = \Delta_{s_1}^- = \emptyset$, $\Delta_{s_1}^+ = \{\langle b_2, a_2 \rangle\}$. Thus, $v^{new} = \{\langle a_1, b_1 \rangle, \langle b_2, a_2 \rangle\}$, leading to that $\emptyset_{post} = \{\langle a_2, b_2 \rangle, \langle b_2, a_2 \rangle\}$ in the rules (r10) and (r11). Therefore, the PUTGET property is violated.

Figure 6 illustrates how the causes of the wrong tuples $\emptyset_{post}(a_2, b_2)$ and $\emptyset_{post}(b_2, a_2)$ are predicted. Here, the *putdelta* program is stratified into P_1, P_2, P_3, P_4 and the PUTGET precondition is stratified into Σ_1, Σ_2, Σ_3, Σ_4.

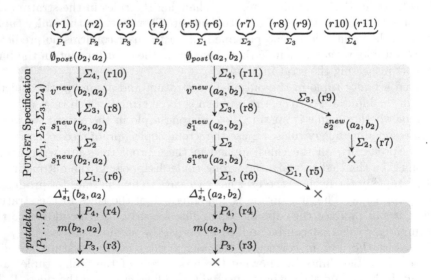

Fig. 6. Debugging demonstration.

For the wrong tuple $\emptyset_{post}(b_2, a_2)$, by using its proof trees at each stratum of $\Sigma_1, \Sigma_2, \Sigma_3$ and Σ_4, we have wrong tuples $v^{new}(b_2, a_2)$, $s_1^{new}(b_2, a_2)$, $s_1^{new}(b_2, a_2)$, and $\Delta_{s_1}^+(b_2, a_2)$, respectively. Since stratum Σ_2 does not contain any rules defining s_1^{new}, the wrong tuple $s_1^{new}(b_2, a_2)$ in the output of Σ_2 is simply derived from this wrong tuple $s_1^{new}(b_2, a_2)$ in the input of Σ_2.

For the wrong tuple $\emptyset_{post}(a_2, b_2)$, at stratum Σ_4, we predict a wrong fact $\neg v^{new}(a_2, b_2)$ in the input of Σ_4. That means $v^{new}(a_2, b_2)$ is missing. At stratum Σ_3, there are two possible proof trees corresponding to rules (r8) and (r9), respectively. Therefore, there are two possible causes of $v^{new}(a_2, b_2)$: $s_1^{new}(a_2, b_2)$ is missing or $s_2^{new}(a_2, b_2)$ is missing. We continue to predict the causes of each of these tuples $s_1^{new}(a_2, b_2)$ and $s_2^{new}(a_2, b_2)$. Eventually, some predicted causes are invalid. For example, at Σ_2, the cause of the missing tuple $s_2^{new}(a_2, b_2)$ is a missing tuple $s_2(a_2, b_2)$ which cannot be fixed because s_2 is an EDB relation. There is only one valid cause: $\Delta_{s_1}^+(a_2, b_2)$ is missing.

Table 1. Debugging results. ✓ indicates that the property is satisfied.

ID	Program	Rules (program & properties)	Counterexample generation time (s)	Counterexample size (tuples)			Number of questions
				DeltaDis	GetPut	PutGet	
1	luxuryitems	12	8.721	✓	✓	2	0
2	ukaz_lok	13	7.162	✓	✓	2	0
3	message	21	10.652	3	2	3	1
4	poi_view	23	10.08	✓	2	3	1
5	all_cars	24	11.116	3	2	3	2
6	newpc	26	10.294	✓	✓	3	1
7	products	28	13.614	✓	✓	4	1
8	purchaseview	29	9.153	✓	5	✓	0
9	vehicle_view	30	Timeout	–	–	–	–
10	koncerty	32	47.951	✓	✓	5	2
11	phonelist	33	11.035	4	3	4	1

After predicting the faults in the output of P_4, i.e., the output of the *putdelta* program, the user interaction is triggered. At stratum P_4, assuming P_4 is correct, the cause of the wrong tuple $\Delta_{s_1}^+(b_2, a_2)$ is a wrong tuple $m(b_2, a_2)$ and the cause of the missing tuple $\Delta_{s_1}^+(a_2, b_2)$ is a missing tuple $m(a_2, b_2)$. Here, a question of confirming whether $m(b_2, a_2)$ is wrong and whether $m(a_2, b_2)$ is missing is raised to the user interface. If the user confirms there is no faulty tuple, the debugging engine will inspect P_4; in contrast, it goes to stratum P_3. For inspecting P_4, since there is only one rule (r4) that is used in the proof tree of $\Delta_{s_1}^+(b_2, a_2)$ and $\Delta_{s_1}^+(a_2, b_2)$, (r4) is a buggy rule. For P_3, because no fault in the input of P_3 is predicted, the engine inspects P_3 without user interaction. Interestingly, both the choices of inspecting P_4 or going to P_3 can detect the bug that can be solved. Specifically, changing $m(X, Y)$ in (r4) to $m(Y, X)$ can make $\Delta_{s_1}^+(b_2, a_2)$ disappear and make $\Delta_{s_1}^+(a_2, b_2)$ appear in the output, and thus PUTGET satisfied. Similarly, changing $m(Y, X)$ in (r3) to $m(X, Y)$ can also correct the program. □

5   Implementation and Experiment

We have implemented a prototype for our debugging approach in Ocaml and integrated it with Rosette [20] and Z3 [1] as the SMT solvers for our counterexample generation. The user can interact with our system via a command-line tool. By the tool, the user can start a debugging session with a counterexample which is automatically generated by the tool or given by the user.

To evaluate our approach, we use non-recursive Datalog programs collected in [21]. These programs are written for implementing practical view update strategies that are required to be well-defined (called the DELTADIS property) and satisfy the round-tripping properties, i.e., GETPUT and PUTGET, with the corresponding view definitions to guarantee the consistency between the views and the source tables. We randomly add bugs to these programs and run an experiment to evaluate the performance of our approach in debugging these programs. Specifically, we measure the time for generating counterexamples, the size of the generated counterexamples, and the number of questions used to ask the user for locating the bugs. The experiment is performed on a computer of 2 CPUs and 4 GB RAM running Ubuntu Server LTS 16.04. We set up a timeout of 1 min for generating counterexamples.

Table 1 summarizes the results of our experiment. The time for generating counterexamples and the size of counterexamples almost increase against the number of rules in the program and the specified properties. The generating time also depends on the difficulty of the bugs and the complexity of Datalog rules. For example, `phonelist` has a smaller generating time than `koncerty` because the rules of `phonelist` are more straightforward. `products` has a bigger generating time than `purchaseview` because PUTGET is usually more complex than GETPUT. For `vehicle_view`, the counterexample generator does not terminate after the maximum allowed running time. The results show that the number of questions used in locating bugs is usually small. This number depends on the complexity of the program and the difficulty of the bugs. Some simple programs such as `luxuryitems` have no question, meanwhile, some bigger programs such as `all_cars` and `koncerty`, which contain more bugs or more user-written rules, need more questions with the user interaction to find the buggy rules.

6   Related Work

Algorithmic debugging [18], also known as declarative debugging, is a semi-automatic debugging technique that is based on the answers of the programmer to a series of questions generated automatically by the algorithmic debugger. Due to its abstraction level, this technique is relevant to declarative programming languages such as Datalog. Some approaches [5,6,14] have been proposed to apply algorithmic debugging to Datalog. These existing approaches can assist the user after a fault (i.e., a counterexample) is detected but suffer from the well-known scalability problems of algorithmic debugging [7] that more user interaction is required in the debugging process. In our approach, we strengthen the algorithmic debugging technique applied to non-recursive Datalog by statically generating minimum-size counterexamples for the debugging process. We exploit provenance techniques [13,15,16] to automatically predict the root causes of the observed faults of the Datalog programs for reducing the human effort of answering the questions raised by the algorithmic debugger.

7 Conclusion

In this paper, we have presented a novel debugging approach to non-recursive Datalog programs. Our framework assists users in checking and generating counterexamples for the programs with properties prespecified by users and then uses counterexamples to guide the users to the location of bugs via a dialog-based interface. The experimental results show the performance of our approach.

Acknowledgments. We would like to thank Meng Wang and the anonymous reviewers for their insightful comments on this paper. This work is partially supported by the Japan Society for the Promotion of Science (JSPS) Grant-in-Aid for Scientific Research (S) No. 17H06099.

References

1. Z3: Theorem prover (2018). https://z3prover.github.io
2. Abiteboul, S., Hull, R., Vianu, V.: Foundations of Databases. Addison-Wesley, Boston (1995)
3. Amaral, C., Florido, M., Santos Costa, V.: PrologCheck – property-based testing in prolog. In: Codish, M., Sumii, E. (eds.) FLOPS 2014. LNCS, vol. 8475, pp. 1–17. Springer, Cham (2014). https://doi.org/10.1007/978-3-319-07151-0_1
4. Bravenboer, M., Smaragdakis, Y.: Strictly declarative specification of sophisticated points-to analyses. In: OOPSLA, pp. 243–262 (2009)
5. Caballero, R., García-Ruiz, Y., Sáenz-Pérez, F.: A theoretical framework for the declarative debugging of Datalog programs. In: Semantics in Data and Knowledge Bases, pp. 143–159 (2008)
6. Caballero, R., García-Ruiz, Y., Sáenz-Pérez, F.: A new proposal for debugging Datalog programs. In: WFLP 2007 (2007)
7. Caballero, R., Riesco, A., Silva, J.: A survey of algorithmic debugging. ACM Comput. Surv. **50**(4), 60:1–60:35 (2017)
8. Calì, A., Gottlob, G., Lukasiewicz, T.: Datalog±: a unified approach to ontologies and integrity constraints. In: ICDT, pp. 14–30 (2009)
9. Ceri, S., Gottlob, G., Tanca, L.: What you always wanted to know about Datalog (and never dared to ask). TKDE **1**(1), 146–166 (1989)
10. Czarnecki, K., Foster, J.N., Hu, Z., Lämmel, R., Schürr, A., Terwilliger, J.F.: Bidirectional transformations: a cross discipline perspective. In: Theory and Practice of Model Transformations, pp. 260–283 (2009)
11. Grebenshchikov, S., Lopes, N.P., Popeea, C., Rybalchenko, A.: Synthesizing software verifiers from proof rules. In: PLDI, pp. 405–416 (2012)
12. Green, T.J., Karvounarakis, G., Ives, Z.G., Tannen, V.: Update exchange with mappings and provenance. In: VLDB, pp. 675–686 (2007)

13. Herschel, M., Hernández, M.A.: Explaining missing answers to SPJUA queries. PVLDB **3**(1), 185–196 (2010)
14. Köhler, S., Ludäscher, B., Smaragdakis, Y.: Declarative Datalog debugging for mere mortals. In: Datalog in Academia and Industry, pp. 111–122 (2012)
15. Köhler, S., Ludäscher, B., Zinn, D.: First-order provenance games. In: In Search of Elegance in the Theory and Practice of Computation, pp. 382–399 (2013)
16. Lee, S., Köhler, S., Ludäscher, B., Glavic, B.: A SQL-middleware unifying why and why-not provenance for first-order queries. In: ICDE, pp. 485–496 (2017)
17. Sáenz-Pérez, F., Caballero, R., García-Ruiz, Y.: A deductive database with Datalog and SQL query languages. In: Yang, H. (ed.) APLAS 2011. LNCS, vol. 7078, pp. 66–73. Springer, Heidelberg (2011). https://doi.org/10.1007/978-3-642-25318-8_8
18. Shapiro, E.Y.: Algorithmic program diagnosis. In: POPL, pp. 299–308 (1982)
19. Shmueli, O.: Equivalence of Datalog queries is undecidable. J. Logic Program. **15**(3), 231–241 (1993)
20. Torlak, E., Bodík, R.: A lightweight symbolic virtual machine for solver-aided host languages. In: PLDI, pp. 530–541 (2014)
21. Tran, V.D., Kato, H., Hu, Z.: Programmable view update strategies on relations. PVLDB **13**(5), 726–739 (2020)

A Symbolic Algorithm for the Case-Split Rule in String Constraint Solving

Yu-Fang Chen[1], Vojtěch Havlena[2], Ondřej Lengál[2(✉)] (iD),
and Andrea Turrini[3,4] (iD)

[1] Academia Sinica, Taipei, Taiwan
[2] FIT, IT4I Centre of Excellence, Brno University of Technology,
Brno, Czech Republic
lengal@fit.vutbr.cz
[3] State Key Laboratory of Computer Science, Institute of Software,
Chinese Academy of Sciences, Beijing, China
[4] Institute of Intelligent Software, Guangzhou, China

Abstract. Case split is a core proof rule in current decision procedures for the theory of string constraints. Its use is the primary cause of the state space explosion in string constraint solving, since it is the only rule that creates branches in the proof tree. Moreover, explicit handling of the case split rule may cause recomputation of the same tasks in multiple branches of the proof tree. In this paper, we propose a symbolic algorithm that significantly reduces such a redundancy. In particular, we encode a string constraint as a regular language and proof rules as rational transducers. This allows to perform similar steps in the proof tree only once, alleviating the state space explosion. In our preliminary experimental results, we validated that our technique (implemented in a Python prototype) works in many practical cases where other state-of-the-art solvers, such as CVC4 or Z3, fail to provide an answer.

1 Introduction

Constraint solving is a technique used as an enabling technology in many areas of formal verification and analysis, such as symbolic execution [21,27], static analysis [23,48], or synthesis [22,38]. For instance, in symbolic execution, feasibility of a path in a program is tested by creating a constraint that encodes the evolution of values of variables on the given path and checking if it is satisfiable. Due to the features used in the analysed programs, checking satisfiability of the constraint can be a complex task. For instance, the solver has to deal with different data types, such as Boolean, Integer, Real, or String. Theories for the first three data types are well known, widely developed, and implemented in tools, while the theory for the String data type has started to be investigated only recently [2,4,5,11,15,16,24,26,31–33,47,50,52], despite having been considered already by A. A. Markov in the late 1960s in connection with Hilbert's 10th problem [18,28,36].

© Springer Nature Switzerland AG 2020
B. C. d. S. Oliveira (Ed.): APLAS 2020, LNCS 12470, pp. 343–363, 2020.
https://doi.org/10.1007/978-3-030-64437-6_18

Most current decision procedures for string constraints involve the so-called *case-split* rule. This rule performs a case split w.r.t. the possible alignment of the variables. The case-split rule is used in most, if not all, (semi-)decision procedures for string constraints, including Makanin's algorithm [34], Nielsen transformation [37] (a.k.a. Levi's lemma [30]), and the procedures implemented in most state-of-the-art solvers such as Z3 [11], CVC4 [31], Z3Str3 [52], Norn [4], and many more. In this paper, we will explain the general idea of our symbolic approach using Nielsen transformation, which is the simplest of the approaches; nonetheless, we believe that the approach is applicable also to other procedures.

Consider the *word equation* $xz = yw$, the primary type of *atomic string constraints* considered in this paper, where x, z, y, and w are *string variables*. When establishing satisfiability of the word equation, Nielsen transformation [37] proceeds by first performing a case split based on the possible alignments of the variables x and y, the first symbol of the left and right-hand sides of the equation, respectively. More precisely, it reduces the satisfiability problem for $xz = yw$ into satisfiability of (at least) one of the following four (non-disjoint) cases (1) y is a prefix of x, (2) x is a prefix of y, (3) x is an empty string, and (4) y is an empty string. For these cases, the Nielsen transformation generates new equations that we describe in the following paragraphs.

For the case (1), all occurrences of x in $xz = yw$ are substituted to yx', where x' is a fresh string variable (we denote this case as $x \hookrightarrow yx'$), i.e., we obtain the equation $yx'z = yw$, which can be simplified to $x'z = w$. In fact, since the transformation $x \hookrightarrow yx'$ removes all occurrences of the variable x, we can just reuse the variable x and perform the transformation $x \hookrightarrow yx$ instead (and take this into account when constructing a model). The case (2) of the Nielsen transformation is just a symmetric counterpart of case (1) discussed above. For cases (3) and (4), the variables x and y, respectively, are replaced by empty strings. Taking into account all four possible transformations of the equation $xz = yw$, we obtain the following four equations:

$$(1)\ xz = w, \qquad (2)\ z = yw, \qquad (3)\ z = yw, \qquad (4)\ xz = w.$$

If $xz = yw$ has a solution, then at least one of the above equations has a solution, too. Nielsen transformation keeps applying the transformation rules on the obtained equations, building a proof tree and searching for a tautology of the form $\varepsilon = \varepsilon$.

Treating each of the obtained equations separately can cause some redundancy. Let us consider the example in Fig. 1, where we apply Nielsen transformation to solve the string constraint $xz = ab \wedge wabyx = awbzv$, where v, w, x, y, and z are string variables and a and b are constant symbols. After processing the first word equation $xz = ab$, we obtain a proof tree with three similar leaf nodes $wabyab = awbv$, $wabya = awbbv$, and $waby = awbabv$, which share the prefixes $waby$ and awb on the left and right-hand side of the equations, respectively. If we continue applying Nielsen transformation on the three leaf nodes, we will create three similar subtrees, with almost identical operations. In particular, the nodes

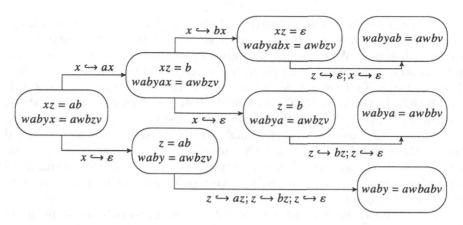

Fig. 1. A partial proof tree of applying Nielsen transformation on $xz = ab \wedge wabyx = awbzv$. The leaves are the outcome of processing the first word equation $xz = ab$. Branches leading to contradictions are omitted.

near the root of such subtrees, which transform $waby \ldots = awb \ldots$, are going to be essentially the same. The resulting proof trees will therefore start to differ only after processing such a common part. Therefore, handling those equations separately will cause some operations to be performed multiple times. In the case the proof tree of each word equation has n leaves and the string constraint is a conjunction of k word equations, we might need to create n^k similar subtrees.

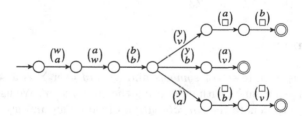

Fig. 2. A finite automaton encoding the three equations $wabyab = awbv$, $wabya = awbbv$, and $waby = awbabv$.

The case split can be performed more efficiently if we process the common part of the said leaves together using a symbolic encoding. In this paper, we use an encoding of a set of equations as a regular language, which is represented by a *finite automaton*. An example is given in Fig. 2, which shows a finite automaton over a 2-track alphabet, where each of the two tracks represents one side of the equation. For instance, the equation $wabyab = awbv$ is represented by the word $\binom{w}{a}\binom{a}{w}\binom{b}{b}\binom{y}{v}\binom{a}{\Box}\binom{b}{\Box}$ accepted by the automaton, where the $\Box$ symbol is a padding used to make sure that both tracks are of the same length.

Given our regular language-based symbolic encoding, we need a mechanism to perform the Nielsen transformation steps on a set of equations encoded as a regular language. We show that the transformations can be encoded as *rational relations*, represented using *finite transducers*, and the whole satisfiability checking problem can be encoded within the framework of *regular model checking* (RMC). In the past, RMC has already been considered for solving string constraints (cf. [7, 49–51]). In those approaches, the languages of the automata are, however, the "models of the formula", so the approaches can be considered "model-theoretic". In our approach, the automata languages are the derived constraints. Hence the approach is closer to "proof-theoretic". We believe this novel aspect has a great potential for further investigation and can bring new ideas to the field of string solving.

We will provide more details on how this is done in Sects. 3 to 5 stepwise. In Sect. 3, we describe the approach for a simpler case where the input is a *quadratic word equation*, i.e., a word equation with at most two occurrences of every variable. In this case, Nielsen transformation is sound and complete. In Sect. 4, we extend the technique to support *conjunctions* of *non-quadratic* word equations. In Sect. 5, we extend our approach to support arbitrary Boolean combinations of string constraints.

We implemented our approach in a prototype Python tool called RETRO and evaluated its performance on two benchmark sets: $Kepler_{22}$ obtained from [29] and PYEX-HARD obtained by running the PyEx symbolic execution engine on Python programs [42] and collecting examples on which CVC4 or Z3 fail. RETRO solved most of the problems in $Kepler_{22}$ (on which CVC4 and Z3 do not perform well). Moreover, it solved over 50 % of the benchmarks in PYEX-HARD that could be solved by neither CVC4 nor Z3.

2   Preliminaries

An *alphabet* Σ is a finite set of *symbols* and a *word* over Σ is a sequence $w = a_1 \ldots a_n$ of symbols from Σ, with ε denoting the *empty word*. We use $w_1.w_2$ (and often just $w_1 w_2$) to denote the *concatenation* of words w_1 and w_2. Σ^* is the set of all words over Σ, $\Sigma^+ = \Sigma^* \setminus \{\varepsilon\}$, and $\Sigma_\varepsilon = \Sigma \cup \{\varepsilon\}$. A *language* over Σ is a subset L of Σ^*. Given a word $w = a_1 \ldots a_n$, we use $|w|$ to denote the length n of w and $|w|_a$ to denote the number of occurrences of the character $a \in \Sigma$ in w. Further, we use $w[i]$ to denote a_i, the i-th character of w, and $w[i:]$ to denote the word $a_i \ldots a_n$. When $i > n$, the value of $w[i]$ and $w[i:]$ is in both cases $\bot$, a special *undefined* value, which is different from all other values and also from itself (i.e., $\bot \neq \bot$). Given an alphabet Σ, we use Σ^k to denote the k-tape alphabet $\underbrace{\Sigma \times \cdots \times \Sigma}_{k}$.

Automata and Transducers. A *(finite) k-tape transducer* is a tuple $\mathcal{T} = (Q, \Delta, \Sigma, Q_i, Q_f)$ where Q is a finite set of *states*, $\Delta \subseteq Q \times \Sigma_\varepsilon^k \times Q$ is a set of *transitions*, Σ is an alphabet, $Q_i \subseteq Q$ is a set of *initial states*, and $Q_f \subseteq Q$ is a set of *final states*. A run π of $\mathcal{T}$ over a k-tuple of words $(w_1, \ldots, w_k)$ is a sequence of transitions $(q_0, a_1^1, \ldots, a_1^k, q_1)$, $(q_1, a_2^1, \ldots, a_2^k, q_2)$, $\ldots$, $(q_{n-1}, a_n^1, \ldots, a_n^k, q_n) \in \Delta$ such that $\forall i : w_i = a_1^i a_2^i \ldots a_n^i$ (note that a_m^i can be ε, so w_i and w_j may be of a different length, for $i \neq j$). The run π is *accepting* if $q_0 \in Q_i$ and $q_n \in Q_f$, and a k-tuple $(w_1, \ldots, w_k)$ is *accepted* by $\mathcal{T}$ if there exists an accepting run of $\mathcal{T}$ over $(w_1, \ldots, w_k)$. The *language* $L(\mathcal{T})$ of $\mathcal{T}$ is defined as the k-ary relation $L(\mathcal{T}) = \{ (w_1, \ldots, w_k) \in (\Sigma^*)^k \mid (w_1, \ldots, w_k) \text{ is accepted by } \mathcal{T} \}$. We call the class of relations accepted by transducers *rational relations*. $\mathcal{T}$ is *length-preserving* if no transition in Δ contains ε. We call the class of relations accepted by length-preserving transducers *regular relations*. A *finite automaton* (FA) is a 1-tape finite transducer. We call the class of languages accepted by finite automata *regular languages*. Given two k-ary relations R_1, R_2, we define their *concatenation* $R_1.R_2 = \{ (u_1 v_1, \ldots, u_k v_k) \mid (u_1, \ldots, u_k) \in R_1 \wedge (v_1, \ldots, v_k) \in R_2 \}$ and given two binary relations R_1, R_2, we define their *composition* $R_1 \circ R_2 = \{ (x, z) \mid \exists y : (x, y) \in R_2 \wedge (y, z) \in R_1 \}$. Given a k-ary relation R we define $R^0 = \{\varepsilon\}^k$, $R^{i+1} = R.R^i$ for $i \geq 0$. *Iteration* of R is then defined as $R^* = \bigcup_{i \geq 0} R^i$. Given a language L and a binary relation R, we define the *R-image* of L as $R(L) = \{ y \mid \exists x \in L : (x, y) \in R \}$.

Proposition 1 ([10]). *(i) The class of binary rational relations is closed under union, composition, concatenation, and iteration and is not closed under intersection and complement. (ii) For a binary rational relation R and a regular language L, the language $R(L)$ is also effectively regular (i.e., it can be computed). (iii) The class of regular relations is closed under Boolean operations.*

String Constraints. Let Σ be an alphabet and $\mathbb{X}$ be a set of *string variables* ranging over Σ^* s.t. $\mathbb{X} \cap \Sigma = \emptyset$. We use $\Sigma_{\mathbb{X}}$ to denote the extended alphabet $\Sigma \cup \mathbb{X}$. An *assignment of* $\mathbb{X}$ is a mapping $I : \mathbb{X} \to \Sigma^*$. A *word term* is a string over the alphabet $\Sigma_{\mathbb{X}}$. We lift an assignment I to word terms by defining $I(\varepsilon) = \varepsilon$, $I(a) = a$, and $I(x.w) = I(x).I(w)$, for $a \in \Sigma$, $x \in \Sigma_{\mathbb{X}}$, and $w \in \Sigma_{\mathbb{X}}^*$. A *word equation* φ_e is of the form $t_1 = t_2$ where t_1 and t_2 are word terms. I is a *model* of φ_e if $I(t_1) = I(t_2)$. We call a word equation an *atomic string constraint*. A *string constraint* is obtained from atomic string constraints using Boolean connectives $(\wedge, \vee, \neg)$, with the semantics defined in the standard manner. A string constraint is *satisfiable* if it has a model. Given a word term $t \in \Sigma_{\mathbb{X}}^*$, a variable $x \in \mathbb{X}$, and a word term $u \in \Sigma_{\mathbb{X}}^*$, we use $t[x \mapsto u]$ to denote the word term obtained from t by replacing all occurrences of x by u, e.g. $(abxcxy)[x \mapsto cy] = abcyccyy$. We call a string constraint *quadratic* if each variable has at most two occurrences, and *cubic* if each variable has at most three occurrences.

2.1 Nielsen Transformation

As already briefly mentioned in the introduction, Nielsen transformation can be used to check satisfiability of a conjunction of word equations. We use the three rules shown in Fig. 3; besides the rules $x \hookrightarrow \alpha x$ and $x \hookrightarrow \varepsilon$ that we have seen

$$\frac{\alpha u = \alpha v}{u = v} \text{ (trim)} \qquad \frac{xu = v}{u[x \mapsto \varepsilon] = v[x \mapsto \varepsilon]} (x \hookrightarrow \varepsilon) \qquad \frac{xu = \alpha v}{x(u[x \mapsto \alpha x]) = v[x \mapsto \alpha x]} (x \hookrightarrow \alpha x)$$

Fig. 3. Rules of Nielsen transformation, for $x \in \mathbb{X}$, $\alpha \in \Sigma_{\mathbb{X}}$, and $u, v \in \Sigma_{\mathbb{X}}^*$. Symmetric rules are omitted.

in the introduction, there is also the (trim) rule, used to remove a shared prefix from both sides of the equation.

Given a system of word equations, multiple Nielsen transformations might be applicable to it, resulting in different transformed equations on which other Nielsen transformations can be performed, as shown in Fig. 1. Trying all possible transformations generates a tree (or a graph in general) whose nodes contain conjunctions of word equations and whose edges are labelled with the applied transformation. The conjunction of word equations in the root of the tree is satisfiable if and only if at least one of the leaves in the graph is a tautology, i.e., it contains a conjunction $\varepsilon = \varepsilon \wedge \cdots \wedge \varepsilon = \varepsilon$.

Lemma 1 (cf. [17,34]). *Nielsen transformation is sound. Moreover, it is complete when the systems of word equations is quadratic.*

Lemma 1 is correct even if we construct the proof tree using the following strategy: every application of $x \hookrightarrow \alpha x$ or $x \hookrightarrow \varepsilon$ is followed by as many applications of the (trim) rule as possible. We use $x \rightarrowtail \alpha x$ to denote the application of one $x \hookrightarrow \alpha x$ rule followed by as many applications of (trim) as possible, and $x \rightarrowtail \varepsilon$ for the application of $x \hookrightarrow \varepsilon$ repeatedly followed by (trim).

2.2   Regular Model Checking

Regular model checking (RMC) [1,12,13] is a framework for verifying infinite state systems. In RMC, each *system configuration* is represented as a word over an alphabet Σ. The set of *initial configurations* $\mathcal{I}$ and *destination configurations* $\mathcal{D}$ are captured as regular languages over Σ. The *transition relation* $\mathcal{T}$ is captured as a binary rational relation over Σ^*. A regular model checking *reachability problem* is represented by the triple $(\mathcal{I}, \mathcal{T}, \mathcal{D})$ and asks whether $\mathcal{T}^{rt}(\mathcal{I}) \cap \mathcal{D} \neq \emptyset$, where $\mathcal{T}^{rt}$ represents the reflexive and transitive closure of $\mathcal{T}$. One way how to solve the problem is to start computing the sequence $\mathcal{T}^{(0)}(\mathcal{I}), \mathcal{T}^{(1)}(\mathcal{I}), \mathcal{T}^{(2)}(\mathcal{I}), \ldots$ where $\mathcal{T}^{(0)}(\mathcal{I}) = \mathcal{I}$ and $\mathcal{T}^{(n+1)}(\mathcal{I}) = \mathcal{T}(\mathcal{T}^{(n)}(\mathcal{I}))$. During computation of the sequence, we can check if we find $\mathcal{T}^{(i)}(\mathcal{I})$ that overlaps with $\mathcal{D}$, and if yes, we can deduce that $\mathcal{D}$ is reachable. On the other hand, if we obtain a sequence such that $\bigcup_{0 \leq i < n} \mathcal{T}^i(\mathcal{I}) \supseteq \mathcal{T}^n(\mathcal{I})$, we know that we have explored all possible system configurations without reaching $\mathcal{D}$, so $\mathcal{D}$ is unreachable.

3   Solving Word Equations Using RMC

In this section, we describe a symbolic RMC-based framework for solving string constraints. The framework is based on encoding a string constraint into a regular language and encoding steps of Nielsen transformation as a rational relation. Satisfiability of a string constraint is then reduced to a reachability problem of RMC.

3.1   Nielsen Transformation as Word Operations

In the following, we describe how Nielsen transformation of a single word equation can be expressed as operations on words. We view a word equation $eq : t_\ell = t_r$ as a pair of word terms $e_{eq} = (t_\ell, t_r)$ corresponding to the two sides of the equation; therefore $e_{eq} \in \Sigma_X^* \times \Sigma_X^*$. Without loss of generality we assume that $t_\ell[1] \neq t_r[1]$; if this is not the case, we pre-process the equation by applying the (trim) Nielsen transformation (cf. Sect. 3) to trim the common prefix of t_ℓ and t_r.

Example 1. The word equation $eq_1 : xay = yx$ is represented by the pair of word terms $e_1 = (xay, yx)$.   □

A rule of Nielsen transformation (cf. Sect. 2.1) is represented using a (partial) function $\tau \colon (\Sigma_X^* \times \Sigma_X^*) \to (\Sigma_X^* \times \Sigma_X^*)$. Given a pair of word terms (t_ℓ, t_r) of a word equation eq, the function τ transforms it into a pair of word terms of a word equation eq' that would be obtained by performing the corresponding step of Nielsen transformation on eq. Before we express the rules of Nielsen transformation, we define functions performing the corresponding substitution. For $x \in X$ and $\alpha \in \Sigma_X$ we define

$$\tau_{x \mapsto \alpha x} = \{ (t_\ell, t_r) \mapsto (t'_\ell, t'_r) \mid t'_\ell = t_\ell[x \mapsto \alpha x] \wedge t'_r = t_r[x \mapsto \alpha x] \} \text{ and}$$
$$\tau_{x \mapsto \varepsilon} = \{ (t_\ell, t_r) \mapsto (t'_\ell, t'_r) \mid t'_\ell = t_\ell[x \mapsto \varepsilon] \wedge t'_r = t_r[x \mapsto \varepsilon] \}. \tag{1}$$

The function $\tau_{x \mapsto \alpha x}$ performs a substitution $x \mapsto \alpha x$ while the function $\tau_{x \mapsto \varepsilon}$ performs a substitution $x \mapsto \varepsilon$.

Example 2. Consider the pair of word terms e_1 from Example 1. The application $\tau_{x \mapsto yx}(e_1)$ would produce the pair $e_2 = (yxay, yyx)$ while the application $\tau_{x \mapsto \varepsilon}(e_1)$ would produce the pair $e_3 = (ay, y)$.   □

The functions introduced above do not take into account the first symbols of each side and do not remove a common prefix of the two sides of the equation, which is a necessary operation for Nielsen transformation to terminate. Let us, therefore, define the following function, which trims (the longest) matching prefix of word terms of the two sides of an equation:

$$\tau_{trim} = \{ (t_\ell, t_r) \mapsto (t'_\ell, t'_r) \mid \exists i (t_\ell[i] \neq t_r[i] \wedge \forall j (j < i \to t_\ell[j] = t_r[j])$$
$$\wedge\ t'_\ell = t_\ell[i:] \wedge t'_r = t_r[i:]) \}. \tag{2}$$

Example 3. Continuing in our running example, the application $\tau_{trim}(e_2)$ produces the pair $e'_2 = (xay, yx)$ while $\tau_{trim}(e_3)$ produces the pair $e'_3 = (ay, y)$.   □

Now we are ready to define functions corresponding to the rules of Nielsen transformation. In particular, the rule $x \rightarrowtail \alpha x$ for $x \in \mathbb{X}$ and $\alpha \in \Sigma_{\mathbb{X}}$ (cf. Sect. 2.1) can be expressed using the function

$$\tau_{x \rightarrowtail \alpha x} = \tau_{trim} \circ \{ (t_\ell, t_r) \mapsto \tau_{x \mapsto \alpha x}(t_\ell, t_r) \mid (t_\ell[1] = \alpha \wedge t_r[1] = x) \vee \\ (t_r[1] = \alpha \wedge t_\ell[1] = x) \} \qquad (3)$$

while the rule $x \rightarrowtail \varepsilon$ for $x \in \mathbb{X}$ can be expressed as the function

$$\tau_{x \rightarrowtail \varepsilon} = \tau_{trim} \circ \{ (t_\ell, t_r) \mapsto \tau_{x \mapsto \varepsilon}(t_\ell, t_r) \mid t_\ell[1] = x \vee t_r[1] = x \}. \qquad (4)$$

If we keep applying the functions defined above on individual pairs of word terms, while searching for the pair $(\varepsilon, \varepsilon)$—which represented the case when a solution to the original equation *eq* exists—, we would obtain the Nielsen transformation graph (cf. Sect. 2.1). In the following, we show how to perform the steps *symbolically* on a representation of a *whole set of word equations* at once.

3.2   Symbolic Algorithm for Word Equations

In this section, we describe the main idea of our symbolic algorithm for solving word equations. We first focus on the case of a single word equation and in subsequent sections extend the algorithm to a richer class.

Our algorithm is based on applying the transformation rules not on a single equation, but on a whole *set of equations* at once. Given a set of equations, the transformation rules are applied atomically, i.e., a single transformation rule is applied on the whole set of equations without interleaving with other

$$\mathcal{T}_{x \rightarrowtail \alpha x} = \bigcup_{x \in \mathbb{X}, \alpha \in \Sigma_{\mathbb{X}}} \tau_{x \rightarrowtail \alpha x}$$

$$\mathcal{T}_{x \rightarrowtail \varepsilon} = \bigcup_{x \in \mathbb{X}} \tau_{x \rightarrowtail \varepsilon}$$

Fig. 4. Transformation relations

transformation rules. For this, we define the relations $\mathcal{T}_{x \rightarrowtail \alpha x}$ and $\mathcal{T}_{x \rightarrowtail \varepsilon}$ that aggregate the versions of $\tau_{x \rightarrowtail \alpha x}$ and $\tau_{x \rightarrowtail \varepsilon}$ for all possible $x \in \mathbb{X}$ and $\alpha \in \Sigma_{\mathbb{X}}$. The signature of these relations is $(\Sigma_{\mathbb{X}}^* \times \Sigma_{\mathbb{X}}^*) \times (\Sigma_{\mathbb{X}}^* \times \Sigma_{\mathbb{X}}^*)$ and they are defined in Fig. 4. Note the following two properties of the relations: (i) they produce outputs of all possible Nielsen transformation steps applicable with the first symbols on the two sides of the equations and (ii) they include the *trimming* operation.

We compose the introduced relations into a single one, denoted as $\mathcal{T}_{step}$ and defined as $\mathcal{T}_{step} = \mathcal{T}_{x \rightarrowtail \alpha x} \cup \mathcal{T}_{x \rightarrowtail \varepsilon}$. The relation $\mathcal{T}_{step}$ can then be used to compute *all successors* of a set of word terms of equations in one step. For a set of word terms S we can compute the $\mathcal{T}_{step}$-image of S to obtain all successors of pairs of word terms in S. The initial configuration, given a word equation $eq : t_\ell = t_r$, is the set $E_{eq} = \{(t_\ell, t_r)\}$.

Example 4. Lifting our running example to the introduced notions over sets, we start with the set $E_{eq} = \{e_1 = (xay, yx)\}$. After applying $\mathcal{T}_{step}$ on E_{eq}, we obtain the set $S_1 = \{e_2' = (xay, yx), e_3' = (ay, y), (axy, yx), (a, \varepsilon)\}$. The pairs e_2' and e_3' were described earlier, the pair (axy, yx) is obtained by the transformation $\tau_{y \rightarrowtail xy}$, and the pair (a, ε) is obtained by the transformation $\tau_{y \rightarrowtail \varepsilon}$. If we continue by computing $\mathcal{T}_{step}(S_1)$, we obtain the set $S_2 = S_1 \cup \{(ax, x)\}$, with the pair (ax, x) obtained from (axy, yx) by using the transformation $\tau_{y \rightarrowtail \varepsilon}$.   □

Using the symbolic representation, we can formulate the problem of checking satisfiability of a word equation eq as the task of

– either testing whether $(\varepsilon, \varepsilon) \in \mathcal{T}_{step}^{rt}(E_{eq})$; this means that eq is satisfiable, or
– finding a set (called *unsat-invariant*) E_{inv} such that $E_{eq} \subseteq E_{inv}$, $(\varepsilon, \varepsilon) \notin E_{inv}$, and $\mathcal{T}_{step}(E_{inv}) \subseteq E_{inv}$, implying that eq is unsatisfiable.

In the following sections, we show how to encode the problem into the RMC framework.

Example 5. To proceed in our running example, when we apply $\mathcal{T}_{step}$ on S_2, we get $\mathcal{T}_{step}(S_2) \subseteq S_2$. Since $e_1 \in S_2$ and $(\varepsilon, \varepsilon) \notin S_2$, the set S_2 is our unsat-invariant, which means eq_1 is unsatisfiable.   □

3.3   Towards Symbolic Encoding

Let us now discuss some possible encodings of the word equations satisfiability problem into RMC. Recall that our task is to find an encoding such that the encoded equation (corresponding to initial configurations in RMC) and satisfiability condition (corresponding to destination configurations) are regular languages and transformation (transition) relation is a rational relation. We start by describing two possible methods of encodings that do not work and then describe the one that we use.

The first idea about how to encode a set of word equations as a regular language is to encode a pair $e_{eq} = (t_\ell, t_r)$ as a word $t_\ell \cdot \ominus \cdot t_r$, where $\ominus \notin \Sigma_X$. One immediately finds out that although the transformations $\tau_{x \rightarrowtail ax}$ and $\tau_{x \rightarrowtail \varepsilon}$ are rational (i.e., expressible using a transducer), the transformation τ_{trim}, which removes the longest matching prefix from both sides, is not (a transducer with an unbounded memory to remember the prefix would be required).

Another attempt of an encoding may be encoding $e_{eq} = (t_\ell, t_r)$ as a rational binary relation, represented, e.g., by a (non-length-preserving) 2-tape transducer (with a tape for t_ℓ and a tape for t_r) and use 4-tape transducers to represent the transformations (with two input tapes for t_ℓ, t_r and two output tapes for t'_ℓ, t'_r). The transducers implementing $\tau_{x \rightarrowtail yx}$ and $\tau_{x \rightarrowtail \varepsilon}$ can be constructed easily and so can be the transducer implementing τ_{trim}, so this solution looks appealing. One, however, quickly realizes an issue with computing $\mathcal{T}_{step}(E_{eq})$. In particular, since E_{eq} and $\mathcal{T}_{step}$ are both represented as rational relations, the intersection $(E_{eq} \times \Sigma_X^* \times \Sigma_X^*) \cap \mathcal{T}_{step}$, which needs to be computed first, may not be rational. Why? Consider $E_{eq} = \{(a^m b^n, c^m) \mid m, n \geq 0\}$ and $\mathcal{T}_{step} = \{(a^m b^n, c^n, \varepsilon, \varepsilon) \mid m, n \geq 0\}$. The intersection $(E_{eq} \times \Sigma_X^* \times \Sigma_X^*) \cap \mathcal{T}_{step} = \{(a^n b^n, c^n, \varepsilon, \varepsilon) \mid n \geq 0\}$ is clearly not rational.

3.4 Symbolic Encoding of Quadratic Equations into RMC

We therefore converge on the following method of representing word equations by a regular language. A set of pairs of word terms is represented as a regular language over a 2-track alphabet with padding $\Sigma_{\mathrm{X},\square}^2$, where $\Sigma_{\mathrm{X},\square} = \Sigma_{\mathrm{X}} \cup \{\square\}$, using an FA. For instance, $e_1 = (xay, yx)$ would be represented by the regular language $\binom{x}{y}\binom{a}{x}\binom{y}{\square}\binom{\square}{\square}^*$. Formally, we first define the *equation encoding function* eqencode: $(\Sigma_{\mathrm{X}}^*)^2 \to (\Sigma_{\mathrm{X},\square}^2)^*$ such that for $\mathsf{t}_\ell = a_1 \ldots a_n$ and $\mathsf{t}_r = b_1 \ldots b_m$ (without loss of generality we assume that $|\mathsf{t}_\ell| \geq |\mathsf{t}_r|$), we have eqencode$(\mathsf{t}_\ell, \mathsf{t}_r) = \binom{a_1}{b_1}\binom{a_2}{b_2} \ldots \binom{a_m}{b_m}\binom{a_{m+1}}{\square} \ldots \binom{a_n}{\square}$. We lift eqencode to sets in the usual way and to relations on pairs of word terms τ as eqencode$(\tau) = \{ (\mathrm{eqencode}(\mathsf{t}_\ell, \mathsf{t}_r), \mathrm{eqencode}(\mathsf{t}'_\ell, \mathsf{t}'_r)) \mid ((\mathsf{t}_\ell, \mathsf{t}_r), (\mathsf{t}'_\ell, \mathsf{t}'_r)) \in \tau \}$.

Let σ be a symbol. We define the *padding* of a k-tuple of words $(w_1, \ldots, w_k)$ with respect to σ as the set $\mathrm{pad}_\sigma(w_1, \ldots, w_k) = \{(w'_1, \ldots, w'_k) \mid w'_i \in w_i.\{\sigma\}^*\}\}$, i.e., it is a set of k-tuples obtained from $(w_1, \ldots, w_k)$ by extending some of the words by an arbitrary number of σ's. We lift pad_σ to a k-ary relation R as $\mathrm{pad}_\sigma(R) = \bigcup_{x \in R} \mathrm{pad}_\sigma(x)$. Finally, we define the function encode, which we use for encoding word equations into regular languages and word operations into rational relations, as $\mathrm{encode} = \mathrm{pad}_{\square} \circ \mathrm{eqencode}$. Properties of encode are given by the following lemmas.

Lemma 2. *If T is a binary regular relation on pairs of word terms, then* encode(T) *is rational. If L is a regular language, then* encode(L) *is regular.*

Lemma 3. *Given a word equation* $eq : \mathsf{t}_\ell = \mathsf{t}_r$ *for* $\mathsf{t}_\ell, \mathsf{t}_\ell \in \Sigma_{\mathrm{X}}^*$, *the set* encode$(eq)$ *is regular.*

Observe that because of the padding part, which introduces unbounded number of padding symbols at the end of an encoded relation, even if T is finite, encode(T) is infinite. Using the presented encoding, when trying to express the $\tau_{x \mapsto ax}$ and $\tau_{x \mapsto \varepsilon}$ transformations, we, however, encounter an issue with the need of an unbounded memory. For instance, for the language $L = \binom{x}{y}^*$, the transducer implementing $\tau_{x \mapsto yx}$ would need to remember how many times it has seen x on the first track of its input (indeed, the image $\{ \mathrm{encode}(u, v) \mid \exists n : u = (yx)^n \wedge v = y^n \square^n \}$ is no longer regular).

We address this issue in several steps: first, we give a rational relation that correctly represents the transformation rules for cases when the equation eq is quadratic, and extend our algorithm to equations with more occurrences of variables in Sect. 4. Let us define the following, more general, restriction of $\tau_{x \mapsto ax}$ to equations with at most $i \in \mathbb{N}$ occurrences of variable x as $\tau_{x \mapsto ax}^{\leq i} = \tau_{x \mapsto ax} \cap \{ ((\mathsf{t}_\ell, \mathsf{t}_r), (w, w')) \mid w, w' \in \Sigma_{\mathrm{X}}^*, |\mathsf{t}_\ell.\mathsf{t}_r|_x \leq i \}$. We define $\tau_{x \mapsto \varepsilon}^{\leq i}$, $\tau_{\bar{x} \mapsto ax}^{\leq i}$, and $\tau_{\bar{x} \mapsto \varepsilon}^{\leq i}$ similarly.

Lemma 4. *Given $i \in \mathbb{N}$, the relations* encode$(\tau_{x \mapsto ax}^{\leq i})$ *and* encode$(\tau_{x \mapsto \varepsilon}^{\leq i})$ *are rational.*

Input: Encoding $\mathcal{I}$ of a formula φ (the initial set), transformers $\mathcal{T}_{x \rightarrowtail \alpha x}$, $\mathcal{T}_{x \rightarrowtail \varepsilon}$, and the destination set $\mathcal{D}$

Output: A model of φ if φ is satisfiable, false otherwise

```
1  reach₀ := ∅;
2  reach₁ := I;
3  processed := reach₀;
4  T := Tₓ↦αₓ ∪ Tₓ↦ε;
5  i := 1;
6  while reachᵢ ⊈ processed do
7  │  if D ∩ reachᵢ ≠ ∅ then
8  │  │    return ExtractModel(reach₁, ..., reachᵢ);
9  │  processed := processed ∪ reachᵢ;
10 │  reachᵢ₊₁ := T(reachᵢ);
11 │  i++;
12 return false;
```

Algorithm 1: Solving a string constraint φ using RMC

In Algorithm 1, we give a high-level algorithm for solving string constraints using RMC. The algorithm is parameterized by the following: a regular language $\mathcal{I}$ encoding a formula φ (the initial set), rational relations $\mathcal{T}_{x \rightarrowtail \alpha x}$ and $\mathcal{T}_{x \rightarrowtail \varepsilon}$, and the destination set $\mathcal{D}$ (also given as a regular language). The algorithm tries to solve the RMC problem $(\mathcal{I}, \mathcal{T}_{x \rightarrowtail \alpha x} \cup \mathcal{T}_{x \rightarrowtail \varepsilon}, \mathcal{D})$ by an iterative unfolding of the transition relation $\mathcal{T}$ computed in Line 4, looking for an element w_i from $\mathcal{D}$. If such an element is found

$$\mathcal{I}^{eq} = \mathsf{encode}(\mathsf{t}_\ell, \mathsf{t}_r)$$

$$\mathcal{D}^{eq} = \left\{ \begin{pmatrix} \square \\ \square \end{pmatrix} \right\}^*$$

$$\mathcal{T}^{eq}_{x \rightarrowtail \alpha x} = \bigcup_{x \in \mathbb{X}, \alpha \in \Sigma_X} \mathsf{encode}(\tau^{\leq 2}_{x \rightarrowtail \alpha x})$$

$$\mathcal{T}^{eq}_{x \rightarrowtail \varepsilon} = \bigcup_{x \in \mathbb{X}} \mathsf{encode}(\tau^{\leq 2}_{x \rightarrowtail \varepsilon})$$

Fig. 5. RMC instantiation for a quadratic equation

in $reach_i$, we extract a model of the original word equation by starting a backward run from w_i, computing pre-images $w_{i-1}, \ldots, w_1$ over transformers $\mathcal{T}_{x \rightarrowtail \alpha x}$ and $\mathcal{T}_{x \rightarrowtail \varepsilon}$ (restricting them to $reach_j$ for every w_j), while updating values of the variables according to the transformation that was performed.

Our first instantiation of the algorithm is for checking satisfiability of a single quadratic word equation $eq : \mathsf{t}_\ell = \mathsf{t}_r$. We instantiate the RMC problem with $(\mathcal{I}^{eq}, \mathcal{T}^{eq}_{x \rightarrowtail \alpha x} \cup \mathcal{T}^{eq}_{x \rightarrowtail \varepsilon}, \mathcal{D}^{eq})$ defined in Fig. 5.

Lemma 5. *The relations $\mathcal{T}^{eq}_{x \rightarrowtail \alpha x}$ and $\mathcal{T}^{eq}_{x \rightarrowtail \varepsilon}$ are rational.*

Lemma 6. *If $eq : \mathsf{t}_\ell = \mathsf{t}_r$ is quadratic then Algorithm 1 instantiated with $(\mathcal{I}^{eq}, \mathcal{T}^{eq}_{x \rightarrowtail \alpha x} \cup \mathcal{T}^{eq}_{x \rightarrowtail \varepsilon}, \mathcal{D}^{eq})$ is sound and complete.*

4 Solving a System of Word Equations Using RMC

In the previous section we described how to solve a single quadratic word equation in the RMC framework. In this section we focus on an extension of this approach to handle a system of word equations $\Phi : \mathsf{t}^1_\ell = \mathsf{t}^1_r \wedge \mathsf{t}^2_\ell = \mathsf{t}^2_r \wedge \ldots \wedge \mathsf{t}^n_\ell = \mathsf{t}^n_r$.

In the first step we need to encode the system Φ as a regular language. For this we extend the encode function to a system of word equations by defining

$$\text{encode}(\Phi) = \text{encode}(t_\ell^1, t_r^1).\{\left(\begin{smallmatrix}\#\\\#\end{smallmatrix}\right)\}.\cdots.\{\left(\begin{smallmatrix}\#\\\#\end{smallmatrix}\right)\}.\text{encode}(t_\ell^n, t_r^n), \qquad (5)$$

where $\#$ is a delimiter symbol, $\# \notin \Sigma_X$. From Lemma 3 we know that $\text{encode}(t_\ell^i, t_r^i)$ is regular for all $1 \leq i \leq n$. Moreover, since regular languages are closed under concatenation (Propostion 1), the set $\text{encode}(\Phi)$ is also regular. Because each equation is now separated by a delimiter, we need to extend the destination set to $\{\left(\begin{smallmatrix}\square\\\square\end{smallmatrix}\right), \left(\begin{smallmatrix}\#\\\#\end{smallmatrix}\right)\}^*$.

For the transition relation, we need to extend $\tau_{x \rightarrowtail \alpha x}^{\leq i}$ and $\tau_{x \rightarrowtail \varepsilon}^{\leq i}$ from Sect. 3 to support delimiters. An application of a rule $x \rightarrowtail \alpha x$ on a system of equations can be described as follows: the rule $x \rightarrowtail \alpha x$ is applied on the first non-empty equation and the rest of the equations are modified according to the substitution $x \mapsto \alpha x$. The substitution on the other equations is performed regardless of their first symbols. The procedure is analogous for the rule $x \rightarrowtail \varepsilon$. A series of applications of the rules can reduce the number of equations, which then leads to a string in our encoding with a prefix from $\{\left(\begin{smallmatrix}\square\\\square\end{smallmatrix}\right), \left(\begin{smallmatrix}\#\\\#\end{smallmatrix}\right)\}^*$. The relation implementing $x \rightarrowtail \alpha x$ or $x \rightarrowtail \varepsilon$ on an encoded system of equations skips this prefix. Formally, the rule $x \rightarrowtail \alpha x$ for a system of equations where every equation has at most i occurrences of every variable is given by the following relation:

$$T_{x \rightarrowtail \alpha x}^{eqs,i} = T_{skip}.\text{encode}(\tau_{x \rightarrowtail \alpha x}^{\leq i}).\left(\{\left(\begin{smallmatrix}\#\\\#\end{smallmatrix}\right) \mapsto \left(\begin{smallmatrix}\#\\\#\end{smallmatrix}\right)\}.\text{encode}(\tau_{trim} \circ \tau_{x \rightarrowtail \alpha x}^{\leq i})\right)^*, \qquad (6)$$

where $T_{skip} = \{\left(\begin{smallmatrix}\square\\\square\end{smallmatrix}\right) \mapsto \left(\begin{smallmatrix}\square\\\square\end{smallmatrix}\right), \left(\begin{smallmatrix}\#\\\#\end{smallmatrix}\right) \mapsto \left(\begin{smallmatrix}\#\\\#\end{smallmatrix}\right)\}^*$. The relation $T_{x \rightarrowtail \varepsilon}^{eqs,i}$ is defined similarly.

Lemma 7. *The relations $T_{x \rightarrowtail \alpha x}^{eqs,i}$ and $T_{x \rightarrowtail \varepsilon}^{eqs,i}$ are rational.*

4.1 Quadratic Case

When Φ is quadratic, its satisfiability problem can be reduced to an RMC problem $(\mathcal{I}_\Phi^{q\text{-}eqs}, T_{x \rightarrowtail \alpha x}^{q\text{-}eqs} \cup T_{x \rightarrowtail \varepsilon}^{q\text{-}eqs}, \mathcal{D}^{q\text{-}eqs})$ where the items are defined in Fig. 6.

Rationality of $T_{x \rightarrowtail \alpha x}^{q\text{-}eqs}$ and $T_{x \rightarrowtail \varepsilon}^{q\text{-}eqs}$ follows directly from Proposition 1. The soundness and completeness of our procedure for a system of quadratic word equations is summarized by the following lemma.

$$\mathcal{I}_\Phi^{q\text{-}eqs} = \text{encode}(\Phi)$$

$$\mathcal{D}^{q\text{-}eqs} = \{\left(\begin{smallmatrix}\square\\\square\end{smallmatrix}\right), \left(\begin{smallmatrix}\#\\\#\end{smallmatrix}\right)\}^*$$

$$T_{x \rightarrowtail \alpha x}^{q\text{-}eqs} = \bigcup_{x \in X, \alpha \in \Sigma_X} T_{x \rightarrowtail \alpha x}^{eqs,2}$$

$$T_{x \rightarrowtail \varepsilon}^{q\text{-}eqs} = \bigcup_{x \in X} T_{x \rightarrowtail \varepsilon}^{eqs,2}$$

Fig. 6. RMC instantiation for a system of quadratic equations

Lemma 8. *If Φ is quadratic then Algorithm 1 instantiated with $(\mathcal{I}_\Phi^{q\text{-}eqs}, T_{x \rightarrowtail \alpha x}^{q\text{-}eqs} \cup T_{x \rightarrowtail \varepsilon}^{q\text{-}eqs}, \mathcal{D}^{q\text{-}eqs})$ is sound and complete.*

Input: System of word equations Φ
Output: Equisatisfiable cubic system of word equations Ψ

1 $\Psi := \Phi$;
2 **while** *There is a word variable x that occurs more than three times in Ψ* **do**
3 | Replace two occurrences of x in Φ by a fresh string variable x' to obtain a new system Ψ';
4 | $\Psi := \Psi' \wedge x = x'$;
5 **return** Ψ;

Algorithm 2: Transformation to a cubic system of equations

4.2 General Case

Let us now consider the general case when the system Φ is not quadratic. In this section, we show that this general case is also reducible to an extended version of RMC.

We first apply Algorithm 2 to a general system of string constraints Φ to get an equisatisfiable cubic system of word equations Φ'. Then we can use the transition relations $T_{x \rightarrowtail \alpha x}^{eqs,3}$ and $T_{x \rightarrowtail \varepsilon}^{eqs,3}$ to construct transformations of the encoded system Φ'.

Lemma 9. *Any system of word equations can be transformed by Algorithm 2 to an equisatisfiable cubic system of word equations.*

One more issue we need to solve is to make sure that we work with a cubic system of word equations in every step of our algorithm. It may happen that a transformation of the type $x \rightarrowtail yx$ increases the number of occurrences of the variable y by one, so if there had already been three occurrence of y before the transformation, the result will not be cubic any more.

More specifically, assume a cubic system of word equations $x.t_\ell = y.t_r \wedge \Phi$, where x and y are string variables and t_ℓ and t_r are word terms. If we apply the transformation $x \rightarrowtail yx$, we will obtain $x(t_\ell[x \mapsto yx]) = t_r[x \mapsto yx] \wedge \Phi[x \mapsto yx]$. Observe that (1) the number of occurrences of y is first *reduced by one* because the first y on the right-hand side of $x.t_\ell = y.t_r$ is removed and (2) then the number of occurrences of y can be at most *increased by two* because there exist at most two occurrences of x in t_ℓ, t_r, and Φ.

$$\mathcal{I}_\Phi^{eqs} = \mathsf{encode}(\Phi')$$

$$\mathcal{D}^{eqs} = \left\{ \begin{pmatrix} \square \\ \square \end{pmatrix}, \begin{pmatrix} \# \\ \# \end{pmatrix} \right\}^*$$

$$T_{x \rightarrowtail \alpha x}^{v_i, eqs} = T_{\mathcal{C}_{v_i}} \circ \bigcup_{x \in \mathbb{X}, \alpha \in \Sigma_{\mathbb{X}}} T_{x \rightarrowtail \alpha x}^{eqs,3}$$

$$T_{x \rightarrowtail \varepsilon}^{v_i, eqs} = T_{\mathcal{C}_{v_i}} \circ \bigcup_{x \in \mathbb{X}} T_{x \rightarrowtail \varepsilon}^{eqs,3}$$

Fig. 7. RMC instantiation for a system of cubic equations

Therefore, after the transformation $x \rightarrowtail yx$, a cubic system of word equations might become *(y-)quartic system of word equations* (at most four occurrences of the variable y and at most three occurrences of any other variable).

Given a fresh variable v, we use $\mathcal{C}_v$ to denote the transformation from a single-quartic system of word equations to a cubic system of equations.

Lemma 10. *The relation $T_{\mathcal{C}_v}$ performing the transformation $\mathcal{C}_v$ on an encoded single-quartic system of equations is rational.*

To express solving a system of string constraints Φ in the terms of a (modified) RMC, we first convert Φ (using Algorithm 2) to an equisatisfiable cubic system Φ'. The satisfiability of a system of word equations Φ can be reduced to a modified RMC problem $(\mathcal{I}_\Phi^{eqs}, \mathcal{T}_{x \rightarrowtail \alpha x}^{v_i, eqs} \cup \mathcal{T}_{x \rightarrowtail \varepsilon}^{v_i, eqs}, \mathcal{D}^{eqs})$ instantiating Algorithm 1 with components given in Fig. 7.

For the modified RMC algorithm, we need to assume $v_i \notin \Sigma_{\mathbb{X}}$. We also need to update Line 4 of Algorithm 1 to $\mathcal{T}^{v_i} := \mathcal{T}_{x \rightarrowtail \alpha x}^{v_i} \cup \mathcal{T}_{x \rightarrowtail \varepsilon}^{v_i}$ and Line 10 to $reach_{i+1} := \mathcal{T}^{v_i}(reach_i)$; $\mathbb{X} := \mathbb{X} \cup \{v_i\}$; to allow using a new variable v_i in every iteration. Rationality of $\mathcal{T}_{x \rightarrowtail \alpha x}^{v_i, eqs}$ and $\mathcal{T}_{x \rightarrowtail \varepsilon}^{v_i, eqs}$ follows directly from Proposition 1.

Lemma 11. *The modified Algorithm 1 instantiated with* $(\mathcal{I}_\Phi^{eqs}, \mathcal{T}_{x \rightarrowtail \alpha x}^{v_i, eqs} \cup \mathcal{T}_{x \rightarrowtail \varepsilon}^{v_i, eqs}, \mathcal{D}^{eqs})$ *is sound if* Φ *is cubic.*

Completeness. Since Nielsen transformation does not guarantee termination for the general case, neither does our algorithm. Investigation of possible symbolic encodings of complete algorithms, e.g. Makanin's algorithm [34], is our future work.

5   Handling a Boolean Combination of String Constraints

In this section, we will extend the procedure from handling a *conjunction* of word equations into a procedure that handles their arbitrary Boolean combination. The negation of word equations can be handled in the standard way. For instance, we can use the approach in [4] to convert a negated word equation $t_\ell \neq t_r$ to the string constraint

$$\bigvee_{c \in \Sigma} (t_\ell = t_r \cdot cx \vee t_\ell \cdot cx = t_r) \qquad \vee \qquad \bigvee_{c_1, c_2 \in \Sigma, c_1 \neq c_2} (t_\ell = x_3 c_1 x_1 \wedge t_r = x_3 c_2 x_2). \quad (7)$$

The first part of the constraint says that either t_ℓ is a strict prefix of t_r or the other way around. The second part says that t_ℓ and t_r have a common prefix x_3 and start to differ in the next symbols c_1 and c_2. For word equations connected using $\wedge$ and $\vee$, we apply distributive laws to obtain an equivalent formula in the conjunctive normal form (CNF) whose size is at worst exponential to the size of the original formula.

Let us now focus on how to express solving a string constraint Φ composed of arbitrary Boolean combination of word equations using a (modified) RMC. We start by removing inequalities in Φ using Eq. 7, then we convert the system without inequalities into CNF, and, finally, apply the procedure in Lemma 9 to convert the CNF formula to an equisatisfiable and cubic CNF Φ'. For deciding satisfiability of Φ' in the terms of RMC, both the transition relations and the destination set remain the same as in Sect. 4.2. The only difference is the initial configuration because the system is not a conjunction of terms any more but rather a general formula in CNF. For this, we extend the definition of encode to a clause $c = (t_\ell^1 = t_r^1 \vee \ldots \vee t_\ell^n = t_r^n)$ as $\mathsf{encode}(c) = \bigcup_{1 \leq j \leq n} \mathsf{encode}(t_\ell^j, t_r^j)$. Then the initial configuration for Φ' is given as

$$\mathcal{I}_{\Phi'}^{sc} = \mathsf{encode}(c_1).\left\{\left(\tfrac{\#}{\#}\right)\right\}.\ldots.\left\{\left(\tfrac{\#}{\#}\right)\right\}.\mathsf{encode}(c_m), \quad (8)$$

where Φ' is of the form $\Phi' : c_1 \wedge \ldots \wedge c_m$ and each clause c_i is of the form $c_i = (t^1_\ell = t^1_r \vee \ldots \vee t^{n_i}_\ell = t^{n_i}_r)$. We obtain the following lemma directly from Proposition 1.

Lemma 12. *The initial set $\mathcal{I}^{sc}_{\Phi'}$ is regular.*

The transition relation and the destination set are the same as the ones in the previous section, i.e., $\mathcal{T}^{v_i,sc}_{x \rightarrowtail \alpha x} = \mathcal{T}^{v_i,eqs}_{x \rightarrowtail \alpha x}$, $\mathcal{T}^{v_i,sc}_{x \rightarrowtail \varepsilon} = \mathcal{T}^{v_i,eqs}_{x \rightarrowtail \varepsilon}$, and $\mathcal{D}^{sc} = \mathcal{D}^{eqs}$. The soundness of our procedure for a Boolean combination of word equations is summarized by the following lemma.

Lemma 13. *Given a Boolean combination of word equations Φ, Algorithm 1 instantiated with $(\mathcal{I}^{sc}_{\Phi'}, \mathcal{T}^{v_i,sc}_{x \rightarrowtail \alpha x} \cup \mathcal{T}^{v_i,sc}_{x \rightarrowtail \varepsilon}, \mathcal{D}^{sc})$ is sound.*

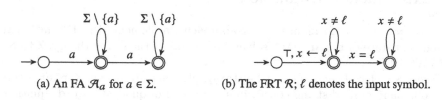

(a) An FA $\mathcal{A}_a$ for $a \in \Sigma$.   (b) The FRT $\mathcal{R}$; ℓ denotes the input symbol.

Fig. 8. Automata accepting L

6   Implementation

We created a prototype Python tool called RETRO, where we implemented the symbolic procedure for solving systems of word equations. RETRO implements a modification of the RMC loop from Algorithm 1. In particular, instead of standard transducers defined in Sect. 2, it uses the so-called *finite-alphabet register transducers* (FRTs), which allow a more concise representation of a rational relation.

Informally, an FRT is a register automaton (in the sense of [25]) where the alphabet is finite. The finiteness of the alphabet implies that the expressive power of FRTs coincides with the class of regular languages, but the advantage of using FRTs is that they allow a more concise representation than FAs.

In particular, transducers (without registers) corresponding to the transformers $\mathcal{T}_{x \rightarrowtail \alpha x}$ and $\mathcal{T}_{x \rightarrowtail \varepsilon}$ contain branching at the beginning for each choice of x and α. Especially in the case of huge alphabets, this yields huge transducers (consider for instance the Unicode alphabet with over 1 million symbols). The use of FRTs yields much smaller automata because the choice of x and α is stored into registers and then processed symbolically. To illustrate the effect of using registers, consider the following example.

Example 6. Consider the language $L = \{ w \in \Sigma^* \mid |w| \geq 1 \wedge |w|_{w[1]} \leq 2 \}$. Figure 8a shows an FA $\mathcal{A}_a$ accepting words starting with a and having at most two occurrences of a (it corresponds to a single choice of the first symbol in L).

We obtain the FA $\mathcal{A}$ for L as the union of all choices, i.e., $\mathcal{A} = \bigcup_{a \in \Sigma} \mathcal{A}_a$ ($\mathcal{A}$ has $1 + 2|\Sigma|$ states). On the other hand, Fig. 8b shows an FRT $\mathcal{R}$ accepting L with just 3 states (for any alphabet size). □

As another feature, RETRO uses deterministic FAs (i.e., FAs having for each state and each symbol at most one successor and having a single initial state) to represent configurations in Algorithm 1. It also uses eager automata minimization, since it has a big impact on the performance, especially on checking the termination condition of the RMC algorithm, which is done by testing language inclusion between the current configuration and all so-far processed configurations.

7   Experimental Evaluation

We compared the performance of our approach (implemented in RETRO) with two current state-of-the-art SMT solvers that support the string theory: Z3 4.8.7 and CVC4 1.7.

The first set of benchmarks is $\texttt{Kepler}_{22}$, obtained from [29]. $\texttt{Kepler}_{22}$ contains 600 hand-crafted string constraints composed of quadratic word equations with length constraints. In Fig. 9, we give a cactus plot of the results of the solvers on the $\texttt{Kepler}_{22}$ benchmark set with the timeout of 20 s. The total numbers of the solved benchmarks within the timeout were: 119 for Z3, 266 for CVC4, and 443 for RETRO (out of which 179 could not be solved by CVC4). On this benchmark set, RETRO can solve significantly more benchmarks than both Z3 and CVC4.

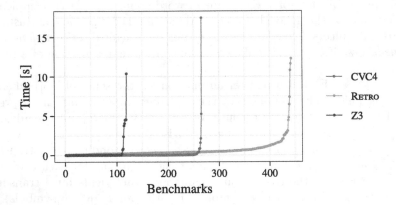

Fig. 9. A cactus plot comparing RETRO, CVC4, and Z3 on the $\texttt{Kepler}_{22}$ benchmark

The other set of benchmarks that we tried is PYEX-HARD. Here we want to see the potential of integrating RETRO with DPLL(T)-based string solvers, like Z3 or CVC4, as a specific string theory solver. The input of this component

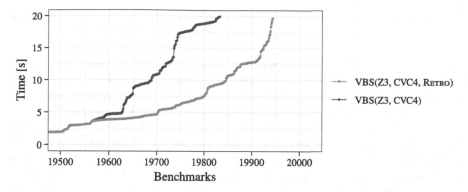

Fig. 10. A cactus plot comparing the Virtual Best Solver with and without RETRO on the PYEX-HARD benchmark. We show ∼500 most difficult benchmarks (from 20,020).

is a conjunction of atomic string formulae (e.g., $xy = zb \wedge z = ax$) that is a model of the Boolean structure of the top-level formula. The conjunction of atomic string formulae is then, in several layers, processed by various string theory solvers, which either add more conflict clauses or return a model. To evaluate whether RETRO is suitable to be used as "one of the layers" of Z3 or CVC4's string solver, we analyzed the PyEx benchmarks [42] and extracted from it 967 difficult instances that neither CVC4 nor Z3 could solve in 10 s. From those instances, we obtained 20,020 conjunctions of word equations that Z3's DPLL(T) algorithm sent to its string theory solver when trying to solve them. We call those 20,020 conjunctions of word equations PYEX-HARD. We then evaluated the three solvers on PYEX-HARD with the timeout of 20 s. Out of these, Z3 could not solve 3,232, CVC4 could not solve 188, and RETRO could not solve 3,099 instances.

Let us now closely look at the hard instances in the PYEX-HARD benchmark set, in particular on the instances that either CVC4 or Z3 could not solve. These benchmarks cannot be handled by the (several layers of) fast heuristics implemented in CVC4 and Z3, which are sufficient to solve many benchmarks without the need to start applying the case-split rule.[1] The set contains the 3,232 benchmarks that Z3 could not solve within 20 s. Out of these, CVC4 could not solve 188 benchmarks (CVC4 could solve every constraint that Z3 could solve), and RETRO could not solve 568 benchmarks. When we compared the solvers on the examples that Z3 and CVC4 failed to solve, RETRO could solve 2,664 examples (82.4 %) out of those where Z3 failed and 111 examples (59.04 %) of those where CVC4 failed. In Fig. 10, we give a cactus plot of the *Virtual Best Solver* on the benchmarks with and without RETRO. Given a set of solvers S, we use $VBS(S)$ to denote the solver that would be obtained by taking, for each benchmark, the

---

[1] For instance, when Z3 receives the word equation $xy = yax$, it infers the length constraint $|x| + |y| = |y| + 1 + |x|$, which implies unsatisfiability of the word equation without the need to start applying the case-split rule at all.

solver that is the fastest on the given benchmark. The graph shows that our approach can significantly help solvers deal with hard equations.

Discussion. From the obtained results, we see that our approach works well in *hard cases*, where the fast heuristics implemented in state-of-the-art solvers are not sufficient to quickly discharge a formula, in particular when the (un)satisfiability proof is complex. Our approach can exploit the symbolic representation of the proof tree and use it to reduce the redundancy of performing transformations. Note that we can still beat the heavily optimized Z3 and CVC4 written in C++ by a Python tool in those cases. We believe that implementing our symbolic algorithm as a part of a state-of-the-art SMT solver would push the applicability of string solving even further, especially for cases of string constraints with a complex structure, which need to solve multiple DPLL(T) queries in order to establish the (un)satisfiability of a string formula.

8   Related Work

The study of solving string constraint traces back to 1946, when Quine [41] showed that the first-order theory of word equations is undecidable. Makanin achieved a milestone result in [34], where he showed that the class of quantifier-free word equation is decidable. Since then, several works, e.g., [4,6,8,15,16, 19,20,32,35,39,40,43,44], consider the decidability and complexity of different classes of string constraints. Efficient solving of satisfiability of string constraints is a challenging problem. Moreover, decidability of the problem of satisfiability of word equations combined with length constraints of the form $|x| = |y|$ has already been open for over 20 years [14].

The strong practical motivation led to the rise of several string constraint solvers that concentrate on solving practical problem instances. The typical procedure implemented within *DPLL(T)-based* string solvers [3,5,9,16,24,45,46,52] is to split the constraints into simpler sub-cases based on how the solutions are aligned, combining with powerful techniques for Boolean reasoning to efficiently explore the resulting exponentially-sized search space. The case-split rule is usually performed explicitly. In contrast, our approach performs case-splits symbolically.

A related topic is about *automata-based* string solvers for analyzing string-manipulating programs. ABC [7] and Stranger [49] soundly over-approximates string constraints using transducers [51]. The main difference of these approaches to ours is that they use transducers to encode possible models (solutions) to the string constraints, while we use automata and transducers to encode the string constraint transformations.

Acknowledgment. We thank the anonymous reviewers for helpful comments on how to improve the paper and Mohamed Faouzi Atig for discussing the topic. This work has been partially supported by the Guangdong Science and Technology Department (grant no. 2018B010107004), by the National Natural Science Foundation of China (grant nos. 61761136011, 61532019, 61836005), the Czech Ministry of Education, Youth and Sports project LL1908 of the ERC.CZ programme, the Czech Science Foundation project 20-07487S, the FIT BUT internal project FIT-S-20-6427, and the project of Ministry of Science and Technology, Taiwan (grant nos. 109-2628-E-001-001-MY3 and 106-2221-E-001-009-MY3).

References

1. Abdulla, P.A.: Regular model checking. STTT **14**(2), 109–118 (2012)
2. Abdulla, P.A., et al.: Flatten and conquer: a framework for efficient analysis of string constraints. In: PLDI, pp. 602–617 (2017)
3. Abdulla, P.A., et al.: Trau: SMT solver for string constraints. In: FMCAD, pp. 1–5 (2018)
4. Abdulla, P.A., et al.: String constraints for verification. In: Biere, A., Bloem, R. (eds.) CAV 2014. LNCS, vol. 8559, pp. 150–166. Springer, Cham (2014). https://doi.org/10.1007/978-3-319-08867-9_10
5. Abdulla, P.A., et al.: Norn: an SMT solver for string constraints. In: Kroening, D., Pǎsǎreanu, C.S. (eds.) CAV 2015. LNCS, vol. 9206, pp. 462–469. Springer, Cham (2015). https://doi.org/10.1007/978-3-319-21690-4_29
6. Abdulla, P.A., Atig, M.F., Diep, B.P., Holík, L., Janků, P.: Chain-free string constraints. In: Chen, Y.-F., Cheng, C.-H., Esparza, J. (eds.) ATVA 2019. LNCS, vol. 11781, pp. 277–293. Springer, Cham (2019). https://doi.org/10.1007/978-3-030-31784-3_16
7. Aydin, A., et al.: Parameterized model counting for string and numeric constraints. In: SIGSOFT, pp. 400–410 (2018)
8. Barceló, P., Figueira, D., Libkin, L.: Graph logics with rational relations. arXiv preprint arXiv:1304.4150 (2013)
9. Barrett, C., et al.: CVC4. In: Gopalakrishnan, G., Qadeer, S. (eds.) CAV 2011. LNCS, vol. 6806, pp. 171–177. Springer, Heidelberg (2011). https://doi.org/10.1007/978-3-642-22110-1_14
10. Berstel, J.: Transductions and context-free languages. Vieweg+Teubner Verlag (1979)
11. Bjørner, N., Tillmann, N., Voronkov, A.: Path feasibility analysis for string-manipulating programs. In: Kowalewski, S., Philippou, A. (eds.) TACAS 2009. LNCS, vol. 5505, pp. 307–321. Springer, Heidelberg (2009). https://doi.org/10.1007/978-3-642-00768-2_27
12. Bouajjani, A., Habermehl, P., Rogalewicz, A., Vojnar, T.: Abstract regular (tree) model checking. STTT **14**(2), 167–191 (2012)
13. Bouajjani, A., Jonsson, B., Nilsson, M., Touili, T.: Regular model checking. In: Emerson, E.A., Sistla, A.P. (eds.) CAV 2000. LNCS, vol. 1855, pp. 403–418. Springer, Heidelberg (2000). https://doi.org/10.1007/10722167_31
14. Büchi, J.R., Senger, S.: Definability in the existential theory of concatenation and undecidable extensions of this theory. In: Mac Lane, S., Siefkes, D. (eds.) The Collected Works of J. Richard Büchi, pp. 671–683. Springer, New York (1990). https://doi.org/10.1007/978-1-4613-8928-6_37
15. Chen, T., Chen, Y., Hague, M., Lin, A.W., Wu, Z.: What is decidable about string constraints with the ReplaceAll function. PACMPL **2**(POPL), 3:1–3:29 (2018)
16. Chen, T., Hague, M., Lin, A.W., Rümmer, P., Wu, Z.: Decision procedures for path feasibility of string-manipulating programs with complex operations. PACMPL **3**(POPL), 49 (2019)

17. Diekert, V.: Makanin's Algorithm, pp. 387–442 (2002)
18. Durnev, V.G., Zetkina, O.V.: On equations in free semigroups with certain constraints on their solutions. J. Math. Sci. **158**(5), 671–676 (2009)
19. Ganesh, V., Berzish, M.: Undecidability of a theory of strings, linear arithmetic over length, and string-number conversion. arXiv preprint arXiv:1605.09442 (2016)
20. Ganesh, V., Minnes, M., Solar-Lezama, A., Rinard, M.: Word equations with length constraints: what's decidable? In: Biere, A., Nahir, A., Vos, T. (eds.) HVC 2012. LNCS, vol. 7857, pp. 209–226. Springer, Heidelberg (2013). https://doi.org/10.1007/978-3-642-39611-3_21
21. Godefroid, P., Klarlund, N., Sen, K.: DART: directed automated random testing. In: PLDI, pp. 213–223 (2005)
22. Gulwani, S., Jha, S., Tiwari, A., Venkatesan, R.: Synthesis of loop-free programs. In: PLDI, pp. 62–73 (2011)
23. Gulwani, S., Srivastava, S., Venkatesan, R.: Program analysis as constraint solving. In: PLDI (2008)
24. Holík, L., Janků, P., Lin, A.W., Rümmer, P., Vojnar, T.: String constraints with concatenation and transducers solved efficiently. PACMPL **2**(POPL), 4 (2018)
25. Kaminski, M., Francez, N.: Finite-memory automata. TCS **134**(2), 329–363 (1994)
26. Kiezun, A., Ganesh, V., Artzi, S., Guo, P.J., Hooimeijer, P., Ernst, M.D.: HAMPI: a solver for word equations over strings, regular expressions, and context-free grammars. TOSEM **21**(4), 25:1–25:28 (2012)
27. King, J.C.: Symbolic execution and program testing. Commun. ACM **19**(7), 385–394 (1976)
28. Kosovskii, N.K.: Properties of the solutions of equations in a free semigroup. J. Math. Sci. **6**(4), 361–367 (1976). https://doi.org/10.1007/BF01084074
29. Le, Q.L., He, M.: A decision procedure for string logic with quadratic equations, regular expressions and length constraints. In: Ryu, S. (ed.) APLAS 2018. LNCS, vol. 11275, pp. 350–372. Springer, Cham (2018). https://doi.org/10.1007/978-3-030-02768-1_19
30. Levi, F.W.: On semigroups. Bull. Calcutta Math. Soc. **36**, 141–146 (1944)
31. Liang, T., Reynolds, A., Tinelli, C., Barrett, C., Deters, M.: A DPLL(T) theory solver for a theory of strings and regular expressions. In: Biere, A., Bloem, R. (eds.) CAV 2014. LNCS, vol. 8559, pp. 646–662. Springer, Cham (2014). https://doi.org/10.1007/978-3-319-08867-9_43
32. Lin, A.W., Barceló, P.: String solving with word equations and transducers: towards a logic for analysing mutation XSS. In: POPL, pp. 123–136 (2016)
33. Lin, A.W., Majumdar, R.: Quadratic word equations with length constraints, counter systems, and Presburger arithmetic with divisibility. In: Lahiri, S.K., Wang, C. (eds.) ATVA 2018. LNCS, vol. 11138, pp. 352–369. Springer, Cham (2018). https://doi.org/10.1007/978-3-030-01090-4_21
34. Makanin, G.S.: The problem of solvability of equations in a free semigroup. Matematicheskii Sbornik **145**(2), 147–236 (1977)
35. Matiyasevich, Y.: Computation paradigms in light of Hilbert's tenth problem. In: Cooper, S.B., Lowe, B., Sorbi, A. (eds.) New computational paradigms, pp. 59–85. Springer, New York (2008). https://doi.org/10.1007/978-0-387-68546-5_4
36. Matiyasevich, Y.V.: A connection between systems of word and length equations and Hilbert's tenth problem. Zap. Nauchnykh Semin. POMI **8**, 132–144 (1968)
37. Nielsen, J.: Die isomorphismen der allgemeinen, unendlichen Gruppe mit zwei Erzeugenden. Mathematische Annalen **78**(1), 385–397 (1917)
38. Osera, P.M.: Constraint-based type-directed program synthesis. In: TyDe, pp. 64–76 (2019)

39. Plandowski, W.: Satisfiability of word equations with constants is in PSPACE. In: FOCS, pp. 495–500 (1999)

40. Plandowski, W.: An efficient algorithm for solving word equations. In: STOC, pp. 467–476 (2006)

41. Quine, W.V.: Concatenation as a basis for arithmetic. JSYML **11**(4), 105–114 (1946)

42. Reynolds, A., Woo, M., Barrett, C., Brumley, D., Liang, T., Tinelli, C.: Scaling up DPLL(T) string solvers using context-dependent simplification. In: Majumdar, R., Kunčak, V. (eds.) CAV 2017. LNCS, vol. 10427, pp. 453–474. Springer, Cham (2017). https://doi.org/10.1007/978-3-319-63390-9_24

43. Robson, J.M., Diekert, V.: On quadratic word equations. In: Meinel, C., Tison, S. (eds.) STACS 1999. LNCS, vol. 1563, pp. 217–226. Springer, Heidelberg (1999). https://doi.org/10.1007/3-540-49116-3_20

44. Schulz, K.U.: Makanin's algorithm for word equations-two improvements and a generalization. In: Schulz, K.U. (ed.) IWWERT 1990. LNCS, vol. 572, pp. 85–150. Springer, Heidelberg (1992). https://doi.org/10.1007/3-540-55124-7_4

45. Trinh, M.T., Chu, D.H., Jaffar, J.: S3: a symbolic string solver for vulnerability detection in web applications. In: CCS, pp. 1232–1243 (2014)

46. Trinh, M.-T., Chu, D.-H., Jaffar, J.: Progressive reasoning over recursively-defined strings. In: Chaudhuri, S., Farzan, A. (eds.) CAV 2016. LNCS, vol. 9779, pp. 218–240. Springer, Cham (2016). https://doi.org/10.1007/978-3-319-41528-4_12

47. Wang, H.-E., Tsai, T.-L., Lin, C.-H., Yu, F., Jiang, J.-H.R.: String analysis via automata manipulation with logic circuit representation. In: Chaudhuri, S., Farzan, A. (eds.) CAV 2016. LNCS, vol. 9779, pp. 241–260. Springer, Cham (2016). https://doi.org/10.1007/978-3-319-41528-4_13

48. Wang, Y., Zhou, M., Jiang, Y., Song, X., Gu, M., Sun, J.: A static analysis tool with optimizations for reachability determination. In: ASE, pp. 925–930 (2017)

49. Yu, F., Alkhalaf, M., Bultan, T.: STRANGER: an automata-based string analysis tool for PHP. In: Esparza, J., Majumdar, R. (eds.) TACAS 2010. LNCS, vol. 6015, pp. 154–157. Springer, Heidelberg (2010). https://doi.org/10.1007/978-3-642-12002-2_13

50. Yu, F., Alkhalaf, M., Bultan, T., Ibarra, O.H.: Automata-based symbolic string analysis for vulnerability detection. FMSD **44**(1), 44–70 (2014). https://doi.org/10.1007/s10703-013-0189-1

51. Yu, F., Shueh, C.Y., Lin, C.H., Chen, Y.F., Wang, B.Y., Bultan, T.: Optimal sanitization synthesis for web application vulnerability repair. In: ISSTA, pp. 189–200 (2016)

52. Zheng, Y., et al.: Z3str2: an efficient solver for strings, regular expressions, and length constraints. FMSD **50**(2–3), 249–288 (2017). https://doi.org/10.1007/s10703-016-0263-6

P³: A Profiler Suite for Parallel Applications on the Java Virtual Machine

Andrea Rosà[✉] and Walter Binder

Faculty of Informatics, Università della Svizzera italiana (USI), Lugano, Switzerland
{andrea.rosa,walter.binder}@usi.ch

Abstract. We present P³, a new profiler suite for parallel applications on the Java Virtual Machine. P³ specifically targets metrics related to parallelism, concurrency, and synchronization. In particular, P³ profiles the use of concurrent entities (e.g., threads, tasks, actors, futures), constructs and classes to implement synchronization (including locks, thread parking, and the synchronizers from the java.util.concurrent package), lock-free operations (such as atomic and volatile memory accesses), as well as synchronized and concurrent collections. To the best of our knowledge, our suite is the first tool detecting the use of volatile memory accesses, futures, synchronizers, and utility classes commonly used in concurrent programming. Moreover, P³ incurs only moderate profiling overhead. P³ can be readily applied to popular benchmark suites and to public code repositories, facilitating new analyses in the wild. We describe the design and implementation of P³ and discuss how our tool was fundamental in the selection of workloads composing the Renaissance benchmark suite. Moreover, we use P³ to analyze the variability of different metrics for multiple iterations of the Renaissance benchmarks.

Keywords: Profiling · Parallelism · Concurrency · Synchronization · Java Virtual Machine

1 Introduction

Developing multi-threaded applications is becoming increasingly important to exploit the massive parallel computing resources of nowadays hardware technologies. While parallel programming offers major benefits in speeding up applications, it can also lead to suboptimal performance if not done with care. To assess the performance of parallel applications and to locate optimization opportunities, it is fundamental to analyze their behavior under multiple aspects, particularly in relation to the use of concurrency and synchronization constructs.

We tackle this problem for multi-threaded applications running on the Java Virtual Machine (JVM). We present P³, a novel profiling suite for parallel applications focused on metrics related to parallelism, concurrency, and synchronization[1]. Specifically, P³ profiles the use of concurrent entities, constructs and

---

[1] P³ stands for "Profiler for Parallel Programs".

© Springer Nature Switzerland AG 2020
B. C. d. S. Oliveira (Ed.): APLAS 2020, LNCS 12470, pp. 364–372, 2020.
https://doi.org/10.1007/978-3-030-64437-6_19

classes to implement synchronization, lock-free operations, as well as synchronized and concurrent collections. Several profilers for parallel applications have been proposed in the literature, such as HPCToolkit [1], Free Lunch [3], and the work of Hofer et al. [4] and Inoue et al. [5]. Our tool enables the collection of metrics that, to the best of our knowledge, are not targeted by other profilers, such as the use of volatile memory accesses, futures and promises, synchronizers, synchronized collections, and concurrent collections. P³ can be run on any standard JVM that supports the JVM Tool Interface (JVMTI).

P³ is composed of several profiling modules that can be enabled individually, each incurring only moderate profiling overhead. In addition, P³ can be immediately applied to popular benchmark suites for the JVM (e.g., Renaissance, DaCapo, ScalaBench, SPECjvm2008) and can be readily used to conduct large-scale analyses on public software repositories via NAB [13]. The main challenges in developing P³ lie in achieving moderate overhead (thus reducing measurement perturbations) while also avoiding loss of accuracy. To this end, P³ resorts to efficient lock-free data structures, a careful architectural design that minimizes computations done in the inserted instrumentation code, and the use of advanced technologies such as reification of reflective information in a separate instrumentation process [8].

This paper makes the following contributions. We present P³, describing the metrics collected by our suite, its architecture and implementation (Sect. 2). We evaluate P³ by presenting a use case where our suite is used to analyze the variability of different metrics for multiple iterations of the Renaissance benchmark suite [7]. We also evaluate the profiling overhead of P³ (Sect. 3). We discuss how P³ was fundamental in conducting previous research, particularly how Renaissance developers used P³ during the development of the suite. We also discuss the limitations of P³ (Sect. 4). Finally, we give our concluding remarks (Sect. 5).

2 Profiler Suite Overview

In this section, we present the metrics collected by P³, its architecture, and we explain some aspects of its implementation.

Metrics. P³ mainly focuses on metrics related to parallelism, concurrency, and synchronization. Metric collection in P³ is organized in *modules* that can be enabled or disabled individually, each associated with different metrics, as reported in Table 1. Overall, the metrics profiled by P³ focus on fundamental entities and constructs for implementing thread-safe parallel applications, which may lead to performance bottlenecks if not used with care and whose understanding is crucial to locate optimization opportunities.

Four modules focus on metrics related to the creation, execution and use of concurrent entities, particularly threads, tasks (i.e., Runnable, Callable, and ForkJoinTask instances), actors (from the Akka library), and futures[2].

---

[2] To profile tasks and actors, P³ integrates modified versions of tgp [10] and AkkaProf [9], respectively. The other metrics are directly profiled by P³.

Six modules focus instead on the use of constructs, patterns, and classes used to implement synchronization on the JVM, i.e., implicit and explicit locks, the wait/notify pattern, thread joining and parking, as well as synchronizers. Three P^3 modules are dedicated to the execution of lock-free operations frequently used to reduce contention in parallel applications, particularly low-level atomic operations (such as compare-and-swap, get-and-swap, get-and-add), the use of atomic classes, and accesses to fields declared volatile. Finally, two modules detect the use of synchronized and concurrent collections offered by the Java Class Library, which are often used by parallel applications on the JVM.

In addition to the above metrics, P^3 can collect useful supporting metrics and context information, particularly the bytecode count (i.e., the number of bytecode instructions executed by the application) and the caller contexts (i.e., the method in which an event occurs). The former can be used to normalize other metrics wrt. a (mostly) platform-independent quantity describing the amount of computations performed by an application, and is useful when comparing metrics in different applications taking into account the amount of computations performed by them [7]. The latter allows P^3 to produce per-method event counters, which allow users to locate the code portions where most events of a given type occur. This information is fundamental to locate optimization opportunities [10].

Table 1. Metrics collected by P^3, broken down by module. The rightmost column reports the profiling overhead (OH) of a module, discussed in Sect. 3.

Module	Metrics	OH
thread	Threads start and termination	1.00
task	Tasks creation and execution (via tgp [10])	1.03
actor	Use of Akka actors (via AkkaProf [9])	1.01
future	Futures and promises from the Java's, Scala's and Twitter's libraries	1.01
ilock	Implicit locks: use of synchronized methods and blocks	1.03
elock	Explicit locks: use of interfaces Lock, ReadWriteLock and Condition	1.01
wait	Calls to Thread.wait, Thread.notify and Thread.notifyAll	1.00
join	Calls to Thread.join	1.01
park	Thread parking and unparking	1.00
synch	Synchronizers: Semaphore, CountDownLatch, CyclicBarrier, Phaser and Exchanger	1.01
cas	Compare-and-swap (CAS), get-and-swap (GAS), get-and-add (GAA)	1.01
atomic	Use of atomic classes: AtomicInt, AtomicLong, AtomicReference	1.01
volatile	Accesses to volatile fields	1.03
scoll	Use of synchronized collections	1.00
ccoll	Use of concurrent collections: BlockingQueue, ConcurrentMap and subtypes	1.01

Architecture. P^3 features a three-component architecture, as shown in Fig. 1. P^3 instruments classes at load-time, performing the instrumentation in a separate process, the *instrumentation server*. When a class is loaded, it is intercepted (step ① in the figure) by a native agent attached to the target application, which sends the class to the instrumentation server ②. Here, the instrumentation logic determines which methods of the class must be instrumented (if any) and instructs the weaver ③ to perform the instrumentation ④. Finally, the (potentially) instrumented class is sent back to the target application ⑤, which links it to the JVM's memory ⑥.

When an event of interest occurs, the instrumentation code registers it in thread-local counters in the memory of the target application ⑦. Before the termination of a thread, such counters are fetched ⑧ and sent ⑨ to another P^3 component running in a separate process, the *analysis server*. The counter processor in the server stores the received counters in appropriate data structures ⑩. When the target application terminates ⑪, the trace handler elaborates the analysis data structures ⑫ and produces traces containing a concise and readable representation of the collected metrics ⑬. To reduce the interference of the servers on application execution, they can be deployed on a different NUMA node or machine from the one where the target application is running.

P^3 provides extensible *plugins* (component Ⓐ in the figure) that can interface with popular benchmark suites for the JVM. Such plugins allow P^3 to determine the start and end of different benchmark iterations, hence enabling the collection of per-iteration metrics, which is useful to differentiate warm-up from steady-state performance. P^3 ships with plugins for the Renaissance [7], DaCapo [2], ScalaBench [11], and SPECjvm2008 [12] benchmark suites; users can implement custom plugins for other suites. When plugins are enabled, thread-local counters are sent to the analysis server also upon iteration start and end, to enable correct per-iteration accounting. In addition, P^3 implements plugins to interface with NAB [13], a framework for automatically conducting dynamic analyses on public code repositories. This makes it possible to readily conduct large-scale analyses with P^3 on software hosted in repositories such as GitHub.

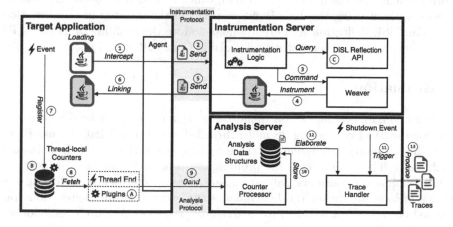

Fig. 1. P^3 architecture.

Implementation. P^3 is built on top of the DiSL framework for Java bytecode instrumentation [6]. DiSL guarantees *complete bytecode coverage*, i.e., all methods with a bytecode representation can be instrumented. This ensures that events of interest can be detected also in the Java Class Library, which is notoriously hard to instrument.

To collect the desired metrics, P^3 instruments multiple code locations, such as invocations to specific methods defined in the Java Class Library (including the special classes sun.misc.Unsafe and LockSupport) and the execution of specific bytecode instructions (such as monitorenter and monitorexit). Moreover, P^3 inspects information contained in the classfile of the class under instrumentation (e.g., to detect synchronized methods) and intercepts thread start and end via a dedicated JVMTI native agent. If the bytecode count is needed, P^3 also instruments all basic blocks to update the counter.

The implementation of P^3 is designed to keep the profiling overhead moderate while not jeopardizing the accuracy. In the target application, events are registered in thread-local primitive counters (component Ⓑ in Fig. 1) that are updated upon each event occurrence without the need of synchronization. This avoids the execution of expensive lock acquisitions and of additional object allocations in the heap. The costly elaboration of such counters is done in a separate process after application execution. Caller contexts (collected only if per-method metrics are needed) are also stored in thread-local data structures.

The instrumentation logic of P^3 often needs to access reflective information of a class[3]. Reflective information is usually not available in frameworks performing the instrumentation in a separate process. This results in the insertion of expensive dynamic checks or the use of the Java Reflection API in the instrumentation code, which are known to greatly increase the profiling overhead. The instrumentation server of P^3 is able to partially access such information by using the DiSL Reflection API [8] (component Ⓒ). The original API provides reflective information on the supertypes of a class. We extended the API to offer information also on the modifiers of a field, which is needed for detecting volatile accesses without using the Java Reflection API in the inserted instrumentation code. The DiSL Reflection API greatly helps reduce the profiling overhead of P^3 (e.g., it lowers the overhead of module volatile from 1613× to 1.03×).

3   Evaluation

In this section, we evaluate P^3 on Renaissance [7], a recently-released benchmark suite for the JVM containing 25 multi-threaded workloads. First, we use P^3 to assess the variability of different metrics for multiple iterations of the Renaissance benchmarks. Then, we discuss the profiling overhead of P^3 on Renaissance.

Our evaluation considers only *steady-state* iterations. Before collecting the metrics of interest, we let the benchmarks run several warm-up iterations (as specified on the suite's website) to let dynamic compilation and GC ergonomics

---

[3] In P^3, this is needed when modules thread, task, actor, future, elock, synch, atomic, volatile or ccoll are active.

stabilize. We use Renaissance v0.10.0 and Java OpenJDK 1.8.0_252. We conduct our analyses on a machine with two NUMA nodes, each containing an Intel Xeon E5-2680 (2.7 GHz) processor with 8 physical cores and 64 GB of RAM, running under Ubuntu 18.04.03 LTS (kernel GNU/Linux 4.15.0-66-generic x86_64). We deploy the instrumentation and analysis servers of P³ on a different NUMA node from the one where the target application is in execution, to reduce interference and measurement perturbation. For the same reason, we ensure that no other CPU-, memory-, or IO-intensive application is in execution during profiling. We disable Turbo Boost and Hyper-Threading.

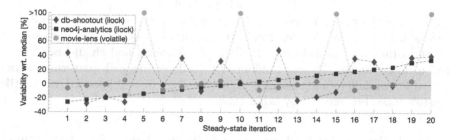

Fig. 2. Variability of metrics over multiple steady-state iterations. We report only benchmarks and metrics showing a variability of ±20% wrt. the median (marked by the gray area) in at least one iteration.

Variability. Benchmarks are often used as reference workloads against which compare the performance of different technologies. For this reason, good benchmarks should exhibit workloads that vary as little as possible in different iterations. In particular, operations related to parallelism, concurrency, and synchronization are those that are more susceptible to variability in a multi-threaded application (due to the intrinsic non-determinism of thread scheduling), and should be analyzed with care.

In this section, we conduct an high-level analysis on the variability of different metrics for multiple iterations of benchmarks in Renaissance, focusing in particular on aspects related to parallelism, concurrency, and synchronization. Our goal is not to fully assess variability; rather, we aim at finding workloads showing symptoms of metric variability across multiple iterations, which should be analyzed in more depth. We apply P³ on Renaissance, collecting, for each benchmark, all metrics reported in Table 1 in 20 different steady-state iterations. For each metric, we then compare the values obtained in each iteration with the median across all steady-state iterations. As the presence of small metric variations in multiple iterations can be considered the norm in multi-threaded workloads, we focus on benchmarks showing a significant variation in at least one iteration, i.e., ±20% wrt. the median.

Among the 25 benchmarks in Renaissance, we found 3 of them exhibiting a significant variability in a single metric. Figure 2 reports the relative value (wrt. the median) of the metric with significant variability in the 3 benchmarks, over different steady-state iterations. In db-shootout, the amount of implicit locks (ilock) used by the benchmark varies significantly across different iterations, being outside the ±20% range in 13 iterations out of 20. On the other hand, neo4j-analytics shows a constantly increasing number of implicit locks used, starting from a value of −26% in the first iteration and reaching a value of +35% wrt. the median in the last iteration. Finally, while the amount of volatile accesses (volatile) in movie-lens is often within the ±20% range, the benchmark exhibits a huge peak of volatile accesses every five iterations (amounting to +342%, +338%, +273% and +248% for iterations #5, 10, 15 and 20, respectively) which is an indication of a repetitive pattern accessing volatile fields frequently.

While the Renaissance benchmarks generally exhibit low metric variability, the three patterns shown in Fig. 2 indicate the presence of occasional or periodic operations that may introduce variability in workloads, and should be investigated in more depth[4]. P^3 was fundamental in detecting such patterns, particularly the variability in movie-lens, as to the best of our knowledge, volatile accesses cannot be detected by other tools.

Overhead. Here, we briefly discuss the profiling overhead of P^3. The rightmost column of Table 1 reports the median profiling overhead of a module across all Renaissance benchmarks. Overhead is presented as *overhead factor*, i.e., the ratio between the instrumented and uninstrumented application execution time. For most modules the overhead does not exceed 1.01×, with the exception of task, ilock and volatile which show an overhead of 1.03×. The relatively higher overhead of these modules can be explained by the complexity of collecting task-related metrics [10] (for task) and the high amount of intrinsic-lock and volatile accesses typically performed by a multi-threaded application (for ilock and volatile). When all modules are active, the median overhead of P^3 is 1.18×.

4   Discussion

Here, we discuss applications of P^3 to previous research work and its limitations.

Applications to Previous Research. P^3 has been used by researchers from both academia and industry. In particular, P^3 has been fundamental in the development of the Renaissance suite. Renaissance developers used P^3 attached to NAB to select candidate workloads hosted in public software repositories showing a high degree of concurrency and synchronization (particularly focusing on metrics in the future, ilock, wait, synch, cas, atomic and ccoll modules). Moreover, they used P^3 to filter out workloads showing low parallelism and concurrency, which did not fall in the scope of the suite. Finally, P^3 was used to obtain key metrics on concurrency and synchronization on the selected benchmarks, which

---

[4] We reported our findings to the Renaissance developers, who are investigating them.

demonstrated the higher diversity of Renaissance wrt. other prevalent benchmark suites for the JVM. All such analyses are detailed in a PLDI publication describing Renaissance [7].

In addition, P³ has been used by the developers of NAB to conduct large-scale analyses on task-parallel workloads running on the JVM (particularly using the task module), as discussed in an ECOOP publication describing NAB [13]. Overall, the availability of previous research work obtained thanks to P³ further demonstrates that our suite can be helpful in conducting novel research.

Limitations. As P³ is based on bytecode instrumentation, it may over-profile some metrics in cases where the just-in-time (JIT) compiler applies on-the-fly optimizations that remove some events of interest (such as the acquisition/release of implicit locks) without also removing the instrumentation code that detects such events. This is a well-known limitation of bytecode instrumentation on the JVM, affecting any profiler relying on such instrumentation strategy. While solving this limitation is challenging, previous work has proposed strategies to partially mitigate this problem for a subset of bytecode instructions [14]. As part of our future work, we plan to integrate similar strategies into P³ to alleviate this limitation.

As discussed in Sect. 3, P³ incurs a median profiling overhead of 1.18× when all modules are active. While this overhead can be considered significant for some applications, activating all modules at the same time is often not needed. On the other hand, individual modules incur only moderate overhead, which can be considered acceptable for most users. We took several measures to mitigate profiling overhead, as discussed in Sect. 2. We are continuously investigating new ways of reducing profiling overhead.

5   Concluding Remarks

We presented P³, a new profiler suite for parallel applications on the JVM, focusing on metrics related to parallelism, concurrency, and synchronization. To the best of our knowledge, our suite is the first tool detecting the use of volatile accesses, futures, synchronizers, as well as synchronized and concurrent collections. P³ incurs only moderate profiling overhead and can be readily applied to prevalent benchmark suites and to public code repositories, facilitating new large-scale analyses. P³ has been fundamental in conducting previous research work. We are confident that our suite can help researchers conduct novel analyses and better understand the behavior of multi-threaded applications.

As part of our future work, we plan to further increase the accuracy of P³ and decrease its profiling overhead, as discussed in Sect. 4. We also plan to expand the metrics profiled by P³ (e.g., including the use of parallel streams) and to further optimize resource usage by merging the instrumentation and analysis server into a single one. P³ is available as an evaluation version at http://inf.usi.ch/postdoc/rosaa/p3/p3-demo.zip.

Acknowledgments. This work has been supported by Oracle (ERO project 1332), by the Hasler Foundation (project 20022) and by the Swiss National Science Foundation (project 200020_188688).

References

1. Adhianto, L., et al.: HPCTOOLKIT: tools for performance analysis of optimized parallel programs. Concurr. Comput. Pract. Exper. **22**(6), 685–701 (2010)
2. Blackburn, S.M., et al.: The DaCapo benchmarks: Java benchmarking development and analysis. In: OOPSLA, pp. 169–190 (2006)
3. David, F., Thomas, G., Lawall, J., Muller, G.: Continuously measuring critical section pressure with the free-lunch profiler. In: OOPSLA, pp. 291–307 (2014)
4. Hofer, P., Gnedt, D., Schörgenhumer, A., Mössenböck, H.: Efficient tracing and versatile analysis of lock contention in Java applications on the virtual machine level. In: ICPE, pp. 263–274 (2016)
5. Inoue, H., Nakatani, T.: How a Java VM can get more from a hardware performance monitor. In: OOPSLA, pp. 137–154 (2009)
6. Marek, L., Villazón, A., Zheng, Y., Ansaloni, D., Binder, W., Qi, Z.: DiSL: a domain-specific language for bytecode instrumentation. In: AOSD, pp. 239–250 (2012)
7. Prokopec, A., et al.: Renaissance: benchmarking suite for parallel applications on the JVM. In: PLDI, pp. 31–47 (2019)
8. Rosà, A., Binder, W.: Optimizing type-specific instrumentation on the JVM with reflective supertype information. J. Visual Lang. Comput. **49**, 29–45 (2018)
9. Rosà, A., Chen, L.Y., Binder, W.: Actor profiling in virtual execution environments. In: GPCE, pp. 36–46 (2016)
10. Rosà, A., Rosales, E., Binder, W.: Analysis and optimization of task granularity on the Java Virtual Machine. ACM Trans. Program. Lang. Syst. **41**(3), 19:1–19:47 (219)
11. Sewe, A., Mezini, M., Sarimbekov, A., Binder, W.: Da Capo con Scala: design and analysis of a Scala benchmark suite for the Java Virtual Machine. In: OOPSLA, pp. 657–676 (2011)
12. Standard Performance Evaluation Corporation (SPEC): SPECjvm2008. https://www.spec.org/jvm2008/
13. Villazón, A., et al.: Automated large-scale multi-language dynamic program analysis in the wild. In: ECOOP, pp. 20:1–20:27 (2019)
14. Zheng, Y., Bulej, L., Binder, W.: Accurate profiling in the presence of dynamic compilation. In: OOPSLA, pp. 433–450 (2015)

Author Index

Aldrich, Jonathan   125
Aspinall, David   67
Atkey, Robert   67

Biernacka, Małgorzata   147
Biernacki, Dariusz   147
Binder, Walter   364
Boulytchev, Dmitry   167, 293
Bravetti, Mario   105

Ceresa, Martín   25
Charatonik, Witold   147
Chen, Yu-Fang   343

Drab, Tomasz   147
Dubey, Shashank Shekhar   231

Fachinetti, Leandro   3
Francalanza, Adrian   105

Gazagnaire, Thomas   231
Golovanov, Iaroslav   105
Gorostiaga, Felipe   25
Groves, Lindsay   125
Guan, Yong   44

Han, Ning   44
Havlena, Vojtěch   343
Hong, Chih-Duo   273
Hou, Chuanjia   251
Hu, Zhenjiang   323
Hüttel, Hans   105

Iwayama, Naoki   86

Jakobsen, Mathias S.   105
Jia, Tong   251

Kato, Hiroyuki   323
Katsura, Hiroyuki   86
Kettunen, Mikkel K.   105
Kienitz, Daniel   67
Kobayashi, Naoki   86
Kokke, Wen   67
Komendantskaya, Ekaterina   67
Kosarev, Dmitry   293

Lengál, Ondřej   343
Li, Ximeng   44
Li, Ying   251
Lin, Anthony W.   273
Liu, Xiaotong   251
Lozov, Petr   293

Mackay, Julian   125
Madhavapeddy, Anil   231
Markgraf, Oliver   273
Midtgaard, Jan   209

Najib, Muhammad   273
Neider, Daniel   273

Palmer, Zachary   3
Perényi, Árpád   209
Potanin, Alex   125

Ravara, António   105
Rosà, Andrea   364
Rozplokhas, Dmitry   167

Sánchez, César   25
Shi, Zhiping   44
Sivaramakrishnan, K. C.   231
Smith, Scott F.   3
Steinhöfel, Dominic   311

Tran, Van-Dang 323
Tsukada, Takeshi 86
Turrini, Andrea 343

Uustalu, Tarmo 186

Voorneveld, Niels 186
Vyatkin, Andrey 167

Wang, Guohui 44
Wu, Ke 3

Yorihiro, Ayaka 3
Yu, Hao 251
Yue, Yang 251

Printed in the United States
By Bookmasters